# Teaching and Learning Classroom Edition

BRIEF FIFTH EDITION

VOLUME 2

D1567537

### David Goldfield
UNIVERSITY OF NORTH CAROLINA, CHARLOTTE

### Carl Abbott
PORTLAND STATE UNIVERSITY

### Virginia DeJohn Anderson
UNIVERSITY OF COLORADO, BOULDER

### Jo Ann E. Argersinger
SOUTHERN ILLINOIS UNIVERSITY

### Peter H. Argersinger
SOUTHERN ILLINOIS UNIVERSITY

### William L. Barney
UNIVERSITY OF NORTH CAROLINA, CHAPEL HILL

### Robert M. Weir
UNIVERSITY OF SOUTH CAROLINA

**Prentice Hall**
New York  Boston  San Francisco
London  Toronto  Sydney  Tokyo
Mexico City  Paris  Cape Town  Hong Kong  Montreal

*For our students, who helped us write this book.*

*Publisher:* Charlyce Jones Owen
*Executive Marketing Manager:* Sue Westmoreland
*Editorial Assistant:* Maureen Diana
*Supplements Editor:* Emsal Hasan
*Operations Supervisor:* Mary Ann Gloriande
*Operations Specialist:* Maura Zaldivar
*Director of Media and Assessment:* Brian Hyland
*Media Project Manager:* Tina Rudowski
*Media Editor:* Sarah Kinney
*Senior Art Director:* Maria Lange
*Creative Director; Interior and Cover Design:* John Christiana
*Contributing Designer:* Michael J. Fruhbeis/
   Frubilicious Design Group

*AV Project Manager:* Mirella Signoretto
*Senior Managing Editor:* Ann Marie McCarthy
*Project Manager:* Denise Brown
*Full-Service Production and Composition:*
   Patty Donovan/Pine Tree Composition, Inc.
*Manager, Rights and Permissions:* Zina Arabia
*Manager, Visual Research:* Beth Brenzel
*Manager, Cover Visual Research and Permissions:*
   Karen Sanatar
*Image Permission Coordinator:* Craig Jones
*Printer/Binder:* Webcrafters
*Cover Printer:* Phoenix Color/Hagerstown

Anna Eleanor Roosevelt, 1884-1962. American humanitarian Eleanor Roosevelt was the wife of U.S. President Franklin D Roosevelt. She served as Chairman of the UN Human rights Commission 1947-1951 and as US representative at the UN General Assembly in 1946.

This book was set in 10/13 New Baskerville.

Credits and acknowledgments borrowed from other sources and reproduced, with permission, in this textbook appear on appropriate page within text (or on page C-1).

**Library of Congress Cataloging-in-Publication Data**

The American journey : a history of the United States / David Goldfield ...
[et al.]. – Teaching and learning classroom ed., 5th ed.
     p. cm.
   "Combined volume."
   Includes bibliographical references and index.
   ISBN-13: 978-0-205-73923-3 (combined)
   ISBN-10: 0-205-73923-7 (combined)
   ISBN-13: 978-0-205-73924-0 (v. 1)
   ISBN-10: 0-205-73924-5 (v. 1)
   ISBN-13: 978-0-205-73917-2 (v. 2)
   ISBN-10: 0-205-73917-2 (v. 2)
   [etc.]
1.  United States–History–Textbooks.  I. Goldfield, David R.
E178.1.A4925 2009b
973–dc22

                                        2008045328

**Prentice Hall**
is an imprint of

www.pearsonhighered.com

10 9 8 7 6 5 4 3 2

Volume 2
ISBN 13: 978-0-205-73917-2
ISBN 10: 0-205-73917-2

CONTENTS

## 19

## TRANSFORMING THE WEST, 1865–1890     558

## 20

## POLITICS AND GOVERNMENT, 1877–1900     586

## Interpreting the Past
**Currency Reform     614**

## 21

## THE PROGRESSIVE ERA, 1900–1917     616

## 22
## CREATING AN EMPIRE, 1865–1917   650

## 23
## AMERICA AND THE GREAT WAR, 1914–1920   678

## 24
## TOWARD A MODERN AMERICA, THE 1920S   708

## Interpreting the Past
### The Scopes Monkey Trial as a Harbinger of Change 738

# 25 THE GREAT DEPRESSION AND THE NEW DEAL, 1929–1939 740

# 26 WORLD WAR II, 1939–1945 774

# 27

## THE COLD WAR AT HOME AND ABROAD, 1946–1952 810

# 28

## THE CONFIDENT YEARS, 1953–1964 840

## Interpreting the Past
**The Quest for African American Equality: Washington, Du Bois, and King 874**

# 29

## SHAKEN TO THE ROOTS, 1965–1980 876

## THE REAGAN REVOLUTION AND A CHANGING WORLD, 1981–1992   910

*Voices from the American Journey: Celia Noup   912*

## COMPLACENCY AND CRISIS, 1993–2007   944

*Voices from the American Journey: John McNamara   946*

## Interpreting the Past

# American Views

# Global Perspectives

SPECIAL FEATURES

# PREFACE

The path that led us to *The American Journey* began in the classroom with our students. Our goal is to make American history accessible to students. The key to that goal—the core of the book—is a strong clear narrative. American history is a compelling story, and we seek to tell it in an engaging, forthright way. But we also provide students with an abundance of tools to help them absorb that story and put it in context. We introduce them to the concerns of the participants in America's history with primary source documents. The voices of contemporaries open each chapter, describing their own personal journeys toward fulfilling their dreams, hopes, and ambitions as part of the broader American journey. These voices provide a personal window on our nation's history, and the themes they express resonate throughout the narrative.

But if we wrote this book to appeal to our students, we also wrote it to engage their minds. We wanted to avoid academic trendiness, particularly the restricting categories that have divided the discipline of history over the last twenty years or so. We believe that the distinctions involved in the debates about multiculturalism and identity, between social and political history, between the history of the common people and the history of the elite, are unnecessarily confusing.

What we seek is integration—to combine political and social history, to fit the experience of particular groups into the broader perspective of the American past, to give voice to minor and major players alike because of their role in the story we have to tell.

## APPROACH

In telling our story, we had some definite ideas about what we might include and emphasize that other texts do not—information we felt that the current and next generations of students will need to know about our past to function best in a new society.

**Chronological Organization** A strong chronological backbone supports the book. We have found that the jumping back and forth in time characteristic of some American history textbooks confuses students. They abhor dates but need to know the sequence of events in history. A chronological presentation is the best way to be sure they do.

**Geographical Literacy** We also want students to be geographically literate. We expect them not only to know what happened in American history, but where it happened as well. Physical locations and spatial relationships were often important in shaping historical events. The abundant maps in *The American Journey*—all numbered and called out in the text—are an integral part of our story.

**Regional Balance** *The American Journey* presents balanced coverage of all regions of the country. In keeping with this balance, the South and the West receive more coverage in this text than in comparable books.

**Point of View** *The American Journey* presents a balanced overview of the American past. But "balanced" does not mean bland. We do not shy away from definite positions on controversial issues, such as the nature of early contacts between Native Americans and Europeans, why the political crisis of the 1850s ended in a bloody Civil War, and how Populism and its followers fit into the American political spectrum. If students and instructors disagree, that's great; discussion and dissent are important catalysts for understanding and learning.

**Religion** This text stresses the importance of religion in American society both as a source of strength and a reflection of some its more troubling aspects.

Historians mostly write for each other. That's too bad. We need to reach out and expand our audience. An American history text is a good place to start. Our students are not only our future historians, but more important, our future. Let their American journey begin.

## PRINT SUPPLEMENTS

**Instructor's Resource Manual** ISBN 10: 0205635679 ISBN 13: 9780205635672.

**Test Item File** ISBN: 0205635709 ISBN 978020563702.

**Transparency Package** ISBN 10: 0132370816 ISBN 13: 9780132370813.

**American Stories: Biographies in United States History (Volume I and II)**

**Retrieving the American Past: A Customized U.S. History Reader** Contact your local Prentice Hall representative for more information about this custom-publishing option.

**Prentice Hall and Penguin Bundle Program** Prentice Hall is pleased to provide adopters of *The American Journey* with an opportunity to receive significant discounts when copies of the text are bundled with Penguin titles in American history. Contact your local Prentice Hall representative for details.

## MULTIMEDIA SUPPLEMENTS

**Pearson MyTest**  This powerful assessment generation program helps instructors easily create and print quizzes and exams. Questions and tests are authored online, allowing ultimate flexibility and the ability to efficiently manage assessments anytime, anywhere. http://www.pearsonmytest.com/

**PEARSON**
**myhistorylab**
www.myhistorylab.com

*MyHistoryLab* means access to a wealth of study resources. Organized by major sections within chapters, these resources will help students to reinforce and apply what they are learning in class and from the text.

## FOR STUDENTS

- Over 300 primary source documents with questions for analysis, classic works from the *History Bookshelf* like Thomas Paine's *Common Sense*, and the e-textbook version of *The American Journey* give students the opportunity to explore historical events in more depth.
- Chapter review materials include a study guide, learning objectives, PPT review presentations, overview activities, and key term flashcards to help students master the contents of the textbook and prepare for exams.
- Hands-on activities and exercises let students explore content in the text in more depth and experience history beyond the textbook. Pearson's *Research Navigator*™ provides help with the research process.

## FOR INSTRUCTORS

For instructors using course management, *MyHistoryLab* means access to the student's resources, *and* all of the instructional material available to use in teaching with the text, including the instructor's manual, the test item file, images, maps, charts, and graphs from the text, video and audio clips, and Powerpoint™ lecture presentations and questions for use with CRS technology in the classroom. These are resources are also available to download from the Pearson Instructor Resource Center online at www.pearsonhighered.com/educator

## ACKNOWLEDGMENTS

We would like to thank the reviewers whose thoughtful and often detailed comments helped shape this fifth edition of *The American Journey, Teaching and Learning Edition.*

Jacqueline Akins, Community College of Philadelphia
James Barrett, University of Illinois—Urbana-Champaign
Caroline Barton, Holmes Community College
Lawrence Culver, Utah State University
Alan Downs, Georgia Southern University
Kimberly Earhart, Mount San Antonio College
E.J. Fabyan, Vincennes University
Jennifer Fry, Kings College
Michael Gabriel, Kutztown University
Mark Goldman, Tallahassee Community College
Kathleen Gorman, Minnesota State University—Mankato
Don Jacobson, Oakton Community College
Hasan Jeffries, The Ohio State University
Thomas Jorsch, Ferris State University
John Klee, Maysville Community and Technical College
Jonathan Mercantini, Canisius College
Loyce Miles, Hinds Community College
James Owens, Oakton Community College
James Page, North Central Texas College
Joshua Schier, Western Michigan University
Larry Wilson, San Jacinto College Central

All of us are grateful to our families, friends, and colleagues for their support and encouragement. Jo Ann and Peter Argersinger would like in particular to thank Anna Champe, Linda Hatmaker, and John Willits; William Barney thanks Pamela Fesmire and Rosalie Radcliffe; Virginia Anderson thanks Fred Anderson, Kim Gruenwald, Ruth Helm, Eric Hinderaker, and Chidiebere Nwaubani; and David Goldfield thanks Frances Glenn and Jason Moscato, Jim Miller, Sylvia Mallory, and Sally Constable played key roles in the book's inception and initial development.

Finally, we would like to acknowledge the members of our Prentice Hall family. They are not only highly competent professionals but also pleasant people. We regard them with affection and appreciation. None of us would hesitate to work with this fine group again. We would especially like to thank our editorial team: Charlyce Jones Owen, publisher, Priscilla McGeehon, VP/Publisher; our marketing team: Sue Westmoreland, executive marketing manager, and Brandy Dawson, Director of Marketing; our production team: Anne Marie McCarthy, Patty Donovan (Pine Tree), Denise Brown, Production Liaison, Maura Zaldovar, manufacturing manager and Mary Ann Gloriande, manufacturing; and Yolanda deRooy, president of Prentice Hall's Humanities and Social Sciences division.

DG
CA
VDJA
JEA
PHA
WLB
RMW

**David Goldfield** received his Ph.D. in history from the University of Maryland. Since 1982 he has been Robert Lee Bailey Professor of History at the University of North Carolina in Charlotte. He is the author or editor of thirteen books on various aspects of southern and urban history. Two of his works—*Cotton Fields and Skyscrapers: Southern City and Region, 1607–1980* (1982) and *Black, White, and Southern: Race Relations and Southern Culture, 1940 to the Present* (1990)—received the Mayflower Award for nonfiction and was nominated for the Pulitzer Prize in history. His most recent book is *Still Fighting the Civil War: The American South and Southern History* (2002). When he is not writing history, Dr. Goldfield applies his historical craft to history museum exhibits, voting rights cases, and local planning and policy issues.

**Carl Abbott** is a professor of Urban Studies and planning at Portland State University. He taught previously in the history departments at the University of Denver and Old Dominion University, and held visiting appointments at Mesa College in Colorado and George Washington University. He holds degrees in history from Swarthmore College and the University of Chicago. He specializes in the history of cities and the American West and serves as co-editor of the Pacific Historical Review. His books include *The New Urban America: Growth and Politics in Sunbelt Cities* (1981, 1987), *The Metropolitan Frontier: Cities in the Modern American West* (1993), *Planning a New West: The Columbia River Gorge National Scenic Area* (1997), and *Political Terrain: Washington, D.C. from Tidewater Town to Global Metropolis* (1999). He is currently working on a comprehensive history of the role of urbanization and urban culture in the history of western North America.

**Virginia DeJohn Anderson** is Professor of History at the University of Colorado at Boulder. She received her B.A. from the University of Connecticut. As the recipient of a Marshall Scholarship, she earned an M.A. degree at the University of East Anglia in Norwich, England. Returning to the United States, she received her A.M. and Ph.D. degrees from Harvard University. She is the author of *New England's Generation: The Great Migration and the Formation of Society and Culture in the Seventeenth Century* (1991) and several articles on colonial history, which have appeared in such journals as the *William and Mary Quarterly* and the *New England Quarterly*. Her most recent book is *Creatures of Empire: How Domestic Animals Transformed Early America* (2004).

**Jo Ann E. Argersinger** received her Ph.D. from George Washington University and is Professor of History at Southern Illinois University. A recipient of fellowships from the Rockefeller Foundation and the National Endowment for the Humanities, she is a historian of social, labor, and business policy. Her publications include *Toward a New Deal in Baltimore: People and Government in the Great Depression* (1988) and *Making the Amalgamated: Gender, Ethnicity, and Class in the Baltimore Clothing Industry* (1999).

**Peter H. Argersinger** received his Ph.D. from the University of Wisconsin and is Professor of History at Southern Illinois University. He has won several fellowships as well as the Binkley-Stephenson Award from the Organization of American Historians, and he is currently president of the Society for Historians of the Gilded Age and Progressive Era. Among his books on political and rural history are *Populism and Politics* (1974), *Structure, Process, and Party* (1992), and *The Limits of Agrarian Radicalism* (1995). His current research focuses on the political crisis of the 1890s.

**William L. Barney** is Professor of History at the University of North Carolina at Chapel Hill. A native of Pennsylvania, he received his B.A. from Cornell University and his M.A. and Ph.D. from Columbia University. He has published extensively on nineteenth century U.S. history and has a particular interest in the Old South and the coming of the Civil War. Among his publications are *The Road to Secession* (1972), *The Secessionist Impulse* (1974), *Flawed Victory* (1975), *The Passage of the Republic* (1987), and *Battleground for the Union* (1989). He is currently finishing an edited collection of essays on nineteenth-century America and a book on the Civil War. Most recently, he has edited *A Companion to 19th-Century America* (2001) and finished *The Civil War and Reconstruction: A Student Companion* (2001).

**Robert M. Weir** is Distinguished Professor of History Emeritus at the University of South Carolina. He received his B.A. from Pennsylvania State University and his Ph.D. from Case Western Reserve University. He has taught at the University of Houston and, as a visiting professor, at the University of Southampton in the United Kingdom. His articles have won prizes from the Southeastern Society for the Study of the Eighteenth Century and the *William and Mary Quarterly*. Among his publications are *Colonial South Carolina: A History*, "The Last of American Freemen": Studies in the Political Culture of the Colonial and Revolutionary South, and, more recently, a chapter on the Carolinas in the new *Oxford History of the British Empire* (1998).

*When writing history, historians use maps, tables, graphs, and visuals to help their readers understand the past. What follows is an explanation of how to use the historian's tools that are contained in this book.*

## TEXT

Whether it is a biography of George Washington, an article on the Civil War, or a survey of American history such as this one, the text is the historian's basic tool for discussing the past. Historians write about the past using narration and analysis. Narration is the story line of history. It describes what happened in the past, who did it, and where and when it occurred. Narration is also used to describe how people in the past lived, how they spent their days and even, when the historical evidence makes it possible for us to know, what they thought, felt, feared, or desired. Using analysis, historians explain why they think events in the past happened the way they did and try to offer an explanation. In this book, narration and analysis are interwoven in each chapter.

## VISUALS

Visual images embedded thoughout the text can provide as much insight into our nation's history as the written word. Within photographs and pieces of fine art lies emotional and historical meaning. Captions provide valuable information, such as in the example below. When studying the images, consider questions such as: "Who are the people?"; "How were they feeling?"; "What event motivated this photograph or painting?"; and "What can be learned from the backdrop surrounding the focal point?" Such analysis allows for a fuller understanding of the people who lived the American journey.

218  **CHAPTER 8**  A NEW REPUBLIC AND THE RISE OF PARTIES

### DEPARTMENTS AND COURTS

In the summer of 1789, Congress authorized the first executive departments: the State Department for foreign affairs, the Treasury for finances, and the War Department for the nation's defense. These departments already existed under the Articles of Confederation, and the only debate about them concerned the extent of presidential control over the officials who would head them. The Constitution was silent on whether the president could dismiss an official without the Senate's consent. Congress decided that the president could do so, setting an important precedent that bolstered presidential power. Department heads would now be closely bound to the president. As a group, they would evolve into the cabinet, the president's chief advisory body.

Greater controversy attended the creation of the federal judiciary. The Constitution called for "one Supreme Court" but left it up to Congress to authorize lower federal courts. The framers were deliberately vague about the federal judiciary, because Antifederalists and proponents of states' rights did not want national courts enforcing a uniform judicial system.

The **Judiciary Act of 1789** represented an artful compromise that balanced the concerns of the Antifederalists and states' rights advocates with the concerns of nationalists who strongly opposed leaving matters of national law up to state courts. It created a hierarchical national judiciary based on thirteen federal district courts, one for each state. Appeals from these courts were to be heard in one of three circuit courts, and the Supreme Court was to have the final say in contested cases. In a major concession to the Antifederalists, however, the act limited jurisdiction in federal courts to legal issues stemming from the Constitution and the laws and treaties of the national government.

**Judiciary Act of 1789** Act of Congress that implemented the judiciary clause of the Constitution by establishing the Supreme Court and a system of lower federal courts.

### REVENUE AND TRADE

The government's most pressing need was for revenue. Aware that Congress under the Articles of Confederation had been crippled by its inability to secure a reliable source of income, Madison acted to put the finances of the new federal government on a firm footing. Nearly everyone agreed that the government's chief source of income should be a tariff on imported goods and tonnage duties (fees based on cargo capacity) on ships entering American ports.

The **Tariff Act of 1789** was designed primarily to raise revenue, not to protect American manufacturers by keeping out foreign goods with high duties. It levied a duty of 5 percent on most imported goods but imposed tariffs as high as 50 percent on a limited number of items, such as steel, salt, cloth, and tobacco. The debate on the Tariff Act provoked some sectional sparring. Manufacturers, who were concentrated in the North, wanted high tariffs for protection against foreign competition. In contrast, farmers and southern planters wanted low tariffs to keep down the cost of the manufactured goods they purchased.

**Tariff Act of 1789** Apart from a few selected industries, this first tariff passed by Congress was intended to raise revenue and not protect American manufactures from foreign competition.

### HAMILTON AND THE PUBLIC CREDIT

The Treasury was the largest and most important new department. To its head, Alexander Hamilton of New York, fell the task of bringing order to the nation's ramshackle finances. The basic problem was the huge debt left over from the Revolution. With interest going unpaid, the debt was growing, and by 1789, it had reached $52 million. Until

Waterborne commerce was the key in the early emergence of New York City as a trading center. Shown here is the Manhattan end of the Brooklyn Ferry in 1790.

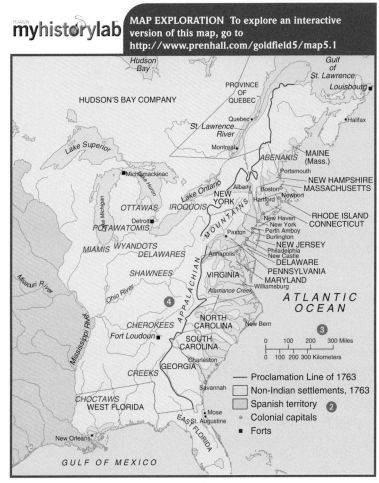

MAP EXPLORATION  To explore an interactive version of this map, go to http://www.prenhall.com/goldfield5/map5.1

**①  MAP 5–1    Colonial Settlement and the Proclamation Line of 1763**    This map depicts the regions claimed and settled by the major groups competing for territory in eastern North America. With the Proclamation Line of 1763, positioned along the crest of the Appalachian Mountains, the British government tried to stop the westward migration of settlers under its jurisdiction and thereby limit conflict with the Indians. The result, however, was frustration and anger on the part of land-hungry settlers.

**⑤    Why do** you think the Proclamation Line of 1763 was positioned along the crest of the Appalachian Mountains?

# MAPS

Maps are important historical tools. They show how geography has affected history and concisely summarize complex relationships and events. Knowing how to read and interpret a map is important to understanding history. Map 5–1 from Chapter 5 shows the British colonies on the eastern seaboard of North America in 1763, about twelve years before the American Revolution. It has three features to help you read it: a caption, a legend, and a scale. The ① **caption** explains the historical significance of the map. Here the caption tells us that in 1763 the British government sought to restrict colonial settlement west of the Appalachian Mountains to prevent conflict between colonists and Indians. Colonial frustration with this policy contributed to the outbreak of the American Revolution.

The legend and the scale appear in the lower right corner of the map. The ② **legend** provides a key to what the symbols on the map mean. The solid line stretching along the Appalachian Mountains from Maine to Georgia represents the Proclamation Line of 1763. Cities are marked with a dot, capitals with a star, and forts by a black square. Spanish territory west of the Mississippi River is represented in gold; territory settled by Europeans is represented in green. The ③ **scale** tells us that 7/8ths of an inch on the map represents 300 miles (about 480 kilometers) on the ground. With this information, estimates of the distance between points on the map are easily made.

The map also shows the ④ **topography** of the region—its mountains, rivers, and lakes. This helps us understand how geography influenced history in this case. For example, the Appalachian Mountains divide the eastern seaboard from the rest of the continent. The mountains obstructed colonial migration to the west for a long time. By running the Proclamation Line along the Appalachians, the British hoped to use this natural barrier to separate Indians and colonists.

A ⑤ **critical-thinking question** asks for careful consideration of the spatial connections between geography and history.

# MAP EXPLORATIONS

Many of the maps in each chapter are provided in a useful interactive version on the text's *Companion Website.* These maps are easily identified by a bar along the top that reads "Map Exploration." An interactive version of *Colonial Settlements and the Proclamation Line of 1763* can be found at www.prenhall.com/goldfield5/map5.1. The interactive version of this particular map provides an opportunity to pan over an enlarged version of the territory in question. Cities, forts, settlements, and terrain are shown in detail. By moving the cursor north, south, east, or west one can gain a bird's-eye view of the entire region.

## STUDY AIDS

Each chapter begins with a collection of historically significant illustrations that provide visual context for the chapter. Expanded pedagogical support helps students orient themselves to the chapter content: Chapter opening questions, organized by the main subtopics of each chapter, that encourage careful consideration of important themes and developments.

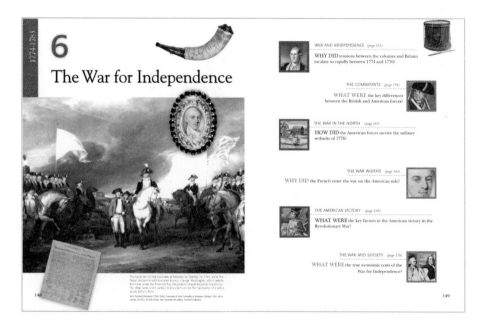

## MARGINAL QUESTIONS

The **Questions** that begin each chapter are repeated at the appropriate place in the margin of the text. Students can use these questions as a review test to confirm their understanding of the chapter content.

## MARGINAL KEY TERMS/GLOSSARY

Significant historical terms are called out in bold type throughout the text, defined in the margin, and listed at the end of each chapter with appropriate page numbers. All **key terms** in the text are listed alphabetically and defined in a glossary at the end of the book.

**WHO WERE** the Regulators, and what were the Regulator movements?

**Pilgrims**  Settlers of Plymouth Colony, who viewed themselves as spiritual wanderers.

QUICK REVIEW

Financial Strain on the Empire

- £146-million-pound national debt after French and Indian War
- Many Britons believed Americans should bear more of the burden of empire
- Economic recession increasedpressure for new taxes

Carl Schurz, *Report on the Condition of the South* (1865)

**Exploring America**
*Ratification of the Constitution*

# QUICK REVIEWS

The **Quick Reviews,** placed at key locations in the margins of each chapter, provide pinpoint summaries of important concepts, events, or topics in American history and serve as a mini-review resource.

# PRIMARY SOURCE DOCUMENTS

Throughout the text there are references to documents related to specific chapter content. These documents are online on the *MyHistorylab* website and include headnotes and questions that can be answered online.

# *MYHISTORYLAB* ACTIVITIES

Interactive and document activities that are included on the *MyHistoryLab* website, *Exploring America* and *From Then to Now,* are highlighted in the margins next to related content.

# OVERVIEW TABLES

The **Overview Tables** in this text are a special features designed to highlight and summarize important topics within a chapter. The Overview table shown here, for example, shows the predominant colonial labor systems in 1750 by geographic area.

| OVERVIEW Predominant Colonial Labor Systems, 1750 | Colony | Labor System |
|---|---|---|
| New England | Massachusetts | Family farms |
| | Connecticut | Family farms |
| | New Hampshire | Family farms |
| | Rhode Island | Family farms |
| Middle Colonies | New York | Family farms, tenancy |
| | Pennsylvania and Delaware | Indentured servitude, tenancy, family farms |
| | New Jersey | Family farms, tenancy |
| South | Maryland | Slavery |
| | Virginia | Slavery |
| | North Carolina | Family farms, slavery |
| | South Carolina | Slavery |

# CHRONOLOGIES

Each chapter includes a **Chronology,** a list of the key events discussed in the chapter arranged in chronological order. The Chronology for Chapter 16 lists the dates of key events during the Reconstruction era from 1861 to 1877. Chronologies provide a review of important events and their relationship to one another.

## CHRONOLOGY

**1861** Tsar Alexander II frees the serfs of Russia.

**1863** Lincoln proposes his Ten Percent Plan.

**1864** Congress proposes the Wade-Davis Bill.

**1865** Sherman issues Field Order No. 15.

Freedmen's Bureau is established.

Andrew Johnson succeeds to the presidency, unveils his Reconstruction plan.

Massachusetts desegregates all public facilities.

Black citizens in several southern cities organize Union Leagues.

Former Confederate states begin to pass black codes.

**1866** Congress passes Southern Homestead Act, Civil Rights Act of 1866.

Ku Klux Klan is founded.

Fourteenth Amendment to the Constitution is passed (ratified in 1868).

President Johnson goes on a speaking tour.

**1867** Congress passes Military Reconstruction Acts, Tenure of Office Act.

**1868** President Johnson is impeached and tried in the Senate for defying the Tenure of Office Act.

Republican Ulysses S. Grant is elected president.

**1869** Fifteenth Amendment passed (ratified 1870).

**1870** Congress passes Enforcement Act.

Republican regimes topple in North Carolina and Georgia.

**1871** Congress passes Ku Klux Klan Act.

**1872** Freedmen's Bureau closes down.

Liberal Republicans emerge as a separate party.

Ulysses S. Grant is reelected.

**1873** Severe depression begins.

Colfax Massacre occurs.

U.S. Supreme Court's decision in the *Slaughterhouse* cases weakens the intent of the Fourteenth Amendment.

Texas falls to the Democrats in the fall elections.

**1874** White Leaguers attempt a coup against the Republican government of New Orleans.

Democrats win off-year elections across the South amid widespread fraud and violence.

**1875** Congress passes Civil Rights Act of 1875.

**1876** Supreme Court's decision in *United States v. Cruikshank* nullifies Enforcement Act of 1870.

Outcome of the presidential election between Republican Rutherford B. Hayes and Democrat Samuel J. Tilden is contested.

**1877** Compromise of 1877 makes Hayes president and ends Reconstruction.

# CONCLUSION AND SUMMARY

The ❶ **conclusion** at the end of each chapter puts the subject of the chapter in the broader perspective of U.S. history. The ❷ **summary** is organized according to the main subtopics of the chapter and serves as an overview of the content in the chapter. Both of these study aids can be used as a review of important concepts.

---

## CONCLUSION ❶

In 1800, the Republicans were an untested party whose rise to power frightened many Federalists into predicting the end of the Union and constitutional government. The Federalists were correct in sensing that their days of power had passed, but they underestimated the ideological flexibility the Republicans would reveal once in office and the imaginative ways in which Jefferson and his successors would wield executive power to expand the size of the original Union. Far from being anarchists and demagogues, the Republicans were shrewd empire builders astute enough to add to their base of political support in the South and West. They also paved the way for the nation to evolve as a democratic republic rather than the more aristocratic republic preferred by the Federalists.

By the mid-1820s, the Republicans were about to join the Federalists as political dinosaurs. With no Federalist threat to enforce party discipline, the Republicans lost their organizational strength. Embracing economic nationalism after the war made the party's original focus on states' rights all but meaningless. Ideologically and organizationally adrift, the party split into regional coalitions in the wake of the Missouri controversy and the panic of 1819. But before it dissolved, the party left as its most enduring legacy the foundations of a continental empire.

## SUMMARY

## SUMMARY

**WHY DID** New Englanders abolish slavery in the decades after the Revolution?

**Washington's America**  The national census of 1790 counted nearly four million Americans, one in four of whom lived in New England. New Englanders found slavery incompatible with the natural rights philosophy that had emerged during the Revolution and abolished it in the 1780s. In other respects, though, politics in New England remained rooted in the Puritan past. The states in the Mid-Atlantic region were the most diverse in the nation, which created a complex political environment. In the South climate and soil conditions favored the production of cash staples for world markets and the use of slavery. And, between the Appalachian Mountains and the Mississippi River stretched the most rapidly growing region of the new nation, the West. Life in the West was harsh and often cruel, and Westerners were willing to strike a deal with almost any outside power to meet their needs.

**WHAT CHALLENGES** faced the Congress that assembled in New York between 1789 and 1791?

**Forging a New Government**  The Congress that assembled in New York from 1789 to 1791 faced a challenge scarcely less daunting than that of the Constitutional Convention of 1787. Led by Madison, the Congress submitted twelve amendments to the Constitution to the states of which ten were ratified. These ten are known as the Bill of Rights. Congress was also busy working out the cabinet and the court system.

**HOW DID** the French Revolution shape the development of party politics in America?

**The Emergence of Parties**  Two parties formed by the end of Washington's first term: the Federalists and the Republicans. In 1792, still in their formative stages, the parties re-elected an unopposed Washington. Control of the West remained an elusive goal throughout Washington's presidency. Among the distractions were wars with the Indians (the Battle of Fallen Timbers) and a Whiskey Rebellion in western Pennsylvania. The first partisan election was the election of 1796, with a divided nation electing Adams over Jefferson.

**WHY WAS** Adams defeated in the election of 1800?

**The Last Federalist Administration**  The Adams administration got off to a rocky start from which it never recovered. His administration dealt with the XYZ Affair, the Quasi-War with France, the Alien and Sedition Acts, and Fries's Rebellion. With Adams's many failed policies and the turmoil surrounding his presidency, the election of 1800 saw Jefferson narrowly elected president and the end of the Federalist party.

# REVIEW QUESTIONS, KEY TERMS, WHERE TO LEARN MORE, AND ADDITIONAL STUDY RESOURCES

At the end of each chapter there are a number of review and enrichment resources. ❶ **Review questions** reconsider the main topics of each chapter. ❷ **Key Terms** reference the page within the chapter where the term is defined. The section called ❸ **Where to Learn More** lists important historical sites and museums around the country and related Websites (which are also found at appropriate places in the margins of the text) that provide first-hand exposure to historical artifacts and settings. The URL for the MyHistoryLab website is also found at the end of each chapter; this website is an excellent resource for additional study aids.

## WHERE TO LEARN MORE ❸

**Ste. Marie among the Hurons, near Midland, Ontario, Canada.** This site contains a reconstructed Jesuit mission from the seventeenth century. There is a museum with information about seventeenth-century France as well as life among the Huron Indians. Further information may be found at **www.saintemarieamongthehurons.on.ca**.

**Taos Pueblo, Taos, New Mexico.** Still a residence for Pueblo Indians, portions of this multistoried pueblo date from the fifteenth century. This is the site from which Popé directed the beginnings of the Pueblo Revolt in 1680. Pictures and other information are available at **www.cr.nps.gov/worldheritage/taos.htm**.

**Carter's Grove Slave Quarter, near Williamsburg, Virginia.** Site includes reconstructed eighteenth-century slave quarters on the original site where slave cabins once stood. Costumed African American interpreters show visitors around and tell stories about actual slaves who lived on the plantation. Information about the house and plantation can be found at **www.williamsburg.com/plant/carter.html**. Pictures of the plantation may also be seen at **www.wise.virginia.edu**.

**Anacostia Museum and Center for African American History and Culture, Washington, D.C.** Part of the Smithsonian Institution, this museum contains exhibits relating to African American art, culture, and history. Information about current and past exhibitions, as well as online resources, can be found at **www.anacostia.si.edu**.

## STUDY RESOURCES

### myhistorylab

For study resources for this chapter, go to www.myhistorylab.com and choose *The American Journey*. You will find a wealth of study and review material for this chapter, including pre- and post-tests, customized study plan, key term review flash cards, interactive map and document activities, and documents for analysis.

## REVIEW QUESTIONS ❶

1. The first phase of Olaudah Equiano's journey into slavery took him from Africa's interior to the coast. What part of this journey most frightened him? Why? How did the development of a transatlantic labor market shape Equiano's experiences in the New World and the Old?

2. English colonists experienced more frequent, and more violent, conflicts with Indians than the settlers of New France did. Why was this so? What factors affected Indian–European relations in the two colonial regions?

3. Why were Catholic missionaries more successful than Protestants in converting Indians to Christianity in early America?

4. When did Chesapeake planters switch from servants to slaves? What factors contributed to their decision to make this change?

5. By about 1750, more slaves in the mainland British colonies were creoles (American-born) than African-born. What effects did this have on the formation of African American communities in America?

6. Different labor systems predominated in various regions of British America. How did the economy of each region help determine its labor system?

7. Tens of thousands of European immigrants came to America in the eighteenth century, but they tended to settle only in certain colonial regions. What destinations did they favor and why?

## KEY TERMS ❷

| | |
|---|---|
| **Bacon's Rebellion** (p. 67) | **Pueblo Revolt** (p. 68) |
| **Beaver Wars** (p. 63) | **Redemptioner** (p. 81) |
| *Encomienda* (p. 62) | *Repartimiento* (p. 62) |
| **King Philip's War** (p. 67) | **Stono Rebellion** (p. 80) |
| **Middle Passage** (p. 72) | |

*Historians find most of their information in written records and original documents that have survived from the past. These include government publications, letters, diaries, newspapers—whatever people wrote or printed, including many private documents never intended for publication. Several features in the text highlight the written record so important to understanding historical events.*

# PERSONAL JOURNEYS

Each chapter begins with a brief firsthand account from an individual which powerfully recounts the personal journey he or she took in their lives. Each of these "voices" relates to the themes that follow in the chapter. For example, in Chapter 18 is an excerpt from a letter written by Mary Antin, a Russian-Jewish immigrant who came to America at the turn of the last century.

**New! Personal Journeys Online**

At the end of each document is a list of additional firsthand accounts that are included on the *Myhistorylab* website.

---

*We were homeless, houseless, and friendless in a strange place. We had hardly money enough to last us through the voyage for which we had hoped and waited for three long years. We had suffered much that the reunion we longed for might come about; we had prepared ourselves to suffer more in order to bring it about, and had parted with those we loved, with places that were dear to us in spite of what we passed through in them, never again to see them, as we were convinced, all for the same dear end. With strong hopes and high spirits that hid the sad parting, we had started on our long journey. And now we were checked so unexpectedly but surely. . . . When my mother had recovered enough to speak, she began to argue with the gendarme, telling him our story and begging him to be kind. The children were frightened and all but I cried. I was only wondering what would happen. . . . Here we had been taken to a lonely place; . . . our things were taken away, our friends separated from us; a man came to inspect us, as if to ascertain our full value; strange-looking people driving us about like dumb animals, helpless and unresisting; children we could not see crying in a way that suggested terrible things; ourselves driven into a little room where a great kettle was boiling on a little stove; our clothes taken off, our bodies rubbed with a slippery substance that might be any bad thing; a shower of warm water let down on us without warning. . . . We are forced to pick out our clothes from among all the others, with the steam blinding us; we choke, cough, entreat the women to give us time; they persist, "Quick! Quick!, or you'll miss the train!", Oh, so we really won't be murdered! They are only making us ready for the continuing of our journey, cleaning us of all suspicions of dangerous sickness. Thank God! . . .*

*Oh, what solemn thoughts I had! How deeply I felt the greatness, the power of the scene! The immeasurable distance from horizon to horizon; . . . the absence of any object besides the one ship; . . . I was conscious only of sea and sky and something I did not understand. And as I listened to its solemn voice, I felt as if I had found a friend, and knew that I loved the ocean.*

— Mary Antin

Mary Antin, *The Promised Land* (Boston: Houghton Mifflin Co., 1912), chap. VIII.

## myhistorylab

Personal Journeys Online

- *Young Chinese immigrant memoir, 1882.* A Chinese immigrant recalls his migration to America and his early days in San Francisco.

- *Letters of Negro Migrants, 1917.* Letters from southern black migrants to the North back home.

MARY ANTIN, a 13-year-old Jewish girl from Russia, describes her family's perilous journey from persecution in tsarist Russia to the ship that would take her from Hamburg, Germany, to faraway America. In 1894, Mary and her mother and sisters set out from their village to join her father in Boston.

Millions of European immigrants made similar journeys across the Atlantic (as did Chinese and Japanese immigrants, across the Pacific), a trip fraught with danger, unpredictable detours, occasional heartbreak, the sundering of family ties, and the fear of the unknown. So powerful was the promise of

# AMERICAN VIEWS

Each chapter contains a selection from a primary source document. The example shown here is the published account of Mary Rowlandson from Lancaster, Massachusetts, who in 1676 was taken captive with two of her children by Indian warriors. Each American Views feature begins with a brief introduction followed by several questions—for discussion or written response—on what the document reveals about key issues and events.

## AMERICAN VIEWS

### Mary Rowlandson Among the Indians

In February 1676, in the midst of King Philip's War, Indian warriors attacked the town of Lancaster, Massachusetts. They killed many inhabitants and took 23 colonists captive, including Mary Rowlandson and three of her children. Rowlandson spent the next three months traveling with various groups of Nipmucs, Narragansetts, and Wampanoags. She suffered physically and emotionally, watching her youngest daughter die in her arms and worrying about her other two children, from whom she was frequently separated. During her captivity, Rowlandson survived by accepting her fate and adapting to the Indians' way of life. Finally, with an English victory imminent, Rowlandson was ransomed and rejoined her husband (who had been away at the time of the attack) and family. In 1682, she published an account of her captivity in which she explored the meaning of her experience. Rowlandson's narrative proved so popular that three editions were printed in the first year.

- **How** did Rowlandson describe the Indians? How did she characterize her encounter with King Philip?
- **In** what ways did Rowlandson accommodate herself to the Indians' way of life? How did she employ her skills to fit in? Did her gender make a difference in her experience of captivity?
- **How** did Rowlandson's Puritan faith shape her narrative?

We travelled on till night; and in the morning, we must go over the River to Philip's crew. When I was in the Cannoo, I could not but be amazed at the numerous crew of Pagans that were on the Bank on the other side. When I came ashore, they gathered all about me, I sitting alone in the midst: I observed they asked one another questions, and laughed, and rejoyced over their Gains and Victories. Then my heart began to fail: and I fell a weeping which was the first time to my remembrance that I wept before them. Although I had met with so much Affliction, and my heart was many times ready to break, yet could I not shed one tear in their sight: but rather had been all this while in a maze, and like one astonished: but now I may say as, Psal. 137.1 *By the rivers of Babylon, there we sat down: yea, we wept when we remembered Zion.* There one of them asked me, why I wept, I could hardly tell what to say: yet I answered, they would kill me: No, said he, none will hurt you. Then came one of them and gave me two spoon-fulls of Meal to comfort me. . . . Then I went to see King Philip, he bade me come in and sit down, and asked me whether I would smoke (a usual Complement now adayes amongst Saints and Sinners) but this no way suited me. For though I had formerly used Tobacco, yet I had left it ever since I was first taken, *It seems to be a bait, the devil lays to make men loose their precious time. . . .*

During my abode in this place, Philip spake to me to make a shirt for his boy, which I did, for which he gave me a shilling: I offered the money to my master, but he bade me keep it: and with it I bought a piece of Horse flesh. Afterwards he asked me to make a Cap for his boy, for which he invited me to Dinner. I went, and he gave me a Pancake, about as big as two fingers; it was made of parched wheat, beaten, and fryed in Bears grease, but I thought I never tasted pleasanter meat in my life. There was a Squaw who spake to me to make a shirt for her *Sannup* [husband], for which she gave me a piece of Bear. Another asked me to knit a pair of Stockins, for which she gave me a quart of Pease. . . . Hearing that my son was come to this place, I went to see him, and found him lying flat upon the ground: I asked him how he could sleep so? He answered me, *That he was not asleep, but at Prayer;* and lay so, that they might not observe what he was doing. I pray God he may remember these things now he is returned in safety.

Source: Neal Salisbury, ed., *The Sovereignty and Goodness of God, Together with the Faithfulness of His Promises Displayed.* . . . (Boston, 1997), pp. 82–83.

# GLOBAL PERSPECTIVES

This feature places the American journey within a broader world-wide context. That journey not only influenced other countries and peoples, but we in turn have been shaped by global economic, migratory, technological, and political trends. The example shown here is about a mass exodus of German-speaking people from the Rhineland to various parts of the world, including the United States.

**New! Critical thinking questions encourage analysis of the global connections.**

## GLOBAL PERSPECTIVES

### THE U.S. RESPONSE TO INDEPENDENCE MOVEMENTS

"*America . . . proclaimed to mankind the inextinguishable rights of human nature, and the only lawful foundations of government. . . . Wherever the standard of freedom and Independence has been or shall be unfurled, there will her heart, her benedictions and her prayers be. But she goes not abroad, in search of monsters to destroy. . . . She well knows that by once enlisting under other banners than her own, were they even the banners of foreign independence, she would involve herself beyond the power of extrication, in all the wars of interest and intrigue, of individual avarice, envy, and ambition, which assume the colors and usurp the standards of freedom. The fundamental maxims of her policy would insensibly change from liberty to force. . . . She might become the dictatress of the world. She would no longer be the ruler of her spirit. . . . [America's] glory is not dominion, but liberty. Her march is the march of the mind.*"

Drawn from the Independence Day speech of Secretary of State John Quincy Adams in 1821, these words gave classic expression to an enduring tension in America's relations with the outside world: Should the United States promote liberty and independence by the force of its example or the force of its arms? Adams was responding to political opponents who were demanding that the United States involve itself in the independence movements in Latin America and Greece. Adams refused to do so. The United States had no vital interests at stake in Greece, and aid to the rebels or premature recognition of the government they were struggling to form carried the risk of embroiling the United States in a conflict with their enemies, the Turks and Russians. Moreover, direct involvement in a European affair would set a dangerous precedent that Europeans could cite to intervene in the Western Hemisphere, where Adams wanted the United States to have a free hand.

As for the Latin American revolutionaries, Adams noted their disregard of the civil rights for which Americans had contended during the Revolution. He had no doubt that the independence movements to the south would eventually succeed, but he believed that the United States could best support them and the cause of liberty by championing and vindicating its own freedom and independence. To intervene abroad in an effort to transform foreign societies was to endanger liberty at home.

At the insistence of President Monroe, Adams extended diplomatic recognition to the new Latin American nations in 1822. In so doing, he insisted that the United States would recognize only governments that promised to adhere to all of their international obligations. Recognition, he stressed, carried no moral approval. This was the recognition policy followed by the U.S. government for ninty years, until President Woodrow Wilson committed it to a policy of liberal interventionism abroad.

- What is your position on the stand taken by Adams against the involvement of the United States in wars of liberty and independence?

# INTERPRETING THE PAST

These two-page features at the end of selected chapters, analyze important topics in U. S. history through images and short document excerpts. A focus question and an introductory narrative give a careful examination of the historical implication of each topic in question. In this example, the accounts of an African and a slave trader on their voyages across the Atlantic from Africa are underscored by the stark images of the slave trade to provide an in-depth perspective on this topic.

---

## INTERPRETING the PAST

### The Voyage to Slavery

**WHAT WERE** the dehumanizing experiences faced by Africans as they were kidnapped and transported to the New World as slaves. Under what conditions were Africans taken for slavery, and what was their fate when they arrived in the New World?

Most Africans were captured by other Africans in interior wars between tribes or specifically for sale as slaves. The slaves were moved to the West Coast of Africa where European and American slavers awaited to purchase a human cargo. Slavers inspected their potential cargo for health and strength. Males were preferred because the work on New World plantations would be hard. Human cargo was packed into ships' holds in the most efficient manner and carried under horrible, inhumane conditions to the New World for sale to the highest bidder. It was not unusual for Africans to prefer death to such a fate and individuals would dive overboard or even throw their children into the sea because drowning was considered a better end to that of slavery. For this reason slaves would be kept below decks in leg irons with the exception of an hour or so of exercise each day. During the exercise period slaves would be forced to jump up and down or "dance" to keep their muscles limber and the sale price for each individual at its highest level. Each day dead slaves would be cast overboard and tales abound of schools of sharks trailing slave ships for hundreds of miles.

### The shrieks of the women, . . .

*Olaudah Equiano, captured in Nigeria at a very early age, later gave this report of the experience crossing the Atlantic in a slave ship in 1789.*

The closeness of the place [ship's hold], and the heat of the climate, added to the number in the ship, which was so crowded that each had scarcely room to turn himself, almost suffocated us. This produced copious perspirations, so that the air soon became unfit for respiration, from a variety of loathsome smells, and brought on a sickness amongst the slaves, of which many died, thus falling victims to the improvident avarice, as I may call it, of their purchasers. This wretched situation was again aggravated by the galling of the chains, now become insupportable; and the filth of the necessary tubs, into which the children often fell, and were almost suffocated. The shrieks of the women, and the groans of the dying, rendered the whole a scene of horror almost inconceivable. Happily perhaps for myself I was soon reduced so low here that it was thought necessary to keep me almost always on deck; and from my extreme youth I was not put in fetters. In this situation I expected every hour to share the fate of my companions, some of whom were almost daily brought upon deck at the point of death, which I began to hope would soon put an end to my miseries. . . . One day, when we had a smooth sea and moderate wind, two of my wearied countrymen who were chained together (I was near them at the time), preferring death to such a life of misery, somehow made through the nettings and jumped into the sea: immediately another quite dejected fellow, who on account of his illness, was suffered to be out of irons, also followed their example; and I believe many more would very soon have done the same if they had not been prevented by the ship's crew who were instantly alarmed. Those of us that were the most active were in a moment put down under the deck, and there was such a noise and confusion amongst the people of the ship as I never heard before, to stop her, and get the boat out to go after the slaves. However two of the wretches were drowned, but they got the other, and afterwards flogged him unmercifully for thus attempting to prefer death to slavery.

*The eighteenth century engraving of a slave ship shows how tightly Africans were packed below the decks of these vessels, evidence that the thirst for profit overrode concerns for their health or welfare.*

*Alexander Falconbridge served as a ship's surgeon aboard a slaver in 1788. He was so horrified by what he witnessed during that time that he became involved in the British abolition movement.*

When the Negroes, whom the black traders have to dispose of, are shown to the European purchasers, they first examine them relative to their age. They then minutely inspect their persons, and inquire into the state of their health; if they are afflicted with any infirmity, or are deformed; or have bad eyes or teeth; if they are lame, or weak in their joints, or distorted in the back, or of a slender make, or are narrow in the chest; in short, if they have been, or are afflicted in any manner, so as to render them incapable of much labour; if any of the foregoing defects are discovered in them, they are rejected. But if approved of, they are generally taken on board the ship the same evening. The purchaser has liberty to return on the following morning, but not afterwards, such as upon re-examination are found exceptionable.

The traders frequently beat those Negroes which are objected to by the captains and use them with great severity. It matters not whether they are refused on account of age, illness, deformity, or for any other reason. At New Calabar, in particular, the traders have frequently been known to put them to death. Instances have happened at that place that the traders, when any of their Negroes have been objected to, have dropped their canoes under the stern of the vessel, and instantly beheaded them, in sight of the captain.

*African men, women, and children are tied together while walking in chains after being captured by slave traders.*

*Looking through the iron bars, one can glimpse the enclosure within Elmina Castle where slaves were confined prior to boarding the ships that would carry them to New World slavery.*

*Two men brand an African woman kneeling helplessly on the ground.*

### The purchaser has liberty to return . . .

88

89

# 16
# Reconstruction

## WHITE SOUTHERNERS AND THE GHOSTS OF THE CONFEDERACY, 1865 *(page 467)*

**HOW DID** Southerners remember the war? How did it shape their response to Reconstruction?

## MORE THAN FREEDOM: AFRICAN AMERICAN ASPIRATIONS IN 1865 *(page 468)*

**WHAT WERE** African Americans' hopes for Reconstruction?

## FEDERAL RECONSTRUCTION, 1865–1870 *(page 474)*

**HOW DID** Presidential Reconstruction differ from Congressional Reconstruction?

## COUNTER-RECONSTRUCTION, 1870–1874 *(page 483)*

**WHAT ROLE** did violence play in the Counter-Reconstruction?

## REDEMPTION, 1874–1877 *(page 487)*

**WHY DID** the federal government abandon African Americans after 1872?

## THE FAILED PROMISE OF RECONSTRUCTION *(page 489)*

**HOW AND** why did reconstruction end?

*Marianna, Florida 1866*

*The white academy opened about the same time the church opened the school for the Negro children. As the colored children had to pass the academy to reach the church it was easy for the white children to annoy them with taunts and jeers. The war passed from words to stones which the white children began to hurl at the colored. Several colored children were hurt and, as they had not resented the rock-throwing in kind because they were timid about going that far, the white children became more aggressive and abusive.*

*One morning the colored children armed themselves with stones and determined to fight their way past the academy to their school. [They] approached the academy in formation whereas in the past they had been going in pairs or small groups. When they reached hailing distance, a half dozen white boys rushed out and hurled their missiles. Instead of scampering away, the colored children not only stood their ground and hurled their missiles but maintained a solemn silence. The white children, seeing there was no backing down as they expected, came rushing out of the academy and charged the colored children.*

*During some fifteen minutes it was a real tug of war. In the close fighting the colored children got the advantage gradually and began to shove the white children back. As they pressed the advantage the white children broke away and ran for the academy. The colored fighters did not follow them but made it hot for the laggards until they also took to their heels. There were many bruises on both sides, but it taught the white youngsters to leave the colored ones alone thereafter.*

— T. Thomas Fortune, Norfolk Journal and Guide

T. Thomas Fortune, "Norfolk Journal and Guide," August 20, 1927, reprinted in Dorothy Sterling, ed., *The Trouble They Seen: Black People Tell the Story of Reconstruction* (Garden City, NY: Doubleday, 1976): 22–24.

## myhistorylab

### Personal Journeys Online

- **N. J. Bell, Southern Railroad Man, 1865.** A railroad conductor recalls the aftermath of the Civil War and its impact on a white family in Wilmington, NC.

- **Adelbert Ames, Letter from the Republican Governor of Mississippi, 1875.** Letter to his wife expressing frustration at the violence against black voters in his state and his hope for federal intervention.

**T. Thomas Fortune,** a New York newspaper editor, recalled this battle between black and white schoolchildren sixty years after it occurred at the beginning of the Reconstruction era. For 10-year-old Thomas, born a slave in Marianna, the incident encapsulated the dilemma of Reconstruction. In the journey from slavery to freedom, education emerged as an important element of full citizenship for African Americans. The eagerness with which black children (and adults) flooded schools, often spaces converted in churches and staffed initially by white missionaries from the North, was matched by the hostility of the white community, which resented any social advance or pretense of equality in the former bondsmen.

Reconstruction was not merely a series of white aggressions against African American aspirations, followed by black retreats. The former slaves did not shy away from asserting their rights. The violence and disorder that punctuated southern society after the Civil War was due in part to the refusal of blacks to relinquish their dreams of equal citizenship, including the right to a decent education.

The position of African Americans in American society was one of the two great issues of the Reconstruction era. Americans of both sections disagreed about how much freedom to grant the former slaves, almost all of whom lived in the South. The other great issue was how and under what terms to readmit the former Confederate states. ✦

## CHRONOLOGY

| | |
|---|---|
| **1861** | Tsar Alexander II frees the serfs of Russia. |
| **1863** | Lincoln proposes his Ten Percent Plan. |
| **1864** | Congress proposes the Wade-Davis Bill. |
| **1865** | Sherman issues Field Order No. 15. |
| | Freedmen's Bureau is established. |
| | Andrew Johnson succeeds to the presidency, unveils his Reconstruction plan. |
| | Massachusetts desegregates all public facilities. |
| | Black citizens in several southern cities organize Union Leagues. |
| | Former Confederate states begin to pass black codes. |
| **1866** | Congress passes Southern Homestead Act, Civil Rights Act of 1866. |
| | Ku Klux Klan is founded. |
| | Fourteenth Amendment to the Constitution is passed (ratified in 1868). |
| | President Johnson goes on a speaking tour. |
| **1867** | Congress passes Military Reconstruction Acts, Tenure of Office Act. |
| **1868** | President Johnson is impeached and tried in the Senate for defying the Tenure of Office Act. |
| | Republican Ulysses S. Grant is elected president. |
| **1869** | Fifteenth Amendment passed (ratified 1870). |

| | |
|---|---|
| **1870** | Congress passes Enforcement Act. |
| | Republican regimes topple in North Carolina and Georgia. |
| **1871** | Congress passes Ku Klux Klan Act. |
| **1872** | Freedmen's Bureau closes down. |
| | Liberal Republicans emerge as a separate party. |
| | Ulysses S. Grant is reelected. |
| **1873** | Severe depression begins. |
| | Colfax Massacre occurs. |
| | U.S. Supreme Court's decision in the *Slaughterhouse* cases weakens the intent of the Fourteenth Amendment. |
| | Texas falls to the Democrats in the fall elections. |
| **1874** | White Leaguers attempt a coup against the Republican government of New Orleans. |
| | Democrats win off-year elections across the South amid widespread fraud and violence. |
| **1875** | Congress passes Civil Rights Act of 1875. |
| **1876** | Supreme Court's decision in *United States v. Cruikshank* nullifies Enforcement Act of 1870. |
| | Outcome of the presidential election between Republican Rutherford B. Hayes and Democrat Samuel J. Tilden is contested. |
| **1877** | Compromise of 1877 makes Hayes president and ends Reconstruction. |

# WHITE SOUTHERNERS AND THE GHOSTS OF THE CONFEDERACY, 1865

Confederate soldiers, generals and troops alike, returned to devastated homes. Yeomen farmers, the backbone of the Confederacy, found uprooted fences, farm animals dead or gone, and buildings destroyed. They and their families wandered about in a living nightmare, seeking shelter where they could. They lived in morbid fear of vengeful former slaves or the hated Yankee soldiers wreaking more damage.

The casualties of war in the South continued long after the hostilities ceased. Although soldiers of both sides would experience difficulty in reentering civilian life, the southerner's case was the more difficult because of the economic devastation, the psychological burdens of defeat, and the break-up of families through death, migration, or poverty. Cities such as Richmond, Atlanta, Savannah, Charleston, and Columbia lay in ruins; farmsteads were stripped of everything but the soil; infrastructure, especially railroads, was damaged or destroyed; factories and machinery were demolished; and at least 5 million bales of cotton, the major cash crop, had gone up in smoke. Add a worthless currency, and the loss was staggering, climbing into hundreds of billions of dollars in today's currency.

**HOW DID** Southerners remember the war? How did it shape their response to Reconstruction?

Carl Schurz, *Report on the Condition of the South* (1865)

This engraving shows Southerners decorating the graves of rebel soldiers at Hollywood Memorial Cemetery in Virginia in 1867. Northerners and southerners alike honored their war dead. But in the South, the practice of commemorating fallen soldiers became an important element in maintaining the myth of the Lost Cause that colored white southerners' view of the war.

**Lost Cause** The phrase many white Southerners applied to their Civil War defeat. They viewed the war as a noble cause but only a temporary setback in the South's ultimate vindication.

**WHERE TO LEARN MORE**

★ Beauvoir, Biloxi, Mississippi.
www.beauvoir.org

Their cause lost and their society destroyed, white southerners lived through the summer and fall of 1865 surrounded by ghosts, the ghosts of lost loved ones, joyful times, bountiful harvests, self-assurance, and slavery. Defeat shook the basic tenets of their religious beliefs. Some praised God for delivering the South from the sin of slavery. But many other white southerners refused to accept their defeat as a divine judgment. Instead, they insisted, God had spared the South for a greater purpose. They came to view the war as the **Lost Cause** and interpreted it, not as a lesson in humility, but as an episode in the South's journey to salvation. White southerners transformed the bloody struggle into a symbol of courage against great odds and piety against sin. Eventually, they believed, redemption would come.

The Lost Cause would not merely exist as a memory, but also as a three-dimensional depiction of southern history, in rituals and celebrations, and as the educational foundation for future generations. The statues of the Confederate common soldier erected typically on the most important site in a town, the courthouse square; the commemorations of Confederate Memorial Day, the birthdays of prominent Confederate leaders, and the reunions of veterans, all marked with flourishing oratory, brass bands, parades, and related spectacles; and the textbooks implanting the white history of the South in young minds and carrying the legacy down through the generations—all of these ensured that the Lost Cause would not only be an interpretation of the past, but also the basic reality of the present and the foundation for the future.

Most white southerners approached the great issues of freedom and reunification with unyielding views. They saw African Americans as adversaries whose attempts at self-improvement were a direct challenge to white people's belief in their own racial superiority. White southerners saw outside assistance to black southerners as another invasion. The Yankees might have destroyed their families, their farms, and their fortunes, but they would not destroy the racial order. The war may have ended slavery, but white southerners were determined to preserve strict racial boundaries.

## MORE THAN FREEDOM: AFRICAN AMERICAN ASPIRATIONS IN 1865

**WHAT WERE** African Americans' hopes for Reconstruction?

Black southerners had a quite different perspective on the Civil War and Reconstruction, seeing the former as a great victory for freedom and the latter as a time of great possibility. To black southerners the Civil War was a war of liberation, not a Lost Cause. The response of southern whites to black aspirations still stunned African Americans, who believed, naively perhaps, that what they sought—education, land, access to employment, and equality in law and politics—were basic rights and modest objectives. The former slaves did not initially even dream of social equality; far less did they plot murder and mayhem, as white people feared. They did harbor two potentially contradictory aspirations. The first was to be left alone, free of white supervision. But the former slaves also wanted land, voting and civil rights, and education. To secure these, they needed the intervention and support of the white power structure.

In 1865, African Americans had reason to hope that their dreams of full citizenship might be realized. They enjoyed a reservoir of support for their aspirations among some Republican leaders. The first step Congress took beyond emancipation was to establish the Bureau of Refugees, Freedmen, and Abandoned Lands in March 1865. Congress envisioned the **Freedmen's Bureau,** as it came to be called, as a multipurpose agency to provide social, educational, and economic services, advice, and protection to former slaves and destitute white southerners. The Bureau marked the federal government's first foray into social welfare legislation. Congress also authorized the bureau to rent confiscated and abandoned farmland to freedmen in 40-acre plots, with an option to buy. This auspicious beginning belied the great disappointments that lay ahead.

## EDUCATION

The greatest success of the Freedmen's Bureau was in education. The bureau coordinated more than fifty northern philanthropic and religious groups, which, in turn, established 3,000 freedmen's schools in the South, serving 150,000 men, women, and children.

Initially, single young women from the Northeast comprised much of the teaching force. By 1871, black teachers outnumbered white teachers in the "colored" schools. The financial troubles of northern missionary societies and white northerners' declining interest in the freedmen's condition opened opportunities for black teachers. Support for them came from black churches, especially the African Methodist Episcopal (AME) Church.

At the end of the Civil War, only about 10 percent of black southerners were literate, compared with more than 70 percent of white southerners. Within a decade,

**Freedmen's Bureau**   Agency established by Congress in March 1865 to provide social, educational, and economic services, advice, and protection to former slaves and destitute whites; lasted seven years.

**WHERE TO LEARN MORE**

Penn Center Historic District, St. Helena Island, South Carolina.
www.penncenter.com

## QUICK REVIEW

**Freedom and Education**

- The Freedman's Bureau established 3,000 freedman's schools
- 1865–1875: Black literacy rises from 10 to 30 percent
- 1860–1880: 1,000 black southerners earn college degrees

The Freedmen's Bureau, northern churches, and missionary societies established more than 3,000 schools, attended by some 150,000 men, women, and children in the years after the Civil War. At first, mostly young white women from the Northeast staffed these schools.

**WHERE TO LEARN MORE**

Hampton University Museum,
Hampton, Virginia.
www.hamptonu.edu/museum

black literacy had risen above 30 percent. Joseph Wilson, a former slave, attributed the rise to "this longing of ours for freedom of the mind as well as the body."

Some black southerners went on to one of the thirteen colleges established by the American Missionary Association and black and white churches. Between 1860 and 1880 more than 1,000 black southerners earned college degrees at institutions still serving students today, such as Howard University in Washington, DC, Fisk University in Nashville, Hampton Institute (now University), Tuskegee Institute, and Biddle Institute (now Johnson C. Smith University) in Charlotte.

Pursuing freedom of the mind involved challenges beyond those of learning to read and write. Many white southerners condemned efforts at "Negro improvement." They viewed the time spent on education as wasted, forcing the former slaves to catch their lessons in bits and pieces between work, often by candlelight or on Sundays. White southerners also harassed white female teachers, questioning their morals and threatening people who rented rooms to them. After the Freedmen's Bureau folded in 1872 and many of the northern societies that supported freedmen's education collapsed or cut back their involvement, education for black southerners became more haphazard.

## "FORTY ACRES AND A MULE"

Although education was important to the freed slaves in their quest for civic equality, land ownership offered them the promise of economic independence. For generations, black people had worked southern farms and had received nothing for their labor.

An overwhelmingly agricultural people, freedmen looked to farm ownership as a key element in their transition from slavery to freedom. "Gib us our own land and we take care of ourselves," a Charleston freedman asserted to a northern visitor in 1865. "But without land, de ole massas can hire or starve us, as dey please." Even before the war's end, rumors circulated through black communities in the South that the government would provide each black family with 40 acres and a mule. These rumors were fueled by General William T. Sherman's **Field Order No. 15** in January 1865, which set aside a vast swath of abandoned land along the South Atlantic coast from the Charleston area to northern Florida for grants of up to 40 acres. The Freedmen's Bureau likewise raised expectations when it was initially authorized to rent 40-acre plots of confiscated or abandoned land to freedmen.

By June 1865, about 40,000 former slaves had settled on Sherman land along the southeastern coast. In 1866, Congress passed the **Southern Homestead Act,** giving black people preferential access to public lands in five southern states. Two years later, the Republican government of South Carolina initiated a land-redistribution program financed by the sale of state bonds. The state used proceeds from the bond sales to purchase farmland, which it then resold to freedmen, who paid for it with state-funded long-term low-interest loans. By the late 1870s, more than 14,000 African American families had taken advantage of this program.

Land ownership did not ensure financial success. Most black-owned farms were small and on marginal land. The value of these farms in 1880 was roughly half that of white-owned farms. Black farmers also had trouble obtaining credit to purchase or expand their holdings. A lifetime of fieldwork left some freedmen without the managerial skills to operate a farm. The hostility of white neighbors also played a role in thwarting black aspirations.

The vast majority of former slaves, however, especially those in the Lower South, never fulfilled their dreams of land ownership. Rumors to the contrary, the federal government never intended to implement a land-redistribution program in the South. General Sherman viewed his field order as a temporary measure to support freedmen for the

**Field Order No. 15** Order by General William T. Sherman in January 1865 to set aside abandoned land along the southern Atlantic coast for forty-acre grants to freedmen, rescinded by President Andrew Johnson later that year.

**Southern Homestead Act** Largely unsuccessful law passed in 1866 that gave black people preferential access to public lands in five southern states.

remainder of the war. President Andrew Johnson nullified the order in September 1865, returning confiscated land to its former owners. Even Republican supporters of black land ownership questioned the constitutionality of seizing privately owned real estate. Most of the land-redistribution programs that emerged after the war, including government-sponsored programs, required black farmers to have capital. But in the impoverished postwar economy of the South, it was difficult for them to acquire it.

Republican Party rhetoric of the 1850s extolled the virtues and dignity of free labor over the degradation of slave labor. Free labor usually meant working for a wage or under some other contractual arrangement. After the war, many white northerners envisioned former slaves assuming the status of free laborers, not necessarily of independent landowners.

Most of the officials of the Freedmen's Bureau shared these views and therefore saw reviving the southern economy as a higher priority than helping former slaves acquire farms. They wanted both to get the crop in the field and start the South on the road to a free labor system. Thus, they encouraged freedmen to work for their former masters under contract and to postpone their quest for land.

At first, agents of the Freedmen's Bureau supervised labor contracts between former slaves and masters. But after 1867, bureau surveillance declined. Agents assumed that both black laborers and white landowners had become accustomed to the mutual obligations of contracts. The bureau, however, underestimated the power of white landowners to coerce favorable terms or to ignore those they did not like. Contracts implied a mutuality that most planters could not accept in their relations with former slaves.

By the late 1870s, most former slaves in the rural South had been drawn into a subservient position in a new labor system called **sharecropping.** The premise of this system was relatively simple: The landlord furnished the sharecroppers with a house, a plot of land to work, seed, some farm animals, and farm implements and advanced them credit at a store the landlord typically owned. In exchange, the sharecroppers promised the landlord a share of their crop, usually one-half. The croppers kept the proceeds from the sale of the other half to pay off their debts at the store and save or spend as they and their families saw fit. In theory, a sharecropper could save enough to secure economic independence.

But white landlords perceived black independence as both contradictory and subversive. With landlords keeping the accounts at the store, black sharecroppers found that the proceeds from their share of the crop never left them very far ahead. Some found themselves in perpetual debt and worked as virtual slaves. Not all white landlords cheated their tenants, but given the sharecroppers' innocence regarding accounting methods and crop pricing, the temptation to do so was great.

## MIGRATION TO CITIES

Even before the hope of land ownership faded, African Americans looked for alternatives to secure their personal and economic independence. Before the war, the city had offered slaves and free black people a measure of freedom unknown in the rural South. After the war, African Americans moved to cities to find families, seek work, escape the tedium and supervision of farm life, or simply to test their right to move about.

Between 1860 and 1870, the African American population in every major southern city rose significantly. In Atlanta, for example, black people accounted for one in five residents in 1860 and nearly one in two by 1870.

Once in the city, freedmen had to find a home and a job. They usually settled on the outskirts of town, where building codes did not apply. Rather than developing one large ghetto, as happened in many northern cities, black southerners lived in small concentrations in and around cities. Sometimes armed with a letter of reference from their

*Documents*

James T. Rapier, *Testimony before U.S. Senate Regarding the Agricultural Labor Force in the South* (1880)

*Documents*

Clinton B. Fisk, *Plain Counsels for Freedmen* (1865)

*Documents*

*A Sharecrop Contract* (1882)

**sharecropping** Labor system that evolved during and after Reconstruction whereby landowners furnished laborers with a house, farm animals, and tools and advanced credit in exchange for a share of the laborers' crop.

**WHERE TO LEARN MORE**

★ Levi Jordan Plantation, Brazoria County, Texas.
www.webarchaeology.com

The black church was the center of African-American life in the postwar urban South. Most black churches were founded after the Civil War, but some, such as the first African Baptist Church in Richmond, shown here in an 1874 engraving, traced their origins to before 1861.

former masters, black people went door to door to seek employment. Many found work serving white families, as guards, laundresses, or maids, for very low wages. Both skilled and unskilled laborers found work rebuilding war-torn cities like Atlanta.

Most rural black southerners, however, worked as unskilled laborers. In both Atlanta and Nashville, black people comprised more than 75 percent of the unskilled workforce in 1870. Their wages were at or below subsistence level. A black laborer in Richmond admitted to a journalist in 1870 that he had difficulty making ends meet on $1.50 a day. "It's right hard," he reported. "I have to pay $15 a month rent, and only two little rooms." His family survived because his wife took in laundry, while her mother watched the children. Considering the laborer's struggle, the journalist wondered, "Were not your people better off in slavery?" The man replied, "Oh, no sir! We're a heap better off now. . . . We're men now, but when our masters had us we was only change in their pockets."

## FAITH AND FREEDOM

Religious faith framed and inspired the efforts of African Americans to test their freedom on the farm and in the city. White southerners used religion to transform the Lost Cause from a shattering defeat to a premonition of a greater destiny. Black southerners, in contrast, saw emancipation in biblical terms as the beginning of an exodus from bondage to the Promised Land.

Some black churches in the postwar South had originated during the slavery era, but most split from white-dominated congregations after the war. White churchgoers deplored the expressive style of black worship, and black churchgoers were uncomfortable in congregations that treated them as inferiors. A separate church also reduced white surveillance.

The church became a primary focus of African American life. It gave black people the opportunity to hone skills in self-government and administration that white-dominated

## GLOBAL PERSPECTIVES

### EMANCIPATION AND FREEDOM IN THE UNITED STATES AND RUSSIA

Tsar Alexander II (1855–1881) freed Russia's serfs in 1861, two years before Abraham Lincoln's Emancipation Proclamation. Although Russian serfs had more rights than American slaves, both were tied to the land and to their landlords/masters. The liberation of the serfs was part of a broader reform plan designed to help modernize Russia.

On becoming tsar in 1855, Alexander II had relaxed the speech, travel, and press restrictions imposed by his predecessors, resulting in an influx of Western ideas into Russia. These ideas helped create widespread public support for the liberation of the serfs. The tsar couched his emancipation proclamation in the ideals of God and country, but its origin lay primarily in Russia's economic aspirations and the tsar's political strategy. While most Americans perceived their liberated slaves as forming an agricultural working class, Alexander made land ownership one of the major attractions of emancipation. The government divided farms equally between the landlords and the former serfs, compensating the owners for the divided property.

In theory at least, Russian serfs seemed in a better position than the southern freedmen to secure economic independence, given the land they received. One Russian official exulted, "The people are erect and transformed; the look, the walk, the speech, everything is changed." But the Russian serfs found their economic situation little improved. The land chosen for redistribution was marginal, and redistribution came with a major catch: The former serfs were required to repay the state on the installment plan. Given the quality of the land, the relatively high interest rates attached to the loans, and the vast numbers of serfs and their families, repayment was unrealistic even in the long term. To ensure that the former serfs would pay up, the tsar allowed local governments to keep the peasants on their land until they fulfilled their financial obligations. In other words, they were as much tied to the land after emancipation as before. And, as a method to improve the quality of agricultural cultivation, the multiplicity of small plots and impoverished peasants was also a failure.

As in the United States, violence marred the transition from bondage to freedom. Rebellions flared in several parts of Russia, but the tsar's armies put these uprisings down quickly. Some of the former serfs managed to escape to towns and cities and become part of the growing laboring class, much as freedmen went to southern cities. In the cities, both former serfs and slaves came closer to the free-labor ideal posited but not supported by their respective governments. In rural areas, reform broke down through a lack of planning and a failure of will.

- After emancipation, did the Russian serf or the American slave have a better opportunity to establish economic independence?

---

society denied them. Within the supportive confines of the congregation, they could assume leadership positions, render important decisions, deal with financial matters, and engage in politics. The church also operated as an educational institution. Local governments, especially in rural areas, rarely constructed public schools for black people; churches often served that function.

The desire to read the Bible inspired thousands of former slaves to attend the church school. The church also spawned other organizations that served the black community, such as burial societies, Masonic lodges, temperance groups, trade unions, and drama clubs. African Americans took great pride in their churches, which became visible measures of their progress. The church and the congregation were a cohesive force in black communities.

Most black churches looked inward to strengthen their members against the harsh realities of postwar southern society. Few ministers dared to engage in or even support protest activities. Some, especially those in the Colored Methodist Episcopal Church, counseled congregants to abide by the rules of second-class citizenship and to trust in God's will to right the wrongs of racism. Northern-based denominations, however,

**HOW DID** Presidential Reconstruction differ from Congressional Reconstruction?

notably the AME Church, were more aggressive advocates of black rights. AME ministers stressed the responsibility of individual black people to realize God's will of racial equality.

The efforts of former slaves in the classroom, on the farm, in cities, and in the churches reflect the enthusiasm and expectations with which black southerners greeted freedom. But the majority of white southerners were unwilling to see those expectations fulfilled. For this reason, African Americans could not secure the fruits of their emancipation without the support and protection of the federal government. The issue of freedom was therefore inextricably linked to the other great issue of the era, the rejoining of the Confederacy to the Union, as expressed in federal Reconstruction policy.

# FEDERAL RECONSTRUCTION, 1865–1870

When the Civil War ended in 1865, no acceptable blueprint existed for reconstituting the Union. President Lincoln believed that a majority of white southerners were Unionists at heart, and that they could and should undertake the task of reconstruction. He favored a conciliatory policy toward the South in order, as he put it in one of his last letters, "to restore the Union, so as to make it . . . a Union of hearts and hands as well as of States." He counted on the loyalists to be fair with respect to the rights of the former slaves.

As early as 1863, Lincoln had proposed to readmit a seceding state if 10 percent of its prewar voters took an oath of loyalty to the Union, and it prohibited slavery in a new state constitution. But this Ten Percent Plan did not require states to grant equal civil and political rights to former slaves, and many Republicans in Congress thought it was not stringent enough. In 1864, a group of them responded with the Wade-Davis Bill, which required a majority of a state's prewar voters to pledge their loyalty to the Union and demanded guarantees of black equality before the law. The bill was passed at the end of a congressional session, but Lincoln kept it from becoming law by refusing to sign it (an action known as a "pocket veto") Lincoln, of course, died before he could implement a Reconstruction plan.

The controversy over the plans introduced during the war reflected two obstacles to Reconstruction that would continue to plague the ruling Republicans after the war. First, neither the Constitution nor legal precedent offered any guidance on whether the president or Congress should take the lead on Reconstruction policy. Second, there was no agreement on what that policy should be. Proposals requiring various preconditions for readmitting a state, loyalty oaths, new constitutions with certain specific provisions, guarantees of freedmen's rights, all provoked vigorous debate.

President Andrew Johnson, some conservative Republicans, and most Democrats believed that because the Constitution made no mention of secession, the southern states had been in rebellion but had never left the Union, and therefore that there was no need for a formal process to readmit them. Moderate and radical Republicans disagreed, arguing that the defeated states had forfeited their rights. Moderates and radicals parted company, however, on the conditions necessary for readmission to the Union. The radicals wanted to treat the former Confederate states as territories, or "conquered provinces," subject to congressional legislation. Moderates wanted to grant the seceding states more autonomy and limit federal intervention in their affairs while they satisfied the conditions of readmission. Neither group held a majority in Congress, and legislators sometimes changed their positions (see the Overview table, Contrasting Views of Reconstruction).

## PRESIDENTIAL RECONSTRUCTION, 1865–1867

When the Civil War ended in April 1865, Congress was not in session and would not reconvene until December. Thus, the responsibility for developing a Reconstruction policy initially fell on Andrew Johnson, who succeeded to the presidency upon Lincoln's assassination. Most northerners and many Republicans approved Johnson's Reconstruction plan when he unveiled it in May 1865. Johnson extended pardons and restored property rights, except in slaves, to southerners who swore an oath of allegiance to the Union and the Constitution. Southerners who had held prominent posts in the Confederacy, however, and those with more than $20,000 in taxable property, had to petition the president directly for a pardon. The plan said nothing about the voting rights or civil rights of former slaves.

Northern Democrats applauded the plan's silence on these issues and its promise of a quick restoration of the southern states to the Union. They expected the southern states to favor their party and expand its political power. Republicans approved the plan because it restored property rights to white southerners, although some wanted it to provide for black suffrage. Republicans also hoped that Johnson's conciliatory terms might attract some white southerners to the Republican Party.

On the two great issues of freedom and reunion, white southerners quickly demonstrated their eagerness to reverse the results of the Civil War. Although most states accepted President Johnson's modest requirements, several objected to one or more of them. Mississippi and Texas refused to ratify the Thirteenth Amendment, which abolished slavery. Alabama accepted only parts of the amendment. South Carolina declined to nullify its secession ordinance. No southern state authorized black voting. When Johnson ordered special congressional elections in the South in the fall of 1865, the all-white electorate returned many prominent Confederate leaders to office.

In late 1865, the newly elected southern state legislatures revised their antebellum slave codes. The updated **black codes** allowed local officials to arrest black people who could not document employment and residence or who were "disorderly" and sentence them to forced labor on farms or road crews. The codes also restricted black people to certain occupations, barred them from jury duty, and forbade them to possess firearms. Apprenticeship laws permitted judges to take black children from parents who could not, in the judges' view, adequately support them. Given the widespread poverty in the South in 1865, the law could apply to almost any freed black family. Northerners looking for contrition in the South found no sign of it. Worse, President Johnson did not seem perturbed about this turn of events.

The Republican-dominated Congress reconvened in December 1865 in a belligerent mood. A consensus formed among radical Republicans, who comprised nearly half of the party's strength in Congress, that to gain readmission, a state would have to extend suffrage to black citizens, protect freedmen's civil rights, and have its white citizens officially acknowledge these rights. Some radicals also supported the redistribution of land to former slaves, but few pressed for social equality. They envisioned a new South of modest farms, some owned by former slaves, and a Republican Party built on an alliance between black people and white loyalists.

But the radicals could not unite behind a program, and it fell to their moderate colleagues to take the first step toward a congressional Reconstruction plan. The moderates shared the radicals' desire to protect the former slaves' civil rights. But they would not support land-redistribution schemes or punitive measures against prominent Confederates, and disagreed on extending voting rights to the freedmen. The moderates' first measure, passed in early 1866, extended the life of the Freedmen's Bureau and authorized it to punish state officials who failed to extend equal civil rights to black citizens. But President Johnson vetoed the legislation.

**black codes**   Laws passed by states and municipalities denying many rights of citizenship to free blacks after the Civil war.

*Documents*

*Mississippi Black Code* (1865)

Selling a Freeman to Pay his Fine at Monticello, Florida. *This 1867 engraving shows how the black codes of the early Reconstruction era reduced former slaves to virtually their pre–Civil War status. Scenes like this convinced northerners that the white South was unrepentant and prompted congressional Republicans to devise their own Reconstruction plans.*

**Fourteenth Amendment** Passed by Congress in 1866, guaranteed every citizen equality before the law by prohibiting states from violating the civil rights of their citizens, thus outlawing the black codes.

*The Fourteenth Amendment* (1868)

Undeterred, Congress passed the Civil Rights Act of 1866 in direct response to the black codes. The act specified the civil rights to which all U.S. citizens were entitled. In creating a category of national citizenship with rights that superseded state laws, the act changed federal-state relations (and in the process overturned the *Dred Scott* decision). President Johnson vetoed the act, but it became law when Congress mustered a two-thirds majority to override his veto, the first time in American history that Congress passed major legislation over a president's veto.

To keep freedmen's rights safe from presidential vetoes, state legislatures, and federal courts, the Republican-dominated Congress moved to incorporate some of the provisions of the 1866 Civil Rights Act into the Constitution. The **Fourteenth Amendment,** which Congress passed in June 1866, addressed the issues of civil and voting rights. It guaranteed every citizen equality before the law. The two key sections of the amendment prohibited states from violating the civil rights of their citizens, thus outlawing the black codes, and gave states the choice of enfranchising black people or losing representation in Congress. Some radical Republicans expressed disappointment that

## AMERICAN VIEWS

### Mississippi's 1865 Black Codes

*W*hite southerners, especially landowners and business owners, feared that emancipation would produce a labor crisis; freedmen, they expected, would either refuse to work or strike hard bargains with their former masters. White southerners also recoiled from the prospect of having to treat their former slaves as full social equals. Thus, beginning in late 1865, several southern states, including Mississippi, enacted laws designed to control black labor, mobility, and social status. Northerners responded to the codes as a provocation, a bold move to deny the result of the war and its consequences.

- **How** did the black codes fit into President Andrew Johnson's Reconstruction program?
- **Some** northerners charged that the black codes were a backdoor attempt at reestablishing slavery. Do you agree?
- **If** southern states enacted black codes to stabilize labor relations, how did the provisions below effect that objective?

#### FROM AN ACT TO CONFER CIVIL RIGHTS ON FREEDMEN, AND FOR OTHER PURPOSES

**Section 1.** All freedmen, free negroes and mulattoes may sue and be sued, implead and be impleaded, in all the courts of law and equity of this State, and may acquire personal property, and choose in action, by descent or purchase, and may dispose of the same in the same manner and to the same extent that white persons may: Provided, That the provisions of this section shall not be so construed as to allow any freedman, free negro or mulatto to rent or lease any lands or tenements except in incorporated cities or towns, in which places the corporate authorities shall control the same.

**Section 7.** Every civil officer shall, and every person may, arrest and carry back to his or her legal employer any freedman, free negro, or mulatto who shall have quit the service of his or her employer before the expiration of his or her term of service without good cause; and said officer and person shall be entitled to receive for arresting and carrying back every deserting employee aforesaid the sum of five dollars, and ten cents per mile from the place of arrest to the place of delivery; and the same shall be paid by the employer, and held as a set off for so much against the wages of said deserting employee: Provided, that said arrested party, after being so returned, may appeal to the justice of the peace or member of the board of police of the county, who, on notice to the alleged employer, shall try summarily whether said appellant is legally employed by the alleged employer, and has good cause to quit said employer. Either party shall have the right of appeal to the county court, pending which the alleged deserter shall be remanded to the alleged employer or otherwise disposed of, as shall be right and just; and the decision of the county court shall be final.

#### FROM AN ACT TO AMEND THE VAGRANT LAWS OF THE STATE

**Section 2.** All freedmen, free negroes and mulattoes in this State, over the age of eighteen years, found on the second Monday in January, 1866, or thereafter, with no lawful employment or business, or found unlawfully assembling themselves together, either in the day or night time, and all white persons assembling themselves with freedmen, Free negroes or mulattoes, or usually associating with freedmen, free negroes or mulattoes, on terms of equality, or living in adultery or fornication with a freed woman, freed negro or mulatto, shall be deemed vagrants, and on conviction thereof shall be fined in a sum not exceeding, in the case of a freedman, free negro or mulatto, fifty dollars, and a white man two hundred dollars, and imprisonment at the discretion of the court, the free negro not exceeding ten days, and the white man not exceeding six months.

Source: "Laws in Relation to Freedmen," 39 Congress, 2 Session, Senate Executive Document 6, Freedmen's Affairs, 182–86.

the amendment, in a reflection of northern ambivalence, failed to give the vote to black people outright.

The amendment also disappointed advocates of woman suffrage, for the first time using the word *male* in the Constitution to define who could vote. Susan B. Anthony, who had campaigned for the abolition of slavery before the war and helped mount a petition drive that collected 400,000 signatures for the Thirteenth Amendment, founded the American Equal Rights Association in 1866 with her colleagues to push for woman suffrage at the state level.

The Fourteenth Amendment had little immediate impact on the South. Although enforcement of black codes diminished, white violence against black people increased. In the 1870s, several decisions by the U.S. Supreme Court weakened the amendment's provisions. Eventually, however, it would play a major role in securing the civil rights of African Americans.

President Johnson encouraged southern white intransigence by openly denouncing the Fourteenth Amendment. In August 1866, at the start of the congressional election campaign, he undertook an unprecedented tour of key northern states to sell his message of sectional reconciliation to the public. Although listeners appreciated Johnson's desire for peace, they questioned his claims of southern white loyalty to the Union. The president's diatribes against the Republican Congress won him followers in those northern states with a reservoir of opposition to black suffrage. But the tone and manner of his campaign offended many as undignified. In the November elections, the Democrats suffered embarrassing defeats in the North as Republicans managed better than two-thirds majorities in both the House and Senate, sufficient to override presidential vetoes. Radical Republicans, joined by moderate colleagues buoyed by the election results and revolted by the president's and the South's intransigence, seized the initiative when Congress reconvened.

**Congressional Reconstruction**   Name given to the period 1867–1870 when the Republican-dominated Congress controlled Reconstruction era policy.

## CONGRESSIONAL RECONSTRUCTION, 1867–1870

The radicals' first salvo in their attempt to take control of Reconstruction occurred with the passing over President Johnson's veto of the Military Reconstruction Acts. The measures, passed in March 1867, inaugurated a period known as **Congressional Reconstruction** or Radical Reconstruction. With the exception of Tennessee, the only southern state that had ratified the Fourteenth Amendment and been readmitted to the Union, Congress divided the former Confederate states into five military districts, each headed by a general (see Map 16–1). The commanders' first order of business was to conduct voter-registration campaigns to enroll black people and bar white people who had held office before the Civil War and supported the Confederacy. The eligible voters would then elect delegates to a state convention to write a new constitution that guaranteed universal manhood suffrage. Once a majority of eligible voters ratified the new constitution and the Fourteenth Amendment, their state would be eligible for readmission to the Union.

The Reconstruction Acts fulfilled the radicals' three major objectives. First, they secured the freedmen's right to vote. Second, they made it likely that southern states would be run by Republican regimes that would enforce the new constitutions, protect former

MAP EXPLORATION  To explore an interactive version of this map go to http://www.prenhall.com/goldfield5/map16.1

**MAP 16–1   Congressional Reconstruction, 1865–1877**   When Congress wrested control of Reconstruction policy from President Andrew Johnson, it divided the South into the five military districts depicted here. The commanding generals for each district held the authority both to hold elections and to decide who could vote.

**What did** each of the former Confederate states have to do to be eligible for readmission to the Union?

slaves' rights, and maintain the Republican majority in Congress. Finally, they set standards for readmission that required the South to accept the preeminence of the federal government and the end of slavery.

To limit presidential interference with their policies, Republicans passed the **Tenure of Office Act,** prohibiting the president from removing certain office-holders without the Senate's consent. Johnson, angered at what he believed was an unconstitutional attack on presidential authority, deliberately violated the act by firing Secretary of War Edwin M. Stanton, a leading radical, in February 1868. The House responded by approving articles of impeachment against a president for the first time in American history. That set the stage for the next step prescribed by the Constitution: a Senate trial to determine whether the president should be removed from office.

Johnson had indeed violated the Tenure of Office Act, a measure of dubious constitutionality even to some Republicans, but enough Republicans felt that his actions fell short of the "high crimes and misdemeanors" standard set by the Constitution for dismissal from office. Seven Republicans deserted their party, and Johnson was acquitted. The seven Republicans who voted against their party did so not out of respect for Johnson but because they feared that a conviction would damage the office of the presidency and violate the constitutional separation of powers. The outcome weakened the radicals and eased the way for Grant, a moderate Republican, to gain the party's nomination for president in 1868.

The Republicans viewed the 1868 presidential election as a referendum on Congressional Reconstruction. They supported black suffrage in the South but equivocated on allowing African Americans to vote in the North. Black northerners could vote in only eight of the twenty-two northern states, and between 1865 and 1869, white northerners rejected equal suffrage referendums in eight of eleven states. Republicans "waved the bloody shirt," reminding voters of Democratic disloyalty, the sacrifices of war, and the peace only Republicans could redeem. Democrats denounced Congressional Reconstruction as federal tyranny and, in openly racist appeals, warned white voters that a Republican victory would mean black rule. Grant won the election, but his margin of victory was uncomfortably narrow. Reflecting growing ambivalence in the North over issues of race and federal authority, New York's Horatio Seymour, the Democratic presidential nominee, probably carried a majority of the nation's white vote. Black voters' overwhelming support for Grant probably provided his margin of victory.

The Republicans retained a strong majority in both houses of Congress and managed to pass another major piece of Reconstruction legislation, the **Fifteenth Amendment,** in February 1869. In response to growing concerns about voter fraud and violence against freedmen, the amendment guaranteed the right of American men to vote, regardless of race. Although the amendment provided a loophole allowing

White man's government cartoon. *Courtesy of the Library of Congress.*

## QUICK REVIEW

### Radical Republican Objectives

- Secure freedmen's right to vote.
- Make it likely that southern states would have Republican governments.
- Require the South to accept preeminence of the federal government and the end of slavery.

**Tenure of Office Act** Passed by the Republican controlled Congress in 1867 to limit presidential interference with its policies, the Act prohibited the president from removing certain office-holders without the Senate's consent.

**Fifteenth Amendment** Passed by Congress in 1869, guaranteed the right of American men to vote, regardless of race.

## OVERVIEW Contrasting Views of Reconstruction: President and Congress

| Politician or Group | Policy on Former Slaves | Policy on Readmission of Former Confederate States |
|---|---|---|
| President Johnson | Opposed to black suffrage | Maintained that rebellious states were already readmitted |
| | Silent on protection of black civil rights | Granted pardons and restoration of property to all who swore allegiance to the United States |
| | Opposed to land redistribution | |
| Radical Republicans | Favored black suffrage | Favored treating rebellious states as territories and establishing military districts* |
| | Favored protection of black civil rights | Favored limiting franchise to black people and loyal white people |
| | Favored land redistribution | |
| Moderate Republicans | Favored black suffrage* | Favored some restrictions on white suffrage** |
| | Favored protection of civil rights | Favored requiring states to meet various requirements before being readmitted* |
| | Opposed land redistribution | Split on military rule |

*After 1866.
**True of most but not all members of the group.

### QUICK REVIEW

**The Tenure of Office Act and Johnson's Impeachment**

- Act prohibited the president from removing certain officeholders without the Senate's consent.
- Johnson deliberately violated the act in February 1868.
- Johnson escaped impeachment by one vote.

**From Then to Now Online**
*African American Voting Rights in the South*

**Address from the Colored Citizens of Norfolk, Virginia, to the People of the United States** (1865)

states to restrict the right to vote based on literacy or property qualifications, it was nonetheless a milestone. It made the right to vote perhaps the most distinguishing characteristic of U.S. citizenship.

The Fifteenth Amendment allowed states to keep the franchise a male prerogative, angering many in the woman-suffrage movement more than had the Fourteenth Amendment. The resulting controversy severed the ties between the movement and Republican politics. Susan B. Anthony broke with her abolitionist colleagues and opposed the amendment. In an appeal brimming with ethnic and racial animosity, Elizabeth Cady Stanton warned that "if you do not wish the lower orders of Chinese, African, Germans and Irish, with their low ideas of womanhood to make laws for you and your daughters . . . awake to the danger . . . and demand that woman, too, shall be represented in the government!" Such language created a major rift in the nascent women's movement.

### SOUTHERN REPUBLICAN GOVERNMENTS, 1867–1870

Away from Washington, the first order of business for the former Confederacy was to draft state constitutions. The documents embodied progressive principles new to the South. They mandated the election of numerous local and state offices. Self-perpetuating local elites could no longer appoint themselves or cronies to powerful positions. The constitutions committed southern states, many for the first time, to public education. Lawmakers enacted a variety of reforms, including social welfare, penal reform, legislative reapportionment, and universal manhood suffrage.

The Republican regimes that gained control in southern states promoted vigorous state government and the protection of civil and voting rights. Three Republican constituencies supported these governments: native whites, native blacks, and northern transplants. The native white group was mostly made up of yeomen farmers. Residing mainly in the upland regions of the South and long ignored by lowland planters and merchants in state government, they were left devastated by the war. They struggled to keep their land and hoped for an easing of credit and for debt-stay laws to help them escape foreclosure. They wanted public schools for their children and good roads to get their crops to market. Some urban merchants and large planters also called themselves Republicans. They were attracted to the party's emphasis on economic development, especially railroad construction, and would become prominent in Republican leadership after 1867, forming a majority of the party's elected officials. Collectively, opponents called these native white southerners **scalawags.**

Northern transplants, or **carpetbaggers,** as many southern whites called them, constituted a second group of southern Republicans. Thousands of northerners came south during and after the war. Many were Union soldiers who simply enjoyed the climate and perhaps married a local woman. Most were drawn by economic opportunity. Land was cheap and the price of cotton high. Although most carpetbaggers had supported the Republican Party before they moved south, few became politically active until the cotton economy nosedived in 1866. Financial concerns were not all that motivated carpetbaggers to enter politics; some hoped to aid the freedmen.

Carpetbaggers never comprised more than 2 percent of any state's population. Most white southerners viewed them as an alien presence, instruments of a hated occupying force. Because many of them tended to support extending political and civil rights to black southerners, carpetbaggers were also often at odds with their fellow white Republicans, the scalawags.

African Americans constituted the Republican Party's largest southern constituency. In three states, South Carolina, Mississippi, and Louisiana, they also constituted the majority of eligible voters. They viewed the franchise as the key to civic equality and economic opportunity and demanded an active role in party and government affairs.

Black people began to take part in southern politics even before the end of the Civil War, especially in cities occupied by Union forces. In February 1865, black people in Norfolk, Virginia, gathered to demand a say in the new government that Union supporters were forming in that portion of the state. In April, they created the Colored Monitor Union club, modeled after regular Republican Party organizations in northern cities, called **Union Leagues.** They demanded "the right of universal suffrage" for "all loyal men, without distinction of color." Black people in other southern cities held similar meetings, seeking inclusion in the democratic process to protect their freedom. Despite white threats, black southerners thronged to Union League meetings in 1867, even

**scalawags**   Southern whites, mainly small landowning farmers and well-off merchants and planters, who supported the Southern Republican party during Reconstruction.

**carpetbaggers**   Northern transplants to the South, many of whom were Union soldiers who stayed in the South after the war.

**Union Leagues**   Republican party organizations in Northern cities that became an important organizing device among freedmen in Southern cities after 1865.

"Time Works Wonders," This Thomas Nast cartoon has Jefferson Davis, former President of the Confederacy, dressed as Iago in William Shakespeare's play *Othello,* declaring with considerable anguish, "For that I suspect the Lusty moor [Othello] hath leap'd into my seat: the thought where of doth like a poisonous mineral gnaw my inwards," Indeed, Hiram Revels occupies Davis's old seat in the U.S. Senate representing the state of Mississippi in 1870.

forging interracial alliances in states such as North Carolina and Alabama. Focusing on political education and recruitment, the leagues successfully mobilized black voters. In 1867, more than 90 percent of eligible black voters across the South turned out for elections. Black women, even though they could not vote, also played a role. During the 1868 presidential campaign, for example, black maids and cooks in the South wore buttons touting the candidacy of the Republican presidential nominee, Ulysses S. Grant.

Black southerners were not content just to vote; they also demanded political office. White Republican leaders in the South often took the black vote for granted. But on several occasions after 1867, black people threatened to run independent candidates, support rival Democrats, or simply stay home unless they were represented among Republican nominees. These demands brought them some success. The number of southern black congressmen in the U.S. House of Representatives increased from two in 1869 to seven in 1873, and more than 600 African Americans, most of them former slaves from plantation counties, were elected to southern state legislatures between 1867 and 1877.

White fears that black officeholders would enact vengeful legislation proved unfounded. African Americans generally did not promote race-specific legislation. Rather, they supported measures such as debt relief and state funding for education that benefited all poor and working-class people. Like all politicians, however, black officials in southern cities sought to enact measures beneficial to their constituents, such as roads and sidewalks.

During the first few years of Congressional Reconstruction, Republican governments walked a tightrope, attempting to lure moderate Democrats and unaffiliated white voters into the party without slighting the black vote. They used the lure of patronage power and the attractive salaries that accompanied public office. In 1868, for example, Louisiana's Republican governor, Henry C. Warmoth, appointed white conservatives to state and local offices, which he divided equally between Confederate veterans and black people, and repealed a constitutional provision disfranchising former Confederate officials.

Republicans also gained support by expanding the role of state government to a degree unprecedented in the South. Southern Republican administrations appealed to hard-pressed upland white constituents by prohibiting foreclosure and passing stay laws that allowed farm owners additional time to repay debts. They undertook building programs that benefited black and white citizens, erecting hospitals, schools, and orphanages. Stepping further into social policy than most northern states at the time, Republican governments in the South expanded women's property rights, enacted legislation against child abuse, and required child support from fathers of mulatto children. In South Carolina, the Republican government provided medical care for the poor; in Alabama, it provided free legal aid for needy defendants.

Despite these impressive policies, southern Republicans were unable to hold their diverse constituency together. The excesses of some state governments, high taxes, contests over patronage, and conflicts over the relative roles of white and black party members opened rifts in Republican ranks. Patronage triggered intraparty warfare. Every office secured by a Democrat created a disappointed Republican. Class tensions erupted in the party as economic development policies sometimes superseded relief and social service legislation supported by small farmers. The failure of Alabama Republicans to deliver on promises of debt relief and land redistribution eroded the party's support among upcountry white voters. There were differences among black voters too. In the Lower South, divisions that had developed in the prewar era between urban, lighter-skinned free black people and darker, rural slaves persisted into the Reconstruction era. In many southern states, black clergy, because of their independence from white support and their important spiritual and educational role, became leaders. But most preached salvation in the next world rather than equality in this one, conceding more to white people than their rank-and-file constituents.

# COUNTER-RECONSTRUCTION, 1870–1874

Republicans might have survived battles over patronage, policy, expenditures, and taxes. But they could not overcome racism and the violence it generated. Racism killed Republican rule in the South because it deepened divisions within the party, encouraged white violence, and eroded support in the North. Southern Democrats discovered that they could use race baiting and racial violence to create solidarity among white people that overrode their economic and class differences. Unity translated into election victories.

Northerners responded to the persistent violence in the South, not with outrage, but with a growing sense of tedium. They came to accept the arguments of white southerners that it was folly to allow black people to vote and hold office. Racism became respectable.

By 1874, Americans were concerned with an array of domestic problems that overshadowed Reconstruction. A serious economic depression left them more preoccupied with survival than racial justice. Corruption convinced many that politics was part of the nation's problems, not a solution to them. With the rest of the nation thus distracted and weary, white southerners reclaimed control of the South.

**WHAT ROLE** did violence play in the Counter-Reconstruction?

## THE USES OF VIOLENCE

Racial violence preceded Republican rule. As African Americans moved about, attempted to vote, haggled over labor contracts, and carried arms as part of the occupying Union

The Klan directed violence at African Americans primarily for engaging in political activity. Here, a black man, John Campbell, vainly begs for mercy in Moore County, North Carolina, in August 1871.

forces, they tested the patience of white southerners, to whom any black assertion of equality seemed threatening.

**Ku Klux Klan**    Perhaps the most prominent of the vigilante groups that terrorized black people in the South during the Reconstruction era, founded by the Confederate veterans in 1866.

White paramilitary groups were responsible for much of the violence directed against African Americans. Probably the best-known of these groups was the **Ku Klux Klan.** Founded in Tennessee by six Confederate veterans in 1866, the Klan was initially a social club. Within a year, the Klan had spread throughout the South. In 1867, when black people entered politics in large numbers, the Klan unleashed a wave of terror against them. The Klan directed much of its violence toward subverting the electoral process. One historian has estimated that roughly 10 percent of all black delegates to the 1867 state constitutional conventions in the South became victims of political violence during the next decade.

Not all Klan attacks had political objectives. Klansmen struck against anyone, black or white, who they believed had violated racial boundaries. A Georgia Klansman murdered a freedman because he could read and write. Klansmen in Florence, South Carolina, killed a black man who rented a plantation "because such a thing ought not to be." And in 1868, Klansmen murdered three southern white Republican Georgia state legislators. Membership in the Klan crossed class lines. Race became an issue on which white people, regardless of differing economic interests, could agree.

*Documents*

Albion W. Tourgee, *Letter on Ku Klux Klan Activities* (1870)

By 1868, white paramilitary organizations permeated the South. Violence was particularly severe in election years in Louisiana, which had a large and active black electorate. The most serious example of political violence in Louisiana, if not in the entire South, occurred in Colfax in 1873, when a white Democratic mob attempted to wrest control of local government from Republicans. For three weeks, black defenders held the town against the white onslaught. When the white mob finally broke through, they massacred the remaining black defenders, including those who had surrendered and laid down their weapons.

Racial violence and the combative reaction it provoked both among black people and Republican administrations energized white voters. Democrats regained power in North Carolina, for example, after the state's Republican governor enraged white voters by calling out the militia to counter white violence during the election of 1870. That same year, the Republican regime in Georgia fell as well.

**QUICK REVIEW**

**The Legislative Responses to Political Violence in the South**

♦ 15th Amendment guaranteed the right to vote.

♦ Enforcement Act of 1870 authorized federal supervision of elections in states that failed to support voting rights.

♦ Ku Klux Klan Act of 1871 permitted federal prosecution of members of groups that denied citizen's civil rights if state authorities failed to act.

The federal government responded with a variety of legislation. One example was the Fifteenth Amendment, ratified in 1869, which guaranteed the right to vote. Another was the Enforcement Act of 1870, which authorized the federal government to appoint supervisors in states that failed to protect voting rights. When violence and intimidation persisted, Congress followed with a second, more sweeping measure, the Ku Klux Klan Act of 1871. This law permitted federal authorities, with military assistance, if necessary, to arrest and prosecute members of groups that denied a citizen's civil rights if state authorities failed to do so. The Klan Act was not successful in curbing racial violence, as the Colfax Massacre in 1873 made vividly clear. But with it, Congress, by claiming the right to override state authority to bring individuals to justice, established a new precedent in federal-state relations.

## NORTHERN INDIFFERENCE

The success of political violence after 1871 reflected both a declining commitment on the part of northern Republicans to support southern Republican administrations and a growing indifference of northerners to the major issues of Reconstruction. That northern base grew increasingly skeptical about Reconstruction policy in general and assistance to the freedmen in particular. Northern Republicans looked around their cities and many saw the local political scene infested with unqualified immigrant voters and corruption. New York City's Democratic boss William M. Tweed and his associates bilked the city of an astounding $100 million dollars. When white southerners charged that unqualified blacks and grasping carpetbaggers corrupted the political process in the South, northerners recognized the argument.

Changing perceptions in the North also indicated a convergence of racial views with white southerners. As radical Republican Congressman from Indiana, George W. Julian admitted in 1865, white northerners "*hate the negro.*" They expressed this hatred in their rejection of black suffrage, racially segregated their African American population, and in periodic violence against black residents, such as during the New York draft riots of 1863. Northerners' views were bolstered by prevailing scientific theories of race that "proved" blacks' limited capacities and, therefore, unfitness for either the ballot or skilled occupations.

By the early 1870s, northern public opinion had shifted greatly with respect to black suffrage, in part because of the growing concern about the immigrant vote in northern cities; whereas in the late 1860s cartoons and the press depicted newly enfranchised African Americans nobly, later representations were hostile as this caricature of the South Carolina legislature by Thomas Nast demonstrates.

QUICK REVIEW

**Sources of Northern Indifference**

◆ Growing skepticism about the potential of Reconstruction

◆ Convergence of racial views of whites in the North and the South

◆ Increased distrust of federal power

Northerners also grew increasingly wary of federal power. The emerging scandals of the Grant administration, fueled, it seemed, by government subsidies to railroads and other private businesses, demanded a scaling back of federal power and discretion. When white southerners complained about federal meddling, again, they found resonance in the North.

The excesses and alleged abuses of federal power inspired a reform movement among a group of northern Republicans and some Democrats. In addition, business leaders decried the ability of wealthy lobbyists to influence economic decisions. An influential group of intellectuals and opinion makers lamented the inability of politicians to understand "natural" laws, particularly those related to race. And some Republicans joined the reform movement out of fear that Democrats would capitalize on the turmoil in the South and the political scandals in the North to reap huge electoral victories in 1872.

## LIBERAL REPUBLICANS AND THE ELECTION OF 1872

Liberal Republicans, as the reformers called themselves, put forward an array of suggestions to improve government and save the Republican Party. They advocated civil service reform to reduce reliance on patronage and the abuses that accompanied office seeking. To limit government and reduce artificial economic stimuli, the reformers called for tariff reduction and an end to federal land grants to railroads. For the South, they recommended a general amnesty for white people and a return to "local self-government" by men of "property and enterprise."

When the Liberals failed to convince other Republicans to adopt their program, they broke with the party. Taking advantage of this split, the Democrats forged an alliance with the Liberals. Together, they nominated journalist Horace Greeley to challenge Ulysses S. Grant for the presidency in the election of 1872. Grant won resoundingly, helped by high turnout among black voters in the South.

The election suggested that the Grant administration had not yet exhausted public tolerance and that the Republican experiment in the South retained some public support. Within a year, however, an economic depression, continued violence in the South, and the persistent corruption of the Grant administration would erode the last remnants of support for Reconstruction and black rights in the South.

## ECONOMIC TRANSFORMATION

After 1873, the Republican Party in the South became a liability for the national party, especially as Americans fastened on economic issues. The major story of the decade would not be equal rights for African Americans, but the changing nature of the American economy. An overextended banking and credit system generated the Panic of 1873 and caused extended suffering, particularly among working-class Americans. But the depression masked a remarkable economic transformation as the nation moved toward a national industrial economy.

The depression and the economic transformation occupied center stage in the American mentality of the mid-1870s, at least in the North. Most Americans had mentally forsaken Reconstruction long before the Compromise of 1877 made its abandonment a political fact. The sporadic violence against black and white Republicans in the South, and the cries of help from freedmen as their rights and persons were abused by white Democrats, became distant echoes from another era, the era of the Civil War, now commemorated and memorialized, but no longer an active part of the nation's present and future. Of course, for white southerners, the past was not yet past. There was still work to do.

# REDEMPTION, 1874–1877

For southern Democrats, the Republican victory in 1872 underscored the importance of turning out larger numbers of white voters and restricting the black vote. They accomplished these goals over the next four years with a surge in political violence, secure in the knowledge that federal authorities would rarely intervene against them. Preoccupied with corruption and economic crisis and increasingly indifferent, if not hostile, to African American aspirations, most Americans looked the other way. The elections of 1876 confirmed the triumph of white southerners.

In a religious metaphor that matched their view of the Civil War as a lost crusade, southern Democrats called their victory "Redemption" and depicted themselves as **Redeemers,** holy warriors who had saved the South from the hell of black Republican rule. Generations of American boys and girls would learn this interpretation of the Reconstruction era, and it would affect race relations for nearly a century.

**WHY DID** the federal government abandon African Americans after 1872?

**Redeemers** Southern Democrats who wrested control of governments in the former Confederacy, often through electoral fraud and violence, from Republican, beginning in 1870.

## THE DEMOCRATS' VIOLENT RESURGENCE

The violence between 1874 and 1876 differed in several respects from earlier attempts to restore white government by force. Attackers operated more openly and more closely identified themselves with the Democratic Party. Mounted, gray-clad ex-Confederate soldiers

As this Thomas Nast cartoon makes clear, the paramilitary violence against black southerners in the early 1870s threatened not only the voting rights of freedmen, but their dreams of education, prosperity, and family life. In this context, the slogan "The Union As It Was" is highly ironic.

flanked Democratic candidates at campaign rallies and "visited" black neighborhoods afterward to discourage black men from voting. With black people intimidated and white people already prepared to vote, election days were typically quiet.

Democrats swept to victory across the South in the 1874 elections. "A perfect reign of terror" redeemed Alabama for the Democrats. The successful appeal to white supremacy inspired a massive white turnout to unseat Republicans in Virginia, Florida (legislature only), and Arkansas. Texas had fallen to the Democrats in 1873. Only South Carolina, Mississippi, and Louisiana, states with large black populations, survived the debacle. But the relentless tide of terror would soon overwhelm them as well.

## THE WEAK FEDERAL RESPONSE

When Governor Daniel H. Chamberlain could no longer contain the violence in South Carolina in 1876, he asked the president for help. Grant acknowledged the gravity of Chamberlain's situation but would offer him only the lame hope that South Carolinians would exercise "better judgment and cooperation" and assist the governor in bringing offenders to justice "without aid from the federal Government."

Congress responded to blacks' deteriorating status in the South with the Civil Rights Act of 1875. The act prohibited discrimination against black people in public accommodations, such as theaters, parks, and trains, and guaranteed freedmen's rights to serve on juries. It had no provision for voting rights, which Congress presumed the Fifteenth Amendment protected. Most judges, however, either interpreted the law narrowly or declared it unconstitutional. In 1883, the U.S. Supreme Court agreed and overturned the act, declaring that only the states, not Congress, could redress "a private wrong, or a crime of the individual."

## THE ELECTION OF 1876 AND THE COMPROMISE OF 1877

Reconstruction officially ended with the presidential election of 1876, in which the Democrat Samuel J. Tilden ran against the Republican Rutherford B. Hayes. When the ballots were counted, it appeared that Tilden, a conservative New Yorker respectable enough for northern voters and Democratic enough for white southerners, had won. But despite a majority in the popular vote, disputed returns in three southern states left him with only 184 of the 185 electoral votes needed to win. The three states—Florida, South Carolina, and Louisiana—were the last in the South still to have Republican adminstrations.

Both camps maneuvered intensively in the following months to claim the disputed votes. Congress appointed a 15-member commission to settle the issue. Because the Republicans controlled Congress, they held a one-vote majority on the commission.

Southern Democrats wanted Tilden to win, but they wanted control of their states more. They were willing to deal. Hayes intended to remove federal support from the remaining southern Republican governments anyway. It thus cost him nothing to promise to do so in exchange for the contested electoral votes. The so-called **Compromise of 1877** installed Hayes in the White House and gave Democrats control of every state government in the South. Southern Democrats emerged the major winners from the Compromise of 1877. President Hayes and his successors into the next century left the South alone. In practical terms, the Compromise signaled the revocation of civil rights and voting rights for black southerners. The Fourteenth and Fifteenth Amendments would be dead letters in the South until well into the twentieth century. On the two great issues confronting the nation at the end of the Civil War, reunion and freedom, the white South had won. It reentered the Union largely on its own terms with the freedom to pursue a racial agenda consistent with its political, economic, and social interests.

**Compromise of 1877** The Congressional settling of the 1876 election which installed Republican Rutherford B. Hayes in the White House and gave Democrats control of all state governments in the South.

## THE MEMORY OF RECONSTRUCTION

Southern Democrats used the memory of Reconstruction to help maintain themselves in power. Reconstruction joined the Lost Cause as part of the glorious fight to preserve the civilization of the Old South. As white southerners elevated Civil War heroes into saints and battles into holy struggles, they equated Reconstruction with Redemption. For white southerners, white Democrats in particular, had rescued the South from a purgatory of black rule and federal oppression. The southern view of Reconstruction permeated textbooks, films, and standard accounts of the period. By the early 1900s, professional historians at the nation's finest institutions concurred in this view, ignoring contrary evidence and rendering the story of African Americans invisible. By that time, therefore, most Americans believed that the policies of Reconstruction had been misguided and had brought great suffering to the white South. The widespread acceptance of this view allowed the South to maintain its system of racial segregation and exclusion without interference from the federal government.

The national historical consensus grew out of a growing national reconciliation concerning the war, a mutual agreement that both sides had fought courageously and that it was time to move on. Hidden in all the goodwill was the tacit agreement between southern and northern whites that the South was now free to work out its own resolution to race relations. Reconstruction rested on a national consensus of African American inferiority.

# THE FAILED PROMISE OF RECONSTRUCTION

If the demise of Reconstruction elicited a resounding indifference from most white Americans, black southerners greeted it with frustration. Their dreams of land ownership faded as a new labor system relegated them to a lowly position in southern agriculture. Redemption reversed their economic and political gains and deprived them of most of the civil rights they had enjoyed under Congressional Reconstruction. Although they continued to vote into the 1890s, they had by 1877 lost most of the voting strength and political offices they held. Rather than becoming part of southern society, they were increasingly set apart from it, valued only for their labor.

**HOW AND** why did Reconstruction end?

Still, the former slaves were better off in 1877 than in 1865. They were free, however limited their freedom. Some owned land; some held jobs in cities. They raised their families in relative peace and experienced the spiritual joys of a full religious life. They socialized freely with relatives and friends, and they moved about. The Reconstruction amendments to the Constitution guaranteed an array of civil and political rights, and eventually these guarantees would form the basis of the civil rights revolution after World War II. But that outcome was long, too long, in the future. By 1877, the "golden moment," an unprecedented opportunity for the nation to live up to its ideals by extending equal rights to all its citizens, black and white alike, had passed.

**Interpreting the Past**
*Realities of Freedom* (pp. 494–495)

## MODEST GAINS AND FUTURE VICTORIES

Black southerners experienced some advances in the decade after the Civil War, but these owed little to Reconstruction. Black families functioned as economic and psychological buffers against unemployment and prejudice. Black churches played crucial roles in their communities. Self-help and labor organizations offered mutual friendship and financial assistance. All of these institutions had existed in the slavery era, although on a smaller scale. And some of them, such as black labor groups, schools, and social welfare associations, endured because comparable white institutions excluded black people.

**Exploring America**
*Did Reconstruction Work for the Freed People?*

## OVERVIEW Constitutional Amendments and Federal Legislation of the Reconstruction Era

| Amendment or Legislation | Purpose | Significance |
|---|---|---|
| Thirteenth Amendment (passed and ratified in 1865) | Prevented southern states from reestablishing slavery after the war | Final step toward full emancipation of slaves |
| Freedmen's Bureau Act (1865) | Oversight of resettlement, labor for former slaves | Involved the federal government directly in relief, education, and assisting the transition from slavery to freedom; worked fitfully to achieve this objective during its seven-year career |
| Southern Homestead Act (1866) | Provided black people preferential access to public lands in five southern states | Lack of capital and poor quality of federal land thwarted the purpose of the act |
| Civil Rights Act of 1866 | Defined rights of national citizenship | Marked an important change in federal-state relations, tilting balance of power to national government |
| Fourteenth Amendment (passed 1866; ratified 1868) | Prohibited states from violating the rights of their citizens | Strengthened the Civil Rights Act of 1866 and guaranteed all citizens equality before the law |
| Military Reconstruction Acts (1867) | Set new rules for the readmission of former Confederate states into the Union and secured black voting rights | Initiated Congressional Reconstruction |
| Tenure of Office Act (1867) | Required congressional approval for the removal of any official whose appointment had required Senate confirmation | A congressional challenge to the president's right to dismiss cabinet members; led to President Andrew Johnson's impeachment trial |
| Fifteenth Amendment (passed 1869; ratified 1870) | Guaranteed the right of all American male citizens to vote regardless of race | The basis for black voting rights |
| Civil Rights Act of 1875 | Prohibited racial discrimination in jury selection, public transportation, and public accommodations | Rarely enforced; Supreme Court declared it Unconstitutional in 1883 |

Black people also scored some modest economic successes during the Reconstruction era, mainly from their own pluck. In the Lower South, black per capita income increased 46 percent between 1857 and 1879, compared with a 35 percent decline in white per capita income. Sharecropping, oppressive as it was, represented an advance over forced and gang labor. Collectively, black people owned more than $68 million worth of property in 1870, a 240 percent increase over 1860, but the average worth of each was only $408.

The Fourteenth and Fifteenth Amendments to the Constitution are among the few bright spots in Reconstruction's otherwise dismal legacy. The Fourteenth Amendment guaranteed former slaves equality before the law; the Fifteenth Amendment protected their right to vote. Both amendments elevated the federal government over the states by protecting freedmen from state attempts to deny them their rights. But the benefits of these two landmark amendments did not accrue to African Americans until well into the twentieth century. White southerners effectively nullified the Reconstruction amendments, and the

U.S. Supreme Court virtually interpreted them, and other Reconstruction legislation, out of existence.

In the **Slaughterhouse cases** (1873), the Supreme Court contradicted the intent of the Fourteenth Amendment by decreeing that most citizenship rights remained under state, not federal, control. In **United States v. Cruikshank** (1876), the Court overturned the convictions of some of those responsible for the Colfax Massacre, ruling that the Enforcement Act applied only to violations of black rights by states, not individuals. Within the next two decades, the Supreme Court would uphold the legality of racial segregation and black disfranchisement, in effect declaring that the Fourteenth and Fifteenth Amendments did not apply to African Americans.

# CONCLUSION

White southerners robbed black southerners of their gains and sought to reduce them again to servitude and dependence, if not to slavery. But in the process, the majority of white southerners lost as well. Yeoman farmers missed an opportunity to break cleanly from the Old South and establish a more equitable society. Instead, they allowed the old elites to regain power and gradually ignore their needs. They preserved the social benefit of a white skin at the cost of almost everything else. Many lost their farms and sank into tenancy. Few had a voice in state legislatures or the U.S. Congress. A new South, rid of slavery and sectional antagonism, had indeed emerged—redeemed, regenerated, and disenthralled. But the old South lingered on.

As federal troops left the South, an era of possibility for American society ended, and a new era began. "The southern question is dead," a Charleston newspaper proclaimed in 1877. "The question of labor and capital, work and wages" had moved to the forefront. The chance to redeem the sacrifice of a bloody civil war with a society that fulfilled the promise of the Declaration of Independence and the Constitution for all citizens slipped away. It would take a new generation of African Americans a long century later to revive it.

# SUMMARY

HOW DID Southerners remember the war? How did it shape their response to Reconstruction?

**The southern white view of the Civil War (and of Reconstruction)** was a need to justify and rationalize the devastation that accompanied defeat. This view, in which the war became the Lost Cause, and Reconstruction became the Redemption, served to forge a community among white southerners at a time of great unrest. The Lost Cause enabled white southerners to move on with their lives and concentrate on rebuilding their shattered region. Elevating the Civil War to a noble, holy enterprise implied a stainless Old South, a civilization worth fighting and dying for. This new history required the return of the freedmen, if not to the status of slaves, then at least to a lowly place in society.

WHAT WERE African Americans' hopes for Reconstruction?

**More than Freedom: African-American Aspirations in 1865** Former slaves wanted to be free of white supervision; they also desired land, voting and civil rights, and education. At the end of the Civil War, African Americans had reason to hope their dreams might be achieved through such actions as the establishment of the Freedmen's Bureau. The vast majority of former slaves was never able to realize their dreams of independent land ownership and continued to work as farm laborers; others migrated to cities. Their religious faith inspired them; they saw their emancipation in biblical terms and the church became the primary focus of the African-American community.

HOW DID Presidential Reconstruction differ from Congressional Reconstruction?

**Federal Reconstruction, 1865–1870** The federal government had two great challenges following the Civil War; supporting the freedom of former slaves and rejoining the Confederacy to the Union. No blueprint for Reconstruction existed; the Constitution was silent on the issue and there was no agreement on policy. Presidential Reconstruction and Congressional Reconstruction brought mixed results. The Civil Rights Act and the Fourteenth and Fifteenth Amendments were key legislative acts during this period; however, by 1870, white Southerners were gradually regaining control of their states and using violence and intimidation to erode gains made by African Americans.

WHAT ROLE did violence play in the Counter-Reconstruction?

**Counter-Reconstruction, 1870–1874** While most of the nation was distracted by political scandals and a serious economic depression, white Southerners regained control of the South. Racial violence through groups like the Ku Klux Klan subverted the electoral process; the success of political violence reflected the erosion of Northern support for Congressional Reconstruction.

WHY DID the federal government abandon African-Americans after 1872?

**Redemption, 1874–1877** After more than fifteen years of Reconstruction, Republicans lost interest in policing their former enemies. By 1877 the Redeemers had triumphed, and all the former Confederate states had returned to the Union in the Compromise of 1877 following the disputed 1876 presidential election. Southern states now had all of their rights and many of their leaders restored to pre-Civil War conditions. Freed slaves remained in mostly subservient positions with few of the rights and privileges enjoyed by other Americans.

HOW AND why did Reconstruction end?

**The Failed Promise of Reconstruction** The tacit agreement between Southern and Northern whites was that the South was now free to work out its own resolution to race relations. The price of sectional reconciliation was that the dream that former slaves held of economic independence and equality would not materialize. The Fourteenth and Fifteenth Amendments were bright spots in the legacy of Reconstruction; the overwhelming majority of African Americans had become landless agricultural workers, eking out a meager income that merchants and landlords often snatched to cover debts. For most, Reconstruction was a failed promise.

# WHERE TO LEARN MORE

**Penn Center Historic District, St. Helena Island, South Carolina.** The Penn School was a sea-island experiment in the education of free black people established by northern missionaries Laura Towne and Ellen Murray in 1862. They operated it until their deaths in the early 1900s. The Penn School became Penn Community Services in 1948, serving as an educational institution, health clinic, and a social service agency. See its website at **www.penncenter.com**

**Hampton University Museum, Hampton, Virginia.** Hampton University was founded by the Freedmen's Bureau in 1868 to provide "practical" training in the agricultural and mechanical fields for former slaves. In addition to a history of the institution, the museum includes one of the oldest collections of African art in the United States. Its website is at **www.hamptonu.edu/museum**

**Beauvoir, Biloxi, Mississippi.** The exhibits at Beauvoir, the home of Jefferson Davis, evoke the importance of the Lost Cause for the white survivors of the Confederacy. Especially interesting is the Jefferson Davis Soldiers Home on the premises and the Confederate Veterans Cemetery. Davis spent his retirement in Beauvoir. Go to **www.beauvoir.org**

**Levi Jordan Plantation, Brazoria County, Texas.** This site provides an excellent depiction and interpretation of the lives of sharecroppers and tenants during and immediately after the Reconstruction era. The site is especially valuable for demonstrating the transition from slavery to sharecropping. Go to **www.webarchaeology.com**

# STUDY RESOURCES

## myhistorylab

For study resources for this chapter, go to www.myhistorylab .com and choose *The American Journey*. You will find a wealth of study and review material for this chapter, including pre- and post-tests, customized study plan, key term review flash cards, interactive map and document activities, and documents for analysis.

# REVIEW QUESTIONS

1. Both Russia and America hoped to develop a free-labor agricultural class after their respective emancipations. Why didn't these governments follow through on their own objectives?

2. Given the different perspectives on the Civil War's outcome and what the social structure of a postwar South should be, was there any common ground between southern white and southern black on which to forge a Reconstruction policy?

3. Black people did achieve some notable gains during Reconstruction, despite its overall failure. What were those gains?

4. In T. Thomas Fortune's recollection of a boyhood incident, why was it important for him and his friends to fight back?

## KEY TERMS

**Black codes** (p. 475)
**Carpetbaggers** (p. 481)
**Compromise of 1877** (p. 488)
**Congressional Reconstruction** (p. 478)
**Field Order No. 15** (p. 470)
**Fifteenth Amendment** (p. 479)
**Fourteenth Amendment** (p. 476)
**Freedmen's Bureau** (p. 469)
**Ku Klux Klan** (p. 485)

**Lost Cause** (p. 468)
**Redeemers** (p. 487)
**Scalawags** (p. 481)
**Sharecropping** (p. 471)
*Slaughterhouse* **cases** (p. 491)
**Southern Homestead Act** (p. 470)
**Tenure of Office Act** (p. 479)
**Union Leagues** (p. 481)
*United States v. Cruikshank* (p. 491)

## Realities of Freedom

FOLLOWING emancipation, what economic and social opportunities actually existed for African Americans in the United States? How did these various opportunities available to freedmen improve their life and that of their families after the official end to slavery?

The Freedmen's Bureau established in 1865 by Congress provided freedmen with clothing, temporary shelter, food, and series of freedmen's schools across the South. Southern response was to fall into the use of terror to deter blacks from becoming economically independent using the agencies of groups like the Ku Klux Klan. Sharecropping was an insidious economic arrangement that also placed both whites and blacks in a form of economic slavery to large land holders in the South of the post-Civil War era.

Share cropping, tenant farming, and peonage were new forms of slavery adopted in the South following the Civil War. The story of African Americans after the end of slavery is complex and varied. Some blacks attempted to seek out better places to establish their new lives while others remained in the security of the only home they had known as slaves.

# *After slavery we had to get in before night . . .*

### An Act to Establish a Bureau for the Relief of Freedmen and Refugees, 1865

Be it enacted, That there is hereby established in the War Department, to continue during the present war of rebellion, and for one year thereafter, a bureau of refugees, freedmen, and abandoned lands, to which shall be committed, as hereinafter provided, the supervision and management of all abandoned lands, and the control of all subjects relating to refugees and freedmen from rebel states, or from any district of country within the territory embraced in the operations of the army, under such rules and regulations as may be prescribed by the head of the bureau and approved by the President. The said bureau shall be under the management and control of a commissioner to be appointed by the President, by and with the advice and consent of the Senate. . .

This illustration depicts former slaves outside their sharecropper cabin in Virginia, ca. 1870.

A SPRING SCENE NEAR RICHMOND, VIRGINIA.—[DRAWN BY W. L. SHEPPARD.]

### "When We Worked on Shares, We Couldn't Make Nothing"

After slavery we had to get in before night too. If you didn't, Ku Klux would drive you in. They would come and visit you anyway. . . . When he got you good and scared he would drive on away. They would whip you if they would catch you out in the night time. . . .

I've forgot who it is that that told us that we was free. Somebody come and told us we're free now. I done forgot who it was.

After freedom, we worked on shares a while. Then we rented. When we worked on shares, we couldn't make nothing, just overalls and something to eat. Half went to the other man and you would destroy your half if you weren't careful. A man that didn't know how to count would always lose. He might lose anyhow. They didn't give no itemized statement. No, you just had to take their word. They never give you no details. They just say you owe so much. No matter how good account you kept, you had to go by their account and now, Brother, I'm tellin' you the truth about this. It's been that way for a long time. You had to take the white man's work on note, and everything. Anything you wanted, you could git if you were a good hand. You could git anything you wanted as long as you worked. If you didn't make no money, that's all right; they would advance you more. But you better not leave him, you better not try to leave and get caught. They'd keep you in debt. They were sharp. Christmas come, you could take up twenty dollar, in somethin' to eat and much as you wanted in whiskey. You could buy a gallon of whiskey. Anything that kept you a slave because he was always right and you were always wrong it there was difference. If there was an argument, he would get mad and there would be a shooting take place.

## Excerpts from a Share Cropper Contract, 1882

To every one applying to rent land upon shares, the following conditions must be read, and agreed to.

To every 30 or 35 acres, I agree to furnish the team, plow, and farming implements, except cotton planters, and I do not agree to furnish a cart to every cropper. The croppers are to have half of the cotton, corn and fodder (and peas and pumpkins and potatoes if any are planted. . .

Croppers are to have no part or interest in the cotton seed raised from the crop planted and worked by them. No vine crops of any description, that is, no watermelons, muskmelons, . . . squashes or anything of that kind, except peas and pumpkins, and potatoes, are to be planted in the cotton or corn. All must work under my direction. All plantation work to be done by the croppers. . . .

No cropper to work off the plantation when there is any work to be done on the land he has rented, or when his work is needed by me or other croppers. Trees to be cut down on Orchard, House field & Evanson fences, leaving such as I may designate . . . .

*Freed women washing laundry along a creek near Circleville, Texas, circa 1866. Other than farming, domestic service was the only work open to freed women after the Civil War.*

### *. . . a bureau of refugees, freedmen, and abandoned lands . . .*

# 17

# A New South: Economic Progress and Social Tradition

THE NEWNESS OF THE NEW SOUTH   *(page 499)*

**HOW NEW**  was the New South?

THE SOUTHERN AGRARIAN REVOLT   *(page 505)*

**WHAT WERE**   the origins and nature of Southern Populism?

 WOMEN IN THE NEW SOUTH   *(page 508)*

**HOW DID**  traditional gender roles shape the opportunities available to women in the New South?

SETTLING THE RACE ISSUE   *(page 511)*

**WHAT ROLE**  did Northerners play in the segregation and disfranchisement of Southern blacks?

*The colored woman of to-day occupies . . . a unique position in this country. . . . She is confronted by both a woman question and a race problem. . . . While the women of the white race can with calm assurance enter upon the work they feel by nature appointed to do [including reform efforts both inside and outside the home], while their men give loyal support and appreciative countenance to [these] efforts, recognizing in most avenues of usefulness the propriety and the need of woman's distinctive co-operation, the colored woman too often finds herself hampered and shamed by a less liberal sentiment . . . on the part of those for whose opinion she cares most. . . .*

*You do not find the colored woman selling her birthright for a mess of pottage. . . . It is largely our women in the South to-day who keep the black men solid in the Republican Party. The black woman can never forget, however lukewarm the party may to-day appear, that it was a Republican president who struck the manacles from her own wrists and gave the possibilities of manhood to her helpless little ones; and to her mind a Democratic Negro is a traitor and a time-server.*

*To be a woman in a . . . [new] age carries with it a privilege and an opportunity never implied before. But to be a woman of the Negro race in America, and to be able to grasp the deep significance of the possibilities of the crisis, is to have a heritage, it seems to me, unique in the ages. In the first place, the race is young and full of the elasticity and hopefulness of youth. All its achievements are before it. . . . Everything to this race is new and strange and inspiring. There is a quickening of its pulses and a glowing of its self-consciousness. Aha, I can rival that! I can aspire to that! I can honor my name and vindicate my race! Something like this, it strikes me, is the enthusiasm which stirs the genius of young Africa in America; and the memory of past oppression and the fact of present attempted repression only serve to gather momentum for its irrepressible power. . . . What a responsibility then to have the sole management of the primal lights and shadows! Such is the colored woman's office. She must stamp weal or woe on the coming history of this people. May she see her opportunity and vindicate her high prerogative.*

◆ Anna J. Cooper,
   *A Voice from the South*, 1892

Anna Julia Cooper, *A Voice from the South* (Xenia, OH: Aldine Printing House, 1892): pp. 134–135, 138–140, 142–145. The book may be accessed from the Internet: http://docsouth.unc.edu/church/cooper/cooper.html

PEARSON
**myhistorylab**

**Personal Journeys Online**

- **Booker T. Washington, *Atlanta Compromise Address*, 1895.** Speech in which Washington accepts segregation and disfranchisement of southern blacks in return for white southerners' economic assistance.

- **W. E. B. Du Bois, *Of Mr. Booker T. Washington and Others*, 1903.** Du Bois declares that Washington's compromise places African Americans in the South on a journey to failure.

ANNA J. COOPER undertook an incredible journey that took her from slavery at her birth in Raleigh, North Carolina, in 1858 to a doctoral degree at the Sorbonne in Paris, France, and to a prominent career as an educator. Throughout her life she remained a firm believer in the role women, especially black women, should play in striking down both white supremacy and male domination. In 1892, Dr. Cooper published *A Voice from the South*, excerpted here. The book appeared at a time when the first African American generation raised in freedom generated a relatively prosperous, educated middle class intent on challenging the limits of race in the New South. The assertiveness of this generation alarmed their white counterparts, who launched a campaign of violence and repression, mainly directed at black men.

By the early 1900s, Cooper was living in Washington, DC and had immersed herself in the woman-suffrage move-ment and the promotion of female education. She would live to see the dawn of a new racial and gender era in the South and in America, but the journey would take many years and many lives. Cooper died at the age of 106 in 1964. ✦

## THE NEWNESS OF THE NEW SOUTH

Despite the destruction of war and the turmoil of Reconstruction, southerners worked to rebuild their stricken region as both a testimony to their ability to rise from the ashes and as a way to secure a measure of economic independence from their former Civil War enemies. Southerners did what other Americans were doing between 1877 and 1900; they built railroads, erected factories, and moved to towns and cities, only on a smaller scale and with more modest results. The changes, nonetheless, brought political and social turmoil, emboldening black people like Cooper to assert their rights, encouraging women to work outside the home and pursue public careers, and frightening some white men.

The New South's "newness" was to be found primarily in its economy, not in its social relations, although the two were complementary. After Reconstruction, new industries absorbed tens of thousands of first-time industrial workers from impoverished rural areas. Southern cities grew faster than those in any other region of the country.

**HOW NEW** was the New South?

**WHERE TO LEARN MORE**

★ Atlanta History Center, Atlanta, Georgia.
www.atlhist.org/exhibitions/html/metropolitan_frontiers.htm

## CHRONOLOGY

**1872** Texas and Pacific Railway connects Dallas to eastern markets.

**1880** First southern local of the Women's Christian Temperance Union is formed in Atlanta.

**1881** Booker T. Washington establishes Tuskegee Institute.

**1882** Agricultural Wheel is formed in Arkansas.

**1883** Laura Haygood founds the home mission movement in Atlanta.

**1884** James B. Duke automates his cigarette factory.

**1886** Dr. John Pemberton creates Coca-Cola.

Southern railroads conform to national track gauge standards.

**1887** Charles W. Macune expands the Southern Farmer's Alliance from its Texas base to the rest of the South.

**1888** The Southern Farmers' Alliance initiates a successful boycott of jute manufacturers.

**1890** Mississippi becomes the first state to restrict black suffrage with literacy tests.

**1892** The Populist Party forms.

**1894** United Daughters of the Confederacy is founded.

**1895** Booker T. Washington delivers his "Atlanta Compromise" address.

**1895** Publication of Theodor Herzl's *The Jewish State* outlining his ideas for a Jewish homeland in Palestine in response to rising anti-Semitism in Europe.

In *Plessy v. Ferguson*, the Supreme Court permits segregation by law.

**1897** First Zionist Congress meets in Switzerland.

**1898** North Carolina Mutual Life Insurance is founded.

**1899** Publication of *Die Grundlagen des neunzehnten Jahrhunderts* ["The Foundations of the Nineteenth Century"] by British scientist Houston Stewart Chamberlain, promoting the superiority of the German "race."

**1903** W. E. B. Du Bois publishes *The Souls of Black Folk*.

**1905** James B. Duke forms the Southern Power Company.

Thomas Dixon publishes *The Clansman*.

**1906** Bloody race riots break out in Atlanta.

**1907** Pittsburgh-based U.S. Steel takes over Birmingham's largest steel producer.

**Solid South** The one-party (Democratic) political system that dominated the South from the 1890s to the 1950s.

## QUICK REVIEW

### Southern Women: 1877-1900

- Most Southern women remained at home or on the farm.
- Middle-class women increasingly active in civic work and reform.
- Young white women found work in mills, factories, and as servants.

**WHERE TO LEARN MORE**

Sloss Furnaces National Historical Landmark, Birmingham, Alabama. www.slossfurnaces.com

*Documents*

John Hill, *Testimony on Southern Textile Industry* (1883)

A burst of railroad construction linked these cities to one another and to the rest of the country, giving them increased commercial prominence. Growing in size and taking on new functions, cities extended their influence into the countryside with newspapers, consumer products, and new values. But this urban influence had important limits. It did not bring electricity, telephones, public health services, or public schools to the rural South. It did not greatly broaden the rural economy with new jobs. And it left the countryside without the daily contact with the outside world that fostered a broader perspective.

The Democratic Party dominated southern politics after 1877, significantly changing the South's political system. Through various deceits, Democrats purged most black people and some white people from the electoral process and suppressed challenges to their leadership. The result was the emergence by 1900 of the **Solid South,** a period of white Democratic Party rule that lasted into the 1950s.

Although most southern women remained at home or on the farm, piecing together families shattered by war, some enjoyed new options after 1877. Middle-class women in the cities, both white and black, became increasingly active in civic work and reform. Tens of thousands of young white women from impoverished rural areas found work in textile mills, in city factories, or as servants. These new options posed a challenge to prevailing views about the role of women but ultimately did not change them.

The status of black southerners changed significantly between 1877 and 1900. The members of the first generation born after Emancipation sought more than just freedom as they came of age. They also expected dignity and self-respect and the right to work, to vote, to go to school, and to travel freely. White southerners responded with the equivalent of a second Civil War, and they won. By 1900, black southerners found themselves more isolated from white southerners and with less political power than at any time since 1865. Despite these setbacks, they succeeded, especially in the cities, in building a rich community life and spawning a vibrant middle class.

## AN INDUSTRIAL AND URBAN SOUTH

Southerners manufactured very little in 1877, less than 10 percent of the national total. By 1900, however, they boasted a growing iron and steel industry, textile mills that rivaled those of New England, a world-dominant tobacco industry, and a timber-processing industry that helped make the South a leading furniture-manufacturing center. A variety of regional enterprises also rose to prominence, among them the maker of what would become the world's favorite soft drink, Coca-Cola.

**Steel mills and textiles.** Birmingham, barely a scratch in the forest in 1870, exemplified one aspect of what was new about the New South. Within a decade, its iron and steel mills were belching the smoke of progress across the northern Alabama hills. By 1889, Birmingham had surpassed the older southern iron center of Chattanooga, Tennessee, and was preparing to challenge Pittsburgh, the nation's preeminent steelmaking city.

The southern textile industry also experienced significant growth during the 1880s. Although the South had manufactured cotton products since the early decades of the nineteenth century, chronic shortages of labor and capital kept the industry small. In the 1870s, however, several factors drew local investors into textile enterprises. The population of the rural South was rising, but farm income was low, ensuring a steady supply of cheap labor. Cotton was plentiful and cheap. Mixing profit and southern patriotism, entrepreneurs promoted a strong textile industry as a way to make the South less dependent on northern manufactured products and capital. By 1900, the South had surpassed New England to become the nation's foremost textile-manufacturing center.

**Tobacco and Coca-Cola.**   The South's tobacco industry, like its textile industry, predated the Civil War. Virginia was the dominant producer, and its main product was chewing tobacco. The discovery of bright-leaf tobacco, a strain suitable for smoking in the form of cigarettes, changed Americans' tobacco habits. In 1884, James B. Duke installed the first cigarette-making machine in his Durham, North Carolina, plant. By 1900, Duke's American Tobacco Company controlled 80 percent of all tobacco manufacturing in the United States.

Although not as important as textiles or tobacco in 1900, a soft drink developed by an Atlanta pharmacist Dr. John Pemberton eventually became the most renowned southern product worldwide. He called his concoction Coca-Cola. It was not an overnight success, and Pemberton, short of cash, sold the rights to it to another Atlantan, Asa Candler, in 1889. By the mid-1890s, Coca-Cola enjoyed a national market.

**Railroads and growth.**   Southern railroad construction boomed in the 1880s, outpacing the rest of the nation. Overall, southern track mileage doubled between 1880 and 1890, with the greatest increases in Texas and Georgia (see Map 17–1). In 1886, the southern railroads agreed to conform to a national standard for track width, firmly linking the region into a national transportation network and ensuring quick and direct access for southern products to the booming markets of the Northeast.

The railroads connected many formerly isolated small southern farmers to national and international agricultural markets. At the same time, it gave them access to a whole new range of products, from fertilizers to fashions. Drawn into commercial agriculture, the farmers were now subject to market fluctuations, their fortunes rising and falling with the market prices for their crops. To an extent unknown before the Civil War, the market now determined what farmers planted, how much credit they could expect, and on what terms. The railroad also opened new areas of the South to settlement and economic development, at the same time as it increased the prominence of interior cities at the expense of older coastal cities.

## THE LIMITS OF INDUSTRIAL AND URBAN GROWTH

Rapid as it was, urban and industrial growth in the South barely kept pace with that in the booming North (see Chapter 18). A weak agricultural economy and a high rural birthrate depressed wages in the South. Southern industrial workers earned roughly half the national average manufacturing wage during the late nineteenth century (see Figure 17–1). Business leaders promoted the advantages of this cheap labor to northern investors. In 1904, a Memphis businessman boasted that his city "can save the northern manufacturer . . . who employs 400 hands, $50,000 a year on his labor bill."

**Effects of low wages.**   Despite their attractiveness to industrialists, low wages undermined the southern economy in several ways. Poorly paid workers did not buy much, keeping consumer demand low and limiting the market for southern manufactured goods. They also could not provide much tax revenue, restricting the southern states' ability to fund services like public education. As a result, investment in education lagged

**QUICK REVIEW**

**Southern Industries**
- Iron and steel.
- Textiles.
- Tobacco.
- Timber.

**QUICK REVIEW**

**Railroads and the South**
- Connected small Southern farmers to national and international markets.
- Opened new areas in the South to settlement and development.
- Increased the importance of interior cities at the expense of older cities.

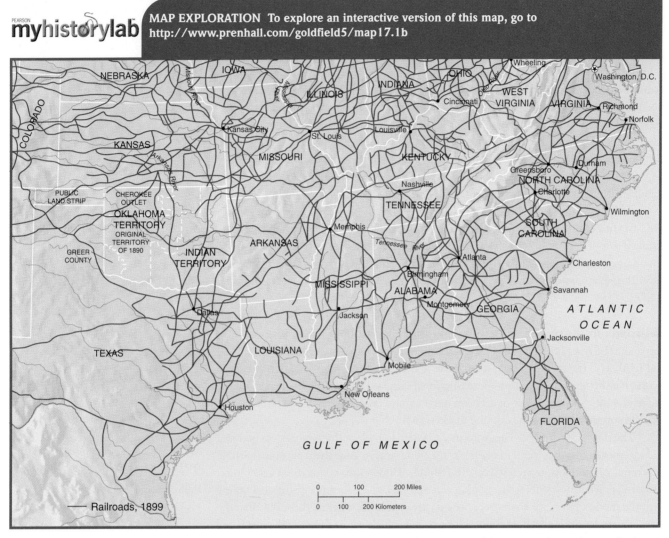

**MAP EXPLORATION** To explore an interactive version of this map, go to
http://www.prenhall.com/goldfield5/map17.1b

MAP 17–1A   **Railroads in the South, 1859 and 1899**   A postwar railroad construction boom promoted commercial agriculture and industry in the South. Unlike the railroads of the prewar South, uniform gauges and connections to major trunk lines in the North linked southerners to the rest of the nation. Northern interests, however, owned the major southern railroads in 1899, and most of the products flowing northward were raw materials to be processed by northern industry or shipped elsewhere by northern merchants.

in the South. Per-pupil expenditure in the region was at least 50 percent below that of the rest of the nation in 1900.

Finally, low wages kept immigrants, and the skills and energy they brought with them, out of the South. Between 1860 and 1900, during one of the greatest waves of immigration the United States has yet experienced, the foreign-born population of the South actually declined from about 10 percent to less than 2 percent.

**Limited capital.**   Why did the South not do better? Why did it not benefit more from the rapid expansion of the national economy in the last three decades of the nineteenth century? The simple answer is that, despite its growing links to the national economy, the South remained a region apart.

The Civil War had wiped out the South's capital resources, leaving it, in effect, an economic colony of the North. Northern goods flowed into the South, but northern capital, technology, and people did not. Northern-based national banks emerged in the wake of the Civil War to fund northern economic expansion. The South, in contrast, had few

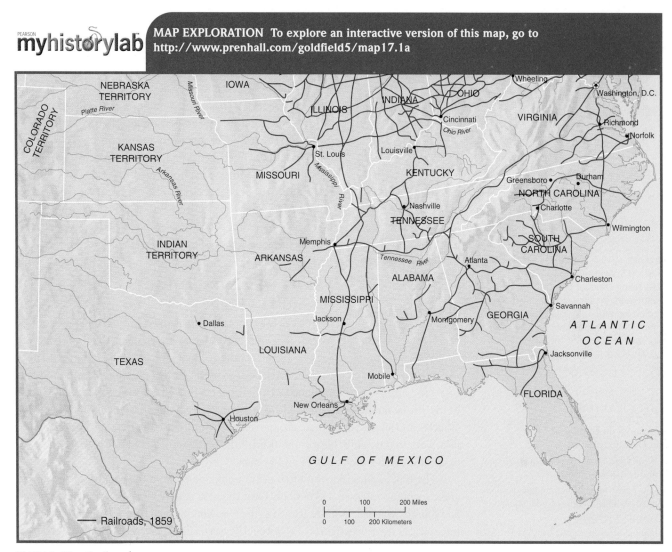

**MAP EXPLORATION** To explore an interactive version of this map, go to
http://www.prenhall.com/goldfield5/map17.1a

— Railroads, 1859

MAP 17–1B    *Continued*

**What effect** did railroads have on the Southern workforce?

banks, and they lacked sufficient capital reserves to fuel an equivalent expansion. In 1880, Massachusetts alone had five times as much bank capital as the entire South.

With limited access to other sources of capital, the South's textile industry depended on thousands of small investors in towns and cities. These investors avoided risk and shunned innovation. Most textile operations remained small-scale. The average southern firm in 1900 was capitalized at $11,000, compared with an average of $21,000 elsewhere.

The lumber industry, the South's largest, typified the shortcomings of southern economic development in the late nineteenth century. It required little capital, relied on unskilled labor, and processed its raw materials on site. After clear-cutting (i.e., felling all the trees) in one region, sawmills moved quickly to the next stand of timber, leaving behind a bare landscape, rusting machinery, and a workforce no better off than before. This process, later repeated by the coal-mining industry, inflicted environmental damage on once remote areas such as Appalachia, and displaced their residents.

**QUICK REVIEW**

**Southern Industry**

- Textile industry depended on thousands of small investors.
- Lumber industry typified the shortcomings of Southern industry.
- Tobacco industry avoided problems that plagued other Southern enterprises.

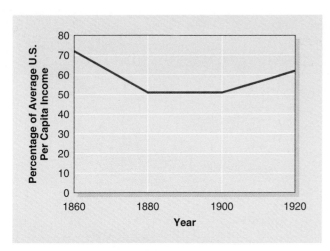

FIGURE 17–1    **Per Capita Income in the South as a Percentage of the U.S. Average, 1860–1920**    This graph illustrates the devastating effect of the Civil War on the southern economy. Southerners began a slow recovery during the 1880s that accelerated after 1900. But even as late as 1920, per capita income in the South was still lower relative to the country as a whole than it had been before the Civil War.

Data Source: Richard A. Easterlin, "Regional Economic Trends, 1840–1950," in *American Economic History*, ed. Seymour E. Harris (1961).

**QUICK REVIEW**

**Restraints on Industrial and Urban Growth**

- Weak agricultural economy and high rural birthrate depressed wages.
- Low wages limited consumption, development of skilled workforce, and immigration into the South.
- Limited access to capital hampered industrial innovation and expansion.

WHERE TO LEARN MORE

Levine Museum of the New South, Charlotte, North Carolina.
www.museumofthenewsouth.org

The tobacco industry, however, avoided the problems that plagued other southern enterprises. James B. Duke's American Tobacco Company was so immensely profitable that he became, in effect, his own bank. With more than enough capital to install the latest technology in his plants, Duke bought out his competitors. In the North, industrialization usually occurred in an urban context and promoted rapid urban growth. In the South, textile mills were typically located in the countryside, often in mill villages where employers could easily recruit families and keep them isolated from the distractions and employment alternatives of the cities. The timber industry similarly remained a rural-based enterprise. Tobacco manufacturing helped Durham and Winston, North Carolina, grow, but they remained small compared to northern industrial cities.

## FARMS TO CITIES: IMPACT ON SOUTHERN SOCIETY

If industrialization in the South was limited compared to the North, it nonetheless had an enormous impact on southern society. In the southern Piedmont, for example, textile mills transformed a portion of the farm population into an industrial workforce. Failed farmers moved to textile villages to earn a living. Entire families secured employment and often a house in exchange for their labor. Widows and single young men also moved to the mills, usually the only option outside farm work in the South. Nearly one-third of the textile-mill labor force by 1900 consisted of children under the age of 14 and women.

In 1880, southern towns often did not differ much from the countryside in appearance, economy, religion, and outlook. Over the next twenty years, the gap between town and country widened. By 1900, a town in the New South would boast a business district and more elegant residences than before. It would have a relatively prosperous economy and more frequent contact with other parts of the country. Its influence would extend into the countryside. Mail, the telegraph, the railroad, and the newspaper brought city life to the attention of farm families. In turn, farm families visited nearby towns and cities more often.

The urban South drew the region's talented and ambitious young people. White men moved to cities to open shops or take jobs as bank clerks, bookkeepers, merchants, and salesmen. White women worked as retail clerks, telephone operators, and office personnel. Black women filled the growing demand for laundresses and domestic servants. And black men also found prospects better in towns than on the farm, despite a narrow and uncertain range of occupations available to them. The excitement that drew some southerners to their new cities repelled others. To them, urbanization and the emphasis on wealth, new technology, and display represented a second Yankee conquest. The cities, they feared, threatened to infect the South with northern values, undermining southern grace, charm, faith, and family.

White southerners in town and country, who not long before had lived similar lives, grew distant. Small landholding white farmers and their families had fallen on hard times. The market that lured them into commercial agriculture threatened to take away their independence. They faced the loss of their land and livelihood. Their way of life no longer served as the standard for the South. New South spokesmen promoted cities and industries and ordered farmers to get on board the train of progress before it left the station without them.

# THE SOUTHERN AGRARIAN REVOLT

Even more than before the Civil War, cotton dominated southern agriculture between 1877 and 1900. And the economics of cotton brought despair to cotton farmers. The size of the cotton crop continued to set annual records after 1877. Fertilizers revived supposedly exhausted soils in North and South Carolina, turning them white with cotton. The railroad opened new areas for cultivation in Mississippi and eastern Texas. But the price of cotton fell while the price of fertilizers, agricultural tools, food, and most other necessities went up (see Figure 17–2). As a result, the more cotton the farmers grew, the less money they made.

**WHAT WERE** the origins and nature of Southern Populism?

## COTTON AND CREDIT

The solution to this agrarian dilemma seemed simple: Grow less cotton. But that course was not possible for several reasons. In a cash-poor economy, credit ruled. Cotton was the only commodity instantly convertible into cash and thus the only commodity accepted for credit. Food crops generated less income per acre than cotton. Local merchants, themselves bound in a web of credit to merchants in larger cities, accepted cotton as collateral. As cotton prices plummeted, the merchants required their customers to grow more cotton to make up the difference. Trapped in debt by low cotton prices and high interest rates, small landowning farmers lost their land in record numbers. Just after the Civil War, less than one-third of white farmers in the South were tenants or sharecroppers. By the 1890s, nearly half were.

## SOUTHERN FARMERS ORGANIZE, 1877–1892

As their circumstances deteriorated, southern farmers fought back. They had lived a communal life of church, family, and kin. Now they would widen the circle of their community to include other farmers sharing the same plight. These were not naive country folk; most owned their own land and participated in the market economy. They just

By the 1890s, textile mills were a common sight in towns throughout the South. The mills provided employment for impoverished rural families, especially women and children.

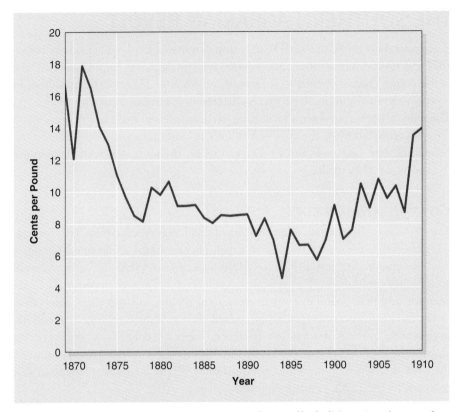

**FIGURE 17–2　The Price of Cotton, 1869–1910**　The steadily declining price of cotton after the Civil War, from 18 cents a pound to 5 cents a pound by the early 1890s, reflected extreme overproduction. Behind the numbers lay an impoverished rural South.
Data Source: U.S. Department of Commerce, *Historical Statistics of the United States: Colonial Times to 1957.*

wanted to make the market fairer, to lower interest rates and ease credit, to regulate railroad freight rates, and to keep the prices of necessities in check.

But these goals required legislation that neither the federal government nor southern state governments were inclined to support. Therefore, southern farmers joined their colleagues nationwide to address common grievances related to pricing, credit, and tax policies. Although some of the southern farmers' problems resulted from conditions peculiar to the South, agricultural distress became widespread after 1870. By 1875, nearly 250,000 southern landowners had joined the National Grange of the Patrons of Husbandry or, more popularly, simply the **Grange** (see Chapter 20). The leaders of the Grange, however, were large landowners. They did not have the same interests as the small farmers who made up the organization's rank and file.

**Salvation and cooperation.**　The most powerful agricultural reform organization, the **Southern Farmers' Alliance,** originated in Texas in the late 1870s. Alliance-sponsored farmers' cooperatives provided their members with discounts on supplies and credit. Members also benefited from marketing their cotton crops collectively.

The Alliance was still very much a Texas organization in 1887 when Charles W. Macune, a Wisconsin native, became its driving force. Macune sent a corps of speakers to create a network of southern cooperatives. Within two years, the Alliance had spread throughout the South and into the North and West. By 1890, it claimed more than a million members. With the exception of a few large landowners and some tenant farmers, almost all were small farmers who owned their own land. The success of the Alliance reflected both the desperate struggle of these small farmers to keep their land and the failure of other organizations to help them.

**Grange**　The National Grange of the Patrons of Husbandry, a national organization of farm owners formed after the Civil War.

**Southern Farmers' Alliance**　The largest of several organizations that formed in the post-Reconstruction South to advance the interests of beleaguered small farmers.

The Alliance operated like a religious denomination. Its leaders preached a message of salvation through cooperation to audiences of as many as 20,000 people at huge revival-like rallies. Qualifications for membership included a belief in the divinity of Jesus and the literal truth of the Bible. Alliance speakers, many of them rural ministers, often held meetings in churches. In their talks, they stressed the importance of doing good as much as good farming. The Alliance lobbied state legislatures to fund rural public schools. To increase the sense of community, the Alliance sponsored picnics, baseball games, and concerts.

The Alliance became for many small farmers a surrogate government and church in a region where public officials and many mainline Protestant ministers ignored their needs. It imposed strict morality on its members, prohibiting drinking, gambling, and sexual misconduct. Alliance leaders criticized the many Baptist, Methodist, and Presbyterian ministers who had strayed from the traditional emphasis on individual salvation and were defending a status quo that benefited large planters and towns.

The Alliance, however, did not accept black members. Black farmers formed the first **Colored Farmers' Alliance** in Texas in 1886. The Colored Alliance had fewer landowners and more tenants and sharecroppers in its ranks than the white organization. It concerned itself with issues relevant to this constituency, such as higher wages for cotton pickers. In 1891, the Colored Alliance attempted a region-wide strike over farm wages but was unable to enforce it in the worsening southern economy.

The white Alliance had better results with a protest over price fixing. To protect cotton shipped to market, farmers wrapped it in a burlap-like material called jute. In 1888, jute manufacturers combined to raise the price from 7 cents to as much as 14 cents a yard. The Alliance initiated a jute boycott throughout the South, telling farmers to use cotton bagging as an alternative. The protest worked, forcing the chastened jute manufacturers to offer farmers their product at a mere 5 cents per yard.

### Storing cotton.

This success encouraged Macune to pursue a more ambitious project. Low cotton prices and a lack of cash kept farmers poor. To address these problems, Macune proposed his **subtreasury plan.** Alliance members were to store their crops in a subtreasury

**Colored Farmers' Alliance**  An organization of Southern black farmers formed in Texas in 1886 in response to the Southern Farmer's Alliance, which did not accept black people as members.

**subtreasury plan**  A program promoted by the Southern Farmer's Alliance in response to low cotton prices and tight credit. Farmers would store their crop in a warehouse until prices rose, in the meantime borrowing up to 80 percent of the value of the stored crops from the government at a low interest rate.

Black sharecroppers in Georgia cotton fields, 1898; the scene is reminiscent of the slavery era. Southern agriculture contradicted New South rhetoric both in social and economic terms.

(i.e., warehouse), keeping their cotton off the market until the price rose. In the meantime, the government would loan the farmers up to 80 percent of the value of the stored crops at a low interest rate of 2 percent per year. This arrangement would free farmers from merchants' high interest rates and crop liens. Macune urged Alliance members to endorse political candidates who supported the subtreasury scheme. Many Democratic candidates for state legislatures throughout the South did endorse it and were elected, with Alliance backing, in 1890. Once in office, however, they failed to deliver.

**Populist party** A major third party of the 1890s, formed on the basis of the Southern Farmers' Alliance and other organizations, mounting electoral challenges against Democrats in the South and the Republicans in the West.

The failure of the subtreasury plan, combined with a steep drop in cotton prices after 1890, undermined the Alliance. Alliance membership declined by two-thirds in Georgia that year. Desperate Alliance leaders merged their organization with a new national political party in 1892, the People's Party, better known as the **Populist party.** The Populists appropriated the Alliance program and challenged Democrats in the South and Republicans in the West. The merger reflected desperation more than calculation. As we will see in Chapter 20, the Populists stirred up national politics between 1892 and 1896. In the South, they challenged the Democratic Party, sometimes courting Republicans, including black voters.

*Documents*

*The People's Party Platform* (1892)

# WOMEN IN THE NEW SOUTH

**HOW DID** traditional gender roles shape the opportunities available to women in the New South?

Because the antebellum reform movements included abolitionism, they had made little headway in the South. As a result, southern women had a meager reform tradition to build on. The war also left them ambivalent about independence. With husbands, fathers, and brothers dead or incapacitated, many women had to care for themselves and their families in the face of defeat and deprivation. Some determined never again to depend on men. Others, responding to the stress of running a farm or business, would have preferred less independence.

The response of southern white men to the war also complicated women's efforts to improve their status. Southern men had been shaken by defeat. They had lost the war and placed their families in peril. Many responded with alcoholism and violence. To regain their self-esteem, they recast the war as a noble crusade rather than a defeat. And they imagined southern white women as paragons of virtue and purity who required men to defend them. Demands for even small changes in traditional gender roles would threaten this image. Southern women understood this and never mounted an extensive reform campaign like their sisters in the North. Some middle-class women were openly hostile to reform, and others adopted conservative causes more inclined to reinforce the role of men in southern society than to challenge it.

## QUICK REVIEW

**Southern Women and Reform**

- Southern women played an active role in the public arena.
- Laura Haygood started the movement to found home mission societies.
- Lily Hammond opened settlement houses in Atlanta in the 1890s.

Despite such limitations, middle-class southern women found opportunities to broaden their social role and enter the public sphere in the two decades after 1880. They found these opportunities primarily in the cities, where servants, stores, and schools freed them of many of the productive functions, such as making clothing, cooking, and childcare, that burdened their sisters in the country and kept them tied to the home.

### CHURCH WORK AND PRESERVING MEMORIES

Southern women waded warily into the public arena, using channels men granted them as natural extensions of the home, such as church work. By the 1880s, evangelical Protestant churches had become prominent in many aspects of southern life. Women took advantage of the church's prominence to build careers using the moral gravity of church affiliation to political advantage. Most of the major reform efforts in the South during this era emanated from the church, and from the women for whom church work was an approved role for their gender.

The movement to found home mission societies, for example, was led by single white women in the Methodist Church. Home missions promoted industrial education among the poor and helped working-class women become self-sufficient. The home mission movement reflected an increased interest in missionary work in white southern evangelical churches. Lily Hammond extended the mission concept when she opened settlement houses in black and white neighborhoods in Atlanta in the 1890s. **Settlement houses,** pioneered in New York in the 1880s, promoted middle-class values in poor neighborhoods and provided them with a permanent source of services. In the North, they were privately sponsored. In the South, they were supported by the Methodist Church and known as Wesley Houses, after John Wesley, the founder of Methodism.

Religion also prompted southern white women to join the **Women's Christian Temperance Union (WCTU).** Temperance reform, unlike other church-inspired activities, involved women directly in public policy. WCTU members visited schools to educate children about the evils of alcohol, addressed prisoners, and blanketed men's meetings with literature. As a result, they became familiar with the South's abysmal school system and its archaic criminal justice system. They soon began advocating education and prison reform as well as legislation against alcohol.

By the 1890s, many WCTU members realized that they could not achieve their goals unless women had the vote. Rebecca Latimer Felton, an Atlanta suffragist and WCTU member, reflected the frustration of her generation of southern women in an address to workingwomen in 1892: "But some will say, you women might be quiet, you can't vote, you can't do anything! Exactly so, we have kept quiet for nearly a hundred years hoping to see relief come to the women of this country, and it hasn't come.

Rebecca Felton's own career highlighted the essentially conservative nature of the reform movement among middle-class white women in the New South. She fought for childcare facilities and sex education, as well as compulsory school attendance, and she pushed for the admission of women to the University of Georgia. But she strongly supported textile operators over textile workers and defended white supremacy. She had no qualms about the lynching of black men, executing them without trial "a thousand times a week if necessary" to preserve the purity of white women. In 1922, she became the first woman member of the U.S. Senate. By any definition, Felton was a reformer, but like most middle-class southern women, she had no interest in challenging the class and racial inequities of the New South.

The dedication of southern women to commemorating the memory of the Confederate cause also indicates the conservative nature of middle-class women's reform in the New South. Ladies' Memorial Associations formed after the war to ensure the proper burial of Confederate soldiers and suitable markings for their graves. The associations joined with men to erect monuments to Confederate leaders and, by the 1880s, to the common soldier. These activities reinforced white solidarity and constructed a common heritage for all white southerners regardless of class or location.

## WOMEN'S CLUBS

A broader spectrum of southern middle-class women joined women's clubs than joined church-sponsored organizations or memorial associations. Most women's clubs began in the 1880s as

**Settlement house**   A multipurpose structure in a poor neighborhood that offered social welfare, educational, and homemaking services to the poor or immigrants usually under private auspices and directed by middle-class women.

**Women's Christian Temperance Union (WCTU)**   Women's organization whose members visited schools to educate children about the evils of alcohol, addressed prisoners, and blanketed men's meetings with literature.

Southern white women played a major role in memorializing the Civil War and Confederate veterans. Here, a float prepared for a Confederate Veterans parade includes the major symbols of the Lost Cause, including the prominent pictures of Robert E. Lee, Thomas "Stonewall" Jackson, and Jefferson Davis, as well as the Confederate Battle Flag. The sponsorship of a casket company affords some irony to the photograph.

literary or self-improvement societies that had little interest in reform. By 1890, most towns and cities boasted at least several women's clubs and perhaps a federated club organization. But by that time, some clubs and their members had also begun to discuss political issues, such as child labor reform, educational improvement, and prison reform.

The activities of black women's clubs paralleled those of white women's clubs. Most African American women in southern cities worked as domestics or laundresses. Black women's clubs supported daycare facilities for working mothers and settlement houses in poor black neighborhoods modeled after those in northern cities. Atlanta's Neighborhood Union, founded by Lugenia Burns Hope in 1908, provided playgrounds and a health center and obtained a grant from a New York foundation to improve black education in the city. Black women's clubs also established homes for single black working women to protect them from sexual exploitation, and they worked for woman suffrage.

# GLOBAL PERSPECTIVES

## ⁂ THE RACE "PROBLEM" IN EUROPE ⁂

*Like the United States, Europe became more race conscious toward the end of the nineteenth century. A combination of factors, including the misapplication of Charles Darwin's* Origin of Species *(1859) to imply a hierarchy of races, increasing mobility and urbanization, rising nationalism, and imperialist ventures in Asia and Africa, generated a greater awareness of racial differences. Scientists and academics singled out the Nordics, Teutons (Germans), and Anglo-Saxons as the "fittest" of the globe's races; they considered such groups as Jews, Slavs, and southern Europeans to be inferior. Although today we would classify all of these as ethnic groups, Europeans at the time called them races. Some Europeans believed that the "superior" races had an obligation to protect and help the "inferior" ones. For others, the racial hierarchy represented nature's ordering of peoples, and human intervention would therefore serve no purpose. These attitudes justified imperialism abroad and discrimination at home.*

These racial attitudes emerged at a time when many European nations had already granted Jewish citizens full legal equality. Freed from occupational, educational, and residential restrictions, the Jewish population flourished as never before, rising and assimilating into European society. Their ascension troubled some Europeans, much as contemporary southern whites felt threatened by African American mobility. During the 1880s and 1890s, Germany and Austria founded right-wing parties that utilized anti-Semitism to win votes among groups that were wary of modern trends such as urbanization and industrialization. For such

people, newly enfranchised Jews were a natural target of hatred and fear. By the 1890s, Europe had a "Jewish problem" that resembled the American South's "Negro problem."

In 1895, Theodor Herzl, an Austrian Jewish journalist, posed an answer to the problem: the voluntary removal of Europe's Jews to Palestine. Surveying the rising tide of European anti-Semitism, Herzl proposed a Jewish nation-state. "Palestine is our ever memorable historic home . . . the great symbol of the solution of the Jewish Question after eighteen centuries of Jewish suffering."

The first Zionist Congress met in Switzerland in 1897, declaring its aim to create a "home in Palestine secured by public law" for world Jewry. Between 1904 and 1914, about 3,000 Jews per year migrated to the Holy Land. Throughout the first half of the twentieth century, Jewish migration to Palestine was restricted, first by the Ottoman Turks and then by the British. Large numbers of Jews settled instead in the northern cities of the United States.

Blacks in the American South also contemplated separate homelands, either in Africa or in the United States. Back-to-Africa movements appeared periodically in the decades after the Civil War. But as with European Jews, the greatest number of migrants went to the cities of the North, especially after the turn of the twentieth century.

- Why did most blacks in the American South and Jews in Europe during the late nineteenth century decide against migrating to a separate homeland?

Only rarely, however, as at some meetings of the Young Women's Christian Association (YWCA) or occasional meetings in support of prohibition, did black and white club members interact. Some white clubwomen expressed sympathy for black women privately, but publicly they maintained white solidarity. Most were unwilling to sacrifice their own reform agenda to the cause of racial reconciliation.

# SETTLING THE RACE ISSUE

The assertiveness of a new generation of African Americans in the 1880s and 1890s, especially in urban areas, provided the impetus and opportunity for white leaders to secure white solidarity. To counter black aspirations, white leaders enlisted the support of young white southerners, convincing them that the struggle for white supremacy would place them beside the larger-than-life heroes of the Civil War generation. African Americans resisted the resulting efforts to deprive them of their remaining freedoms. Although some left the South, many more built new lives and communities within the restricted framework white southerners allowed them.

**WHAT ROLE** did Northerners play in the segregation and disfranchisement of Southern blacks?

## The Fluidity of Southern Race Relations, 1877–1890

Race relations remained remarkably fluid in the South between the end of Reconstruction and the early 1890s. Despite the departure of federal troops and the end of Republican rule, many black people continued to vote and hold office. Some Democrats even courted the black electorate. Although segregation ruled in churches, schools, and in some organizations and public places after the Civil War, black people and white people continued to mingle, do business with each other, and often maintain cordial relations.

In 1885, T. McCants Stewart, a black journalist from New York, traveled to his native South Carolina, expecting a rough reception once his train headed south from Washington, DC. To his surprise, the conductor allowed him to remain in his seat while white riders sat on baggage or stood. He provoked little reaction among white passengers when he entered the dining car. Some of them struck up a conversation with him. In Columbia, South Carolina, Stewart found that he could move about with no restrictions. "I can ride in first-class cars. . . . I can go into saloons and get refreshments even as in New York. I can stop in and drink a glass of soda and be more politely waited upon than in some parts of New England."

Other black people corroborated Stewart's experiences in different parts of the South. During the 1880s, black people joined interracial labor unions and continued to be active in the Republican Party. They engaged in business with white people. In the countryside, African Americans and white people hunted and fished together, worked side by side at sawmills, and traded with each other. Cities were segregated more by class than by race, and people of both races sometimes lived in the same neighborhoods. To be sure, black people faced discrimination in employment and voting and random retaliation for perceived violations of racial barriers. But the barriers were by no means fixed.

## The White Backlash

The black generation that came of age in this environment demanded full participation in American society. For many in the generation of white southerners who came of age in the same period, this assertiveness rankled. These young white people, raised on the myth of the Lost Cause, were continually reminded of the heroism and sacrifice of their fathers during the Civil War. For them, black people replaced the Yankees as the enemy; they saw it as their mission to preserve white purity and dominance. The South's deteriorating rural economy and the volatile politics of the late 1880s and early 1890s exacerbated the growing tensions between assertive black people and threatened white people. So too did the growth of industry and cities in the South. In the cities, black and white people came into close contact, competing for jobs and jostling each other for seats on streetcars and trains. Racist rhetoric and violence against black people accelerated in the 1890s.

## LYNCH LAW

In 1892, three prominent black men, Tom Moss, Calvin McDowell, and William Stewart, opened a grocery on the south side of Memphis, an area with a large African American population. The People's Grocery prospered, while a white-owned store across the street struggled. The proprietor of the white-owned store, W. H. Barrett, was incensed. He obtained an indictment against Moss, McDowell, and Stewart for maintaining a public nuisance. Outraged black community leaders called a protest meeting at the grocery, during which two people made threats against Barrett. Barrett learned of the threats, notified the police, and warned the gathering at the People's Grocery that white people planned to attack and destroy the store. Nine sheriff's deputies, all white, approached the store to arrest the men who had threatened Barrett. Fearing Barrett's threatened white assault, the people in the grocery fired on the deputies, unaware who they were, and wounded three. When the deputies identified themselves, thirty black people surrendered, including Moss, McDowell, and Stewart, and were imprisoned. Four days later, deputies removed the three owners from jail, took them to a deserted area, and shot them dead.

The men at the People's Grocery had violated two of the unspoken rules that white southerners imposed on black southerners to maintain racial barriers: They had prospered, and they had forcefully challenged white authority. During 1892, a year of political agitation and economic depression, 235 **lynchings** occurred in the South. White mobs lynched nearly 2,000 black southerners between 1882 and 1903. Most lynchers were

**lynching** Execution, usually by a mob, without trial.

Lynching became a public spectacle, a ritual designed to reinforce white supremacy. Note the matter-of-fact satisfaction of the spectators at this gruesome murder of a black man.

working-class whites with rural roots, who were struggling in the depressed economy of the 1890s and enraged at the fluidity of urban race relations. The most common justification for lynching was the presumed threat posed by black men to the sexual virtue of white women. Sexual "crimes" could include remarks, glances, and gestures. Yet only 25 percent of the lynchings that took place in the thirty years after 1890 had an alleged sexual connection. Certainly, the men of the People's Grocery had committed no sex crime. Lynchers did not carry out their grisly crimes to end a rape epidemic; they killed to keep black men in their place and to restore their own sense of manhood and honor.

Ida B. Wells, who owned a black newspaper in Memphis, used her columns to publicize the People's Grocery lynchings. The great casualty of the lynchings, she noted, was her faith that education, wealth, and upright living guaranteed black people the equality and justice they had long sought. The reverse was true. The more black people succeeded, the greater was their threat to white people. She investigated other lynchings, countering the claim that they were the result of assaults on white women. When she suggested that, on the contrary, perhaps some white women were attracted to black men, the white citizens of Memphis destroyed her press and office. Exiled to Chicago, Wells devoted herself to the struggle for racial justice.

## SEGREGATION BY LAW

Southern white lawmakers sought to cement white solidarity and ensure black subservience in the 1890s by instituting **segregation** by law and the **disfranchisement** of black voters. Racial segregation restricting black Americans to separate and rarely equal public facilities had prevailed nationwide before the Civil War. After 1870, the custom spread rapidly in southern cities.

During the same period, many northern cities and states, often in response to protests by African Americans, were ending segregation. Roughly 95 percent of the nation's black population, however, lived in the South. Integration in the North, consequently, required white people to give up very little to black people. And as African American aspirations increased in the South during the 1890s while their political power waned, they became more vulnerable to segregation by law at the state level. At the same time, migration to cities, industrial development, and technologies such as railroads and elevators increased the opportunities for racial contact and muddled the rules of racial interaction.

Much of the new legislation focused on railroads, a symbol of modernity and mobility in the New South. Local laws and customs could not control racial interaction on interstate railroads. White passengers objected to black passengers' implied assertion of economic and social equality when they sat with them in dining cars and first-class compartments. Black southerners, by contrast, viewed equal access to railroad facilities as a sign of respectability and acceptance. When southern state legislatures required railroads to provide segregated facilities, black people protested.

Segregation laws required the railroads to provide "separate but equal" accommodations for black passengers. Railroads balked at the expense involved in doing so and provided black passengers with distinctly inferior facilities. Many lines refused to sell first-class tickets to black people and treated them roughly if they sat in first-class seats or tried to eat in the dining car. In 1890, Homer Plessy, a black Louisianan, refused to leave the first-class car of a railroad traveling through the state. Arrested, he filed suit, arguing that his payment of the first-class fare entitled him to sit in the same first-class accommodations as white passengers.

The U.S. Supreme Court ruled on the case, ***Plessy v. Ferguson,*** in 1896. In a seven-to-one decision, the Court held that Louisiana's railroad segregation law did not violate the

Ida B. Wells-Barnett, from *A Red Record* (1895)

**segregation**   A system of racial control that separated the races, initially by custom but increasingly by law, during and after Reconstruction.

**disfranchisement**   The use of legal means to bar individuals or groups from voting.

***Plessy v. Ferguson***   Supreme Court decision holding that Louisiana's railroad segregation law did not violate the Constitution as long as the railroads or the state provided equal accommodations.

Ida B. Wells, an outspoken critic of lynching, fled to Chicago following the People's Grocery lynchings in Memphis in 1892 and became a national civil-rights leader.

*Plessy v. Ferguson* (1896)

**Jim Crow laws**    Segregation laws that became widespread in the South during the 1890s.

**poll taxes**    Taxes imposed on voters as a requirement for voting.

**grandfather clause**    Rule that required potential voters to demonstrate that their grandfathers had been eligible to vote; used in some Southern states after 1890 to limit the black electorate.

Constitution as long as the railroads or the state provided equal accommodations for black passengers. The decision left unclear what "equal" meant. In the Court's view, "Legislation is powerless to eradicate racial instincts," meaning that segregation of the races was natural and transcended constitutional considerations. The only justice to vote against the decision was John Marshall Harlan, a Kentuckian and former slave owner. He predicted that the decision would result in an all-out assault on black rights.

Harlan's was a prophetic dissent. Both northern and southern states enacted new segregation laws in the wake of *Plessy v. Ferguson*. In practice, the separate facilities for black people these laws required, if provided at all, were rarely equal.

The segregation statutes came to be known collectively as **Jim Crow laws,** after the blackface stage persona of Thomas Rice, a white northern minstrel-show performer in the 1820s. Reflecting white stereotypes of African Americans, Rice had caricatured Crow as a foolish, elderly, lame slave who spoke in an exaggerated dialect.

Economic segregation followed social segregation. Before the Civil War, black men had dominated such crafts as carpentry and masonry. By the 1890s, white men were replacing them in these trades and excluding them from new ones, such as plumbing and electrical work. Trade unions, composed primarily of craft workers, began systematically to exclude African Americans. Although the steel and tobacco industries hired black workers, most other manufacturers turned them away. Confined increasingly to low or unskilled positions in railroad construction, the timber industry, and agriculture, black people underwent deskilling, a decline in workforce expertise, after 1890. With lower incomes from unskilled labor, they faced reduced opportunities for better housing and education.

## DISFRANCHISEMENT

With economic and social segregation came political isolation. The authority of post-Reconstruction Redeemer governments had rested on their ability to limit and control the black vote. Following the political instability of the late 1880s and the 1890s, however, white leaders determined to disfranchise black people altogether, thereby reinforcing white solidarity and eliminating the need to consider black interests. Support for disfranchisement was especially strong among large landowners in the South's plantation districts, where heavy concentrations of black people threatened their political domination. Urban leaders, especially after the turmoil of the 1890s, looked on disfranchisement as a way to stabilize politics and make elections more predictable.

The movement to reduce or eliminate the black vote in the South began in the 1880s and continued through the early 1900s (see Overview table, The March of Disfranchisement across the South, 1889–1908). Democrats enacted a variety of measures to attain their objectives without violating the letter of the Fifteenth Amendment. They complicated the registration and voting processes. States enacted **poll taxes,** requiring citizens to pay to vote. They adopted the secret ballot, which confused and intimidated illiterate black voters accustomed to using ballots with colors to identify parties. States set literacy and educational qualifications for voting or required prospective registrants to "interpret" a section of the state constitution. To avoid disfranchising poor, illiterate white voters with these measures, states enacted **grandfather clauses,** granting the vote automatically to anyone whose grandfather could have voted prior to 1867 (the year Congressional Reconstruction began). The grandfathers of most black men in the 1890s had been slaves, ineligible to vote.

Lawmakers sold white citizens on franchise restrictions with the promise that they would apply only to black voters and would scarcely affect white voters. This promise proved untrue. Alarmed by the Populist uprising, Democratic leaders used disfranchisement to gut dissenting parties. During the 1880s, minority parties in the South consistently polled an average of 40 percent of the statewide vote; by the mid-1890s, the figure had diminished to 30 percent despite the Populist insurgency. Turnout dropped even more dramatically. In Mississippi, for example, voter turnout in gubernatorial races during the 1880s averaged 51 percent; during the 1890s, it was 21 percent. Black turnout in Mississippi, which averaged 39 percent in the 1880s, plummeted to near zero in the 1890s. Overall turnout, which averaged 64 percent during the 1880s, fell to only 30 percent by 1910.

Black people protested disfranchisement vigorously. When 160 South Carolina delegates gathered to amend the state constitution in 1895, the six black delegates among them mounted a passionate but futile defense of their right to vote. Black delegate W. J. Whipper noted the irony of white people clamoring for supremacy when they already held the vast majority of the state's elected offices. Robert Smalls, the state's leading black politician, urged delegates not to turn their backs on the state's black population (see American Views, Robert Smalls Argues Against Disfranchisement). Such pleas fell on deaf ears.

## A NATIONAL CONSENSUS ON RACE

How could the South get away with it? How could southerners openly segregate, disfranchise, and lynch African Americans without a national outcry? Apparently, the majority of Americans in the 1890s subscribed to the notion that black people were inferior to white people and deserved to be treated as second-class citizens. Contemporary depictions of black people show scarcely human stereotypes: black men with bulbous lips and bulging eyes, fat black women wearing turbans and smiling vacuously, and black children contentedly eating watermelon or romping with jungle animals. Among the widely read books of the era was *The Clansman*, a glorification of the rise of the Ku Klux Klan. D. W. Griffith transformed *The Clansman* into an immensely popular motion picture epic under the title *Birth of a Nation*.

Intellectual and political opinion in the North bolstered southern policy. So-called scientific racism purported to establish white superiority and black inferiority on biological grounds. Northern-born professional historians reinterpreted the Civil War and Reconstruction in the white South's favor. Respected journals openly supported disfranchisement and segregation. The *New York Times*, summarizing this national consensus in 1903, noted that "practically the whole country" supported the "southern solution" to the race issue, because "there was no other possible settlement."

# "JIM CROW" CARS

## For Virginia Afro-Americans, as Well as Those of Kentucky, Tennessee and Several Other Southern States.

## An Attempt to Extend the Provisions of the Outrageous Law to Street Cars.

## The Constitutionality of the Law to be Attacked in the Courts by an Electric Street Car Company and Prominent Virginia Afro-Americans.

Richmond, Va.—Since Sunday week, July 1, the "Jim Crow" car law passed by the Virginia legislature last January, and signed by Gov. Tyler in spite of the remonstrance of nearly every influential colored man in Virginia, has been in force. It requires every railroad and, some attorneys say, every street car company in the state to provide separate cars for the exclusive use of colored people. Negroes are not allowed to ride on the cars intended for the use of the whites, and vice versa; but any Negro forcing himself upon a car for whites, and refusing to leave when requested to do so, may be forcibly ejected

Segregation by law accelerated after the 1896 *Plessy v. Ferguson* decision, but public conveyances often failed to abide by the "equal" portion of the separate-but-equal ruling. African Americans in the South fought racial separation and exclusion vigorously, as this excerpt from a black newspaper in Cleveland attests. July 14, 1900.

## OVERVIEW The March of Disfranchisement Across the South, 1889–1908

| Year | State | Strategies |
| --- | --- | --- |
| 1889 | Florida | Poll tax |
| 1889 | Tennessee | Poll tax |
| 1890 | Mississippi | Poll tax, literacy test, understanding clause |
| 1891 | Arkansas | Poll tax |
| 1893, 1901 | Alabama | Poll tax, literacy test, grandfather clause |
| 1894, 1895 | South Carolina | Poll tax, literacy test, understanding clause |
| 1894, 1902 | Virginia | Poll tax, literacy test, understanding clause |
| 1897, 1898 | Louisiana | Poll tax, literacy test, grandfather clause |
| 1899, 1900 | North Carolina | Poll tax, literacy test, grandfather clause |
| 1902 | Texas | Poll tax |
| 1908 | Georgia | Poll tax, literacy test, understanding clause, grandfather clause |

**From Then to Now Online**
*The Confederate Flag Battle*

**Exploring America**
*Racism in America*

These views permeated Congress, which made no effort to block the institution-alization of white supremacy in the South after 1890, and the courts, which upheld discriminatory legislation. As the white consensus on race emerged, the status of African Americans slipped in the North as well as the South. Although no northern states threatened to deny black citizens the right to vote, they did increase segregation. The booming industries of the North generally did not hire black workers. Antidiscrimination laws on the books since the Civil War went unenforced. In 1904, 1906, and 1908, race riots erupted in Springfield, Ohio; Greensburg, Indiana; and Springfield, Illinois, matching similar disturbances in Wilmington, North Carolina; and Atlanta, Georgia.

The offices of the North Carolina Mutual Life Insurance Company, around 1900. Founded by John Merrick, C. C. Spaulding, and Dr. A. M. Moore (all of whom appear in the picture), this Durham-based insurance company became one of the most successful black enterprises in the country.

## AMERICAN VIEWS

### Robert Smalls Argues against Disfranchisement

Born in Beaufort, South Carolina, in 1839, Robert Smalls worked as a slave pilot in Charleston harbor. In 1862, he emancipated himself, with his family and friends, when he delivered a Confederate steamer, The Planter, to the Union fleet blockading the harbor. He entered politics in 1864 as a delegate from his state to the Republican National Convention. He helped write South Carolina's Reconstruction constitution, which, among its provisions, guaranteed the right of former slaves to vote and hold office. Smalls won election to the state house of representatives in 1869, the state senate in 1871, and the U.S. House of Representatives in 1875. With opportunities for African Americans to hold public office declining following Reconstruction, Smalls secured appointment as collector of the port of Beaufort, a federal post he occupied until his death in 1915. In the speech excerpted here, delivered to the South Carolina Constitutional Convention of 1895, he bitterly assails the state's plan to disfranchise black voters.

- **From** the white perspective, what is Smalls's most telling argument against the disfranchisement and the planned strategies to implement it?
- **How** does Smalls depict the black citizens of South Carolina?
- **Why** were white political leaders unmoved by Smalls's plea?

Mr. President, this convention has been called for no other purpose than the disfranchisement of the negro. . . .

The negroes are paying taxes in the south on $263,000,000 worth of property. In South Carolina, according to the census, the negroes pay tax on $12,500,000 worth of property. That was in 1890. You voted down without discussion . . . a proposition for a simple property and education qualification [for voting]. What do you want? . . . In behalf of the 600,000 negroes in the State and the 132,000 negro voters all that I demand is that a fair and honest election law be passed. We care not what the qualifications imposed are, all that we ask is that they be fair and honest,

and honorable, and with these provisos we will stand or fall by it. You have 102,000 white men over 21 years of age, 13,000 of these cannot read nor write. You dare not disfranchise them, and you know that the man who proposes it will never be elected to another office in the State of South Carolina. . . . Fifty-eight thousand negroes cannot read nor write. This leaves a majority of 14,000 white men who can read and write over the same class of negroes in this State. We are willing to accept a scheme that provides that no man who cannot read nor write can vote, if you dare pass it. How can you expect an ordinary man to "understand and explain" any section of the Constitution, to correspond to the interpretation put upon it by the manager of election, when by a very recent decision of the supreme court, composed of the most learned men in the State, two of them put one construction upon a section, and the other justice put an entirely different construction upon it. To embody such a provision in the election law would be to mean that every white man would interpret it aright and every negro would interpret it wrong. . . . Some morning you may wake up to find that the bone and sinew of your country is gone. The negro is needed in the cotton fields and in the low country rice fields, and if you impose too hard conditions upon the negro in this State there will be nothing else for him to do but to leave. What then will you do about your phosphate works? No one but a negro can work them; the mines that pay the interest on your State debt. I tell you the negro is the bone and sinew of your country and you cannot do without him. I do not believe you want to get rid of the negro, else why did you impose a high tax on immigration agents who might come here to get him to leave?

Now, Mr. President we should not talk one thing and mean another. We should not deceive ourselves. Let us make a Constitution that is fair, honest and just. Let us make a Constitution for all the people, one we will be proud of and our children will receive with delight.

Source: *The Columbia State*, October 27, 1895.

## RESPONSE OF THE BLACK COMMUNITY

American democracy had, it seemed, hung out a "whites only" sign. How could African Americans respond to the growing political, social, and economic restrictions on their lives? Given white America's hostility, protest proved ineffective, even dangerous. African Americans organized more than a dozen boycotts of streetcar systems in the urban South between 1896 and 1908 in an effort to desegregate them, but not one succeeded. The Afro-American Council, formed in 1890 to protest the deteriorating conditions of black life, accomplished little and disbanded in 1908. W. E. B. Du Bois organized an annual Conference on Negro Problems at Atlanta University beginning in 1896, but it produced no effective plan of action.

A few black people chose to leave the South. Most black people who moved in the 1890s stayed within the South, settling in places like Mississippi, Louisiana, and Texas, where they could find work with timber companies or farming new lands that had opened to cotton and rice cultivation.

**An urban middle class.**   More commonly, black people withdrew to develop their own rich community life within the restricted confines white society permitted them. Particularly in the cities of the South, they could live relatively free of white surveillance and even white contact. In 1890, fully 70 percent of black city dwellers lived in the South; and between 1860 and 1900, the proportion of black people in the cities of the South rose from one in six to more than one in three. The institutions, businesses, and families that black people had begun painstakingly building during Reconstruction continued to grow, and in some cases flourish, after 1877.

By the 1880s, a new black middle class had emerged in the South. Urban-based, professional, business-oriented, and serving a primarily black clientele, its members fashioned an interconnected web of churches, fraternal and self-help organizations, families, and businesses. Black Baptists, AME, and AME Zion churches led reform efforts that sought to eliminate drinking, prostitution, and other vices in black neighborhoods.

African American fraternal and self-help groups, led by middle-class black people, functioned as surrogate welfare organizations for the poor. Fraternal orders also served as the seedbed for such business ventures as the North Carolina Mutual Life Insurance Company, founded in Durham in 1898. Within two decades, North Carolina Mutual became the largest black-owned business in the nation and helped transform Durham into the "capital of the black middle class." Durham's thriving black business district included several black-owned insurance firms, banks, and a textile mill. Most southern cities boasted active black business districts by the 1890s.

The African American middle class worked especially hard to improve black education (see Figure 17–3). Declining black political power encouraged white leaders to reduce funding for black public education. Black students in cities had only makeshift facilities; those in the countryside had almost no facilities. By the early 1900s, the student-teacher ratio in Nashville's segregated school system was 33 to one for white schools but 71 to one for black schools. To improve these conditions, black middle-class leaders solicited educational funds from northern philanthropic organizations.

**Black women's roles.**   After disfranchisement, middle-class black women assumed an even more pivotal role in the black community. They often used their relations with prominent white women and organizations such as the WCTU and the Young Women's Christian Association (YWCA) to press for public commitments to improve the health and education of African Americans. Absent political pressure from black men, and given the danger of African American males asserting themselves in the tense racial climate after 1890, black women became critical spokespersons for their race.

**QUICK REVIEW**

**Responses**

◆ Desegregation efforts in the South failed.
◆ A few black people chose to leave the South.
◆ Most black people withdrew into their own communities.

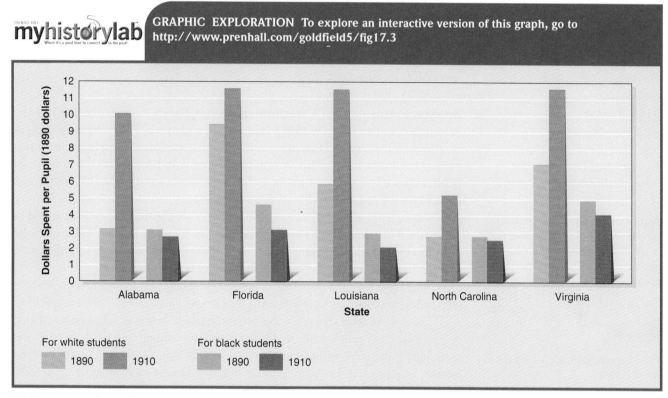

**GRAPHIC EXPLORATION** To explore an interactive version of this graph, go to
http://www.prenhall.com/goldfield5/fig17.3

**FIGURE 17–3   Disfranchisement and Educational Spending in the South, 1890–1910**   By barring black people from the political process, franchise restrictions limited their access to government services. Educational expenditures, which increased for white people but decreased for black people following disfranchisement, provide one measure of the result.

Data Source: Robert A. Margo, "Disfranchisement, School Finance, and the Economics of Segregated Schools in the United States South, 1890–1910," Ph.D. diss., Harvard University, 1982.

The extension of black club work into rural areas of the South, where the majority of the African American population lived, to educate families about hygiene, nutrition, and childcare, anticipated similar efforts among white women after 1900. But unlike their white counterparts, these middle-class black women worked with limited

Booker T. Washington at his desk, Tuskegee Institute, 1902.

resources in a context of simmering racial hostility and political and economic impotence. In response, they nurtured a self-help strategy to improve the conditions of the people they sought to help. One of the most prominent African American leaders of the late nineteenth and early twentieth centuries, Booker T. Washington, adopted a similar approach to racial uplift.

**Booker T. Washington's accommodation.**    Born a slave in Virginia in 1856, Washington and his family worked in the salt and coal mines of West Virginia after the Civil War. Ambitious and flushed with the postwar enthusiasm for advancement that gripped freedmen, he enrolled in Hampton Normal and Agricultural Institute, the premier black educational institution in the South. Washington worked his way through Hampton, graduated, taught for a time, and then, in 1881, founded the Tuskegee Institute for black students in rural Alabama. Washington thought that his students would be best served if they learned a trade and workplace discipline. By learning industrial skills, he maintained, black people could acquire self-respect and economic independence. As a result, Tuskegee emphasized vocational training over the liberal arts.

Washington argued that African Americans should accommodate themselves to segregation and disfranchisement until they could prove their economic worth to American society. In exchange for this accommodation, however, white people should help provide black people with the education and job training they would need to gain their independence. Washington articulated this position, known as the **Atlanta Compromise,** in a speech at the Atlanta Cotton States and International Exposition in 1895. Despite his conciliatory public stance, Washington secretly helped to finance legal challenges to segregation and disfranchisement. The social and economic realities of the South, meanwhile, frustrated his educational mission. Increasingly, black people were shut out of the kinds of jobs for which Washington hoped to train them. Facing a depressed rural economy and growing racial violence, they had little prospect of advancement.

**W. E. B. Du Bois attacks the Atlanta Compromise.**    Another prominent African American leader, W. E. B. Du Bois, challenged Washington's acceptance of black social inequality. Born in Massachusetts in 1868, Du Bois was the first African American to earn a doctorate at Harvard. Du Bois promoted self-help, education, and black pride. In *The Souls of Black Folk,* published in 1903, he described the strengths of black culture and attacked Washington's Atlanta Compromise. Du Bois was a cofounder, in 1910, of the **National Association for the Advancement of Colored People (NAACP),** an interracial organization dedicated to restoring African American political and social rights.

Despite their differences, which reflected their divergent backgrounds, Washington and Du Bois agreed on many issues. Both had reservations about allowing illiterate black people to vote, and both believed that black success in the South required some white assistance. But it became apparent to Du Bois that white people did not care to elevate black southerners. In 1906, after a bloody race riot in Atlanta, Du Bois left the South, a decision millions of black southerners would make over the next two decades.

# CONCLUSION

In many respects, the South was more like the rest of the nation in 1900 than at any other time since 1860. Southern cities hummed with activity, and industries from textiles to steel dotted the southern interior. Young men and women migrated to southern cities to pursue opportunities unavailable to their parents. Advances in the production and marketing of cigarettes and soft drinks would soon make southern entrepreneurs and

## Sidebar

**QUICK REVIEW**

**Booker T. Washington**

- Born a slave in Virginia in 1856.
- Founded Tuskegee Institute in 1881.
- Advocated the Atlanta Compromise.

**Atlanta Compromise**   Booker T. Washington's policy accepting segregation and disfranchisement for African Americans in exchange for white assistance in education and job training.

Booker T. Washington, *Atlanta Exposition Address* (1895)

**National Association for the Advancement of Colored People (NAACP)** Interracial organization co-founded by W. E. B. Du Bois in 1910 dedicated to restoring African-American political and social rights.

**QUICK REVIEW**

**W. E. B. Du Bois**

- Born in Massachusetts in 1868.
- First African-American to earn a doctorate at Harvard.
- Promoted self-help, education, and black pride.
- Opponent of Washington's Atlanta Compromise.

W. E. B. Du Bois, *Of Mr. Booker T. Washington and Others* (1903)

their products household names. Southerners ordered fashions from Sears, Roebuck catalogs and enjoyed electric lights, electric trolleys, and indoor plumbing as much as other urban Americans.

Americans idealized the South—not the urban industrial South, but a mythical South of rural grace and hospitality. National magazines and publishers rushed to print stories about this land of moonlight and magnolias, offering it as a counterpoint to the crowded, immigrant-infested, factory-fouled, money-grubbing North. It was this fantasy South that white people in both the North and the South imagined as they came to a common view on race and reconciled their differences. Northern journalists offered admiring portraits of such southern heroes as Robert E. Lee, of whom one declared in 1906, "the nation has a hero to place beside her greatest." The Republican-dominated Congress agreed to care for the graves of the Confederate dead and ordered the return to the South of captured Confederate flags. White southerners cultivated national reconciliation but remained fiercely dedicated to preserving the peculiarities of their region: a one-party political system, disfranchisement of African Americans, and segregation by law. The region's urban and industrial growth, impressive from the vantage of 1865, paled before that of the North. The South remained a colonial economy characterized more by deep rural poverty than urban prosperity.

How one viewed the New South depended on one's vantage point. White northerners accepted at face value the picture southerners painted for them of a chastened and prosperous, yet still attractive, region. Middle-class white people in the urban South enjoyed the benefits of a national economy and a secure social position. Middle-class white women enjoyed increased influence in the public realm, but not to the extent of their northern sisters. And the institutionalization of white supremacy gave even poor white farmers and factory workers a place in the social hierarchy a rung or two above the bottom.

For black people, the New South proved a crueler ruse than Reconstruction. No one now stepped forward to support their cause and stem the erosion of their economic independence, political freedom, and civil rights. Yet they did not give up the American dream, nor did they give up the South for the most part. They built communities and worked as best they could to challenge restrictions on their freedom.

The New South was thus both American and southern. It shared with the rest of the country a period of rapid urban and industrial growth. But the legacy of war and slavery still lay heavily on the South, manifesting itself in rural poverty, segregation, and black disfranchisement. The burdens of this legacy would limit the attainments of both black and white southerners for another half-century, until Americans finally rejected racial inequality as an affront to their national ideals.

# SUMMARY

## HOW NEW was the New South?

**The Newness of the New South** The "newness" of the New South was to be found primarily in its economic shift toward industrialization and urbanization rather than its social relations. Urban and rural white leaders had used the banner of white supremacy to constrict African-American social and economic roles; the Solid South, a white Democratic voting bloc emerged. Industry from textiles to steel dotted the Southern landscape, young men and women migrated to cities, and railroads connected the growing urban centers. Economically, the South remained behind the booming North; a weak agricultural economy, high birthrate, and low wages were some of the undermining factors.

## WHAT WERE the origins and nature of Southern Populism?

**The Southern Agrarian Revolt** More than even before the Civil War, cotton dominated Southern agriculture; the price of cotton was low, and the prices of fertilizer, tools and necessities rose. Curtailing production to raise prices was not an option; the credit-based economy of the South was dependent upon cotton. Black and white sharecroppers and tenant farmers fought back by organizing, scoring limited successes; it took higher cotton prices and returning prosperity in the late 1890s to bring relief to farmers.

## HOW DID traditional gender roles shape the opportunities available to women in the New South?

**Women in the New South** White women in the South were cast in the roles of paragons of virtue and purity who needed men to defend them. With these limitations, middle-class women entered the public arena slowly. Women's involvement in church organizations, temperance, and as protectors of Southern history allowed them involvement without challenging the class and racial inequalities of the New South, while women's club activities addressed their self-improvement and allowed them to help other women.

## WHAT ROLE did Northerners play in the segregation and disfranchisement of Southern blacks?

**Settling the Race Issue** The generation of black people who had come of age by the 1890s demanded full participation; white Southerners raised on the myth of the Lost Cause resented the changed status of black people. Economic and political violence worsened the tensions, and violence, including lynchings, accelerated. Segregation and disfranchisement laws were passed; the U.S. Supreme Court condoned separate accommodations in the case *Plessy* v. *Ferguson*. The majority of white Americans, North and South, ascribed to the notion of black inferiority; no national debate resulted in response to the new restrictions. African Americans responded by creating their own community life within these new confines. Booker T. Washington and W. E. B. Du Bois differed on the approaches black people should take to accommodate and improve themselves.

# WHERE TO LEARN MORE

**Levine Museum of the New South, Charlotte, North Carolina.** The museum has exhibits on various New South themes and a permanent exhibit on the history of Charlotte and the Carolina Piedmont. **www.museumofthenewsouth.org**

**Atlanta History Center, Atlanta, Georgia.** The major exhibit, "Metropolitan Frontiers, 1835– 2000," includes a strong segment on the New South era, including the development of separate black and white economies in Atlanta. The Herndon home, on the grounds of the center, has an exhibit on black upper-class life in Atlanta from 1880 to 1930. **www.atlhist.org/exhibitions/html/metropolitan_frontiers.htm**

**Sloss Furnaces National Historical Landmark, Birmingham, Alabama.** The site recalls the time when Birmingham challenged Pittsburgh as the nation's primary steel-producing center. **www.slossfurnaces.com**

# STUDY RESOURCES

### PEARSON
# myhistorylab

For study resources for this chapter, go to www.myhistorylab .com and choose *The American Journey*. You will find a wealth of study and review material for this chapter, including pre- and post-tests, customized study plan, key term review flash cards, interactive map and document activities, and documents for analysis.

# REVIEW QUESTIONS

1. In what ways did the growing activism of white middle-class women, the increasing assertiveness of young urban black people, and the persistence of the agricultural depression affect the politics of the South in the late 1880s and early 1890s?

2. We associate segregation and disfranchisement with reactionary political and social views. Yet many white people who promoted both seriously believed them to be reforms. How could white people hold such a view?

3. What strategies did black southerners employ in response to the narrowing of economic and political opportunities in the New South?

4. What accounted for Anna J. Cooper's optimism for African American women in the South at a time when southern whites were beginning an extensive legal and physical assault on black civil rights?

5. Why did racial "problems" emerge as a major issue in Europe and the United States in the late nineteenth century?

## KEY TERMS

**Atlanta Compromise** (p. 520)
**Colored Farmers' Alliance** (p. 507)
**Disfranchisement** (p. 513)
**Grandfather clause** (p. 514)
**Grange** (p. 506)
**Jim Crow laws** (p. 514)
**Lynching** (p. 512)
**National Association for the Advancement of Colored People (NAACP)** (p. 520)

**Plessy v. Ferguson** (p. 513)
**Poll taxes** (p. 514)
**Populist party** (p. 508)
**Segregation** (p. 513)
**Settlement house** (p. 509)
**Solid South** (p. 500)
**Southern Farmers' Alliance** (p. 506)
**Subtreasury plan** (p. 507)
**Women's Christian Temperance Union (WCTU)** (p. 509)

# 18
# Industry, Immigrants and Cities

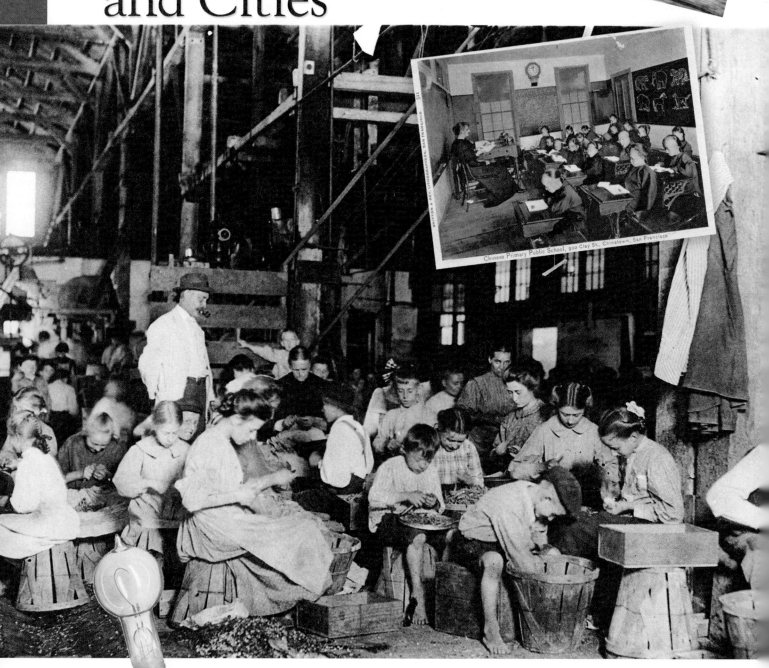

Chinese Primary Public School, 920 Clay St., Chinatown, San Francisco

NEW INDUSTRY    *(page 528)*

**HOW DID** workers respond to the changing demands of the workplace in the late nineteenth century?

NEW IMMIGRANTS  *(page 539)*

**WHAT IMPACT** did new immigration have on cities in the North?

 NEW CITIES  *(page 549)*

**WHO MADE UP** the new middle class?

*We were homeless, houseless, and friendless in a strange place. We had hardly money enough to last us through the voyage for which we had hoped and waited for three long years. We had suffered much that the reunion we longed for might come about; we had prepared ourselves to suffer more in order to bring it about, and had parted with those we loved, with places that were dear to us in spite of what we passed through in them, never again to see them, as we were convinced, all for the same dear end. With strong hopes and high spirits that hid the sad parting, we had started on our long journey. And now we were checked so unexpectedly but surely. . . . When my mother had recovered enough to speak, she began to argue with the gendarme, telling him our story and begging him to be kind. The children were frightened and all but I cried. I was only wondering what would happen. . . . Here we had been taken to a lonely place; . . . our things were taken away, our friends separated from us; a man came to inspect us, as if to ascertain our full value; strange-looking people driving us about like dumb animals, helpless and unresisting; children we could not see crying in a way that suggested terrible things; ourselves driven into a little room where a great kettle was boiling on a little stove; our clothes taken off, our bodies rubbed with a slippery substance that might be any bad thing; a shower of warm water let down on us without warning. . . . We are forced to pick out our clothes from among all the others, with the steam blinding us; we choke, cough, entreat the women to give us time; they persist, "Quick! Quick!, or you'll miss the train!", Oh, so we really won't be murdered! They are only making us ready for the continuing of our journey, cleaning us of all suspicions of dangerous sickness. Thank God! . . .*

*Oh, what solemn thoughts I had! How deeply I felt the greatness, the power of the scene! The immeasurable distance from horizon to horizon; . . . the absence of any object besides the one ship; . . . I was conscious only of sea and sky and something I did not understand. And as I listened to its solemn voice, I felt as if I had found a friend, and knew that I loved the ocean.*

◆ Mary Antin

Mary Antin, *The Promised Land* (Boston: Houghton Mifflin Co., 1912), chap. VIII.

**PEARSON**
## myhistorylab™

### Personal Journeys Online

- *Young Chinese immigrant memoir, 1882.* A Chinese immigrant recalls his migration to America and his early days in San Francisco.

- *Letters of Negro Migrants, 1917.* Letters from southern black migrants to the North back home.

◆ MARY ANTIN, a 13-year-old Jewish girl from Russia, describes her family's perilous journey from persecution in tsarist Russia to the ship that would take her from Hamburg, Germany, to faraway America. In 1894, Mary and her mother and sisters set out from their village to join her father in Boston.

Millions of European immigrants made similar journeys across the Atlantic (as did Chinese and Japanese immigrants, across the Pacific), a trip fraught with danger, unpredictable detours, occasional heartbreak, the sundering of family ties, and the fear of the unknown. So powerful was the promise of

# CHRONOLOGY

**1869** The Knights of Labor is founded in Philadelphia.

**1870** John D. Rockefeller organizes the Standard Oil Company.

Congress passes the Naturalization Act barring Asians from citizenship.

**1871** Unification of Germany in the wake of rising nationalism following the Franco-Prussian War

**1876** The Centennial Exposition opens in Philadelphia.

Beginning of the rule of dictator Porfirio Diaz in Mexico, whose regime is ended by the Mexican Revolution.

**1877** Execution of ten Molly Maguires in Pennsylvania.

The Great Uprising railroad strike, the first nationwide work stoppage in the United States, provokes violent clashes between workers and federal troops.

**1879** Thomas Edison unveils the electric light bulb.

**1880** Founding of the League of American Wheelmen helps establish bicycling as one of urban America's favorite recreational activities.

**1881** Assassination of Tsar Alexander II begins a series of pogroms that triggers a wave of Russian Jewish immigration to the United States.

**1882** Congress passes the Chinese Exclusion Act.

First country club in the United States founded in Brookline, Massachusetts.

**1883** National League merges with the American Association and opens baseball to working-class fans.

**1884** Berlin Conference on Africa to set rules for competing European powers annexing African territory.

**1886** The Neighborhood Guild, the nation's first settlement house, opens in New York City.

Riot in Chicago's Haymarket Square breaks the Knights of Labor.

American Federation of Labor is formed.

**1887** Anti-Catholic American Protective Association is formed.

**1888** Wanamaker's department store introduces a "bargain room," and competitors follow suit.

**1889** Jane Addams opens Hull House, the nation's most celebrated settlement house, in Chicago.

**1890** Jacob A. Riis publishes *How the Other Half Lives*.

**1891** African American Chicago physician Daniel Hale Williams establishes Provident Hospital, the nation's first interracially staffed hospital.

**1892** General Electric opens the first corporate research and development division in the United States.

Strike at Andrew Carnegie's Homestead steelworks fails.

**1894** Pullman Sleeping Car Company strike fails.

Immigration Restriction League is formed.

**1895** American-born Chinese in California form the Native Sons of the Golden State to counter nativism.

**1897** George C. Tilyou opens Steeplechase Park on Coney Island in Brooklyn, New York.

First Zionist Congress meets in Switzerland proclaiming its aim to create a home in Palestine for the Jewish people.

**1898** Congress passes the Erdman Act to provide for voluntary mediation of railroad labor disputes.

---

American life for the migrants that they willingly risked these obstacles to come to the United States.

For Mary, America did indeed prove to be *The Promised Land*, as she titled her emigration memoir, published in 1912. At the age of 15, she published her first poem in the *Boston Herald* and, after attending Barnard College in New York City, she wrote on immigrant issues, lectured widely, and worked for Theodore Roosevelt's Progressive Party. She fought against immigration-restriction legislation and promoted public education as the main channel of upward mobility for immigrants.

Mary and her family were part of a major demographic and economic transformation in the United States between 1870 and 1900. Rapid industrial development changed the nature of the workforce and the workplace. Large factories staffed by semiskilled laborers displaced the skilled artisans and small shops that had dominated American industry before 1870. Industrial development also accelerated urbanization. Between the Civil War and 1900, the proportion of the nation's population living in cities, swelled by migrants from the countryside and immigrants from Europe and Asia, increased from 20 to 40 percent, a rate of growth twice that of the population as a whole. During the 1880s alone, more than 5 million immigrants came to the United States, twice as many as in any previous decade.

The changes in American life were exhilarating for some, tragic for others. New opportunities opened as old opportunities disappeared. Vast new wealth was created, but poverty increased. New technologies eased life for some but left others untouched. It would be the great dilemma of early-twentieth-century America to reconcile these contradictions and satisfy the American quest for a decent life for all within the new urban industrial order.

Late-nineteenth-century America is often called the **Gilded Age.** The term is taken from the title of a novel by Mark Twain that satirizes the materialistic excesses of the day. It serves as a shorthand description of the shallow worship of wealth, and the veneer of respectability and prosperity covering deep economic and social divisions, that characterized the period. ✦

# NEW INDUSTRY

**HOW DID** workers respond to the changing demands of the workplace in the late nineteenth century?

**Gilded Age** Term applied to late-nineteenth-century America that refers to the shallow display and worship of wealth characteristic of that period.

Mark Twain and Charles Dudley Warner, *The Gilded Age* (1880)

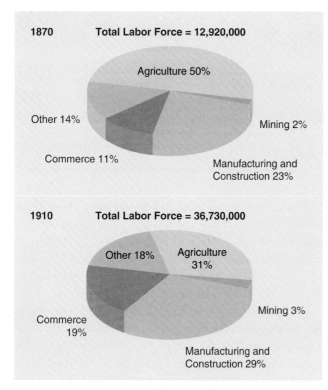

**1870**    **Total Labor Force = 12,920,000**

Agriculture 50%

Other 14%

Mining 2%

Commerce 11%

Manufacturing and Construction 23%

**1910**    **Total Labor Force = 36,730,000**

Other 18%   Agriculture 31%

Mining 3%

Commerce 19%

Manufacturing and Construction 29%

FIGURE 18–1 **Changes in the American Labor Force, 1870–1910** The transformation of the American economy in the late nineteenth century changed the nature and type of work. By 1910, the United States was an urban, industrial nation with a matching workforce that toiled in factories and commercial establishments (including railroads) and, less frequently, on farms.

Between 1870 and 1900, the United States transformed itself from an agricultural nation, a nation of farmers, merchants, and artisans, into the world's foremost industrial power, producing more than one-third of the world's manufactured goods. By the early twentieth century, factory workers made up one-fourth of the workforce, and agricultural workers had dropped from a half to less than a third (see Figure 18–1).

Although the size of the industrial workforce increased dramatically, the number of firms in any given industry shrank. Mergers, changes in corporate management and the organization of the workforce, and a compliant government left a few companies in control of vast segments of the American economy. Workers, reformers, and eventually government challenged this concentration of economic power.

## INVENTING TECHNOLOGY: THE ELECTRIC AGE

Technology played a major role in transforming factory work and increasing the scale of production. Steam engines, like the giant Corliss engine at the Centennial Exposition and, later, electricity, freed manufacturers from dependence on water power. Factories no longer had to be located by rivers. Technology also enabled managers to substitute machines for workers, skewing the balance of power in the workplace toward employers. And it transformed city life, making available a host of new conveniences. By the early twentieth century, electric lights, appliances, ready-made clothing, and store-bought food eased middle-class life. Electric trolleys whisked clerks, salespeople, bureaucrats, and bankers to new urban and suburban subdivisions. Electric streetlights lit up city streets at night.

For much of the nineteenth century, the United States was dependent on the industrial nations of Europe for technological innovation. American engineers often went to England and Germany for education and training, and the textile industry, railroads, and the early steel industry benefited from German and English inventions. In the late nineteenth century, the United States changed from a technology borrower to a technology innovator. By 1910, a million patents had been issued in the United States, 900,000 of them after 1870.

Nothing represented this shift better than Thomas A. Edison's development of a practical electric light bulb and electric generating system. Edison's invention transformed electricity into a new and versatile form of industrial energy. It also reflected a change in the relationship between science and technology. Until the late nineteenth century, advances in scientific theory usually followed technological innovation, rather than the other way around.

Edison's initial success touched off a wave of research and development in Germany, Austria, Great Britain, France, and the United States. Whoever could light the world cheaply and efficiently held the key to an enormous fortune. Ultimately, the prize fell not to Edison but to Elihu Thomson. Thomson purchased Edison's General Electric Company in 1892 and established the country's first corporate research and development division. His scientists produced what was then the most efficient light bulb design, and by 1914, General Electric was producing 85 percent of the world's light bulbs.

Following this precedent, other American companies established research and development laboratories. Standard Oil, U.S. Rubber, the chemical giant Du Pont, and the photographic company Kodak all became world leaders in their respective industries because of innovations their laboratories developed.

The process of invention that emerged in the United States gave the country a commanding technological lead. But the modernization of industry that made the United States the world's foremost industrial nation after 1900 reflected organizational as well as technological innovation. As industries sought efficient ways to apply technology and expand their markets within and beyond national borders, their workforces expanded, and their need for capital mounted. Coping with these changes required significant changes in corporate management.

**WHERE TO LEARN MORE**

Edison National Historic Site, West Orange, New Jersey.
www.nps.gov/edis

## THE CORPORATION AND ITS IMPACT

The modern corporation provided the structural framework for the transformation of the American economy. A corporation is an association of individuals that is legally authorized to act as a fictional "person" and thus relieves its individual members of certain legal liabilities. This form of business organization had existed since colonial times but became a significant factor in the American economy with the growth of railroad companies in the 1850s. A key feature of a corporation is the separation of ownership from management. A corporation can raise capital by selling ownership shares, or stock, to people who have no direct role in running it. The shareholders benefit from dividends drawn on profits and, if the corporation thrives, from the rising value of its stock.

The corporation had two major advantages over other forms of business organization that made it attractive to investors. First, unlike a partnership, which dissolves when a partner dies, a corporation can outlive its founders. This durability permits long-term planning. Second, a corporation's officials and shareholders are not personally liable for its debts. If it goes bankrupt, they stand to lose only what they have invested in it.

As large corporations emerged in major American industries, they had a ripple effect on the economy. To build plants, merge with or acquire other companies, develop new technology, and hire workers, large corporations needed huge supplies of capital. They turned to the banks to help meet these needs, and the banks grew in response. The corporations stimulated technological change as they looked for ways to speed production, improve products, and lower costs. As they grew, they generated jobs.

Large industrial corporations also changed the nature of work. By the early twentieth century, control of the workplace was shifting to managers, and semiskilled and unskilled workers were replacing skilled artisans. These new workers, often foreign-born, performed repetitive tasks for low wages.

**QUICK REVIEW**

**Corporations**

- Corporation: an association with legal rights and liabilities separate from those of its members.
- Became a significant factor with the growth of railroads in the 1850s.
- Key feature of the corporation is the separation of ownership and management.

Electricity conquered space and the night. The yellow glow of incandescent bulbs, the whiz of trolleys, and the rumble of elevated railways energize the Bowery, an emerging entertainment district in lower Manhattan at the end of the nineteenth century.

W. Louis Sonntag, Jr., *The Bowery at Night,* watercolor, 1895. Copyright Museum of the City of New York. 32.275.2

Because corporations usually located factories in cities, they stimulated urban growth. Large industrial districts sprawled along urban rivers and rail lines. By 1900, fully 90 percent of all manufacturing occurred in cities.

Two organizational strategies, vertical integration and horizontal integration, helped successful corporations reduce competition and dominate their industries. **Vertical integration** involved the consolidation of all functions related to a particular industry, from the extraction and transport of raw materials to manufacturing and finished-product distribution and sales. Vertical integration reduced a company's dependence on outside suppliers, cutting costs and delays. Geographical dispersal went hand in hand with vertical integration. Different functions, a factory and its source of raw materials, for example, were likely to be in different places, a development made possible by such advances in communication as the telephone. The multiplication of functions also prompted the growth of corporate bureaucracy.

**Horizontal integration** involved the merger of competitors in the same industry. John D. Rockefeller's Standard Oil Company pioneered horizontal integration in the 1880s.

He began investing in Cleveland oil refineries by his mid-twenties and formed Standard Oil in 1870. Using a variety of tactics, including threats, deceit, and price wars, Rockefeller rapidly acquired most of his competitors. Supported by investment

**vertical integration**  The consolidation of numerous production functions, from the extraction of the raw materials to the distribution and marketing of the finished products, under the direction of one firm.

**horizontal integration**  The merger of competitors in the same industry.

bankers like J. P. Morgan, Standard Oil controlled 90 percent of the nation's oil refining by 1890. Acquiring oil fields and pipelines as well as refineries, it achieved both vertical and horizontal integration.

The invention of the internal combustion engine and the growth of automobile and truck manufacturing after 1900 suddenly made an inconsequential by-product of the refining process, gasoline, an indispensable fuel. By that time, the refining and production of oil had spread to Texas and Oklahoma, with the discovery of oil at Spindletop Hill, near Beaumont, Texas. The Texas oil fields dwarfed the Pennsylvania basin and soon surpassed their eastern rivals in output, spawning towns from the Gulf Coast to the Permian Basin in West Texas, and new companies such as the Texas Oil Company (Texaco) and Gulf Oil, breaking Rockefeller's near-monopoly. The petroleum industry represented one of the earliest shifts of industrial wealth from the Northeast and Midwest to the South and Southwest.

A family takes a spin in their Model T Ford with the boys up front. The Ford Motor Company built affordable machines for the expanding middle-class, changing patterns of recreation and expanding work commutes and tourism.

Other entrepreneurs achieved similar dominance in other industries and amassed similarly enormous fortunes. The concentration of industry in the hands of a few powerful corporate monopolies or **trusts,** as they came to be known, alarmed many Americans. Giant corporations set prices, influenced politicians, and threatened to restrict opportunities for small entrepreneurs like the shopkeepers, farmers, and artisans who abounded at mid-century. Impersonal and governed by profit, the modern corporation challenged the ideal of the self-made man and the belief that success and advancement would reward hard work. These concerns eventually prompted the federal and state governments to respond with antitrust and other regulatory laws (see Chapters 20 and 21).

Tabloid newspapers reinforced distrust of the corporations with exposés of the sharp business practices of corporate barons and accounts of the sumptuous lifestyles of the corporate elite. Public concern notwithstanding, however, the giant corporations helped increase the efficiency of the American economy, raise the national standard of living, and transform the United States into a major world power. Corporate expansion generated jobs that attracted rural migrants and immigrants by the millions from Europe and Asia to American cities.

## THE CHANGING NATURE OF WORK

From the perspective of the workers, immigrant and native-born alike, the growth of giant corporations was a mixed blessing. The corporations provided abundant jobs, but they firmly controlled working conditions.

As late as the 1880s, shops of skilled artisans were responsible for most manufacturing in the United States. Since the mid-century, however, industrialists had been introducing ways to simplify manufacturing processes so that they could hire low-skilled workers. This deskilling process accelerated in the 1890s in response to new technologies, new workers, and workplace reorganization.

Mechanization and technological innovation did not reduce employment, although they did eliminate some jobs, most of them skilled. On the contrary, the birth of whole new industries—steel, automobiles, electrical equipment, cigarettes, food canning, and machine tools—created a huge demand for workers. Innovations in existing industries, like railroads, similarly spurred job growth.

**QUICK REVIEW**

**Captains of Industry**
- John D. Rockefeller (oil).
- James B. Duke (tobacco).
- Andrew Carnegie (steel).

**trusts**    A combination of corporations cooperating in order to reduce competition and control prices.

Ironically, it was a shortage of skilled workers as much as other factors that encouraged industrialists to mechanize. Unskilled workers cost less than the scarce artisans. And with massive waves of immigrants arriving from Europe and Asia between 1880 and 1920 (joined after 1910 by migrants from the American South), the supply of unskilled workers seemed limitless.

**Low salaries and long hours.** The new workers shared little of the wealth generated by industrial expansion and enjoyed few of the gadgets and products generated by the new manufacturing. Nor did large corporations put profits into improved working conditions. In 1881, on-the-job accidents maimed or killed 30,000 railroad workers. Safety equipment existed that could have prevented many of these injuries, but the railroads refused to purchase it. At a U.S. Steel plant in Pittsburgh, injuries or death claimed one out of every four workers between 1907 and 1910.

Factory workers typically worked 10 hours a day, six days a week in the 1880s. Steel workers put in 12 hours a day. The mills operated around the clock, so once every two weeks, when the workers changed shifts, one group had to take a "long turn" and stay on the job for 24 hours.

Long hours affected family life. By Sunday, most factory workers were too tired to do more than sit around home. During the week, they had time only to eat and sleep. Workers lived as close to the factory as possible, to reduce the time and expense of getting to work.

Big factories were not characteristic of all industries after 1900. In some, like the "needle," or garment, trade, operations remained small scale. But salaries and working conditions in these industries were, if anything, worse than in the big factories. The garment industry was dominated by small manufacturers who assembled clothing for retailers from cloth provided by textile manufacturers. The manufacturers squeezed workers into small, cramped, poorly ventilated **sweatshops.** These might be in attics or lofts or even in the workers' own dwellings. Workers pieced together garments on the manufacturer's sewing machines. A government investigator in Chicago in the 1890s described one sweatshop in a three-room tenement where the workers, a family of eight, both lived and worked: "The father, mother, two daughters, and a cousin work together making trousers at seventy-five cents a dozen pairs. . . . They work seven days a week. . . . Their destitution is very great."

## CHILD LABOR

Child labor was common in the garment trade and other industries. Shocked reformers in the 1890s told of the devastating effect of factory labor on children's lives, citing cases like that of a 7-year-old girl whose legs were paralyzed and deformed because she toiled "day after day with little legs crossed, pulling out bastings from garments."

By 1900, Pennsylvania and a few other states had passed legislation regulating child labor, but enforcement of these laws was lax. Parents desperate for income often lied about their children's age, and government officials were often sympathetic toward mill or mine owners, who paid taxes and provided other civic benefits.

## WORKING WOMEN

Women accompanied children into the workforce outside the home in increasing numbers after 1870. The comparatively low wages of unskilled male workers often required women family members to work as well. Between 1870 and 1920, the number of women and children in the workforce more than doubled.

**QUICK REVIEW**

**Factory Life**

- Job conditions were often dangerous.
- Factory workers worked ten hours a day, six days a week.
- Workers lived as close to factories as possible to reduce travel time.

**sweatshops** Small, poorly ventilated shops or apartments crammed with workers, often family members, who pieced together garments.

Noted urban and labor photographer Lewis Hine's crusade against child labor included this photo of breaker boys at a Pennsylvania coal mine, 1910. The boys worked ina constant cloud of coal dust picking out refuse from coal coming down chutes. Note the overseer with a stick at right.

Like child labor, the growing numbers of women in the workforce alarmed middle-class reformers. They worried about the impact on family life and on the women themselves. Streets in working-class districts teemed with unsupervised children. Working-class men were also concerned. The trend toward deskilling favored women. Employers, claiming that women worked only for supplemental money, paid them less than men. In one St. Louis factory in 1896, women received $4 a week for work for which men were paid $16 a week. Women chafed under this wage system but had no recourse other than to quit.

Most women worked out of economic necessity. In 1900, fully 85 percent of wage-earning women were unmarried and under the age of 25. They supported siblings and contributed to their parents' income. A typical female factory worker earned $6 a week in 1900. On this wage, a married woman might help pull her family up to subsistence level. For a single woman on her own, however, it allowed little more, in the writer O. Henry's words, "than marshmallows and tea." Her lodging rarely consisted of more than one room.

Over time, more work options opened to women, but low wages and poor working conditions persisted. Women entered the needle trades after widespread introduction of the sewing machine in the 1870s. Factories gradually replaced sweatshops in the garment industry after 1900, but working conditions improved little.

On the factory floor, young women had less room for negotiation because the customer was far removed from the manufacturing process, but they banded together, sometimes in labor unions after 1900, to demand and receive concessions from management. Working women, no less than working men, refused to be inanimate recipients of bosses' decrees and working conditions. The factory, though less so than the department store, was a space for negotiation between worker and management. And if a young woman could obtain some basic skills, other opportunities loomed as well.

The introduction of the typewriter transformed office work, dominated by men until the 1870s, into a female preserve. Women were alleged to have the dexterity and tolerance for repetition that the new technology required. But they earned only half the salary of the men they replaced. Middle-class parents saw office work as clean and honorable compared with factory or sales work. Consequently, clerical positions drew growing numbers of native-born women into the urban workforce after 1890.

**From Then to Now Online**
*The Nature of Work*

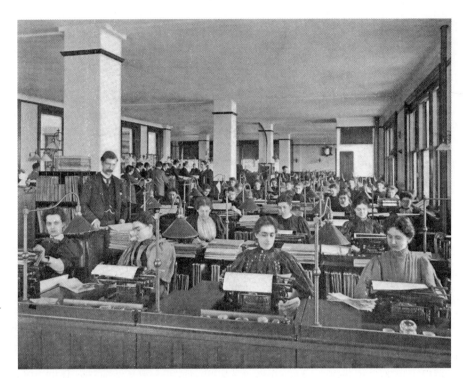

Before the typewriter was invented, most office workers were men. However, employers believed that women exhibited greater dexterity with the new machines, and besides, they could pay them less. Note the male supervisor.

*Documents*

M. Carey Thomas, *Higher Education for Women* (1901)

## QUICK REVIEW

### Working Women in 1900

- 85 percent of wage-earning women unmarried and under 25.
- Typical female factory worker earned $6 per week.
- Some working-class women turned to prostitution.

## QUICK REVIEW

### Stereotypes

- Most Americans believed that a woman's proper role was to care for her home and her family.
- Stereotypes reinforced notion that working women were promiscuous.
- Sexual harassment at work was rarely punished.

*Documents*

Jacob Riis, *How the Other Half Lives* (1890)

By the turn of the century, women were gaining increased access to higher education. Coeducational colleges were rare, but by 1900 there were many women-only institutions. By 1910, women comprised 40 percent of all American college students, compared to 20 percent in 1870. Despite these gains, many professions, including those of physician and attorney, remained closed to women. Men still accounted for more than 95 percent of all doctors in 1900. Women also were rarely permitted to pursue doctoral degrees.

Most women college graduates found employment in such "nurturing" professions as nursing, teaching, and library work. Between 1900 and 1910, the number of trained women nurses increased sevenfold. In response to the growing problems of urban society, a relatively new occupation, social work, opened to women. There were 1,000 women social workers in 1890 and nearly 30,000 by 1920. Reflecting new theories on the nurturing role of women, school boards after 1900 turned exclusively to female teachers for the elementary grades. Despite these gains, women's work remained segregated. More than 90 percent of all wage-earning women in 1900 worked at occupations in which women comprised the great majority of workers. Some reforms meant to improve working conditions for women reinforced this state of affairs. Protective legislation restricted women to "clean" occupations and limited their ability to compete with men in other jobs.

Women also confronted negative stereotypes. Most Americans in 1900 believed a woman's proper role was to care for home and family. The single working woman faced doubts about her virtue. The system of "treating" on dates reinforced stories about loose salesgirls, flirtatious secretaries, and easy factory workers. Newspapers and magazines published exposés of working girls descending into prostitution. These images encouraged sexual harassment at work, which was rarely punished.

## RESPONSES TO POVERTY AND WEALTH

Concerns about working women merged with larger anxieties about the growing numbers of impoverished workers in the nation's cities during the 1890s and the widening gap between rich and poor. While industrial magnates flaunted their fabulous wealth, working men and women led hard lives on meager salaries and in crowded dwellings.

The new industrial age created great wealth and abject poverty, and the city became the stage upon which these hard economic lessons played out. Here a "modest" Fifth Avenue mansion in turn-of-the-century New York City; farther downtown, Jacob Riis found this tenement courtyard.

Getty Images Inc., Hulton Archive Photos. Photograph by Jacob A. Riis, 22 Baxter Street Court. The Jacob A. Riis Collection, Museum of the City of New York

The urban poor included workers as well as the unemployed, aged, widowed, and disabled. The industrial economy strained working-class family life. Workplace accidents and deaths left many families with only one parent. Infant mortality among the working poor was nearly twice the citywide norm in 1900. Epidemic diseases, especially typhoid, an illness spread by impure water, devastated crowded working-class districts.

Inadequate housing was the most visible badge of poverty. Crammed into four- to six-story buildings on tiny lots, **tenement** apartments in urban slums were notorious for their lack of ventilation and light. Authorities did nothing to enforce laws prohibiting overcrowding for fear of leaving people homeless. The population density of New York's tenement district in 1894 was 986.4 people per acre, the highest in the world at the time. (Today, the densest areas of American cities rarely exceed 400 people per acre, and only Calcutta, India, and Lagos, Nigeria, approach the crowding of turn-of-the-century New York; today Manhattan has 84 residents per acre.)

One early attempt to deal with these conditions was the settlement house. The settlement house movement, which originated in England, sought to moderate the effects of poverty through neighborhood reconstruction. New York's Neighborhood Guild, established in 1886, was the first settlement house in the country; Chicago's **Hull House,** founded in 1889 by Jane Addams, a young Rockford (Illinois) College graduate, became the most famous. Addams had visited settlement houses in England and thought the idea would work well in American cities.

**tenements**   Four- to six-story residential dwellings, once common in New York, built on tiny lots without regard to providing ventilation or light.

## QUICK REVIEW

### Settlement Houses

- Effort moderate effects of poverty through neighborhood reconstruction
- Neighborhood Guild (1886) in New York was first settlement house in the United States
- Jane Addams' Hull House (1889) in Chicago was most famous settlement house

**Hull House**   Chicago settlement house that became part of a broader neighborhood revitalization project led by Jane Addams.

## OVERVIEW　Workers Organize

| Organization | History | Strategies |
|---|---|---|
| Knights of Labor | Founded in 1869; open to all workers; declined after 1886 | Disapproved of strikes; supported a array of labor reforms, including cooperatives; favored broad political involvement |
| American Federation of Labor | Founded in 1886; open only to craft workers and organized by craft; hostile to blacks and women; became the major U.S. labor organization after 1880s | Opposed political involvement; supported a limited number of labor reforms; approved of strikes |

**Gospel of Wealth**　Thesis that hard work and perseverance lead to wealth, implying that poverty is a character flaw.

**Social Darwinism**　The application of Charles Darwin's theory of biological evolution to society, holding that the fittest and wealthiest survive, the weak and the poor perish, and government action is unable to alter this "natural" process.

**The Gospel of Wealth.**　Late-nineteenth-century political ideology discouraged more comprehensive efforts to remedy urban poverty until the Progressive Era (discussed in Chapter 21). According to the **Gospel of Wealth,** a theory popular among industrialists, intellectuals, and some politicians, any intervention on behalf of the poor was of doubtful benefit. Hard work and perseverance, in this view, led to wealth. Poverty, by implication, resulted from the flawed character of the poor.

A flawed attempt to apply Charles Darwin's theory of biological evolution to human society emerged as a more common justification than the Gospel of Wealth for the growing gap between rich and poor. According to the theory of **Social Darwinism,** the human race evolves only through competition. The fit survive, the weak perish, and humanity moves forward. Wealth reflects fitness; poverty, weakness. For governments or private agencies to interfere with this natural process is futile. Thus, Columbia University president Nicholas Murray Butler, claiming that "nature's cure for most social and political diseases is better than man's," warned against charity for the poor in 1900. Standard Oil's John D. Rockefeller concurred, asserting that the survival of the fittest—Darwin never used that phrase—is "the working out of a law of nature and a law of God."

## WORKERS ORGANIZE

The growing power of industrial corporations and the declining power of workers generated social tensions reminiscent of the sectional crisis that triggered the Civil War. Wild swings in the business cycle, the fluctuation between periods of growth and contraction in the economy, aggravated these tensions. Two prolonged depressions, one beginning in 1873 and the other in 1893, threw as many as 2 million laborers out of work. Skilled workers, their security undermined by deskilling, were hit particularly hard. Their hopes of becoming managers or starting their own businesses disappearing, they saw the nation "drifting," as a carpenter put it in 1870, "to that condition of society where a few were rich, and the many very poor."

Beginning after the Civil War and continuing through World War I, workers fought their loss of independence to industrial capital by organizing and striking (see the Overview table, Workers Organize). Violence often accompanied these actions.

**Great Uprising**　Unsuccessful railroad strike of 1877 to protest wage cuts and the use of federal troops against strikers; the first nationwide work stoppage in American history.

More widespread and violent was the railroad strike of 1877, sometimes referred to as the **Great Uprising.** The four largest railroads, in the midst of a depression and in the wake of a series of pay cuts over the preceding four years, agreed to slash wages yet again. When Baltimore & Ohio Railroad workers struck in July to protest the cut, President Rutherford B. Hayes dispatched federal troops to protect the line's property. The use of federal troops infuriated railroad workers throughout the East and Midwest, and they stopped work. Violence erupted in Pittsburgh when the state militia opened fire on strikers and their families, killing 25, including a woman and three children. As news of the violence spread, so did the strike, as far as Galveston, Texas, and San Francisco. Over the next two weeks, police and federal troops continued to clash with strikers. By the time this first nationwide work stoppage in American history ended, more than 100 had been killed. The wage cuts remained.

Despite its ultimate failure, the Great Uprising was notable for the way workers cooperated with one another across ethnic and, in some cases, racial lines. The experience proved important in the next major upheaval, nine years later.

The **Knights of Labor,** a union of craft workers founded in Philadelphia in 1869, grew dramatically after the Great Uprising under the leadership of Terence V. Powderly. Reflecting the views of many skilled workers, the Knights saw "an inevitable . . . conflict between the wage system of labor and [the] republican system of government." Remarkably inclusive for its time, the Knights welcomed black workers and women to its ranks. Victories in several small railroad strikes in 1884 and 1885 boosted its membership to nearly 1 million workers by 1886.

In that year, the Knights led a movement for an eight-hour workday. Ignoring the advice of the national leadership to avoid strikes, local chapters staged more than 1,500 strikes involving more than 340,000 workers. Employers fought back. They persuaded the courts to order strikers back to work and used local authorities to arrest strikers for trespassing or obstructing traffic. In early May 1886, police killed four unarmed workers during a skirmish with strikers in Chicago. Rioting broke out when a bomb exploded at a meeting in Haymarket Square to protest the slayings. The bomb killed seven policemen and four strikers and left 100 people wounded. Eight strike leaders were tried for the deaths, and despite the lack of evidence linking them to the bomb, four were executed.

The Haymarket Square incident, and a series of disastrous walkouts that followed it, weakened the Knights of Labor. By 1890, it had fewer than 100,000 members. Thereafter, the **American Federation of Labor** (AFL), found in 1886, became the major organizing body for skilled workers.

**Knights of Labor**   Labor union founded in 1869 that included skilled and unskilled workers irrespective of race or gender.

*Address* by George Engel, Condemned Haymarket Anarchist (1886)

**American Federation of Labor (AFL)**   Union formed in 1886 that organized skilled workers along craft lines and emphasized a few workplace issues rather than a broad social program.

During the Great Uprising of 1877, federal troops clashed with striking workers. Here the Maryland militia fires at strikers in Baltimore, killing 12. As Reconstruction ended, government attention shifted from the South to quelling labor unrest.

**collective bargaining** Representatives of a union negotiating with management on behalf of all members.

Documents

Andrew Carnegie, *Wealth* (1889)

The AFL was much less ambitious, and less inclusive, than the Knights of Labor. Led by a British immigrant, Samuel Gompers, it emphasized **collective bargaining,** negotiations between management and union representatives, to secure workplace concessions. The AFL also discouraged political activism. With this business unionism, the AFL proved more effective than the Knights of Labor at meeting the needs of skilled workers, but it left out the growing numbers of unskilled workers, black workers, and women workers, to whom the Knights had given a glimmer of hope.

Rather than including all workers in one large union, the AFL organized skilled workers by craft. It then focused on a few basic workplace issues important to each craft. The result was greater cohesion and discipline. In 1889 and 1890, more than 60 percent of AFL-sponsored strikes were successful, a remarkable record in an era when most strikes failed. Responding to this success, employers determined to break the power of craft unions just as they had destroyed the Knights. In 1892, Andrew Carnegie dealt the steelworkers' union a major setback in the Homestead strike. Carnegie's manager, Henry Clay Frick, announced to workers at Carnegie's Homestead plant in Pennsylvania that he would negotiate only with workers individually and not renew the union's collective bargaining contract. Expecting a strike, Frick locked the union workers out of the plant and hired 300 armed guards to protect the nonunion ("scab") workers he planned to hire in their place. Union workers, with the help of their families and unskilled workers, seized control of Homestead's roads and utilities. In a bloody confrontation, they drove back Frick's forces. Nine strikers and seven guards died. But Pennsylvania's governor called out the state militia to open the plant and protect the nonunion workers. After four months, the union capitulated. With this defeat, skilled steelworkers lost their power on the shop floor. Eventually, mechanization cost them their jobs.

In 1894, workers suffered another setback in the Pullman strike, against George Pullman's Palace Sleeping Car Company. The strike began when the company cut wages for workers at its plant in the "model" suburb it had built outside Chicago, without a corresponding cut in the rent it charged workers for their company-owned housing. When Pullman rejected their demands, the workers appealed for support to the American Railway Union (ARU), led by Eugene V. Debs. On behalf of the Pullman strikers, Debs ordered a boycott of any trains with Pullman cars, disrupting train travel in several parts of the country. The railroads claimed to be innocent victims of a local dispute, and with growing public support, they fired workers who refused to handle trains with Pullman cars. Debs called for all ARU members to walk off the job, crippling rail travel nationwide. When Debs refused to honor a federal court injunction against the strike, President Cleveland, at the railroads' request, ordered federal troops to enforce it. Debs was arrested, and the strike and the union were broken.

These setbacks, and the depression that began in 1893, left workers and their unions facing an uncertain future. But growing public opposition to the use of troops, the high-handed tactics of industrialists, and the rising concerns of Americans about the power of big business sustained the unions. Workers would call more than 22,000 strikes over the next decade, the majority of them union-sponsored. Still, no more than 7 percent of the American workforce was organized by 1900. By that time, a dramatic change in the industrial workforce was afoot. As the large factories installed labor- and time-saving machinery, unskilled foreign-born labor flooded onto the shop floor. For many reasons, not least of which were the adjustments required for life in a new country, labor radicalism was not a high priority for many of the newcomers. Immigrants transformed not only the workplace, but also the cities where they settled and the nation many eventually adopted. In the process, they changed themselves.

## QUICK REVIEW

### Pullman Strike

- 1894 strike against Pullman's Palace Sleeping Car Company.
- Pullman workers sought solidarity with Eugene Debs' American Railway Union.
- President Cleveland ordered federal troops to enforce injunction against strike.

# NEW IMMIGRANTS

The late nineteenth century was a period of unprecedented worldwide population movements. The United States was not the only New World destination for the migrants of this period. Many also found their way to Brazil, Argentina, and Canada. The scale of overseas migration to the United States after 1870, however, dwarfed all that preceded it. Between 1870 and 1910, the country received more than 20 million immigrants. Before the Civil War, most immigrants came from northern Europe. Most of the new immigrants, by contrast, came from southern and eastern Europe. Swelling their ranks were migrants from Mexico and Asia, as well as internal migrants moving from the countryside to American cities (see Map 18–1 and Figure 18–2).

**WHAT IMPACT** did new immigration have on cities in the North?

## OLD WORLD BACKGROUNDS

The people of southern and eastern Europe had long been accustomed to migrating within Europe on a seasonal basis to find work to support their families. In the final quarter of the nineteenth century, however, several factors drove migrants beyond the borders of Europe and into the Western Hemisphere.

**WHERE TO LEARN MORE**

Statue of Liberty National Monument and Ellis Island, New York, New York.
www.nps.gov/stli

**MAP EXPLORATION** To explore an interactive version of this map, go to http://www.prenhall.com/goldfield5/map18.1

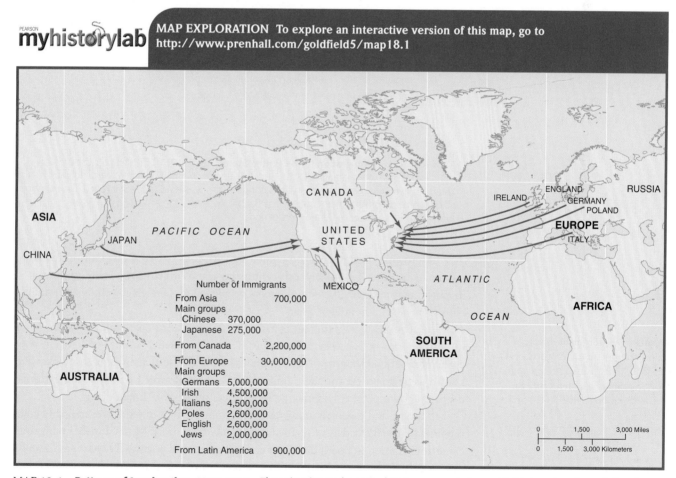

**MAP 18–1   Patterns of Immigration, 1820–1914**   The migration to the United States was part of a worldwide transfer of population that accelerated with the industrial revolution and the accompanying improvement in transportation.

**What forces** propelled so many people to emigrate from European countries?

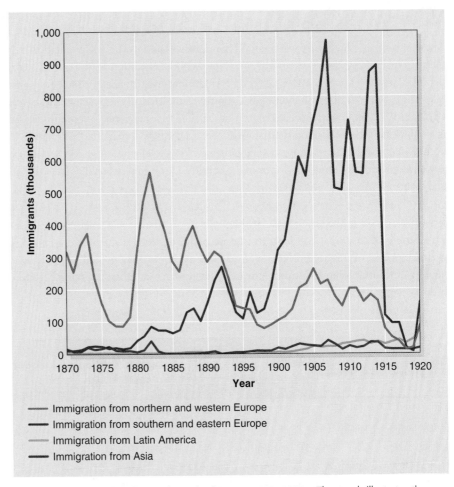

FIGURE 18–2   **Immigration to the United States, 1870–1915**   The graph illustrates the dramatic change in immigration to the United States during the late nineteenth and early twentieth centuries. As immigration from northern and western Europe slackened, the numbers of newcomers from southern and eastern Europe swelled. Latin American and Asian immigration also increased during this period.

**pogroms**   Government-directed attacks against Jewish citizens, property, and villages in tsarist Russia beginning in the 1880s; a primary reason for Russian Jewish migration to the United States.

A growing rural population combined with unequal land distribution to create economic distress in late-nineteenth-century Europe. With land ownership concentrated in increasingly fewer hands, more and more people found themselves working ever smaller plots as laborers rather than owners.

For Russian Jews, religious persecution compounded economic hardship. After the assassination of Tsar Alexander II in 1881, which was falsely blamed on Jews, the government sanctioned a series of violent attacks on Jewish settlements; these attacks were known as **pogroms.** At the same time, the government forced Jews into fewer towns, deepening their poverty and making them easier targets for violence.

Chinese and Japanese immigrants also came to the United States in appreciable numbers for the first time during the late nineteenth century. Most Chinese immigrants came from Canton in South China, a region of great rural poverty. They worked on railroads and in mines throughout the West and as farm laborers in California. Many eventually settled in cities such as San Francisco, where they established residential enclaves referred to as Chinatowns. The Chinese population in the United States peaked at about 125,000 in 1882.

Japanese began immigrating to the United States in the late 1880s, driven by a land shortage even more acute than the one in Europe. The first wave came by way of Hawaii to work on farms in California, taking the place of Chinese workers who had moved to the cities. By 1900, there were some 50,000 Japanese immigrants in the United States, nearly all on the West Coast.

Some immigrants came from right on our borders. In the late nineteenth century, Mexicans came across the border to work on the ranches and cotton farms of South and West Texas. Unlike their counterparts from Asia and Europe, these migrants settled primarily in rural areas. Whether on farms, in squalid quarters in the *barrios* of El Paso or San Antonio, or in the smaller urban centers in South Texas, such as Laredo, living and working conditions were harsh. By the turn of the century, Mexican laborers in urban areas began to organize into unions.

Wherever they came from, most migrants saw their route as a two-way highway. They intended to stay only a year or two, long enough to earn money to buy land or, more likely, to start a business back home and improve life for themselves and their families. Roughly half of all immigrants to the United States between 1880 and World War I returned to their country of origin. Some made several round trips. Jews, unwelcome in the lands they left, were the exception. No more than 10 percent of Jewish immigrants returned to Europe, and very few Jews from Russia, who accounted for almost 80 percent of Jewish immigrants after 1880, went back home.

Most of the newcomers were young men. (Jews, again, were the exception: Reflecting their intention to stay in their new home, they tended to migrate in families.) Immigrants easily found work in the nation's booming cities. The quickest way to make money was in the large urban factories, with their voracious demands for unskilled labor. Except for the Japanese, few immigrants came to work on farms after 1880.

By 1900, women began to equal men among all immigrant groups as young men who had decided to stay sent for their families. In a few cases, entire villages migrated, drawn by the good fortune of one or two compatriots, a process called **chain migration.** The success of Francesco Barone, a Buffalo tavern owner, induced 8,000 residents of his former village in Sicily to migrate to that city, many arriving on tickets Barone purchased.

Immigrants tended to live in neighborhoods among people from the same homeland. Their native culture helped shape their response to their new home.

The desire of the new immigrants to retain their cultural traditions led contemporary observers to doubt their ability to assimilate into American society. Even sympathetic observers, such as social workers, marveled at the utterly foreign character of immigrant districts.

## CULTURAL CONNECTIONS IN A NEW WORLD

Immigrants maintained their cultural traditions through the establishment of religious and communal institutions. Charitable organizations were frequently connected to religious institutions. The church or synagogue became the focal point for immigrant neighborhood life. Much more than a place of worship, it was a school for transmitting Old World values and language to American-born children. The church or synagogue also functioned as a recreational facility and a gathering place for community leaders. In Jewish communities, associations called *landsmanshaften* arranged for burials, jobs, housing, and support for the sick, poor, and elderly. Because religious institutions were so central to their lives, immigrant communities insisted on maintaining control over them.

Religious institutions played a less formal role among Chinese and Japanese neighborhoods. For them, the family functioned as the source of religious activity and communal organization. Chinatowns were organized in clans of people with the same surname. An umbrella organization called the Chinese Consolidated Benevolent Association emerged; it functioned like the Jewish *landsmanshaften*. Perhaps most important, the association

**WHERE TO LEARN MORE**

★ Pasa al Norte, El Paso, Texas. Utminers.utep .edu/panihm/default.htm

**chain migration**   Process common to many immigrant groups whereby one family member brings over other family members, who in turn bring other relatives and friends and occasionally entire villages.

## QUICK REVIEW

### Maintenance of Cultural Traditions

◆ Religious and communal institutions played a key role in maintaining immigrants' cultural traditions.

◆ Churches were often the focal point of immigrant life.

◆ The family was the most important institution in Chinese and Japanese communities.

shipped the bones of deceased members back to China for burial in ancestral cemeteries. A similar association, the Japanese Association of America, governed the Japanese community in the United States. This organization was sponsored by the Japanese government, which was sensitive to mistreatment of its citizens abroad and anxious that immigrants set a good example. The Japanese Association, unlike other ethnic organizations, actively encouraged assimilation and stressed the importance of Western dress and learning English.

Ethnic newspapers, theaters, and schools supplemented associational life for immigrants. These institutions reinforced Old World culture while informing immigrants about American ways. Thus, the *Jewish Daily Forward*, first published in New York in 1897, reminded readers of the importance of keeping the Sabbath while admonishing them to adopt American customs.

## THE JOB

If immigrant culture provided newcomers with a supportive environment, work offered the ultimate reward for coming to America. All immigrants perceived the job as the way to independence and as a way out, either back to the Old World or into the larger American society.

Immigrants typically got their first job with the help of a countryman. Italian, Chinese, Japanese, and Mexican newcomers worked with contractors who placed them in jobs. These middlemen often provided housing, loans, and other services for recent arrivals. They exacted a fee, sometimes extortionate, for their services. In an era before employment agencies, however, they efficiently matched immigrants with jobs. Other immigrant groups, such as Poles and Russian Jews, often found work through their ethnic associations or village or family connections. Family members sometimes exchanged jobs with one another.

The type of work available to immigrants depended on their skills, the local economy, and local discrimination. Mexican migrants to southern California, for example, concentrated in railroad construction. Mostly unskilled, they replaced Chinese laborers when the federal government prohibited Chinese immigration after 1882. Mexicans built the interurban rail lines of Los Angeles in 1900 and established communities at their construction camps. Los Angeles businessmen barred Mexicans from other occupations. Similarly, Chinese immigrants were confined to work in laundries and restaurants within the boundaries of Los Angeles's Chinatown.

The Japanese who came to Los Angeles around 1900 were forced into sectors of the economy that native-born white people had either shunned or failed to exploit. The Japanese turned this discrimination to their benefit when they transformed the cultivation of market-garden crops into a major agricultural enterprise. By 1904, Japanese farmers owned more than 50,000 acres in California.

Stereotypes also channeled immigrants' work options, sometimes benefiting one group at the expense of another. Jewish textile entrepreneurs, for example, sometimes hired only Italians because they thought them less prone to unionization than Jewish workers. Other Jewish bosses hired only Jewish workers, hoping that ethnic loyalty would overcome the lure of the unions. Pittsburgh steelmakers preferred Polish workers to the black workers who began arriving in northern cities in appreciable numbers after 1900. This decision began the decades-long tradition of handing down steel mill jobs through the generations in Polish families.

Jews, alone among European ethnic groups, found work almost exclusively with one another. Among the factors contributing to this pattern may have been the discrimination Jews faced in eastern Europe, the existence of an established Jewish community when they arrived, and their domination of the needle trades. Jews comprised three-quarters of the

*Documents*

Lee Chew, *Life of a Chinese Immigrant* (1903)

more than half-million workers in New York City's garment industry in 1910. Jews were also heavily concentrated in the retail trade.

Like their native-born counterparts, few married immigrant women worked outside the home, but unlike the native-born, many Italian and Jewish women did piecework for the garment industry in their apartments. Unmarried Polish women often worked in factories or as domestic servants. Japanese women, married and single, worked with their families on farms. Until revolution in China in 1911 began to erode traditional gender roles, married Chinese immigrant women typically remained at home.

The paramount goal for many immigrants was to work for themselves rather than for someone else. Most new arrivals, however, had few skills, and no resources beyond their wits, with which to realize their dreams. Major banks at the time were unlikely to extend even a small business loan to a budding ethnic entrepreneur. Family members and small ethnic-based community banks provided the initial stake for most immigrant businesses.

Immigrants could not fully control their own destinies in the United States, any more than native-born Americans could. The vagaries of daily life, including death, disease, and bad luck, thwarted many immigrants' dreams. Hard work did not always ensure success. Add to these the difficulty of cultural adjustment to an unfamiliar environment, and the newcomer's confident hopes could fade quickly. Almost all immigrants, however, faced an obstacle that by its nature white native-born Americans did not. They faced it on the job, in the city at large, and even in their neighborhoods: the antiforeign prejudice of American nativism.

## NATIVISM

**Exploring America**
*The Unwelcome Mat*

Despite the openness of America's borders in the nineteenth century, and contrary to the nation's reputation as a refuge from foreign persecution and poverty, immigrants did not always receive a warm reception. From the 1830s to 1860, nativist sentiment, directed mainly at Irish Catholic immigrants, expressed itself in occasional violence and

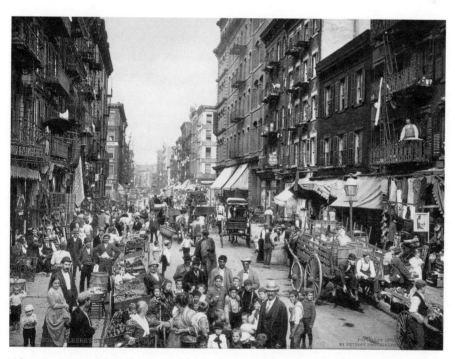

Mulberry Street, New York, 1905. The vibrant, predominantly Russian-Jewish Lower East Side of New York at first reflected more the culture of the homeland than of the United States. Language, dress, ways of doing business, keeping house, and worshiping, all followed Old World patterns. Gradually, thanks especially to the influence of school-age children, a blend of Russian Jewish and American traditions emerged.

# AMERICAN VIEWS

## ⟬ Tenement Life ⟭

In 1890, the Danish immigrant Jacob A. Riis published How the Other Half Lives, an exposé of living conditions among immigrants in New York City's Lower East Side neighborhood. The book, complete with vivid photographs, caused a sensation. At a time when newspapers and magazines competed for readers with lurid tales of urban life, Riis's detailed and gruesome depictions shocked readers and provided an impetus for housing reform in New York and, eventually, across the urban nation. Riis's scientific tone, devoid of sensationalism, rendered the scenes that much more dramatic. For a nation that valued family life and the sanctity of childhood, Riis's accounts of how the environment, inside and outside the tenement, destroyed young lives provided moving testimony that for some and perhaps many immigrants, the "promise" had been taken out of the Promised Land.

- **What** is Jacob Riis's attitude toward the tenement dwellers?
- **Considering** the destitute character of the family Riis describes, what sort of assistance do you think they receive?
- **Why** do you suppose the authorities were reluctant to enforce sanitary, capacity, and building regulations in these neighborhoods?

Look into any of these houses, everywhere the same piles of rags, of malodorous bones and musty paper all of which the sanitary police flatter themselves they have banished. . . . Here is a "parlor" and two pitch-dark coops called bedrooms. Truly, the bed is all there is room for. The family teakettle is on the stove, doing duty for the time being as a wash-boiler. By night it will have returned to its proper use again, a practical illustration of how poverty . . . makes both ends meet. One, two, three beds are there, if the old boxes and heaps of foul straw can be called by that name; a broken stove with crazy pipe from which the smoke leaks at every joint, a table of rough boards propped up on boxes, piles of rubbish in the corner. The closeness and smell are appalling. . . .

Well do I recollect the visit of a health inspector to one of these tenements on a July day when the thermometer outside was climbing high in the nineties; but inside, in that awful room, with half a dozen persons washing, cooking, and sorting rags, lay the dying baby alongside the stove, where the doctor's thermometer ran up to 115 degrees! Perishing for the want of a breath of fresh air in this city of untold charities! . . .

A message came one day last spring summoning me to a Mott Street tenement in which lay a child dying from some unknown disease. With the "charity doctor" I found the patient on the top floor, stretched upon two chairs in a dreadfully stifling room. She was gasping in the agony of peritonitis [abdominal infection] that had already written its death-sentence on her wan and pinched face. The whole family, father, mother, and four ragged children, sat around looking on with the stony resignation of helpless despair that had long since given up the fight against fate as useless. A glance around the wretched room left no doubt as to the cause of the children's condition. "Improper nourishment," said the doctor, which translated to suit the place, meant starvation. The father's hands were crippled from lead poisoning. He had not been able to work for a year. A contagious disease of the eyes, too long neglected, had made the mother and one of the boys nearly blind. The children cried with hunger. . . . For months the family had subsisted on two dollars a week from the priest, and a few loaves and a piece of corned beef which the sisters sent them on Saturday. The doctor gave direction for the treatment of the child, knowing that it was possible only to alleviate its sufferings until death should end them, and left some money for food for the rest. An hour later, when I returned, I found them feeding the dying child with ginger ale, bought for two cents a bottle at the pedlar's cart down the street. A pitying neighbor had proposed it as the one thing she could think of as likely to make the child forget its misery.

Source: Jacob A. Riis, *How the Other Half Lives: Studies Among the Tenements of New York* (New York: Charles Scribner's Sons, 1890).

job discrimination. Anti-immigrant sentiment gave rise to an important political party, the Know-Nothings, in the 1850s.

When immigration revived after the Civil War, so did antiforeign sentiment. But late-nineteenth-century **nativism** differed in two ways from its antebellum predecessor. First, the target was no longer Irish Catholics, but the even more numerous Catholics and Jews of southern and eastern Europe, people whose languages and usually darker complexions set them apart from the native-born majority. Second, late-nineteenth-century nativism had a pseudoscientific underpinning. As we saw in Chapter 17, the "scientific" racism of the period maintained that some people are inherently inferior to others. There was, in this view, a natural hierarchy of race. At the top, with the exception of the Irish, were northern Europeans, especially those of Anglo-Saxon ancestry. Below them in descending order were French, Slavs, Poles, Italians, Jews, Asians, and Africans. Social Darwinism, which justified the class hierarchy, reinforced scientific racism.

When the "inferior" races began to arrive in the United States in significant numbers after 1880, nativists sounded the alarm. A prominent Columbia University professor wrote in 1887 that Hungarians and Italians were "of such a character as to endanger our civilization." Nine years later, the director of the U.S. census warned that eastern and southern Europeans were "beaten men from beaten races. They have none of the ideas and aptitudes which fit men to take up readily and easily the problem of self-care and self-government." The result of unfettered migration would be "race suicide."

The popular press translated these scientific pronouncements into blunter language. In the mid-1870s, a Chicago newspaper described recently arrived immigrants from Bohemia (the present-day Czech Republic) as "depraved beasts, harpies, decayed physically and spiritually, mentally and morally, thievish and licentious." The rhetoric of the scientific press was scarcely less extreme. *Scientific American* magazine warned immigrants to "assimilate" quickly or "share the fate of the native Indians" and face "a quiet but sure extermination."

Such sentiments generated proposals to restrict foreign immigration. The treatment of the Chinese provided a precedent. Chinese immigrants had long worked for low wages, under harsh conditions, in mining and railroad construction in the West. Their different culture and their willingness to accept low wages provoked resentment among native- and European-born workers. Violence against Chinese laborers increased during the 1860s and 1870s. In 1870, the Republican-dominated Congress passed the Naturalization Act, which limited citizenship to "white persons and persons of African descent." The act was specifically intended to prevent Chinese from becoming citizens, a ban not lifted until 1943, but it affected other Asian groups also. The Chinese Exclusion Act of 1882, passed following another decade of anti-Chinese pressure, made the Chinese the only ethnic group in the world that could not immigrate freely into the United States.

Labor competition also contributed to the rise of new anti-immigrant organizations. A group of skilled workers and small businessmen formed the American Protective Association (APA) in 1887 and claimed half a million members a year later. The APA sought to limit Catholic civil rights in the United States to protect the jobs of Protestant workingmen.

THROWING DOWN THE LADDER BY WHICH THEY ROSE.

"Throwing Down the Ladder by Which They Rose," Thomas Nast's 1870 attack on nativism. White workers, many of them immigrants themselves, objected to labor competition from Chinese immigrants and eventually helped to persuade Congress to pass the Chinese Exclusion Act in 1882.

**nativism** Favoring the interests and culture of native-born inhabitants over those of immigrants.

**WHERE TO LEARN MORE**

★ Angel Island State Park, San Francisco Bay. www.AngelIsland.org

**myhistorylab**

**Exploring America**
*The Chinese Exclusion Act*

The Immigration Restriction League (IRL), formed in 1894 in the midst of a depression, took a more modest and indirect approach. The IRL proposed to require prospective immigrants to pass a literacy test that most southern and eastern Europeans would presumably fail.

The IRL ultimately failed to have its literacy requirement enacted. The return of prosperity and the growing preference of industrialists for immigrant labor put an end to calls for formal restrictions on immigration for the time being. Less than 30 years later, however, Congress would enact major restrictive legislation aimed at southern and eastern European immigrants. In the meantime, IRL propaganda encouraged northern universities to establish quotas limiting the admission of new immigrants, especially Jews.

Immigrants and their communal associations fought attempts to restrict immigration. The Japanese government even hinted at violent retaliation if Congress ever enacted restrictive legislation on Japanese similar to that imposed on the Chinese. But most immigrants believed that the more "American" they became, the less prejudice they would encounter. Accordingly, leaders of immigrant groups stressed the importance of assimilation.

Assimilation connotes the loss of one culture in favor of another. The immigrant experience of the late nineteenth and early twentieth centuries might better be described as a process of adjustment between old ways and new. It was a dynamic process that resulted in entirely new cultural forms. The Japanese, for example, had not gone to Los Angeles to become truck farmers, but circumstances led them to that occupation, and they used their cultural heritage of hard work, strong family ties, and sober living to make a restricted livelihood successful. Sometimes economics and the availability of alternatives resulted in modifications of traditions that nonetheless maintained their spirit. In the old country, Portuguese held *festas* every Sunday honoring a patron saint. In New England towns, they confined the tradition to their churches instead of parading through the streets. And instead of baking bread themselves, Portuguese immigrant women were happy to buy all the bread they needed from local bakers.

Despite the antagonism of native-born white people toward recent immigrants, the greatest racial divide in America remained that between black and white. Newcomers quickly caught on to this distinction and sought to assert their "whiteness" as a common bond with other European immigrant groups and a badge of acceptance into the larger society. For immigrants, therefore, becoming "white," distancing themselves from African American culture and people, was often part of the process of adjusting to American life, especially as increasing numbers of black southerners began moving to northern cities.

## ROOTS OF THE GREAT MIGRATION

Nearly 90 percent of African Americans still lived in the South in 1900, most in rural areas. Between 1880 and 1900, however, black families began to move into the great industrial cities of the Northeast and Midwest. They were drawn by the same economic promise that attracted overseas migrants and were pushed by growing persecution in the South. Job opportunities probably outweighed all other factors in motivating what became known as the **Great Migration.**

In most northern cities in 1900, black people typically worked as common laborers or domestic servants. They competed with immigrants for jobs, and in most cases they lost. Immigrants even claimed jobs that black workers had once dominated, such as barbering and service work in hotels, restaurants, and transportation.

Black women had very few options in the northern urban labor force outside of domestic service, although they earned higher wages than they had for similar work in southern cities. The retail and clerical jobs that attracted young working-class white women remained closed to black women. Employers rejected them for any job involving direct contact with the public.

## GLOBAL PERSPECTIVES

### ✺ THE ERA OF GLOBAL MIGRATIONS ✺

The massive wave of immigration from Europe and Asia to the United States was part of a worldwide migration in the late nineteenth century. Italian peasants, for example, migrated to major cities in their newly unified country, to Berlin and London, to South America, and to Canada and Australia as well as to the United States. A major objective of the migrants was to improve their lot so that they and their families would have a better life. Countries undergoing industrialization, particularly those in the Western Hemisphere, provided opportunities that did not exist in China, Japan, Italy, and Eastern Europe.

In Italy, too little land, too many people, and the lack of educational and social opportunities aided the migration stream. Italy experienced a sudden surge in fertility in the 1880s. That, combined with a declining mortality rate, resulted in sharply reduced resources and land, especially in the mostly rural regions of southern Italy and Sicily. It was a region where tax policies favored the wealthy landlords. High tariffs protected northern Italian industry but not southern enterprises, resulting in high unemployment. Adding to the misery, a blight eradicated vineyards in southern Italy, and, in 1905, a series of earthquakes rattled the region. In 1908, a tsunami in the Straits of Messina between Sicily and the Italian mainland leveled the city of Messina. None of these economic, political, and natural misfortunes by themselves caused people to pull up roots in a very rooted society. But in combination, their effect was powerful.

The same combination spurred immigration from other countries. Economic policies that ruined farm workers in southern China touched off migrations to the West Coast of the United States. In Japan, soaring inflation and unemployment during the 1870s and 1880s, worsened by a destructive typhoon in 1884, prompted nearly 30,000 Japanese to leave for Hawaii. Russian Jewish migrants feared not only for their livelihoods but their lives. Emigration was more of a necessity than a choice in these cases.

While opportunities provided the attraction, and economic, political, and religious oppression at home provided the push, technology enhanced the means to get to far-flung places. The migration of labor was something that had gone on since ancient times. But by the late nineteenth century, the advent of railroads and steamships shrunk the world, making jobs accessible anywhere. These new modes of transportation, combined with inexpensive newspapers, letters from countrymen, and the telegraph, also spread information quickly and more widely than ever before. As Mary Antin wrote about her Russian town in the early 1890s, "America was in everybody's mouth."

- Why did such massive immigration occur in the late nineteenth century?

The lack of options black migrants confronted in the search for employment matched similar frustrations in their quest for a place to live. Even more than foreign immigrants, they were restricted to segregated urban ghettos. Small black ghettos existed in antebellum northern cities. As black migration to northern cities accelerated after 1900, the pattern of residential isolation became more pronounced. The black districts in northern cities were more diverse than those in southern cities. Migration brought rural southerners, urban southerners, and West Indians together with the black northerners already living there. People of all social classes lived in these districts.

The difficulties that black families faced to make ends meet paralleled in some ways those of immigrant working-class families. Restricted job options, however, limited the income of black families, even with black married women five times more likely to work than married white women. In black families, moreover, working teenage children were less likely to stay home and contribute their paychecks to the family income.

Popular culture reinforced the marginalization of African Americans. Vaudeville and minstrel shows, popular urban entertainments around 1900, featured songs belittling black people and black characters with names like Useless Peabody and Moses Abraham

An African-American religious meeting, New York City, early 1900s. Black migrants from the South found vibrant communities in northern cities typically centered around black churches and their activities. Like immigrants from Asia and Europe, who sought to transplant the culture of their homelands within the urban United States, black migrants reestablished southern religious and communal traditions in their new homes.

Highbrow. Immigrants frequented these shows and absorbed the culture of racism from them. The new medium of film perpetuated the negative stereotypes.

In the North as in the South, African Americans sought to counter the hostility of the larger society by building their own communal institutions. An emerging middle-class leadership sought to develop black businesses. Despite these efforts, chronic lack of capital kept black businesses mostly small and confined to the ghetto. Immigrant groups often pooled extended-family capital resources or tapped ethnic banks. With few such resources at their disposal, black businesses failed at a high rate. Most black people worked outside the ghetto for white employers. Economic marginalization often attracted unsavory businesses—dance halls, brothels, and bars—to black neighborhoods. One recently arrived migrant from the South complained that in his Cleveland neighborhood, his family was surrounded by loafers, "gamblers [and] pocket pickers; I can not raise my children here like they should be."

Other black institutions proved more lasting than black businesses. In Chicago in 1891, black physician Daniel Hale Williams established Provident Hospital, the nation's first interracially staffed hospital, with the financial help of wealthy white Chicagoans. Although it failed as an interracial experiment, the hospital thrived, providing an important training ground for black physicians and nurses.

Black branches of the Young Men's and Young Women's Christian Association provided living accommodations, social facilities, and employment information for black young people. Many black migrants to northern cities, perhaps a majority, were single, and the Y provided them with guidance and a "home." White people funded many black Y projects but did not accept black members in their chapters. By 1910, black settlement houses modeled on the white versions appeared in several cities.

# NEW CITIES

Despite the hardships associated with urban life, the American city continued to act, in the words of the contemporary novelist Theodore Dreiser, as a "giant magnet." Immigration from abroad and migration from American farms to the cities resulted in an urban explosion during the late nineteenth century (see Map 18–2). In 1850, six cities had a population exceeding 100,000; by 1900, thirty-eight did. In 1850, only 5 percent of the nation's population lived in cities of more than 100,000 inhabitants; by 1900, the figure was 19 percent. The nation's population tripled between 1860 and 1920, but the urban population increased ninefold.

**WHO MADE UP** the new middle class?

Adna Weber, *The Growth of Cities in the Nineteenth Century* (1899)

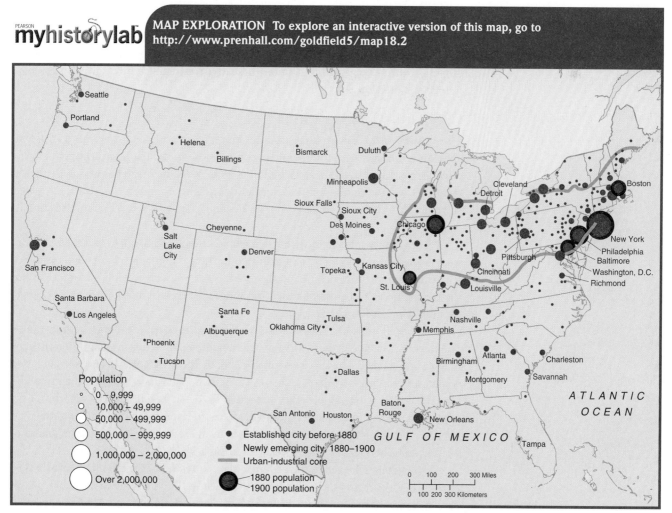

**MAP EXPLORATION** To explore an interactive version of this map, go to http://www.prenhall.com/goldfield5/map18.2

Population
- ° 0 – 9,999
- ○ 10,000 – 49,999
- ○ 50,000 – 499,999
- ○ 500,000 – 999,999
- ○ 1,000,000 – 2,000,000
- ○ Over 2,000,000

- Established city before 1880
- Newly emerging city, 1880–1900
- Urban-industrial core

1880 population
1900 population

MAP 18–2   **The Growth of American Cities, 1880–1900**   Several significant trends stand out on this map. First is the development of an urban-industrial core, stretching from New England to the Midwest, where the largest cities were located. And second is the emergence of relatively new cities in the South and West, reflecting the national dimensions of innovations in industry and transportation.

**What were** the economic forces that contributed to the growth of some cities and the decline of others?

In Europe, a few principal cities, such as Paris and Berlin, absorbed most of the urban growth during this period. In the United States, by contrast, growth was more evenly distributed among many cities. Despite the relative evenness of growth, a distinctive urban system had emerged by 1900, with New York and Chicago anchoring an urban-industrial core extending in a crescent from New England to the cities bordering the Great Lakes. This region included nine of the nation's ten largest cities in 1920. Western cities like Denver, San Francisco, and Los Angeles emerged as dominant urban places in their respective regions but did not challenge the urban core for supremacy. Southern cities, limited in growth by low consumer demand, low wages, and weak capital formation, were drawn into the orbit of the urban core. Atlanta, an offspring of the railroad, prospered as the region's major way station for funneling wealth into the urban North. Dallas emerged as Atlanta's counterpart in the western South (see Chapter 17).

Urban growth highlighted the growing divisions in American society. The crush of people and the emergence of new technologies expanded the city outward and upward as urban dwellers sorted themselves by social class and ethnic group. While the new infrastructure of water and sewer systems, bridges, and trolley tracks kept steel mills busy, it also fragmented the urban population by allowing settlements well beyond existing urban boundaries. The way people satisfied their needs for food, clothing, and shelter stimulated the industrial economy while distinguishing one class from another. Although urban institutions emerged to counter these divisive trends, they could not overcome them completely.

## CENTERS AND SUBURBS

The centers of the country's great cities changed in scale and function in this era, achieving a prominence they would eventually lose in the twentieth century. Downtowns expanded up and out as tall buildings arose, monuments to business and finance, creating towering urban skylines. Residential neighborhoods were pushed out, leaving the center dominated by corporate headquarters and retail and entertainment districts.

Corporate heads administered their empires from downtown, even if their factories were located on the urban periphery or in other towns and cities. Banks and insurance companies clustered in such financial centers as Atlanta's Five Points district to service the corporations. Department stores and shops clustered in retail districts in strategic locations along electric trolley lines.

As retail and office uses crowded out dwellings from the city center, a new phenomenon emerged: the residential neighborhood. Advances in transportation technology, first the horsedrawn street railway and, by the 1890s, the electric trolley, eased commuting for office workers. Some in the growing and increasingly affluent middle class left the crowded, polluted city altogether to live in new residential suburbs. These people did not abandon the city; they still looked to it for its jobs, schools, libraries, and entertainment, but they rejected it as a place to live, leaving it to the growing ranks of working-class immigrants and African Americans.

The suburb emerged as the preferred place of residence for the urban middle class after 1870. As early as 1873, Chicago boasted nearly 100 suburbs with a combined population of more than 50,000. Smaller cities like Cleveland, Richmond, Memphis, Omaha, and San Francisco also sprouted large suburban communities. The ideals that had promoted modest suburban growth earlier in the nineteenth century—privacy, aesthetics, and home ownership—became increasingly important to the growing numbers of middle-class families after 1880. Consider the Russells of Short Hills, New Jersey. Short Hills lay 18 miles by railroad from New York City. William Russell; his wife, Ella Gibson Russell;

*Documents*

Lincoln Steffens, from *The Shame of the Cities* (1904)

and their six children moved there from Brooklyn in the late 1880s, seeking a "pleas-ant, cultured people whose society we could enjoy" and a cure for Russell's rheumatism. Russell owned and managed a small metal brokerage in New York. Ella Russell cared for their six children with the help of a servant and also found time for several clubs and charities.

The design of the Russell home reflected the principles Catharine Beecher and Harriet Beecher Stowe outlined in their suburban home bible, *American Woman's Home* (1869). The kitchen, according to Beecher and Stowe, should be organized for expedi-ence and hygiene. The home's utilities should be confined to a central core, freeing wall areas for other functions. The new technology of central heating made it unnecessary to divide a house into many small rooms, each with its own fireplace or stove. Taking advantage of this change, Beecher and Stowe recommended that a home's ground floor have fewer but larger rooms, to encourage the family to pursue their individual activi-ties in a common space. Parlors and reception rooms disappeared, along with such for-mer standards as the children's wing, the male "smoking room," and the female parlor.

The once-prevailing view that women were too frail for vigorous exercise was changing. Thus, the entire Russell family was to be found enjoying the tennis, swim-ming, and skating facilities at the Short Hills Athletic Club. Because the community bordered on undeveloped woodland traversed by trails, "wheel clubs" appeared in the 1880s to organize families for bicycle outings. The emphasis on family togetherness also reflected the changing role of men in late-nineteenth-century society. Women's roles also broadened, as Ella Russell's club work attested.

Suburbs differed, not only from the city, but also from one another. With the growth after 1890 of the electric trolley, elevated rail lines, and other relatively inexpensive forms of commuter travel, suburbs became accessible to a broader spectrum of the middle class. The social structure, architecture, and amenities of suburbs varied, depending on the rail service and distance from the city. The commuter railroad remained popular among peo-ple like the Russells who could afford the time and expense of commuting to and from the city center.

The suburb underscored the growing fragmentation of life in and around American cities in the late nineteenth century. Residence, consumer habits, and leisure activities reflected growing social and class divisions. Yet, at the same time, the growing material-ism of American society promised a common ground for its disparate ethnic, racial, and social groups.

## THE NEW MIDDLE CLASS

From the colonial era, America's urban middle class had included professionals, physicians, lawyers, ministers, educators, editors, as well as merchants, shopkeepers, and skilled arti-sans (until they dropped from the middle class in the late nineteenth century). In the late nineteenth century, industrial technology and urban growth expanded the urban middle class to include salespeople, factory supervisors, managers, civil servants, technicians, and a broad range of "white-collar" office workers, such as insurance agents, bank tellers, and legal assistants. This newer middle class set national trends in residential patterns, consumption, and leisure.

The more affluent members of the new middle class, like the Russells, repaired to new subdivisions within and outside the city limits. Simple row houses sheltered the growing numbers of clerks and civil servants who remained in the city. These dwellings contrasted sharply with the crowded one- or two-room apartments that confined the working class. Rents for these apartments ran as much as $3 a week, at a time when few workers made more than $9 or $10.

**QUICK REVIEW**

**The New Middle Class**
- Middle class expanded to include new "white-collar" workers, such as salespeople, managers and technicians
- Affluent middle class lived in suburbs
- Less wealthy middle-class workers remained in cities
- New middle class set trends in residential patterns, consumption, and leisure

## A CONSUMER SOCIETY

The new middle class transformed America into a consumer society. In earlier times, land had been a symbol of prestige. Now it was consumer goods. And the new industries obliged with a dazzling array of merchandise and technologies. By 1910, the new middle class lived in all-electric homes with indoor plumbing. A typical kitchen might include an electric coffeepot, a hot plate, a chafing dish, and a toaster. The modern city dweller worked by the clock, not by the sun. Eating patterns changed: Cold packaged cereals replaced hot meats at breakfast; fast lunches of Campbell's soup, "a meal in itself," or canned stews weaned Americans from the heavy lunch. Jell-O appeared in the 1890s, touted as America's "most quick and easy" dessert.

The middle class liked anything that saved time: trolleys, trains, electric razors, vacuum cleaners. The telephone replaced the letter for everyday communication; it was quicker and less formal. By 1900, some 1.4 million phones were in service, and many middle-class homes had one.

The middle class liked its news in an easy-to-read form. Urban tabloids multiplied after 1880, led by Joseph Pulitzer's *New York World* and William Randolph Hearst's *New York Journal*. The newspapers organized the news into topical sections, used bold headlines and graphics to catch the eye, ran human interest stories to capture the imagination, inaugurated sports pages to attract male readers, and offered advice columns for women. And they opened their pages to a wide range of attractive advertising, much of it directed to women, who did about 90 percent of the shopping in American cities by 1900.

As the visual crowded out the printed in advertising, newspapers, and magazines, these materials became accessible to a wider urban audience. Although mainly middle class in orientation, the tabloid press drew urban society together with new features such as the comic strip, which first appeared in the 1890s, and heart-rending personal sagas drawn from real life. Immigrants, who might have had difficulty reading small-type newspapers, received their initiation into the mainstream of American society through the tabloids.

In a similar manner, the department store, essentially a middle-class retail establishment, became one of the city's most democratic forums and the focus of the urban downtown after 1890. Originating in the 1850s and 1860s with the construction of retail palaces such as Boston's Jordan Marsh, Philadelphia's Wanamaker & Brown, New York's Lord & Taylor, and Chicago's Marshall Field, the department store came to epitomize the bounty of the new industrial capitalism. They exuded limitless abundance with their extensive inventories, items for every budget, sumptuous surroundings, and efficient, trained personnel.

At first, most department-store customers were middle-class married women. Not expected to work and with disposable income and flexible schedules, these women had the means and time to wander department store aisles. The stores catered to their tastes, and the current emphasis on home and domesticity, with such items as prefabricated household furnishings, ready-made clothing, toys, and stationery. Industry churned out uniform, high-quality products in abundance, and middle-class salaries absorbed them. Department stores maintained consumers' interest with advertising campaigns arranged around holidays like Easter and Christmas, the seasons, and the school calendar. Each event required new clothing and accessories, and the ready-made clothing industry changed fashions accordingly.

Soon the spectacle and merchandise of the department store attracted shoppers from all social strata, not just the middle class. Although many less affluent women came merely to "window-shop" (a new expression inspired by the large plate-glass display windows retailers installed in their stores to attract customers), some came to buy. After 1890, department stores increasingly hired young immigrant women to cater to their growing foreign-born clientele.

The department store, the turn-of-the-century shopping mall, provided inexpensive amusement for young working-class people, especially immigrants. Mary Antin recalled how she and her teenage friends and sister would spend their Saturday nights patrolling "a dazzlingly beautiful palace called a 'department store.'" It was there that Mary and her sister "exchanged our hateful homemade European costumes . . . for real American machine-made garments, and issued forth glorified in each other's eyes."

By 1900, department stores had added sporting goods and hardware sections and were attracting customers from a wide social spectrum.

## THE GROWTH OF LEISURE ACTIVITIES

The expanding floor space devoted to sporting goods reflected the growth of leisure in urban society. And like other aspects of that society, leisure and recreation both separated and cut across social classes. The leisure activities of the wealthy increasingly removed them from the rest of urban society. As such sports as football became important extracurricular activities at Harvard, Yale, and other elite universities, intercollegiate games became popular occasions for the upper class to congregate and, not incidentally, to discuss business. The elite also gathered at the athletic clubs and country clubs that emerged as open spaces disappeared in the city. High fees and strict membership criteria kept these clubs exclusive. The clubs offered a suburban retreat, away from the diverse middle- and working-class populations, where the elite could play in privacy.

Middle-class urban residents could not afford country clubs, but they rode electric trolleys to the end of the line to enjoy suburban parks and bicycle and skating clubs. Reflecting the emphasis on family togetherness in late-nineteenth-century America, both men and women participated in these sports. Bicycling in particular became immensely popular.

If college football was the rage among the elite, baseball was the leading middle-class spectator sport. Organized baseball originated among the urban elite before the Civil War. The middle class took over the sport after the war. Baseball epitomized the nation's transition from a rural to an urban industrial society. Reflecting rural tradition, it was played on an expanse of green, usually on the outskirts of the city. It was leisurely; unlike other games, it had no time limit. Reflecting industrial society, however, it had clearly defined rules and was organized into leagues. Professional leagues were profit-making enterprises, and, like other enterprises, they frequently merged. Initially, most professional baseball games were played on weekday afternoons, making it hard for working-class spectators to attend. After merging with the American Association in 1883, the National League adopted some of its innovations to attract more fans, including beer sales, cheap admission, and, despite the objections of Protestant churches, Sunday games.

The tavern, or saloon, was the workingman's club. Typically an all-male preserve, the saloon provided drink, cheap food, and a place to read a newspaper, socialize, and learn about job opportunities. Alcoholism was a severe problem in cities, especially, though not exclusively, among working-class men, fueling the prohibition movement of the late nineteenth century.

Amusement parks, with their mechanical wonders, were another hallmark of the industrial city. Declining trolley fares made these parks accessible to the working class around 1900. Unlike taverns, they provided a place for working-class men and women to meet and date.

The most renowned of these parks was Brooklyn's Coney Island. In 1897, George C. Tilyou opened Steeplechase Park on Coney Island. Together with such attractions as mechanical horses and 250,000 of Thomas Edison's light bulbs, Steeplechase dazzled patrons with its technological wonders. It was quickly followed by Luna Park and Dreamland, and the Coney Island attractions became collectively known as "the poor man's

**QUICK REVIEW**

**Department Stores**

- Originated in the 1850s and 1860s.
- First customers were married, middle-class women.
- By 1900 department stores attracted customers from a wide social spectrum

Richard K. Fox, from *Coney Island Frolics* (1883)

paradise." Immigrant entrepreneurs, seeing a good thing, flocked to Coney Island to set up sideshows, pool halls, taverns, and restaurants.

After 1900, the wonders of Coney Island began to lure people from all segments of an increasingly diverse city. Sightseers came from around the world. In much the same manner, baseball was becoming a national pastime as games attracted a disparate crowd of people with little in common but their devotion to the home team.

Increasing materialism had revealed great fissures in American urban society by 1900. Yet places like department stores, baseball parks, and amusement parks provided democratic spaces for some interaction. Newspapers and schools also offered diverse groups the vicarious opportunity to share similar experiences.

## THE IDEAL CITY

For all its problems, the American city was undeniably the locus of the nation's energy; in some ways, with the passing of the frontier, it had replaced the West in the national imagination as the environment where possibility was boundless. This sense of limitless energy and innovation appeared most notably in urban skylines where skyscrapers reached heavenward as graceful cathedrals of commerce. The tall buildings bespoke a confidence that declared even the sky was not the limit.

Few landscapes expressed this ideal better than the 1893 World's Columbian Exposition in Chicago, a World's Fair to celebrate the 400th anniversary of the European discovery of America. The Fair demonstrated how with foresight, planning, and copious funds, it was possible to create a safe and esthetic urban environment, quite different from the gritty industrial city just beyond its borders. Dubbed the White City, the exposition epitomized cleanliness, grandeur, beauty, and order in its architecture. That it was sheer fantasy, a temporary respite from the reality beyond the gates, did not faze the millions who attended. The White City represented the possibility, and in America, anything was possible.

# CONCLUSION

The new industrial order, the changing nature of work, the massive migrations of populations from the countryside and abroad, and the rise of great cities changed the American landscape in the late nineteenth century. By 1900, the factory worker and the department store clerk were more representative of the new America than the farmer and small shopkeeper. Industry and technology had created thousands of new jobs, but they also eliminated the autonomy many workers had enjoyed and limited their opportunities to advance.

Immigrants thronged to the United States to realize their dreams of economic and religious freedom. They found both to varying degrees but also discovered a darker side to the promise of American life. The great cities thrilled newcomers with their possibilities and their abundance of goods and activities. But the cities also bore witness to the growing divisions in American society. As the new century dawned, the prospects for urban industrial America seemed limitless, yet the stark contrasts that had appeared so vividly inside and outside the Centennial Exposition persisted and deepened.

Still, it would be wrong to depict the nation in 1900 as merely a larger and more divided version of what it had been in 1876. Although sharp ethnic, racial, and class differences persisted, the nation seemed better poised to address them in 1900 than it had a quarter-century earlier. Labor unions, ethnic organizations, government legislation, and new urban institutions promised ways to remedy the worst abuses of the new urban, industrial economy.

# SUMMARY

HOW DID workers respond to the changing demands of the workplace in the late nineteenth century?

**New Industry** The Gilded Age of the late 1800s saw America transformed into the world's foremost industrial power. Technological and scientific advances, the modernization of industry, and the development of the modern corporation created changes in work life and urban living. The demand for workers drew immigrants to America and women and children into the work place. In the new urban landscape poverty abounded; the growing gap between rich and poor was seen as a result of Social Darwinism and survival of the fittest. Industrial tensions resulted in workers organizing into unions, and labor strikes, some violent, resulted as employers fought back to break the power of the unions.

WHAT IMPACT did new immigration have on cities in the North?

**New Immigrants** The period saw a dramatic rise in immigration to the United States, as the number of people moving to America from northern and western Europe slackened, the numbers from southern and eastern Europe, Latin America, and Asia increased. Work, and the resulting independence it would bring, was the goal; immigrants maintained their religious and cultural traditions while some Americans attempted to restrict their numbers through legislation. African Americans moved into the industrial cities of the North and Midwest drawn by the same promise that attracted overseas immigrants.

WHO MADE UP the new middle class?

**New Cities** Cities acted like giant magnets; an urban-industrial core extended from New England to the Great Lakes; the crush of people and the emergence of new technologies expanded the city outward and upward. Urban dwellers sorted themselves by social class and ethnic groups; residential neighborhoods, downtowns, and suburbs became fixtures of the modern city. The new middle class transformed America into a consumer society and leisure activities, spectator sports, and amusement parks became hallmarks of urban life.

# WHERE TO LEARN MORE

**Edison National Historic Site, West Orange, New Jersey.** The site contains the Edison archives, including photographs, sound recordings, and industrial and scientific machinery. Its 20 historic structures dating from the 1880–1887 period include Edison's home and laboratory. **www.nps.gov/edis**

**Pasa al Norte.** This museum, located in El Paso, Texas, serves as the Mexico–United States International Immigration History Center. Its exhibits focus on the importance of El Paso ("the Southwest Ellis Island") as a port-of-entry between the United States and Mexico from the late sixteenth century to the present. **Utminers.utep.edu/panihm/default.htm**

**Missouri Historical Society, St. Louis, Missouri.** The Society displays a long-term exhibition accompanied by public programs called "St. Louis in the Gilded Age," which focuses on the changes generated by industrialization and urban development in St. Louis from 1865 to 1900. **www.mohistory.org**

**Angel Island State Park, San Francisco Bay.** Angel Island served as a detention center from 1910 to 1940 for Asian immigrants who were kept there for days, months, and, in some cases, years while immigration officials attempted to ferret out illegal entries. Exhibits depict the era through pictures and artifacts. **www.Angelisland.org**

**Statue of Liberty National Monument and Ellis Island, New York, New York.** More than 12 million immigrants were processed at Ellis Island between 1892 and 1954. The exhibits provide a fine overview of American immigration history during this period. There is an ongoing oral history program as well. **www.nps.gov/stli**

# STUDY RESOURCES

### PEARSON myhistorylab

For study resources for this chapter, go to www.myhistorylab.com and choose *The American Journey*. You will find a wealth of study and review material for this chapter, including pre- and posttests, customized study plan, key term review flash cards, interactive map and document activities, and documents for analysis.

# REVIEW QUESTIONS

1. Were there ways to achieve the benefits of industrialization without its social costs, or did the nation's political and economic systems make that impossible?

2. How did working-class women respond to the new economy? How did their participation and responses differ from that of working-class men?

3. What factors accounted for immigration becoming a global phenomenon during the late nineteenth century?

4. The growing fragmentation of urban life reflected deep divisions in modern urban industrial society. At the same time, there were forces that tended to overcome these divisions. What were these forces, and were they sufficient to bridge the divisions?

5. How did Old World conditions influence Mary Antin's adjustment to American life? Would individuals from other immigrant groups have expressed similar sentiments, or was Mary's reaction specific to her Jewish background?

## KEY TERMS

**American Federation of Labor** (p. 537)
**Chain migration** (p. 541)
**Collective bargaining** (p. 538)
**Gilded Age** (p. 528)
**Gospel of Wealth** (p. 536)
**Great Migration** (p. 546)
**Great Uprising** (p. 536)
**Horizontal integration** (p. 530)
**Hull House** (p. 535)
**Knights of Labor** (p. 537)
**Nativism** (p. 545)
**Pogroms** (p. 540)
**Social Darwinism** (p. 536)
**Sweatshops** (p. 532)
**Tenements** (p. 535)
**Trusts** (p. 531)
**Vertical integration** (p. 530)

# 19
# Transforming the West

SUBJUGATING NATIVE AMERICANS   *(page 561)*

**WHAT WERE** the main objectives of federal Indian policy in the late nineteenth century?

EXPLOITING THE MOUNTAINS: THE MINING BONANZA   *(page 569)*

**WHAT WERE** the environmental consequences of the expansion of mining in the nineteenth century?

USING THE GRASS: THE CATTLE KINGDOM   *(page 573)*

**WHAT FACTORS** contributed to the development of the range cattle industry?

WORKING THE EARTH: HOMESTEADERS AND AGRICULTURAL EXPANSION   *(page 577)*

**HOW DID** new technology contribute to the growth of Western agriculture?

*After a pleasant ride of about six miles we attained a very high elevation, and, passing through a gorge of the mountains, we entered a level, circular valley, about three miles in diameter, surrounded on every side by mountains. The track is on the eastern side of the plain, and at the point of junction extends in nearly a southwest and northeast direction. Two lengths of rails are left for today's work. . . . At a quarter to nine A.M. the whistle of the C.P. [Central Pacific Railroad] is heard, and soon arrives, bringing a number of passengers. . . . Two additional trains arrive from the East. At a quarter to eleven the Chinese workmen commenced leveling the bed of the road with picks and shovels, preparatory to placing the ties. . . . At a quarter past eleven the Governor's train arrived. The engine was gayly decorated with little flags and ribbons, the red, white, and blue. At 12 M. the rails were laid, and the iron spikes driven. The last tie that was laid is 8 feet long, 8 inches wide, and 6 inches thick. It is of California laurel, finely polished, and is ornamented with a silver escutcheon bearing the following inscription: "The last tie laid on the Pacific Railroad, May 10th, 1869." . . .*

*The point of contact is 1,085 4/5 miles from Omaha, leaving 690 miles for the C.P. portion of the work. The engine Jupiter, of the C.P., and engine 119, of the U.P.R.R. [Union Pacific Railroad] moved up within thirty feet of each other. . . . Three cheers were given for the Government of the United States, for the railroad, for the President, for the Star Spangled Banner, for the laborers, and for those who furnished the means respectively. The four spikes, two gold and two silver, were furnished by Montana, Idaho, California, and Nevada. They were about seven inches long, and a little larger than the iron spike. Dr. Harkness, of Sacramento, on presenting to Governor Stanford a spike of pure gold, delivered a short and appropriate speech. The Hon. F.A. Tuttle, of Nevada, presented Dr. Durant with a spike of silver, saying: 'To the iron of the East, and the gold of the West, Nevada adds her link of silver to span the continent and wed the oceans.' . . . The two locomotives then moved up until they touched each other, . . . and at one P.M., under an almost cloudless sky, and in the presence of about one thousand one hundred people, the completion of the greatest railroad on earth was announced.*

Andrew J. Russell, "The Completion of the Pacific Railroad," *Frank Leslie's Illustrated Newspaper,* June 5, 1869.

PEARSON
### myhistory𝒮lab

**Personal Journeys Online**

- Eugene Chihuahua, *Leaving the West,* 1885. An Apache's account of being forced from his home into imprisonment.

- Emma Hill, *Settling in Kansas,* 1873. A woman's account of pioneer hardships.

- Carl and Fredrik Bergman, *Times Look Quite Promising,* 1884-1893. Swedish immigrants describe their experiences in Texas.

ANDREW J. RUSSELL'S short journey on the morning of May 10, 1869, from Ogden to Promontory Summit, Utah, enabled him to document what he called "the completion of the greatest work of the age, by which this vast continent is spanned, from ocean to ocean, by the iron path of travel and commerce."

The construction of the transcontinental railroad set a precedent for western development. The two railroads that met in a desolate sagebrush basin were huge corporate enterprises, not individual efforts, and corporations would dominate western growth as much as they did eastern industrialization. The crowd of onlookers had good reason to give three cheers for the federal government, for it played a crucial role in railroad construction, as in virtually all aspects of western development. Congress had authorized the Union Pacific and Central Pacific to build the railroad link, given them the right-of-way for their tracks, and provided huge land grants and financial subsidies.

The railroads' dependence on capital investment, engineering knowledge, technological innovations, and labor skills also typified western development. Their labor forces both reflected and reinforced the region's racial and ethnic diversity. European immigrants, Mexicans, Paiute Indians, both male and female, and especially Chinese, recruited in California and Asia, chiseled the tunnels through the mountains, built the bridges over the gulches, and laid the ties and rails across the plains. But Russell had the Chinese workers step back so as not to appear in the famous photographs he took at Promontory, an indication of the racism that marred so many western achievements.

Laying track as quickly as possible to collect the subsidies awarded by the mile, the railroad corporations adopted callous and reckless construction tactics, resulting in waste, deaths (perhaps as many as a thousand Chinese), and environmental destruction, all consequences that would similarly characterize other forms of economic development in the West. And as with most American undertakings in the West, the construction provoked conflict with the Cheyenne, Sioux, and other tribes.

The most important feature of the railroad, however, was that traffic moved in both directions. The transcontinental and subsequent railroads helped move soldiers, miners, cattle raisers, farmers, merchants, and other settlers into the West, but they also enabled the West to send precious metals, livestock, lumber, and wheat to the growing markets in the East. Thus the railroad both integrated the West into the rest of the nation and made it a crucial part of the larger economic revolution that transformed America after the Civil War. ✦

# SUBJUGATING NATIVE AMERICANS

The initial obstacle to exploiting the West was the people already living there, who used its resources in their own way and held different concepts of progress and civilization. As whites pressed westward, they attempted to subjugate the Indians, displace them from their lands, and strip them of their culture.

**WHAT WERE** the main objectives of federal Indian policy in the late nineteenth century?

## CHRONOLOGY

| | | | |
|---|---|---|---|
| **1858** | Gold is discovered in Colorado, Nevada, and British Columbia. | **1876** | Indians devastate U.S. troops in the Battle of the Little Bighorn. |
| **1860** | Gold is discovered in Idaho. | **1879** | Defeat of Araucanian Indians opens the pampas to settlement in Argentina "Exodusters" migrate to Kansas. |
| **1862** | Homestead Act is passed. | | |
| | Gold is discovered in Montana. | **1885** | Chinese massacred at Rock Springs, Wyoming. |
| **1864** | Militia slaughters Cheyennes at Sand Creek, Colorado. | **1887** | Dawes Act is passed. |
| **1867** | Cattle drives make Abilene the first cow town. | **1890** | Government troops kill 200 Sioux at Wounded Knee, South Dakota. |
| **1868** | Fort Laramie Treaty is signed. | | |
| **1869** | First transcontinental railroad is completed. | **1892** | Mining violence breaks out at Coeur d'Alene, Idaho. |
| **1872** | Canada enacts homestead law. | **1893** | Western Federation of Miners is organized. |
| **1874** | Gold is discovered in the Black Hills. | | |
| | Turkey Red wheat is introduced in Kansas. | | |
| | Barbed wire is patented. | | |

This photograph, taken by A. J. Russell, records the celebration at the joining of the Central Pacific and Union Pacific railroads on May 10, 1869, at Promontory Summit Utah. Railroads transformed the American West, linking the region to outside market spurring rapid settlement, and threatening Indian survival.

**W**  WHERE TO LEARN MORE

Golden Spike National Historic Site, near Promontory, Utah.
www.nps./gov/gosp

**W**  WHERE TO LEARN MORE

National Museum of the American Indian, Smithsonian Institution, Washington DC.
www.nmai.si.edu

**QUICK REVIEW**

**Indians in the West**

- Desert tribes had to contend with a harsh environment.
- The cultures of many Southwest tribes emphasized communal solidarity.
- The most numerous Indian groups in the West lived on the Great Plains.

## TRIBES AND CULTURES

Throughout the West, Indians had adapted to their environment, developing subsistence economies ranging from simple gathering to complex systems of irrigated agriculture. Each activity encouraged their sensitivity to the natural world, and each had social and political implications.

In the Northwest, abundant food from rich waters and dense forests gave rise to complex and stable Indian societies. During summer fishing runs, the Tillamooks, Chinooks, and other tribes caught salmon that, after being dried in smokehouses, sustained them throughout the year. During the mild winters, they developed artistic handicrafts, elaborate social institutions, and a satisfying religious life.

At the opposite environmental extreme, in the dry and barren Great Basin of Utah and Nevada, Shoshones and Paiutes ate grasshoppers and other insects to supplement their diet of rabbits, mice, and other small animals. Such harsh environments restricted the size, strength, and organizational complexity of societies. In the Southwest, the Pueblos dwelled in permanent towns of adobe buildings and practiced intensive agriculture. Because tribal welfare depended on maintaining complex irrigation systems, the Zunis, Hopis, and other Pueblos emphasized community solidarity rather than individual ambition. Town living encouraged social stability and the development of effective governments, elaborate religious ceremonies, and creative arts.

The most numerous Indian groups lived on the Great Plains. The largest of these tribes were the Lakotas, or Sioux, who ranged from western Minnesota through the Dakotas; the Cheyennes and Arapahos, who controlled much of the central plains between the Platte and Arkansas rivers; and the Comanches, preeminent on the southern plains. Two animals dominated the lives of these peoples: the horse, which enabled them to move freely over the plains and to use the energy stored in the valuable grasses, and the buffalo, which provided meat, hides, bones and horns for tools, and a focus for spiritual life.

**Clashing values.**    Despite their diversity, all tribes emphasized community welfare over individual interest. They based their economies on subsistence rather than profit. They tried to live in harmony with nature to ward off sickness, injury, death, or misfortune.

And they were intensely religious, absorbed with the need to establish proper relations with supernatural forces that linked human beings with all other living things. These connections also shaped Indians' attitude toward land, which they regarded, like air and water, as part of nature to be held and used communally, not as an individual's personal property from which others could be excluded.

White and Indian cultural values were incompatible. Disdaining Native Americans and their religion, white people condemned them as "savages" to be converted or exterminated. Rejecting the concept of communal property, most settlers demanded land for the exclusive use of ambitious individuals. Ignoring the need for natural harmony, they followed their own culture's goal of extracting wealth from the land for a market economy.

## FEDERAL INDIAN POLICY

The government had in the 1830s adopted the policy of separating whites and Indians (see Chapter 10). Eastern tribes were moved west of Missouri and resettled on land then scorned as "the Great American Desert," unsuitable for white habitation and development. This division presumed a permanent frontier with perpetual Indian ownership of western America. It collapsed in the 1840s, when the United States acquired Texas, California, and Oregon, and migrants crossed Indian lands to reach the West Coast. Rather than curbing white entry into Indian country, the government built forts along the overland trails and ordered the army to punish Indians who threatened travelers.

White migration devastated the Indians, already competing among themselves for the limited resources of the Plains. Migrants' livestock destroyed crucial timber and pastures along streams in the semiarid region; trails disrupted buffalo grazing patterns and eliminated buffalo from tribal hunting ranges. The Plains Indians also suffered from diseases the white migrants introduced. Smallpox, cholera, measles, whooping cough, and scarlet fever, for which Indians had no natural immunity, swept through the tribes, killing up to 40 percent of their population. Emigrants along the Platte River routes came across "villages of the dead."

By the early 1850s, white settlers sought to occupy Indian territory. Recognizing that the Great American Desert could support agriculture, they pressed on the eastern edge of the plains and demanded the removal of the Indians. Simultaneously, railroad companies developed plans to lay tracks across the plains. To promote white settlement, the federal government decided to relocate the tribes to separate specific reserves. In exchange for accepting such restrictions, the tribes were promised annual payments of livestock, clothing, and other materials. To implement this policy, the government negotiated treaties extinguishing Indian rights to millions of acres (see Map 19–1) and ordered the army to keep Indians on their assigned reservations.

These actions alarmed Native Americans. One Cherokee complained of a government official "with a pocket full of money and his mouth full of lies. Some chiefs he will bribe, some he will flatter and some he will make drunk; and the result . . . will be called a treaty." And the treaties the army enforced were not always what the Indians, however reluctantly, had accepted. White negotiators sometimes omitted from the formal documents provisions that Indians had insisted upon, and at times Congress sharply reduced the annual payments or the size of the reservations promised in the treaties.

## WARFARE AND DISPOSSESSION

Most smaller tribes accepted the government's conditions, but larger tribes resisted. From the 1850s to the 1880s, warfare engulfed the advancing frontier. Indians sometimes initiated conflict, especially in the form of small raids, but invading Americans bore

Helen Hunt Jackson, *A Century of Dishonor* (1881)

◻ Indian lands ceded 1865–1894
◻ Indian reservations
*Pimas* Indian groups
✳ Indian battles

**MAP 19–1    Indian Land Cessions, 1860–1894**    As white people pushed into the West to exploit its resources, Indians were steadily forced to cede their lands. By 1900 they held only scattered parcels, often in areas considered worthless by white people. Restricted to these reservations, tribes endured official efforts to suppress Indian customs and values.

**How did** federal Indian policy change over the course of the nineteenth century? How did the government respond to Indian efforts to resist dispossession?

ultimate responsibility for these wars. As General Philip Sheridan declared of the Indians: "We took away their country and their means of support, broke up their mode of living, their habits of life, introduced disease and decay among them, and it was for this and against this that they made war. Could anyone expect less?"

One notorious example of white aggression occurred in 1864, at Sand Creek, Colorado. Gold discoveries had attracted a flood of white miners and settlers onto land only recently guaranteed to the Cheyennes and Arapahos. Rather than enforcing the Indians' treaty rights, however, the government compelled the tribes to relinquish their lands, except for a small tract designated as the Sand Creek reservation. But white settlers wanted to eliminate the Indian presence altogether. John Chivington, a Methodist minister who had organized Denver's first Sunday school, led a militia force to the Sand Creek camp of a band of Cheyennes under Black Kettle, an advocate of peace and accommodation. The militia attacked Black Kettle's sleeping camp without warning. With howitzers and rifles, the soldiers fired into the camp and then assaulted any survivors with swords and knives. One white trader later described the helpless Indians: "They were scalped, their brains knocked out; the [white] men used their knives, ripped open women, clubbed little children, knocked them in the head with their guns, beat their brains out, mutilated their bodies in every sense of the word."

The **Sand Creek Massacre** appalled many easterners. The Cheyennes, protested the commissioner of Indian affairs, were "butchered in cold blood by troops in the service of the United States." Westerners, however, justified the brutality as a means to secure their own opportunities. One western newspaper demanded, "Kill all the Indians that can be killed. Complete extermination is our motto."

Other tribes were more formidable. None was more powerful than the Sioux, whose military skills had been honed in conflicts with other tribes. General William T. Sherman, who had marched through Georgia against Confederates, knew that the odds were different in the West. Fifty Plains Indians, he declared, could "checkmate" 3,000 soldiers. General Philip Sheridan calculated that the army suffered proportionately greater losses fighting Indians than either the Union or the Confederacy had suffered in the Civil War.

With the army unable to defeat the Sioux and their allies, and with many easterners shocked by both the military's indiscriminate aggression and the expense of the fighting, the government sued for peace. Describing white actions as "uniformly unjust," a federal peace commission in 1868 negotiated the **Second Treaty of Fort Laramie,** in which the United States abandoned the Bozeman Trail and other routes and military posts on Sioux territory, one of the few times Indians forced whites to retreat. The United States also guaranteed the Sioux permanent ownership of the western half of South Dakota and the right to inhabit and hunt in the Powder River country in Wyoming and Montana, an area to be henceforth closed to all white people.

For several years, peace prevailed on the northern plains, but in 1872, the Northern Pacific Railroad began to build westward on a route that would violate Sioux territory. Rather than stopping the railroad, the government sent an army to protect the surveyors. Sherman drew up plans for the war that he expected the construction to provoke. He regarded railroad expansion as the most important factor in defeating the Indians, for it would allow troops to travel as far in a day as they could march in weeks. Other technological developments, from the telegraph to rapid-fire weapons, also undercut the skills of the Indian warrior.

The destruction of the buffalo also threatened Native Americans. From 1872 to 1874, white hunters killed 4 million buffalo. Railroad survey and construction parties disrupted grazing areas, and hunters working for the railroads killed hordes of buffalo, both

**Sand Creek Massacre** The near annihilation in 1864 of Black Kettle's Cheyenne band by Colorado troops under Colonel John Chivington's orders to "kill and scalp all, big and little."

**Second Treaty of Fort Laramie** The treaty acknowledging U.S. defeat in the Great Sioux War in 1868 and supposedly guaranteeing the Sioux perpetual land and hunting rights in South Dakota, Wyoming, and Montana.

**Exploring America**
*Dakota Sioux Conflict*

**WHERE TO LEARN MORE**

★ Little Bighorn Battlefield National
Monument, Crow Agency, Montana.
www.nps.gov/libi/home.htm

**Battle of the Little Bighorn**    Battle in
which Colonel George A. Custer and the
Seventh Cavalry were defeated by the
Sioux and Cheyennes under Sitting Bull
and Crazy Horse in Montana in 1876.

**From Then to Now Online**
*The Legacy of Americanization*

Red Cloud, Oglala Lakota chief in the 1880s. In the 1860s, he led the Sioux to military victory over the United States, forcing the government, in the Treaty of Fort Laramie, to abandon army posts and withdraw from Sioux territory.

to feed construction crews and to prevent the animals from obstructing rail traffic. Hide hunters slaughtered even more of the beasts for their skins, leaving the bodies to rot. Federal officials encouraged the buffalo's extermination because it would destroy the Indians' basis for survival.

The climactic provocation of the Sioux began in 1874, when Colonel George A. Custer led an invasion to survey the Black Hills for a military post and to confirm the presence of gold. The Oglala Sioux, under Crazy Horse, repulsed one prong of this offensive at the Battle of the Rosebud in June 1876 and then joined a larger body of Sioux under Sitting Bull and their Cheyenne and Arapaho allies to overwhelm a second American column, under Custer, at the **Battle of the Little Bighorn.**

But the Indians could not follow up their dramatic victory. They had to divide their forces to find fresh grass for their horses and to hunt for food. Not similarly handicapped but supplied and equipped by an industrializing nation, the U.S. Army relentlessly pursued the separate bands to exhaustion. In the end, the conquest of the northern plains came, not through any decisive victory, but through attrition and the inability of the traditional Indian economy to support resistance to the technologically and numerically superior white forces.

In the Southwest, the Navajos and the Comanches were subdued, as the Sioux had been, by persistent pursuit that prevented them from obtaining food. The last to submit were the Apaches, under Geronimo. In 1886, he and 36 followers, facing 5,000 U.S. troops, finally surrendered. Geronimo and other Apaches were sent to a military prison in Florida; the tribes were herded onto barren reservations. The Oglala chief Red Cloud concluded of the white invasion: "They made us many promises, more than I can remember, but they never kept but one. They promised to take our land, and they took it."

## LIFE ON THE RESERVATION: AMERICANIZATION

Conquering the tribes and seizing their land were only the initial objectives of government policy. The next goal was to require Indians to adopt white ways, instilled by education and religion and enforced when necessary by the military. This goal did not involve assimilation but merely "Americanization," an expression of cultural conquest.

The government received aid from many Christian denominations, which had long proposed nonviolent methods of controlling Indians. Reformers wanted to change Indian religious and family life, train Indian children in Protestant beliefs, and force Indians to accept private ownership and market capitalism.

Confined to reservations, Indians were a captive audience for white reformers. Furthermore, with their very survival dependent on government rations and annual payments stipulated by treaties, Indians were "compelled by sheer necessity," as one federal official said, to accept government orders "or starve." Government agents of the Bureau of Indian Affairs used their power to undermine tribal authority and destroy traditional Indian government, prohibiting tribal councils from meeting and imprisoning tribal leaders.

White activists sought to destroy Indian religion because it was "pagan" and because it helped Indians resist assimilation. Protestant religious groups persuaded the Bureau of Indian Affairs to frame a criminal code prohibiting tribal religious practices. Established in 1884, the code remained in effect until 1933. To enforce the ban, the government withheld rations and disrupted the religious ceremonies that transmitted traditional values. In 1890, to suppress the Ghost Dance religion, the army even used artillery and killed at least 200 Sioux men, women, and children at Wounded Knee, South Dakota, in what became known as the **Wounded Knee Massacre.**

The government and religious groups also used education to eliminate Indian values and traditions. They isolated Indian children from tribal influences at off-reservation boarding schools. Troops often seized Indian children for these schools, where they were confined until after adolescence. The schoolchildren were forced to speak English, attend Christian services, and profess white American values (see American Views: Zitkala-Sa's View of Americanization).

Finally, the government and the religious reformers imposed the economic practices and values of white society on Indians. Government agents taught Indian men how to farm and distributed agricultural implements; Indian women were taught household tasks. These tactics reduced the status of Indian women, whose traditional responsibility for agriculture had guaranteed them respect and authority. Nor could men farm successfully on reservation lands that whites had already rejected as unproductive. Whites, however, believed that the real obstacle to economic prosperity for the Indians was their rejection of private property. The Indians' communal values, the reformers argued, inhibited the pursuit of personal success that lay at the heart of capitalism.

To force such values on Indians, Congress in 1887 passed the **Dawes Act,** which divided tribal lands among individual Indians. Western settlers who had no interest in the Indians supported the law because it provided that reservation lands not allocated to individual Indians would be opened to white settlers. Under this "reform," the amount of land held by Indians declined by more than half by 1900.

*Congressional Report on Indian Affairs* (1887)

Chief Red Cloud, *Tragedy at Wounded Knee* (1890)

**Wounded Knee Massacre**   The U.S. Army's brutal winter massacre in 1890 of at least two hundred Sioux men, women, and children as part of the government's assault on the tribe's Ghost Dance religion.

**Dawes Act**   An 1887 law terminating tribal ownership of land and allotting some parcels of land to individual Indians with the remainder opened for white settlement.

D. W. C. Duncan, *How Allotment Impoverishes the Indian* (1906)

Dressed in their school uniforms, Indian children sit under the U.S. flag. Government and missionary schools sought to promote "Americanization" and suppress native cultures. Such education, said one member of Congress, "is the solution of the vexed Indian problem."

Western History Collections, University of Oklahoma Library, "Phillips #436."

## AMERICAN VIEWS

### Zitkala-Sa's View of Americanization

*Zitkala-Sa, or Red Bird, was an 8-year-old Sioux girl when she was taken from her South Dakota reservation in 1884 and placed in a midwestern missionary school, where she encountered what she called the "iron routine" of the "civilizing machine." Here she recalls her first day at the school.*

- **What** lessons were the missionaries trying to teach Zitkala-Sa by their actions?
- **What** lessons did Zitkala-Sa learn?

Soon we were being drawn rapidly away by the white man's horses. When I saw the lonely figure of my mother vanish in the distance, a sense of regret settled heavily upon me. . . . I no longer felt free to be myself, or to voice my own feelings. The tears trickled down my cheeks, and I buried my face in the folds of my blanket. Now the first step, parting me from my mother, was taken, and all my belated tears availed nothing. . . . Trembling with fear and distrust of the palefaces . . . I was as frightened and bewildered as the captured young of a wild creature. . . .

[At the missionary school,] the constant clash of harsh noises, with an undercurrent of many voices murmuring an unknown tongue, made a bedlam within which I was securely tied. And though my spirit tore itself in struggling for its lost freedom, all was useless. . . .

We were placed in a line of girls who were marching into the dining room. . . . A small bell was tapped, and each of the pupils drew a chair from under the table. Supposing this act meant they were to be seated, I pulled out mine and at once slipped into it from one side. But when I turned my head, I saw that I was the only one seated, and all the rest at our table remained standing. Just as I began to rise, looking shyly around to see how chairs were to be used, a second bell was sounded. All were seated at last, and I had to crawl back into my chair again. I heard a man's voice at one end of the hall, and I looked around to see him. But all others hung their heads over their plates. As I glanced at the long chain of tables, I caught the eyes of a paleface woman upon me. Immediately I dropped my eyes, wondering why I was so keenly watched by the strange woman. The man ceased his mutterings, and then a third bell was tapped. Every one picked up his knife and fork and

began eating. I began crying instead, for by this time I was afraid to venture anything more.

But this eating by formula was not the hardest trial in that first day. Late in the morning, my friend Judewin gave me a terrible warning. Judewin knew a few words of English; and she had overheard the paleface woman talk about cutting our long, heavy hair. Our mothers had taught us that only unskilled warriors who were captured had their hair shingled by the enemy. Among our people, short hair was worn by mourners, and shingled hair by cowards!

. . . I remember being dragged out, though I resisted by kicking and scratching wildly. In spite of myself, I was carried downstairs and tied fast in a chair. I cried aloud, shaking my head all the while until I felt the cold blades of the scissors against my neck, and heard them gnaw off one of my thick braids. Then I lost my spirit. . . . My long hair was shingled like a coward's. In my anguish I moaned for my mother, but no one came to comfort me. Not a soul reasoned quietly with me, as my own mother used to do; for now I was only one of many little animals driven by a herder. . . .

I blamed the hard-working, well-meaning, ignorant [missionary] woman who was inculcating in our hearts her superstitious ideas. Though I was sullen in all my little troubles, as soon as I felt better I was . . . again actively testing the chains which tightly bound my individuality like a mummy for burial. . . .

Many specimens of civilized peoples visited the Indian school. The city folks with canes and eyeglasses, the countrymen with sunburnt cheeks and clumsy feet, forgot their relative social ranks in an ignorant curiosity. Both sorts of these Christian palefaces were alike as at seeing the children of savage warriors so docile and industrious. . . .

In this fashion many [whites] have passed idly through the Indian schools during the last decade, afterward to boast of their charity to the North American Indian. But few there are who have paused to question whether real life or long-lasting death lies beneath this semblance of civilization.

Source: Zitkala-Sa, "The School Days of an Indian Girl" (1900). Reprinted in *American Indian Stories* (Glorieta, NM.: Rio Grande Press, 1976).

White acquisition and exploitation of Indian land seemed to be the only constant in the nation's treatment of Native Americans. Assimilation failed, because most Indians clung to their own values and rejected as selfish, dishonorable, and obsessively materialistic those favored by whites. As Big Bear, a chief of the Otoe-Missouria, defiantly declared, "You cannot make white men of us. That is one thing you can't do." But if it was not yet clear what place Native Americans would have in America, it was at least clear by 1900 that they would no longer stand in the way of western development.

# EXPLOITING THE MOUNTAINS: THE MINING BONANZA

In the later nineteenth century, the West experienced several stages of economic development that transformed the environment, produced economic and social conflict, and integrated the region into the modern national economy. The first stage of development centered on mining, which attracted eager prospectors into the mountains and deserts in search of gold and silver. They founded communities, stimulated the railroad construction that brought further development, and contributed to the disorderly heritage of the frontier. But few gained the wealth they expected.

**WHAT WERE** the environmental consequences of the expansion of mining in the nineteenth century?

## RUSHES AND MINING CAMPS

The first important gold rush in the Rocky Mountains came in Colorado in 1859. More than 100,000 prospectors crowded into Denver and nearby mining camps. Simultaneously, the discovery of the famous Comstock Lode in Nevada produced an eastward rush of miners from California and booming mining camps like Virginia City. Strikes in the northern Rockies followed in the 1860s. Boise and Lewiston in Idaho and Helena in Montana became major mining centers, and other camps prospered briefly before fading into ghost towns. The last of the frontier gold rushes came in 1874 on the Sioux reservation in the Black Hills of South Dakota, where the roaring mining camp of Deadwood flourished. Later, other minerals shaped frontier development: silver in Nevada, silver and lead in Colorado and Idaho, silver and copper in Arizona and Montana.

Mining camps were often isolated by both distance and terrain. They frequently consisted only of flimsy shanties, saloons, crude stores, dance halls, and brothels, all hastily built by entrepreneurs. Such towns reflected the speculative, exploitive, and transitory character of mining. And yet they did contribute to permanent settlement by encouraging agriculture, industry, and transportation in the surrounding areas.

The camps had an unusual social and economic structure. Their population was overwhelmingly male. In 1860, for example, about 2,300 men and only 30 women lived in the Nevada camps of Virginia City and Gold Hill. Women found far fewer economic opportunities than men did on the mining frontier. Some became prospectors, but most stayed within conventional domestic spaces. Several opened lodging houses or hotels. Those with less capital worked as seamstresses and cooks and took in washing. The few married women often earned more than their husbands by boarding other miners willing to pay for the trappings of family life.

**Prostitution.**   But the largest source of paid employment for women was prostitution, a flourishing consequence of the gender imbalance and the limited economic options for women. Many who entered brothels already suffered from economic hardship or a broken family. Some Chinese women were virtually sold into prostitution. Prostitution then

*Documents*

Bill Haywood, *Miners and Cowboys* (1887)

usually worsened their distress. By the 1890s, as men gained control of the vice trade from the madams, violence, suicide, alcoholism, disease, drug addiction, and poverty overcame most prostitutes.

Public authorities showed little concern for the abuse and even murder of prostitutes, although they fined and taxed "sporting women" to raise revenue. Condemning such moral indifference, middle-class Protestant women in Denver and other cities established "rescue homes" to protect or rehabilitate prostitutes and dance-hall girls from male vice and violence. But their attempts to impose piety and purity had little success; male community leaders valued social order less than they did economic opportunity.

**Saloon society.**   The gender imbalance in the mining camps also made saloons prevalent among local businesses. An 1879 business census of Leadville, Colorado, reported 10 dry-goods stores, 4 banks, and 4 churches, but 120 saloons, 19 beer halls, and 118 gambling houses. Saloons were social centers in towns where most miners lived in crowded and dirty tents and rooming houses.

The male-dominated saloon society of the mining camps generated social conflict. Disputes over mining claims could become violent, adding to the disorder. The California mining town of Bodie experienced 29 killings between 1877 and 1883, a homicide rate higher than that of any U.S. city a century later. But such killings occurred only within a small group of males, young, single, surly, and armed, who were known as the Badmen of Bodie. Daily life for most people was safe.

**Collective violence.**   Indeed, personal and criminal violence, which remains popularly associated with the West, was less pervasive than collective violence. This, too, affected mining camps and was aggravated by their ethnic and racial diversity. Irish, Germans, English, Chinese, Australians, Italians, Slavs, and Mexicans, among others, rushed into the mining regions. In many camps, half the population was foreign-born and another fourth consisted of first-generation Americans. The European immigrants who sometimes encountered nativist hostility in the East experienced less animosity in the West, but nonwhite minorities often suffered. In particular, white people frequently drove Mexicans and Chinese from their claims or refused to let them work in higher-paid occupations in the mining camps. The Chinese had originally migrated to the California gold fields and thereafter spread to the new mining areas of the Rockies and the Great Basin, where they worked in mining when possible, operated laundries and restaurants, and held menial jobs like hauling water and chopping wood. In 1870, more than a quarter of Idaho's population and nearly 10 percent of Montana's was Chinese. Where they were numerous, the Chinese built their own communities and maintained their customs.

But racism and fear of economic competition sparked hostility and violence against the Chinese almost everywhere. The worst anti-Chinese violence occurred in Rock Springs, Wyoming, in 1885 when whites killed 28 Chinese workers and drove away all 700 residents from the local Chinatown. Although the members of the mob were well known, the grand jury, speaking for the white majority, found no cause for legal action. Such community sanction for violence against racial minorities made mob attacks one of the worst features of the mining camps.

## LABOR AND CAPITAL

New technology had dramatic consequences for both miners and the mining industry. Initially, mining was an individual enterprise in which miners used simple tools, such as picks, shovels, and wash pans, to work shallow surface deposits known as placers. Placer mining attracted prospectors with relatively little capital or expertise, but surface deposits

Opening restaurants and boarding houses, some women earned money from their domestic skills in the mining camps.

were quickly exhausted. More complex and expensive operations were needed to reach the precious metal buried in the earth.

Hydraulic mining, for example, required massive capital investment to build reservoirs, ditches, and troughs to power high-pressure water cannons that would pulverize hillsides and uncover the mineral deposits. Quartz, or lode, mining, sometimes called hard-rock mining, required still more money, technology, and time to sink a shaft into the earth, timber underground chambers and tunnels, install pumps to remove underground water and hoists to lower men and lift out rock, and build stamp mills and smelters to treat the ore.

Such complex, expensive, and permanent operations necessarily came under corporate control. Often financed with eastern or British capital, the new corporations integrated the mining industry into the larger economy. Hard-rock mining produced more complex ores than could be treated in remote mining towns. With the new railroad network, they were shipped to smelting plants as far away as Kansas City and St. Louis and then to refineries in eastern cities. Western ores thus became part of national and international business. The mining industry's increasing development of lower-grade deposits led to greater capital investment and larger operations that employed more workers and machinery.

**Effects of corporate mining.**   Quartz mining thus helped usher the mining frontier into a more stable period. But the new corporate mining had disturbing effects. Its impact on the environment was horrendous. Hydraulic mining washed away hillsides, depositing debris in canyons and valleys to a depth of 100 feet or more, clogging rivers and causing floods, and burying thousands of acres of farmland. Such damage provoked an outcry and eventually led to government regulation. Fewer westerners worried about sterile slag heaps or the toxic fumes that belched from smelters and killed vegetation. They were the signs of progress. "The thicker the fumes," declared one proud Butte newspaper, "the greater our financial vitality."

Corporate mining also hurt miners, transforming them into wage workers with restricted opportunities. Miners' status declined as new machinery, such as power drills, reduced the need for skilled laborers and enabled employers to hire cheaper workers from eastern and southern Europe. Mining corporations, moreover, did little to protect miners' health or safety. Miners died in cave-ins, explosions, and fires or from the great

## QUICK REVIEW

### Technology and Mining

- Mining began as an individual enterprise.
- Deeper mining required expensive equipment.
- As mining became more complex and costly, it came under corporate control.

Edward Gould Buffum, *Six Months in the Gold Mines* (1850)

Chinese miners in Idaho operate the destructive water cannons used in hydraulic mining. Technological changes made most miners wage workers for companies

Idaho State Historical Society

heat and poisonous gases in underground mines. Others contracted silicosis, lead poisoning, or other diseases or were crippled or killed by machines.

**Unions and union busting.**    To protect themselves, miners organized unions. These functioned as benevolent societies, aiding injured miners or their survivors, establishing hospitals and libraries, and providing an alternative to the saloons with union halls serving as social and educational centers. Unions also promoted miners' interests by striking against wage cuts and campaigning for mine safety. They convinced states to pass mine safety laws and, beginning in the 1880s, to appoint mine inspectors. The chief role of these state officials was, in the words of a Colorado inspector, to decide "How far should an industry be permitted to advance its material welfare at the expense of human life?"

The industry itself, however, often provided the answer to this question, for mining companies frequently controlled state power and used it to crush unions. Thus, in 1892, in the Coeur d'Alene district of Idaho, mining companies locked out strikers and imported a private army, which battled miners in a bloody gunfight. Management next persuaded the governor and the president to send in the state militia and the U.S. Army. State officials then suppressed the strike and the union by confining all union members and their sympathizers in stockades.

Strikes, union busting, and violence continued for years. When mining companies in Utah, Colorado, and Montana pursued the same aggressive tactics of lockouts and wage cuts, the local miners' unions in the West united for strength and self-protection. In 1893, they formed one of the nation's largest and most militant unions, the Western Federation of Miners.

Violence and conflict were attributable not to frontier lawlessness but to the industrialization of the mines. Both management's tactics—blacklisting union members, locking out strikers, obtaining court injunctions against unions, and using soldiers against workers—and labor's response mirrored conditions in the industrial East. In sum, western

## QUICK REVIEW

### Miners' Unions

- Paid benefits to injured miners or their survivors.
- Served as social and educational centers.
- Promoted miners' interests on the job.

mining, reflecting the industrialization of the national economy, had been transformed from a small-scale prospecting enterprise characterized by individual initiative and simple tools into a large-scale corporate business characterized by impersonal management, outside capital, advanced technology, and wage labor.

# USING THE GRASS: THE CATTLE KINGDOM

The development of the range-cattle industry opened a second stage of exploitation of the late-nineteenth-century West. It reflected the needs of an emerging eastern urban society, the economic possibilities of the grasslands of the Great Plains, the technology of the expanding railroad network, and the requirements of corporations and capital. It also brought "cow towns" and urban development to the West. The fabled cowboy, though essential to the story, was only a bit player.

**WHAT FACTORS** contributed to the development of the range cattle industry?

## CATTLE DRIVES AND COW TOWNS

The cattle industry originated in southern Texas, where the Spanish had introduced cattle in the eighteenth century. Developed by Mexican ranchers, "Texas longhorns" proved well adapted to the plains grasslands. By the 1860s, they numbered about 5 million head. As industrial expansion in the East and Midwest enlarged the urban market for food, the potential value of Texas steers increased. And the extension of the railroad network into the West opened the possibility of tapping that market. The key was to establish a shipping point on the railroads west of the settled farming regions, a step first taken in 1867 by Joseph McCoy, an Illinois cattle shipper. McCoy selected Abilene, Kansas. But Abilene was the western railhead of the Kansas Pacific Railroad and was ringed by lush grasslands for cattle. Texans opened the **Chisholm Trail** through Indian Territory to drive their cattle northward to Abilene. Within three years, a million and a half cattle reached Abilene, divided into herds of several thousand, each directed by a dozen cowhands on a "long drive" taking two to three months.

Joseph G. McCoy, *Historic Sketches of the Cattle Trade of the West and Southwest* (1874)

**Chisholm Trail** The route followed by Texas cattle raisers driving their herds north to markets at Kansas railheads.

**Cow town life.** The cattle trade attracted other entrepreneurs who created a bustling town. As both railroads and settlement advanced westward, a series of other cow towns— Ellsworth, Wichita, Dodge City, Cheyenne—attracted the long drives, cattle herds, and urban development.

As with the mining camps, the cow towns' reputation for violence was exaggerated. They adopted gun-control laws, prohibiting the carrying of handguns within city limits, and established police forces to maintain order. The primary duties of law officers were arresting drunks, fixing sidewalks, and collecting fines. The cow towns regulated, rather than prohibited, prostitution and gambling, for merchants viewed these vices as necessary to attract the cattle trade. Thus, the towns taxed prostitutes and gamblers and charged high fees for liquor licenses. By collecting such "sin taxes," Wichita was able to forgo general business taxes, thereby increasing its appeal to prospective settlers.

Not all cow towns became cities like Wichita, most, like Abilene, dwindled into small towns serving farm populations. But cow towns, again like mining camps, contributed to the growth of an urban frontier. Railroads often determined the location and growth of western cities, providing access to markets for local products, transporting supplies and machinery for residents, and attracting capital for commercial and industrial development. The West, in fact, had become the most urban region in the nation by 1890, with two-thirds of its population living in communities of at least 2,500 people.

## RISE AND FALL OF OPEN-RANGE RANCHING

The significance of the long drive to the cow towns faded as cattle raising expanded beyond Texas. Indian removal and extension of the railroads opened land for ranching in Kansas, Nebraska, Wyoming, Colorado, Montana, and the Dakotas. Cattle reaching Kansas were increasingly sold to stock these northern ranges rather than for shipment to the packinghouses. Ranches soon spread across the Great Plains and into the Great Basin, the Southwest, and even eastern Oregon and Washington. This expansion was helped by the initially low investment that ranching required.

By the early 1880s, the high profits from this enterprise and an expanding market for beef attracted speculative capital and reshaped the industry. Eastern and European capital flooded the West, with British investors particularly prominent. Some investors went into partnership with existing ranchers, providing capital in exchange for expertise and management. Wisconsin investors formed the Three Rivers Land and Cattle Company of New Mexico, for example, by buying into a ranch owned by Susan Barber, whom they then employed as general manager. Barber was unusual in the male-dominated industry, but the managerial skills she demonstrated were necessary for success. On a larger scale, British and American corporations acquired, expanded, and managed huge ranches.

**Effects of corporate control.**   Large companies soon dominated the industry, just as they had gained control of mining. On the plains, cattle companies often worked together to enhance their power, especially by restricting access to the range and by intimidating small competitors. Some large companies illegally enclosed the open range, building fences to exclude newcomers and minimize labor costs by reducing the number of cowboys needed to control the cattle. One Wyoming newspaper complained: "Some morning we will wake up to find that a corporation has run a wire fence about the boundary lines of Wyoming, and all within the same have been notified to move."

Such tensions sometimes exploded in instances of social violence as serious as those that disrupted the mining frontier. Attempts by large ranchers to fence off public

### QUICK REVIEW

#### Cattle Ranching

* Indian removal and the arrival of the railroad opened land for ranching.
* High profits in the industry attracted speculative capital and large companies.
* The industry collapsed in the 1880s due to overgrazing.

Cowboys gather around the chuck wagon at the XIT Ranch in Texas. Poor pay and arduous work defined the lives of most cowboys.

## GLOBAL PERSPECTIVES

### THE WEST ABROAD

Americans have always liked to think of the American West as a distinctive region whose prospectors, cowboys, and homesteaders helped shape an exceptional national experience. In fact, however, other countries also experienced comparable developments in the late nineteenth century. While the United States and other countries romanticized their frontier experiences, common environmental, economic, and social forces diminished their distinctiveness.

An obvious demonstration that the frontier was not uniquely American was the interlocking western development in the United States and Canada. The mining frontier crossed the border and included gold rushes in British Columbia from 1858 to 1867 and the Yukon in the 1890s. Canadian goldfields imported California's mining regulations and also followed the pattern of corporate supplanting placer mining. As for cattle raising, one Alberta rancher said in 1884: "We adopted pretty much the same system as was carried on across the border." Ranchers used Canada's public domain for pasture, while cowboys had familiar clothing, work, and wages. Stock associations developed to safeguard ranchers' interests, and gradually big eastern Canadian and British firms dominated the industry.

Like its American counterpart, the Canadian government promoted the construction of a transcontinental railroad, the Canadian Pacific, with land grants and subsidies. It enacted a homestead law providing free land in 1872. It encouraged European immigrants to settle and then witnessed land booms, commercial wheat production, and falling crop prices.

Canada experienced less violence and disorder than the United States, largely because of its Indian policy.

Although it too established reservations, Canada treated Indians with respect, created a system of incorruptible agents, and used the North West Mounted Police to prevent the exploitation of Indians by settlers. The Mounted Police also maintained law and order on the mining and ranching frontiers.

While Canada most closely paralleled the American experience, Australia, too, had similarities. Its gold rush began in 1851, attracted miners, technology, and capital from California, and saw violence against Chinese. As in North America, corporate mining soon replaced the original "diggers." In 1861 Australia enacted homestead-type laws to assist small farmers who eventually developed into major wheat producers. And in the 1870s a large-scale pastoral economy, though based on sheep, not cattle, emerged in its vast arid region.

Argentina had no mining frontier, but after suppressing the Araucanian Indians in 1879 to open the pampas to settlement, it developed first a cattle ranching and then an agricultural frontier. Argentine gauchos, like American cowboys, came to symbolize the national character, though they too soon became ranch hands dependent on wages. The government promoted railroad construction in the 1880s, and European immigration helped people the prairies, spurring wheat production and the adoption of the new farming technologies.

- How might transnational factors such as economic, technological, and demographic changes contribute to understanding the development of the American West in the late nineteenth century?

lands in Texas provoked the Fence-Cutters War of 1883–84. Montana's largest cattlemen organized an armed force known as "Stuart's Stranglers" and, in America's worst vigilante violence, killed over a hundred people they viewed as challenging their power.

The corporate cattle boom overstocked the range and threatened the industry itself. Overgrazing replaced nutritious grasses with sagebrush, Russian thistle, and other plants that livestock found unpalatable. Droughts in the mid-1880s further withered vegetation and enfeebled the animals. Millions of cattle starved or froze to death in terrible blizzards in 1886 and 1887. These ecological and financial disasters destroyed the open-range cattle industry. The surviving ranchers reduced their operations, restricted the size of their herds, and tried to ensure adequate winter feed by growing hay. To further reduce their dependence on natural vegetation, they introduced drought-resistant sorghum and new grasses; to reduce their dependence on rainfall, they drilled wells and installed windmills to pump water.

## COWHANDS AND CAPITALISTS

**WHERE TO LEARN MORE**

★ National Cowboy Hall of Fame, Oklahoma City, Oklahoma. www.cowboyhalloffame.org/ index2.html

One constant in the cattle industry was the cowboy, but his working conditions and opportunities changed sharply over time and corresponded little to the romantic image of a dashing individual free of social constraints. Cowboys' work was hard, dirty, seasonal, tedious, sometimes dangerous, and poorly paid. Many early cowboys were white southerners unwilling or unable to return home after the Civil War. Black cowhands made up perhaps 25 percent of the trail-herd outfits. Many others, especially in Texas and the Southwest, were Mexicans. Indeed, Mexicans developed most of the tools, techniques, and trappings that characterized the cattle industry: from boots, chaps, and the "western" saddle to roundups and roping. As the industry expanded northward, more cowboys came from rural Kansas, Nebraska, and neighboring states.

Initially, in the frontier-ranching phase dominated by the long drive, cowboys were seasonal employees who worked closely with owners. Often the sons or neighbors of ranchers, they frequently expected to become independent stock raisers themselves. They typically enjoyed the rights to "maverick" cattle, or put their own brand on unmarked animals they encountered, and to "run a brand," or to own their own cattle while working for a ranch. These informal rights provided opportunities to acquire property and move up the social ladder.

As ranching changed with the appearance of large corporate enterprises, so did the work and work relationships of cowhands. The power and status of employer and employees diverged, and the cowboys' traditional rights disappeared. Employers redefined mavericking as rustling and prohibited cowhands from running a brand of their own. One cowboy complained that these restrictions deprived a cowhand of his one way "to get on in the world." But that was the purpose: Cowboys were to be workers, not potential ranchers and competitors. To increase labor efficiency, some companies prohibited their cowboys from drinking, gambling, and carrying guns.

**Unions and strikes.**   Cowboys sometimes responded to these structural transformations the same way skilled workers in the industrial East did, by forming unions and striking. The first strike occurred in Texas in 1883, when the Panhandle Stock Association, representing large operators, prohibited ranch hands from owning their own cattle and imposed a standard wage. More than 300 cowboys struck seven large ranches for higher wages and the right to brand mavericks for themselves and to run small herds on the public domain. Ranchers evicted the cowboys, hired scabs, and used the Texas Rangers to drive the strikers from the region.

Other strikes also failed because corporate ranches and their stock associations had great influence and cowhands faced long odds in their efforts to organize. They were isolated across vast spaces and had little leverage in the industry. years' experience," they conceded, "We are dependent on you."

The transformation of the western cattle industry and its integration into a national economy dominated by corporations thus made the cherished image of cowboy independence and rugged individualism more myth than reality. One visitor to America in the late 1880s commented: "Out in the fabled West, the life of the 'free' cowboy is as much that of a slave as is the life of his Eastern brother, the Massachusetts mill-hand. And the slave-owner is in both cases the same, the capitalist."

# WORKING THE EARTH: HOMESTEADERS AND AGRICULTURAL EXPANSION

Even more than ranching and mining, agricultural growth boosted the western economy and bound it tightly to national and world markets. In this process, the government played a significant role, as did the railroads, science and technology, eastern and foreign capital, and the dreams and hard work of millions of rural settlers. The development of farming produced remarkable economic growth, but it left the dreams of many unfulfilled.

**HOW DID** new technology contribute to the growth of Western agriculture?

## SETTLING THE LAND

To stimulate agricultural settlement, Congress passed the most famous land law, the **Homestead Act** of 1862 (see the Overview table, Government Land Policy). The measure offered 160 acres of land free to anyone who would live on the plot and farm it for five years. The act promised opportunity and independence to ambitious farmers.

**Homestead Act** 1862 law providing 160 acres of free land to anyone who would live on and farm the land for five years.

**Limits of the Homestead Act.**   Despite the apparently liberal land policy, however, prospective settlers found less land open to public entry than they expected. Federal land laws did not apply in much of California and the Southwest, where Spain and Mexico had previously transferred land to private owners. Elsewhere, the government had given away millions of acres to railroads or authorized selling millions more for educational and other purposes. Moreover, other laws provided for easy transfer of public lands to cattle companies, to other corporations exploiting natural resources, and to land speculators.

*The Homestead Act* (1862)

Thus, settlers in Kansas, Nebraska, Minnesota, and the Dakotas in the late 1860s and early 1870s often found most of the best land unavailable for homesteading and much of the rest remote from transportation facilities and markets. Although 375,000 farms were claimed by 1890 through the Homestead Act, a success by any measure, most settlers had to purchase their land.

Charles and Nellie Wooster, *Letters from the Frontier* (1872)

Mexican-American ranch family, Mora Valley, New Mexico Territory, 1895. Note the leather boots on the baby's feet: this family perhaps has aspirations for their young son.

Source: Photographic Archives, Palace of the Governors, Museum of New Mexico, Santa Fe, New Mexico.

## OVERVIEW    Government Land Policy

| Legislation | Result |
| --- | --- |
| Railroad land grants (1850–1871) | Granted 181 million acres to railroads to encourage construction and development |
| Homestead Act (1862) | Gave 80 million acres to settlers to encourage settlement |
| Morrill Act (1862) | Granted 11 million acres to states to sell to fund public agricultural colleges |
| Other grants | Granted 129 million acres to states to sell for other educational and related purposes |
| Dawes Act (1887) | Allotted some reservation lands to individual Indians to promote private property and weaken tribal values among Indians and offered remaining reservation lands for sale to whites (by 1906, some 75 million acres had been acquired by whites) |
| Various laws | Permitted direct sales of 100 million acres by the Land Office |

The Homestead Act also reflected traditional eastern conceptions of the family farm, which were inappropriate in the West. A farm of 160 acres would have suited conditions in eastern Kansas or Nebraska, but farther west, larger-scale farming was necessary. And the law ignored the need for capital that was required for successful farming.

**Promoting settlement.**    Nevertheless, many interests promoted settlement. Newspaper editors trumpeted the prospects of their region. Land companies, eager to sell their speculative holdings, sent agents through the Midwest and Europe to encourage migration. Steamship companies, hoping to sell transatlantic tickets, advertised the opportunities in the American West across Europe. Religious and ethnic groups encouraged immigration.

Most important, railroad advertising and promotional campaigns attracted people to the West. Not only would the railroads profit from selling their huge land reserves to settlers, but a successful agricultural economy would produce crops to be shipped east and a demand for manufactured goods to be shipped west on their lines. The railroads therefore advanced credit to prospective farmers, provided transportation assistance, and extended technical and agricultural advice.

Thus encouraged, migrants poured into the West, occupying and farming more acres between 1870 and 1900 than Americans had in the previous 250 years (see Figure 19–1). Farmers settled in every region. Most, however, streamed into the Great Plains states, from the Dakotas to Texas.

White migrants predominated in the mass migration, but African Americans initiated one of its most dramatic episodes, a millenarian folk movement they called the Exodus. Seeking to escape the misery and repression of the post-Reconstruction South, these poor "Exodusters" established several dozen black communities in 1879 in Kansas and Nebraska on the agricultural frontier.

Many of the new settlers came from Europe, bringing with them not only their own attitudes toward the land but also special

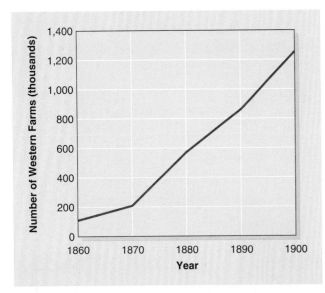

**FIGURE 19–1    The Growth of Western Farming,**
**1860–1900**   Indian removal, railroad expansion, and liberal land policies drew farm families into the West from much of Europe as well as the East. Technological innovations like barbed wire and farm machinery soon enabled them to build farms, but economic, social, and environmental challenges remained.
Data Source: Historical Statistics of the United States (1975).

crops, skills, settlement patterns, and agricultural practices. Peasants from Norway, Sweden, and Denmark flocked to Minnesota. Germans, Russians, and Irish put down roots across Texas, Kansas, Nebraska, and the Dakotas. French, Germans, and Italians developed vineyards, orchards, and nurseries in California, where laborers from Japan and Mexico arrived to work in fields and canneries.

**Hispanic losses.**   Migrants moved into the West in search of opportunity, which they sometimes seized at the expense of others already there. In the Southwest, Hispanics had long lived in village communities largely outside a commercial economy, farming small tracts of irrigated land and herding sheep on communal pastures. As Anglos, or white Americans, arrived, their political and economic influence undermined traditional Hispanic society. Congress restricted the original Hispanic land grants to only the villagers' home lots and irrigated fields, throwing open most of their common lands to newcomers. Hispanic title was confirmed to only 2 million of the 37.5 million acres at stake. Anglo ranchers and settlers manipulated the federal land system to control these lands.

Spanish Americans resisted these losses in court or through violence. One militant group, organized as *Las Gorras Blancas* ("the White Caps"), staged night raids to cut fences erected by Anglo ranchers and farmers and to attack the property of railroads, the symbol of the encroaching new order. Such resistance, however, had little success.

As their landholdings shrank, Hispanic villagers could not maintain their pastoral economy. Few turned to homesteading, for that would have required dispersed settlement and abandoning the village and its church, school, and other cultural institutions. Thus many Hispanics became seasonal wage laborers in the Anglo-dominated economy, sometimes working as stoop labor in the commercial sugar-beet fields that emerged in the 1890s, sometimes working on the railroads or in the mines. Such seasonal labor enabled Hispanics to maintain their villages and provided sufficient income to adopt some Anglo technology, such as cook stoves and sewing machines. But if Hispanics retained some cultural autonomy, they had little influence over the larger processes of settlement and development that restricted their opportunities and bound them to the western and national economy.

## HOME ON THE RANGE

In settling the West, farm families encountered many difficulties, especially on the Great Plains, where they had to adapt to a radically new environment. The scarcity of trees on the plains meant that there was little wood for housing, fuel, and fencing. Until they had reaped several harvests and could afford to import lumber, pio-

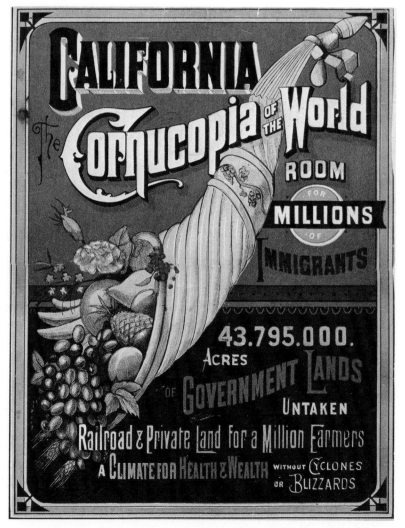

An 1880s poster advertises the availability of land for settlement and highlights the healthy, agreeable climate in California.

Sunday school meeting in Custer County, Nebraska, in 1888. Sunday schools were important social as well as religious institutions on the Great Plains, where, as one newspaper reported, rural families often felt like "strangers in a strange land."

neer families lived in houses made of sod. Though inexpensive and sturdy, sod houses were also dark and dirty. Snakes, mice, and insects often crawled out of the walls and roofs.

**Women's work.**   Within these rough houses, women worked to provide food, clothing, and medicine to ensure the family's survival. Their efforts were greatly constrained by the harsh environment. For fuel, families often had to rely on buffalo or cattle "chips," dried dung. The scarcity of water also complicated women's domestic labor. They often had to transport water over long distances, pulling barrels on "water sleds" or carrying pails on neck yokes. They melted snow for wash water and used the same water over again for different chores. Where possible, they also helped to dig wells by hand.

Some women farmed the land themselves. Single women could claim land under the Homestead Act, and in some areas, women claimants made up 18 percent of the total and succeeded more frequently than men in gaining final title. At times, married women operated the family farm by themselves while their husbands worked elsewhere to earn the money needed for seeds, equipment, and building supplies.

**Isolation and community.**   Isolation and loneliness troubled many early settlers on the plains. Women especially suffered because they frequently had less contact with other people than farm men, who conducted their families' business in town and participated in such public activities as political meetings.

Over time, conditions improved. As population increased, women in particular worked to bind isolated households into communities by organizing social activities and institutions. They held fairs, dances, and picnics and established churches, schools, and libraries, thereby gaining both companionship and a sense of purpose.

Churches, in turn, also promoted community. Indeed, many were "union" churches, open to people of all denominations. In addition to holding religious services, revivals, and camp meetings, churches were often the center of social life, especially by sponsoring sociables and children's organizations. Nondenominational Sunday schools helped bind together differing nationalities and church preferences, and because they did not require the services of an ordained minister they often enabled women to initiate and lead community activities.

Other institutions also encouraged community action. Rural families created their own agricultural cooperatives and other economic and social organizations, like local Grange lodges. External developments also served the rural population. Rural Free Delivery, for example, eventually brought letters, newspapers, magazines, and advertisements to farm families' doorsteps; mail-order companies made available to farm people such helpful goods as stoves, sewing machines, and shoes. Such changes helped incorporate westerners into the larger society.

## FARMING THE LAND

Pioneer settlers had to make daunting adjustments to develop the agricultural potential of their new land. Advances in science, technology, and industry made such adjustments possible. The changes not only reshaped the agricultural economy but also challenged traditional rural values and expectations.

**Growing crops.**  Fencing was an immediate problem, for crops needed protection from livestock. But without timber, farmers could not build wooden fences. Barbed wire, developed in the mid-1870s, solved the problem. By 1900, farmers were importing nearly 300 million pounds of barbed wire each year from eastern and midwestern factories.

The aridity of most of the West also posed difficulties. In California, Colorado, and a few other areas, settlers used streams fed by mountain snow packs to irrigate land. Elsewhere, enterprising farmers developed variants of the "dry farming" practices that the Mormons had introduced in Utah to maximize the limited rainfall. Some farmers erected windmills to pump underground water. The scarce rainfall also discouraged the cultivation of many of the crops that supported traditional general agriculture and encouraged farmers to specialize in a single cash crop for market. Government agencies and agricultural colleges contributed to the success of such adaptations, and private engineers and inventors also fostered agricultural development. Related technological advancements included grain elevators that would store grain for shipment and load it into rail cars mechanically and mills that used corrugated, chilled-iron rollers rather than millstones to process the new varieties of wheat.

Mechanization and technological innovations made possible the large-scale farming practiced in semiarid regions. Farmers required special plows to break the tough sod, new harrows to prepare the soil for cultivation, grain drills to plant the crop, and harvesting and threshing machines to bring it in. Thanks to more and better machines, agricultural efficiency and productivity shot up. By the 1890s, machinery permitted the farmer to produce 18 times more wheat than hand methods had. Nearly 1,000 corporations were manufacturing agricultural machinery to meet the demands of farmers, who purchased implements in steadily mounting quantities.

**Growing tensions.**  These developments reflected both the expansion of agriculture and its increasing dependence on the larger society. Western commercial farmers needed the high demand of eastern and midwestern cities and the expanding world market. The rail network provided essential transportation for their crops; the nation's industrial sector produced necessary agricultural machinery. Banks and loan companies extended the credit and capital that allowed farmers to take advantage of mechanization and other new advances; and many other businesses graded, stored, processed, and sold their crops. In short, because of its market orientation, mechanization, and specialization, western agriculture relied on other people or impersonal forces as it was incorporated into the national and international economy.

Farm workers harvested sheaves of grain with a horse drawn Marsh harvester, manufactured by a Chicago company. With this plow, farmers could harvest ten acres per day. It saved several bushels per acre by binding the grain before it touched the ground.

When conditions were favorable—good weather, good crops, and good prices—western farmers prospered. Too often, however, they faced adversity. The early years of settlement were unusually wet, but even then periodic droughts brought crop failures. Other natural hazards also disrupted production. Especially alarming were plagues of grasshoppers. Grasshoppers ate crops, clothing, and bedding; they attacked sod houses and chewed woodwork and furniture.

In the late 1880s, drought coincided with a slump in crop prices. The large European market that had encouraged agricultural expansion in the 1870s and early 1880s contracted after 1885, when several nations erected trade barriers to U.S. commodities. More important, America's production competed with that from Argentina, Canada, Australia, and Russia, and a world surplus of grain drove prices steadily downward.

Squeezed between high costs for credit, transportation, and manufactured goods and falling agricultural prices, western farmers faced disaster. They responded by lashing back at their points of contact with the new system. They especially condemned the railroads, believing that the companies charged excessive and discriminatory freight rates.

Farmers censured the grain elevators in the local buying centers. Often owned by eastern corporations, including the railroads, elevators allegedly exploited their local monopoly to cheat farmers by fixing low prices or misrepresenting the quality of wheat. A Minnesota state investigation found that systematic fraud by elevators cost farmers collectively a massive sum. Farmers also denounced the bankers and mortgage lenders who had provided the credit for them to acquire land, equipment, and machinery. Much of the money had come from eastern investors seeking the higher interest rates in the West. With failing crops and falling prices, however, the debt burden proved calamitous for many farmers. Beginning in 1889, many western farms were foreclosed.

Stunned and bitter, western farmers concluded that their problems arose because they had been incorporated into the new system, an integrated economy directed by forces beyond their control. And it was a system that did not work well. "There is," one of them charged, "something radically wrong in our industrial system. There is a screw loose."

# CONCLUSION

The farmers' complaints indicted the major processes by which the West was developed and exploited in the late nineteenth century. Railroad expansion, population movements, eastern investment, corporate control, technological innovations, and government policies had incorporated the region fully into the larger society. Indians experienced this incorporation most thoroughly and most tragically, losing their lands, their traditions, and often their lives.

Cowboys and miners also learned that the frontier merely marked the cutting edge of eastern industrial society. Both groups were wageworkers, often for corporations controlled by eastern capital, and if industrial technology directly affected miners more than cowhands, neither could escape integration into the national economy by managerial decisions, transportation links, and market forces. Most settlers in the West were farmers, but they too learned that their distinctive environment did not insulate them from assimilation into larger productive, financial, and marketing structures.

Western developments, in short, reflected and interacted with those of eastern industrial society. The processes of incorporation drained away westerners' hopes along with their products, and many of the discontented would demand a serious reorganization of relationships and power. Led by angry farmers, they turned their attention to politics and government, where they encountered new obstacles and opportunities.

# SUMMARY

WHAT WERE the main objectives of federal Indian policy in the late nineteenth century?

**Subjugating Native Americans** As white people pressed westward, the initial obstacle to exploiting the West was the people who already lived there. The native peoples used the land in their own way, had different concepts of progress and civilization, and had developed a variety of economies and cultures. From the 1850s to the 1880s, warfare engulfed the advancing frontier; railroad expansion, the destruction of the buffalo, and technological development undercut the ability of the Native Americans to resist. The conquest gradually forced Indians onto reservations, but efforts to "Americanize" the Indian way of life were less successful.

WHAT WERE the environmental consequences of the expansion of mining in the nineteenth century?

**Exploiting the Mountains: The Mining Bonanza** The first stage of the economic development of the West centered on mining as swarms of eager prospectors were attracted into the mountains and deserts in search of gold and silver. The male-dominated saloon society of the mining camps generated violence and social conflicts. Mining was transformed from an individual effort into a corporate one; as minerals became more difficult to uncover, mining became technologically complex and expensive. Corporate mining permanently changed the landscape of the West through its environmental impact.

WHAT FACTORS contributed to the development of the range cattle industry?

**Using the Grass: The Cattle Kingdom** The development of the range cattle industry opened a second stage in the exploitation of the West. It reflected the needs of the Eastern urban society for food and the ability of the expanding rail network to deliver it. The cattle kingdom spread from Texas throughout the Great Plains; after the era of the long drives, cattle ranching became an increasingly corporate endeavor. While the romantic image of the cowboy is one of a rugged individualist freed of societal constraints, the actual work was hard, dirty, seasonal, dangerous, and poorly paid.

HOW DID new technology contribute to the growth of Western agriculture?

**Working the Earth: Homesteaders and Agricultural Expansion** Even more than ranching and mining, agricultural growth boosted the West's economy and bound it to national and world markets. Government played a significant role in the expansion of farming, as did railroads, science and technology, Eastern capital, and hard work. The Homestead Act, along with land, railroad, and steamship companies, encouraged Western migration. Settlers encountered many difficulties: a radically new environment, the need for new farming techniques, weather conditions, loneliness, and isolation. These were combined with farmers becoming part of a global economic system; farmers reached the conclusion that something was terribly wrong with the system, and that bankers, grain elevator operators, and the railroads were to blame.

# WHERE TO LEARN MORE

**Little Bighorn Battlefield National Monument, Crow Agency, Montana.** The site of Custer's crushing defeat includes a monument to the Seventh Cavalry atop Last Stand Hill. A newly authorized Indian Memorial will include sacred texts, artifacts, and pictographs of the Plains Indians. **www.nps.gov/libi/home.htm**

**National Museum of the American Indian, Smithsonian Institution, Washington DC.** This spectacular museum opened in 2004 and reflects the world view of Native Americans, with exhibits on spirituality and identity, performances of traditional dances, and important lecture series. **www.nmai.si.edu**

**National Cowboy Hall of Fame, Oklahoma City, Oklahoma.** This large institution contains an outstanding collection of western art, displays of cowboy and Indian artifacts, and both kitschy exhibitions of the mythic Hollywood West and serious galleries depicting the often hard realities of the cattle industry. Its many public programs also successfully combine fun with learning. **www.cowboyhalloffame.org/index2.html**

**Golden Spike National Historic Site, near Promontory, Utah.** The completion of the transcontinental railroad here in 1869 is reenacted from May to October, using reproductions of the original locomotives. Visitors can drive the route of the railroad, now a National Backway Byway through abandoned mining and railroad towns, from Promontory to Nevada. Virtual tour, history, and tourist links. **www.nps./gov/gosp**

# STUDY RESOURCES

## myhistorylab

For study resources for this chapter, go to www.myhistorylab.com and choose *The American Journey*. You will find a wealth of study and review material for this chapter, including pre- and post-tests, customized study plan, key term review flash cards, interactive map and document activities, and documents for analysis.

# REVIEW QUESTIONS

1. Why was the completion of the first transcontinental railroad, described by Andrew J. Russell, celebrated from Boston to San Francisco? How did western railroads shape the settlement and development of the West and affect the East as well?

2. What factors were most influential in the subjugation of American Indians?

3. What were the major goals of federal Indian policy, and how did they change?

4. How did technological developments affect Indians, miners, and farmers in the West?

5. How did the federal government help transform the West?

6. In what ways did European investors, markets, and migrants influence the development of the American West?

## KEY TERMS

Chisholm Trail (p. 573)
Dawes Act (p. 567)
Homestead Act (p. 577)
Little Bighorn, Battle of the (p. 566)
Sand Creek Massacre (p. 565)

Second Treaty of Fort Laramie (p. 565)
Wounded Knee Massacre (p. 567)

# 20
# Politics and Government

Grover Cleveland and Allen G. Thurman as the Democratic party candidates for President and Vice President on a lithograph campaign poster by Kurz & Allison, 1888.

586

## THE STRUCTURE AND STYLE OF POLITICS  *(page 589)*

**HOW DID** parties mobilize voters in the late nineteenth century?

## THE LIMITS OF GOVERNMENT  *(page 594)*

**HOW EFFECTIVE** was the federal government in addressing the problems of America's industrializing economy?

## PUBLIC POLICIES AND NATIONAL ELECTIONS  *(page 596)*

**WHY WERE** monetary issues so important to so many Americans at the end of the nineteenth century?

## THE CRISIS OF THE 1890s  *(page 601)*

**WHAT FACTORS** contributed to the rise and fall of the Populist Party?

The largest political procession of the season in Fort Wayne, so far, was that of the Republicans Saturday night. They turned out in very large numbers and paraded on the principal streets preparatory to the speaking which came later at the Rifles' armory. The following were in line:

First Regiment Band

Railroad Men's Club

Soldiers' and Sons' Union Club

Tippecanoe Club

Chase Club

Lincoln Club

McKinley Club

Colored Drum Corps

Colored Republicans' Club

Republican Voters

The McKinley Club wore tin hats and the Tippecanoe club carried torches that spouted fire at intervals. One of the prettiest illuminations was the railroad lantern light of the Railroad Men's Republican club. The numerous lights of the colors used in the railway service make as pretty a sight as can be seen anywhere.

Most of the clubs were in fine uniforms and made a grand appearance. Numerous banners and transparencies announcing mottoes of the campaign were carried. One banner bore the words, "Cleveland's record—Glad Lincoln was shot—Pronounced the war a failure."

The great parade was viewed by thousands of people who thronged the streets all along the line of march.

The hall was crowded and the meeting was most enthusiastic. Music was furnished by the band and Emerson quartette of Huntington. . . . The quartette just took the cake. Anything more enjoyable and mirth-provoking than their glees rendered as they render them would be hard to find. After music by the quartette, which was enthusiastically encored, Dr. Stemen, the presiding officer, introduced the speaker of the evening, Hon. L.R. Stookey, of Warsaw, Ind. Mr. Stookey is a ready and rapid speaker. He paid a glowing tribute to the soldiers, and referred in scathing terms to Grover Cleveland's treatment of them and his insulting vetoes of pension bills. He spoke . . . [of a law providing for election supervisors at the polls] and what we ask is that it shall apply without limitation north and south whenever there is an attempt or danger of attempt, to deny equal rights of all to cast their free ballot and have it counted as cast.

When he concluded the Emerson quartette gave another selection and responded to an encore. The audience then began to call loudly for "You," "You." Mr. A.J. You, our candidate for congress, was then introduced and made a stirring address. Mr. You has been speaking nearly every day and evening and is holding out first rate and proving himself one of the most popular candidates in the field.

He was repeatedly and enthusiastically cheered during his speech. Another selection by the quartette, and the house resounded with calls for "Brown," "Brown." Rev. W.H. Brown, for years the pastor of the A.M.E. church, of this city, took the platform and though he protested that *the hour was too late to permit another speech made it clearly evident in the course of a twenty minute speech that the colored people of the country understand the situation and intend to stand by the party that broke the chains and gave freedom to the slave. The meeting then adjourned to music by the Glee club.*

Source: *Fort Wayne* (Ind.) *Weekly Gazette,* October 20, 1892.

### myhistorylab

**Personal Journeys Online**

- Susan B. Anthony, *Speech to the National American Woman Suffrage Association,* 1894. Asking Congress for political justice.

- Henry Vincent, *Marching through Iowa,* 1894. The journey of Kelly's "industrial army."

- William Jennings Bryan, 1896. Campaigning across America.

**THE FORT WAYNE GAZETTE,** a fiercely Republican newspaper, proudly reported on the activities of the local Republicans in Indiana during the political campaign in 1892. The pageantry and hoopla made politics a major source of popular entertainment for Republicans and Democrats alike. But the extreme campaign rhetoric and outright misrepresentation of opponents indicated the intensity of partisan emotions. So did the military-style campaign, with uniformed marchers organized into companies, brigades, and divisions; with signs, slogans, and speeches referring to soldiers and the Civil War; with rallies held in armories. These campaign features also pointed to the enduring importance of the Civil War as a basis for partisan divisions and loyalties and marked electoral politics as a rough-and-tumble masculine business.

At the same time, contemporary issues did matter. Stookey's stump appeal for election supervisors to protect voters' rights at the polls similarly pointed to an important policy issue while hinting at the sometimes violent nature of elections, including the suppression of voters. It also emphasized that suffrage was often a contested issue.

The prominent role of Rev. Brown, the content of his speech, and the participation of the Colored Drum Corps and the Colored Republicans' Club in the parade show that partisan divisions in the United States overlapped with racial, religious, and other social divisions. Black voters, for instance, would "stand by the party that broke the chains and gave freedom to the slave."

While the *Gazette* lavished praise on the Republican campaign, its Democratic counterpart, the *Fort Wayne Sentinel,* extolled the success of the Democratic campaign. Such partisanship permeated journalism as well as nearly all aspects of public life, including government agencies.

These features of late-nineteenth-century politics would eventually be transformed in significant ways. But while they endured, they shaped not only campaigns and elections but also the form and role of government. Only a national crisis in the 1890s would finally cause some Americans to demand more of their political leaders and institutions. ✦

## THE STRUCTURE AND STYLE OF POLITICS

Politics in the late nineteenth century was an absorbing activity. Campaigns and elections expressed social values as they determined who held the reins of government. Political parties dominated political life. They organized campaigns, controlled balloting, and held the unswerving loyalty of most of the electorate. While the major parties worked to maintain a sense of unity and tradition among their followers, third

**HOW DID** parties mobilize voters in the late nineteenth century?

## CHRONOLOGY

| | |
|---|---|
| **1867** Patrons of Husbandry (the Grange) is founded. | **1890** Sherman Antitrust Act is passed. |
| **1869** Massachusetts establishes the first state regulatory commission. | McKinley Tariff Act is passed. |
| | Sherman Silver Purchase Act is passed. |
| **1873** Silver is demonetized in the "Crime of '73." | National American Woman Suffrage Association is organized. |
| **1874** Woman's Christian Temperance Union is organized. | |
| **1875** U.S. Supreme Court, in *Minor v. Happersett*, upholds denial of suffrage to women. | Wyoming enters the Union as the first state with woman suffrage. |
| **1876** Greenback Party runs presidential candidate. | **1892** People's Party is organized. |
| **1877** Rutherford B. Hayes becomes president after disputed election. | Cleveland is elected to his second term as president. |
| | **1893** Depression begins. |
| Farmers' Alliance is founded. | Sherman Silver Purchase Act is repealed. |
| Supreme Court, in *Munn v. Illinois*, upholds state regulatory authority over private property. | **1894** Coxey's Army marches to Washington. |
| | Pullman strike ends in violence. |
| **1878** Bland-Allison Act requires the government to buy silver. | **1895** Supreme Court, in *Pollock v. Farmers' Loan and Trust Company*, invalidates the federal income tax. |
| **1880** James A. Garfield is elected president. | |
| **1881** Garfield is assassinated; Chester A. Arthur becomes president. | Supreme Court, in *United States v. E. C. Knight Company*, limits the Sherman Antitrust Law to commerce, excluding industrial monopolies. |
| **1883** Pendleton Civil Service Act is passed. | |
| **1884** Grover Cleveland is elected president. | **1896** William Jennings Bryan is nominated for president by Democrats and Populists. |
| **1886** Supreme Court, in *Wabash v. Illinois*, rules that only the federal government, not the states, can regulate interstate commerce. | William McKinley is elected president. |
| | **1900** Currency Act puts U.S. currency on the gold standard. |
| **1887** Interstate Commerce Act is passed. | |
| **1888** Benjamin Harrison is elected president. | |

parties sought to activate those the major parties left unserved. Other Americans looked outside the electoral arena to achieve their political goals.

## CAMPAIGNS AND ELECTIONS

Political campaigns and elections generated remarkable public participation and enthusiasm. They constituted a major form of entertainment at a time when recreational opportunities were limited. Campaign pageantry absorbed communities large and small. Attending party meetings and conventions, listening to lengthy speeches appealing to group loyalties and local pride, gathering at the polls to watch the voting and the counting, celebrating victory and drowning the disappointment of defeat—all these provided social enjoyment and defined popular politics.

Virtually all men participated in politics. In many states, even immigrants not yet citizens were eligible to vote and flocked to the polls. African Americans voted regularly in the North and irregularly in the South before being disfranchised at the end of the century. Overall, turnout was remarkably high, averaging nearly 80 percent of eligible voters in presidential elections between 1876 and 1900, a figure far greater than ever achieved thereafter (see Figure 20–1).

Political parties mobilized this huge electorate. With legal regulations and public machinery for elections negligible, parties dominated the campaigns and elections.

Until the 1890s, most states had no laws to ensure secrecy in voting, and balloting often took place in open rooms or on sidewalks. Election clerks and judges were not public officials but partisans chosen by the political parties.

Nor did public authorities issue official ballots. Instead voters used party tickets—strips of paper printed by the parties—listing only the names of the candidates of the party issuing them and varying in size and color. Casting a ballot thus revealed the voter's party allegiance. Fighting and intimidation were so commonplace at the polls that one state supreme court ruled in 1887 that they were "acceptable" features of elections.

As the court recognized, the open and partisan aspects of the electoral process did not necessarily lead to election fraud, however much they shaped the nature of political participation. In these circumstances, campaigns and elections provided opportunities for men to demonstrate publicly their commitment to their party and its values, thereby reinforcing their partisan loyalties.

Nonvoting women, too, often exhibited their partisanship in this exciting political environment. Women wrote partisan literature and gave campaign speeches. Sometimes partisan women acted together with men; other times they worked through separate women's organizations. In these partisan groups women discussed and circulated party literature and devised plans to influence elections.

## PARTISAN POLITICS

A remarkably close balance prevailed between the two major parties in the elections of this era. Democrats and Republicans had virtually the same level of electoral support, one reason they worked so hard to get out the vote (see Map 20–1). Control of the presidency and Congress shifted back and forth. Rarely did either party control both branches of government at once.

The party balance gave great influence to New York, New Jersey, Ohio, and Indiana, whose evenly divided voters controlled electoral votes that could swing an election either way. Both parties tended to nominate presidential and vice presidential candidates

**From Then to Now Online**
*Political Parties*

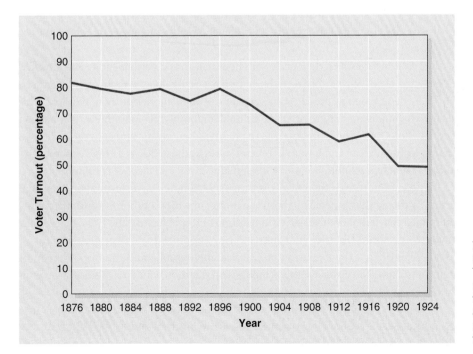

**FIGURE 20–1 Voter Turnout in Presidential Elections, 1876–1924**
The exciting partisan politics of the late nineteenth century produced very high voter turnouts, but as party competition declined and states enacted more restrictive voter regulations, popular participation in elections fell in the twentieth century.

MAP EXPLORATION  To explore an interactive version of this map, go to http://www.prenhall.com/goldfield5/map20.1

**myhistorylab**

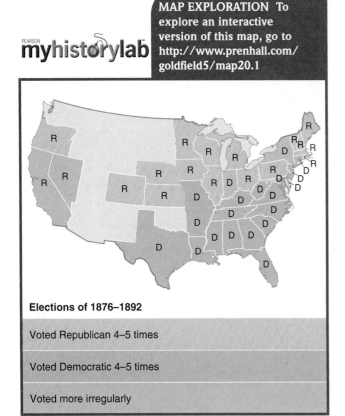

**Elections of 1876–1892**

Voted Republican 4–5 times

Voted Democratic 4–5 times

Voted more irregularly

**MAP 20–1　The Two-Party Stalemate of the Late Nineteenth Century**　Strong parties, staunch loyalties, and an evenly divided electorate made for exciting politics but often stalemated government in the late nineteenth century. Most states voted consistently for one of the major parties, leaving the few swing states like New York and Indiana the scenes of fierce partisan battles.

**QUICK REVIEW**

**Party Identities**

◆ Republican self-image: party of national-ism and national unity.

◆ Republican vision of Democrats: alliance of embittered South and Northern slums.

◆ Democratic self-image: party of limited government and personal liberties.

*Documents*

George Washington Plunkitt, *Honest Graft* (1905)

from those states to woo their voters. The parties also concen-trated campaign funds and strategy on the swing states.

**Party loyalty.**　Interrelated regional, ethnic, religious, and local factors determined the party affiliations of most Americans. Economic issues, although important to the politics of the era, generally did not decide party ties. Farmers, for example, despite their many shared economic concerns, affiliated with both major parties. Like religious belief and ethnic identity, partisan loyalty was largely a cultural trait passed from parents to children, a situation that helps to explain the electoral stability of most communities.

Republicans were strongest in the North and Midwest, where they benefited from their party's role as the defender of the Union in the Civil War. But not all northerners voted for the Grand Old Party, or GOP. The Republican Party appealed primarily to old-stock Americans and other Protestants, including those of German and Scandinavian descent. African Americans, loyal to the party that had emancipated and enfranchised the slaves of the South, also supported the GOP where they could vote. Democrats were strongest in the South, where they stood as the defenders of the traditions of the region's white population. But Democrats also drew support in the urban Northeast, especially from Catholics and recent immigrants.

**Party identities.**　Each major party consisted of a complex coalition of groups with differing traditions and interests. This internal diversity often provoked conflict and threatened party stability. To hold its coalition together, each party identified itself with a theme that appealed broadly to all its constituents, while suggesting that it was menaced by the members and objectives of the opposing party.

Republicans identified their party with nationalism and national unity and attacked the Democrats as an "alliance between the embittered South and the slums of the Northern cities." They combined a "bloody shirt" appeal to the memories of the Civil War with campaigns for immigration restriction and cultural uniformity. Seeing a threat to American society in efforts by Catholic immigrants to preserve their ethnic and cultural traditions, for example, Republican legislatures in several states in the 1880s and 1890s enacted laws regulating parochial schools, the use of foreign languages, and alcohol consumption.

Democrats portrayed themselves as the party of limited government and "personal liberties," a theme that appealed to both the racism of white southerners and the resent-ment immigrants felt about the nativist meddling of Republicans. The Democrats' com-mitment to personal liberties had limits. They supported the disfranchisement of African Americans, the exclusion of Chinese immigrants, and the dispossession of American Indians. Nevertheless, their emphasis on traditional individualism and localism proved popular.

The partisan politics of both major parties culminated in party machines, espe-cially at the local level. Led by powerful bosses, the machines controlled not only city politics but also municipal government. Party activists used well-organized ward clubs to mobilize working-class voters, who were rewarded with municipal jobs and baskets of food or coal doled out by the machine. Such assistance was often necessary, given the lack of public welfare systems, but to buy votes the machine also sold favors. Public contracts and franchises were peddled to businesses whose high bids covered kickbacks to the machine.

**Third parties.**  The partisan politics of the era left room for several third parties, organized around specific issues or groups. The **Prohibition Party** persistently championed the abolition of alcohol but also supported electoral reforms such as woman suffrage, economic reforms such as railroad regulation and income taxes, and social reforms including improved race relations. The **Greenback Party** of the 1870s denounced "the infamous financial legislation which takes all from the many to enrich the few." Its policies of labor reform and currency inflation (to stimulate and democratize the economy) attracted supporters from Maine to Texas. Other significant third parties included the Anti-Monopoly Party, the Union Labor Party, and, most important, the People's or **Populist Party** of the 1890s. Although third parties often won temporary success at the local or regional level, they never permanently displaced the major parties or undermined traditional voter allegiances.

## ASSOCIATIONAL POLITICS

Much political activity was neither partisan nor electoral. Associations of like-minded citizens, operating as pressure groups, played an increasingly important role in late-nineteenth-century politics. These organizations worked to achieve public policies beneficial to their members. Farmers organized many such groups, most notably the Patrons of Husbandry, known familiarly as the Grange (see Chapter 17). Its campaign for public regulation of the rates charged by railroads and grain elevators helped convince midwestern states to pass the so-called **Granger laws.**

Industrialists also formed pressure groups. Organizations such as the American Iron and Steel Association and the American Protective Tariff League lobbied Congress for high tariff laws and made campaign contributions to friendly politicians of both parties. At the state level business groups used their political clout to block the reform efforts of farmers and workers, sometimes in the legislatures but otherwise in the courts.

A small group of conservative reformers known derisively as **Mugwumps** (the term derives from the Algonquian word for "chief") devoted most of their effort to campaigning for honest and efficient government through civil service reform. Other pressure groups focused on cultural politics. The rabidly anti-Catholic American Protective Association, for example, agitated for laws restricting immigration, taxing church property, and inspecting Catholic religious institutions.

Christian lobbyists committed their political energies to demanding laws imposing their view of personal moral behavior. The greatest success for such Christian lobbyists was the Comstock Law, passed by Congress in 1873, which outlawed the possession or sale of "obscene" materials, including any contraceptive information or devices. Directly affecting the lives of many Americans, the Comstock Law clearly revealed the importance of this type of political activism.

**Prohibition Party**  A venerable third party still in existence that has persistently campaigned for the abolition of alcohol but has also introduced many important reform ideas into American politics.

**Greenback Party**  A third party of the 1870s and 1880s that garnered temporary support by advocating currency inflation to expand the economy and assist debtors.

**Populist Party**  A major third party of the 1890s formed on the basis of the Farmers' Alliance and other reform organizations.

**Granger laws**  State laws enacted in the Midwest in the 1870s that regulated rates charged by railroads, grain elevator operators, and other middlemen.

**Mugwumps**  Elitist and conservative reformers who favored sound money and limited government and opposed tariffs and the spoils system.

The Grange rejected partisanship but not politics. This sympathetic cartoon shows a Granger trying to warn Americans blindly absorbed in partisan politics of the dangers of onrushing industrialization.

Women lobbying a Congressional committee to support woman suffrage. Susan B. Anthony noted with regret that "to all men women suffrage is only a side issue."

**National American Woman Suffrage Association** The organization, formed in 1890, that coordinated the ultimately successful campaign to achieve women's right to vote.

Ⓦ **WHERE TO LEARN MORE**

★ Frances Willard's Rest Cottage, Evanston, Illinois.
www.wctu.org/house.html

**Women as activists.** Women also sought power and influence through associational politics. The leading organizations merged in 1890 as the **National American Woman Suffrage Association.** Despite the opposition of male politicians of both major parties, suffragists had succeeded by the mid-1890s in gaining full woman suffrage in four western states, Wyoming, Colorado, Idaho, and Utah, and partial suffrage (the right to vote in school elections) in several other states, east and west.

Other women shaped public issues through social service organizations. Although the belief that women belonged in the domestic sphere limited their involvement in electoral politics, it furnished a basis for political action focused on welfare and moral reform. With petition campaigns, demonstrations, and lobbying, women's social service organizations sought to remedy poverty and disease, improve education and recreation, and provide day nurseries for the children of workingwomen.

Under the leadership of Frances Willard, the WCTU built on traditional women's concerns to develop an important critique of American society. Reversing the conventional view, Willard argued that alcohol abuse was a result, not a cause, of poverty and social disorder. Under the slogan of "Home Protection," the WCTU inserted domestic issues into the political sphere with a campaign for social and economic reforms far beyond temperance. It pushed for improved health conditions, reached out to the Knights of Labor to support workplace reforms, and lobbied for federal aid to education, particularly as a means to provide schooling for black children in the South. It eventually supported woman suffrage as well, on the grounds that women needed the vote to fulfill their duty to protect home, family, and morality.

**HOW EFFECTIVE** was the federal government in addressing the problems of America's industrializing economy?

**laissez-faire** The doctrine that government should not intervene in the economy, especially through regulation.

## THE LIMITS OF GOVERNMENT

Despite the popular enthusiasm for partisan politics and the persistent pressure of associational politics, government in the late nineteenth century was neither active nor productive by present standards. The receding governmental activism of the Civil War and Reconstruction years coincided with a resurgent belief in localism and **laissez-faire** policies. In addition, a Congress and presidency divided between the two major parties, a small and inefficient bureaucracy, and judicial restraints joined powerful private interests to limit the size and objectives of the federal government.

## THE WEAK PRESIDENCY

The presidency was a weak and restricted institution. The impeachment of President Johnson at the outset of Reconstruction had undermined the office. President Grant clearly subordinated it to the legislative branch by deferring to Congress on appointments and legislation. Other factors contributed as well. The men who filled the office between 1877 and 1897 were all honest and generally capable. Each had built a solid political record at the state or federal level. But they were all conservatives, with a narrow view of the presidency, and proposed few initiatives. The presidents of this era viewed their duties as chiefly administrative. They made little effort to reach out to the public or to exert legislative leadership. (See Global Perspectives, Why Great Men Are Not Chosen Presidents.)

The presidency was also hampered by its limited control over bureaus and departments, which responded more directly to Congress, and by its small staff, consisting of no more than a half-dozen secretaries, clerks, and telegraphers.

## THE INEFFICIENT CONGRESS

Congress was the foremost branch of the national government. It exercised authority over the federal budget, oversaw the cabinet, debated public issues, and controlled legislation. Its members were often state and national party leaders, who were strong-willed and, as one senator conceded, "tolerated no intrusion from the President or from anybody else."

But Congress was scarcely efficient. Its chambers were noisy and chaotic, and members rarely devoted their attention to the business at hand. The repeated shifts in party control impeded effective action. So, too, did the loss of experienced legislators to rapid turnover. In some Congresses, a majority of members were first-termers. Procedural rules, based on precedents from a simpler time and manipulated by determined partisans, hindered congressional action. Some rules restricted the introduction of legislation; others prevented its passage. The most notorious rule required that a quorum be not only present but voting. When the House was narrowly divided along party lines, the minority could block all business simply by refusing to answer when the roll was called.

But as a nationalizing economy required more national legislation, the amount of business before Congress grew relentlessly (see Figure 20-2). The expanding scale of congressional work prompted a gradual reform of procedures and the centralization of power in the Speaker of the House and the leading committees. These changes did not, however, create a coherent program for government action.

## THE FEDERAL BUREAUCRACY AND THE SPOILS SYSTEM

Reflecting presidential weakness and congressional inefficiency, the federal bureaucracy remained small and limited in the late nineteenth century. There were little more than 50,000 government employees in 1871, and three-fourths of them were local postmasters scattered across the nation.

HER PLATFORM GOING TO PIECES.

"BETWEEN THE TWO I SHALL HAVE A HEAVY FALL."

Anticipating a floor fight at the Democratic convention over the tariff issue, cartoonist Bernhard Gillam depicts the female persona of the Democratic party anxiously holding on to the platform which is being broken into two pieces. Speaker of the House John Carlisle of Kentucky (left) leads the tariff reform movement (lower tariffs or free trade) in the name of labor interests. Representative (and former speaker of the house) Samuel Randall of Pennsylvania pulls for tariff protectionism in the name of business interests ("monopolists"). In reality, the Democratic party decided not to decide the issue at the convention, and included only la vague statement in its national party platform.

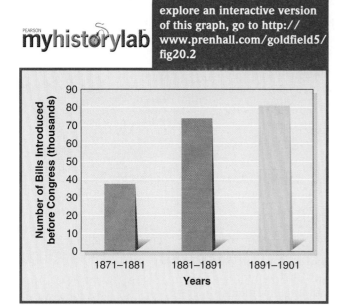

**GRAPHIC EXPLORATION  To explore an interactive version of this graph, go to http://www.prenhall.com/goldfield5/fig20.2**

FIGURE 20–2   **Increase in Congressional Business, 1871–1901**   Industrialization, urbanization, and western expansion brought increased demands for government action, but the party stalemate, laissez-faire attitudes, and inefficient public institutions often blocked effective responses.

**QUICK REVIEW**

**The Spoils System**

◆ Fifty thousand federal employees in 1871.

◆ Politicians awarded government jobs to party workers.

◆ Critics charged that the system was corrupt.

The system for selecting and supervising federal officials had developed gradually in the first half of the century. Known as the spoils system, its basic principle was that victorious politicians awarded government jobs to party workers, often with little regard for qualifications, and ousted the previous employees. The spoils system played a crucial role in all aspects of politics. It enabled party leaders to strengthen their organizations, reward loyal party service, and attract the political workers needed to mobilize the electorate. Supporters described it as a democratic system that offered opportunities to many citizens and prevented the emergence of an entrenched bureaucracy.

Critics, however, charged that the system was riddled with corruption, abuse, and inefficiency. Rapid turnover bred instability; political favoritism bred incompetence. Certainly, the spoils system was ineffective for filling positions that required special clerical skills, such as typing, or scientific expertise. Even worse, the spoils system absorbed the president and Congress in unproductive conflicts over patronage.

## INCONSISTENT STATE GOVERNMENT

State governments were more active than the federal government. Considered closer and more responsible to the people, they had long exercised police power and regulatory authority. They collected taxes for education and public works, and they promoted private enterprise and public health. Still, they did little by today's standards. Few people thought it appropriate for government at any level to offer direct help to particular social groups. Some state governments contracted in the 1870s and 1880s, following the wartime activism of the 1860s, and new state constitutions restricted the scope of public authority.

Nonetheless, state governments gradually expanded their role in response to the stresses produced by industrialization. Following the lead of Massachusetts in 1869, most states had by the turn of the century created commissions to investigate and regulate industry. Public intervention in other areas of the economy soon followed. In Minnesota, for example, the state helped farmers by establishing a dairy commission, prohibiting the manufacture or sale of margarine, creating a bureau of animal industry, and employing state veterinarians.

Not all such agencies and laws were effective, nor were all state governments as diligent as Minnesota's. Southern states, especially, lagged, and one midwesterner complained that his legislature "meets in ignorance, sits in corruption, and dissolves in disgrace every two years." Still, the widening scope of state action represented a growing acceptance of public responsibility for social welfare and economic life and laid the foundation for more effective steps in the early twentieth century.

# PUBLIC POLICIES AND NATIONAL ELECTIONS

**WHY WERE** monetary issues so important to so many Americans at the end of the nineteenth century?

Several great issues dominated the national political arena in the late nineteenth century, including civil service reform, tariffs, and business and financial regulation. Rarely, however, did these issues clearly and consistently separate the major political parties. Instead, they divided each party into factions along regional, interest, and economic lines. As a consequence, these leading issues often played only a small role in determining elections and were seldom resolved by government action.

## GLOBAL PERSPECTIVES

### WHY GREAT MEN ARE NOT CHOSEN PRESIDENTS

*U.S. politics and government were subjects of great interest to Europeans. Accustomed to monarchs, prime ministers, parliaments, and efficient civil service bureaucracies, they found perplexing the decentralized U.S. system of federalism, the emphasis on localism and laissez-faire, and the popular frenzy and organizational thrust of partisan politics. Nothing was more fascinating than the character of U.S. political leaders, who seemed to Europeans to be consistently unimaginative and dull. As one noted, "The only thing remarkable about them is that being so commonplace they should have climbed so high."*

Lord James Bryce of Great Britain provided the classic European perspective on the U.S. presidency in 1888. "Europeans often ask," Bryce observed, "how it happens that this great office . . . is not more frequently filled by great and striking men?" This seemed particularly puzzling given that the United States boasted of an open society that rewarded ability, not one bound by the hereditary distinctions of aristocracy.

Most important in explaining the absence of "brilliancy" among U.S. presidents, Bryce ventured, was the political system of the United States, with its party-dominated politics and its limited government.

In America party loyalty and party organization have been hitherto so perfect that any one put forward by the party will get the full party vote if his character is good and his "record," as they call it,

unstained. . . . Even those who admit his mediocrity will vote straight when the moment for voting comes. Besides, the ordinary American voter does not object to mediocrity. He has a lower conception of the qualities requisite to make a statesman than those who direct public opinion in Europe have. He likes his candidates to be sensible, vigorous, and, above all, what he calls "magnetic," and does not value, because he sees no need for, originality or profundity, a fine culture or a wide knowledge. . . .

After all, . . . a President need not be a man of brilliant intellectual gifts. Englishmen, imagining him as something like their prime minister, assume that he ought to be a dazzling orator, able to sway legislatures or multitudes, possessed also of the constructive powers that can devise a great policy or frame a comprehensive piece of legislation. They forget that the President does not sit in Congress, . . . submit bills nor otherwise influence the action of the legislature. His main duties are to be prompt and firm in securing the due execution of the laws and maintaining the public peace. . . . Eloquence, . . . imagination, profundity of thought or extent of knowledge . . . are not necessary.

- How might the "ordinary American voter" in the late nineteenth century have defended the U.S. political system from Bryce's indictment?

## CIVIL SERVICE REFORM

Reform of the spoils system emerged as a prominent issue during the Hayes administration. The Mugwumps and other reformers wanted a professional civil service, based on merit and divorced from politics. They wanted officeholders to be selected on the basis of competitive written examinations and protected from removal on political grounds. They expected such a system to promote efficiency, economy, and honesty in government. But they also expected it to increase their own influence and minimize that of "mere politicians."

The weakness of the civil service reformers was dramatically underscored in 1880 when the Republicans, to improve their chances of carrying the crucial state of New York, nominated Chester A. Arthur of New York for vice president on a ticket headed by James Garfield of Ohio. They won, and Garfield immediately found himself enmeshed in the demands of the unreformed spoils system. Within a few months of his inauguration in 1881, Garfield was assassinated by a disappointed and crazed office seeker, and Arthur became president.

**WHERE TO LEARN MORE**

★ Rutherford B. Hayes Presidential Center, Fremont, Ohio.
www.rbhayes.org

**Pendleton Civil Service Act** A law of 1883 that reformed the spoils system by prohibiting government workers from making political contributions and creating the Civil Service Commission to oversee their appointment on the basis of merit rather than politics.

Public dismay over this tragedy finally spurred changes in the spoils system. In 1883 Congress passed the **Pendleton Civil Service Act,** prohibiting federal employees from soliciting or receiving political contributions from government workers and creating the Civil Service Commission to administer competitive examinations to applicants for government jobs. The act gave the commission jurisdiction over only about 10 percent of federal positions but provided that presidents could extend its authority. A professional civil service free from partisan politics gradually emerged, strengthening the executive branch's ability to handle its increasing administrative responsibilities.

The new emphasis on merit and skill rather than party ties opened new opportunities to women. Federal clerks were nearly exclusively male as late as 1862, but by the early 1890s, women held a third of the clerical positions in the executive departments in Washington. These workers constituted the nation's first substantial female clerical labor force. Their work in public life challenged the conventional belief that a woman's ability and personality limited her to the domestic sphere.

## THE POLITICAL LIFE OF THE TARIFF

Americans debated heatedly over tariff legislation throughout the late nineteenth century. This complex issue linked basic economic questions to partisan, ideological, and regional concerns. Tariffs on imported goods provided revenue for the federal government and protected American industry from European competition. They promoted industrial growth but often allowed favored industries to garner high profits. By the 1880s, tariffs covered 4,000 items and generated more revenue than the government needed to carry on its limited operations.

Reflecting its commitment to industry, the Republican Party vigorously championed protective tariffs. Party leaders also claimed that American labor benefited from tariff protection. Most Democrats, by contrast, favored tariff reduction, a position that reflected their party's relatively laissez-faire outlook. They argued that lower tariffs would encourage foreign trade and, by reducing the treasury surplus, minimize the temptation for the government to pursue activist policies. They pointed out the discriminatory effects of high tariffs, which benefited some interests, such as certain manufacturers, but hurt others, such as some farmers, while raising the cost of living for all (see the Overview, Arguments in the Tariff Debates).

In the 1880s many Americans feared that corporate power had too much influence in government and was endangering popular liberty. The question, as posed by this cartoon, as "What are you going to do about it?"

## OVERVIEW   Arguments in the Tariff Debates

| Area Affected | High-Tariff Advocates | Low-Tariff Advocates |
| --- | --- | --- |
| Industry | Tariffs promote industrial growth. | Tariffs inflate corporate profits. |
| Employment | Tariffs stimulate job growth. | Tariffs restrict competition. |
| Wages and prices | Tariffs permit higher wages. | Tariffs increase consumer prices. |
| Government | Tariffs provide government revenue. | Tariffs violate the principle of laissez-faire and produce revenues that tempt the government to activism. |
| Trade | Tariffs protect the domestic market. | Tariffs restrict foreign trade. |

The differences between the parties, however, were often more rhetorical than substantial. They disagreed only about how high tariffs should be and what interests they should protect. Congressmen of both parties voted for tariffs that would benefit their districts.

In the 1884 campaign, the Republican presidential candidate, James G. Blaine, maintained that prosperity and high employment depended on high tariffs. The Democrats' platform endorsed a lowered tariff, but their candidate, New York governor Grover Cleveland, generally ignored the issue. Unable to address this and other important issues, both parties resorted to scandal mongering. One observer called the election "a more bitter, personal, and disgusting campaign than we have ever seen."

Cleveland continued to avoid the tariff issue for three years after his election, until the growing treasury surplus and rising popular pressure for tariff reduction prompted him to act. He devoted his entire 1887 annual message to attacking the "vicious, inequitable, and illogical" tariff, apparently making it the dominant issue of his 1888 reelection campaign. Once again, however, the distinctive political attribute of the period—intense and organized campaigning between closely balanced parties—forced both Democrats and Republicans to blur their positions. Cleveland proposed a Democratic platform that ignored his recent message and did not even use the word *tariff*. Cleveland won slightly more popular votes than his Republican opponent, Benjamin Harrison of Indiana, but Harrison carried the electoral college, indicating the decisive importance of strategic campaigning, local issues, and large campaign funds rather than great national issues.

The triumphant Republicans raised tariffs to prohibitive levels with the McKinley Tariff Act of 1890. McKinley praised the law as "protective in every paragraph and American on every page," but it provoked a popular backlash that helped return the Democrats to power. Still, the Democrats made little effort to push tariff reform.

**WHERE TO LEARN MORE**

★ President Benjamin Harrison's Home, Indianapolis, Indiana. www.presidentbenjaminharrison.org

**QUICK REVIEW**

**Tariffs and Politics**

◆ Tariffs provided revenues and protected American industries from competition.

◆ Republicans were strong supporters of protective tariffs.

◆ Congressmen voted for tariffs that benefited their home districts.

## THE BEGINNINGS OF FEDERAL REGULATION

While business leaders pressed for protective tariffs and other public policies that promoted their interests, they otherwise used their great political influence to ensure governmental laissez-faire. Popular pressure nonetheless compelled Congress to take the first steps toward the regulation of business with the passage of the Interstate Commerce Act in 1887 and the Sherman Antitrust Act in 1890.

Popular concern focused first on the railroads, the preeminent symbol of big business. Both farm groups and business shippers complained of discriminatory rates levied by railroads. Consumers condemned the railroads' use of pooling arrangements to

**Interstate Commerce Act**   The 1887 law that expanded federal power over business by prohibiting pooling and discriminatory rates by railroads and establishing the first federal regulatory agency, the Interstate Commerce Commission.

**Interstate Commerce Commission (ICC)**   The first federal regulation agency, established in 1887 to oversee railroad practices.

**QUICK REVIEW**

**Interstate Commerce Commission (ICC)**

◆ Established by Interstate Commerce Act (1887).

◆ Commission was first federal regulatory agency.

◆ In first fifteen years, only one court case was decided in favor of the ICC.

**Sherman Antitrust Act**   The first federal antitrust measure, passed in 1890; sought to promote economic competition by prohibiting business combinations in restraint of trade or commerce.

**sound money**   Misleading slogan that referred to a conservative policy of restricting the money supply and adhering to the gold standard.

suppress competition and raise rates. The resulting pressure was responsible for the Granger laws enacted in several midwestern states in the 1870s to regulate railroad freight and storage rates. At first, the Supreme Court upheld this legislation, ruling in *Munn v. Illinois* (1877) that state governments had the right to regulate private property when it was "devoted to a public use." But in 1886, the Court ruled in *Wabash, St. Louis, and Pacific Railway Company v. Illinois* that only the federal government could regulate interstate commerce. This decision effectively ended state regulation of railroads but simultaneously increased pressure for congressional action. With the support of both major parties, Congress in 1887 passed the **Interstate Commerce Act.**

The act prohibited rebates, discriminatory rates, and pooling and established the **Interstate Commerce Commission (ICC)** to investigate and prosecute violations. The ICC was the first federal regulatory agency. But its powers were too limited to be effective. Railroads continued their objectionable practices and frustrated the commission by refusing to provide required information and endlessly appealing its orders to a conservative judiciary. In its first 15 years, only one court case was decided in favor of the ICC.

Many people saw railroad abuses as indicative of the dangers of corporate power in general and demanded a broader federal response. As with railroad regulation, the first antitrust laws—laws intended to break up or regulate corporate monopolies—were passed by states. Exposés of the monopolistic practices of such corporations as Standard Oil forced both major parties to endorse national antitrust legislation during the campaign of 1888. In 1890, Congress enacted the **Sherman Antitrust Act** with only a single vote in opposition. But this near unanimity concealed real differences over the desirability and purpose of the law. Although it emphatically prohibited any combination in restraint of trade (any attempt to restrict competition), the law was vaguely written and too weak to prevent abuses. The courts further weakened the act, and presidents of both parties made little effort to enforce it. Essentially still unfettered, large corporations remained a threat in the eyes of many Americans.

## THE MONEY QUESTION

Persistent wrangling over questions of currency and coinage made monetary policy the most divisive political issue. Despite the sometimes arcane and difficult nature of the money question, millions of Americans adopted positions on it and defended them with religious ferocity.

Creditors, especially bankers, as well as conservative economists and many business leaders favored limiting the money supply. They called this a **sound money** policy and insisted that it would ensure economic stability, maintain property values, and retain investor confidence. Farmers and other debtors complained that this deflationary monetary policy would depress already low crop prices, drive debtors further into debt, and restrict economic opportunities. They favored expanding the money supply to match the country's growing population and economy. They expected this inflationary policy to raise prices, stimulate the economy, reduce debt burdens, and increase opportunities.

The conservative leadership of both major parties supported the sound money policy, but their rank-and-file membership, especially in the West and the South, included many inflationists. As a result, the parties avoided confronting each other on the money issue.

The conflict between advocates of sound money and inflation centered on the use of paper money, or "greenbacks," and silver coinage. In 1875, sound money advocates in Congress enacted a deflationary law that withdrew some greenbacks from circulation and required that the remainder be convertible into gold after 1878. This action forced the money issue into electoral politics. Outraged inflationists organized the Greenback

Party. The Greenbackers polled more than a million votes in 1878 and elected 14 members of Congress, nearly gaining the balance of power in the House. As the depression faded, however, so did interest in the greenback issue, and the party soon withered.

**The silver issue.**   Inflationists then turned to the silver issue, which would prove more enduring and disruptive. Historically, the United States had been on a bimetallic standard, using both gold and silver as the basis of its currency. But after the 1840s, the market price of silver rose above the currency value assigned to it by the government. Silver miners and owners began to sell the metal for commercial use rather than to the government for coinage, and little silver money circulated. In 1873, Congress passed a law "demonetizing" silver, thereby making gold the only standard for U.S. currency. Gold-standard supporters hoped that the law would promote international trade by aligning U.S. financial policy with that of Great Britain, which insisted on gold-based currency. But they also wanted to prevent new silver discoveries in the American West from expanding the money supply.

Indeed, silver production soon boomed, flooding the commercial market and dropping the value of the metal. Dismayed miners wanted the Treasury Department to purchase their surplus silver on the old terms and demanded a return to the bimetallic system. More important, the rural debtor groups seeking currency inflation joined in this demand, seeing renewed silver coinage as a means to reverse the long deflationary trend in the economy.

Again, both major parties equivocated. Eastern conservatives of both parties denounced silver; southerners and westerners demanded **free silver,** meaning unlimited silver coinage. By 1878, a bipartisan coalition succeeded in passing the Bland-Allison Act. This compromise measure required the government to buy and coin at least $2 million of silver a month. However, the government never exceeded the minimum, and the law had little inflationary effect.

After hard times hit rural regions in the late 1880s, inflationists secured passage of the Sherman Silver Purchase Act of 1890. The Treasury now had to buy a larger volume of silver and pay for it with treasury notes redeemable in either gold or silver. But this, too, produced little inflation, because the government did not coin the silver it purchased, redeemed the notes only with gold, and, as western silver production increased further, had to spend less and less to buy the stipulated amount of silver. Debtors of both parties remained convinced that the government favored the "classes rather than the masses." Gold-standard advocates (again, of both parties) were even less happy with the law and planned to repeal it at their first opportunity. The division between the two groups was deep and bitter.

**free silver**   Philosophy that the government should expand the money supply by purchasing and coining all the silver offered to it.

**QUICK REVIEW**

**The Money Question**

◆ Bimetallic standard: use of both gold and silver as basis of currency, practice of United States prior to 1873.

◆ Advocates of "gold standard" hoped to promote international trade and economic stability.

◆ Advocates of "free silver" hoped to stimulate economy, reduce debt, and create opportunity.

# THE CRISIS OF THE 1890s

In the 1890s, social, economic, and political pressures created a crisis for both the political system and the government. A third-party political challenge generated by agricultural discontent disrupted traditional party politics. A devastating depression spawned social misery and labor violence. Changing public attitudes led to new demands on the government and a realignment of parties and voters. These developments, in turn, set the stage for important political, economic, and social changes in the new century.

**WHAT FACTORS** contributed to the rise and fall of the Populist Party?

## FARMERS PROTEST INEQUITIES

The agricultural depression that engulfed the Great Plains and the South in the late 1880s brought misery and despair to millions of rural Americans. Falling crop prices and rising debt overwhelmed many people already exhausted from overwork and alarmed by the new corporate order. "At the age of 52 years, after a long life of toil, economy, and self-denial, I find myself and family virtual paupers," lamented one Kansan. His family's farm, rather than being "a house of refuge for our declining years, by a few turns of the monopolistic crank has been rendered valueless." To a large extent, the farmers' plight stemmed from bad weather and international over-production of farm products. Seeking relief, however, the farmers naturally focused on the inequities of railroad discrimination, tariff favoritism, a restrictive financial system, and apparently indifferent political parties.

**Credit inequities.**    Angry farmers particularly singled out the systems of money and credit that worked so completely against agricultural interests. Government rules for national banks directed credit into the urbanized North and East at the expense of the rural South and West and prohibited loans on farm property and real estate. As a result, farmers had to turn to other sources of credit and pay higher interest rates. In the West, farmers borrowed from mortgage companies to buy land and machinery, but declining crop prices made it difficult for them to pay their debts, and mortgage foreclosures then crushed the hopes of many. In the South, the credit shortage interacted with the practices of cotton marketing and retail trade to create the sharecropping system, which trapped more and more farmers, black and white, in a vicious pattern of exploitation. Moreover, the government's policies of monetary deflation worsened the debt burden for all farmers.

**Freight rates and tariffs.**    Farmers protested other features of the nation's economic system as well. Railroad freight rates were two or three times higher in the West and South than in the North and East. The near-monopolistic control of grain elevators and cotton brokerages in rural areas left farmers feeling exploited. Protective tariffs on agricultural machinery and other manufactured goods further raised their costs. The failure of political parties and the government to devise effective regulatory and antitrust measures or to correct the inequities in the currency, credit, and tariff laws capped the farmers' anger. By the 1890s, many were convinced that the nation's economic and political institutions were aligned against them.

**Farmers' Alliance**  A broad mass movement in the rural South and West during the late nineteenth century, encompassing several organizations and demanding economic and political reforms.

**Farmers organize.**    In response, farmers turned to the **Farmers' Alliance,** the era's greatest popular movement of protest and reform. Originating in Texas, the Southern Farmers' Alliance spread throughout the South and across the Great Plains to the Pacific coast. African American farmers organized the Colored Farmers' Alliance. The Northwestern Farmers' Alliance reached westward and northward from Illinois to Nebraska and Minnesota. In combination, these groups constituted a massive grassroots movement committed to economic and political reform.

The Farmers' Alliance restricted membership to men and women of the "producing class" and urged them to stand "against the encroachments of monopolies and in opposition to the growing corruption of wealth and power." At first, the Alliance organized farmers' cooperatives to market crops and purchase supplies. Although some co-ops worked well, most soon failed because of the opposition of established business interests. In Leflore County, Mississippi, when members of the Colored Farmers' Alliance shifted their trade to an Alliance store, local merchants provoked a conflict in which state troops killed 25 black farmers, including the local leaders of the Colored Alliance.

The Alliance also developed ingenious proposals to remedy rural credit and currency problems. In the South, the Alliance pushed the subtreasury system, which called on the government to warehouse farmers' cotton and advance them credit based on its value (see Chapter 17). In the West, the Alliance proposed a system of federal loans to farmers, using land as security. These proposals were immensely popular among farmers, but the major parties and Congress rejected them. The Alliance also took up earlier calls for free silver, government control of railroads, and banking reform, again to no avail.

## THE PEOPLE'S PARTY

In the West, discontented agrarians organized independent third parties to achieve reforms the major parties had ignored. State-level third parties appeared in the elections of 1890 under many names. All eventually adopted the labels "People's" or "Populist," which were first used by a Kansas party formed by members of the Farmers' Alliance, the Knights of Labor, the Grange, and the old Greenback Party. The new party's campaign, marked by grim determination and fierce rhetoric, set the model for Populist politics.

The Populist parties proved remarkably successful. They gained control of the legislatures of Kansas and Nebraska and won congressional elections in Kansas, Nebraska, and Minnesota. Their victories came at the expense of the Republicans, who had traditionally controlled politics in these states, and contributed to a massive defeat of the GOP in the 1890 midterm elections. Thereafter, Populists won further victories throughout the West. In the mountain states, where their support came more from miners than from farmers, they won governorships in Colorado and Montana. On the Pacific coast, angry farmers found allies among urban workers in Seattle, Tacoma, Portland, and San Francisco, where organized labor had campaigned for reform since the 1880s. The Populists elected a governor in Washington, congressmen in California, and legislators in all three states.

*The People's Party Platform* (1892)

With their new political power, farmers enacted reform legislation in many western states. New laws regulated banks and railroads and protected debtors by capping interest rates and restricting mortgage foreclosures. Others protected unions and mandated improved workplace conditions. Still others made the political system more democratic. Populists were instrumental, for example, in winning woman suffrage in Colorado and Idaho, although the united opposition of Democrats and Republicans blocked their efforts to win it in other states.

In the South, the angry farmers did not initially form third parties but instead attempted to seize control of the dominant Democratic Party by forcing its candidates to pledge support to the Alliance platform. The rural southern electorate then swept these "Alliance Democrats" into office. But most of these Democrats then repudiated their Alliance pledges and remained loyal to their party and its traditional opposition to governmental activism. Betrayed again by the political system, disgruntled Alliance members began organizing their own Populist parties, but they faced obstacles that western farmers did not. A successful challenge to the entrenched Democrats would require the political cooperation of both white and black farmers, but that would expose Populists to demagogic attacks from Democrats for undermining white supremacy, frightening away potential white supporters.

Some Southern Populists, black and white, did appeal for racial cooperation in political if not social action. In Georgia, the Populist leader Tom Watson supported a biracial party

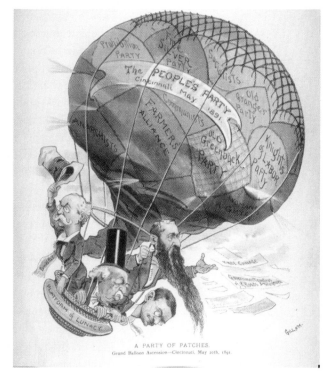

A PARTY OF PATCHES.
Grand Balloon Ascension—Cincinnati, May 20th, 1891.

Established interests ridiculed the Populists unmercifully. This hostile cartoon depicts the People's Party as an odd assortment of radical dissidents committed to a "Platform of Lunacy."

organization and counseled white people to accept black people as partners in their common crusade. "You are kept apart," Watson told black and white southerners, "that you may be separately fleeced of your earnings. You are made to hate each other because upon that hatred is rested the keystone of the arch of financial despotism which enslaves you both."

But steeped in racism, most white southerners recoiled from the prospect of interracial unity. And for their part, most black people remained loyal to the Republican Party for its role in abolishing slavery and for the few patronage crumbs the party still threw their way. Moreover, primarily tenants and farm laborers, their interests were not identical to those of white landowning farmers who formed the core of the Populist Party. Unwilling or unable to mobilize black voters and largely unsuccessful in dislodging white voters from the Democratic Party, Populists in the South achieved but limited political success, making significant inroads only in the legislatures of Texas, Alabama, and Georgia, and sending Tom Watson to Congress.

**National action.**    Populists soon realized that successful reform would require national action. They met in Omaha, Nebraska, on July 4, 1892, to organize a national party and nominated former Greenbacker James B. Weaver for president. The party platform, known as the **Omaha Platform,** rejected the laissez-faire policies of the old parties: It demanded government ownership of the railroads and the telegraph and telephone systems, a national currency issued by the government rather than by private banks, the subtreasury system, free silver, a graduated income tax, and the redistribution to settlers of land held by railroads and speculative corporations. Accompanying resolutions endorsed the popular election of senators, the secret ballot, and other electoral reforms to make government more democratic and responsive to popular wishes.

The Populists left Omaha to begin an energetic campaign. Weaver toured the western states and with movement leader Mary Lease invaded the Democratic stronghold of the South where some Populists tried to mobilize black voters. Southern Democrats, however, used violence and fraud to intimidate Populist voters and cheat Populist candidates out of office. Some local Populist leaders were murdered, and Weaver was driven from the South. Southern Democrats also appealed effectively to white supremacy, undermining the Populist effort to build a biracial reform coalition.

Elsewhere, too, Populists met disappointment. Midwestern farmers unfamiliar with Alliance ideas and organization ignored Populist appeals and stood by their traditional political allegiances. So did most eastern working-class voters, who learned little of the Populist program beyond its demand for inflation, which they feared would worsen their own conditions.

The Populists lost the election but showed impressive support. They garnered more than a million votes, carried several western states, and won hundreds of state offices throughout the West and in pockets of the South. Populist leaders immediately began working to expand their support, to the alarm of both southern Democrats and northern Republicans.

## THE CHALLENGE OF THE DEPRESSION

The emergence of a significant third-party movement was but one of many developments that combined by the mid-1890s to produce a national political crisis. A harsh and lengthy depression began in 1893, cruelly worsening conditions not only for farmers but for most other Americans. Labor unrest and violence engulfed the nation, reflecting workers' distress but frightening more comfortable Americans. The persistent failure of the major parties to respond to serious problems contributed mightily to the growing popular discontent. Together these developments constituted an important challenge to America's new industrial society and government.

Although the Populists lost in 1892, the election nonetheless reflected the nation's spreading dissatisfaction. Voters decisively rejected President Harrison and the incumbent Republicans in Congress, putting the Democrats in control of Congress and Grover Cleveland back in the White House. But the conservative Cleveland was almost oblivious to the mounting demand for reform. He delivered an inaugural address championing laissez-faire and rejecting government action to solve social or economic problems.

Cleveland's resolve was immediately tested when the economy collapsed in the spring of 1893. Railroad overexpansion, a weak banking system, tight credit, and plunging agricultural prices all contributed to the disaster. So too did a depression in Europe, which reduced American export markets and prompted British investors to sell their American investments for gold. Hundreds of banks closed, and thousands of businesses, including the nation's major railroads, went bankrupt. By winter, 20 percent of the labor force was unemployed, and the jobless scavenged for food in a country that had no public unemployment or welfare programs.

Churches, local charity societies, and labor unions tried to provide relief but were overwhelmed. Most state governments offered little relief beyond encouraging private charity to the homeless.

**Appeals for federal action.**    If Cleveland and Congress had no idea how the federal government might respond to the depression, other Americans did. Jacob Coxey, a Populist businessman from Ohio, proposed a government public-works program for the unemployed to be financed with paper money. This plan would improve the nation's infrastructure, create jobs for the unemployed, and provide an inflationary stimulus to counteract the depression's deflationary effects. In short, Coxey advocated positive government action to combat the depression.

Coxey organized a march of the unemployed to Washington as "a petition with boots on" to support his ideas. **Coxey's Army** of the unemployed, as the excited press dubbed it, marched through the industrial towns of Ohio and Pennsylvania and into Maryland, attracting attention and support. Other armies formed in eastern cities from Boston to Baltimore and set out for the capital. Some of the largest armies organized in the western cities of Denver, San Francisco, and Seattle.

Lewis Fry, the organizer of the Los Angeles army, declared: "If the government has a right to make us die in time of war, we have the right to demand of her the right to live in time of peace." Fry's 500 marchers captured a train to cross the Southwest and were feted and fed by townspeople from Tucson to El Paso. When the Southern Pacific uncoupled the train's locomotive and left the marchers stranded without food or water in West Texas, the governor of Texas threatened to hold the railroad responsible for murder "by torture and starvation." Texas citizens quickly raised funds to speed the army on to St. Louis. From there it marched to Washington on foot.

The sympathy and assistance with which Americans greeted these industrial armies reflected more than anxiety over the depression and unemployment. As one economist noted, what distinguished the Populists and Coxeyites from earlier reformers was their appeal for federal action. Their substantial public support suggested a deep dissatisfaction with the failure of the government to respond to social and economic needs.

Nonetheless, the government acted to suppress Coxey. When he reached Washington with 600 marchers, police and soldiers arrested him and his aides, beat sympathetic bystanders in a crowd of 20,000, and herded the marchers into detention camps. Unlike the lobbyists for business and finance, Coxey was not permitted to reach Congress to deliver his statement urging the government to assist "the poor and oppressed."

**QUICK REVIEW**

**The Depression of 1893**

♦ Harsh and lengthy depression began in 1893.

♦ By winter 1893, 20 percent of the labor force was unemployed.

♦ Most state governments offered little relief.

**Coxey's Army**    A protest march of unemployed workers, led by Populist businessman Jacob Coxey, demanding inflation and a public works program during the depression of the 1890s.

Jacob Coxey's "Army" of the unemployed marches to Washington, D.C., in 1894. Many such "industrial armies" were organized during the depressed 1890s, revealing dissatisfaction with traditional politics and limited government.

**Protecting big business.**   The depression also provoked labor turmoil. In 1894, there were some 1,400 industrial strikes, involving nearly 700,000 workers, the largest number of strikers in any year in the nineteenth century. Cleveland had no response except to call for law and order. One result was the government's violent suppression of the Pullman strike (see Chapter 18).

In a series of decisions in 1895, the Supreme Court strengthened the bonds between business and government. First, it upheld the use of a court-ordered injunction to break the Pullman strike. As a result, injunctions became a major weapon for courts and corporations against labor unions, until Congress finally limited their use in 1932. Next, in *United States v. E. C. Knight Company*, the Court gutted the Sherman Antitrust Act by ruling that manufacturing, as opposed to commerce, was beyond the reach of federal regulation. Finally, the Court invalidated an income tax that agrarian Democrats and Populists had maneuvered through Congress. Not until 1913, and then only with an amendment to the Constitution, would it be possible to adopt an equitable system of taxation.

Surveying these developments, farmers and workers increasingly concluded that the government protected powerful interests while ignoring the plight of ordinary Americans. Certainly the callous treatment shown workers contrasted sharply with Cleveland's concern for bankers as he managed the government's monetary policy in the depression. Cleveland blamed the economic collapse on the Sherman Silver Purchase Act, which he regarded as detrimental to business confidence and a threat to the nation's gold reserve. He persuaded Congress in 1893 to repeal the law, enraging southern and western members of his own party. These Silver Democrats condemned Cleveland for betraying the public good to "the corporate interests."

Cleveland's policy failed to end the depression. By 1894, the Treasury began borrowing money from Wall Street to bolster the gold reserve. These transactions benefited a syndicate of bankers headed by J. P. Morgan. It seemed to critics that an indifferent Cleveland was helping rich bankers profit from the nation's economic agony.

## THE BATTLE OF THE STANDARDS AND THE ELECTION OF 1896

The government's unpopular actions, coupled with the unrelenting depression, alienated workers and farmers from the Cleveland administration and the Democratic Party. In the off-year elections of 1894, the Democrats suffered the greatest loss of congressional seats in American history. Populists increased their vote by 42 percent, making especially significant gains in the South. But the real beneficiaries of the popular hatred of Cleveland and his policies were the Republicans. They gained solid control of Congress as well as state governments across the North and West. All three parties began to plan for the presidential election of 1896.

As hard times persisted, the silver issue came to overshadow all others. Some Populist leaders, hoping to broaden the party's appeal, began to emphasize silver rather than the more radical but divisive planks of the Omaha Platform. Many southern and western Democrats, who had traditionally favored silver inflation, also decided to stress the issue, both to undercut the Populists and to distance themselves and their party from the despised Cleveland.

**McKinley and the Republicans.** William McKinley, governor of Ohio and author of the McKinley Tariff Act of 1890, emerged as the front-runner of a crowd of hopeful Republican presidential candidates. The Republicans nominated McKinley on the first ballot at their 1896 convention. Their platform called for high tariffs but also endorsed the gold standard, placating eastern delegates but prompting several western Silver Republicans to withdraw from the party.

**Bryan and the Silverites.** When the Democratic convention met, embattled supporters of the gold standard soon learned that the silver crusade had made them a minority in the party. With a fervor that conservatives likened to "scenes of the French Revolution," the Silver Democrats revolutionized their party. They adopted a platform repudiating Cleveland and his policies and endorsing free silver, the income tax, and tighter regulation of trusts and railroads. A magnificent speech supporting this platform by William Jennings Bryan helped convince the delegates to nominate him for president.

Holding their convention last, the Populists faced a terrible dilemma. The Democratic nomination of Bryan on a silver platform undercut their hopes of attracting disappointed reformers from the major parties. Bryan, moreover, had already worked closely with Nebraska Populists, who now urged the party to endorse him rather than split the silver vote and ensure the victory of McKinley and the gold standard. Other Populists argued that fusing—joining with the Democrats—would cost the Populists their separate identity and subordinate their larger political principles to the issue of free silver. After anguished discussion, the Populists nominated Bryan for president.

William Jennings Bryan in 1896. A powerful orator of great human sympathies, Bryan was adored by his followers as "the majestic man who was hurling defiance in the teeth of the money power." Nominated three times for the presidency by the Democrats, he was never elected.

## AMERICAN VIEWS

### A Populist Views American Government

An educator, merchant, and former editor, Lorenzo D. Lewelling became one of the most articulate champions of the Populist Party and its principles. Elected governor of Kansas in 1892, he headed what was heralded as "The First People's Party Government on Earth." On January 9, 1893, Lewelling delivered his inaugural address, in which he declared, "I appeal to the people of this great commonwealth to array themselves on the side of humanity and justice." The following passages from the speech sketch out Lewelling's views of the 1890s and his "dream of the future."

- **How** does Lewelling's rhetoric reflect the deep divisions of the 1890s?
- **What** is Lewelling's view of the proper role of government?
- **For what** does Lewelling criticize the government of the 1890s?
- **What** does Lewelling mean by his statement that "the rich have no right to the property of the poor"?

The survival of the fittest is the government of brutes and reptiles, and such philosophy must give place to a government which recognizes human brotherhood. It is the province of government to protect the weak, but the government today is resolved into a struggle of the masses with the classes for supremacy and bread, until business, home, and personal integrity are trembling in the face of possible want in the family. Feed a tiger regularly and you tame and make him harmless, but hunger makes tigers of men. If it be true that the poor have no right to the property of the rich let it also be declared that the rich have no right to the property of the poor.

It is the mission of Kansas to protect and advance the moral and material interests of all its citizens. It is its especial duty at the present time to protect the producer from the ravages of combined wealth. National legislation has for twenty years fostered and protected the interests of the few, while it has left the South and West to supply the products with which to feed and clothe the world, and thus to become the servants of wealth.

The demand for free coinage has been refused. The national banks have been permitted to withdraw their circulation, and thus the interests of the East and West have been diverged until the passage of the McKinley bill culminated in their diversement. The purchasing power of the dollar has become so great [that] corn, wheat, beef, pork, and cotton have scarcely commanded a price equal to the cost of production.

The instincts of patriotism have naturally rebelled against these unwarranted encroachments of the power of

**Money and oratory.** The campaign was intense and dramatic, with each side demonizing the other. Eastern financial and business interests contributed millions of dollars to McKinley's campaign. Standard Oil alone provided $250,000, about the same amount as the Democrats' total national expenses. McKinley's campaign used these funds to organize an unprecedented campaign. Shifting the emphasis from parades to information, Republicans issued 250 million campaign documents in a dozen languages, warning of economic disaster should Bryan be elected and the bimetallic standard be restored, but promising that McKinley's election would finally end the depression. Republicans were aided by a national press so completely sympathetic that many newspapers not only shaped their editorials but distorted their news stories to Bryan's disadvantage.

Lacking the Republicans' superior resources, the Democrats relied on Bryan's superb speaking ability and youthful energy. Bryan was the first presidential candidate to campaign systematically, speaking hundreds of times to millions of voters. The intense campaign brought a record voter turnout. McKinley won decisively by capturing the East and Midmoney. Sectional hatred has also been kept alive by the old powers, the better to enable them to control the products and make the producer contribute to the millionaire; and thus, while the producer labors in the field, the shop, and the factory, the millionaire usurps his earnings and rides in gilded carriages with liveried servants. . . .

The problem of today is how to make the State subservient to the individual, rather than to become his master. Government is a voluntary union for the common good. It guarantees to the individual life, liberty, and the pursuit of happiness. The government then must make it possible for the citizen to enjoy liberty and pursue happiness. If the government fails of these things, it fails in its mission. . . . If old men go to the poor-house and young men go to prison, something is wrong with the economic system of the government.

What is the State to him who toils, if labor is denied him and his children cry for bread? What is the State to the farmer who wearily drags himself from dawn till dark to meet the stern necessities of the mortgage on the farm? What is the State to him if it sanctions usury and other legal forms by which his home is destroyed and his innocent ones become a prey to the fiends who lurk in the shadow of civilization? What is the State to the business man, early grown gray, broken in health and spirit by successive failures; anxiety like a boding owl his constant companion by day and the disturber of his dreams by night? How is life to be sustained, how is liberty to be enjoyed, how is happiness to be pursued under such adverse conditions as the State permits if it does not sanction? Is the State powerless against these conditions?

This is the generation which has come to the rescue. Those in distress who cry out from the darkness shall not be heard in vain. Conscience is in the saddle. We have leaped the bloody chasm and entered a contest for the protection of home, humanity, and the dignity of labor.

The grandeur of civilization shall be emphasized by the dawn of a new era in which the people shall reign, and if found necessary they will "expand the powers of government to solve the enigmas of the times." The people are greater than the law or the statutes, and when a nation sets its heart on doing a great and good thing it can find a legal way to do it.

I have a dream of the future. I have the evolution of an abiding faith in human government, and in the beautiful vision of a coming time I behold the abolition of poverty. A time is foreshadowed when the withered hand of want shall not be outstretched for charity; when liberty, equality, and justice shall have permanent abiding places in the republic.

Source: *People's Party Paper* (Atlanta), January 20, 1893.

west as well as Oregon and California (see Map 20–2). Bryan carried the traditionally Democratic South and the mountain and plains states, where Populists and silverites dominated. He failed to gain support in either the Midwest or the cities of the East. His silver campaign had little appeal to industrial workers. The elections of 1894 and 1896 ended the close balance between the major parties. Cleveland's failures, coupled with an economic recovery in the wake of the election of 1896, gained the Republicans a reputation as the party of prosperity and industrial progress, firmly establishing them in power for years to come. By contrast, the Democratic Party receded into an ineffectual sectional minority dominated by southern conservatives, despite Bryan's liberal views.

The People's Party simply dissolved. Demoralized by fusion with the Democrats, who had earlier violently repressed them, many southern Populists dropped out of politics. The Democrats' disfranchisement laws, directed at discontented poor white southerners as well as poor black southerners, further undermined the Populists in the South. In the West, the silver tide of 1896 carried many Populists into office, but with their party collapsing, they had no hope of reelection. By 1898, the Populist Party had virtually disappeared. Its reform

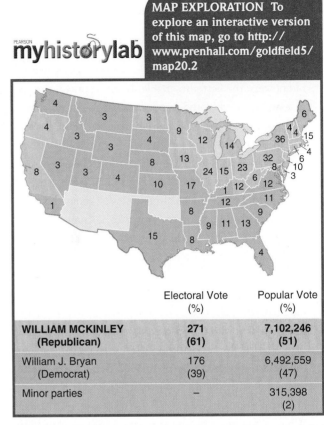

MAP EXPLORATION To explore an interactive version of this map, go to http://www.prenhall.com/goldfield5/map20.2

myhistorylab

|  | Electoral Vote (%) | Popular Vote (%) |
|---|---|---|
| **WILLIAM MCKINLEY** (Republican) | **271** **(61)** | **7,102,246** **(51)** |
| William J. Bryan (Democrat) | 176 (39) | 6,492,559 (47) |
| Minor parties | – | 315,398 (2) |

MAP 20–2   **The Election of 1896**   William Jennings Bryan carried most of the rural South and West, but his free silver campaign had little appeal to more urban and industrial regions, which swung strongly to Republican candidate William McKinley.

**Was the** election of 1896 closer than the electoral vote would suggest?

legacy, however, proved more enduring. The issues it raised would continue to shape state and national politics.

McKinley plunged into his presidency. Unlike his predecessors, he had a definite, if limited, program, consisting of tariff protection, sound money, and overseas expansion. He worked actively to see it through Congress and to shape public opinion, thereby helping establish the model of the modern presidency. He had promised prosperity, and it returned, although not because of the record high tariff his party enacted in 1897 or the Currency Act of 1900, which firmly established the gold standard. Prosperity returned, instead, because of reviving markets and a monetary inflation that resulted from the discovery of vast new deposits of gold in Alaska, Australia, and South Africa. The silverites had recognized that an expanding industrial economy required an expanding money supply. Ironically, the new inflation was greater than the inflation that would have resulted from free silver. With the return of prosperity and the decline of social tensions, McKinley easily won reelection in 1900, defeating Bryan a second time.

# CONCLUSION

In late-nineteenth-century America, politics and government often seemed at cross-purposes. Political contests were exciting events, absorbing public attention, attracting high voter turnout, and often raising issues of symbolic or substantive importance. Closely balanced political parties commanded the zealous support of their constituents and wielded power and influence. The institutions of government, by contrast, were limited in size, scope, and responsibility. A weakened presidency and an inefficient Congress, hampered by a restrictive judiciary, were often unable to resolve the very issues that were so dramatically raised in the political arena. The persistent disputes over tariff and monetary policy illustrate this impasse. But the issue that most reflected it was civil service reform. The patronage system provided the lifeblood of politics but also disrupted government business.

Localism, laissez-faire, and other traditional principles that shaped both politics and government were becoming increasingly inappropriate for America's industrializing society. New challenges were emerging that state and local governments could not effectively solve on their own. The national nature of the railroad network, for example, finally brought the federal government into the regulatory arena, however imperfectly, with the Interstate Commerce Act of 1887. Both the depression of the 1890s and the popular discontent articulated most clearly by the Populist rejection of laissez-faire underscored the need for change and discredited the limited government of the Cleveland administration.

By the end of the decade, the political system had changed. The Republicans had emerged as the dominant party, ending the two-party stalemate of previous decades. Campaign hoopla in local communities had given way to information-based campaigns directed by and through national organizations. A new, activist presidency was emerging. And the disruptive currency issue faded with the hard times that had brought it forth. Still greater changes were on the horizon. The depression and its terrible social and economic consequences undermined traditional ideas about the responsibilities of government and increased public support for activist policies. The stage was set for the Progressive Era.

# Summary

HOW DID parties mobilize voters in the late nineteenth century?

**The Structure and Style of Politics** Politics in the late nineteenth century expressed social values as it determined who held the reins of government. While the two major political parties dominated, third parties sought to activate those the Democrats and Republicans left unserved. Virtually all men participated in politics; the voter turnout of that era has never been equaled. Religious, ethnic, and regional factors determined party ties, but third parties, such as the Populists, emerged around issues. Women also participated in politics and some states now allowed full or partial suffrage.

HOW EFFECTIVE was the federal government in addressing the problems of America's industrializing economy?

**The Limits of Government** Government in the late nineteenth century was neither active nor productive by present standards; localism and laissez-faire policies were resurgent. Congress and a presidency divided between the two political parties, a small and inefficient federal bureaucracy, and judicial restraints joined powerful private interests to limit the size and objectives of the federal government.

WHY WERE monetary issues so important to so many Americans at the end of the nineteenth century?

**Public Policies and National Elections** The spoils system, the system for selecting and supervising federal employees, was finally reformed as a result of the assassination of President Garfield. The Pendleton Civil Service Act emphasized merit and skill; it also opened new opportunities for women. Americans heatedly debated the tariff policies; popular pressure compelled Congress to take the first steps toward the regulation of business; the most divisive political issue of the era was monetary policies with inflationists wanting more money, especially silver, in circulation.

WHAT FACTORS contributed to the rise and fall of the Populist Party?

**The Crisis of the 1890s** Protests from Midwestern farmers over freight rates, tariffs, and the money supply resulted in popular movements of protest and reform. The Populists, a third party, funneled the discontent into politics; their emergence was but one of the many developments combining to produce a national political crisis. A severe economic depression, labor unrest, and government inaction, along with the silver issue, underscored the need for change. The presidential election of 1896 was an intense campaign with record voter turnout; with William McKinley's victory over William Jennings Bryan, the Republicans became established as the party of prosperity and individual progress.

# WHERE TO LEARN MORE

**Rest Cottage, Evanston, Illinois.** Frances Willard's home, from which she directed the Woman's Christian Temperance Union, is carefully preserved as a museum. The Willard Memorial Library contains more memorabilia and papers of Willard and the WCTU. **www.wctu.org/house.html**

**President Benjamin Harrison's Home, Indianapolis, Indiana.** President Harrison's brick Italianate mansion, completed in 1875, has been completely restored with the family's furniture and keepsakes. The former third-floor ballroom serves as a museum with exhibits of many artifacts of the Harrisons' public and private lives. **www.presidentbenjaminharrison.org**

**Susan B. Anthony House National Historic Landmark, Rochester, New York.** This modest house was the home of the prominent suffragist and contains Anthony's original furnishings and personal photographs. **www.susanbanthonyhouse .org/main.html**

**Rutherford B. Hayes Presidential Center, Fremont, Ohio.** This complex contains President Hayes's home, office, and extensive grounds together with an excellent library and museum holding valuable collections of manuscripts, artifacts, and photographs illustrating his personal interests and political career. **www.rbhayes.org**

# STUDY RESOURCES

## myhistorylab

For study resources for this chapter, go to www.myhistorylab .com and choose *The American Journey*. You will find a wealth of study and review material for this chapter, including pre- and post-tests, customized study plan, key term review flash cards, interactive map and document activities, and documents for analysis.

# REVIEW QUESTIONS

1. What social and institutional factors shaped the disorderly nature of elections in the late nineteenth century? How did they operate in U.S. politics?

2. What social and institutional factors determined the role of government? How and why did the role of government change during this period?

3. What factors determined the party affiliation of American voters? Why did so many third parties develop during this era?

4. How might the planks of the Omaha Platform have helped solve farmers' troubles?

5. What factors shaped the conduct and outcome of the election of 1896? How did that contest differ from earlier elections?

## KEY TERMS

Coxey's Army (p. 605)
Farmers' Alliance (p. 602)
Free silver (p. 601)
Granger laws (p. 593)
Greenback Party (p. 593)
Interstate Commerce Act (p. 600)
Interstate Commerce Commission (ICC) (p. 600)
Laissez-faire (p. 594)
Mugwumps (p. 593)

National American Woman Suffrage Association (p. 594)
Omaha Platform (p. 604)
Pendleton Civil Service Act (p. 598)
Populist Party (p. 593)
Prohibition Party (p. 593)
Sherman Antitrust Act (p. 600)
Sound money (p. 600)

# INTERPRETING the PAST

## Currency Reform

**EXPLAIN AND DESCRIBE** the powerful political lure of currency reform in American presidential campaigns between 1874 and 1900. Where did various political groups and candidates stand on this issue and to whom did they attempt to appeal?

During the Civil War farmers in the Midwest had gone deeply into debt to expand their crop production and meet the profitable demand for grain and other crops created by war. The wild financial swings of booms and busts between 1865 and 1900 caused farmers to borrow heavily again to meet the demand for grains created by various world events. Farmers frequently had to borrow to obtain the seeds and materials to plant their crops. If crop prices were low at harvest or a crop failure

occurred, farmers were in deep financial trouble. Radical variations in international crop prices impacted the farmer's bottom line. Looking for simplistic explanations to complicated problems, farmers decided that the railroads and eastern financial interests were in a conspiracy to reduce them to economic slavery to the industrial East. Simplistic explanations led to simplistic answers and currency reform became the central focus of many farmer political movements. After silver was dropped from the list of authorized coins for the U.S., farmers demanded the free coinage of silver to create an artificial inflation that would raise crop prices and free them from debt, or so they believed. Currency reform became an emotional issue in politics between 1874 and 1900.

## We demand a national currency . . .

### Coinage Act, February 12, 1873

SEC. 14. That the gold coins of the United States shall be a One-dollar piece . . . a quartereagle, or two-and-a-half dollar piece; a three dollar piece; a half-eagle, or five-dollar piece; an eagle, or ten-dollar piece; and a double eagle, or twenty dollar piece . . . which coins shall be a legal tender in all payments at their nominal value. . . .

SEC. 15. That the silver coins of the United States shall be . . . a half dollar, or fifty-cent piece, a quarter-dollar, or twenty five-cent piece, a dime, or ten cent piece; . . . and said coins shall be a legal tender at their nominal value for any amount not exceeding five dollars in any one payment. . . .

SEC. 17. That no coins, either of gold, silver, or minor coinage, shall hereafter be issued from the mint other than those of the denominations, standards, and weights herein set forth.

### Populist Platform, 1892

Silver, which has been accepted as coin since the dawn of history, has been demonetized to add to the purchasing power of gold by decreasing the value of all forms of property as well as human labor, and the supply of currency is purposely abridged to fatten usurers, bankrupt enterprise, and enslave industry. A vast conspiracy against mankind has been organized on two continents, and it is rapidly taking possession of the world. If not met and overthrown at once it forebodes terrible social convulsions, the destruction of civilization, or the establishment of an absolute despotism.

We demand a national currency, safe, sound, and flexible issued by the general government only, a full legal tender for all debts, public and private. . . . We demand free and unlimited coinage of silver and gold at the present legal ratio of 16 to 1.

*This Republican campaign poster of 1896 depicts William McKinley standing on sound money and promising a revival of prosperity. The depression of the 1890s shifted the electorate into the Republican column.*

With silver remonetized, and gold at a premium, not one-tenth the hardships could result that now afflict us. . . . The bimetallic standard will make the United States the most prosperous nation on the globe.

## William Jennings Bryan, "Cross of Gold Speech," Democratic National Convention, July 9, 1896

You come to us and tell us that the great cities are in favor of the gold standard. I tell you that the great cities rest upon these broad and fertile prairies. Burn down your cities and leave our farms, and your cities will spring up again as if by magic. But destroy our farms and the grass will grow in the streets of every city in the country. . . .

If they dare to come out in the open field and defend the gold standard as a good thing, we shall fight them to the uttermost, having behind us the producing masses of the nation and the world. Having behind us the commercial interests and the laboring interests and all the toiling masses, we shall answer their demands for a gold standard by saying to them, you shall not press down upon the brow of labor this crown of thorns. You shall not crucify mankind upon a cross of gold.

## William H. Harvey, *Coin's Financial School,* 1893

It is proposed by the bimetallists to remonetize silver, and add it to the quantity of money that is to be used for measuring the value of all other property. . . .

You increase the value of all property by adding to the number of money units in the land. You make it possible for the debtor to pay his debts; business to start anew, and revivify all the industries of the country, which must remain paralyzed so long as silver as well as all other property is measured by a gold standard. . . .

The money lenders in the United States, who own substantially all our money, have a selfish interest in maintaining the gold standard. They, too, will not yield. . . .

*Cartoonist Grant Hamilton emphasizes the free silver issue in this cartoon, criticizing William Jennings Bryan as "worth 53 cents only in free silver."*

*Burn down your cities . . .*

# 21
# The Progressive Era

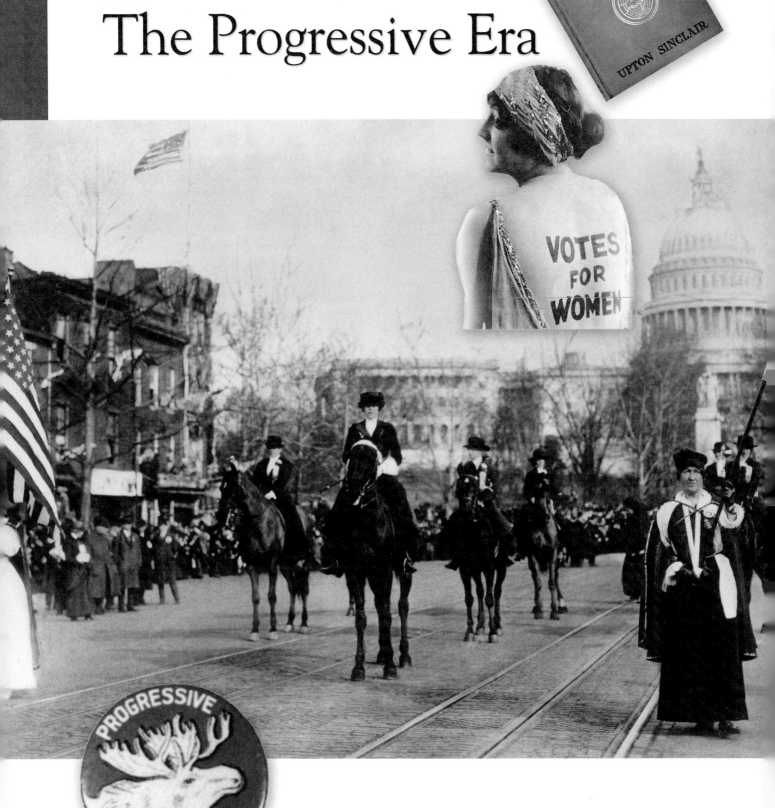

THE JUNGLE

UPTON SINCLAIR

VOTES FOR WOMEN

PROGRESSIVE

A women's suffrage parade in Washington D.C., 1913.

THE FERMENT OF REFORM *(page 620)*

## WHAT VALUES and beliefs bound progressives together?

REFORMING SOCIETY *(page 627)*

## WHAT ROLE did women play in progressive reform movements?

REFORMING POLITICS AND GOVERNMENT *(page 633)*

## WHAT STEPS were taken toward woman suffrage during the Progressive Era?

THEODORE ROOSEVELT AND THE
PROGRESSIVE PRESIDENCY *(page 637)*

## HOW DID Theodore Roosevelt envision the power of the president?

WOODROW WILSON AND PROGRESSIVE REFORM *(page 641)*

## HOW DID Woodrow Wilson's vision of reform differ from Theodore Roosevelt's?

*Five thousand women, marching in the woman suffrage pageant yesterday, practically fought their way foot by foot up Pennsylvania avenue, through a surging mass of humanity that completely defied the Washington police, swamped the marchers, and broke their procession into little companies. The women, trudging stoutly along under great difficulties, were able to complete their march only when troops of cavalry from Fort Myer were rushed into Washington to take charge of Pennsylvania avenue. No inauguration has ever produced such scenes, which in many instances amounted to little less than riots. . . .*

*The parade in itself, in spite of the delays, was a great success . . . . As a spectacle the pageant was entrancing. Beautiful women, posing in classic robes, passed in a bewildering array, presenting an irresistible appeal to the artistic, and completely captivating the hundred thousand spectators. . . .*

*Miss Margaret Foley, bearing aloft a large "Votes for Women" flag, and Mrs. G. Farquhar, carrying an American flag, led the procession. . . . After the float reading, "We Demand an Amendment to the United States Constitution Enfranchising the Women of This Country," came a body of ushers clad in light blue capes. . . . Two large floats . . . represented the countries in which women are working for equal rights, followed by a large body of women on foot dressed in street clothes, who bore the banners and pennants of scores of suffrage associations throughout the world. . . . The Homemakers . . . were dressed in long purple robes over their street clothes. Following them came a float, "In Patriotic Service," . . . and Miss Lillian Wald, the walking leader of a large body of women who followed the float, dressed as trained nurses, with gray caps and coats.*

*Miss Margaret Gage and Maurice Cohen, wearing college gowns with mortar boards, represented "Education," which was followed by nearly 1,000 women of the college section. . . . A group of young girls in blue capes represented the wage-earners, followed by "A Labor Story," which depicted the crowded condition of tenements, with women and children bendng over sewing machines, dirty and disheveled, in squalid quarters. . . . [Then followed] the women in the government section, all wearing light blue capes, . . . the business women, dressed in similar manner, . . . the teachers, . . . the social workers, . . . the white and pink costumed delegation of "writers," . . . club women and women clergy.*

*The greatest ovation was given to "General" Rosalie Jones, who led her little band of hikers from New York over rough roads and through snow and rain to march for the "cause." . . .*

*But there were hostile elements in the crowd through which the women marched. . . . Passing through two walls of antagonistic humanity, the marchers for the most part kept their temper. They suffered insult and closed their ears to jibes and jeers. . . .*

*The pageant moved up Pennsylvania avenue with great difficulty and surrounded with some danger. Crowds surged into the streets, completely overwhelming the police and stopping the pageant's progress. Mounted police charged into the crowds, but failed at times to drive them back, even with the free use of clubs. In more than an hour the pageant had moved only ten blocks. . . .*

*When the surging multitude was driven back in one place it flowed back into the street at another. The pageant slowly moved along, sometimes not more than a dozen feet at a time. . . .*

*As a result of the unruly spirit of the biggest crowd that ever witnessed a parade on Pennsylvania Avenue, or of the inactivity of the police, who seemed powerless to protect the marching suffragists, the Emergency Hospital last night was filled to overflowing. . . .*

*Washington Post,* March 4, 1913.

## PEARSON myhistorylab

### Personal Journeys Online

- Mother Jones, *Marching Against Child Labor,* 1903. Account of Mother Jones leading a group of children to see President Roosevelt.

- Alice Hamilton, *Investigating Industrial Health,* 1943. Hamilton's recollection of her pioneering efforts in Chicago to investigate and improve industrial health conditions.

- Al Smith, *Enacting Reform Legislation,* 1929. Smith's account of overcoming opposition to reform laws in the wake of the Triangle Fire in 1911.

"**GENERAL**" **ROSALIE JONES'S** march and the jumbled news accounts from the *Washington Post* reporters convey the intensity of the dramatic woman suffrage parade on March 3, 1913. But the women's difficult journey down Pennsylvania Avenue that day, suggestive of the much longer journey to achieve woman suffrage, illustrated critical features of life in the **Progressive Era.**

Important movements challenged traditional relationships and attitudes—here involving women's role in American life—and often met strong resistance. "Progressives" seeking reforms organized their supporters across lines of class, education, occupation, geography, gender, and, at times, race and ethnicity—as the variety of groups in the suffrage parade demonstrates. Rather than rely on traditional partisan politics, reformers adopted new political techniques, including lobbying and demonstrating, as nonpartisan pressure groups. Reform work begun at the local and state levels—where the suffrage movement had already met some success—inexorably moved to the national level as the federal government expanded its authority and became the focus of political interest. Finally,

**Progressive Era**   An era in the United States (roughly between 1900 and 1917) in which important movements challenged traditional relationships and attitudes.

this suffrage demonstration reveals the exceptional diversity of the progressive movement, for the women were marching, in part, against Woodrow Wilson, who had campaigned for the presidency as a progressive.

However, woman suffrage did not define progressivism. Indeed, in a sense, there was no "progressive movement," for progressivism had no unifying organization, central leadership, or consensus on objectives. Instead, it represented the coalescing of different and sometimes even contradictory movements that sought changes in the nation's social, economic, and political life. But reformers did share certain convictions. They believed that industrialization and urbanization had produced serious social disorders, from city slums to corporate abuses. They believed that new ideas and methods were required to correct these problems. In particular, they rejected the ideology of individualism in favor of broader concepts of social responsibility, and they sought to achieve social order through organization and efficiency. Finally, most progressives believed that government itself, as the organized agent of public responsibility, should address social and economic problems.

## CHRONOLOGY

| | |
|---|---|
| **1893–1898** | Depression grips the nation. |
| **1893** | New Zealand establishes woman suffrage. |
| **1894** | New Zealand establishes maximum hours and compulsory arbitration. |
| **1898** | South Dakota adopts initiative and referendum. |
| | New Zealand initiates old age pensions. |
| | National Consumers' League is organized. |
| **1899** | Anti-Cigarette League of America is established. |
| **1900** | Robert La Follette is elected governor of Wisconsin. |
| **1901** | United States Steel Corporation is formed. |
| | President William McKinley is assassinated; Theodore Roosevelt becomes president. |
| | Socialist Party of America is organized. |
| | New York Tenement House Law is enacted. |
| | Galveston, Texas, initiates the city commission plan. |
| **1902** | Antitrust suit is filed against Northern Securities Company. |
| | *McClure's* initiates muckraking journalism. |
| | Mississippi enacts the first direct-primary law. |
| | National Reclamation Act is passed. |
| | Roosevelt intervenes in coal strike. |
| **1903** | Women's Trade Union League is organized. |
| **1904** | National Child Labor Committee is formed. |
| | Roosevelt is elected president. |

| | |
|---|---|
| **1905** | Industrial Workers of the World is organized. |
| **1906** | Hepburn Act strengthens the Interstate Commerce Commission. |
| | Meat Inspection Act extends government regulation. |
| | Pure Food and Drug Act is passed. |
| **1908** | *Muller v. Oregon* upholds maximum workday for women. |
| | William Howard Taft is elected president. |
| **1910** | National Association for the Advancement of Colored People is organized. |
| | Ballinger-Pinchot controversy erupts. |
| **1912** | Children's Bureau is established. |
| | Progressive Party organizes and nominates Roosevelt. |
| | Woodrow Wilson is elected president. |
| **1913** | Sixteenth and Seventeenth Amendments are ratified. |
| | Underwood-Simmons Tariff Act establishes an income tax. |
| | Federal Reserve Act creates the Federal Reserve System. |
| **1914** | Federal Trade Commission is established. |
| | Harrison Act criminalizes narcotics. |
| **1915** | National Birth Control League is formed. |
| **1916** | Keating-Owen Act prohibits child labor. |
| **1917** | Congress enacts literacy test for immigrants. |
| **1918** | Woman Suffrage is adopted in England. |
| **1919** | Eighteenth Amendment is ratified. |
| **1920** | Nineteenth Amendment is ratified. |

# THE FERMENT OF REFORM

**WHAT VALUES** and beliefs bound progressives together?

The diversity of progressivism reflected the diverse impulses of reform. Reformers responded to the tensions of industrialization and urbanization by formulating programs according to their own interests and priorities. Nearly every movement for change encountered fierce opposition. But in raising new issues and proposing new ideas, progressives helped America grapple with the problems of industrial society. (See Overview, Major Progressive Organizations and Groups.)

*Documents*

Herbert Croly, *Progressive Democracy* (1914)

## THE CONTEXT OF REFORM: INDUSTRIAL AND URBAN TENSIONS

The origins of progressivism lay in the crises of the new urban-industrial order that emerged in the late nineteenth century. The severe depression and mass suffering of the 1890s, the labor violence and industrial armies, the political challenges of Populism and an obviously ineffective government shattered the complacency many middle-class Americans had felt about their nation and made them aware of social and economic

## OVERVIEW    Major Progressive Organizations and Groups

| Group | Activity |
| --- | --- |
| Social Gospel movement | Urged churches and individuals to apply Christian ethics to social and economic problems |
| Muckrakers | Exposed business abuses, public corruption, and social evils through investigative journalism |
| Settlement House movement | Attempted through social work and public advocacy to improve living and working conditions in urban immigrant communities |
| National Consumers' League (1898) | Monitored businesses to ensure decent working conditions and safe consumer products |
| Women's Trade Union League (1903) | United workingwomen and their middle-class allies to promote unionization and social reform |
| National Child Labor Committee (1904) | Campaigned against child labor |
| Country Life movement | Attempted to modernize rural social and economic conditions according to urban-industrial standards |
| National American Woman Suffrage Association | Led the movement to give women the right to vote |
| Municipal reformers | Sought to change the activities and structure of urban government to promote efficiency and control |
| Conservationists | Favored efficient management and regulation of natural resources rather than uncontrolled development or preservation |

inequities that rural and working-class families had long recognized. Many Americans began to question the validity of social Darwinism and the laissez-faire policies that had justified unregulated industrial growth. They began to reconsider the responsibilities of government and, indeed, of themselves for social order and betterment.

By 1900, returning prosperity had eased the threat of major social violence, but the underlying problems intensified. Big business, which had disrupted traditional economic relationships in the late nineteenth century, suddenly became bigger in a series of mergers between 1897 and 1903, resulting in huge new business combinations. Such gigantic corporations threatened to squeeze opportunities for small firms and workers, dominate markets, and raise social tensions. They also inspired calls for public control.

Industrial growth affected factory workers most directly. Working conditions were difficult and often dangerous. Wages were minimal; an economist in 1905 calculated that 60 percent of all adult male breadwinners made less than a living wage. Family survival, then, often required women and children to work, often in the lowest paid, most exploited positions. Poor ventilation, dangerous fumes, open machinery, and the absence of safety programs threatened not only workers' health but their lives as well. Such conditions were gruesomely illustrated in 1911, when a fire killed 146 workers, most of them young women, trapped inside the factory of the Triangle Shirtwaist Company in New York because management had locked the exits. The fire chief found "skeletons bending over sewing machines." The United States had the highest rate of industrial accidents in the world. Half a million workers were injured and 30,000 killed at work each year. These terrible conditions cried out for reform.

**QUICK REVIEW**

**Triangle Shirtwaist Fire**

- 1911: Fire kills 146 workers.
- Managers had locked the exits.
- The United States had the highest rate of industrial accidents in the world.

Other Americans saw additional social problems in the continuing flood of immigrants who were transforming America's cities. From 1900 to 1917, more than 14 million immigrants entered the United States. Most of the arrivals were so-called new immigrants from southern and eastern Europe, rather than the British, Irish, Germans, and Scandinavians who had arrived earlier. Several hundred thousand Japanese also arrived, primarily in California, as did increasing numbers of Mexicans. Crowding into urban slums, immigrants overwhelmed municipal sanitation, education, and fire protection services.

## CHURCH AND CAMPUS

**Social Gospel movement**  Movement created by reform-minded Protestant ministers seeking to introduce religious ethics into industrial relations and appealing to churches to meet their social responsibilities.

Many groups, drawing from different traditions and inspirations, responded to these economic and social issues. Reform-minded Protestant ministers were especially influential, creating the **Social Gospel movement,** which sought to introduce religious ethics into industrial relations and appealed to churches to meet their social responsibilities. Washington Gladden, a Congregational minister in Columbus, Ohio, was one of the earliest Social Gospelers. Shocked in 1884 by a bloody strike crushed by wealthy members of his own congregation, Gladden began a ministry to working-class neighborhoods that most churches ignored. He endorsed unions and workers' rights and proposed replacing a cruelly competitive wage system with profit sharing.

The Social Gospel was part of an emerging liberal movement in American religion. Scholars associated with this movement discredited the literal accuracy of the Bible and emphasized instead its general moral and ethical lessons. As modernists, they abandoned theological dogmatism for a greater tolerance of other faiths and became more interested in social problems. By linking reform with religion (as "applied Christianity," in the words of Washington Gladden), the Social Gospel movement gave progressivism a powerful moral drive that affected much of American life.

**muckraking**  Journalism exposing economic, social, and political evils, so named by Theodore Roosevelt for its "raking the muck" of American society.

The Social Gospel movement provided an ethical justification for government intervention to improve the social order. Scholars in the social sciences also gradually helped turn public attitudes in favor of reform by challenging the laissez-faire views of the social Darwinists and traditional academics. In *Applied Sociology* (1906), Lester Ward called for social progress through rational planning and government intervention rather than through unrestrained and unpredictable competition. Economists rejected laissez-faire principles in favor of state action to accomplish social evolution. Industrialization, declared economist Richard T. Ely, "has brought to the front a vast number of social problems whose solution is impossible without the united efforts of church, state, and science."

## MUCKRAKERS

Journalists also spread reform ideas by developing a new form of investigative reporting known as **muckraking.** Technological innovations had recently made possible the mass circulation of magazines, and editors competed to attract an expanding urban readership. Samuel S. McClure sent his reporters to uncover political and corporate corruption for *McClure's Magazine*.

Overcome with grief, families of the victims of the Triangle Shirtwaist fire later received from the factory owners $75 for each life lost. Still mourning, family members asked, "Justice, what justice?"

Sensational exposés sold magazines, and soon *Cosmopolitan, Everybody's,* and other journals began publishing investigations of business abuses, dangerous working conditions, and the miseries of slum life.

Muckraking novels also appeared. *The Octopus* (1901), by Frank Norris, dramatized the Southern Pacific Railroad's stranglehold on California's farmers, and *The Jungle* (1906), by Upton Sinclair, exposed the nauseating conditions in Chicago's meatpacking industry.

## THE GOSPEL OF EFFICIENCY

Many progressive leaders believed that efficiency and expertise could control or resolve the disorder of industrial society. President Theodore Roosevelt praised the "gospel of efficiency." Like many other progressives, he admired the success of corporations in applying management techniques to guide economic growth. Drawing from science and technology as well as from the model of the corporation, many progressives attempted to manage or direct change efficiently. They used scientific methods to collect extensive data and relied on experts for analysis and recommendations. "Scientific management," a concept often used interchangeably with "sound business management," seemed the key to eliminating waste and inefficiency in government, society, and industry.

Business leaders especially advocated efficiency, order, and organization. Industrialists were drawn to the ideas of Frederick Taylor, a proponent of scientific management, for cutting factory labor costs. Taylor proposed to increase worker efficiency through imposed work routines, speedups, and mechanization. Workers, Taylor insisted, should "do what they are told promptly and without asking questions. . . . It is absolutely necessary for every man in our organization to become one of a train of gear wheels." By assigning workers simple and repetitive tasks on machines, Taylorization made their skills expendable and enabled managers to control the production, pace of work, and hiring and firing of personnel. Stripped of their influence and poorly paid, factory workers shared little of the wealth generated by industrial expansion and scientific management.

Sophisticated managers of big business saw some forms of government intervention as another way to promote order and efficiency. In particular, they favored regulations that could bring about safer and more stable conditions in society and the economy. Government regulations, they reasoned, could reassure potential consumers, open markets, mandate working conditions that smaller competitors could not provide, or impose systematic procedures that competitive pressures would otherwise undercut.

## LABOR DEMANDS ITS RIGHTS

Industrial workers with different objectives also hastened the ferment of reform. Workers resisted the new rules of efficiency experts and called for improved wages and working conditions and reduced work hours. They and their middle-class sympathizers sought to achieve some of these goals through state intervention,

> ### QUICK REVIEW
>
> **Scientific Management**
>
> ♦ Progressive leaders praised the "gospel of efficiency."
>
> ♦ Promoted application of scientific management to government, society, and industry.
>
> ♦ Saw application of scientific method as the key to reform.

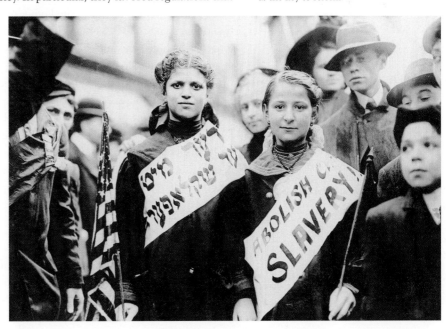

The campaign against child labor attracted passionate support from many Americans. Here two girls, wearing "Abolish Child Slavery" banners in Yiddish and English, participate in a labor parade in New York City on May 1, 1909.

**Wobblies**   Popular name for the members of the Industrial Workers of the World (IWW).

demanding laws to compensate workers injured on the job, curb child labor, and regulate the employment of women.

Workers also organized unions to improve their lot. The American Federation of Labor (AFL) claimed 4 million members by 1920, recruiting mainly skilled workers, particularly native-born white males. New unions organized the factories and sweatshops where most immigrants and women worked. Despite strong employer resistance, the International Ladies Garment Workers Union (1900) and the Amalgamated Clothing Workers (1914) organized the garment trades, developed programs for social and economic reforms, and led their members—mostly young Jewish and Italian women—in spectacular strikes.

A still more radical union tried to organize miners, lumberjacks, and Mexican and Japanese farm workers in the West, black dockworkers in the South, and immigrant factory hands in New England. Founded in 1905, the Industrial Workers of the World (IWW), whose members were known as **"Wobblies,"** used sit-down strikes, sit-ins, and mass rallies, tactics adopted by other industrial unions in the 1930s and the civil rights movement in the 1960s.

## EXTENDING THE WOMAN'S SPHERE

Women reformers and their organizations played a key role in progressivism. Women responded not merely to the human suffering caused by industrialization and urbanization but also to related changes in their own status and role. By the early twentieth century, more women than before were working outside the home—in the factories, mills, and sweatshops of the industrial economy and as clerks in stores and offices. In 1910, more than one-fourth of all workers were women, increasing numbers of them married. Their importance in the workforce and participation in unions and strikes challenged assumptions that woman's "natural" role was to be a submissive housewife.

The women's clubs that had begun multiplying in the late nineteenth century became seed-beds of progressive ideas in the early twentieth century. Often founded for cultural purposes, women's clubs soon adopted programs for social reform and gave their members a route to public influence.

Women also joined or created other organizations that pushed beyond the limits of traditional domesticity. "Woman's place is in the home," observed one progressive, but "no longer is the home encompassed by four walls." By threatening healthy and happy homes, urban problems required that women become "social housekeepers" in the community.

Although most progressive women stressed women's special duties and responsibilities as social housekeepers, others began to demand women's equal rights. In 1914, for example, critics of New York's policy of dismissing women teachers who married formed a group called the Feminist Alliance and demanded "the removal of all social, political, economic and other discriminations which are based upon sex, and the award of all rights and duties in all fields on the basis of individual capacity alone." With these new organizations and ideas, women gave important impetus and direction to the reform sentiments of the early twentieth century.

## TRANSATLANTIC INFLUENCES

A major source of America's progressive impulse lay outside its borders. European nations were already grappling with many of the problems that stemmed from industrialization and urbanization, and they provided guidance, examples, and possible solutions. Progressive reformers soon learned that America's political, economic, and social structures made it necessary to modify, adapt, or even abandon these imported ideas, but their influence was obvious.

University study in Europe taught Americans the limits of their traditional laissez-faire attitudes and the possibilities of state action. Trained in Germany, the economist Richard T. Ely returned to academic posts in America to teach that government "is the agency through which we must work." International influences were especially strong in the Social Gospel movement, symbolized by William T. Stead, a British social evangelist, whose idea of a "Civic Church" (a partnership of churches and reformers) captured great attention in the United States. Muckrakers not only exposed American problems but looked for foreign solutions. *Everybody's* sent Charles E. Russell around the world in 1905 to describe the social advances in Europe and New Zealand. (See Global Perspectives, The New Zealand Way.)

By 1912, American consumer activists, trade unionists, factory inspectors, and feminists regularly participated in international conferences on labor legislation, child welfare, social insurance, and housing reform and returned home with new ideas and strategies. State governments organized commissions to analyze European policies and agencies for lessons that might be applicable in the United States.

## SOCIALISM

The growing influence of socialist ideas also promoted the spirit of progressivism. Socialism never attracted a large following in the United States, but its criticism of the industrial economy gained increasing attention in the early twentieth century. American socialists condemned social and economic inequities, criticized limited government, and demanded public ownership of railroads, utilities, and communications. They also campaigned for tax reforms, better housing, factory inspections, and recreational facilities for all.

The most prominent socialist was the dynamic and engaging Eugene V. Debs. An Indiana labor leader who had converted to socialism while imprisoned for his role in the 1894 Pullman strike, Debs had evangelical energy and a generous spirit. He decried what he saw as the dehumanization produced by industrial capitalism and hoped for an egalitarian society where everyone would have the opportunity "to develop the best there is in him for his own good as well as the good of society."

Eugene V. Debs, *The Outlook for Socialism in the United States* (1900)

In 1901, Debs helped organize the Socialist Party of America; thereafter, he worked tirelessly to attract followers to a vision of socialism deeply rooted in American political and religious traditions. In the next decade, the party won many local elections, especially in Wisconsin and New York, where it drew support from German and Russian immigrants, and in Oklahoma, where it attracted poor tenant farmers.

Most progressives considered socialist ideas too drastic. Nevertheless, socialists contributed importantly to the reform ferment, not only by providing support for reform initiatives but often also by prompting progressives to push for changes to undercut increasingly attractive radical alternatives.

## OPPONENTS OF REFORM

Not all Americans supported progressive reforms. Social Gospelers faced opposition from Protestant traditionalists emphasizing what they termed fundamental beliefs. Particularly strong among evangelical denominations with rural roots, these **fundamentalists** stressed personal salvation rather than social reform. Indeed, the urban and industrial crises that inspired Social Gospelers to preach reform drove many evangelical leaders to endorse social and political conservatism.

Business interests, angered by exposés of corporate abuse and corruption, attacked the muckrakers. Business groups such as the American Bankers' Association accused muckrakers of promoting socialism. Major corporations like Standard Oil created public relations bureaus to improve their image and identify business, not its critics, with the

**fundamentalists** Religious conservatives who believe in the literal accuracy and divine inspiration of the Bible.

## GLOBAL PERSPECTIVES

### THE NEW ZEALAND WAY

In its very name, the Progressive Era seems characteristically American, but its major developments were actually part of a worldwide phenomenon in which the peoples of many different nations promoted significant reforms, especially through the expansion of government responsibility and power. While Europeans provided an important range of reform ideas and models for Americans, it was often New Zealand, described by one muckraker as the "practical utopia of the South Seas," that "blazed the world's way" in social and economic reforms.

Small, rural, sparsely populated, only slightly industrialized, and still a colony of Great Britain, New Zealand might seem an unlikely candidate to lead progressive reform, but one American minister predicted in 1900 that "we fool Americans will go on for fifty or seventy-five years before we . . . undertake what they have already achieved in New Zealand." New Zealanders were less driven by a desire to correct the evils of industrialization and urbanization—poverty, sweatshops, slums, labor exploitation, social conflict—than by a determination to prevent their emergence in the first place. As the charismatic Liberal leader Richard Seddon declared, "If we deal with [these problems] now, the curse of the older countries will never come to New Zealand."

With the election of a Liberal government in 1891, New Zealand launched two decades of reform. It began the serious regulation of working conditions in 1891. In 1894 the General Assembly mandated regular factory inspections and established maximum hours, first for women and then for men, and prohibited child labor in factories. Other laws in the 1890s established minimum wages for women. The Industrial Conciliation and Arbitration Act of 1894 both encouraged unionization and required compulsory arbitration to deal with industrial disputes and assure social peace and progress. A model system of workers' compensation was established in 1901.

New Zealand also pioneered in political and social reform. In 1893 it became the first country to establish woman suffrage in national elections. With one member of the parliament reasoning that "it is the duty of the State to make proper provision for the aged," New Zealand initiated old age pensions in 1898. Early in the twentieth century it expanded state-funded, rather than contributory, pensions to cover widows with children, injured miners, and other groups. Beginning in 1905, it developed public housing programs, providing first rental housing for low-income families and then government loans for the purchase of homes. The Public Health Act of 1900 initiated a series of laws expanding government responsibility for proper sanitation, safe water, vaccinations, and the regulation of food and drugs.

New Zealand reformers urged the United States to follow the "New Zealand Way" and adopt these and other reforms, and many American progressives did look to that small country for guidance. "If a British colony dares to lead," noted one progressive journalist, "surely it is not visionary to expect our Republic to fall in line."

• What economic, social, and political factors might explain why progressive reform emerged more slowly and less completely in the United States than in New Zealand?

public interest. Advertising boycotts discouraged magazines from running critical stories, and credit restrictions forced some muckraking journals to suspend publication. By 1910, the heyday of muckraking was over.

Labor unions likewise encountered resistance. Led by the National Association of Manufacturers, business groups denounced unions as corrupt and radical, hired thugs to disrupt them, organized strikebreaking agencies, and used blacklists to eliminate union activists. The antiunion campaign peaked in Ludlow, Colorado, in 1914, when John D. Rockefeller's Colorado Fuel and Iron Company used armed guards and the state militia to shoot and burn striking workers and their families. The courts aided employers by issuing injunctions against strikes and prohibiting unions from using boycotts, one of their most effective weapons.

Progressives campaigning for government intervention and regulation also met stiff resistance. Many Americans objected to what they considered unwarranted interference in private economic matters. Again, the courts often supported these attitudes. In *Lochner v. New York* (1905), the Supreme Court even overturned a maximum-hours law on the grounds that it deprived employers and employees of their "freedom of contract." Progressives continually struggled against such opponents, and progressive achievements were limited by the persistence and influence of their adversaries.

# REFORMING SOCIETY

With their varied motives and objectives, progressives worked to transform society by improving living conditions, educational opportunities, family life, and social and industrial relations. (See Overview, Major Laws and Constitutional Amendments of the Progressive Era.) They sought what they called social justice, but their plans for social reform sometimes also smacked of social control. Organized women dominated the movement to reform society, but they were supported, depending on the goal, by Social Gospel ministers, social scientists, urban immigrants, labor unions, and even some conservatives eager to regulate personal behavior.

**WHAT ROLE** did women play in progressive reform movements?

## SETTLEMENT HOUSES AND URBAN REFORM

The spearheads for social reform were settlement houses—community centers in urban immigrant neighborhoods. Reformers created 400 settlement houses, largely modeled after Hull House in Chicago, founded in 1889 by Jane Addams.

Most settlements were led and staffed primarily by middle-class young women, seeking to alleviate poverty and do useful professional work when most careers were closed to them. Settlement work did not immediately violate prescribed gender roles because it initially focused on the "woman's sphere"—family, education, domestic skills, and cultural "uplift."

However, settlement workers soon saw that the root problem for immigrants was widespread poverty that required more than changes in individual behavior. Unlike earlier reformers, they regarded many of the evils of poverty as products of the social environment rather than of moral weakness. Thus, settlement workers campaigned for stricter building codes to improve slums, better urban sanitation systems to enhance public health, public parks to revive the urban environment, and laws to protect women and children.

Their crusades for sanitation and housing reform demonstrated the impact that social reformers often had on urban life. Settlement worker Mary McDowell became known as the "Garbage Lady" for her success in improving Chicago's massive environmental problems. Similarly, Lawrence Veiller was convinced by his work at the University Settlement in New York City that "the improvement of the homes of the people was the starting point for everything." Based on the findings of settlement workers, Veiller drafted a new housing code limiting the size of tenements and requiring toilet facilities, ventilation, and fire protection. In 1901, the New York Tenement House Law became a model for other cities.

## PROTECTIVE LEGISLATION FOR WOMEN AND CHILDREN

While settlement workers initially undertook private efforts to improve society, many reformers eventually concluded that only

*Greene, in New York (N.Y.) Telegram*

**A WOMAN'S WORK IS NEVER DONE**

Women's activism was critically important in reconstructing American life during the Progressive Era. Busily engaged in social housekeeping, Mother America uses corrective legislation to clean the dirty laundry of industrialization and injustice.

## OVERVIEW   Major Laws and Constitutional Amendments of the Progressive Era

| Legislation | Effect |
|---|---|
| New York Tenement House Law (1901) | Established a model housing code for safety and sanitation |
| Newlands Act (1902) | Provided for federal irrigation projects |
| Hepburn Act (1906) | Strengthened the Interstate Commerce Commission |
| Pure Food and Drug Act (1906) | Regulated the production and sale of food and drug products |
| Meat Inspection Act (1906) | Authorized federal inspection of meat products |
| Sixteenth Amendment (1913) | Authorized a federal income tax |
| Seventeenth Amendment (1913) | Mandated the direct popular election of senators |
| Underwood-Simmons Tariff Act (1913) | Lowered tariff rates and levied the first regular federal income tax |
| Federal Reserve Act (1913) | Established the Federal Reserve System to supervise banking and provide a national currency |
| Federal Trade Commission Act (1914) | Established the FTC to oversee business activities |
| Harrison Act (1914) | Regulated the distribution and use of narcotics |
| Smith-Lever Act (1914) | Institutionalized the county agent system |
| Keating-Owen Act (1916) | Indirectly prohibited child labor |
| Eighteenth Amendment (1919) | Instituted prohibition |
| Nineteenth Amendment (1920) | Established woman suffrage |

Jane Addams, *Twenty Years at Hull House* (1910)

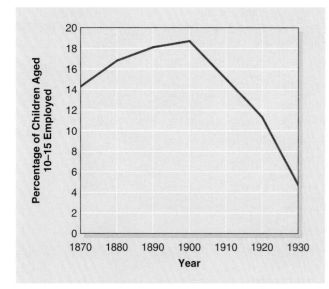

FIGURE 21–1   **Child Labor, 1870–1930**   Nearly 2 million children worked in factories and fields in 1900, twice as many as in 1870. Progressives' efforts to curtail child labor through laws for compulsory education and a minimum working age encountered resistance, and change came slowly.

Data source: U.S. Bureau of the Census.

government intervention could achieve social justice. The National Child Labor Committee, organized in 1904, led the campaign to curtail child labor (see Figure 21–1). Reformers documented the problem with extensive investigations and also benefited from the public outrage stirred by socialist John Spargo's muckraking book *The Bitter Cry of the Children* (1906). In 1900, most states had no minimum working age; by 1914, every state but one had such a law. Effective regulation, however, required national action, for many state laws were weak or poorly enforced.

Social reformers also lobbied for laws regulating the wages, hours, and working conditions of women and succeeded in having states from New York to Oregon pass maximum-hours legislation. After the Supreme Court upheld such laws in *Muller v. Oregon* (1908), 39 states enacted new or stronger laws on women's maximum hours between 1909 and 1917. Fewer states established minimum wages for women.

Protective legislation for women posed a troubling issue for reformers. In California, for example, middle-class clubwomen favored protective legislation on the grounds of women's presumed weakness. They wanted to preserve "California's potential motherhood." More radical progressives, as in the socialist-led Women's Trade Union League of Los Angeles, supported such legislation to help secure economic independence and equality in the labor market for women, increase the economic strength of the working class, and serve as a precedent for laws improving conditions for all workers.

Progressive Era lawmakers adopted the first viewpoint. They limited protective legislation to measures reflecting the belief that women needed paternalist protection, even by excluding them from certain occupations. Laws establishing a minimum wage for women, moreover, usually set a wage level below subsistence rates. Rather than assuring women's economic independence, then, protective legislation in practice reinforced women's subordinate place in the labor force.

Social justice reformers forged the beginnings of the welfare state in further legislation. Prompted by both humanitarian and paternalistic urgings, many states began in 1910 to provide "mothers' pensions" to indigent widows with dependent children. Twenty-one states, led by Wisconsin in 1911, enacted workers' compensation programs, ending the custom of holding workers themselves liable for injuries on the job.

Compared to the social insurance programs in western Europe, however, these were feeble responses to the social consequences of industrialization. Proposals for health insurance, unemployment insurance, and old-age pension programs went nowhere. Business groups and other conservative interests curbed the movement toward state responsibility for social welfare.

## RESHAPING PUBLIC EDUCATION

Concerns about child labor overlapped with increasing attention to the public schools. The rapid influx of immigrants, as well as the demands of the new corporate workplace, generated interest in education not only as a means of advancement but also as a tool for assimilation and the training of future workers.

Between 1880 and 1920, compulsory school attendance laws, kindergartens, age-graded elementary schools, professional training for teachers, vocational education, parent-teacher associations, and school nurses became standard elements in American education. School reformers believed these measures to be both educationally sound and important for countering slum environments. Others supported the kindergarten as "the earliest opportunity to catch the little Russian, the little Italian, the little German, Pole, Syrian, and the rest and begin to make good American citizens of them."

The famous photographer Lewis Hine used his camera to document child labor. The eleven-year old boys at this North Carolina textile mill in 1908 earned sixty cents a day.

Public education in the South lagged behind the North. Northern philanthropy and southern reformers brought some improvements after 1900, as per capita expenditures for education doubled, school terms were extended, and high schools spread across the region. But the South frittered away its limited resources on a segregated educational system that shortchanged both races. Black southerners particularly suffered, for the new programs increased the disparity in funding for white and black schools. South Carolina spent 12 times as much per white pupil as per black pupil.

Racism also underlay important changes in the schooling of Native Americans. The earlier belief that education would promote equality and facilitate assimilation gave way to a conviction that Indians were inferior and fit merely for manual labor. Educators now rejected the notion of a common school education for Indian children in favor of manual training that would enable Indians to fill menial jobs and whites to "turn their attention to more intellectual employments." Educators also renounced the practice of integrating Indian children into previously all-white classrooms, a policy begun in 1891.

## CHALLENGING GENDER RESTRICTIONS

Most progressives held fairly conservative, moralistic views about sexuality and gender roles. Margaret Sanger, however, radically challenged conventional ideas about the social role of women. Despite great opposition, she initiated the modern birth control movement. A public-health nurse and an IWW organizer, she soon made the struggle for reproductive rights her personal crusade. Sanger saw in New York's immigrant neighborhoods the plight of poor women worn out from repeated pregnancies or injured or dead from self-induced knitting-needle abortions. Despite federal and state laws against contraceptives, Sanger began promoting birth control as a way to avert such tragedies. Prohibiting contraceptives meant "enforced motherhood," Sanger declared. "Women cannot be on an equal footing with men until they have full and complete control over their reproductive function."

Sanger's crusade attracted support from many women's and labor groups, but it also infuriated those who regarded birth control as a threat to the family and morality. Indicted for distributing information about contraception, Sanger fled to Europe. Other women took up the cause, forming the National Birth Control League in 1915 to campaign for the repeal of laws restricting access to contraceptive information and devices.

## REFORMING COUNTRY LIFE

Although most progressives focused on the city, others sought to reform rural life, both to modernize its social and economic conditions and to integrate it more fully into the larger society. They worked to improve rural health and sanitation, to replace inefficient one-room schools with modern consolidated ones under professional control, and to extend new roads and communication services into the countryside. To further these goals, President Theodore Roosevelt created the Country Life Commission in 1908. The country lifers had a broad program for social and economic change, involving expanded government functions, activist government agencies staffed by experts, and the professionalization of rural social services.

Agricultural scientists, government officials, and many business interests also sought to promote efficient, scientific, and commercial agriculture. A key innovation was the county-agent system: The U.S. Department of Agriculture and business groups placed an agent in each county to teach farmers new techniques and to encourage changes in the rural social values that had previously spawned the Populist radicalism that most progressives decried. Few farmers, however, welcomed these efforts. Most farmers believed that their problems stemmed, not from rural life, but from industrial society and its nefarious trusts, banks, and middlemen. Rural Americans did not want their lives revolutionized.

Even so, rural people were drawn into the larger urban-industrial society during the Progressive Era. Government agencies, agricultural colleges, and railroads and banks steadily tied farmers to urban markets. Telephones and rural free delivery of mail lessened countryside isolation but quickened the spread of city values. Improved roads and the coming of the automobile eliminated many rural villages and linked farm families directly with towns and cities. Consolidated schools wiped out the social center of rural neighborhoods and carried children out of their communities, eventually encouraging an ever-growing migration to the city.

## MORAL CRUSADES AND SOCIAL CONTROL

Moral reform movements, although often appearing misguided or unduly coercive today, generally reflected the progressive hope to protect people in a debilitating environment. In practice, however, these efforts to shape society tended toward social control. Morerover, these efforts often meshed with the restrictive attitudes that conservative Americans held about race, religion, immigration, and morality. The result was widespread attempts to restrict certain groups and control behavior.

**Controlling immigrants.**    Many Americans wanted to limit immigration for racist reasons. Nativist agitation in California prompted the federal government to secure restrictions on Japanese immigration in 1907. Californians, including local progressives, also hoped to curtail the migration of Mexicans.

Nationally, public debate focused on restricting the flow of new immigrants from southern and eastern Europe. Some labor leaders believed that immigration held down wages and impeded unionization; many sociologists thought it created serious social problems; other Americans disliked the newcomers on religious, cultural, or ethnic grounds. Many backed their prejudice with a distorted interpretation of Darwinism, labeling the Slavic and Mediterranean peoples "inferior races."

Other nativists demanded the "Americanization" of immigrants already in the country. The Daughters of the American Revolution sought to inculcate loyalty, patriotism, and conservative values. Settlement workers and Social Gospelers promoted a gentler kind of Americanization through English classes and home mission campaigns, but they too attempted to transfer their own values to the newcomers.

**Prohibition.**    Closely linked to progressives' worries about immigrants was their campaign for **prohibition.** This movement engaged many of the progressives' basic impulses. Social workers saw liquor as a cause of crime, poverty, and family violence; employers blamed it for causing industrial accidents and inefficiency; Social Gospel ministers condemned the "spirit born of hell" because it impaired moral judgment and behavior. But also important was native-born Americans' fear of new immigrants—"the dangerous classes, who are readily dominated by the saloon." Many immigrants, in fact, viewed liquor and the neighborhood saloon as vital parts of daily life, and so prohibition became a focus of nativist hostility, cultural conflict, and Americanization pressures. In the South, racism also figured prominently. Alexander McKelway, the southern secretary for the National Child Labor Committee, endorsed prohibition as a way to maintain social order and white supremacy.

Protestant fundamentalists also stoutly supported prohibition, working through the Anti-Saloon League, founded in 1893. Their nativism and antiurban bias surfaced

James H. Patten, *Chairman of the National Legislative Committee of the American Purity Federation, Testimony Before Congress* (1910)

**QUICK REVIEW**

**Opposition to Immigration**

◆ Nativists in California wanted to restrict the entry of Japanese and Mexicans.

◆ The national debate focused on immigrants from southern and eastern Europe.

◆ Some nativists demanded the "Americanization" of immigrants.

**Exploring America**
*Americanization*

**prohibition**    A ban on the production, sale, and consumption of liquor, achieved temporarily through state laws and the Eighteenth Amendment.

in demands for prohibition to prevent the nation's cities from lapsing into "raging mania, disorder, and anarchy."

With these varied motivations, prohibitionists campaigned for local and state laws against the manufacture and sale of alcohol. Beginning in 1907, they proved increasingly successful, especially in the South, Midwest, and Far West. By 1917, 26 states had prohibition laws. Congress then approved the **Eighteenth Amendment,** which made prohibition the law of the land by 1920.

Less controversial were drives to control or prohibit narcotics and cigarettes. Patent (over-the-counter) medicines commonly contained opium, heroin, and cocaine (popularly used for hay fever), and physicians known as "dope doctors" openly dispensed drugs to paying customers. Fears that addiction was spreading in "the fallen and lower classes"—and particularly among black people and immigrants—prompted Congress in 1914 to pass the Harrison Act, prohibiting the distribution and use of narcotics for other than medicinal purposes. The Anti-Cigarette League of America, organized in 1899 and having 300,000 members by 1901, led the charge against cigarettes.

**Suppressing prostitution.** Reformers also sought to suppress the "social evil" of prostitution. Like crowded slums, sweatshops, and child labor, the "vice districts" where prostitution flourished were seen as part of the exploitation and disorder in the industrial cities. Women's low wages as factory workers and domestic servants explained some of the problem, as a muckraking article entitled "The Daughters of the Poor" pointed out. But nativism spurred public concern, as when New York officials insisted that most prostitutes and brothel owners, some of whom "have been seducers of defenseless women all their lives," were foreign-born.

The response to prostitution was typical of progressivism: investigation and exposure, a reliance upon experts—boards of health, medical groups, clergy—for recommendations, and enactment of new laws. The progressive solution emerged in state and municipal action abolishing the "red light" districts previously tolerated and in a federal law, the Mann Act of 1910, prohibiting the interstate transport of women "for immoral purposes."

**Eighteenth Amendment**
Constitutional revision, adopted in 1919, that prohibited the production and sale of alcohol in the United States.

The Flanner House, a black settlement house in Indianapolis, provided the black community with many essential services, including health care. In addition to this baby clinic, pictured in 1918, it established a tuberculosis clinic at a time when the city's public hospitals refused to treat black citizens afflicted with the disease.

## For Whites Only?

Racism permeated the Progressive Era. In the South, progressivism was built on black disfranchisement and segregation. Like most white southerners, progressives believed that racial control was necessary for social order and that it enabled reformers to address other social problems. Such reformers also invoked racism to gain popular support for their objectives. In Georgia, for instance, child labor reformers warned that while white children worked in the Piedmont textile mills, black children were going to school: Child labor laws and compulsory school attendance laws were necessary to maintain white supremacy.

Governors Hoke Smith of Georgia and James Vardaman, "the White Chief," of Mississippi typified the link between racism and reform in the South. These men supported progressive reforms but also viciously attacked black rights. Their racist demagogy incited antiblack violence throughout the South.

Even in the North, race relations deteriorated. Civil rights laws went unenforced, restaurants and hotels excluded black customers, and schools were segregated. A reporter in Pennsylvania found that "this disposition to discriminate against Negroes has greatly increased within the past decade." Antiblack race riots exploded in New York in 1900 and in Springfield, Illinois—Abraham Lincoln's hometown—in 1908.

**Black activism.** Although most white progressives promoted or accepted racial discrimination, and most black southerners had to adapt to it, black progressive activism was growing. Even in the South, some African Americans struggled to improve conditions. In Atlanta, for example, black women created progressive organizations and established settlement houses, kindergartens, and daycare centers.

In the North, African Americans more openly criticized discrimination and rejected Booker T. Washington's philosophy of accommodation. Ida Wells-Barnett, the crusading journalist who had fled the South for Chicago (see Chapter 17), became nationally prominent for her militant protests. She fought fiercely against racial injustices, especially school segregation, agitated for woman suffrage, and organized kindergartens and settlement houses for Chicago's black migrants.

Still more important was W. E. B. Du Bois, who campaigned tirelessly against all forms of racial discrimination. In 1905, Du Bois and other black activists met in Niagara Falls, Canada, to make plans to promote political and economic equality. In 1910, this **Niagara Movement** joined with a small group of white reformers, including Jane Addams, to organize the National Association for the Advancement of Colored People. The NAACP sought to overthrow segregation and establish equal justice and educational opportunities. As its director of publicity and research, Du Bois launched an influential magazine, *The Crisis*, to shape public opinion. "Agitate," he counseled, "protest, reveal the truth, and refuse to be silenced." By 1918, the NAACP had 44,000 members in 165 branches.

*Platform Adopted by the National Negro Committee* (1909)

**Niagara Movement** African-American group organized in 1905 to promote racial integration, civil and political rights, and equal access to economic opportunity.

# REFORMING POLITICS AND GOVERNMENT

Progressives of all kinds worked to reform politics and government. But their political activism was motivated by different concerns, and they sometimes pursued competing objectives. Many wanted to change procedures and institutions to promote greater democracy and responsibility. Others hoped to improve the efficiency of government, eliminate corruption, or increase their own influence. All justified their objectives as necessary to adapt the political system to the nation's new needs.

**WHAT STEPS** were taken toward woman suffrage during the Progressive Era?

Carrying ballot boxes on a stretcher to ridicule American pretensions to a healthy democracy without woman suffrage, these activists marched in a dramatic parade in New York City in 1915. Combining such tactics with traditional appeals to patriotism and women's moral purity, woman suffragists eventually achieved the greatest democratic reform of the Progressive Era.

## WOMAN SUFFRAGE

One of the most important achievements of the era was woman suffrage. The movement had begun in the mid-nineteenth century, but suffragists had been frustrated by the prevailing belief that women's proper sphere was the home and the family. Males dominated the public sphere, including voting. Woman suffrage, especially when championed as a step toward women's equality, seemed to challenge the natural order of society, and it generated much opposition, not only among men but among traditionalist-minded women as well.

Most women progressives viewed suffrage as the key issue of the period. Already taking active leadership in broad areas of public affairs—especially by confronting and publicizing social problems and then lobbying legislators and other officials to adopt their proposed solutions—they thought it ridiculous to be barred from the ballot box. But most of all, the vote meant power, both to convince politicians to take seriously their demands for social reforms and to participate fully in electoral as in other forms of politics, thereby advancing the status of women.

In the early twentieth century, suffragists began to outflank their traditional opposition. Under a new generation of leaders, such as Carrie Chapman Catt and Harriot Stanton Blatch, they adopted activist tactics, including parades, mass meetings, and "suffrage tours" by automobile. They also organized by political districts and attracted workingwomen and labor unions. By 1917, the National American Woman Suffrage Association had over 2 million members.

Some suffrage leaders adopted new arguments to gain more support. Rather than insisting on the justice of woman suffrage or emphasizing equal rights, they spoke of the special moral and maternal instincts women could bring to politics if allowed to vote. Many suffragists, particularly among working-class groups, remained committed to the larger possibilities they saw in suffrage, but the new image of the movement increased public support by appealing to conventional views of women.

Gradually, the suffrage movement began to prevail (see Map 21–1). In 1910, Washington became the first state since the mid-1890s to approve woman suffrage, followed

*Documents*

Helen M. Todd, *Getting Out the Vote* (1911)

**MAP EXPLORATION**  To explore an interactive version of this map, go to http://www.prenhall.com/goldfield5/map21.1

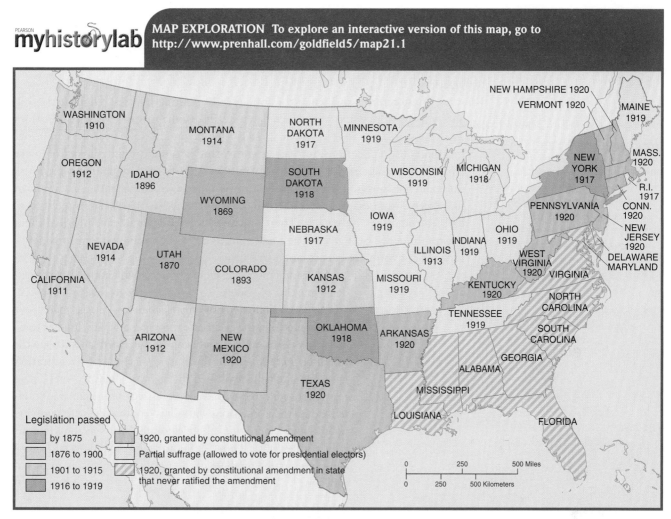

MAP 21–1   **Woman Suffrage in the United States before the Ratification of the Nineteenth Amendment**   Beginning with Wyoming in 1869, woman suffrage slowly gained acceptance in the West, but women in the South and much of the East got the ballot only when the Nineteenth Amendment was ratified in 1920.

**How might** you explain the relatively early dates at which women in the West got the right to vote? Why was woman suffrage slower in coming to the East and South?

by California in 1911 and Arizona, Kansas, and Oregon in 1912. Suffragists also mounted national actions, such as the dramatic inaugural parade in March 1913 described at the beginning of this chapter. The violence surrounding that event outraged public opinion, revived interest in a federal constitutional amendment to grant women the vote, and prompted women to send petitions and organize pilgrimages to Washington from across the country. By 1919, thirty-nine states had established full or partial woman suffrage, and Congress finally approved an amendment. Ratified by the states in 1920, the **Nineteenth Amendment** marked a critical advance in political democracy.

## ELECTORAL REFORM

Other electoral reforms changed the election process and the meaning of political participation. The so-called **Australian ballot** adopted by most states during the 1890s provided for secret voting, freeing voters from intimidation and discouraging vote buying and other corruption.

**QUICK REVIEW**

**Votes for Women**

- Woman suffrage movement began in the mid-nineteenth century.
- Early twentieth-century leaders adopted activist tactics.
- Nineteenth Amendment ratified in 1920.

**Nineteenth Amendment**   Constitutional revision that in 1920 established women citizens' right to vote.

**Australian ballot**   Secret voting and the use of official ballots rather than party tickets.

Government responsibility for the ballot soon led to public regulation of other parts of the electoral process previously controlled by parties. Beginning with Mississippi in 1902, nearly every state provided for direct primaries to remove nominations from the boss-ridden caucus and convention system. Many states also reformed campaign practices.

These reforms weakened the influence of political parties. Their decreasing ability to mobilize voters was reflected in a steady decline in voter participation, from 79 percent in 1896 to 49 percent in 1920 (see Figure 20–1). These developments had ominous implications, for parties and voting had traditionally linked ordinary Americans to their government. As parties slowly contracted, nonpartisan organizations and pressure groups, promoting narrower objectives, gained influence. Many of these special-interest groups represented the same middle- or upper-class interests that had led the attack on parties. Their organized lobbying would steadily give them greater influence over government and contribute to the declining popular belief in the value of voting or participation in politics.

Disfranchisement more obviously undermined American democracy. In the South, Democrats—progressive and conservative alike—eliminated not only black voters but also many poor white voters from the electorate through poll taxes, literacy tests, and other restrictions. Republicans in the North adopted educational or literacy tests in ten states, enacted strict registration laws, and gradually abolished the right of aliens to vote. These restrictions reflected both the progressives' anti-immigrant prejudices and their obsessions with social control and with purifying politics and "improving" the electorate. Such electoral reforms reduced the political power of ethnic and working-class Americans, often stripping them of their political rights and means of influence.

## MUNICIPAL REFORM

Antiparty attitudes also affected progressives' efforts to reform municipal government, which they regarded as inefficient and corrupt, at least partly because of the power of urban political machines. Muckrakers had exposed crooked alliances between city bosses and business leaders that resulted in wasteful or inadequate municipal services. In some cities, urban reformers attempted to break these alliances and improve conditions for those suffering most from municipal misrule.

More elitist progressives attempted to change the structure of urban government by replacing ward elections, which could be controlled by the neighborhood-based city machine, with at-large elections. To win citywide elections required greater resources and therefore helped swell middle-class influence at the expense of the working class. So did nonpartisan elections, which reformers introduced to weaken party loyalties.

Urban reformers developed two other structural innovations: the city commission and the city manager. Both attempted to institutionalize efficient, businesslike government staffed by professional administrators. By 1920, hundreds of cities had adopted one of the new plans, which business groups often pro-

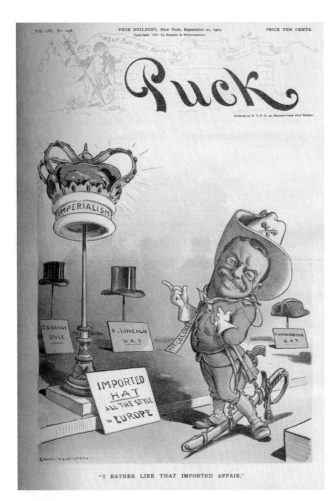

Pro-Democratic *Puck* portrays President Theodore Roosevelt as Louis XIV, whose authoritarian reign (1643–1715) made him a symbol of absolute monarchy. "The Sun King" famously declared, "The state, it is I" (expressed in this cartoon caption in the original French). Opponents of the Republican chief executive complained that his assertive rule usurped the authority of Congress and upset the constitutional balance of power.

moted. Again, then, reform often shifted political power from ethnic and working-class voters, represented however imperfectly by partisan elections, to smaller groups with greater resources.

## PROGRESSIVE STATE GOVERNMENT

Progressives also reshaped state government. Some tried to democratize the legislative process, regarding the legislature—the most important branch of state government in the nineteenth century—as ineffective and even corrupt, dominated by party bosses and corporate influences. The Missouri legislature reportedly "enacted such laws as the corporations paid for, and such others as were necessary to fool the people." Populists had first raised such charges in the 1890s and proposed two novel solutions. The **initiative** enabled reformers to propose legislation directly to the electorate, bypassing an unresponsive legislature; the **referendum** permitted voters to approve or reject legislative measures. South Dakota Populists established the first system of "direct legislation" in 1898, and progressives adopted these innovations in 20 other states between 1902 and 1915.

Other innovations also expanded the popular role in state government. The **Seventeenth Amendment,** ratified in 1913, provided for the election of U.S. senators directly by popular vote instead of by state legislatures. Beginning with Oregon in 1908, ten states adopted the **recall,** enabling voters to remove unsatisfactory public officials from office.

As state legislatures and party machines were curbed, dynamic governors such as Robert La Follette in Wisconsin, Charles Evans Hughes in New York, and Hiram Johnson in California pushed progressive programs into law. Elected governor in 1900, "Fighting Bob" La Follette turned Wisconsin into "the laboratory of democracy." Overcoming fierce opposition from "stalwart" Republicans, La Follette established direct primaries, railroad regulation, the first state income tax, workers' compensation, and other important measures before being elected to the U.S. Senate in 1906. La Follette also stressed efficiency and expertise. The Legislative Reference Bureau that he created to advise on public policy was staffed by university professors. He used regulatory commissions to oversee railroads, banks, and other interests. Most states followed suit, and expert commissions became an important feature of state government, gradually gaining authority at the expense of elected local officials.

**initiative** Procedure by which citizens can introduce a subject for legislation, usually through a petition signed by a specific number of voters.

**referendum** Submission of a law, proposed or already in effect, to a direct popular vote for approval or rejection.

**Seventeenth Amendment** Constitutional change that in 1913 established the direct popular election of U.S. senators.

**recall** The process of removing an official from office by popular vote, usually after using petitions to call for such a vote.

# THEODORE ROOSEVELT AND THE PROGRESSIVE PRESIDENCY

When an anarchist assassinated William McKinley in 1901, Theodore Roosevelt entered the White House, and the progressive movement gained its most prominent leader. The son of a wealthy New York family, Roosevelt had pursued a career in Republican politics, serving as a New York legislator, U.S. civil service commissioner, and assistant secretary of the navy. After his exploits in the Spanish-American War (see Chapter 22), he was elected governor of New York in 1898 and vice president in 1900. His public life was matched by an active private life, in which he both wrote works of history and obsessively pursued what he called the "strenuous life": boxing, wrestling, hunting, rowing, even ranching and chasing rustlers in Dakota Territory. Roosevelt's flamboyance and ambitions made him the most popular politician of the time and enabled him to dramatize the issues of progressivism and to become the first modern president.

**HOW DID** Theodore Roosevelt envision the power of the president?

## TR and the Modern Presidency

Roosevelt rejected the limited role of Gilded Age presidents. He believed that the president could do anything to meet national needs that the Constitution did not specifically prohibit. "Under this interpretation of executive power," he later recalled, "I did and caused to be done many things not previously done. . . . I did not usurp power, but I did greatly broaden the use of executive power." Indeed, the expansion of government power and its consolidation in the executive branch were among his most significant accomplishments.

Rather than defer to Congress, Roosevelt exerted legislative leadership. He spelled out his policy goals in more than 400 messages to Congress, sent drafts of bills to Capitol Hill, and intervened to win passage of "his" measures. Roosevelt generally avoided direct challenges to the conservative Old Guard Republicans who controlled Congress, but his activities helped shift the balance of power within the national government.

Roosevelt also reorganized the executive branch. He believed in efficiency and expertise, which he attempted to institutionalize in special commissions and administrative procedures. To promote rational policymaking and public management, he staffed the expanding federal bureaucracy with able professionals.

Finally, Roosevelt encouraged the development of a personal presidency by exploiting the public's interest in their exuberant young president. He established the first White House press room and skillfully handled the mass media. His endless and well-reported activities, from playing with his children in the White House to wrestling, hiking, and horseback-riding with various notables, made him a celebrity, known as TR or Teddy. The publicity not only kept TR in the spotlight but also enabled him to mold public opinion.

## Roosevelt and Labor

One sign of TR's vigorous new approach to the presidency was his handling of a coal strike in 1902. Members of the United Mine Workers Union walked off their jobs, demanding higher wages, an eight-hour day, and recognition of their union. The mine owners closed the mines and waited for the union to collapse. But led by John Mitchell, the strikers held their ranks. The prospect of a freezing winter frightened consumers. Management's stubborn arrogance contrasted with the workers' orderly conduct and willingness to negotiate and hardened public opinion against the owners.

Although his legal advisers told him that the government had no authority to intervene, Roosevelt invited both the owners and the union leaders to the White House and declared that the national interest made government action necessary. Mitchell agreed to negotiate with the owners or to accept an arbitration commission appointed by the president. The owners, however, refused even to speak to the miners and demanded that Roosevelt use the army to break the union, as Cleveland had done in the Pullman strike in 1894.

Roosevelt was not a champion of labor, and he had favored shooting the Pullman strikers. But as president, he believed his role was to mediate social conflict for the public good. Roosevelt announced that he would use the army to seize and operate the mines, not to crush the union. Reluctantly, the owners accepted the arbitration commission they had previously rejected. The commission gave the miners a 10 percent wage increase and a nine-hour day, but not union recognition, and permitted the owners to raise coal prices by 10 percent. Roosevelt's intervention set important precedents for an active government role in labor disputes and a strong president acting as a steward of the public.

## MANAGING NATURAL RESOURCES

Federal land policy had helped create farms and develop transportation, but it had also ceded to speculators and business interests much of the nation's forests, mineral deposits, waterpower sites, and grazing lands. Reckless exploitation of these resources alarmed a new generation that believed the public welfare required the **conservation** of natural resources through efficient and scientific management. Conservationists achieved early victories in the Forest Reserve Act (1891) and the Forest Management Act (1897), which authorized the federal government to withdraw timberlands from development and to regulate grazing, lumbering, and hydroelectric sites in the forests.

Roosevelt built on these beginnings and on his friendship with Gifford Pinchot to make conservation a major focus of his presidency. Appointed in 1898 to head the new Division of Forestry (renamed the Forest Service in 1905), Pinchot brought rational management and regulation to resource development. With his advice, TR used presidential authority to triple the size of the forest reserves to 150 million acres, set aside another 80 million acres valuable for minerals and petroleum, and establish dozens of wildlife refuges. In 1908, Roosevelt held a White House conference of state and federal officials that led to the creation of the National Conservation Commission, 41 state conservation commissions, and widespread public support for the conservation movement.

Not everyone, of course, agreed with TR's conservationist policies. Some favored **preservation,** hoping to set aside land as permanent wilderness, whereas Roosevelt favored a scientific and efficient rather than uncontrolled use of resources. Preservationists won some victories, saving a stand of California's giant redwoods and helping create the National Park Service in 1916, but more Americans favored the utilitarian emphasis of the early conservationists.

Other interests opposed conservation completely. While some of the larger timber and mineral companies supported conservation as a way to guarantee long-run profits, smaller western entrepreneurs often cared only about quick returns. Many westerners, moreover, resented having easterners make key decisions about western growth and saw conservation as a perpetuation of this colonial subservience.

But westerners were happy to take federal money for expensive irrigation projects that private capital would not underwrite. They favored the 1902 National Reclamation Act, which established what became the **Bureau of Reclamation.** Its engineers were to construct dams, reservoirs, and irrigation canals, and the government was to sell the irrigated lands in tracts no larger than 160 acres. With massive dams and networks of irrigation canals, it reclaimed fertile valleys from the desert, but by not enforcing the 160-acre limitation it helped create powerful corporate farms in the West.

Westerners also welcomed Roosevelt's policies of conservation and rational development when they restricted Indian control of land and resources. Based on racist assumptions that Indians wasted natural resources, these policies sought to break up many reservations to open the land to whites for "efficient" development. Roosevelt also supported irrigation projects on Indian land that diverted Indian rivers to make water available to whites, not only in agriculture but in growing cities like Phoenix. Tribal protests were ignored.

## CORPORATE REGULATION

Nothing symbolized Roosevelt's active presidency better than his popular reputation as a "trust buster." TR regarded the formation of large business combinations favorably, but he realized he could not ignore the public anxiety about corporate power. Rather than invoking "the foolish antitrust law," he favored government regulation to prevent corporate abuses

**conservation**  The efficient management and use of natural resources, such as forests, grasslands, and rivers, as opposed to preservation or uncontrolled exploitation.

**Exploring America**
*Hetch Hetchy*

 WHERE TO LEARN MORE

John Muir National Historic Site, Martinez, California.
www.nps.gov/jomu

**Preservation**  Protecting forests, land, and other features of the natural environment from development or destruction, often for aesthetic appreciation.

**myhistorylab**

**From Then to Now Online**
*The Environmental Movement*

**Bureau of Reclamation**  Federal agency established in 1902 providing public funds for irrigation projects in arid regions.

and defend the public interest. "Misconduct," not size, was the issue. Roosevelt preferred to use government agencies to work with corporations to avoid lawsuits. But he did sue some "bad trusts."

In 1902, the Roosevelt administration filed its most famous antitrust suit, against the Northern Securities Company, a holding company organized by J. P. Morgan to control the railroad network of the Northwest. For TR, this suit was an assertion of government power that reassured a worried public and encouraged corporate responsibility. In 1904, the Supreme Court ordered the dissolution of the Northern Securities Company. Ultimately, Roosevelt brought 44 antitrust suits against business combinations, but except for a few like Standard Oil, he avoided the giant firms. Many of the cases had inconclusive outcomes, but Roosevelt was more interested in establishing a regulatory role for government than in breaking up big businesses.

Elected president in his own right in 1904 over the colorless and conservative Democratic candidate, Judge Alton B. Parker, Roosevelt responded to the growing popular demand for reform by pushing further toward a regulatory government. In 1906, Congress passed the Hepburn Act, the Pure Food and Drug Act, and the Meat Inspection Act. All three were compromises between reformers seeking serious government control of the industries involved and political defenders and lobbyists of the industries themselves.

Despite the compromises and weaknesses in the three laws, TR contended that they marked "a noteworthy advance in the policy of securing federal supervision and control over corporations." In 1907 and 1908, he pushed for an eight-hour workday, stock market regulation, and inheritance and income taxes. Republican conservatives in Congress blocked such reforms, and tensions increased between the progressive and conservative wings of the party.

## TAFT AND THE INSURGENTS

TR handpicked his successor as president: a loyal lieutenant, William Howard Taft. If Roosevelt thought that Taft would be a successful president, continuing his policies and holding the Republican Party together, he was wrong. Taft's election in 1908, over Democrat William Jennings Bryan in his third presidential campaign, led to a Republican political disaster.

Taft did preside over important progressive achievements. His administration pursued a more active and successful antitrust program than Roosevelt's. He supported the Mann-Elkins Act (1910), which extended the ICC's jurisdiction to telephone and telegraph companies. Taft set aside more public forest lands and oil reserves than Roosevelt had. He also supported a constitutional amendment authorizing an income tax, which went into effect in 1913 under the **Sixteenth Amendment.** One of the most important accomplishments of the Progressive Era, the income tax would provide the means for the government to expand its activities and responsibilities.

Nevertheless, Taft soon alienated progressives and floundered into a political morass. His problems were twofold. First, the Republicans were divided. Midwestern reform Republicans, led by La Follette, clashed with conservative Republicans, led by Senator Nelson Aldrich of Rhode Island. Second, Taft was politically inept. He was unable to mediate between the two Republican factions, and the party split apart.

Reformers wanted to restrict the power of the Speaker of the House, "Uncle Joe" Cannon, a reactionary who systematically blocked progressive measures and loudly declared, "I am goddamned tired of listening to all this babble of reform." After seeming to promise support, Taft backed down when conservatives threatened to defeat important legislation. The insurgents in Congress eventually restricted the speaker's

**Sixteenth Amendment**
Constitutional revision that in 1913 authorized a federal income tax.

powers, but they never forgave what they saw as Taft's betrayal. The tariff also alienated progressives from Taft. He had campaigned in 1908 for a lower tariff to curb inflation—and to the approval of midwestern Republicans. But when they introduced tariff reform legislation, the president failed to support them, and Aldrich's Senate committee added 847 amendments, many of which raised tariff rates. Progressives concluded that Taft had sided with the Old Guard against real change.

This perception solidified when Taft stumbled into a controversy over conservation. Gifford Pinchot had become embroiled in a complex struggle with Richard Ballinger, Taft's secretary of the interior. Ballinger, who was closely tied to western mining and lumbering interests, favored private development of public lands. When Pinchot challenged Ballinger's role in a questionable sale of public coal lands in Alaska to a J. P. Morgan syndicate, Taft upheld Ballinger and fired Pinchot. Progressives concluded that Taft had repudiated Roosevelt's conservation policies.

The Progressives determined to replace Taft, whom they now saw as an obstacle to reform. In 1911, the National Progressive League organized to champion La Follette for the Republican nomination in 1912. Roosevelt rejected an appeal for support, convinced that a challenge to the incumbent president was both doomed and divisive. Besides, his own position was closer to Taft's than to what he called "the La Follette type of fool radicalism." But Taft's political blunders increasingly angered Roosevelt. Condemning Taft as "disloyal to our past friendship," TR began to campaign for the Republican nomination himself. In 13 state primaries, he won 278 delegates, to only 46 for Taft. But most states did not then have primaries; as a result, Taft was able to dominate the Republican convention and win renomination. Roosevelt's forces formed a third party—the Progressive Party—and nominated the former president. The Republican split almost guaranteed victory for the Democratic nominee, Woodrow Wilson.

# WOODROW WILSON AND PROGRESSIVE REFORM

The pressures for reform called forth many new leaders. The one who would preside over progressivism's culmination, and ultimately its collapse, was Woodrow Wilson. Elected president in 1912 and 1916, he mediated among differing progressive views to achieve a strong reform program, enlarge the power of the executive branch, and make the White House the center of national politics.

**HOW DID** Woodrow Wilson's vision of reform differ from Theodore Roosevelt's?

## THE ELECTION OF 1912

Despite the prominence of Roosevelt and La Follette, progressivism was not simply a Republican phenomenon. As the Republicans quarreled during Taft's administration, Democrats pushed progressive remedies and achieved major victories in the state and congressional elections of 1910. To improve the party's chances in 1912, William Jennings Bryan announced that he would step aside. The Democratic spotlight shifted to the governor of New Jersey, Woodrow Wilson.

Wilson first entered public life as a conservative, steeped in the limited-government traditions of his native South. As president of Princeton University, beginning in 1902, he became a prominent representative of middle-class respectability and conservative causes. In 1910, New Jersey's Democratic bosses selected him for governor

Theodore Roosevelt, from *The New Nationalism* (1910)

A portrait of Woodrow Wilson by Edward Charles Tarbell. A strong president, Wilson led Congress to enact sweeping and significant legislation.

**New Nationalism**    Theodore Roosevelt's 1912 program calling for a strong national government to foster, regulate, and protect business, industry, workers, and consumers.

**New Freedom**    Woodrow Wilson's 1912 program for limited government intervention in the economy to restore competition by curtailing the restrictive influences of trusts and protective tariffs, thereby providing opportunities for individual achievement.

to head off the progressives, but once in office, Wilson championed popular reforms and immediately began to campaign as a progressive for the party's 1912 presidential nomination.

Wilson's progressivism differed from that of Roosevelt in 1912. TR emphasized a strong government to promote economic and social order. He defended big business as inevitable and healthy provided that government control ensured that it would benefit the entire nation. Roosevelt called this program the **New Nationalism,** reflecting his belief in a powerful state and a national interest. He also supported demands for social welfare, including workers' compensation and the abolition of child labor.

Wilson was horrified by Roosevelt's vision. His **New Freedom** program rejected what he called TR's "regulated monopoly." Wilson wanted "regulated competition," with the goverment's role limited to breaking up monopolies through antitrust action and preventing artificial barriers like tariffs from blocking free enterprise. Wilson opposed social welfare legislation as paternalistic, reaching beyond the proper scope of the federal government, which he hoped to minimize.

Roosevelt's endorsement of social legislation attracted many women into political action. As Jane Addams observed, "their long concern for the human wreckage of industry has come to be considered politics." (See American Views, Jane Addams and the Progressive Party.) The Progressive Party also endorsed woman suffrage, accepted women as convention delegates, and pledged to give women equal representation on party committees.

Despite his personal popularity, however, TR was unable to add progressive Democrats to the Republicans who followed him into the Progressive Party, and thus was doomed to defeat. Other reform voters embraced the Socialist candidate, Eugene V. Debs, who captured 900,000 votes—6 percent of the total. Taft played little role in the campaign.

Wilson won an easy electoral college victory, though he received only 42 percent of the popular vote and fewer popular votes than Bryan had won in any of his three campaigns (see Map 21–2). Roosevelt came in second, Taft third. The Democrats also gained control of Congress, giving Wilson the opportunity to enact his New Freedom program.

Woodrow Wilson, from *The New Freedom* (1913)

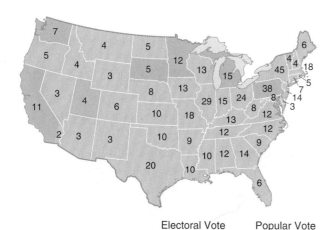

| | Electoral Vote (%) | Popular Vote (%) |
|---|---|---|
| **WOODROW WILSON** (Democrat) | 435 (82) | 6,296,547 (42) |
| Theodore Roosevelt (Progressive) | 88 (17) | 4,118,571 (27) |
| William Taft (Republican) | 8 (1) | 3,486,720 (23) |
| Eugene Debs (Socialist) | – | 900,672 (6) |

MAP 21–2  **The Election of 1912**  The split within the Republican Party enabled Woodrow Wilson to carry most states and become president even though he won only a minority of the popular vote.

**How is** it possible that Woodrow Wilson received 82 percent of the electoral vote but only 42 percent of the popular vote?

## AMERICAN VIEWS

### Jane Addams and the Progressive Party

*J*ane Addams, the founder of Hull House in Chicago, was active not merely in a range of social reform movements but also in nearly every facet of progressive politics. An ardent suffragist, Addams seconded the presidential nomination of Theodore Roosevelt at the founding convention of the Progressive Party in 1912, while a "Jane Addams Chorus" sang "Onward, Christian Soldiers" and "The Battle Hymn of the Republic." In this reminiscence from her second autobiography, Addams describes the convention and her part in the party's campaign that year.

- **Why** did settlement workers like Addams see the Progressive Party as the climax to their struggle for social justice?
- **How** did Addams's political interests fit into Roosevelt's program of the New Nationalism?
- **How** does Addams's rhetoric reflect the moral impulses underlying much of progressive reform?
- **Why** does Addams believe that women were attracted to the Progressive Party?

It was in August, 1912, that the Progressive Party was organized.

Suddenly, as if by magic, the city of Chicago became filled with men and women from every state in the Union who were evidently haunted by the same social compunctions and animated by like hopes; they revealed to each other mutual sympathies and memories. They urged methods which had already been tried in other countries, for righting old wrongs and for establishing standards in industry. For three days together they defined their purposes and harmonized their wills into gigantic cooperation. . . .

They believed that the program of social legislation placed before the country by the Progressive Party was of great significance to the average voter quite irrespective of the party which might finally claim his allegiance.

The platform, in the hope that the political organization of the nation might never again get so far away from the life of the people, advocated equal suffrage, direct primaries, the initiative and referendum. . . . In spite of our belief in our leader [Theodore Roosevelt], I was there, and I think the same was true of many others, because the platform expressed the social hopes so long ignored by the politicians; although we appreciated to the full our good fortune in securing on their behalf the magnetic personality of the distinguished candidate. Perhaps we felt so keenly the uplifting sense of comradeship with old friends and coworkers not only because we had all realized how inadequate we were in small groups but because the very sentiments of compassion and desire for social justice were futile unless they could at last find expression as an integral part of . . . government. At any rate, it was evident that measures of industrial amelioration and demands for social justice, so long discussed by small groups, were at last thrust into the stern arena of political action. . . .

### IMPLEMENTING THE NEW FREEDOM

As president, Wilson built on Roosevelt's precedent to strengthen executive authority. He proposed a full legislative program and worked forcefully to secure its approval. When necessary, he appealed to the public for support, ruthlessly used patronage, or compromised with conservatives. With such methods and a solid Democratic majority, Wilson gained approval of important laws.

Wilson turned first to the traditional Democratic goal of reducing the high protective tariff, the symbol of special privileges for industry. He forced through the **Underwood-Simmons Tariff Act** of 1913, the first substantial reduction in duties since before the Civil War. The act also levied the first income tax under the recently ratified Sixteenth Amendment. Conservatives condemned the "revolutionary" tax, but it was designed simply to compensate for lower tariff rates. The top tax rate paid by the wealthiest was a mere 7 percent.

**Underwood-Simmons Tarriff Act**
The 1913 reform law that lowered tariff rates and levied the first regular federal income tax.

The Progressive Convention has been described many times, and perhaps never quite adequately. It was a curious moment of release from inhibitions, and it did not seem in the least strange that reticent men and women should speak aloud of their religious and social beliefs, confident that they would be understood.

The women who identified themselves with the Progressive Convention inevitably experienced moments of heart searching and compunction. It is hard to understand it now, after we have possessed the ballot for a decade and have come to deem it a virtue "to enter politics," but at the moment we felt it necessary to give to the public our reasons for thus identifying ourselves with a political party. We said that when a great party pledges itself to the protection of children, to the care of the aged, to the relief of overworked girls, to the safeguarding of burdened men, it is inevitable that it should appeal to women and should seek to draw upon the great reservoir of their moral energy so long undesired and unutilized in practical politics; that one is the corollary of the other; a program of human welfare, the necessity for women's participation.

The real interest in the measures advocated in the party platform came however during the campaign itself when it was possible to place them before many groups throughout the country. Sometimes the planks in our platform were sharply challenged, but more often regarded with approval and occasionally with enthusiasm. I recall a meeting in Leadville, Colorado, made up altogether of miners who were much surprised to find that politics had anything to do with such affairs. They had always supposed that hours of labor were matters to be fought for and not voted upon. It was very exhilarating to talk to them, and it seemed to me that I had never before realized how slow we had been to place the definite interests of the workingmen in such shape that they could be voted upon. As a campaign speaker I was sent from town to town in both Dakotas, in Iowa, Nebraska, Oklahoma, Colorado, Kansas, and Missouri. The comradeship which a like-minded group always affords, combined with the heartiness of western good will, kept my spirits at high tide in spite of the fatigue of incessant speaking. . . .

The campaign renewed one's convictions that if the community as a whole were better informed as to the ethical implications of industrial wrongs whole areas of life could be saved from becoming brutalized or from sinking into hard indifference. . . . At moments we believed that we were witnessing a new pioneering of the human spirit, that we were in all humility inaugurating an exploration into the moral resources of our fellow citizens.

Source: Jane Addams, *The Second Twenty Years at Hull-House* (New York: Macmillan, 1930).

---

Wilson next reformed the nation's banking and currency system, which was inadequate for a modernizing economy. Wilson skillfully maneuvered a compromise measure through Congress, balancing the demands of agrarian progressives for government control with the bankers' desires for private control. The **Federal Reserve Act** of 1913 created 12 regional Federal Reserve banks that, although privately controlled, were to be supervised by the Federal Reserve Board, appointed by the president. The law also provided for a flexible national currency and improved access to credit.

Wilson's third objective was new legislation to break up monopolies. Initially, he supported the Clayton antitrust bill, which prohibited unfair trade practices and sharply restricted holding companies. But when business leaders and other progressives strenuously objected, Wilson reversed himself. Opting for continuous federal regulation rather than for the dissolution of trusts, Wilson endorsed the creation of the **Federal Trade Commission (FTC)** to oversee business activity and prevent illegal restrictions on competition.

 *Documents*

Louis Brandeis, *Other People's Money and How the Bankers Use It* (1913)

**Federal Reserve Act**   The 1913 law that revised banking and currency by extending limited government regulation through the creation of the Federal Reserve System.

**Federal Trade Commission**
Government agency established in 1914 to provide regulatory oversight of business activity.

The Federal Trade Commission Act of 1914 dismayed many of Wilson's early supporters because it embraced the New Nationalism's emphasis on positive regulation. Roosevelt's 1912 platform had proposed a federal trade commission; Wilson now accepted what he had earlier denounced as a partnership between trusts and the government that the trusts would dominate. Indeed, Wilson's conservative appointments to the FTC ensured that the agency would not seriously interfere with business, and by the 1920s, the FTC had become virtually a junior partner of the business community.

The fate of the Clayton antitrust bill after Wilson withdrew his support reflected his new attitude toward big business. Congressional conservatives gutted the bill with crippling amendments before permitting it to become law in 1914.

These measures indicate the limited nature of Wilson's vision of reform. In fact, he now announced that no further reforms were necessary—astonishing many progressives whose objectives had been completely ignored. Wilson refused to support woman suffrage and helped kill legislation abolishing child labor and expanding credits to farmers. Race relations provided a flagrant instance of Wilson's indifference to issues of social justice. Raised in the South, he believed in segregation and backed the southern Democrats in his cabinet when they introduced formal segregation within the government itself.

## THE EXPANSION OF REFORM

Wilson had won in 1912 only because the Republicans had split. By 1916, Roosevelt had returned to the GOP, and Wilson realized that he had to attract some of TR's former followers. Wilson therefore abandoned his opposition to social and economic reforms and promoted measures he had previously condemned. But he had also grown in the White House and now recognized that some problems could be resolved only by positive federal action.

To assist farmers, Wilson in 1916 convinced Congress to pass the Federal Farm Loan Act. This law, which Wilson himself had earlier rejected twice, provided farmers with federally financed long-term agricultural credits. The Warehouse Act of 1916 improved short-term agricultural credit. The Highway Act of 1916 provided funds to construct and improve rural roads through the adoption of the dollar-matching principle by which the federal government would expand its power over state activities in the twentieth century.

Wilson and the Democratic Congress also reached out to labor. Wilson signed the Keating-Owen Act prohibiting the interstate shipment of products made by child labor. In 1902, Wilson had denounced Roosevelt's intervention in the coal strike, but in 1916 he broke a labor-management impasse and averted a railroad strike by helping pass the Adamson Act establishing an eight-hour day for railroad workers. Wilson also pushed the Kern-McGillicuddy Act, which achieved the progressive goal of a workers' compensation system for federal employees. Together, these laws marked an important advance toward government regulation of the labor market.

Wilson also promoted activist government when he nominated Louis Brandeis to the Supreme Court. Known as "the people's lawyer," Brandeis had successfully defended protective labor legislation before the conservative judiciary. The nomination outraged conservatives, including William Howard Taft and the American Bar Association. Brandeis was the first Jew nominated to the court, and anti-Semitism motivated some of his opponents. Wilson overcame a vicious campaign against Brandeis and secured his confirmation.

By these actions, Wilson brought progressivism to a culmination of sorts and consolidated reformers behind him for a second term. Less than a decade earlier, Wilson the private citizen had assailed government regulation and social legislation; by 1916, he had guided an unprecedented expansion of federal power. His own transformation symbolized the development of progressivism.

## CONCLUSION

Progressivism had its ironies and paradoxes. It called for democratic reforms—and did achieve woman suffrage, direct legislation, and popular election of senators—but helped disfranchise black southerners and northern immigrants. It advocated social justice but often enforced social control. It demanded responsive government but helped create bureaucracies largely removed from popular control. It endorsed the regulation of business in the public interest but forged regulatory laws and commissions that tended to aid business.

Both the successes and the failures of progressivism revealed that the nature of politics and government had changed significantly. Americans had come to accept that government action could resolve social and economic problems, and the role and power of government expanded accordingly. The emergence of an activist presidency, capable of developing programs, mobilizing public opinion, directing Congress, and taking forceful action, epitomized this key development.

These important features would be crucial when the nation fought World War I, which brought new challenges and dangers to the United States. The Great War would expose many of the limitations of progressivism and the naiveté of the progressives' optimism.

# SUMMARY

## WHAT VALUES and beliefs bound progressives together?

**The Ferment of Reform** Progressivism was a diverse movement; reformers responded to the tensions of industrialization and urbanization by developing programs to give women the right to vote, expose business abuses, end child labor, make government more efficient, manage natural resources, and bring about social reform. The Social Gospel movement sought to introduce religious ethics into industrial relations. As businesses adopted Taylorization to improve workplace efficiency, workers resisted these new rules of efficiency. Opponents of reform held to traditional values and religious fundamentalism; businesses, angered by muckraking, used public relations as well as less desirable tactics to counter their critics.

## WHAT ROLE did women play in progressive reform movements?

**Reforming Society** Progressives worked to transform society by improving living conditions, educational opportunities, family life, and social and industrial relations. Settlement houses were the spearheads of social reform in urban immigrant neighborhoods, while the country lifers worked to transform rural society. Other progressives sought government intervention to limit immigration, impose prohibition, or improve schools. The Niagara Movement sought to extend equal justice to African Americans, who often suffered from the hostility or indifference of white progressives.

## WHAT STEPS were taken toward woman suffrage during the Progressive Era?

**Reforming Politics and Government** Progressives clamored for the reform of politics and the government; many wanted to change procedures and institutions to promote greater democracy; others hoped to improve the efforts of government and eliminate corruption. One of the most important achievements was woman suffrage; the Nineteenth Amendment gave women across America the right to vote. The initiative, referendum, recall, and direct election of senators were all introduced into the American political landscape during this period.

## HOW DID Theodore Roosevelt envision the power of the president?

**Theodore Roosevelt and the Progressive Presidency** Progressive proponent Theodore Roosevelt entered the White House upon the assassination of President McKinley in 1901. He rejected the limited role of the Gilded Age presidents and expanded executive authority. Called the first "modern president," Roosevelt's flamboyance and ambitions made him the most popular president of the time and enabled him to take aggressive approaches toward a coal strike, conservation, "busting" trusts, and regulating business abuses.

## HOW DID Woodrow Wilson's vision of reform differ from Theodore Roosevelt's?

**Woodrow Wilson and Progressive Reform** Progressivism was not limited to the Republican party; Democrats also pushed progressive remedies. President Woodrow Wilson, elected in 1912, introduced the New Freedom program; though he believed government's role should be more limited, he took steps to reduce the high protective tariff, create the Federal Reserve, regulate business through the Federal Trade Commission, assist farmers, help workers, and build highways. Wilson's Progressivism resulted in an unprecedented expansion of federal power.

# WHERE TO LEARN MORE

**John Muir National Historic Site, Martinez, California.** The architecture and furnishings of this 17-room house reflect the interests of John Muir, the writer and naturalist who founded the Sierra Club and led the preservationists in the Progressive Era. **www.nps.gov/jomu**

**Sewall-Belmont House National Historic Site, Washington, DC.** Headquarters of the National Woman's Party, this 200-year-old house on Capitol Hill has memorabilia of the woman suffrage movement, including posters, flags, and photographs of the early marches, and an extensive feminist library focused on the struggle for equal suffrage. Beginning in 1923 Alice Paul campaigned from this building for the Equal Rights Amendment. **http://www.sewallbelmont.org**

**Hull House, Chicago, Illinois.** This pioneering settlement house is now a museum on the campus of the University of Illinois, Chicago. **www.uic.edu/jaddams/hull/hull_house.html**

**Lower East Side Tenement Museum, New York City, New York.** A six-story tenement building containing 22 apartments, this museum vividly illustrates the congested and unhealthy living conditions of urban immigrants from the 1870s to the early twentieth century. See **www.tenement .org** for a virtual tour.

# STUDY RESOURCES

## PEARSON myhistorylab

For study resources for this chapter, go to www.myhistorylab .com and choose *The American Journey*. You will find a wealth of study and review material for this chapter, including pre- and post-tests, customized study plan, key term review flash cards, interactive map and document activities, and documents for analysis.

# REVIEW QUESTIONS

1. How and why did the presidency change during the Progressive Era?

2. How did the progressive concern for efficiency affect social reform efforts, public education, government administration, and rural life?

3. How and why did the relationship between business and government change during this time?

4. Why did social reform and social control often intermingle in the Progressive Era? Can such objectives be separate?

5. What factors, old and new, stimulated the reform movements of progressivism?

6. How did the role of women change during the Progressive Era? How did the changes affect progressivism?

7. Why did the demand for woman suffrage provoke such determined support and such bitter opposition, as illustrated by the 1913 parade and riot in Washington, DC?

## KEY TERMS

**Australian ballot** (p. 635)
**Bureau of Reclamation** (p. 639)
**Conservation** (p. 639)
**Eighteenth Amendment** (p. 632)
**Federal Reserve Act** (p. 645)
**Federal Trade Commission** (p. 645)
**Fundamentalists** (p. 625)
**Initiative** (p. 637)
**Muckraking** (p. 622)
**New Freedom** (p. 642)
**New Nationalism** (p. 642)
**Niagara Movement** (p. 633)
**Nineteenth Amendment** (p. 635)
**Preservation** (p. 639)
**Progressive Era** (p. 619)
**Prohibition** (p. 631)
**Recall** (p. 637)
**Referendum** (p. 637)
**Seventeenth Amendment** (p. 637)
**Sixteenth Amendment** (p. 640)
**Social Gospel Movement** (p. 622)
**Underwood-Simmons Tariff Act** (p. 644)
**Wobblies** (p. 624)

# 22
# Creating An Empire

*Havana, Cuba October 1901*

*When the Spanish-American war was declared the United States . . . assumed a position as protector of the interests of Cuba. It became responsible for the welfare of the people, politically, mentally, and morally. The mere fact of freeing the island from Spanish rule has not ended the care which this country should give. . . . The effect will be to uplift the people, gaining their permanent friendship and support and greatly increasing our own commerce. At present there are two million people requiring clothing and food, for but a small proportion of the necessaries of life are raised on the island. It is folly to grow food crops when sugar and tobacco produce such rich revenues in comparison. The United States should supply the Cubans with their breadstuffs, even wine, fruit, and vegetables, and should clothe the people. . . . The money received for their crops will be turned over in a great measure in buying supplies from the United States. . . .*

*Naturally the manufacturers of the United States should have precedence in furnishing machinery, locomotives, cars, and rails, materials for buildings and bridges, and the wide diversity of other supplies required, as well as fuel for their furnaces. With the present financial and commercial uncertainty at an end the people of the island will . . . come into the American market as customers for products of many kinds.*

*The meeting of the Constitutional Convention on November 5th will be an event in Cuban history of the greatest importance, and much will depend upon the action and outcome of this convention as to our future control of the island. . . . I considered it unwise to interfere, and I have made it a settled policy to permit the Cubans to manage every part of their constitution-making. This has been due to my desire to prevent any possible charge of crimination being brought against the United States in the direction of their constitutional affairs. . . .*

*There is no distrust of the United States on the part of the Cubans, and I know of no widespread antipathy to this country, its people, or its institutions. There are, of course, a handful of malcontents, as there must be in every country. . . .*

*I could not well conceive how the Cubans could be otherwise than grateful to the United States for its efforts in their behalf. . . . In the brief time since the occupation of the island by American troops the island has been completely rehabilitated—agriculturally, commercially, financially, educationally, and governmentally. This improvement has been so rapid and so apparent that no Cuban could mistake it. To doubt in the face of these facts that their liberators were not still their faithful friends would be impossible.*

Major-General Leonard Wood, "The Future of Cuba," *The Independent* 54 (January 23, 1902): 193–194; idem, "The Cuban Convention," *The Independent* 52 (November 1, 1900): 265–266. ◆

## PEARSON myhistorylab

Personal Journeys Online

- **Josiah Strong, *Our Country*, 1885.** An appeal for Anglo-Saxon imperialism by an American minister.

- **Charles Denby, *Shall We Keep the Philippines?*, 1898.** An argument for an economic empire by an American diplomat.

- **Vincent F. Howard, *Imperialism*, 1900.** A poem denouncing the imperialist journey.

◆ **GENERAL LEONARD WOOD'S** reports on Cuba, then under his control as military governor, captured the complex mixture of attitudes and motives that underlay the journey of the United States from a developing nation to a world power. Plans for economic expansion, a belief in national mission, a sense of responsibility to help others, scarcely hidden religious impulses and racist convictions—all combined in an uneasy mixture of self-interest and idealism.

The tension between what a friend of Wood's called the "righteous" and the "selfish" aspects of expanding American influence lay beneath the surface in Wood's reports. His claim that he was not interfering with Cuba's constitutional convention was disingenuous, for he had already undertaken to limit those who could participate as voters or delegates and was even then devising means to restrict the convention's autonomy. And in his repeated insistence that the Cubans were grateful for the intervention of "their faithful friends," the Americans, Wood obviously protested too much: Cubans, as well as Filipinos, Puerto Ricans, and others, rarely perceived American motives or American actions as positively as did Wood and other proponents of American expansion. Victory in the Spanish-American War had provided the United States with an extensive empire, status as a world power, and opportunities and problems that would long shape U.S. foreign policy. ◆

# CHRONOLOGY

| | |
|---|---|
| **1861–1869** | Seward serves as secretary of state. |
| **1867** | United States purchases Alaska from Russia. |
| **1870** | Annexation of the Dominican Republic is rejected. |
| **1879** | France conquers Algeria. |
| **1881** | Naval Advisory Board is created. |
| **1882** | Great Britain occupies Egypt. |
| **1887** | United States gains naval rights to Pearl Harbor. |
| **1890** | Alfred Thayer Mahan publishes *The Influence of Sea Power upon History*. |
| **1893** | Harrison signs but Cleveland rejects a treaty for the annexation of Hawaii. |
| **1893–1897** | Depression increases interest in economic expansion abroad. |
| **1894–1895** | Sino-Japanese War is fought. |
| **1895** | United States intervenes in Great Britain–Venezuelan boundary dispute. |
| | Cuban insurrection against Spain begins. |
| **1896** | William McKinley is elected president on an imperialist platform. |
| **1898** | Spanish-American War is fought. |
| | Hawaii is annexed. |
| | Anti-Imperialist League is organized. |
| | Treaty of Paris is signed. |
| **1899–1902** | Filipino-American War is fought. |

| | |
|---|---|
| **1899** | Open Door note is issued. |
| **1900** | Boxer Rebellion against foreign influence breaks out in China. |
| **1901** | Theodore Roosevelt becomes president. |
| **1903** | Platt Amendment restricts Cuban autonomy. |
| | Panama "revolution" is abetted by the United States. |
| **1904** | United States acquires the Panama Canal Zone. |
| | Roosevelt Corollary is announced. |
| **1904–1905** | Russo-Japanese War is fought. |
| **1905** | Treaty of Portsmouth ends the Russo-Japanese War through U.S. mediation. |
| **1906–1909** | United States occupies Cuba. |
| **1907–1908** | Gentlemen's Agreement restricts Japanese immigration. |
| **1909** | United States intervenes in Nicaragua. |
| **1912–1933** | United States occupies Nicaragua. |
| **1914** | Panama Canal opens. |
| **1914–1917** | United States intervenes in Mexico. |
| **1915–1934** | United States occupies Haiti. |
| **1916–1924** | United States occupies the Dominican Republic. |
| **1917** | Puerto Ricans are granted U.S. citizenship. |
| **1917–1922** | United States occupies Cuba. |

# THE ROOTS OF IMPERIALISM

**WHAT ARGUMENTS** were made in favor of American expansion in the late nineteenth century?

Henry Cabot Lodge, *The Business World vs. the Politicians* (1895)

**imperialism** The policy and practice of exploiting nations and peoples for the benefit of an imperial power either directly through military occupation and colonial rule or indirectly through economic domination of resources and markets.

Albert Beveridge, *The March of the Flag* (1898)

**WHERE TO LEARN MORE**

★ Mission Houses, Honolulu, Hawaii. www.missionhouses.org

The United States had a long-established tradition of expansion across the continent. Indeed, by the 1890s, Republican Senator Henry Cabot Lodge of Massachusetts boasted that Americans had "a record of conquest, colonization, and territorial expansion unequalled by any people in the nineteenth century." Lodge now urged the country to build an overseas empire, emulating the European model of **imperialism** based on the acquisition and exploitation of colonial possessions. Other Americans favored a less formal empire, in which United States interests and influence would be ensured through extensive trade and investments rather than through military occupation. Still others advocated a cultural expansionism in which the nation exported its ideals and institutions. All such expansionists could draw from many sources to support their plans. (see Overview, Rationales for Imperialism).

## IDEOLOGICAL AND RELIGIOUS ARGUMENTS

Scholars, authors, politicians, and religious leaders provided interlocking ideological arguments for the new imperialism. Some intellectuals, for example, invoked social Darwinism, maintaining that the United States should engage in a competitive struggle for wealth and power with other nations. "The survival of the fittest," declared one writer, was "the law of nations as well as a law of nature." As European nations expanded into Asia and Africa in the 1880s and 1890s, seeking colonies, markets, and raw materials, these advocates argued, the United States had to adopt similar policies to ensure national success.

Related to social Darwinism was a pervasive belief in racial inequality and in the superiority of people of English, or Anglo-Saxon, descent. To many Americans, the industrial progress, military strength, and political development of England and the United States were proof of an Anglo-Saxon superiority that carried with it a responsibility to extend the blessings of their rule to less able people. As a popular expression put it, colonialism was the "white man's burden," carrying with it a duty to aid and uplift other peoples. Such attitudes led some expansionists to favor imposing American ideas and practices on other cultures regardless of their own values and customs.

Reflecting this aggressiveness, as well as Darwinian anxieties, some Americans endorsed expansion as consistent with their ideals of masculinity. Forceful expansion would be a manly course, relying upon and building strength and honor among American males. Men who confronted the challenges of empire would thereby improve their ability to compete in the international arena. "Pride of race, courage, manliness," predicted one enthusiast, would be both the causes and the consequences of an assertive foreign policy.

American missionaries also promoted expansionist sentiment. Hoping to evangelize the world, American religious groups increased the number of Protestant foreign missions sixfold from 1870 to 1900. Women in particular organized foreign missionary societies and served in the missions. Missionaries publicized their activities throughout the United States, generating interest in foreign developments and support for what one writer called the "imperialism of righteousness." Abroad they pursued a religious transformation that often resembled a cultural conversion, for they promoted trade, developed business interests, and encouraged westernization through technology and education as well as religion. Sometimes, as in the Hawaiian Islands, American missionaries even promoted annexation by the United States.

## OVERVIEW  Rationales for Imperialism

| Category | Beliefs |
|---|---|
| Racism and Social Darwinism | The conviction that Anglo-Saxons were racially superior and should dominate other peoples, either to ensure national success, establish international stability, or benefit the "inferior" races by imposing American ideas and institutions on them |
| Righteousness | The conviction that Christianity, and a supporting American culture, should be aggressively spread among the benighted peoples of other lands |
| Mahanism | The conviction, following the ideas advanced by Alfred Thayer Mahan, that U.S. security required a strong navy and economic and territorial expansion |
| Economics | A variety of arguments holding that American prosperity depended on acquiring access to foreign markets, raw materials, and investment opportunities |

Indeed, the American religious press endlessly repeated the themes of national destiny, racial superiority, and religious zeal. Missionaries contributed to the imperial impulse by describing their work in terms of the conquest of enemy territory. Thus, while missionaries were motivated by what they considered to be idealism and often brought real benefits to other lands, especially in education and health, religious sentiments reinforced the ideology of American expansion.

## STRATEGIC CONCERNS

Other expansionists were motivated by strategic concerns, shaped by what they saw as the forces of history and geography. America's location in the Western Hemisphere, its coastlines on two oceans, and the ambitions and activities of other nations, particularly Germany and Britain, convinced some Americans that the United States had to develop new policies to protect and promote its national security and interests. Alfred Thayer Mahan, a naval officer and president of the Naval War College, emphasized the importance of a strong navy for national greatness in his book *The Influence of Sea Power upon History*. To complement the navy, Mahan proposed that the United States build a canal across the isthmus of Panama to link its coasts, acquire naval bases in the Caribbean and the Pacific to protect the canal, and annex Hawaii and other Pacific islands to promote trade and service the fleet.

**Mahanism** found a receptive audience. President Benjamin Harrison declared in 1891 that "as to naval stations and points of influence, we must look forward to a departure from the too conservative opinions which have been held heretofore." Still more vocal advocates of Mahan's program were a group of nationalistic Republicans, predominantly from the Northeast. They included politicians like Henry Cabot Lodge and Theodore Roosevelt, journalists like Whitelaw Reid and Albert Shaw, and diplomats and lawyers like John Hay and Elihu Root. (see American Views, An Imperialist Views the World).

Even so, Mahan was not solely responsible for the large-navy policy popular among imperialists. Its origins went back to 1881, when Congress established the Naval Advisory Board, which successfully lobbied for larger naval appropriations. An extensive program to replace the navy's obsolete wooden ships with modern cruisers and battleships was well under way by 1890, when Mahan's book appeared. The United States soon possessed the formidable navy the expansionists wanted. This larger navy, in turn, demanded strategic bases and coaling stations.

**Mahanism** The ideas advanced by Alfred Thayer Mahan, stressing U.S. naval, economic, and territorial expansion.

Emily Hartwell, an American missionary, and her Chinese converts ("Bible Women") in the Foochow Mission in 1902. American missionaries wanted to spread the Gospel abroad but inevitably spread American influence as well. Hartwell used the ethnocentric and militant rhetoric of the imperialism of righteousness in appealing to Americans for money and prayers for her "picket duty on the very outskirts of the army of the Lord."

## ECONOMIC DESIGNS

One reason for the widespread support for a larger navy was its use to expand and protect America's international trade. Nearly all Americans favored economic expansion through foreign trade. Such a policy promised national prosperity: more markets for manufacturers and farmers, greater profits for merchants and bankers, more jobs for workers. Far fewer favored the acquisition of colonies that was characteristic of European imperialism. (See Global Perspectives, European Colonial Imperialism.)

The United States had long aggressively fostered American trade, especially in Latin America and East Asia. As early as 1844, the United States had negotiated a trade treaty with China, and ten years later a squadron under Commodore Matthew Perry had forced the Japanese to open their ports to American products. In the late nineteenth century, the dramatic expansion of the economy caused many Americans to favor more government action to open foreign markets to American exports.

Exports, especially of manufactured goods, which grew ninefold between 1865 and 1900, did increase greatly in the late nineteenth century. Still, periodic depressions fed the fears of overproduction. The massive unemployment and social unrest that accompanied these economic crises also provided social and political arguments for economic relief through foreign trade.

In the depression of the 1890s, with the secretary of state seeing "symptoms of revolution" in the Pullman strike and Coxey's Army of unemployed workers (see Chapter 20), the interest in foreign trade became obsessive. More systematic government efforts to promote trade seemed necessary, a conclusion strengthened by new threats to existing American markets. In that tumultuous decade, European nations raised tariff barriers against American products, and Japan and the European imperial powers began to restrict commercial opportunities in the areas of China that they controlled. Many American leaders decided that the United States had to adopt decisive new policies or face economic catastrophe.

**WHAT ROLE** did public opinion play in the emergence of American imperialism?

# FIRST STEPS

Despite the growing ideological, strategic, and economic arguments for imperialism, the government only fitfully interested itself in foreign affairs before the mid-1890s. It did not pursue a policy of isolationism from international affairs, for the nation maintained normal diplomatic and trade ties and at times vigorously intervened in Latin America and East

Asia. But in general the government deferred to the initiative of private interests, reacted haphazardly to outside events, and did little to create a professional foreign service. In a few bold if inconsistent steps, however, the United States moved to expand its influence.

## SEWARD AND BLAINE

Two secretaries of state, William H. Seward, secretary under Presidents Abraham Lincoln and Andrew Johnson (1861–1869), and James G. Blaine, secretary under Presidents James Garfield and Benjamin Harrison (1881, 1889–1892), laid the foundation for a larger and more aggressive U.S. role in world affairs. Seward possessed an elaborate imperial vision, based on his understanding of commercial opportunities, strategic necessities, and national destiny. His interest in opening East Asia to American commerce and establishing American hegemony over the Caribbean anticipated the subsequent course of American expansion. Seward purchased Alaska from Russia in 1867, approved the navy's occupation of the Midway Islands in the Pacific, pushed American trade on a reluctant Japan, and repeatedly tried to acquire Caribbean naval bases (see Map 22–1).

**W** WHERE TO LEARN MORE

★ James G. Blaine House, Augusta, Maine.
http://www.blainehouse.org

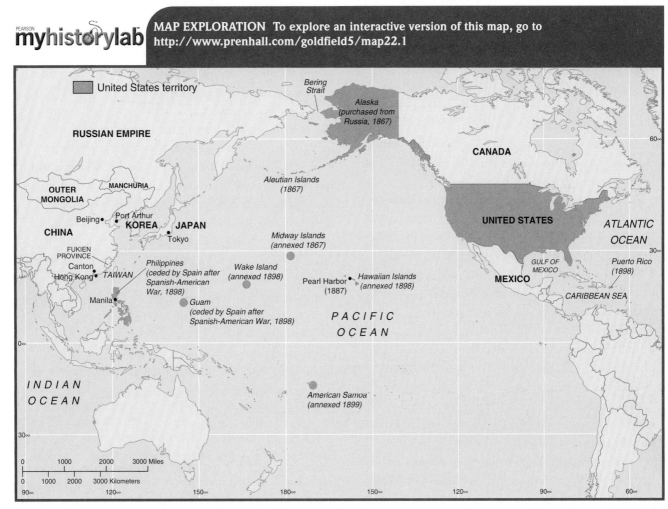

MAP EXPLORATION  To explore an interactive version of this map, go to
http://www.prenhall.com/goldfield5/map22.1

MAP 22–1  **United States Expansion in the Pacific, 1867–1899**  Pursuing visions of a commercial empire in the Pacific the United States steadily expanded its territorial possessions as well as its influence there in the late nineteenth century.

**What did** the United States gain from its expansion in the Pacific?

## AMERICAN VIEWS

### An Imperialist Views the World

Theodore Roosevelt, Henry Cabot Lodge, Alfred Thayer Mahan, and other influential imperialists frequently corresponded with one another, expressing their views forcefully if not always in depth. The following excerpts are from Roosevelt's private letters to Lodge and Mahan in 1897, while he was assistant secretary of the navy and before the Spanish-American War.

- **In what** ways does Roosevelt reflect the influence of Mahan?
- **What** is Roosevelt's view of war?
- **How** does Roosevelt view European nations?
- **How** does he view the independence of other nations in the Western Hemisphere?

I suppose that I need not tell you that as regards Hawaii I take your views absolutely, as indeed I do on foreign policy generally. If I had my way we would annex those islands tomorrow. If that is impossible I would establish a protectorate over them. I believe we should build the Nicaraguan canal at once, and in the meantime that we should build a dozen new battleships, half of them on the Pacific Coast; and these battleships should have a large coal capacity and a consequent increased radius of action. . . . I think President Cleveland's action [in rejecting the annexation of Hawaii] was a colossal crime, and we should be guilty of aiding him after the fact if we do not reverse what he did. I earnestly hope we can make the President [McKinley] look at things our way. Last Saturday night Lodge pressed his views upon him with all his strength.

I agree with all you say as to what will be the result if we fail to take Hawaii. It will show that we either have lost, or else wholly lack, the masterful instinct which alone can make a race great. I feel so deeply about it I hardly dare express myself in full. The terrible part is to see that it is the men of education who take the lead in trying to make us prove traitors to our race.

I fully realize the importance of the Pacific coast. . . . But there are big problems in the West Indies also. Until we

definitely turn Spain out of those islands (and if I had my way that would be done tomorrow), we will always be menaced by trouble there. We should acquire the Danish Islands [in the West Indies], and by turning Spain out should serve notice that no strong European power, and especially not Germany, should be allowed to gain a foothold by supplanting some weak European power. I do not fear England; Canada is a hostage for her good behavior.

I wish we had a perfectly consistent foreign policy, and that this policy was that every European power should be driven out of America, and every foot of American soil, including the nearest islands in both the Pacific and the Atlantic, should be in the hands of independent American states, and so far as possible in the possession of the United States or under its protection.

To speak with a frankness which our timid friends would call brutal, I would regard a war with Spain from two standpoints: first, the advisability on the grounds both of humanity and self-interest of interfering on behalf of the Cubans, and of taking one more step toward the complete freeing of America from European dominion; second, the benefit done our people by giving them something to think of which isn't material gain, and especially the benefit done our military forces by trying both the Navy and the Army in actual practice. I should be very sorry not to see us make the experiment of trying to land, and therefore feed and clothe, an expeditionary force [on Cuba], if only for the sake of learning from our own blunders. I should hope that the force would have some fighting to do. It would be a great lesson, and we would profit much by it.

I wish there was a chance that the [U.S. battleship] Maine was going to be used against some foreign power; by preference Germany—but I am not particular, and I'd take even Spain if nothing better offered.

Source: Reprinted by permission of the publisher from *The Letters of Theodore Roosevelt*, Vol. I 1868–1898, selected and edited by Elting E. Morison (Cambridge, MA: Harvard University Press, 1951)

## GLOBAL PERSPECTIVES

### EUROPEAN COLONIAL IMPERIALISM

The United States was not alone in expanding its role in the world. Beginning in the 1870s, leading European nations engaged in a competitive struggle to partition much of Africa and Asia in pursuit of their imperial ambitions. Like Americans, Europeans advanced many justifications for imperialism. Many favored colonies to acquire markets, resources, and investment opportunities; others saw in colonies strategic advantages or international prestige. Some interwove racist and religious attitudes to justify European empire building as "an instrument for the good of humanity."

But advanced industrialization, more than the questionable blessings of religion and race, accounted for European success. Railroads, steamships, and ocean cables facilitated transportation and communication, and modern weaponry easily overcame native resistance. In the Battle of Omdurman in 1898, a British expedition armed with machine guns massacred 11,000 Sudanese tribesmen trying to defend their independence while itself suffering only 28 casualties. Said one observer: "It was not a battle but an execution."

Before the 1870s Africa had largely escaped European colonialism, but within 30 years European powers had divided much of the continent. France gained most of northwestern Africa, conquering Algeria in 1879, occupying Tunisia in 1881, and dividing Morocco with Spain. Britain acquired territory from the Mediterranean Sea to the Cape. To control the area around the Suez Canal, viewed as the empire's lifeline to India, the British occupied Egypt in 1882 and then seized the Sudan. With unimaginable brutality, Belgium's King Leopold colonized the Congo in central Africa. Germany established colonies in southwestern Africa and, like Italy, in East Africa.

European powers also advanced on Asia. To its earlier control of India, Great Britain added Burma and Malaya. France extended its authority over Indochina in the 1880s and 1890s by gaining control of Vietnam and Laos. Russia expanded its empire into contiguous territories, securing Turkestan in Central Asia and then reaching toward East Asia, particularly the Manchurian region of China. Other nations also sought spheres of influence in China, acquiring ports, naval stations, and railroad and mining concessions.

Competitive imperialism risked conflict, between expansive nations as well as with colonized peoples, but such risks did not deter aspiring imperialists. In 1887 the Japanese foreign minister insisted: "We have to establish a new, European-style empire on the edge of Asia." And in 1895 an American leader declared of European imperialism: "The United States must not fall out of the line of march."

- While many Americans distinguished their foreign policy goals from European imperialism, how might the nation's expansion into the American West and its treatment of Native Americans correspond to such colonialism?

Blaine was an equally vigorous, if inconsistent, advocate of expansion. He worked to extend what he called America's "commercial empire" in the Pacific. In an effort to induce Latin American nations to import manufactured products from the United States rather than Europe, Blaine proposed a customs union to reduce trade barriers, expecting it to strengthen U.S. control of hemispheric markets. Wary of economic subordination to the colossus of the north, however, the Latin American nations rejected Blaine's plan but did agree to establish what eventually came to be known as the **Pan American Union.** Based in Washington, it helped to promote hemispheric understanding and cooperation.

If U.S. officials were increasingly assertive toward Latin America and Asia, however, they remained little involved in Europe and were wholly indifferent to Africa, which the European powers were then carving up into colonies. In short, despite some important precedents for the future, much of American foreign policy remained undeveloped, sporadic, and impulsive.

**Pan American Union** International organization originally established as the Commercial Bureau of American Republics by Secretary of State James Blaine's first Pan-American Conference in 1889 to promote cooperation among nations of the Western Hemisphere through commercial and diplomatic negotiations.

## HAWAII

Blaine regarded Hawaii as "indispensably" part of "the American system." As early as 1842, the United States had announced its opposition to European control of Hawaii, a key waystation in the China trade and where New England missionaries and whalers were already active. Although Hawaii continued to be ruled by native monarchs, American influence grew, particularly as other Americans arrived to establish sugar plantations and eventually dominate the economy. Treaties in 1875 and 1887 integrated the islands into the American economy and gave the United States control over Pearl Harbor on the island of Oahu. In 1887, the United States rejected a proposal from Britain and France for a joint guarantee of Hawaii's independence and endorsed a new Hawaiian constitution that gave political power to wealthy white residents. The obvious next step was U.S. annexation, which Blaine endorsed in 1891.

A combination of factors soon impelled American planters to bid for annexation. The McKinley Tariff Act of 1890 effectively closed the U.S. market to Hawaiian sugar producers, threatening their economic ruin. At the same time, Queen Liliuokalani moved to restore native control of Hawaiian affairs. To ensure market access and protect their political authority, the American planters decided to seek annexation to the United States. In 1893, they overthrew the queen. John Stevens, the American diplomatic representative, ordered U.S. marines to help the rebels, then declared an American protectorate over the new Hawaiian government. A delegation from the new provisional government, which did not include any native Hawaiians, went to Washington to draft a treaty for annexation. President Harrison signed the pact but could not get Senate approval before the new Cleveland administration took office.

Grover Cleveland immediately called for an investigation of the whole affair. Soon convinced that "the undoubted sentiment of the people is for the Queen, against the provisional Government, and against annexation," Cleveland apologized to the queen for the "flagrant wrong" done her by the "reprehensible conduct" of U.S. diplomats and troops. But the American-dominated provisional government refused to step down, and Cleveland's rejection of annexation set off a noisy debate in the United States.

Many Republicans strongly supported annexation, which they regarded as merely part of a larger plan of expansion.

Democrats generally opposed annexation. Most Democrats believed that "the mission of our nation is to build up and make a greater country out of what we have, instead of annexing islands." The Hawaiian episode of 1893 thus foreshadowed the arguments over imperialism at the end of the century and emphasized the policy differences between Democrats and the increasingly expansionist Republicans.

## CHILE AND VENEZUELA

American reactions to developments in other countries in the 1890s also reflected an increasingly assertive national policy and excitable public opinion. In 1891, American sailors on shore leave in Chile became involved in a drunken brawl that left two of them dead, 17 injured, and dozens in jail. Encouraged by a combative navy, President Harrison threatened military retaliation against Chile, provoking an outburst of bellicose nationalism in the United States. Harrison relented only when Chile apologized and paid an indemnity.

COASTING.
The old horse was too slow for Uncle Sam.

As other imperial powers look on, the United States abandons its traditional principles to rush headlong into world affairs. Uncle Sam would not always find it a smooth ride.

A few years later, the United States again threatened war over a minor issue but against a more formidable opponent. Although opposed to annexing Hawaii, President Cleveland adopted an increasingly aggressive policy in Latin America. In 1895, he intervened in a boundary dispute between Great Britain and Venezuela over British Guiana. Cleveland was motivated not only by the long-standing U.S. goal of challenging Britain for Latin American markets but also by ever more expansive notions of the Monroe Doctrine and the authority of the United States. Secretary of State Richard Olney sent Britain a blunt note demanding arbitration of the disputed territory and stoutly asserting American supremacy in the Western Hemisphere. Cleveland urged Congress to establish a commission to determine the boundary and enforce its decision by war if necessary. As war fever swept the United States, Britain agreed to arbitration, recognizing the limited nature of the issue that so convulsed Anglo-American relations.

Cleveland's assertion of U.S. hemispheric dominance angered Latin Americans, and their fears deepened when the United States decided arbitration terms with Britain without consulting Venezuela, which protested before bowing to American pressure. The United States had intervened less to protect Venezuela from the British bully than to advance its own hegemony. The further significance of the Venezuelan crisis, Captain Mahan noted, lay in its "awakening of our countrymen to the fact that we must come out of our isolation . . . and take our share in the turmoil of the world."

# THE SPANISH-AMERICAN WAR

The forces pushing the United States toward imperialism and international power came to a head in the Spanish-American War. Cuba's quest for independence from the oppressive colonial control of Spain activated Americans' long-standing interest in the island. Many sympathized with the Cuban rebels' yearning for freedom, others worried that disorder in Cuba threatened their own economic and political interests, and some thought that intervention would increase the influence of the United States in the Caribbean and along key Pacific routes to Asian markets. But few foresaw that the war that finally erupted in 1898 would dramatically change U.S. relationships with the rest of the world and give the United States a colonial empire.

**WHAT WERE** the most important consequences of the Spanish-American War?

*The Spanish-American War* (1898)

## THE CUBAN REVOLUTION

The last major European colony in Latin America, Cuba held an economic potential that attracted American business interests and a strategic significance for any Central American canal. In the late nineteenth century, American investors expanded their economic influence in Cuba, while Cubans themselves rebelled repeatedly but unsuccessfully against increasingly harsh Spanish rule. Cuban discontent erupted again in 1895, when the Cuban patriot José Martí launched another revolt.

The rebellion was a classic guerrilla war, with the rebels controlling the countryside and the Spanish army the towns and cities. American economic interests were seriously affected, for both Cubans and Spaniards destroyed American property and disrupted American trade. But the brutality with which Spain attempted to suppress the revolt promoted American sympathy for the Cuban insurgents. Determined to cut the rebels off from their peasant supporters, the Spanish herded most civilians into "reconcentration camps," where tens of thousands died of starvation and disease.

American sympathy was further aroused by the sensationalist **yellow press.** To attract readers and boost advertising revenues, the popular press of the day adopted bold headlines, fevered editorials, and real or exaggerated stories of violence, sex, and corruption.

**yellow press**   A deliberately sensational journalism of scandal and exposure designed to attract an urban mass audience and increase advertising revenues.

Failure to intervene to protect the innocent from Spanish lust and cruelty, insisted the yellow journalists, would be dishonorable and cowardly.

The nation's religious press, partly because it reflected the prejudice of many Protestants against Catholic Spain, also advocated American intervention. The *Catholic Herald* of New York sarcastically referred to the "bloodthirsty preachers" of the Protestant churches, but such preachers undeniably influenced American opinion against Spain.

As the Cuban rebellion dragged on, more and more Americans advocated intervention to stop the carnage, protect U.S. investments, or uphold various principles. In the election of 1896, both major parties endorsed Cuban independence.

## GROWING TENSIONS

In his 1897 inaugural address, President William McKinley outlined an expansionist program ranging from further enlargement of the navy to the annexation of Hawaii and the construction of a Central American canal in Nicaragua, but his administration soon focused on Cuba. McKinley's principal complaint was that chronic disorder in Cuba disrupted American investments and agitated public opinion. Personally opposed to military intervention, McKinley first used diplomacy to press Spain to adopt reforms that would settle the rebellion. In late 1897, Spain modified its brutal military tactics and offered limited autonomy to Cuba. But Cubans insisted on complete independence, a demand that Spain refused to grant.

Relations between the United States and Spain deteriorated. On February 15, 1898, the U.S. battleship *Maine* blew up in Havana harbor, killing 260 men. The Spanish were not responsible for the tragedy, which a modern naval inquiry has attributed to an internal accident. But many Americans agreed with Theodore Roosevelt, the assistant secretary of the navy, who called it "an act of dirty treachery on the part of the Spaniards" and told McKinley that only war was "compatible with our national honor." Thus understandings of appropriate male conduct also influenced decisions as to how the nation should act.

Popular anger was inflamed, but the sinking of the *Maine* by itself did not bring war, though it did restrict McKinley's options and pressure him to be more assertive toward Spain. Other pressures soon began to build on the president. Increasingly, business interests favored war as less disruptive than a volatile peace that threatened their investments. Further, McKinley feared that a moderate policy would endanger Republican congressional candidates.

At the end of March 1898, McKinley sent Spain an ultimatum. He demanded an armistice in Cuba, an end to the reconcentration policy, and the acceptance of American arbitration, which implied Cuban independence. Desperately, Spain made concessions, abolishing reconcentration and declaring a unilateral armistice. But McKinley had already begun war preparations. He submitted a war message to Congress on April 11, asking for authority to use force against Spain. Congress declared war on Spain on April 25, 1898.

A few national leaders welcomed the war as a step toward imperialism, but there was little popular support for an imperialist foreign policy. Most interventionists were not imperialists, and Congress added the **Teller Amendment** to the war resolution, disclaiming any intention of annexing Cuba and promising that Cubans would govern themselves. Congress also refused to approve either a canal bill or the annexation of Hawaii. Nevertheless, the Spanish-American War did turn the nation toward imperialism.

**Teller Amendment** A congressional resolution adopted in 1898 renouncing any American intention to annex Cuba.

## WAR AND EMPIRE

The decisive engagement of the war took place not in Cuba but in another Spanish colony, the Philippines, and it involved the favored tool of the expansionists, the new navy (see Map 22–2). Once war was declared, Commodore George Dewey led the U.S.

**PEARSON**
**myhistorylab**    **MAP EXPLORATION** To explore an interactive version of this map, go to
http://www.prenhall.com/goldfield5/map22.2

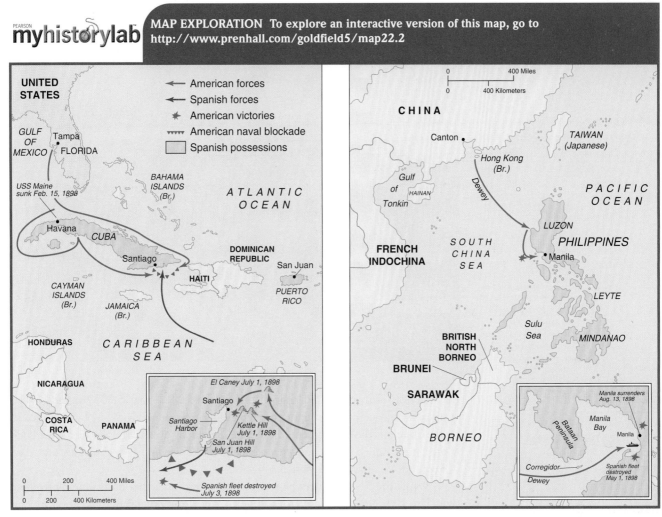

MAP 22–2    **The Spanish–American War**    The United States gained quick victories in both theaters of the Spanish–American War. Its naval power proved decisive, with Commodore Dewey destroying one enemy fleet in the Philippines, and a second U.S. naval force cutting off the Spanish in Cuba.

**Why did** the United States want to control the Philippines?

Asiatic squadron into Manila Bay and destroyed the much weaker Spanish fleet on May 1, 1898. This dramatic victory galvanized expansionist sentiment in the United States. With Dewey's triumph, exulted one expansionist, "We are taking our proper rank among the nations of the world. We are after markets, the greatest markets now existing in the world." To expand this foothold in Asia, McKinley ordered troops to the Philippines, postponing the military expedition to Cuba itself.

Dewey's victory also precipitated the annexation of Hawaii, which had seemed unlikely only weeks before. Annexationists now pointed to the islands' strategic importance as stepping stones to Manila. In July, Congress approved annexation, a decision welcomed by Hawaii's white minority. Native Hawaiians solemnly protested this step taken "without reference to the consent of the people of the Hawaiian Islands." Filipinos would soon face the same American imperial impulse.

Military victory also came swiftly in Cuba, once the U.S. Army finally landed in late June. Victory came despite bureaucratic bungling in the War Department, which left

*Documents*

William McKinley, *Decision on the Philippines* (1900)

Source: Theodore Roosevelt and the Rough Riders. Ironically, their horses were left behind in Florida and TR complained of the Army's "Confusion and lack of system and general mismanagement."

Most Americans enthusiastically greeted the declaration of war against Spain. Rallies and parades, such as this "Off to War Parade" in Denver, encouraged the war spirit.

the American army poorly led, trained, and supplied. More than 5,000 Americans died of diseases and accidents brought on by such mismanagement; only 379 were killed in battle. State militias supplemented the small regular army, as did volunteer units, such as the famous Rough Riders, a cavalry regiment of cowboys and eastern dandies organized by Leonard Wood and Theodore Roosevelt.

While the Rough Riders captured public attention, other units were more effective. The 10th Negro Cavalry, for example, played the crucial role in capturing San Juan Hill, a battle popularly associated with the Rough Riders. Nevertheless, the Rough Riders gained the credit, thanks in part to Roosevelt's self-serving and well-promoted account of the conflict, which one humorist proposed retitling *Alone in Cuba*.

U.S. naval power again proved decisive. In a lopsided battle on July 3, the Spanish squadron in Cuba was destroyed, isolating the Spanish army and guaranteeing its defeat. U.S. forces then seized the nearby Spanish colony of Puerto Rico without serious opposition. Humbled, Spain signed an armistice ending the war on August 12.

## THE TREATY OF PARIS

The armistice required Spain to accept Cuban independence, cede Puerto Rico and Guam (a Pacific island between Hawaii and the Philippines) to the United States, and allow the Americans to occupy Manila, pending the final disposition of the Philippines at a formal peace conference. The acquisition of Puerto Rico and Guam indicated the expansionist nature the conflict had assumed for the United States. So did the postponement of the Philippine issue. McKinley knew that delay would permit the advocates of expansion to build public support for annexation. Because the U.S. Army did not capture Manila until after the armistice had been signed, he could not claim the islands by conquest, as Spain pointed out.

McKinley defended his decision to acquire the Philippines with self-righteous imperialist rhetoric, promising to extend Christian influence and American values. But he was motivated primarily by a determination to use the islands to strengthen America's political and commercial position in East Asia. Moreover, he believed the Filipinos poorly suited to self-rule, and he feared that Germany or Japan might seize the Philippines if the United States did not. Meeting in Paris in December, American and Spanish negotiators settled the final terms for peace. Spain agreed—despite Filipino demands for independence—to cede the Philippines to the United States.

The decision to acquire the Philippines sparked a dramatic debate over the ratification of the Treaty of Paris. Imperialists invoked the familiar arguments of economic expansion, national destiny, and strategic necessity, while asserting that Americans had religious and racial responsibilities to advance civilization by uplifting backward peoples.

Opponents of the treaty raised profound questions about national goals and ideals. They included such prominent figures as the civil-service reformer Carl Schurz, the steel baron Andrew Carnegie, the social reformer Jane Addams, the labor leader Samuel Gompers, and the author Mark Twain. Their organizational base was the Anti-Imperialist League, which campaigned against the treaty, distributing pamphlets, petitioning Congress, and holding rallies. The League's criticisms reflected a conviction that imperialism was a repudiation of the moral and political traditions embodied in the Declaration of Independence. The acquisition of overseas colonies, they argued, conflicted with the nation's commitment to liberty and its claim to moral superiority.

But other arguments were less high-minded. Many anti-imperialists objected to expansion on the racist grounds that Filipinos were inferior and unassimilable. Gompers feared that cheap Asian labor would undercut the wages and living standards of American workers. The *San Francisco Call*, representing California-Hawaiian sugar interests, wanted no competition from the Philippines.

Finally, on February 6, 1899, the Senate narrowly ratified the treaty. All but two Republicans supported the pact; most Democrats opposed it, although several voted in favor after William Jennings Bryan suggested that approval was necessary to end the war and detach the Philippines from Spain. Thereafter, he hoped, a congressional resolution would give the Filipinos their independence. But by a single vote, the Republicans defeated a Democratic proposal for Philippine independence once a stable government had been established; the United States would keep the islands.

Bryan attempted to make the election of 1900 a referendum on "the paramount issue" of imperialism, promising to free the Philippines if the Democrats won. But other issues determined the outcome. Some of the most ardent anti-imperialists were conservatives who remained loyal to McKinley because they could not tolerate Bryan's economic policies. Republicans

Mark Twain, *Incident in the Philippines* (1924)

## QUICK REVIEW

### The Anti-Imperialist League

- Central to campaign against the Treaty of Paris (ratified 1899).
- League members saw treaty as a repudiation of American moral and political traditions.
- Many anti-imperialists objected to expansion on racist grounds.

Republicans countered William Jennings Bryan's attempt to make imperialism an issue in 1900 by wrapping themselves in patriotism and the American flag. "Take Your Choice," a cartoon from *Judge*, posed President McKinley raising Old Glory over the Philippines with a disheveled and frantic Bryan chopping down the symbol of American pride and power.

also benefited from the prosperity the country experienced under McKinley after the hard 1890s, and they played on the nationalist emotions evoked by the war, especially by nominating the "hero of San Juan Hill," Theodore Roosevelt, for vice president. Bryan lost again, as in 1896, and under Republican leadership, the United States became an imperial nation.

# IMPERIAL AMBITIONS: THE UNITED STATES AND EAST ASIA, 1899–1917

WHAT WAS the nature of U.S. involvement in Asia?

In 1899, as the United States occupied its new empire, Assistant Secretary of State John Bassett Moore observed that the nation had become "a world power.... Where formerly we had only commercial interests, we now have territorial and political interests as well." American policies to promote these expanded interests focused first on East Asia and Latin America, where the Spanish-American War had provided the United States with both opportunities and challenges. In Asia, the first issue concerned the fate of the Philippines, but looming beyond it were American ambitions in China, where other imperial nations had their own goals.

## THE FILIPINO-AMERICAN WAR

Filipino nationalists, like the Cuban insurgents, were already fighting Spain for their independence before the sudden American intervention. The Filipino leader, Emilio Aguinaldo, welcomed Dewey's naval victory as the sign of a *de facto* alliance with the United States; he then issued a declaration of independence and proclaimed the Philippine Republic. His own troops captured most of Luzon, the Philippines' major island, before the U.S. Army arrived. When the Treaty of Paris provided for U.S. ownership rather than independence, Filipinos felt betrayed. Mounting tensions erupted in a battle between American and Filipino troops outside Manila on February 4, 1899, sparking a long and brutal war.

Ultimately, the United States used nearly four times as many soldiers to suppress the Filipinos as it had to defeat Spain in Cuba and, in a tragic irony, employed many of the same brutal methods for which it had condemned Spain. U.S. military commanders adopted ever harsher measures, often directed at civilians, who were crowded into concentration camps in which perhaps 200,000 died. American troops often made little effort to distinguish between soldiers and noncombatants, viewing all Filipinos with racial antagonism. After reporting one massacre of a thousand men, women, and children, an American soldier declared, "I am in my glory when I can sight my gun on some dark skin and pull the trigger."

A California newspaper defended such actions with remarkable candor: "There has been too much hypocrisy about this Philippine business.... Let us all be frank. WE DO NOT WANT THE FILIPINOS. WE DO WANT THE PHILIPPINES. All of our troubles in this annexation matter have been caused by the presence in the Philippine Islands of the Filipinos.... The more of them killed the better. It seems harsh. But they must yield before the superior race."

Other Americans denounced the war. The Anti-Imperialist League revived, citing the war as proof of the corrosive influence of imperialism on the nation's morals and principles. Women figured prominently in mass meetings and lobbying efforts to have the troops returned, their moral stature further undercutting the rationale for colonial wars. By 1902, the realities of imperial policy—including American casualties far exceeding those of the Spanish-American War—disillusioned most of those who had clamored to save Cuba.

By that time, however, the American military had largely suppressed the rebellion, and the United States had established a colonial government headed by an American governor general appointed by the president. Filipino involvement in the government was limited on educational and religious grounds. Compared to the brutal war policies, U.S. colonial rule was relatively benign, though paternalistic. William Howard Taft, the first governor general, launched a program that brought the islands new schools and roads, a public health system, and an economy tied closely to both the United States and a small Filipino elite. Independence would take nearly half a century.

## CHINA AND THE OPEN DOOR

America's determined involvement in the Philippines reflected its preoccupation with China. By the mid-1890s, other powers threatened prospects for American commercial expansion in China. Japan, after defeating China in 1895, annexed Formosa (Taiwan) and secured economic privileges in the mainland province of Fukien (Fujian); the major European powers then competed aggressively to claim other areas of China as their own **spheres of influence.**

These developments alarmed the American business community. It was confident that, given an equal opportunity, the United States would prevail in international trade because of its efficient production and marketing systems. But the creation of exclusive spheres of influence limited the opportunity to compete. In early 1898, business leaders organized the Committee on American Interests in China to lobby Washington to promote American trade in the shrinking Chinese market. The committee persuaded the nation's chambers of commerce to petition the McKinley administration to act. This campaign influenced McKinley's interest in acquiring the Philippines, but the Philippines, in the words of Mark Hanna, were only a "foothold"; China was the real target.

In 1899, the government moved to advance American interests in China. Without consulting the Chinese, Secretary of State John Hay asked the imperial powers to maintain an **Open Door** for the commercial and financial activities of all nations within their Chinese spheres of influence. Privately, Hay had already approved a plan to seize a Chinese port for the United States, if necessary to join in the partition of China, but equal opportunity for trade and investment would serve American interests far better. It would avoid the expense of military occupation, avert further domestic criticism of U.S. imperialism, and guarantee a wider sphere for American business.

The other nations replied evasively, except for Russia, which rejected the Open Door concept. In 1900, an antiforeign Chinese nationalist movement known as the Boxers laid siege to the diplomatic quarter in Beijing. The defeat of the Boxer Rebellion by a multinational military force, to which the United States contributed troops, again raised the prospect of a division of China among the colonial powers. Hay sent a second Open Door note, reaffirming "the principle of equal and impartial trade" and respect for China's territorial integrity.

"L'ETAT, C'EST MOI."

President Theodore Roosevelt is portrayed as Louis XIV, a symbol of absolute monarchy who famously declared, "The state, it is I" (L'etat, c'est moi). Roosevelt's opponents complained that his assertive rule upset the constitutional balance of power:

### QUICK REVIEW

**Filipino-American War**
- Filipinos felt betrayed by Treaty of Paris.
- February 4, 1899: fighting between American and Filipino troops sparked war.
- 1902: U.S. colonial rule is established after a brutal war.

**spheres of influence** Regions dominated and controlled by an outside power.

**Open Door** American policy of seeking equal trade and investment opportunities in foreign nations or regions.

Katharine Mullikin Lowry, *Besieged in Pekin* (1900)

**A FAIR FIELD AND NO FAVOR.**
UNCLE SAM: "I'm out for commerce, not conquest."

The United States usually preferred the "annexation of trade" to the annexation of territory. The Open Door policy promised to advance American commercial expansion, but Uncle Sam had to restrain other imperialists with colonial objectives.

**QUICK REVIEW**

**Trade with China**

◆ American business interests lobbied for access to China's markets.

◆ 1899: Secretary of State John Hay calls for an Open Door policy.

◆ Open Door became a central doctrine of American foreign policy.

**Gentlemen's Agreement** A diplomatic agreement in 1907 between Japan and the United States curtailing but not abolishing Japanese immigration.

Despite Hay's notes, China remained a tempting arena for imperial schemes. But the Open Door became a cardinal doctrine of American foreign policy in the twentieth century, a means by which the United States sought to dominate foreign markets. The United States promoted an informal or economic empire, as opposed to the traditional territorial colonial empire identified with European powers. Henceforth, American economic interests expected the U.S. government to oppose any developments that threatened to close other nations' economies to American penetration and to advance "private enterprise" abroad.

## RIVALRY WITH JAPAN AND RUSSIA

At the turn of the twentieth century, both the Japanese and the Russians were more deeply involved in East Asia than was the United States. Japan and Russia expressed little support for the Open Door, which they correctly saw as favoring American interests over their own. But in pursuing their ambitions in China, the two countries came into conflict with each other. Alarmed at the threat of Russian expansion in Manchuria and Korea, Japan in 1904 attacked the Russian fleet at Port Arthur and defeated the Russian army in Manchuria.

American sympathies in the Russo-Japanese War lay with Japan, for the Russians were attempting to close Manchuria to foreign trade. President Theodore Roosevelt privately complained that a reluctant American public opinion meant that "we cannot fight to keep Manchuria open." He welcomed the Japanese attack in the belief that "Japan is playing our game." But he soon began to fear that an overwhelming Japanese victory would threaten American interests as much as Russian expansionism did, so he skillfully mediated an end to the war. In the Treaty of Portsmouth in 1905, Japan won control of Russia's sphere of influence in Manchuria, half the Russian island of Sakhalin, and recognition of its domination of Korea.

The treaty marked Japan's emergence as a great power, but, ironically, it worsened relations with the United States. Anti-American riots broke out in Tokyo. The Japanese people blamed Roosevelt for obstructing further Japanese gains and blocking a Russian indemnity that would have helped Japan pay for the war. Tensions were further aggravated by San Francisco's decision in 1906 to segregate Asian and white schoolchildren. Japan regarded this as a racist insult, and Roosevelt worried that "the infernal fools in California" would provoke war. Finally, he persuaded the city to rescind the school order in exchange for his limiting Japanese immigration, which lay at the heart of California's hostility. Under the **Gentlemen's Agreement,** worked out through a series of diplomatic notes in 1907 and 1908, Japan agreed to deny passports to workers trying to come to the United States, and the United States promised not to prohibit Japanese immigration overtly or completely.

The United States and Japan entered into other agreements aimed at calming their mutual suspicions in East Asia but failed to mend the deteriorating relationship.

Increasingly, Japan began to exclude American trade from its territories in East Asia and to press for further control over China. Elihu Root, Roosevelt's secretary of state, insisted that the Open Door and American access had to be maintained but asserted also that the United States did not want to be "a protagonist in a controversy in China with Russia and Japan or with either of them." The problem was that the United States could not sustain the Open Door without becoming a protagonist in China. This paradox, and the unwillingness to commit military force, would plague American foreign policy in Asia for decades.

# IMPERIAL POWER: THE UNITED STATES AND LATIN AMERICA, 1899–1917

**HOW DID** Latin Americans respond to U.S. intervention in the region?

In Latin America, where no major powers directly challenged American objectives as Japan and Russia did in Asia, the United States was more successful in exercising imperial power (see Map 22–3). In the two decades after the Spanish-American War, the United States intervened militarily in Latin America no fewer than 20 times to promote its own strategic and economic interests (see Overview, U.S. Interventions in Latin America, 1891–1933). Intervention at times achieved American goals, but it often ignored the wishes and interests of Latin Americans, provoked resistance and disorder, and aroused lasting ill will.

## U.S. RULE IN PUERTO RICO

Military invasion during the Spanish-American War and the Treaty of Paris brought Puerto Rico under American control, with mixed consequences. A military government improved transportation and sanitation and developed public health and education. But to the dismay of Puerto Ricans, who had been promised that American rule would bestow "the advantages and blessings of enlightened civilization," their political freedoms were curtailed.

In 1900, the United States established a civil government, but it was under U.S. control, with popular participation even less than under Spain. In the so-called Insular Cases (1901), the Supreme Court upheld the authority of Congress to establish an inferior status for Puerto Rico as an "unincorporated territory" without promise of statehood. Disappointed Puerto Ricans pressed to end this colonial status, some advocating independence, others statehood or merely greater autonomy. This division would continue for decades to come. In 1917, the United States granted citizenship and greater political rights to Puerto Ricans, but their island remained an unincorporated territory under an American governor appointed by the president.

Economic development also disappointed most islanders, for American investors quickly gained control of the best land and pursued large-scale sugar production for the U.S. market. The landless peasants struggled to survive as workers on large plantations. Increasingly, Puerto Ricans left their homes to seek work in the United States.

## CUBA AS A U.S. PROTECTORATE

Despite the Teller Amendment, the Spanish-American War did not leave Cuba independent. McKinley opposed independence and distrusted the Cuban rebels. Accordingly, a U.S. military government was established in the island. Only in 1900, when the Democrats made an issue of imperialism, did the McKinley administration move toward permitting a Cuban government and withdrawing American troops. McKinley summoned a Cuban convention to draft a constitution under the direction of the American military governor, General Leonard Wood. Reflecting the continuing U.S. fear of Cuban autonomy, the constitution restricted suffrage on the basis of property and education, leaving few Cubans with the right to vote.

**MAP EXPLORATION** To explore an interactive version of this map, go to
http://www.prenhall.com/goldfield5/map22.3

**PEARSON
myhistorylab**

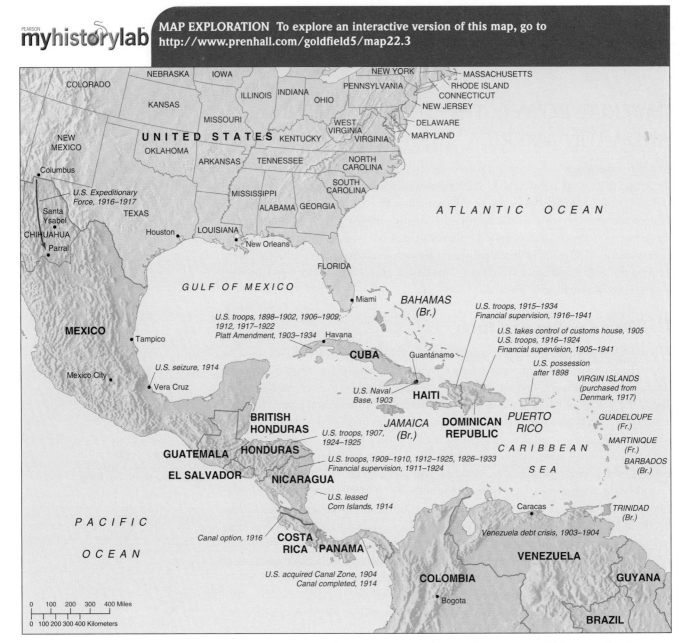

**MAP 22–3    The United States in the Caribbean**    For strategic and economic reasons, the United States repeatedly intervened in the Caribbean in the first three decades of the twentieth century. Such interventions protected the U.S. claim to dominance but often provoked great hostility among Latin Americans.

**What were** the arguments for and against the repeated United States interventions in the Caribbean?

**Platt Amendment**    A stipulation the United States had inserted into the Cuban constitution in 1901 restricting Cuban autonomy and authorizing U.S. intervention and naval bases.

Even so, before removing its troops, the United States wanted to ensure its control over Cuba. It therefore made U.S. withdrawal contingent on Cuba's adding to its constitution the provisions of the **Platt Amendment,** drawn up in 1901 by the U.S. secretary of war. The Platt Amendment restricted Cuba's autonomy in diplomatic relations with other countries and in internal financial policies, required Cuba to lease naval bases to the United States, and most important, authorized U.S. intervention to maintain

## OVERVIEW   U.S. Interventions in Latin America, 1891–1933

| Country | Type of Intervention | Year |
| --- | --- | --- |
| Chile | Ultimatum | 1891–1892 |
| Colombia | Military intervention | 1903 |
| Cuba | Occupation | 1898–1902, 1906–1909, 1912, 1917–1922 |
| Dominican Republic | Military and administrative intervention | 1905–1907 |
|  | Occupation | 1916–1924 |
| Haiti | Occupation | 1915–1934 |
| Mexico | Military intervention | 1914, 1916–1917 |
| Nicaragua | Occupation | 1912–1925, 1927–1933 |
| Panama | Acquisition of Canal Zone | 1904 |
| Puerto Rico | Military invasion and territorial acquisition | 1898 |

order and preserve Cuban independence. As General Wood correctly observed, "There is, of course, little or no independence left Cuba under the Platt Amendment."

During their occupations of Cuba, the Americans modernized its financial system, built roads and public schools, and developed a public-health and sanitation program that eradicated the deadly disease of yellow fever. But most Cubans thought that these material benefits did not compensate for their loss of political and economic independence. The Platt Amendment remained the basis of U.S. policy toward Cuba until 1934.

## THE PANAMA CANAL

The Spanish-American War intensified the long American interest in a canal through Central America to eliminate the lengthy and dangerous ocean route around South America. Its commercial value seemed obvious, but the war emphasized its strategic importance. McKinley declared that a canal was now "demanded by the annexation of the Hawaiian Islands and the prospective expansion of our influence and commerce in the Pacific."

Theodore Roosevelt moved quickly to implement McKinley's commitment to a canal after becoming president in 1901. First, Roosevelt persuaded Britain to renounce its treaty right to a joint role with the United States in any canal venture. Where to build the canal was a problem. One possibility was Nicaragua, where a sea-level canal could be built. Another was Panama, then part of Colombia. A canal through Panama would require an elaborate system of locks. But the French-owned Panama Canal Company had been unsuccessfully trying to build a canal in Panama and was now eager to sell its rights to the project before they expired in 1904.

In 1902, Congress directed Roosevelt to purchase the French company's claims for $40 million and build the canal in Panama if Colombia ceded a strip of land across the isthmus on reasonable terms. Otherwise, Roosevelt was to negotiate with Nicaragua for the alternative route. In 1903, Roosevelt pressed Colombia to sell a canal zone to the United States for $10 million and an annual payment of $250,000. Colombia, however, rejected the proposal, fearing the loss of its sovereignty in Panama and hoping for more money.

**From Then to Now Online**
*The Panama Canal*

Theodore Roosevelt, *Third Annual Message to Congress* (1903)

**QUICK REVIEW**

**Acquisition of the Canal Zone**

◆ Possible canal sites were located in Nicaragua and Panama (then part of Colombia).

◆ 1903: Colombia rejects Roosevelt's offer to purchase canal zone in Panama.

◆ 1903–1904: U.S. forces support Panamanian rebellion against Colombia and take control of canal zone.

**Roosevelt Corollary**    President Theodore Roosevelt's policy asserting U.S. authority to intervene in the affairs of Latin American nations; an expansion of the Monroe Doctrine.

**dollar diplomacy**    The U.S. policy of using private investment in other nations to promote American diplomatic goals and business interests.

Roosevelt was furious. After threatening "those contemptible little creatures" in Colombia, he began writing a message to Congress proposing military action to seize the isthmus of Panama. Instead of using direct force, however, Roosevelt worked with Philippe Bunau-Varilla, a French official of the Panama Canal Company, to exploit long-smoldering Panamanian discontent with Colombia. Roosevelt ordered U.S. naval forces to Panama; from New York, Bunau-Varilla coordinated a revolt against Colombian authority directed by officials of the Panama Railroad, owned by Bunau-Varilla's canal company. The bloodless "revolution" succeeded when U.S. forces prevented Colombian troops from landing in Panama, although the United States was bound by treaty to maintain Colombian sovereignty in the region. Bunau-Varilla promptly signed a treaty accepting Roosevelt's original terms for a canal zone and making Panama a U.S. protectorate, which it remained until 1939. Panamanians themselves denounced the treaty for surrendering sovereignty in the zone to the United States, but the United States took formal control of the canal zone in 1904 and completed construction of the Panama Canal in 1914.

## THE ROOSEVELT COROLLARY

To protect the security of the canal, the United States increased its authority in the Caribbean. The objective was to establish conditions there that would both eliminate any pretext for European intervention and promote American control over trade and investment. The inability of Latin American nations to pay their debts to foreign lenders raised the possibility of European intervention, as evidenced by a German and British blockade of Venezuela in 1903 to secure repayment of debts to European bankers. "If we intend to say hands off to the powers of Europe," Roosevelt concluded, "then sooner or later we must keep order ourselves."

Toward that end, in 1904, Roosevelt announced a new policy, the so-called **Roosevelt Corollary** to the Monroe Doctrine. "Chronic wrongdoing," he declared, would cause the United States to exercise "an international police power" in Latin America. The Monroe Doctrine had expressed American hostility to European intervention in Latin America; the Roosevelt Corollary attempted to justify U.S. intervention and authority in the region. Roosevelt invoked his corollary immediately, imposing American management of the debts and customs duties of the Dominican Republic in 1905. Commercial rivalries and political intrigue in that poor nation had created disorder, which Roosevelt suppressed for both economic and strategic reasons. Financial insolvency was averted, popular revolution prevented, and possible European intervention forestalled.

Latin Americans vigorously resented the United States' unilateral claim to authority. By 1907, the so-called Drago Doctrine (named after Argentina's foreign minister) was incorporated into international law, prohibiting armed intervention to collect debts. Still, the United States would continue to invoke the Roosevelt Corollary to advance its interests in the hemisphere.

## DOLLAR DIPLOMACY

Roosevelt's successor as president, William Howard Taft, hoped to promote U.S. interests in less confrontational ways. He proposed "substituting dollars for bullets"—using government action to encourage private American investments in Latin America to supplant European interests, promote development and stability, and earn profits for American bankers. Under this **dollar diplomacy,** American investments in the Caribbean increased dramatically during Taft's presidency from 1909 to 1913, and the State Department helped arrange for American bankers to establish financial control over Haiti and Honduras.

THE BIG STICK IN THE CARIBBEAN SEA

The Big Stick in the Caribbean Sea
The Roosevelt Corollary proclaimed the intention of the United States to police Latin America. Enforcement came, as this cartoon shows, with Roosevelt and subsequent presidents sending the U.S. Navy to one Caribbean nation after another.

But Taft did not shrink from employing military force to protect American property or to establish the conditions he thought necessary for American investments. In fact, Taft intervened more frequently than Roosevelt had, with Nicaragua a major target. In 1909, Taft sent U.S. troops there to aid a revolution fomented by an American mining corporation and to seize the Nicaraguan customs houses. Under the new government, American bankers then gained control of Nicaragua's national bank, railroad, and customs service. To protect these arrangements, U.S. troops were again dispatched in 1912. To control popular opposition to the American client government, the marines remained in Nicaragua for two decades.

Dollar diplomacy increased American power and influence in the Caribbean and tied underdeveloped countries to the United States economically and strategically. By 1913, American investments in the region reached $1.5 billion, and Americans had captured more than 50 percent of the foreign trade of Costa Rica, Cuba, the Dominican Republic, Guatemala, Haiti, Honduras, Nicaragua, and Panama. But this policy failed to improve conditions for most Latin Americans. U.S. officials remained primarily concerned with promoting American control and extracting American profits from the region. Not surprisingly, dollar diplomacy proved unpopular in Latin America.

## WILSONIAN INTERVENTIONS

Taking office in 1913, the Democrat Woodrow Wilson repudiated the interventionist policies of his Republican predecessors. He promised that the United States would "never again seek one additional foot of territory by conquest" but would instead work to promote "human rights, national integrity, and opportunity" in Latin America.

Nonetheless, Wilson soon became the most interventionist president in American history. Convinced that the United States had to expand its exports and investments abroad and that U.S. dominance of the Caribbean was strategically necessary, he also held the racist belief that Latin Americans were inferior and needed paternalistic guidance from the United States. In providing that guidance, through military force if necessary,

**QUICK REVIEW**

**American Economic Involvement in Latin America**

- 1913: U.S. investment in region reaches 1.5 billion.

- Americans captured large share of Latin America's foreign trade.

- American investment failed to improve conditions for most Latin Americans.

Wilson came close to assuming that American principles and objectives were absolutes, and that different cultural traditions and national aspirations were simply wrong.

**Caribbean interventions.** In 1915, Wilson ordered U.S. marines to Haiti. They went to restore order and preserve "gravely menaced" American interests. The United States saved and even enhanced those interests by establishing a protectorate over Haiti and drawing up a constitution that increased U.S. property rights and commercial privileges. The U.S. Navy selected a new Haitian president, granting him nominal authority over a client government. Real authority, however, rested with the American military, which controlled Haiti until 1934, protecting the small elite who cooperated with American interests and exploited their own people.

Wilson also intervened elsewhere in the Caribbean. In 1916, when the Dominican Republic refused to cede control of its finances to U.S. bankers, Wilson ordered the marines to occupy the country. The marines ousted Dominican officials, installed a military government to rule "on behalf of the Dominican government," and ran the nation until 1924. In 1917, the United States intervened in Cuba, which remained under American control until 1922.

**Interfering with Mexico.** Wilson also involved himself in the internal affairs of Mexico. The lengthy dictatorship of Porfirio Díaz had collapsed in 1911 in revolutionary disorder. The popular leader Francisco Madero took power and promised democratic and economic reforms that alarmed both wealthy Mexicans and foreign investors, particularly Americans. In 1913, General Victoriano Huerta seized control in a brutal counterrevolution backed by the landed aristocracy and foreign interests. Appalled by the violence of Huerta's power grab and aware that opponents had organized to reestablish constitutional government, Wilson refused to recognize the Huerta government.

Wilson authorized arms sales to the Constitutionalist forces led by Venustiano Carranza, pressured Britain and other nations to deprive Huerta of foreign support, and blockaded the Mexican port of Vera Cruz. In 1914 Wilson exploited a minor incident to have the marines attack and occupy Vera Cruz. This assault damaged his image as a promoter of peace and justice, and even Carranza and the Constitutionalists denounced the American occupation as unwarranted aggression. After, Carranza toppled Huerta, Wilson shifted his support to Francisco ("Pancho") Villa, who seemed more susceptible to American guidance. But Carranza's growing popular support in Mexico and Wilson's preoccupation with World War I in Europe finally led the United States to grant de facto recognition to the Carranza government in October 1915.

Villa then began terrorizing New Mexico and Texas, hoping to provoke an American intervention that would undermine Carranza. In 1916, Wilson ordered troops under General John J. Pershing to pursue Villa into Mexico, leading Carranza to fear a permanent U.S. occupation of northern Mexico. Soon the American soldiers were fighting the Mexican army rather than Villa's bandits. On the brink of full-fledged war, Wilson finally ordered U.S. troops to withdraw in January 1917 and extended full recognition to the Carranza government. Wilson lamely defended these steps as showing that the United States had no intention of imposing on Mexico "an order and government of our own choosing." That had been Wilson's original objective, however. His aggressive tactics had not merely failed but also embittered relations with Mexico.

**QUICK REVIEW**

**Woodrow Wilson and Mexico**

- Initially supported Venustiano Carranza and the Constitutionalists.
- Switched to support of Francisco "Pancho" Villa when Carranza proved too independent.
- Ended up fighting both Villa and Carranza.
- Extended full recognition to Carranza's government in January 1917.

## CONCLUSION

By the time of Woodrow Wilson's presidency, the United States had been expanding its involvement in world affairs for half a century. Several themes had emerged from this activity: increasing American domination of the Caribbean, continuing interest in East Asia, the creation of an overseas empire, and the evolution of the United States into a major world power. Underlying these developments were an uneasy mixture of ideas and objectives. The American involvement in the world reflected a traditional, if often misguided, sense of national rectitude and mission. Generous humanitarian impulses vied with ugly racist prejudices as Americans sought both to help other peoples and to direct them toward U.S. concepts of religion, sanitation, capitalist development, and public institutions. American motives ranged from ensuring national security and competing with European colonial powers to the conviction that the United States had to expand its economic interests abroad. But if imperialism, both informal and at times colonial, brought Americans greater wealth and power, it also increased tensions in Asia and contributed to anti-American hostility and revolutionary ferment in Latin America. It also entangled the United States in the Great Power rivalries that would ultimately result in two world wars.

# SUMMARY

**WHAT ARGUMENTS** were made in favor of American expansion in the late nineteenth century?

**The Roots of Imperialism** The United States had a long tradition of expansion across the continent; now America embarked on building an overseas empire. Some Americans favored acquiring and exploiting colonies; others wanted an empire based on trade and investments; still others advocated the United States exporting its ideas and institutions. Social Darwinism, Protestant evangelism, and naval expansion were all rationales for America becoming a world power.

**WHAT ROLE** did public opinion play in the emergence of American imperialism?

**First Steps** Despite the growing pro-imperialist arguments, America was generally passive toward foreign affairs until the end of the nineteenth century. The purchase of Alaska from Russia, the growing American commercial influence in Hawaii, and the assertion of hemispheric domination in Latin America demonstrated America's increasingly assertive national policy throughout the late 1800s.

**WHAT WERE** the most important consequences of the Spanish-American War?

**The Spanish-American War** The war originated in Cuba's quest for independence from Spain. Spain's brutality in suppressing the revolt prompted American sympathy; the sensationalist yellow press fanned the flames for war. The Spanish-American War made America an imperialist nation; the Battle of Manila Bay gave America a foothold in the Philippines; Hawaii was annexed as part of America's "Manifest Destiny"; and a short campaign in Cuba resulted in the defeat of Spanish

troops there. The Treaty of Paris gave America Puerto Rico and Guam and set the stage for the acquisition of the Philippines; anti-imperialists questioned national goals and America's commitment to liberty and freedom.

**WHAT WAS** the nature of U.S. involvement in Asia?

**Imperial Ambitions: The United States and East Asia, 1899–1917** The Filipino-American War resulted from the betrayed hope of the Filipino people for independence following the Treaty of Paris. A brutal war fought to put down rebellion resulted in America's establishing a colonial government in the Philippines. America's involvement in the Philippines reflected its interest in China; European nations and Japan claimed areas of influence in China, limiting America's options to develop trade. Involvement in China brought the United States into conflict with Japan and Russia; Japan's emergence as a great power saw growing discord between the two countries.

**HOW DID** Latin Americans respond to U.S. intervention in the region?

**Imperial Power: The United States and Latin America, 1899–1917** Following the Spanish-American War, America often intervened in Latin America to promote its own strategic and economic interests; trade expanded and ill will increased. Puerto Rico became a territory, Cuba, a U.S. protectorate, and land in Panama was acquired to build a canal; each was part of America's exercise of imperial power. President Theodore Roosevelt's Corollary to the Monroe Doctrine announced America's role as a policeman and debt collector; President Taft attempted dollar diplomacy; President Wilson intervened in the Caribbean, and his tactics in Mexico created lasting ill will.

# WHERE TO LEARN MORE

**Mission Houses, Honolulu, Hawaii.** Built between 1821 and 1841, these buildings were homes and shops of missionaries sent to Hawaii by the American Board of Commissioners for Foreign Missions. Their exhibits include furnishings and memorabilia of a group important in developing American ties with Hawaii. www.missionhouses.org

**Funston Memorial Home, Iola, Kansas.** Operated as a museum by the Kansas State Historical Society, this is the boyhood home of General Frederick Funston, prominent in the Spanish-American War and the Filipino-American War. For a virtual tour, together with military information, political cartoons, Roosevelt correspondence, and Funston links, see http://skyways.lib.ks.us/museums/funston

**James G. Blaine House, Augusta, Maine.** The Executive Mansion of Maine's governor since 1919, this house was formerly Blaine's home and still contains his study and furnishings from the time he served as secretary of state and U.S. senator. http://www.blainehouse.org

# STUDY RESOURCES

## myhistorylab

For study resources for this chapter, go to www.myhistorylab.com and choose *The American Journey*. You will find a wealth of study and review material for this chapter, including pre- and post-tests, customized study plan, key term review flash cards, interactive map and document activities, and documents for analysis.

# REVIEW QUESTIONS

1. After the Spanish-American War, General Leonard Wood asserted that Cubans believed that their American "liberators" were "still their faithful friends." Why might Cubans not have agreed with Wood?

2. What factors, old and new, shaped American foreign policy in the late nineteenth century? How were they interrelated?

3. How were individual politicians and diplomats able to affect America's foreign policy? How were they constrained by governmental institutions, private groups, and public opinion?

4. To what extent was the United States' emergence as an imperial power a break from, as opposed to a culmination of, its earlier policies and national development?

5. How effective were U.S. interventions in Latin America? What were the objectives and consequences?

6. In what ways did the policies of other nations shape the development of American foreign policy?

## KEY TERMS

**Dollar diplomacy** (p. 672)
**Gentlemen's Agreement** (p. 668)
**Imperialism** (p. 654)
**Mahanism** (p. 655)
**Open Door** (p. 667)
**Pan American Union** (p. 659)

**Platt Amendment** (p. 670)
**Roosevelt Corollary** (p. 672)
**Spheres of Influence** (p. 667)
**Teller Amendment** (p. 662)
**Yellow press** (p. 661)

# 23

# America and the Great War

Women war workers in an engineering shop, 1917

WAGING NEUTRALITY *(page 681)*

**WHY WERE** Americans so reluctant to get involved in World War I?

WAGING WAR IN AMERICA *(page 686)*

**HOW DID** the war effort threaten civil liberties?

WAGING WAR AND PEACE ABROAD *(page 691)*

**WHAT HOPES** did Wilson have for the Treaty of Versailles?

WAGING PEACE AT HOME *(page 697)*

**WHAT CHALLENGES** did America face in the aftermath of the war?

*The present German submarine warfare against commerce is a warfare against mankind. . . . It is a war against all nations. . . . Each nation must decide for itself how it will meet it. . . . There is one choice we cannot make, we are incapable of making: we will not choose the path of submission and suffer the most sacred rights of our nation and our people to be ignored or violated. . . . The world must be made safe for democracy. Its peace must be planted upon the tested foundations of political liberty.*

Excerpted from President Woodrow Wilson's Request for Declaration of War, April 2, 1917. Woodrow Wilson Presidential Library

*If it is important for us to speak and vote our convictions in matters of internal policy, though we may unfortunately be in disagreement with the President, it is infinitely more important for us to speak and vote our convictions when the question is one of peace or war, certain to involve the lives and fortunes of many of our people and, it may be, the destiny of all of them and of the civilized world as well.*

*Mr. President, many of my colleagues on both sides of this floor have from day to day offered for publication in the Record messages and letters received from their constituents. I have received some 15,000 letters and telegrams [and] 9 out of 10 are an unqualified endorsement of my course in opposing war with Germany. . . .*

*The poor, sir, who are the ones called upon to rot in the trenches, have no organized power, have no press to voice their will upon the questions of peace or war; but, oh, Mr. President, at some time they will be heard.*

*The failure to treat the belligerent nations of Europe alike . . . is wholly accountable for our present dilemma. We should not seek to hide our blunder behind the smoke of battle to inflame the mind of our people by half truths into a frenzy of war in order that they may never appreciate the real cause of it until it is too late. I do not believe that our national honor is served by such a course.*

Excerpts from Wisconsin Senator Robert M. La Follette's three-hour speech opposing the war, April 4, 1917—Congressional Record—Senate, April 4, 1917, 224–225.

PEARSON
**myhistorylab**

**Personal Journeys Online**

- Jane Addams, *Peace and Bread in Time of War,* **1922. Describing the transition of President Wilson from an advocate of peace to one of war.**

- **Letter from former president Theodore Roosevelt to Sir Edward Grey, 1915.**

- **Promoting American preparedness and support of the Allies.**

**ESCORTED BY THE U.S. CAVALRY** on the evening of April 2, 1917, Woodrow Wilson drove through a misty rain eerily illuminated by searchlights down Pennsylvania Avenue to Capitol Hill to deliver his war address. Throughout the day the Emergency Peace Federation had frantically lobbied Congress, but sentiment in both houses was growing for war. When Wilson promised to make the world "safe for democracy," many members of Congress, waving small American flags, broke into cheers, and pro-war Senator Henry Cabot Lodge personally congratulated Wilson.

Although widely recognized for his oratorical talents, Senator La Follette proved unable to sway the forces for war in Congress. Indeed, his speech aroused such anger in the Senate chamber that he was handed a noose as he exited the room. Both the Senate and the House unanimously supported Wilson's request and the United States entered the war on April 6. Denounced in the press, Senator La Follette and his family were ostracized for his anti-war views, providing a sobering indication of the treatment Americans would face who dared to oppose the war against Germany.

## CHRONOLOGY

| | |
|---|---|
| **1914** World War I begins in Europe. | East St. Louis race riot erupts. |
| President Woodrow Wilson declares U.S. neutrality. | Bolshevik Revolution occurs in Russia. |
| **1915** Germany begins submarine warfare. | **1918** Wilson announces his Fourteen Points. |
| *Lusitania* is sunk. | Sedition Act is passed. |
| Woman's Peace Party is organized. | Eugene Debs is imprisoned. |
| **1916** Gore-McLemore resolutions are defeated. | The United States intervenes militarily in Russia. |
| Sussex Pledge is issued. | Armistice ends World War I. |
| Preparedness legislation is enacted. | **1919** Paris Peace Conference is held. |
| Woodrow Wilson is reelected president. | Steel, coal, and other strikes occur. |
| **1917** The February Revolution ends tsarist regime in Russia. | Red Scare breaks out. |
| Germany resumes unrestricted submarine warfare. | Prohibition amendment is adopted. |
| The United States declares war on Germany. | Wilson suffers a massive stroke. |
| Selective Service Act establishes the military draft. | **1920** Palmer Raids round up radicals. |
| Espionage Act is passed. | League of Nations is defeated in the U.S. Senate. |
| Committee on Public Information, War Industries Board, Food Administration, and other mobilization agencies are established. | Woman suffrage amendment is ratified. |
| | U.S. troops are withdrawn from Russia. |
| American Expeditionary Force arrives in France. | Warren Harding is elected president. |
| | **1921** United States signs a separate peace treaty with Germany. |

Two years later on July 10, 1919, Wilson made the same journey down Pennsylvania Avenue to Capitol Hill. He asked the Senate to ratify a peace treaty that most Americans favored and that he promised would prevent future wars. But Wilson's reception in the Senate was chilly; some even refused to stand when he entered the room and many others received the address in silence. The Senate ultimately rejected the treaty and Wilson's peace.

Between these two presidential appearances, Americans experienced the horrors of the Great War, confronting and overcoming challenges but also sacrificing some of their national ideals and aspirations. Not only was the war the United States' first major military conflict on foreign soil, but it also changed American life.

Many of the changes, from increased efficiency to Americanization, reflected prewar progressivism, and the war years did promote some reforms. But the war also diverted reform energies into new channels, subordinated generous impulses to attitudes that were more coercive and strengthened the conservative opposition to reform. The results were often reactionary and contributed to a post-war mood that not only curtailed further reform but also helped defeat the peace treaty upon which so much had been gambled. ✦

# WAGING NEUTRALITY

Few Americans were prepared for the Great War that erupted in Europe in August 1914, but fewer still foresaw that their own nation might become involved in it. With near unanimity, they supported neutrality. But American attitudes, decisions, and actions, both public and private, undercut neutrality, and the policies of governments in Berlin, London, and Washington drew the United States into the war.

**WHY WERE** Americans so reluctant to get involved in World War I?

## THE ORIGINS OF CONFLICT

There had been plenty of warning. Since the 1870s, the competing imperial ambitions of the European powers had led to economic rivalries, military expansion, diplomatic

*The Great War* (1914)

maneuvering, and international tensions. A complex system of alliances divided the continent into two opposing blocs. In central Europe, the expansionist Germany of Kaiser Wilhelm II allied itself with the multinational Austro-Hungarian Empire. Confronting them, Great Britain and France entered into alliances with tsarist Russia. A succession of crises threatened this precarious balance of power, and in May 1914, an American diplomat reported anxiously, "There is too much hatred, too many jealousies." He predicted "an awful cataclysm."

The cataclysm began a month later. On June 28, a Serbian terrorist assassinated Archduke Franz Ferdinand, the heir to the Austro-Hungarian throne, in Sarajevo. With Germany's support, Austria declared war on Serbia on July 28. Russia then mobilized its army against Austria to aid Serbia, its Slavic client state. To assist Austria, Germany declared war on Russia and then on Russia's ally, France. Hoping for a quick victory, Germany struck at France through neutral Belgium; in response, Britain declared war on Germany on August 4. Soon Turkey and Bulgaria joined Germany and Austria to form the **Central Powers.** The **Allies**—Britain, France, and Russia—were joined by Italy and Japan.

Mass slaughter enveloped Europe as huge armies battled to a stalemate. The British and French faced the Germans along a line of trenches stretching across France and Belgium from the English Channel to Switzerland. Little movement occurred despite great efforts and terrible casualties from artillery, machine guns, and poison gas. The belligerents subordinated their economies, politics, and cultures to military demands. The Great War, said one German soldier, had become "the grave of nations."

## AMERICAN ATTITUDES

Although the United States had also competed for markets, colonies, and influence, few Americans had expected this calamity. Most believed that the United States had no vital interest in the war and would not become involved.

However, neither the American people nor their president stayed strictly neutral. German Americans often sympathized with Germany, and many Irish Americans hoped for a British defeat that would free Ireland from British rule. But most Americans sympathized with the Allies. Ethnic, cultural, and economic ties bound most Americans to the British and French. Politically, too, most Americans felt a greater affinity for the democratic Western Allies—tsarist Russia repelled them—than for Germany's more authoritarian government and society.

Wilson himself admired Britain's culture and government and distrusted Germany's imperial ambitions. Like other influential Americans, Wilson believed that a German victory would threaten America's economic, political, and perhaps even strategic interests. Robert Lansing, counselor of the State Department; Walter Hines Page, the ambassador to England; and Colonel Edward House, Wilson's closest adviser on foreign affairs—all assisted British diplomats, undercut official U.S. protests against British violations of American neutrality, and encouraged Wilson's suspicions of Germany.

British propaganda bolstered American sympathies. British writers, artists, and lecturers depicted the Allies as fighting for civilization against a brutal Germany that mutilated nuns and babies. Although German troops, like most other soldiers, did commit outrages, they were not guilty of the systematic barbarity claimed by Allied propagandists. Britain, however, shaped America's view of the conflict.

Sympathy for the Allies, however, did not mean that Americans favored intervention. Indeed, few Americans doubted that neutrality was the appropriate course and peace the proper goal. The carnage in France solidified their convictions. Wilson was determined to pursue peace as long as his view of national interests allowed.

---

**Central Powers** Germany and its World War I allies in Austria, Turkey, and Bulgaria.

**Allies** In World War I, Britain, France, Russia, and other nations fighting against the Central Powers but not including the United States.

### QUICK REVIEW

**The Outbreak of War**

- June 28, 1914: Archduke Franz Ferdinand assassinated.
- July 28, 1914: Austria declares war on Serbia with German support.
- Chain reaction draws all European powers into the war.

### QUICK REVIEW

**Ties to the Allies**

- Ethnic, cultural, and economic ties bound most Americans to the British and French.
- Americans felt affinity for Western democracies.
- Sympathy with Allies did not mean Americans favored intervention.

## THE ECONOMY OF WAR

Economic issues soon threatened American neutrality. International law permitted neutral nations to sell or ship war matériel to belligerents, and with the economy mired in a recession when the war began, many Americans looked to war orders to spur economic recovery. But the British navy prevented trade with the Central Powers. Only the Allies could buy American goods.

Some Americans worried that this one-sided war trade undermined genuine neutrality. Congress even considered an embargo on munitions. But few Americans supported the idea.

A second economic issue complicated matters. To finance their war purchases, the Allies borrowed from American bankers. Initially, Secretary of State Bryan persuaded Wilson to prohibit loans to the belligerents as "inconsistent with the true spirit of neutrality." But as the importance of the war orders to both the Allies and the American economy became clear, Wilson ended the ban. By April 1917, American loans to the Allies exceeded $2 billion, nearly a hundred times the amount lent to Germany. These financial ties, like the war trade they underwrote, linked the United States to the Allies and convinced Germany that American neutrality was only a formality.

## THE DIPLOMACY OF NEUTRALITY

The same imbalance characterized American diplomacy. Wilson insisted on American neutral rights but acquiesced in British violations of those rights, while sternly refusing to yield on German actions.

When the war began, the United States asked belligerents to respect the 1909 **Declaration of London** on neutral rights. Germany agreed to do so; the British refused. Instead, skirting or violating established procedures, Britain blockaded Germany, mined the North Sea, and forced neutral ships into British ports to search their cargoes and confiscate material deemed useful to the German war effort. Wilson branded Britain's blockade illegal and unwarranted, but by October he had conceded many of America's neutral rights in order to avoid conflict with Britain.

**Declaration of London** Statement drafted by an international conference in 1909 to clarify international law and specify the rights of neutral nations.

The British then prohibited food and other products that Germany had imported during peacetime, thereby interfering further with neutral shipping. But when the Wilson administration finally protested, it undermined its own position by noting that "imperative necessity" might justify a violation of international law. This statement virtually authorized the British to violate American rights.

**Submarine warfare.**   This policy tied the United States to the British war effort and provoked a German response. With its army stalemated on land and its navy no match for Britain's, Germany decided in February 1915 to use its submarines against Allied shipping in a war zone around the British Isles. Neutral ships risked being sunk by mistake, partly because British ships illegally flew neutral flags. Germany maintained that the blockade and the acquiescence of neutral countries in British violations of international law made submarine warfare necessary.

In May 1915, a German submarine sank a British passenger liner, the *Lusitania*. It had been carrying arms, and the German embassy had warned Americans against traveling on the ship, but the loss of life—1,198 people, including 128 Americans—caused Americans to condemn Germany. Yet only six of a thousand editors surveyed called for war, and even the combative Theodore Roosevelt estimated that 98 percent of Americans still opposed war. Wilson saw that he had to "carry out the double wish of our people, to maintain a firm front in respect of what we demand of Germany and yet do nothing that might by any possibility involve us in the war."

**QUICK REVIEW**

**Anglo-American Ties**

- 1915: U.S. gives tacit support to British naval blockade of Germany.
- May 1915: German submarine sinks the *Lusitania*.
- Americans demanded a tough stand against Germany, but did not want to be drawn into the war.

***Sussex* Pledge**    Germany's pledge during World War I not to sink merchant ships without warning, on the condition that Britain also observe recognized rules of international laws.

**preparedness**    Military buildup in preparation for possible U.S. participation in World War I.

This was a difficult stance. Wilson demanded that Germany abandon its submarine campaign. His language was so harsh that Bryan resigned, warning that by requiring more of Germany than of Britain, the president violated neutrality and threatened to draw the nation into war. Bryan protested Britain's use of American passengers as shields to protect contraband cargo and proposed prohibiting Americans from traveling on belligerent ships. His proposal gained support in the South and West and was introduced as a resolution in both the Senate and the House in February 1916.

Wilson moved to defeat the resolutions, insisting that they impinged on presidential control of foreign policy and on America's neutral rights. In truth, the resolutions abandoned no vital national interest and offered to prevent another provocative incident. Moreover, neither law nor tradition gave Americans the right to travel safely on belligerent ships. Wilson's assertion of such a right committed him to a policy that could only lead to conflict.

Arguments over submarine warfare climaxed in April 1916. A German submarine torpedoed the French ship *Sussex*, injuring four Americans. Wilson threatened to break diplomatic relations if Germany did not abandon unrestricted submarine warfare against all merchant vessels, enemy as well as neutral. This threat implied war. Germany promised not to sink merchant ships without warning but made its ***Sussex* Pledge** contingent on the United States' requiring Britain also to adhere to "the rules of international law universally recognized before the war." Peace for America would depend on the British adopting a course they had already rejected. Wilson's diplomacy had left the nation's future at the mercy of others.

## The Battle over Preparedness

The threat of war sparked a debate over military policy. Theodore Roosevelt and a handful of other politicians, mostly northeastern Republicans convinced that Allied victory was in the national interest, advocated what they called **preparedness**, a program to expand the armed forces and establish universal military training. Conservative business groups also joined the agitation. The National Security League, consisting of eastern bankers and industrialists, combined demands for preparedness with attacks on progressive reforms.

But most Americans, certain that their nation would not join the bloody madness, opposed expensive military preparations. Many supported the peace movement. Most opponents agreed that military spending would undermine domestic reform and raise taxes while enriching arms merchants and financiers.

Wilson also opposed preparedness initially, but he reversed his position when the submarine crisis with Germany intensified. He also began to champion military expansion lest Republicans accuse him in the 1916 election of neglecting national defense.

## The Election of 1916

Wilson's preparedness plans stripped the Republicans of one issue in 1916, and his renewed support of progressive reforms (see Chapter 21) helped to hold Bryan Democrats in line. Wilson continued his balancing act in the campaign itself, at first stressing Americanism and preparedness but then emphasizing peace. The slogan "He Kept Us Out of War" appealed to the popular desire for peace, and the Democratic campaign became one long peace rally.

The Republicans were divided. They had hoped to regain their progressive members after Roosevelt urged the Progressive Party to follow him back into the GOP. But many joined the Democratic camp instead, including several Progressive Party leaders, who endorsed Wilson for having enacted the party's demands of 1912. Roosevelt's frenzied interventionism had alienated many midwestern Republicans opposed to preparedness

A preparedness parade winds its way through Mobile, Alabama, on July 4, 1916. By 1916, President Wilson, invoking the spirit of patriotism, had given his support to the preparedness program of military expansion.

University of South Alabama Achives.

and cost him any chance of gaining the nomination for himself. Instead, the GOP nominated Charles Evans Hughes, a Supreme Court justice and former New York governor. The platform denounced Wilson's "shifty expedients" in foreign policy and promised "strict and honest neutrality." Unfortunately for Hughes, Roosevelt's attacks on Wilson for not pursuing a war policy persuaded many voters that the GOP was a war party.

The election was the closest in decades (see Map 23–1). When California narrowly went for Wilson, it decided the contest. The results reflected sectional differences, with the South and West voting for Wilson and most of the Northeast and Midwest for Hughes. The desire for peace, all observers concluded, had determined the election.

## DESCENT INTO WAR

Still, Wilson knew that war loomed, and he made a last effort to avert it. In 1915 and 1916, he had tried to mediate the European conflict, using Colonel House as a secret intermediary. Now he again appealed for an end to hostilities. In January 1917, he sketched out the terms of what he called a "peace without victory." Anything else, he warned, would only lead to another war. The new world order should be based on national equality and **self-determination,** arms reductions, freedom of the seas, and an international organization to ensure peace. It was a distinctly American vision.

Neither the Allies nor the Central Powers were interested. Each side had sacrificed too much to settle for anything short of outright victory. To break the deadlock, Germany resumed unrestricted submarine warfare. German generals believed that even if the United States declared war, it could do little more in the short run to injure Germany than it was already doing. German submarines, they hoped, would end the war by cutting the Allies off from U.S. supplies before the United States could send an army to Europe. On January 31, Germany announced its decision to unleash its submarines in a broad war zone.

**self-determination**  The right of a people or a nation to decide its own political allegiance or form of government without external influence.

### QUICK REVIEW

#### The Zimmermann Note

- Proposed alliance between Germany and Mexico in event of war between Germany and United States.

- Mexico would recover territory in Texas, New Mexico, and Arizona.

- Publication of note increased support for American intervention.

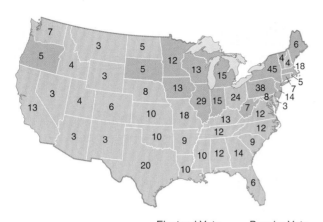

| | Electoral Vote (%) | Popular Vote (%) |
|---|---|---|
| **WOODROW WILSON (Democrat)** | **277 (52)** | **9,127,695 (49.4)** |
| Charles E. Hughes (Republican) | 254 (48) | 8,533,507 (46.2) |
| A.L. Benson (Socialist) | – | 585,113 (3.2) |
| Other parties (Socialist Labor, Prohibition) | – | 233,909 (1.3) |

MAP 23–1 **The Election of 1916** Woodrow Wilson won reelection in 1916, despite a reunified Republican Party, by sweeping the South and West on campaign appeals to peace and progressive reform.

**How was** Woodrow Wilson able to win reelection in 1916 despite the reunification of the Republican party?

**Wilson commits to war.** Wilson was now virtually committed to a war many Americans opposed. He broke diplomatic relations with Germany and asked Congress to arm American merchant vessels. When the Senate refused, Wilson invoked an antipiracy law of 1819 and armed the ships anyway. Although no American ships had yet been sunk, he also ordered the naval gun crews to fire at submarines on sight. The secretary of the navy warned Wilson that these actions violated international law and were a step toward war; Wilson called his policy "armed neutrality." Huge rallies across America demanded peace.

Several developments soon shifted public opinion. On March 1, Wilson released an intercepted message from the German foreign minister, Arthur Zimmermann, to the German minister in Mexico. It proposed that in the event of war between the United States and Germany, Mexico should ally itself with Germany; in exchange, Mexico would recover its "lost territory in Texas, New Mexico, and Arizona." The Zimmermann note produced a wave of hostility toward Germany and increased support for intervention in the war, especially in the Southwest, which had opposed involvement. When submarines sank four American freighters in mid-March, anti-German feeling broadened.

On April 2, 1917, Wilson delivered his war message, declaring that neutrality was no longer possible, given Germany's submarine "warfare against mankind." To build support for joining a war that most people had long regarded with revulsion and as alien to American interests, Wilson set forth the nation's war goals as simple and noble. The United States would not fight for conquest or domination but for "the ultimate peace of the world and for the liberation of its peoples." After vigorous debate, the Senate passed the war resolution 82 to 6 and the House 373 to 50. On April 6, 1917, the United States officially entered the Great War.

# WAGING WAR IN AMERICA

HOW DID the war effort threaten civil liberties?

Mobilizing for military intervention was a massive undertaking. The government reorganized the economy to emphasize centralized management, developed policies to control public opinion and suppress dissent, and transformed the role of government itself.

## MANAGING THE WAR ECONOMY

Surveying the nation's economy in May 1917, Secretary of War Newton Baker noted that war no longer involved merely soldiers and weapons. "It is the conflict of smokestacks now, the combat of the driving wheel and the engine." To harness those factories and machines for the war, federal and state governments developed a complex structure of agencies and controls for every sector of the economy, from industry and agriculture to transportation and labor (see Overview Major Government Wartime Agencies). Supervised by the Council of National Defense, these agencies shifted resources to war-related enterprises, increased production of goods and services, and improved transportation and distribution.

## OVERVIEW   Major Government Wartime Agencies

| Agency | Purpose |
| --- | --- |
| War Industries Board | Reorganized industry to maximize wartime production |
| Railroad Administration | Modernized and operated the nation's railroads |
| Food Administration | Increased agricultural production, supervised food distribution and farm labor |
| National War Labor Board | Resolved labor-management disputes, improved labor conditions, and recognized union rights as means to promote production and efficiency |
| Committee on Public Information | Managed propaganda to build public support for the war effort |

**Organizing industry.**   The most important agency was the **War Industries Board (WIB),** established in July 1917 to set industrial priorities, coordinate military purchasing, and supervise business. Led by financier Bernard Baruch, the WIB exercised unprecedented power over industry by setting prices, allocating scarce materials, and standardizing products and procedures to boost efficiency. Yet Baruch was not an industrial dictator; he aimed at business-government integration. The WIB promoted major business interests, helped suspend antitrust laws, and guaranteed huge corporate profits. Some progressives began to see the dangers, and business leaders the advantages, of government economic intervention.

The Railroad Administration also linked business ambitions to the war economy. Under William McAdoo, it operated the nation's railroads as a unified system to move supplies and troops efficiently. Centralized management eliminated competition, permitted improvements in equipment, and brought great profits to the owners but higher prices to the general public.

**Ensuring food supplies.**   Equally effective and far more popular was the Food Administration, headed by Herbert Hoover. Hoover had organized relief supplies for war-torn Belgium and now controlled the production and distribution of food for the United States and its allies. He persuaded millions of Americans to accept meatless and wheatless days, so that the Food Administration could feed military and foreign consumers. Half a million women went door to door to secure food-conservation pledges from housewives. City residents planted victory gardens in parks and vacant lots, and President Wilson even pastured sheep on the White House lawn.

Hoover also worked closely with agricultural processors and distributors, ensuring profits in exchange for cooperation. Farmers profited from the war, too. To encourage production, Hoover established high prices for commodities, and agricultural income rose by 30 percent. State and federal governments provided commercial farmers with sufficient farm labor despite the military draft and competition from high-wage war industries.

**Overseeing labor relations.**   The National War Labor Board supervised labor relations. In exchange for labor's cooperation, this agency guaranteed the rights of unions to organize and bargain collectively. With such support, unions sharply increased their membership. The labor board also encouraged improved working conditions, higher wages, and shorter hours. War contracts stipulated an eight-hour day, and by the end of the war, nearly half the nation's workers had achieved the 48-hour week. Wages rose, too, but often only as fast as inflation. These improvements limited labor disputes during

**War Industries Board (WIB)**   The federal agency that reorganized industry for maximum efficiency and productivity during World War I.

**QUICK REVIEW**

**The War Industries Board**
- Promoted business interests.
- Helped suspend anti-trust laws.
- Guaranteed huge profits.

*Documents*

Anna Howard Shaw, *Woman's Committee of the Council of National Defense* (1917)

the war, and Secretary of War Baker praised labor as "more willing to keep in step than capital." But when such unions as the Industrial Workers of the World did not keep in step, the government suppressed them.

Although these and other government regulatory agencies were dismantled when the war ended, their activities reinforced many long-standing trends in the American economy, from the consolidation of business to the commercialization of agriculture and the organization of labor. They also set a precedent for governmental activism that would prove valuable during the crises of the 1930s and 1940s.

## WOMEN AND MINORITIES: NEW OPPORTUNITIES, OLD INEQUITIES

**Women and war work.** The reorganization of the economy also had significant social consequences, especially for women and African Americans. In response to labor shortages, public officials and private employers exhorted women to join the work force. Women now took jobs previously closed to them. More than 100,000 women worked in munitions plants and 40,000 in the steel industry. Women constituted 20 percent or more of all workers making electrical machinery, leather and rubber goods, and food. They operated drills and lathes, controlled cranes in steel mills, and repaired equipment in machine shops.

Many working women simply shifted to other jobs, where their existing skills earned better wages and benefits. The reshuffling of jobs among white women opened new vacancies for black women in domestic, clerical, and industrial employment. As black women replaced white women in the garment and textile industries, social reformers spoke of "a new day for the colored woman worker." But their optimism was unwarranted. Racial as well as gender segregation continued to mark employment, and wartime improvements were temporary.

**Woman suffrage and prohibition.** The war did help middle-class women reformers achieve two long-sought objectives: woman suffrage and prohibition. Women's support for the war effort prompted more Americans to support woman suffrage. Congress approved the suffrage amendment, which was ratified in 1920. Convinced that abstaining from alcohol would save grain and make workers and soldiers more efficient, Congress also passed the Prohibition amendment, which was ratified in 1919.

**African Americans and war work.** The war also changed the lives of African Americans. The demand for industrial labor caused a huge migration of black people from the rural South, where they had little opportunity, few rights, and no hope. In northern cities, they worked in shipyards, steel mills, and packing houses. Half a million African Americans moved north during the war, doubling and tripling the black populations of Chicago, Detroit, and other industrial cities.

Unfortunately, black people often encountered the kind of racial discrimination and violence in the North that they had hoped to leave behind in the South. Fearful and resentful white people started race riots in northern cities. In East St. Louis,

With women's labor crucial for the war effort, both government agencies and private industry recruited women for factory work. Here, four women, wearing "womanall" worksuits, pause at their jobs at the Westinghouse Electric Company in 1918.

Hagley Museum and Library, Wilmington Delaware.

Illinois, where thousands of black southerners sought defense work, a white mob, in July 1917, murdered at least 39 black people, sparing, as an investigating committee reported, "neither age nor sex in their blind lust for blood."

*Letters from the Great Migration* (1917)

## FINANCING THE WAR

To finance the war, the government borrowed money and raised taxes. Business interests favored the first course, but southern and western progressives argued that taxation was more efficient and equitable and would minimize war profiteering. Despite conservative and business opposition to progressive taxation, the tax laws of 1917 and 1918 established a graduated tax structure with higher taxes on large incomes, corporate profits, and wealthy estates. Conservative opposition, however, would frustrate progressives' hopes for permanent tax reforms.

The government raised two-thirds of the war costs by borrowing. Most of the loans came from banks and wealthy investors, but the government also campaigned to sell **Liberty Bonds** to the general public. Celebrities went to schools, churches, and rallies to persuade Americans to buy bonds as their patriotic duty. "Every person who refuses to subscribe," Secretary of the Treasury McAdoo told a California audience, "is a friend of Germany." Using techniques of persuasion and control from advertising and mass entertainment, the Wilson administration thus enlisted the emotions of loyalty, fear, patriotism, and obedience for the war effort.

**Liberty Bonds**   Interest-bearing certificates sold by the U.S. government to finance the American World War I effort.

## CONQUERING MINDS

The government also tried to promote a war spirit among the American people by establishing propaganda agencies and enacting legislation to control social attitudes and behavior. This program drew from the restrictive side of progressivism: its impulses toward social control, behavior regulation, and nativism. It also reflected the interests of more conservative forces. The Wilson administration adopted this program of social mobilization because many Americans opposed the war.

Black women work in a brickyard for wartime construction. Mobilization opened new jobs for women, but racial subordination and segregation persisted. Black women often performed the hardest and least desirable work.

**Government propaganda.** To rally Americans behind the war effort, Wilson established the **Committee on Public Information (CPI)** under journalist George Creel. Despite its title, the CPI sought to manipulate, not inform, public opinion. The CPI flooded the country with press releases, advertisements, cartoons, and canned editorials. The CPI made newsreels and war movies to capture public attention. It scheduled 75,000 speakers, who delivered a million speeches to 400 million listeners. It hired artists to design posters, professors to write pamphlets in 23 languages, and poets to compose war poems for children.

Other government agencies launched similar campaigns. The Woman's Committee of the Council of National Defense established the Department of Educational Propaganda and Patriotic Education. The agency worked to win over women who opposed the war, particularly in the rural Midwest, West, and South. It formed women's speakers bureaus, developed programs for community meetings at country schools, and distributed millions of pamphlets.

Government propaganda had three themes: national unity, the loathsome character of the enemy, and the war as a grand crusade for liberty and democracy. Obsessed with national unity and conformity, Creel promoted fear, hatred, and prejudice in the name of a triumphant Americanism. Germans were depicted as brutal, even subhuman, rapists and murderers. The campaign suggested that any dissent was unpatriotic, if not treasonous, and dangerous to national survival. This emphasis on unreasoning conformity helped prompt hysterical attacks on German Americans, radicals, and pacifists.

## SUPPRESSING DISSENT

The Wilson administration also suppressed dissent, now officially branded disloyalty. For reasons of their own, private interests helped shape a reactionary repression that tarnished the nation's professed idealistic war goals. The campaign also established unfortunate precedents for the future.

Congress rushed to stifle antiwar sentiment. The **Espionage Act** provided heavy fines and up to 20 years in prison for obstructing the war effort, a vague phrase but "omnipotently comprehensive," warned an Idaho senator who opposed the law. In fact, the Espionage Act became a weapon to crush dissent and criticism. Eventually, Congress passed the still more sweeping **Sedition Act of 1918,** which provided severe penalties for speaking or writing against the draft, bond sales, and war production and for criticizing government personnel or policies.

Postmaster General Albert Burleson banned antiwar or radical newspapers and magazines from the mail. Even more zealous in attacking radicals and presumed subversives was the reactionary attorney general, Thomas Gregory, who made little distinction between traitors and pacifists, war critics, and radicals. Eugene Debs was sentenced to ten years in prison for a "treasonous" speech in which he declared it "extremely dangerous to exercise the right of free speech in a country fighting to make democracy safe in the world." By war's end, a third of the Socialist Party's national leadership was in prison, leaving the party in a shambles.

Gregory also enlisted the help of private vigilantes, including the several hundred thousand members of the reactionary American Protective League, which sought to purge radicals and reformers from the nation's economic and political life. They wiretapped telephones, intercepted private mail, burglarized union offices, broke up German-language newspapers, harassed immigrants, and staged mass raids, seizing thousands of people who they claimed were not doing enough for the war effort.

State and local authorities also suppressed what they saw as antiwar, radical, or pro-German activities. They established 184,000 investigative and enforcement agencies, known as councils of defense or public-safety committees. They encouraged

**Committee on Public Information (CPI)** Government agency during World War I that sought to shape public opinion in support of the war effort through newspapers, pamphlets, speeches, films, and other media.

George Creel, *How We Advertised America* (1920)

*Boy Scouts Support the War Effort* (1917)

**Espionage Act** Law whose vague prohibition against obstructing the nation's war effort was used to crush dissent and criticism during World War I.

**Sedition Act of 1918** Broad law restricting criticism of America's involvement in World War I or its government, flag, military, taxes, or officials.

Eugene Debs, *Statement to the Court* (1918)

Newton D. Baker, *The Treatment of German-Americans* (1918)

Americans to spy on one another, required people to buy Liberty Bonds, and prohibited teaching German in schools or using the language in religious services and telephone conversations. Indeed, suppression of all things German reached extremes. Germanic names of towns, streets, and people were changed; sauerkraut became liberty cabbage, and the hamburger the liberty sandwich. Members of the business community exploited the hysteria to promote their own interests at the expense of farmers, workers, and reformers. On the Great Plains from Texas to North Dakota, the business target was the Nonpartisan League, a radical farm group demanding state control or ownership of banks, grain elevators, and flour mills. Although the League supported the war, oversubscribed bond drives, and had George Creel affirm its loyalty, conservatives depicted it as seditious to block its advocacy of political and economic reforms, including the confiscation of large fortunes to pay for the war. Nebraska's council of defense barred League meetings. Public officials and self-styled patriots broke up the League's meetings and whipped and jailed its leaders.

In the West, business interests targeted labor organizations, especially the Industrial Workers of the World. In Arizona, for example, the Phelps-Dodge Company broke a mine strike in 1917 by depicting the Wobblie miners as bent on war-related sabotage. A vigilante mob, armed and paid by the mining company, seized 1,200 strikers, many of them Wobblies and one-third of them Mexican Americans, and herded them into the desert without food or water.

The government itself assisted the business campaign. It used the army to break loggers' support for the IWW in the Pacific Northwest, and it raided IWW halls across the country in September 1917. The conviction of nearly 200 Wobblies on charges of sedition in three mass trials in Illinois, California, and Kansas crippled the nation's largest industrial union.

In the end, the government was primarily responsible for the war hysteria. It encouraged suspicion and conflict through inflammatory propaganda, repressive laws, and violation of basic civil rights, by supporting extremists who used the war for their own purposes, and by tolerating mob violence against German Americans. This ugly mood would infect the postwar world.

"Beat Back the Hun," a poster to induce Americans to buy Liberty Bonds, demonizes the enemy in a raw, emotional appeal. Liberty bond drives raised the immense sum of $23 billion.

## WAGING WAR AND PEACE ABROAD

While mobilizing the home front, the Wilson administration undertook an impressive military effort to help the Allies defeat the Central Powers. Wilson also struggled to secure international acceptance for his plans for a just and permanent peace.

### THE WAR TO END ALL WARS

When the United States entered the war, the Allied position was dire. The losses from three years of trench warfare had sapped military strength and civilian morale. French soldiers mutinied and refused to continue an assault that had cost 120,000 casualties in five days; the German submarine campaign was devastating the British. On the eastern front, the Russian army had collapsed, and the Russian government had gradually disintegrated after the overthrow of the tsarist regime.

**WHAT HOPES** did Wilson have for the Treaty of Versailles?

**WHERE TO LEARN MORE**

Wisconsin Veterans Museum, Madison, Wisconsin.
http://museum.dva.state.wi.us

**Selective Service Act of 1917**    The law establishing the military draft for World War I.

**WHERE TO LEARN MORE**

National Infantry Museum, Fort Benning, Georgia. www.benningmwr.com/index.cfm

**myhistorylab**

**From Then to Now Online**
*Women and War*

*Documents*

*American Troops in the Trenches* (1918)
Eugene Kennedy, *A "Doughboy" Describes the Fighting Front* (1918)

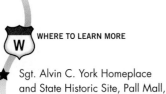

**WHERE TO LEARN MORE**

Sgt. Alvin C. York Homeplace and State Historic Site, Pall Mall, Tennessee. www.alvincyork.org

**Bolshevik**    Member of the Communist movement in Russia that established the Soviet government after the 1917 Russian Revolution.

In May, Congress passed the **Selective Service Act of 1917,** establishing conscription. More than 24 million men eventually registered for the draft, and nearly 3 million entered the army when their numbers were drawn in a national lottery. Almost 2 million more men volunteered, as did more than 13,000 women, who served in the navy and marines. Nearly one-fifth of America's soldiers were foreign-born (Europeans spoke of the "American Foreign Legion"); 367,000 were black. Many Native Americans served with distinction as well; in recognition, Indian veterans were made citizens in 1919, a status extended to all Indians five years later.

Civilians were transformed into soldiers in hastily organized training camps, operated according to progressive principles. Prohibition prevailed in the camps; the poorly educated and largely working-class recruits were taught personal hygiene; worries about sin and inefficiency produced massive campaigns against venereal disease; and immigrants were taught English and American history. Some units were ethnically segregated: At Camp Gordon, Georgia, Italians and Slavs had separate units, with their own officers.

Racial segregation was more rigid, not only in training camps and military units but in assignments as well. The navy assigned black sailors to menial positions, and the army similarly used black soldiers primarily as gravediggers and laborers. But one black combat division was created, and four black regiments fought under French command. France decorated three of these units with its highest citations for valor. White American officers urged the French not to praise black troops, treat black officers as equals, or permit fraternization. But white racism could not diminish the extraordinary record of one of the most famous of the black units in France—the 369th Infantry Regiment, also known as the "Harlem Hellfighters." The 369th spent 191 days in combat and was the first Allied unit to reach the Rhine.

Women were recruited as noncombatant personnel, such as clerks, translators, and switchboard operators, thereby enabling more men to be assigned to combat duty. The navy awarded them equal rank with males performing the same tasks, and they were eligible after the war for veterans benefits. The army was a different story. Although they served in uniform and under military discipline, women had no formal military status, were ineligible for benefits, and often had their skills and contributions devalued.

**Into action in France.**    The first American troops landed in France in June 1917. Months of training, under French direction, then followed as the Americans learned about trench warfare: using bayonets, grenades, and machine guns and surviving poison-gas attacks. Finally in October, the 1st Division, the Big Red One, moved into the trenches.

Full-scale American intervention began in the late spring of 1918 (see Map 23–2). Further savage fighting at Belleau Wood blocked the Germans again, prompting a French officer to declare, "You Americans are our hope, our strength, our life." In July, the AEF helped defeat another German advance, at Rheims. The influx of American troops had tipped the balance toward Allied victory. By July 18, the German chancellor later acknowledged, "even the most optimistic among us knew that all was lost. The history of the world was played out in three days."

**The Russian front.**    In July, Wilson also agreed to commit 15,000 American troops to intervene in Russia. Russia's provisional government had collapsed when the radical **Bolshevik** faction of the communist movement had seized power in November 1917. Under V. I. Lenin, the Bolsheviks signed an armistice with Germany in early 1918, which freed German troops for the summer offensive in France. The Allied interventions were initially designed to reopen the eastern front and later to help overthrow the Bolshevik government.

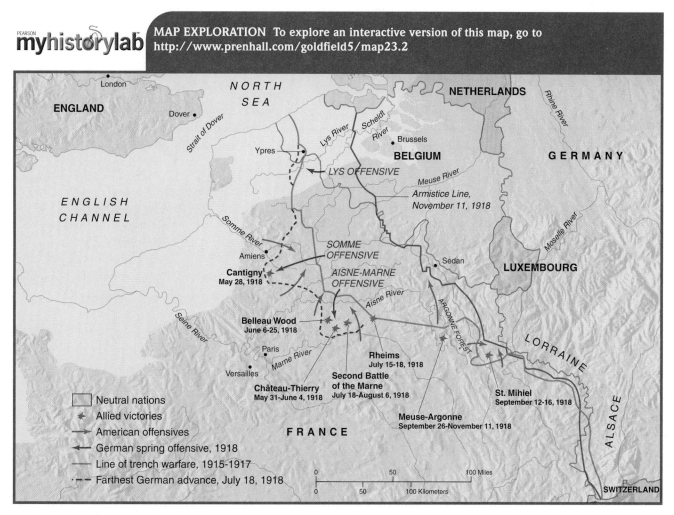

**MAP EXPLORATION** To explore an interactive version of this map, go to
http://www.prenhall.com/goldfield5/map23.2

**MAP 23–2   The Western Front, 1918**   After three years of trench warfare, the arrival of large numbers of American troops in 1918 enabled the Allies to launch an offensive that drove back the Germans and forced an armistice.

**At the** time of the armistice, how far back had the Germans been forced to retreat from their farthest advance?

Lenin's call for the destruction of capitalism and imperialism alarmed the Allied leaders. One Wilson adviser urged the "eradication" of the Russian government. Soon, American and British troops were fighting Russians in an effort to influence Russia's internal affairs. U.S. forces remained in Russia even after Germany surrendered in 1918. They did not leave until 1920. These military interventions failed, but they contributed to Russian distrust of the West.

**The Western front.**   The Allies were more successful on the western front. Having stopped the German offensive in July, they launched their own advance. The decisive battle began in late September when an American army over 1 million strong attacked German trenches in the Argonne Forest. Many Americans were still inexperienced; some had been drafted only in July and had spent more time traveling than training. Nevertheless, they advanced steadily, despite attacks with poison gas and heavy artillery.

The battle for the Argonne raged for weeks. A German general reported that his exhausted soldiers faced Americans who "were fresh, eager for fighting, and brave." But he found their sheer numbers most impressive. Eventually, this massive assault overwhelmed the Germans. Despite severe casualties, the AEF had helped the British and French to

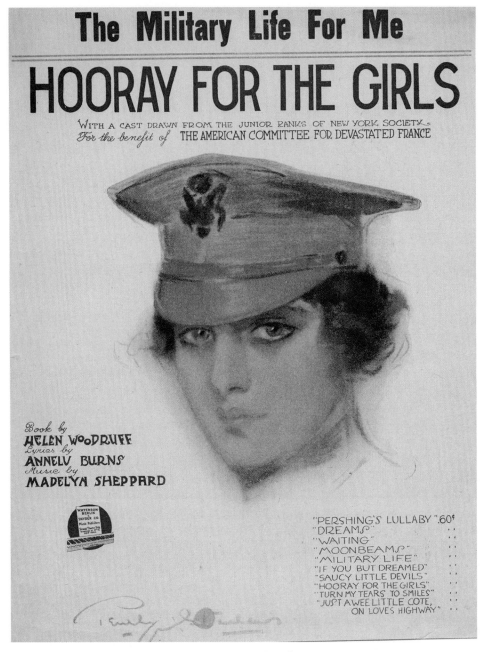

"I want to be a soldier" was this popular song describing women's war-time roles.

defeat the enemy. (See American Views, Letter from Albert Smith, October 15, 1918.) With its allies surrendering, its own army in retreat, and revolution breaking out among the war-weary residents of its major cities, Germany asked for peace. On November 11, 1918, an armistice ended the Great War. More than 115,000 Americans were among the 8 million soldiers and 7 million civilians dead.

## THE FOURTEEN POINTS

The armistice was only a step toward final peace. President Wilson had already enunciated America's war objectives on January 8, 1918, in a speech outlining what became known as the Fourteen Points. In his 1917 war message, Wilson had advocated a more

*Documents*

Woodrow Wilson, *The Fourteen Points* (1918)

democratic world system, and this new speech spelled out how to achieve it. But Wilson also had a political purpose. The Bolsheviks had published the Allies' secret treaties dividing up the expected economic and territorial spoils of the war. Lenin had called for an immediate peace based on the liberation of all colonies, self-determination for all peoples, and the rejection of annexations and punitive indemnities. Wilson's Fourteen Points reassured the American and Allied peoples that they were fighting for more than imperialist gains and offered an alternative to what he called Lenin's "crude formula" for peace.

Eight of Wilson's points proposed creating new nations, shifting old borders, or ensuring self-determination for peoples previously subject to the Austrian, German, or Russian empire. The point about Russia would haunt Wilson after the Allied interventions there began, for it called on all nations to evacuate Russian territory and permit Russia "an unhampered and unembarrassed opportunity for the independent determination of her own political development" under "institutions of her own choosing." Another five points invoked principles to guide international relations: freedom of the seas, open diplomacy instead of secret treaties, reduction of armaments, free trade, and the fair settlement of colonial claims. Wilson's fourteenth and most important point proposed a league of nations to carry out these ideals and ensure international stability.

Wilson and the German government had these principles in mind when negotiating the armistice. The Allies, however, had never explicitly accepted the Fourteen Points, and framing a final peace treaty would be difficult. While Wilson favored a settlement that would promote international stability and economic expansion, he recognized that the Allies sought "to get everything out of Germany that they can." Indeed, after their human and economic sacrifices, Britain and France wanted tangible compensation, not pious principles.

Convinced of the righteousness of his cause, Wilson decided to attend the peace conference in Paris, although no president had ever gone to Europe while in office. But Wilson weakened his position before he even set sail. First, he urged voters to support

### QUICK REVIEW

**Wilson's Fourteen Points**

- Wilson articulated U.S. war aims in his Fourteen Points.
- The Allies did not explicitly support Wilson's program.
- Domestic political failures undermined Wilson's position at the Paris peace conference.

American soldiers advancing through smoke and shattered trees of the Argonne Forest in October 1918. The Great War was a conflict of relentless attrition, marked by the horrors of poison gas, artillery bombardment, pandemic disease, and what one American called the "unburied dead."

U.S. Army Signal Corps. National Archives III-SC 94980.

Democratic candidates in the November 1918 elections to indicate approval of his peace plan. But the electorate, responding primarily to domestic problems like inflation, gave the Republicans control of both houses of Congress. This meant that any treaty would have to be approved by Senate Republicans angry that Wilson had tried to use war and peace for partisan purposes. Second, Wilson refused to consult with Senate Republicans on plans for the peace conference and failed to name important Republicans to the Paris delegation. It was going to be Wilson's treaty, and Republicans would feel no responsibility to approve it.

## THE PARIS PEACE CONFERENCE

The peace conference opened on January 18, 1919. Meeting at the Palace of Versailles, the delegations were dominated by the principal Allied leaders: Wilson of the United States, David Lloyd George of Britain, Georges Clemenceau of France, and Vittorio Orlando of Italy. The Central Powers and Bolshevik Russia were excluded. The treaty would be one-sided except to the extent that Wilson could insist on the liberal terms of the Fourteen Points against French and British intransigence.

For months, the conference debated Wilson's other goals and the Allies' demands for compensation and security. Lloyd George later commented, with reference to the self-righteous Wilson and the assertive Clemenceau, "I think I did as well as might be expected, seated as I was between Jesus Christ and Napoleon Bonaparte." Under protest, Germany signed the **Treaty of Versailles** on June 28, 1919. Its terms were far more severe than Wilson had proposed or Germany had anticipated. Germany had to accept sole responsibility for starting the war, a stipulation that all Germans bitterly resented. It was required to pay huge reparations to the Allies, give up land to France, Poland, Belgium, and Denmark, cede its colonies, limit its army and navy to small self-defense forces, destroy military bases, and promise not to manufacture or purchase armaments.

Wilson gained some acceptance of self-determination. As the German, Austro-Hungarian, Turkish, and Russian empires had collapsed at the end of the war, nationalist groups had proclaimed their independence. On one hand, the peace settlement formally recognized these new nation-states: Poland, Finland, Estonia, Latvia, and Lithuania in eastern Europe and Austria, Hungary, Czechoslovakia, and Yugoslavia in central Europe. On the other hand, France, Italy, Romania, and Japan all annexed territory regardless of the wishes of the inhabitants. Germans were placed under Polish control in Silesia and Czech control in Bohemia. Austria was not allowed to merge with Germany. And the conference sanctioned colonialism by establishing a trusteeship system that enabled France, Britain, and Japan to take over German colonies and Turkish territory.

The Allied leaders endorsed the changes in eastern Europe in part because the new states there were anticommunist and would constitute a barrier against Bolshevism. Communist movements in early 1919 in Germany, Austria, and Hungary caused the Allies to fear that "the Russian idea was still rising in power," and they hoped to isolate and weaken Bolshevik Russia. Allied armies were in Russia during the peace conference, and Wilson and the other leaders agreed to provide further aid to fight the Bolsheviks. This hostility to Russia, like the punitive terms for Germany and the concessions to imperial interests, boded ill for a stable and just postwar order. (see Global Perspectives, War and Revolution: The Bolsheviks and the International Community.)

But Wilson hoped that the final section of the Versailles treaty would resolve the flaws of the agreement by establishing his great international organization to preserve peace: the **League of Nations.** The Covenant, or constitution, of the League was built

**Treaty of Versailles**  The treaty ending World War I and creating the League of Nations.

**League of Nations**  International organization created by the Versailles Treaty after World War I to ensure world stability.

into the treaty. Its crucial feature, Article Ten, bound the member nations to guarantee each other's independence—a provision that was Wilson's concept of collective security. "At least," he told an aide, "we are saving the Covenant, and that instrument will work wonders, bring the blessing of peace, and then when the war psychosis has abated, it will not be difficult to settle all disputes that baffle us now."

# WAGING PEACE AT HOME

Wilson was determined to defeat the opposition to the peace treaty. But many Americans were engaged in their own struggles with the new conditions of a nation suddenly at peace but driven by economic, social, and political conflict. Wilson's battle for the League of Nations would fail tragically. The other conflicts would rage until the election of 1920 restored a normalcy of sorts.

**WHAT CHALLENGES** did America face in the aftermath of the war?

## Battle over the League

Most Americans favored the Versailles treaty. A survey of 1,400 newspapers found fewer than 200 opposed. Thirty-three governors and 32 state legislatures endorsed the League of Nations. But when Wilson called for the Senate to accept "the moral leadership . . . and confidence of the world" by ratifying the treaty, he met resistance. Some Republicans wanted to prevent the Democrats from campaigning in 1920 as the party responsible for a victorious war and a glorious peace. But most Republican opponents of the treaty raised serious questions, often reflecting national traditions in foreign relations. Nearly all Democrats favored the treaty, but they were a minority; some Republicans would have to be converted for the treaty to be approved.

Progressive Republican senators, such as Robert La Follette and Hiram Johnson, led one group of opponents. Called the **Irreconcilables,** they opposed participation in the League of Nations, which they saw as designed to perpetuate the power of imperialist countries. Article Ten, they feared, would require the United States to help suppress rebellions in Ireland against British rule or to enforce disputed European borders. Johnson declared, "I am opposed to American boys policing Europe and quelling riots in every new nation's backyard." Most of the Irreconcilables gave priority to restoring civil liberties and progressive reform at home.

A larger group of opponents had reservations about the treaty's provisions. These **Reservationists** were led by Henry Cabot Lodge, the chair of the Senate Foreign Relations Committee. They regarded Article Ten as eroding congressional authority to declare war. They also fretted that the League might interfere with domestic questions, such as immigration laws. Many progressives criticized the treaty's compromises on self-determination, reparations, and colonies. Linking these failures with Wilson's domestic policies, one former supporter concluded; "The administration has become reactionary, and deserves no support from any of us."

**Irreconcilables**   Group of U.S. senators adamantly opposed to ratification of the Treaty of Versailles after World War I.

**Reservationists**   Group of U.S. senators opposing approval of the Treaty of Versailles, without significant amendments.

With the defeat of Germany, Americans wanted their soldiers home. And although many returning African-American soldiers were denied celebratory homecomings and would face discrimination and hostility, their role in World War I brought fresh confidence and respect to the African-American community. Few units stirred the patriotism and pride as did the valiant 369th Infantry Regiment, decorated by the French government for heroism and "gallantry under fire." Here African-American friends and families turn out to welcome home the "Men of Bronze," as they were also called.

## AMERICAN VIEWS

### ∽ Letter from Albert Smith, October 15, 1918 ∽

Ultimately numbering over 2 million men, the American troops sent to Europe were organized as the American Expeditionary Forces (AEF) under the command of General Pershing. By August 1918, Pershing had enough troops to form the American First Army, which fought on its own front. In this letter to his brother, Albert Smith describes the largest campaign of the American forces—the Meuse-Argonne campaign—which proved both decisive and costly for the Allies. In the struggle, the AEF cooperated with an African American unit under French command, and the campaign produced one of the greatest heroes of World War I: Private Alvin York of Pall Mall, Tennessee, who would receive the Medal of Honor and promotion to sergeant for personally killing 20 Germans and destroying 35 German machine guns.

Smith's letter glowingly refers to the heroic actions of American doughboys—both white and black. Moreover, even as he discourages his own brother from joining the war, he also takes great pride in his own role on the front lines.

- **What** does Smith's letter illustrate about the impact of total war on soldiers and civilians?
- **How** does Smith suggest both his confidence about defeating the Germans and his war weariness?
- **How** did Smith adapt to the new tools of war, especially the use of gas and machine guns?

France
Oct, 15, 1918
Mr. Mcgregor Smith
Cookeville, Tenn.

**Dear "Greg";**

I received a letter from you a few weeks ago but have not had time to answer for we have been exceedingly busy. We are speedy clearing France of the Huns and making Europe safe for you Kids to come over next spring. This will be the most peaceable country in the world in about sixty days. You just think that you want to come over here we wont need you. I wanted to come over pretty badly and was happy as a lark the day we left New York but that will be nothing to the state of my feeling when I start back to the states. If the Statue of liberty ever sees me again it will have to about face and come down south to find me after she sees me pass going into the harbor at New York on my way home. This is the wettest muddiest country I ever saw, it has been raining steadily for seven weeks. I stepped in a mud hole the other night and went up to my waist in mud and didnt get to change clothes and in fact I haven't changed yet. I haven't changed for over two month and haven't even had my clothes off for that length of time. I have not had a bath for six weeks and none in sight for I haven't the slightest idea of using what little drinking water

Lodge's opposition was shaped by both partisanship and deep personal hostility. Wilson reciprocated, and when Lodge proposed reservations or amendments to the treaty, Wilson refused to compromise. He proposed "a direct frontal attack" on his opponents. If they wanted war, he said, he would "give them a belly full." In early September 1919, Wilson set out across the country to win popular support for the League. In three weeks, he traveled 8,000 miles and delivered 37 speeches.

In poor health following a bout with influenza, Wilson collapsed in Pueblo, Colorado. Taken back to Washington, Wilson on October 2 suffered a massive stroke that paralyzed his left side and left him psychologically unstable and temporarily blind. Wilson's physician and his wife, Edith Galt Wilson, kept the nature of his illness secret from the public, Congress, and even the vice president and cabinet. Rumors circulated that Edith Wilson was running the administration, but she was not. Instead, it was immobilized.

By February 1920, Wilson had partially recovered, but he remained suspicious and quarrelsome. Bryan and other Democratic leaders urged him to accept Lodge's reserva-

**QUICK REVIEW**

**Defeat of the Treaty**

- Most Democrats favored the treaty.
- Republicans led by Henry Cabot Lodge wanted amendments.
- Wilson's refusal to compromise doomed the treaty.

I get in my canteen for batheing purposes. I shave as often as possible for the beard on my face keeps my Gas mask from being effective and the germans use quite a bit of gas. Gas and machine gun is their only effective weapons. I have been on every front in France. You cant imagine how torn up this country really is. Every where there are wire entanglements and trenches and dug outs. Even out of the war zone there are entanglements and dugouts to protect the civilians from air raids. . . . The hardest fight we were in was in the Argenne [Argonne] Forest. Our batteries were the one that destroyed the machine gun nest at Montfaucon. I was at the Forward observation post the night the barrage was laid during the big drive of the last few weeks. The barrage that night was the heaviest one ever laid in France. I saw every bit of it and saw the infantry go over the top. That certainly was a night that I will always remember. Our doughboy are the greatest men in the world, they certainly have "Fritz" bluffed. During Aug. When we were in a drive against mount Sac [Montsec] the strongest fortified hill in France we supported a regiment of Negro infantry and when they went over the top and up the hill they were saying to them germans "take yo hats off white folks no Kazerade to late now." They sure did slaughter the Huns. The southern boys are certainly hard fighters. The third Tenn. Infantry is the hardest fighting regiment over here. I understand that they have been cited by the British for bravery. At Cambrai they were the Americans that advanced thru the heart of the city and cleared the place of machine guns.

Don't worry about coming over here stay in school that is your service to your country. I am in good health and ready to come home after the war but not before, I will do my bit here. I was appointed for the officers, training camp this month for the third time but refused it, I will go later on in the year I want to stay on the front as long as the war lasts. Be good and study HARD have a good time and write often,

Love to all,

Albert

Corp. Albert P. Smith

Hq. Co. 115 F.A. American Expdt. France

Source: www.historychannel.com/letters/albert_smith.html

tions to gain ratification of the treaty. Wilson refused. Isolated and inflexible, he ordered Democratic senators to vote with the Irreconcilables against the treaty as amended by Lodge. On March 19, 1920, the Senate killed the treaty.

## ECONOMIC READJUSTMENT AND SOCIAL CONFLICT

The League was not the only casualty of the struggle to conclude the war. Grave problems shook the United States in 1919 and early 1920. An influenza epidemic had erupted in Europe in 1918 among the massed armies. It now hit the United States, killing perhaps 700,000 Americans, far more than had died in combat. Frightened officials closed public facilities and banned public meetings in futile attempts to stop the contagion.

Meanwhile, the Wilson administration had no plans for an orderly reconversion of the wartime economy, and chaos ensued. The government canceled war contracts and dissolved the regulatory agencies. Noting that "the war spirit of cooperation and

## GLOBAL PERSPECTIVES

### WAR AND REVOLUTION: THE BOLSHEVIKS AND THE INTERNATIONAL COMMUNITY

An uneasy amalgam of distinctive nationalities, the Russian Empire at the start of World War I covered vast territories and included 178 million people. A poor, agrarian country, Russia suffered from autocratic tsarist rule. Long-standing economic problems and political aspirations, especially among land-starved peasants, combined to make Russia a cauldron of tensions inflamed by its involvement in the Great War. The Russian army reflected the discontent that plagued the empire; 400,000 soldiers were killed during the first six months of war, and thereafter desertion became a significant problem.

Food shortages provoked protests among peasants and workers—all challenging tsarist rule. Uprisings in February 1917 immobilized Petrograd, the capital, and persuaded the military to mutiny. The February Revolution ended the Romanov dynasty and brought to power a Provisional Government dominated by liberal reformers. Despite recognition and financial aid from its Allies—the United States, France, and Britain—the new government was politically vulnerable and unable to solve the country's pressing problems.

As frustrations mounted, support for the Bolshevik faction of the Communist Party grew. The Bolsheviks envisioned a world without classes or war—a vision that appealed to a war-weary society with a disintegrating economy. In October 1917, the Provisional Government collapsed and the Bolsheviks came to power.

Promising peace, land, and workers' control, the Bolsheviks were led by V. I. Lenin, a lawyer who had worked for a socialist revolution in Russia since the turn of the century. On March 3, 1918, Russia and Germany signed the Treaty of Brest-Litovsk, an armistice that cost Russia significant territory. But Lenin defended the treaty because Germany still occupied large parts of Russia and the counter-revolutionary, or "White," forces were gathering momentum.

The Allies decried both the Bolshevik revolution and the separate peace with Germany, which enabled Germany to strengthen its forces on the western front. Russia's withdrawal from the war emboldened the "Whites," the opponents of the Bolshevik "Reds," and encouraged the Allies to assist them with financial support and troops. But the Allied invasions of Russia were failures, serving only to convince Lenin that the Allies were imperialists bent on overthrowing the world's only socialist state. In the tumultuous postwar period, Lenin's call for workers to overthrow their governments, European and American leaders believed, fed the postwar labor unrest that wracked industrialized nations. Woodrow Wilson fumed that the "poison" of Bolshevism was "running through the veins of the world." Wilson feared that returning African American troops would serve as the "greatest medium in conveying bolshevism to America," but other policymakers targeted aliens, immigrants, and labor activists, culminating in the "Red Scare."

The fears stirred by the Bolshevik Revolution, however, did not provoke similar governmental extremism in either Great Britain or France, both of which would recognize the Soviet Union by 1924. But America, as the British ambassador noted, was singularly "frightened" of the revolution, and the United States would withhold recognition until 1933.

- What was the impact of the Bolshevik revolution on the war and peace? How did the Allies respond to the Bolsheviks who came to power in Russia in 1917?

---

J. Grimke, *Address of Welcome to the Men Who Have Returned from the Battlefront* (1919)

sacrifice" had disappeared with the Armistice, Bernard Baruch decided to "turn industry absolutely free" and abolished the War Industries Board as of January 1, 1919. Other agencies followed in such haste that turmoil engulfed the economy.

The government also demobilized the armed forces. With no planning or assistance, veterans were hustled back into civilian life. There they competed for scarce jobs with workers recently discharged from the war industries.

As unemployment mounted, the removal of wartime price controls brought runaway inflation. The cost of food, clothing, and other necessities more than doubled over prewar rates. The return of the soldiers caused a serious housing shortage, and rents skyrocketed. Democratic leaders urged Wilson to devote less time to the League of Nations and more to the cost of living and the tensions it unleashed. Farmers also suffered from economic readjustments. Net farm income declined by 65 percent between 1919 and 1921. Farmers who had borrowed money for machinery and land to expand production for the war effort were left impoverished and embittered.

**Postwar battles: gender and race.**    Women also lost their wartime economic advances. Returning soldiers took away their jobs. Male trade unionists insisted that women go back to being housewives. At times, male workers struck to force employers to fire women and barred women from unions in jobs where union membership was required for employment. Indeed, state legislatures passed laws prohibiting women from working in many of the occupations they had successfully filled during the war. By 1919, half of the women newly employed in heavy industry during the war were gone; by 1920, women constituted a smaller proportion of the workforce than they had in 1910.

The postwar readjustments also left African Americans disappointed. During the war, they had agreed with W. E. B. Du Bois to "forget our special grievances and close our ranks shoulder to shoulder with our own white fellow citizens." Participation in the war effort, they had hoped, might be rewarded by better treatment thereafter. Now, the meagerness of their reward became clear.

Housing shortages and job competition interacted with racism in 1919 to produce race riots in 26 towns and cities, resulting in at least 120 deaths. In Chicago, 38 people were killed and more than 500 injured in a five-day riot that began when white thugs stoned to death a black youth swimming too near "their" beach. White rioters then fired a machine gun from a truck hurtling through black neighborhoods. But black residents fought back, no longer willing, the *Chicago Defender* reported, "to move along the line of least resistance as did their sires." The new militancy reflected both their experiences in the military and in industry and their exposure to propaganda about freedom and democracy. Racial conflict was part of a postwar battle between Americans hoping to preserve the new social relations fostered by the war effort and those wanting to restore prewar patterns of power and control.

**Fighting for industrial democracy.**    Even more pervasive discontents roiled as America adjusted to the postwar world. More than 4 million angry workers launched a wave of 3,600 strikes in 1919. They were reacting not only to the soaring cost of living, which undermined the value of their wages, but also to employers' efforts to reassert their authority and destroy the legitimacy labor had won by its participation in the war effort. The abolition of government controls on industry enabled employers not only to raise prices but also to rescind their recognition of unions and reimpose objectionable working conditions. Employers also protected their rising profits by insisting that wages remain fixed. In response, strikers demanded higher wages, better conditions, and recognition of unions and the right of collective bargaining.

The greatest strike involved the American Federation of Labor's attempt to organize steelworkers, who endured dangerous conditions and 12-hour shifts. When the steel companies refused to recognize the union or even discuss issues, 365,000 workers went out on strike in September 1919. Employers hired thugs to beat the strikers, used strikebreakers to take their jobs, and exploited ethnic and racial divisions. To undercut support for the workers, management portrayed the strikers as disruptive radicals influenced by Bolshevism. After four months, the strike failed.

Employers used the same tactic to defeat striking coal miners, whose wages had fallen behind the cost of living. Refusing to negotiate with the United Mine Workers,

**QUICK REVIEW**

**Labor Unrest**

- ◆ Efforts to roll back war-time gains upset workers.
- ◆ 4 million workers launched 3,600 strikes in 1919.
- ◆ The largest strike involved efforts to organize steelworkers.

Postwar labor unrest met determined suppression. Here, mounted police attack steelworkers in Pittsburgh in 1919. The strikers were seeking union recognition and an end to twelve-hour days.

coal operators claimed that Russian Bolsheviks had financed the strike to destroy the American economy. Attorney General Mitchell Palmer secured an injunction against the strike under the authority of wartime legislation. Because the government no longer controlled coal prices or enforced protective labor rules, miners complained bitterly that the war had ended for corporations but not for workers.

Two municipal strikes in 1919 also alarmed the public when their opponents depicted them as revolutionary attacks on the social order. In Seattle, the Central Labor Council called a general strike to support 35,000 shipyard workers striking for higher wages and shorter hours. When 60,000 more workers from 110 local unions also walked out, the city ground to a halt. The strikers behaved peacefully and protected public health and safety by operating garbage and fire trucks and providing food, water, and electricity. Nevertheless, Seattle's mayor, business leaders, and newspapers attacked them as Bolsheviks and anarchists. Threatened with military intervention, the labor council called off the strike, but not before it had caused a public backlash against unions across the nation.

In Boston, the police commissioner fired police officers for trying to organize a union to improve their inadequate pay. In response, the police went on strike. As in Seattle, Boston newspapers, politicians, and business leaders attributed the strike to Bolshevism. The entire police force was fired; many of their replacements were war veterans.

## THE RED SCARE

**Red Scare**  Post-World War I public hysteria over Bolshevik influence in the United States directed against labor activism, radical dissenters, and some ethnic groups.

The strikes contributed to an anti-Bolshevik hysteria that swept the country in 1919. The **Red Scare** reflected fears that the Bolshevik revolution in Russia might spread to the United States. Steeped in the antiradical propaganda of the war years, many Americans were appalled by Russian Bolshevism, described by the *Saturday Evening Post* as a "compound of slaughter, confiscation, anarchy, and universal disorder." But the Red Scare also reflected the willingness of antiunion employers, ambitious politicians, sen-

At the peak of the Red Scare, few major newspapers questioned the wholesale assault on civil liberties and instead placed fears of Bolshevism above rights of individuals, especially workers, immigrants, and radicals. In this 1919 cartoon, the Philadelphia Inquirer, using the American flag as a protective cover, registers its support for the exile of radical immigrants and ideas.

sational journalists, zealous veterans, and racists to exploit the panic to advance their own purposes.

Fed by misleading reports about Russian Bolshevism and its influence in the United States, the Red Scare reached panic levels by mid-1919. Bombs mailed anonymously to several prominent people on May Day seemed proof enough that a Bolshevik conspiracy threatened America. The Justice Department, Congress, and patriotic organizations like the American Legion joined with business groups to suppress radicalism, real and imagined. Wilson and Attorney General Mitchell Palmer called for more stringent laws and refused to release political prisoners jailed during the war. State governments harassed and arrested hundreds.

Palmer created a new agency, headed by J. Edgar Hoover, to suppress radicals and impose conformity. Its war on radicalism became the chief focus of the Justice Department. As an ambitious and ruthless bureaucrat, Hoover had participated in the government's assault on aliens and radicals during the war. Now he collected files on labor leaders and other "radical agitators" from Senator Robert La Follette to Jane Addams, issued misleading reports on communist influence in labor strikes and race riots, and contacted all major newspapers "to acquaint people like you with the real menace of evil-thinking, which is the foundation of the Red Movement."

Lithuanian born anarchist and birth control advocate Emma Goldman (1869–1940) was deported to the Soviet Union on the SS Buford, known as the Red Ark. Goldman returned to the U.S. for the first time 15 years later, on February 2, 1934, on a 90 day permit approved by President Roosevelt.

In November 1919, Palmer and Hoover began raiding groups suspected of subversion. A month later, they deported 249 alien radicals, including the anarchist Emma Goldman, to Russia. In January 1920, Palmer and Hoover rounded up more than 4,000 suspected radicals in 33 cities. Often without warrants, they broke into union halls, club rooms, and private homes, assaulting and arresting everyone in sight. People were jailed without access to lawyers; some were beaten into signing false confessions. The *Washington Post* declared, "There is no time to waste on hairsplitting over infringement of liberty."

Other Americans began to recoil from the excesses and illegal acts. Support for the Red Scare withered. Palmer's attempt to inflame public emotion backfired. When his predictions of a violent attempt to overthrow the government on May 1, 1920, came to naught, most Americans realized that no menace had ever existed. They agreed with the *Rocky Mountain News:* "We can never get to work if we keep jumping sideways in fear of the bewhiskered Bolshevik." But if the Red Scare faded in mid-1920, the hostility to immigrants, organized labor, and dissent it reflected would endure for a decade.

## THE ELECTION OF 1920

The Democratic coalition that Wilson had cobbled together on the issues of progressivism and peace came apart after the war. Workers resented the administration's hostility to the postwar strikes. Ethnic groups brutalized by the Americanization of the war years blamed Wilson for the war or condemned his peace settlement. Farmers grumbled about wartime price controls and postwar falling prices. Wartime taxes and the social and economic turmoil of 1919–1920 alienated the middle class. Americans were weary of great crusades and social sacrifices; in the words of Kansas journalist William Allen White, they were "tired of issues, sick at heart of ideals, and weary of being noble." They yearned for what the Republican presidential candidate, Warren Harding of Ohio, called "normalcy."

The Republican ticket in 1920 symbolized the reassurance of simpler times. Harding was a genial politician who devoted more time to golf and poker than to public policy. An Old Guard conservative, he had stayed with the GOP when Theodore Roosevelt led the progressives out in 1912. His running mate, Calvin Coolidge, governor of Massachusetts, owed his nomination to his handling of the Boston police strike.

Wilson called the election of 1920 "a great and solemn referendum" on the League of Nations, but such lofty appeals fell flat. Harding was ambiguous about the League, and the Democratic national platform endorsed it but expressed a willingness to accept amendments or reservations. The Democratic nominees, James Cox, former governor of Ohio, and the young Franklin D. Roosevelt, Wilson's assistant secretary of the navy, favored the League, but it was not a decisive issue in the campaign.

Harding won in a landslide reflecting the nation's dissatisfaction with Wilson and the Democratic Party. Not even his closest backers considered Harding qualified for the White House, but, as Lippmann said, the nation's "public spirit was exhausted" after the war years. The election of 1920 was "the final twitch" of America's "war mind."

A 1920 campaign poster of Republican candidates Warren Harding, Calvin Coolidge portrayed with American flags and a mighty eagle.

## CONCLUSION

Participation in the war, moreover, had changed the U.S. government, economy, and society. Some of these changes, including the centralization of the economy and an expansion of the regulatory role of the federal government, were already under way; some offered opportunities to implement progressive principles or reforms. Woman suffrage and prohibition gained decisive support because of the war spirit. But other consequences of the war betrayed both progressive impulses and the democratic principles the war was allegedly fought to promote. The suppression of civil liberties, manipulation of human emotions, repression of radicals and minorities, and exploitation of national crises by narrow interests helped disillusion the public. The repercussions of the Great War would linger for years, at home and abroad.

# SUMMARY

WHY WERE Americans so reluctant to get involved in World War I?

**Waging Neutrality** Few Americans were prepared for the Great War that erupted in Europe in 1914; fewer still envisioned the United States becoming involved in the war. The Central Powers and the Allies were involved in mass slaughter and stalemate in Europe; America had no vital interest in the war, but it did not stay strictly neutral. The economy of America became closely tied with Britain and the Allies, the President sympathized with the Allied cause, and German submarine warfare tied the United States to the British war effort. The desire for peace determined the results of the 1916 election; in 1917 America entered the war as Germany decided to resume unrestricted submarine warfare and the contents of the Zimmermann note, linking Germany to Mexico's recovering the Southwest, were exposed.

HOW DID the war effort threaten civil liberties?

**Waging War in America** In addition to mobilizing for military invention, the government reorganized the economy to emphasize centralized management and developed policies to control public opinion and suppress dissent. In response to labor shortages women and minorities entered the work force, obtaining jobs which had previously been closed to them; individual citizens planted victory gardens and bought Liberty Bonds to help the war effort. Government propaganda to rally Americans painted the enemy as subhuman; dissent was viewed as unpatriotic; Americans were encouraged to spy on one another; basic civil rights were violated.

WHAT HOPES did Wilson have for the Treaty of Versailles?

**Waging War and Peace Abroad** The American involvement in the Great War turned the tide and ensured Allied victory. Having stopped the German advance on the Western Front, the Allies, with fresh American troops, began a counteroffensive that ended the war with an armistice on November 11, 1918. President Wilson envisioned the postwar world based on the Fourteen Points and attended the Paris Peace Conference convinced of the righteousness of his peace plans. The Allied leaders were more interested in revenge and retribution than righteousness. The Treaty of Versailles imposed harsh restrictions on Germany; the specter of Bolshevism hung over the peace conference; fear of communism influenced decisions made by the delegates.

WHAT CHALLENGES did America face in the aftermath of the war?

**Waging Peace at Home** While most Americans favored the Versailles treaty, the senators who had to vote on the treaty were largely opposed to it. The Irreconcilables opposed participation in the League of Nations, and the Reservationists feared the power of the League and the erosion of Congressional authority. The Treaty of Versailles was never approved by the United States. The vote in the Senate was not the only war casualty: An influenza epidemic, the reconversion to a peacetime economy, housing shortages, unemployment, labor unrest, and the Red Scare wearied Americans. By 1920, Americans wanted a return to "normalcy" and elected Warren Harding as president in a landslide victory.

# WHERE TO LEARN MORE

**National Infantry Museum, Fort Benning, Georgia.**
This sprawling collection of weapons, uniforms, and equipment includes exhibits on World War I. **www.benningmwr.com/index.cfm**

**General John J. Pershing Boyhood Home, Laclede, Missouri.** Maintained by the Missouri State Park Board, Pershing's restored nineteenth-century home exhibits some of his personal belongings and papers. **www.mostateparks.com/pershingsite.htm**

**Sgt. Alvin C. York Homeplace and State Historic Site, Pall Mall, Tennessee.** The home of America's greatest military hero of World War I contains fascinating artifacts, including York's letters written in the trenches. **www.alvincyork.org**

**Wisconsin Veterans Museum, Madison, Wisconsin.**
The most stunning museum of its size in the United States, this large building combines impressive collections of artifacts ranging from uniforms to tanks, with substantive exhibits and video programs based on remarkable historical research. It both documents and explains the participation of Wisconsin soldiers in the nation's wars, including the Spanish-American War and World War I. **http://museum.dva.state.wi.us**

# STUDY RESOURCES

## myhistorylab

For study resources for this chapter, go to www.myhistorylab.com and choose *The American Journey*. You will find a wealth of study and review material for this chapter, including pre- and post-tests, customized study plan, key term review flash cards, interactive map and document activities, and documents for analysis.

# REVIEW QUESTIONS

1. Why did Senator Robert La Follette oppose the war against Germany? How did many Americans regard the war and possible U.S. intervention?

2. What were the major arguments for and against U.S. entry into the Great War? What position do you find most persuasive? Why?

3. How and why did the United States shape public opinion in World War I? What were the consequences, positive and negative, of the propaganda of the Committee on Public Information, the Food Administration, and other government agencies?

4. How did the war affect women and minorities?

5. Evaluate the role of Woodrow Wilson at the Paris Peace Conference. What obstacles did he face? How successful was he in shaping the settlement?

6. Discuss the arguments for and against American ratification of the Treaty of Versailles.

## KEY TERMS

**Allies** (p. 682)
**Bolshevik** (p. 692)
**Central Powers** (p. 682)
**Committee on Public Information (CPI)** (p. 690)
**Declaration of London** (p. 683)
**Espionage Act** (p. 690)
**Irreconcilables** (p. 697)
**League of Nations** (p. 696)
**Liberty Bonds** (p. 689)

**Preparedness** (p. 684)
**Red Scare** (p. 702)
**Reservationists** (p. 697)
**Sedition Act of 1918** (p. 690)
**Selective Service Act of 1917** (p. 692)
**Self-determination** (p. 685)
***Sussex* Pledge** (p. 684)
**Treaty of Versailles** (p. 696)
**War Industries Board (WIB)** (p. 687)

# 24

# Toward a Modern America

THE ECONOMY THAT ROARED  *(page 711)*

**WHAT CONTRIBUTED** to the economic boom of the 1920s?

THE BUSINESS OF GOVERNMENT  *(page 716)*

**WHAT WAS** the relationship between big business and government in the 1920s?

CITIES AND SUBURBS  *(page 719)*

**WHAT LED** to the Great Migration?

MASS CULTURE IN THE JAZZ AGE  *(page 722)*

HOW DID new systems of distribution, marketing, and mass communication shape American culture?

CULTURE WARS  *(page 726)*

**WHAT EXPLAINS** the resurgence of the Ku Klux Klan in the 1920s?

A NEW ERA IN THE WORLD?  *(page 732)*

WHAT ROLE did the United States play in international diplomacy in the decade after World War I?

HERBERT HOOVER AND THE FINAL TRIUMPH OF THE NEW ERA  *(page 734)*

**WHAT FACTORS** contributed to Herbert Hoover's victory in 1928 over his Democratic opponent, Alfred E. Smith? In what ways did Hoover epitomize the policies of the New Era?

*Happy times were here again. American industry, adopting Henry Ford's policy of mass production and low prices, was making it possible for everybody to have his share of everything. The newspapers, the statesmen, the economists, all agreed that American ingenuity had solved the age-old problem of poverty. There could never be another depression. . . .*

*The war had done something to Henry, it had taught him a new way to deal with his fellow men. . . . He became more abrupt in his manner, more harsh in his speech. "Gratitude?" he would say. "There's no gratitude in business. Men work for money." . . . From now on he was a business man, and held a tight rein on everything. This industry was his, he had made it himself, and what he wanted of the men he hired was that they should do exactly as he told them. . . .*

*Every worker had to be strained to the uttermost limit, every one had to be giving the last ounce of energy he had in his carcass. . . . They were tired when they started in the morning, and when they quit they were grey and staggering with fatigue, they were empty shells out of which the last drop of juice had been squeezed. . . .*

*Henry Ford was now getting close to his two million cars a year goal. . . . From the moment the ore was taken out of the ship at the River Rouge plant [in Detroit], through all the processes turning it into steel and shaping it into automobile parts with a hundred-ton press, and putting five thousand parts together into a car which rolled off the assembly line under its own power—all those processes were completed in less than a day and a half!*

*Some forty-five thousand different machines were now used in the making of Ford cars, in sixty establishments scattered over the United States. . . . Henry Ford was remaking the roads of America, and in the end he would remake the roads of the world—and line them all with filling stations and hot-dog stands of the American pattern.*

Upton Sinclair, *The Flivver King: A Story of Ford-America* (Chicago: Charles H. Kerr, 1999).

**myhistorylab**

### Personal Journeys Online

- Chicago Daily Tribune, "Capt. Charles Lindbergh, Lone U.S. Flyer, Wings Way from New York to Paris in 33 Hours 29 Minutes," 1927. Photographic essay of Lindbergh's accomplishment.

- Elsie Johnson McDougald, "The Double Task: The Struggle of Negro Women for Sex and Race Emancipation," 1925. Article attacks racial stereotypes and discusses the diversity among African American women in New York City.

**UPTON SINCLAIR,** one of America's most famous muckraking journalists, won his greatest recognition with the 1906 publication of his novel *The Jungle*, which graphically depicted the wretched conditions endured by Chicago's immigrant meatpacking workers. In *The Flivver King*, Sinclair wove together a dramatic and historical account of industrial America, as embodied in the rise of the automobile industry and the revolutionizing vision of Henry Ford, the entrepreneur who captured the American mind and symbolized modern America to the world.

"Machinery," proclaimed Henry Ford, "is the new Messiah." Ford had introduced the assembly line at his automobile factory on the eve of World War I, and by 1925 it was turning out a Model T car every ten seconds. The term "mass production" originated in Henry Ford's 1926 description of the system of flow-production techniques popularly called

"Fordism." The system symbolized the nation's booming economy: in the 1920s, Europeans used the word *Fordize* as a synonym for *Americanize*.

Henry Ford was conflicted about the progress he championed—the changes he saw and had helped facilitate. Launching a crusade against the new direction America was headed, Ford decided, according to Sinclair, that "what America needed was to be led back to its past." Embracing nativism and Protestantism, Ford, an ardent anti-Semite, targeted Jewish Americans in his diatribes, blaming them for radicalism and labor organization, and he singled out the "International Jew" for allegedly controlling the international financial community.

Henry Ford and Fordism reflected the complexity of the 1920s. Economic growth and technological innovation were paired with social conflict as traditions were destroyed, values were displaced, and new people were incorporated into a society increasingly industrialized, urbanized, and dominated by big business. Industrial production and national wealth soared, buoyed by new techniques and markets for consumer goods. Business values pervaded society, and government promoted business interests.

But not all Americans prospered. Many workers were unemployed, and the wages of still more were stagnant or falling. Farmers endured grim conditions and worse prospects. Social change brought pleasure to some and deep concern to others. City factories like the Ford Works attracted workers from the countryside, increasing urbanization; rapid suburbanization opened other horizons. Leisure activities flourished, and new mass media promoted modern ideas and stylish products. Workers would have to achieve personal satisfaction through consumption and not production. But such experiences often proved unsettling, and some Americans, like Ford, sought reassurance by imposing their cultural or religious values on everyone around them. ✦

## THE ECONOMY THAT ROARED

Following a severe postwar depression in 1920 and 1921, the American economy boomed through the remainder of the decade. Gross domestic product soared nearly 40 percent; output per worker-hour, or productivity, rose 72 percent in manufacturing; average per capita income increased by a third. Although the prosperity was not evenly distributed and some sectors of the economy were deeply troubled, most Americans welcomed the industrial expansion and business principles of the New Era.

**WHAT CONTRIBUTED** to the economic boom of the 1920s?

### BOOM INDUSTRIES

Many factors spurred the economic expansion of the 1920s. The huge wartime and postwar profits provided investment capital that enabled business to mechanize. Mass

## CHRONOLOGY

| | |
|---|---|
| **1915** Ku Klux Klan is founded anew. | **1923** Harding dies; Calvin Coolidge becomes president. |
| **1919** Volstead Act is passed. | **1924** National Origins Act sharply curtails immigration. |
| **1920** Urban population exceeds rural population for the first time. | Coolidge is elected president. |
| Warren Harding is elected president. | **1925** Scopes trial is held in Dayton, Tennessee. |
| Prohibition takes effect. | F. Scott Fitzgerald publishes *The Great Gatsby*. |
| First commercial radio show is broadcast. | **1927** Charles A. Lindbergh flies solo across the Atlantic. |
| Sinclair Lewis publishes *Main Street*. | **1928** Kellogg-Briand Pact is signed. |
| **1921** Sheppard-Towner Maternity and Infancy Act is passed. | Herbert Hoover is elected president. |
| Washington Naval Conference limits naval armaments. | **1929** Ernest Hemingway publishes *A Farewell to Arms*. |
| **1922** Fordney-McCumber Act raises tariff rates. | |
| Sinclair Lewis publishes *Babbitt*. | |
| Country Club Plaza in Kansas City opens. | |

**WHERE TO LEARN MORE**

★ Henry Ford Museum and Greenfield Village, Dearborn, Michigan. www.hfmgv.org

Robert and Helen Lynd, *The Automobile Comes to Middletown* (1924)

production spread quickly in American industry; machine-made standardized parts and the assembly line increased efficiency and production. Businesses steadily adopted the scientific management principles of Frederick W. Taylor (see Chapter 21). The nation more than doubled its capacity to generate electricity during the decade, further bolstering the economy.

The automobile industry drove the economy. Its productivity increased constantly, and sales rose from about 1.9 million vehicles in 1920 to nearly 5 million by 1929, when 26 million vehicles were on the road (see Figure 24–1). The automobile industry also employed one of every 14 manufacturing workers and stimulated other industries, from steel to rubber and glass. It created a huge new market for the petroleum industry and fostered oil drilling in Oklahoma, Texas, and Louisiana. It launched new businesses, from service stations (over 120,000 by 1929) to garages. It also encouraged the construction industry, a mainstay of the 1920s economy. Large increases in road building and residential housing, prompted by growing automobile ownership and migration to cities and suburbs, provided construction jobs, markets for lumber and other building materials, and profits.

The Great War also stimulated the chemical industry. The government confiscated chemical patents from German firms that had dominated the field and transferred them to U.S. companies like DuPont. With this advantage, DuPont in the 1920s became one of the nation's largest industrial firms, a chemical empire producing plastics, finishes, dyes, and organic chemicals. Led by such successes, the chemical industry became a $4 billion giant employing 300,000 workers by 1929.

The new radio and motion picture industries also flourished. Commercial broadcasting began with a single station in 1920. By 1927, there were 732 stations, and Congress created the Federal Radio Commission to prevent wave-band interference. The rationale for this agency, which was reorganized as the Federal Communications Commission (FCC) in 1934, was that the airwaves belong to the American people

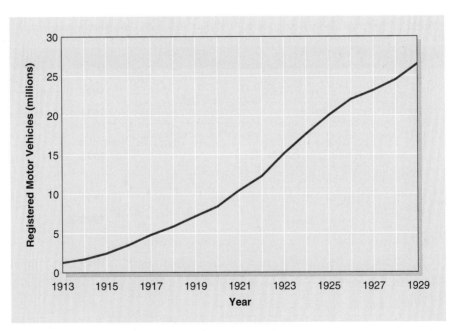

**FIGURE 24–1 Registered Motor Vehicles, 1913–1929** The rapid adoption of automobiles shaped the 1920s, stimulating demand for steel and gasoline, encouraging the use of credit, facilitating urbanization, promoting tourism, and suggesting new cultural horizons.
Data Source: U.S. Bureau of Public Roads

and not to private interests. Nevertheless, corporations quickly dominated the new industry.

The motion-picture industry became one of the nation's five largest businesses, with 20,000 movie theaters selling 100 million tickets a week. Hollywood studios were huge factories, hiring directors, writers, camera crews, and actors to produce films on an assembly-line basis. While Americans watched Charlie Chaplin showcase his comedic genius in such films as *The Gold Rush* (1925), corporations like Paramount were integrating production with distribution and exhibition to maximize control and profit and eliminate independent producers and theaters. The advent of talking movies later in the decade brought still greater profits and power to the major studios, which alone could afford the increased engineering and production costs.

## CORPORATE CONSOLIDATION

A wave of corporate mergers, rivaling the one at the turn of the century, swept over the 1920s economy. Great corporations swallowed up thousands of small firms. Particularly significant was the spread of **oligopoly**—the control of an entire industry by a few giant firms. The number of automobile manufacturers dropped from 108 to 44, while only three companies—Ford, General Motors, and Chrysler—produced 83 percent of the nation's cars. In the electric light and power industry, nearly 4,000 local utility companies were merged into a dozen holding companies. Mergers also expanded oligopolistic control over other industries. By 1929, the nation's 200 largest corporations controlled nearly half of all nonbanking corporate wealth.

**oligopoly**   An industry, such as steel making or automobile manufacturing, that is controlled by a few large companies.

## OPEN SHOPS AND WELFARE CAPITALISM

Business also launched a vigorous assault on labor. In 1921, the National Association of Manufacturers organized an **open-shop** campaign to break union-shop contracts, which required all employees to be union members. Denouncing collective bargaining as un-American, businesses described the open shop, in which union membership was not required and usually prohibited, as the "American plan." They forced workers to sign so-called **yellow-dog contracts** that bound them to reject unions to keep their jobs. Business also used boycotts to force employers into a uniform antiunion front. Bethlehem Steel, for example, refused to sell steel to companies employing union labor. Where unions existed, corporations tried to crush them, using spies or hiring strikebreakers.

**open-shop**   Factory or business employing workers whether or not they are union members; in practice, such a business usually refuses to hire union members and follows antiunion policies.

**yellow-dog contracts**   Employment agreements binding workers not to join a union.

Some companies advocated a paternalistic system called **welfare capitalism** as an alternative to unions. Eastman Kodak, General Motors, U.S. Steel, and other firms provided medical services, insurance programs, pension plans, and vacations for their workers and established employee social clubs and sports teams. These policies were designed to undercut labor unions and persuade workers to rely on the corporation. Welfare capitalism, however, covered scarcely 5 percent of the workforce and often benefited only skilled workers already tied to the company through seniority.

**welfare capitalism**   A paternalistic system of labor relations emphasizing management responsibility for employee well-being.

Corporations in the 1920s also promoted company unions, management-sponsored substitutes for labor unions. But company unions were usually forbidden to handle wage and hour issues. Their function was to implement company policies and undermine real unionism.

Partly because of these pressures, membership in labor unions fell from 5.1 million in 1920 to 3.6 million in 1929. But unions also contributed to their own decline. Conservative union leaders neglected ethnic and black workers in mass-production industries. Nor did they try to organize women, by 1930 nearly one-fourth of all workers. And they failed to respond effectively to other changes in the labor market. The growing

An Assembly Line
of the
Ford Motor Company

Ford Motor Company's assembly line at the River Rouge plant in Detroit. The increasing mechanization of work, linked to managerial and marketing innovations, boosted productivity in the 1920s and brought consumer goods within the reach of far more Americans than before.

State Historical Society of Wisconsin.

numbers of white-collar workers regarded themselves as middle class and beyond the scope of union action.

With increasing mechanization and weak labor unions, workers suffered from job insecurity and stagnant wages. Unemployment reached 12 percent in 1921 and remained a persistent concern of many working-class Americans during the decade. And despite claims to the contrary, hours were long: The average workweek in manufacturing remained more than 50 hours.

The promise of business to pay high wages proved hollow. Real wages (purchasing power) did improve, but most of the improvement came before 1923 and reflected falling prices more than rising wages. The failure to raise wages when productivity was increasing threatened the nation's long-term prosperity. In short, rising national income largely reflected salaries and dividends, not wages.

Some workers fared worse than others. Unskilled workers, especially southern and eastern Europeans, black migrants from the rural South, and Mexican immigrants, saw their already low wages decline relative to those of skilled workers. Southern workers earned much less than northerners, even in the same industry, and women were paid much less than men even for the same jobs. Overall, the gap between rich and poor widened during the decade (see Figure 24–2). By 1929, fully 71 percent of American families earned less than what the U.S. Bureau of Labor Statistics regarded as necessary for a decent living standard. The maldistribution of income meant that eventually Americans would be unable to purchase the products they made.

Consumer credit, rare before the 1920s, expanded during the decade. Credit offered temporary relief by permitting consumers to buy goods on time. General Motors introduced consumer credit on a national basis to create a mass market for expensive automobiles. By 1927, two-thirds of automobiles were purchased on the installment plan. By 1929, providing consumer credit had become the nation's tenth-largest business. Nevertheless, installment loans did not in the long run raise the purchasing power of an income; they simply added interest charges to the price of products.

## QUICK REVIEW

**Signs of Underlying Economic Weakness**

- Unemployment remained high.
- Wages did not rise with increased prosperity.
- The gap between rich and poor grew.
- Consumption fueled by expanding consumer credit.

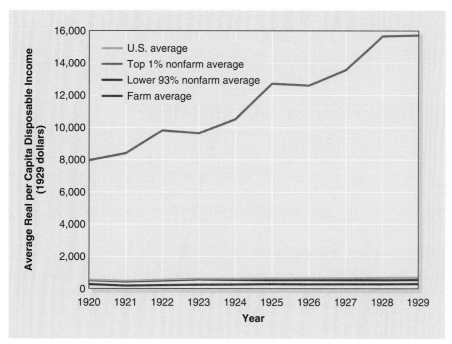

**FIGURE 24–2   Growing Income Inequality in the 1920s**   Despite the aura of prosperity in the 1920s, the vast majority of Americans received little or no increase in their real income. Farm families dragged the average down further, while the wealthiest Americans doubled their own incomes.

Data Source: Charles Holt, "Who Benefited from the Prosperity of the Twenties?" *Explorations in Economic History*, 14 (1977).

## SICK INDUSTRIES

Despite the general appearance of prosperity, several "sick" industries dragged on the economy. Coal mining, textile and garment manufacturing, and railroads suffered from excess capacity (too many mines and factories), shrinking demand, low returns, and management-labor conflicts. For example, U.S. coal mines had a capacity of a billion tons, but scarcely half of that amount was needed because of increasing use of oil, natural gas, and hydroelectricity. Using company police, strikebreakers, and injunctions, mine operators broke the United Mine Workers and slashed wages by up to one-third. Unemployment in the industry approached 30 percent.

Similarly, the textile industry coped with overcapacity and declining demand by shifting operations from New England to the cheap-labor South, employing girls and young women for 56-hour weeks at 18 cents an hour. Textile companies, aided by local authorities, suppressed strikes in Tennessee and North Carolina.

The textile industry, despite substandard wages and repressive policies, remained barely profitable. American agriculture never recovered from the 1921 depression. Agriculture surpluses and shrinking demand forced down prices. After the war, foreign markets dried up, and domestic demand for cotton slackened. Moreover, farmers' wartime expansion left them heavily mortgaged in the 1920s. Small farmers, unable to compete with larger, better-capitalized farmers, suffered most. Many lost their land and became tenants or farm hands.

Racial discrimination worsened conditions for black and Hispanic tenants, sharecroppers, and farm workers. In the South, African American sharecroppers trapped in grinding poverty endured segregation, disfranchisement, and violence. Mexican immigrants and Hispanic Americans labored as migrant farm workers in

**QUICK REVIEW**

**Sick Industries**

♦ Coal mining.

♦ Textiles.

♦ Agriculture.

the Southwest and California. Exploited by the contract-labor system pervasive in large-scale agriculture, they suffered from poor wages, miserable living conditions, and racism.

# THE BUSINESS OF GOVERNMENT

**WHAT WAS** the relationship between big business and government in the 1920s?

The Republican surge in national politics also shaped the economy. In the 1920 election, the Republican slogan was "Less government in business, more business in government." By 1924, Calvin Coolidge, the decade's second Republican president, proclaimed, "This is a business country . . . and it wants a business government." Under such direction, the federal government advanced business interests at the expense of other objectives.

## REPUBLICAN ASCENDANCY

Republicans in 1920 had retained control of Congress and put Warren Harding in the White House. Harding was neither capable nor bright. Moreover, Harding recognized his own limitations and promised to appoint "the best minds" to his cabinet. Some of his appointees were highly accomplished, and two of them, Secretary of Commerce Herbert Hoover and Secretary of the Treasury Andrew Mellon, shaped economic policy throughout the 1920s.

A self-described progressive dedicated to efficiency, Hoover made the Commerce Department the government's most dynamic office. He cemented its ties with the leading sectors of the economy, expanded its collection and distribution of industrial information, pushed to exploit foreign resources and markets, and encouraged innovation. Hoover's goal was to foster prosperity by making business efficient, responsive, and profitable.

Andrew Mellon had a narrower goal. A wealthy banker and industrialist, he pressed Congress to reduce taxes on businesses and the rich. He argued that lower taxes would enable wealthy individuals and corporations to increase their capital investments, thereby creating new jobs and general prosperity. But Mellon's hope that favoring the rich would cause prosperity to trickle down to the working and middle classes proved ill-founded. Nevertheless, despite the opposition of progressives in Congress, Mellon succeeded in lowering maximum tax rates and eliminating wartime excess-profits taxes in 1921.

The Harding administration promoted business interests in other ways, too. The tariff of 1922 raised import rates to protect industry from foreign competition. But high tariffs made it difficult for European nations to earn the dollars to repay their war debts to the United States. High rates also impeded American farm exports and raised consumer prices.

The Harding administration aided the business campaign against unions and curtailed government regulation. By appointing advocates of big business to the Federal Trade Commission and the Federal Reserve Board, among others, Harding made government the collaborator rather than the regulator of business.

Finally, Harding reshaped the Supreme Court into a still more aggressive champion of business. He named the conservative William Howard Taft as chief justice and matched him with three other justices. All were, as one of them proclaimed, sympathetic to business leaders "beset and bedeviled with vexatious statutes, prying commissions, and government intermeddling of all sorts." The Court struck down much of the government economic regulation adopted during the Progressive Era, invalidated restraints on child labor and a minimum wage law for women, and approved restrictions on labor unions.

**WHERE TO LEARN MORE**

Calvin Coolidge Homestead, Plymouth, Vermont.
www.calvin-coolidge.org/pages/homestead
www.dhca.state.vt.us./HistoricSites/sites.htm

**WHERE TO LEARN MORE**

Warren G. Harding House, Marion, Ohio.
www.ohiohistory.org/places/harding

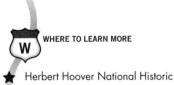

**WHERE TO LEARN MORE**

Herbert Hoover National Historic Site, West Branch, Iowa.
www.hoover.archives.gov

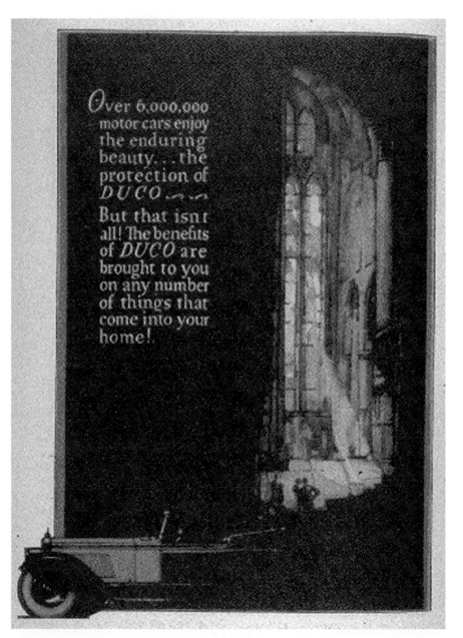

DuPont became one of the nation's largest industrial corporations in the 1920s by developing new consumer products and marketing them aggressively. This advertisement for Duco automobile finishes blends images of a cathedral and an auto showroom, placing consumerism in a favorable light.

## GOVERNMENT CORRUPTION

The green light that Harding Republicans extended to private interests led to corruption and scandals. Harding appointed many friends and cronies who saw public service as an opportunity for graft. Attorney General Daugherty's associates in the Justice Department took bribes in exchange for pardons and government jobs. The head of the Veterans Bureau went to prison for cheating disabled veterans of $200 million. Albert Fall, the secretary of the interior, leased petroleum reserves set aside by progressive conservationists to oil companies in exchange for cash, bonds, and cattle for his New Mexico ranch. Exposed for his role in the Teapot Dome scandal, named after a Wyoming oil reserve, Fall became the first cabinet officer in history to go to jail. Daugherty escaped a similar fate by destroying records and invoking the Fifth Amendment.

Harding was appalled by the scandals. "My God, this is a hell of a job!" he told William Allen White. "I have no trouble with my enemies. . . . But my damned friends, . . . they're the ones that keep me walking the floor nights!" Harding died shortly thereafter, probably of a heart attack.

## COOLIDGE PROSPERITY

On August 3, 1923, Vice President Calvin Coolidge was sworn in as president. Coolidge's calm appearance hid a furious temper and a mean spirit. Coolidge supported business with ideological conviction. He opposed the activist presidency of the Progressive Era, cultivating instead a deliberate inactivity calculated to lower expectations of government.

Like Harding, Coolidge installed business supporters in the regulatory agencies. To chair the Federal Trade Commission he appointed an attorney who had condemned the agency as "an instrument of oppression and disturbance and injury instead of help to business." Under this leadership, the FTC described its new goal as "helping business to help itself," which meant approving trade associations and agreements to suppress competition. This attitude, endorsed by the Supreme Court, aided the mergers that occurred after 1925. The *Wall Street Journal* crowed, "Never before, here or anywhere else, has a government been so completely fused with business."

"Coolidge prosperity" determined the 1924 election. The Democrats, hopelessly divided, took 103 ballots to nominate the colorless, conservative Wall Street lawyer John W. Davis. A more interesting opponent for Coolidge was Robert La Follette, nominated by discontented farm and labor organizations that formed a new Progressive Party. La Follette campaigned against "the power of private monopoly over the political and economic life of the American people." The Republicans, backed by immense contributions from business, denounced La Follette as an agent of Bolshevism. The choice, Republicans insisted, was "Coolidge or Chaos." Thus instructed, Americans chose Coolidge, though barely half the electorate bothered to vote.

## THE FATE OF REFORM

But progressive reform was not completely dead. A small group in Congress, led by La Follette and George Norris, attacked Mellon's regressive tax policies and supported measures regulating agricultural processors, protecting workers' rights, and maintaining public ownership of a hydroelectric dam at Muscle Shoals, Alabama, that conservative Republicans wanted to privatize. Yet the reformers' successes were few and often temporary.

The fate of women's groups illustrates the difficulties reformers faced in the 1920s. At first, the adoption of woman suffrage prompted politicians to champion women's reform issues. In 1920, both major parties endorsed many of the goals of the new **League of Women Voters.** Within a year, many states had granted women the right to serve on juries, several enacted equal-pay laws, and Wisconsin adopted an equal-rights law. Congress passed the **Sheppard-Towner Maternity and Infancy Act,** the first federal social-welfare law, in 1921. It provided federal funds for infant and maternity care, precisely the type of protective legislation that the suffragists had described as women's special interest. Women also ran for political office and by 1922 there were fifteen women mayors of small towns throughout the nation.

But thereafter women reformers gained little. As it became clear that women did not vote as a bloc but according to their varying social and economic backgrounds, Congress lost interest in women's issues. In 1929, Congress killed the Sheppard-Towner Act. Nor could reformers gain ratification of a child-labor amendment after the Supreme Court invalidated laws regulating child labor. Conservatives attacked women reformers as "Bolsheviks."

**League of Women Voters**   League formed in 1920 advocating for women's rights, among them the right for women to serve on juries and equal pay laws.

**Sheppard-Towner Maternity and Infancy Act**   The first federal social welfare law, passed in 1921, providing federal funds for infant and maternity care.

# CITIES AND SUBURBS

The 1920 census was the first to report that more Americans lived in urban than in rural areas. The trend toward urbanization accelerated in the 1920s as millions of Americans fled the depressed countryside for the booming cities. This massive population movement interacted with technological innovations to reshape cities, build suburbs, and transform urban life (see Map 24–1).

**WHAT LED** to the Great Migration?

## EXPANDING CITIES

Urbanization affected every region of the country. In absolute terms, the older industrial cities of the Northeast and upper Midwest grew the most, attracting migrants from the rural South and distressed Appalachia. New York remained the nation's foremost metropolis.

Rural southerners also headed for southern cities. In fact, the South was the nation's most rapidly urbanizing region. Migrants from the countryside poured into Atlanta,

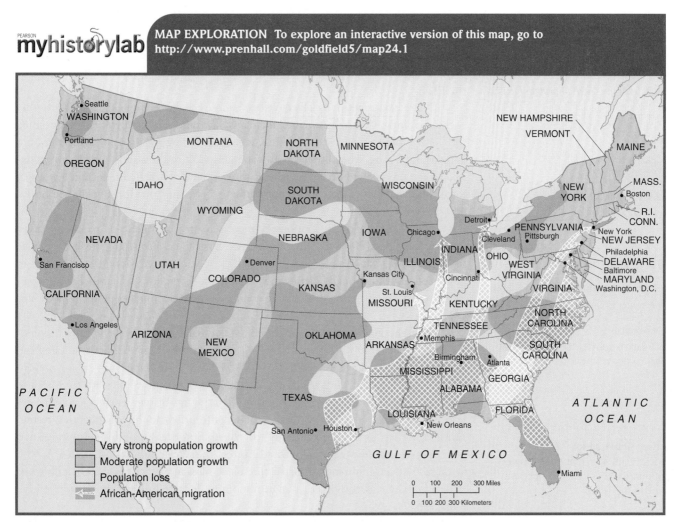

**MAP EXPLORATION  To explore an interactive version of this map, go to http://www.prenhall.com/goldfield5/map24.1**

Very strong population growth
Moderate population growth
Population loss
African-American migration

**MAP 24–1    Population Shifts, 1920–1930**    Rural Americans fled to the cities during the 1920s, escaping a declining agricultural economy to search for new opportunities. African Americans in particular left the rural South for eastern and midwestern cities, but the urban population also jumped in the West and in the South itself.

**Why did** certain states and areas gain population during this period and why did others see population decreases?

Birmingham, Memphis, and Houston. Little more than jungle before 1914, Miami became the fastest growing city in the United States during the 1920s—"the Magic City."

In the West, Denver, Portland, and Seattle (each a regional economic hub) and several California cities grew rapidly. Los Angeles grew by 115 percent and by 1930 was the nation's fifth-largest city, with over 1.2 million people.

The population surge transformed the urban landscape. As land values soared, developers built skyscrapers, giving Cleveland, Kansas City, San Francisco, and many other cities modern skylines. By the end of the decade, American cities had nearly 400 skyscrapers taller than 20 stories.

## THE GREAT BLACK MIGRATION

**Great Migration** The mass movement of African Americans from the rural South to the urban North, spurred especially by new job opportunities during World War I and the 1920s.

A significant feature of the rural-to-urban movement was the **Great Migration** of African Americans from the South. Like other migrants, they were responding chiefly to economic factors. Southern segregation and violence made migration attractive, but job opportunities made it possible. Prosperity created jobs, and with the decline in European immigration, black workers filled the positions previously given to new immigrants. Though generally the lowest paid and least secure jobs, they were better than sharecropping in the rural South. The migrants often found adjustment to their new environment difficult. Southern rural black culture clashed with industrial work rhythms and discipline and with urban living. Still, more than 1.5 million African Americans moved to northern cities in the 1920s.

*Letters from the Great Migration* (1917)

There black ghettos usually developed, more because of prejudice than the wishes of the migrants. Although African Americans, like European immigrants, often wanted to live together to sustain their culture, racist restrictions meant that segregation, not congregation, most shaped their urban community. With thousands of newcomers limited to certain neighborhoods, housing shortages developed. High rents and low wages forced black families to share inferior and unsanitary housing that threatened their health and safety.

Charles S. Johnson, *The City Negro* (1925)

However, the Great Migration also increased African Americans' racial consciousness, autonomy, and power. In 1928, for instance, black Chicagoans, using the ballot denied to African Americans in the South, elected the first black man to Congress since the turn of the century. Mutual-aid societies and fraternal orders proliferated. Churches were particularly influential. A reporter in 1926 counted 140 black churches in a 150-block area of Harlem.

QUICK REVIEW

**Restrictions on Immigration**

◆ Emergency Quota Act of 1921 reduced immigration and established quotas for nationalities.

◆ National Origins Act of 1924 restricted immigration on the basis of national origins.

◆ Other steps targeted Japanese residents in the West.

Another organization also appealed to poor black ghetto dwellers. The Universal Negro Improvement Association (UNIA), organized by Marcus Garvey, a Jamaican immigrant to New York, rejected the NAACP's goal of integration. A black nationalist espousing racial pride, Garvey exhorted black people to migrate to Africa to build a "free, redeemed, and mighty nation." In the meantime, he urged them to support black businesses. UNIA organized many enterprises, including groceries, restaurants, laundries, a printing plant, and the Black Star Steamship Line, intended as a commercial link between the United States, the West Indies, and Africa. UNIA attracted half a million members, the first black mass movement in American history. When Garvey was convicted of mail fraud and deported, however, the movement collapsed.

**Harlem Renaissance** A new African-American cultural awareness that flourished in literature, art, and music in the 1920s.

Racial pride also found expression in the **Harlem Renaissance,** an outpouring of literature, painting, sculpture, and music. Inspired by African American culture and black urban life, writers and artists created works of power and poignancy. The poetry of Langston Hughes reflected the rhythm and mood of jazz and the blues. Other leading authors of the Harlem Renaissance who asserted their independence included

**Exploring America**
*Harlem Renaissance*

Claude McKay, who wrote of the black working class in *Home to Harlem* (1928), Zora Neale Hurston, James Weldon Johnson, and Dorothy West.

## BARRIOS

Hispanic migrants also entered the nation's cities in the 1920s, creating their own communities, or barrios. Fifty thousand Puerto Ricans settled in New York, mostly in East ("Spanish") Harlem, where they found low-paying jobs. Far more migrants arrived from Mexico. Although many worked as migrant farm laborers, they often lived in cities in the off-season. Others permanently joined the expanding urban economy in industrial and construction jobs. The barrios, with their own businesses, churches, and cultural organizations, created a sense of permanency.

These communities enabled the newcomers to preserve their cultural values and build social institutions, such as *mutualistas* (mutual aid societies), that helped them obtain credit, housing, and healthcare. But the barrios also reflected the hostility that Hispanics encountered in American cities. Los Angeles maintained separate schools for Mexicans, and a social worker reported that "America has repulsed the Mexican immigrant in every step he has taken" toward integration. As new migrants streamed in, conditions in the barrios deteriorated, for few cities provided adequate public services for them.

Some Hispanics fought discrimination. La Orden de Hijos de America ("The Order of the Sons of America"), organized in San Antonio in 1921, campaigned against inequities in schools and the jury system. In 1929, it helped launch the larger League of United Latin American Citizens (LULAC), which would help advance civil rights for all Americans.

## THE ROAD TO SUBURBIA

As fast as the cities mushroomed in the 1920s, the suburbs grew twice as fast. Automobiles created the modern suburb. Nineteenth-century suburbs were small and linear, stretching along the street railway system. The new developments were sprawling and dispersed, for the automobile enabled people to live in formerly remote areas. A single-family house surrounded by a lawn became the social ideal, a pastoral escape from the overcrowded and dangerous city. Many suburbs excluded African Americans, Hispanics, Jews, and working-class people.

Suburbanization and the automobile brought other changes. The government provided federal money to states to build highways, and by the end of the decade, road construction was the largest single item in the national budget. Autos and suburbs also stimulated the growth of new industries. In 1922, J. C. Nichols opened the Country Club Plaza, the first suburban shopping center, in Kansas City; it provided free off-street parking. Department stores and other large retailers began leaving the urban cores for the suburbs, where both parking and more affluent customers were waiting. Drive-in restaurants began with Royce Hailey's Pig Stand in Dallas in 1921. That same year, the first fast-food franchise chain, White Castle, appeared, with its standardized menu and building, serving hamburgers "by the sack" to Americans in record numbers.

*Zora Neale Hurston, folklorist, anthropologist, and novelist, wrote with wit and verve about the African-American South she so closely studied. Part of the dynamic community known as the Harlem Renaissance, Hurston won recognition in 1925 for her short story "Spunk." Her collective work, especially her later novel,* Their Eyes Were Watching God, *both reflected and advanced the creative pulse of what one black intellectual regarded as the first opportunity for African Americans to realize "group expression and self-determination."*

# MASS CULTURE IN THE JAZZ AGE

HOW DID new systems of distribution, marketing, and mass communication shape American culture?

The White Castle chain symbolized a new society and culture. Urbanization and the automobile joined with new systems of distributing, marketing, and communications to mold a mass culture of standardized experiences and interests. Not all Americans participated equally in the new culture, however, and some attacked it.

## ADVERTISING THE CONSUMER SOCIETY

Advertising and its focus on increasing consumption shaped the new society. Advertisers exhorted consumers via newspapers, billboards, streetcar signs, junk mail, radio, movies, and even skywriting. They sought to create a single market where everyone, regardless of region and ethnicity, consumed brand-name products. Advertisers attempted to stimulate new wants by ridiculing previous models or tastes as obsolete, acclaiming the convenience of a new brand, or linking the latest fashion with status or sex appeal.

The home became a focus of consumerism. Middle- and upper-class women purchased mass-produced household appliances, such as electric irons, toasters, vacuum cleaners, washing machines, and refrigerators. Working-class women bought packaged food, ready-made clothing, and other consumer goods to lighten their workload. Advertisers attempted to redefine the housewife's role as primarily that of a consumer, purchasing goods for her family.

A shifting labor market also promoted mass consumption. The increasing number of white-collar workers had more time and money for leisure and consumption. Factory workers, whose jobs often provided little challenge, less satisfaction, and no prospect

*Advertisements* (1925, 1927)

*Motion Picture Diaries* (1920s)

Making tortillas—the staple of the Mexican diet—these Mexican American women used stone mortars in the 1920s to grind the corn by hand at the El Sol del Mayo tortilla plant in East Los Angeles. Spurned by Anglo society, Mexican Americans found support, jobs, and community in the barrios where they lived and worked. The barrios also enabled some Mexican Americans, like plant owner Maria Zuevedo, to become small business owners. They provided products and services that satisfied the traditional cultural values of the Mexican community.

for advancement, found in consumption not only material rewards but, thanks to advertisers' claims, some self-respect and fulfillment as stylish and attractive people worthy of attention.

Under the stimulus of advertising, consumption increasingly displaced the traditional virtues of thrift, prudence, and avoidance of debt. Installment buying became common. By 1928, fully 85 percent of furniture, 80 percent of radios, and 75 percent of washing machines were bought on credit. But with personal debt rising more than twice as fast as incomes, even aggressive advertising and the extension of credit could not indefinitely prolong the illusion of a healthy economy.

## LEISURE AND ENTERTAINMENT

During the 1920s, Americans also spent more on recreation and leisure, important features of the new mass society. Millions of people packed into movie theaters whose ornate style symbolized their social importance.

Movies helped to spread common values and to set national trends in dress, language, and behavior. Studios made films to attract the largest audiences and fit prevailing stereotypes. Cecil B. De Mille titillated audiences while reinforcing conventional standards with religious epics like *The Ten Commandments* (1923) and *The King of Kings* (1927). Set in ancient times, such movies depicted both sinful pleasures and the eventual triumph of moral order.

Radio also helped to mold popular culture. The first radio network, the National Broadcasting Company (NBC), was formed in 1926. Soon it was charging $10,000 to broadcast a commercial to a national market. Networks provided standardized entertainment, personalities, and news to Americans across the nation. Radio incorporated listeners into a national society.

The phonograph, another popular source of entertainment, allowed families to listen to music of their choice in their own homes. The phonograph business boomed. Manufacturers turned out more than 2 million phonographs and 100 million records annually. The popularity of the trumpet player Louis Armstrong and other jazz greats gave the decade its nickname, the **Jazz Age.**

Jazz derived from African American musical traditions. The Great Migration spread it from New Orleans and Kansas City to cities throughout the nation. Its improvisational and rhythmic characteristics differed sharply from older and more formal music and were often condemned by people who feared that jazz would undermine conventional restraints on behavior. (See Global Perspectives, The International Journey of Jazz.)

Professional sports also became more commercialized. Millions of Americans, attracted by the popularity of such celebrities as Babe Ruth of the New York Yankees, crowded into baseball parks to follow major league teams. Ruth treated himself as a commercial commodity, hiring an agent, endorsing Cadillacs and alligator shoes, and defending a salary in 1932 that dwarfed that of President Hoover by declaring, "I had a better year than he did."

Large crowds turned out to watch boxers Jack Dempsey and Gene Tunney pummel each other; those who could not get tickets listened to radio announcers describe

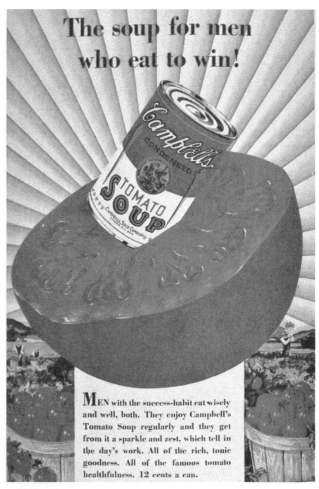

The soup for men who eat to win!

MEN with the success-habit eat wisely and well, both. They enjoy Campbell's Tomato Soup regularly and they get from it a sparkle and zest, which tell in the day's work. All of the rich, tonic goodness. All of the famous tomato healthfulness. 12 cents a can.

Advertisements for brand-name products, like this 1929 ad for Campbell's tomato soup, often tried to link simple consumption with larger issues of personal success and achievement.

**Jazz Age** The 1920s, so called for the popular music of the day as a symbol of the many changes taking place in the mass culture.

*Documents*

*Family Planning* (1926)
Eleanor Wembridge, *Petting and Necking* (1925)

*Documents*

Paul Morand, *Speakeasies in New York* (1929)

*Violinist Carroll Dickerson, at the Sunset Café in 1922, led one of the jazz bands that flourished in Chicago's many clubs, pointing up the central role of African Americans in the Jazz Age. Variety magazine dubbed Chicago the "hottest café town" in the United States, but the Illinois Vigilance Association despaired that "in Chicago alone" it had "traced the fall of 1,000 girls to jazz music" in just two years.*

WHERE TO LEARN MORE

F. Scott and Zelda Fitzgerald Museum, Montgomery, Alabama. www.alabamatravel.org/central/szfm.html

Documents

Sinclair Lewis, *Our Ideal Citizen* (1922)

Documents

H.L. Mencken, *The Sahara of the Bozart* (1920)

each blow. College football attracted frenzied followers among people with no interest in higher education.

## THE NEW MORALITY

The promotion of consumption and immediate gratification weakened traditional self-restraint and fed a desire for personal fulfillment. The failure of wartime sacrifices to achieve promised glories deepened Americans' growing disenchantment with traditional values. The social dislocations of the war years and growing urbanization accelerated moral and social change. Sexual pleasure became an increasingly open objective. Popularization of Sigmund Freud's ideas weakened prescriptions for sexual restraint; the growing availability of birth-control information enabled women to enjoy sex with less fear of pregnancy. Traditionalists worried as divorce rates, cigarette consumption, and hemlines went up while respect for parents, elders, and clergy went down.

Young people seemed to embody the new morality. Rejecting conventional standards, they embraced the era's frenzied dances, bootleg liquor, smoking, more revealing clothing, and sexual experimentation. They welcomed the freedom from parental control that the automobile afforded. The "flapper"—a frivolous young woman with short hair and a skimpy skirt who danced, smoked, and drank in oblivious self-absorption—was a major obsession in countless articles bearing such titles as "These Wild Young People" and "The Uprising of the Young."

But the new morality was neither as new nor as widespread as its advocates and critics believed. Signs of change had appeared before the Great War in the popularity of new clothing fashions, social values, and public amusements among working-class and ethnic groups. And if it now became fashionable for the middle class to adopt such attitudes and practices, most Americans still adhered to traditional beliefs and values. Moreover, the new morality offered only a limited freedom. It certainly did not promote social equality for women, who remained subject to traditional double standards, with marriage and divorce laws, property rights, and employment opportunities biased against them.

## GLOBAL PERSPECTIVES

### THE INTERNATIONAL JOURNEY OF JAZZ

A central part of American culture in the 1920s, jazz expanded its global reach in the decade known for mass production and mass consumerism. Just as Henry Ford sold his Model T cars abroad, jazz musicians took their distinctively American form of music south to Latin America and east to England, France, the Soviet Union, and China.

Jazz caught the imagination of the world. For many at home and abroad, the jarring spontaneity of jazz signaled a new age. It was, according to George Gershwin, the result of "energy stored up in America." For the composer John Alden Carpenter, it represented "the first art innovation originating in America to be accepted seriously in Europe." A German critic could not have agreed more, exclaiming, "Jazz is the expression of a Kultur epoch. . . . Jazz is a musical revelation, a religion, a philosophy of the world, just like Expressionism and Impressionism."

Jazz also had its detractors—both in the United States and abroad. At home, one of the principal architects of mass production, Henry Ford, labeled jazz "musical slush" that encouraged the youth to imitate the "drivel of morons." A noted French poet called jazz "a triumph of barbaric folly," and an English observer worried that jazz—the "aboriginal music of the Negro"—might threaten American music.

Still, the enthusiasm for jazz was so strong that white jazz musicians claimed credit for its origins—at least until the 1930s, when the historical role of African Americans in creating jazz was more fully acknowledged in the United States and Europe. Black musicians had given Europe its first taste of jazz during World War I with James Reese Europe's 369th Division Band. Throughout the 1920s, other African American bands and performers traveled abroad, spreading the international message of jazz while escaping the racism of their home country. Sam Wooding's orchestra toured Europe and the Soviet Union; Herb Flemming's band, the Red Devils, and Benny Peyton's band along with remarkable performers like Josephine Baker dazzled audiences with dance and music in Buenos Aires, Paris, and London.

Jazz underscored to America and the world that an important part of the American heritage derived from an African—not European—heritage. But as the popularity of jazz grew internationally, the music no longer belonged exclusively to Americans, or even African Americans. Other countries appropriated the music and shaped it on their own terms. Still, the origins of jazz—this movement that captured the world's attention—belonged to black musicians who regarded jazz as a special expression of the African American community.

- How did the influence of jazz affect America domestically and internationally?

## THE SEARCHING TWENTIES

Many writers rejected what they considered the materialism, conformity, and provincialism of mass culture. Their criticism made the postwar decade one of the most creative periods in American literature. The brutality and hypocrisy of the war stimulated the critics' disillusionment and alienation. What Gertrude Stein called the Lost Generation considered, in the words of F. Scott Fitzgerald, "all Gods dead, all wars fought, all faiths in man shaken." Ernest Hemingway, wounded as a Red Cross volunteer during the war, rejected idealism in his novel A Farewell to Arms (1929), declaring that he no longer saw any meaning in "the words sacred, glorious, and sacrifice."

Novelists also turned their attention to American society. In The Great Gatsby (1925), Fitzgerald traced the self-deceptions of the wealthy. Sinclair Lewis ridiculed middle-class society and its narrow business culture in Babbitt (1922), whose title character provided a new word applied to the smug and shallow. In 1930, Lewis became the first American to win the Nobel Prize in literature.

Other writers condemned the mediocrity and intolerance of mass society. The critic Harold Stearns edited *Civilization in the United States* (1922), a book of essays. Its depiction of a repressive society sunk in hypocrisy, conformity, and materialism prompted his departure for Paris, where he lived, like Hemingway and Fitzgerald, as an expatriate, alienated from America. H. L. Mencken made his *American Mercury* the leading magazine of cultural dissenters. Conventional and conservative himself, Mencken heaped vitriol on the "puritans," "peasants," and "prehensile morons" he saw everywhere in American life.

# CULTURE WARS

**WHAT EXPLAINS** resurgence of the Ku Klux Klan in the 1920s?

Despite the blossoming of mass culture and society in the 1920s, conflicts divided social groups. Some of these struggles involved reactions against the new currents in American life, including technological and scientific innovations, urban growth, and materialism. But movements to restrict immigration, enforce prohibition, prohibit the teaching of evolution, and even sustain the Ku Klux Klan did not have simple origins, motives, or consequences. The forces underlying the culture wars of the 1920s would surface repeatedly in the future (see Overview, Issues in the Culture Wars of the 1920s).

### NATIVISM AND IMMIGRATION RESTRICTION

U.S. Congress, *Debating Immigration Restriction* (1921)

For years, many Americans, from racists to reformers, had campaigned to restrict immigration. In 1917, Congress required immigrants to pass a literacy test. But renewed immigration after the war revived the anti-immigration movement, and the propaganda of the war and the Red Scare years generated public support for more restriction. Depict-

Evangelist Aimee Semple McPherson

## OVERVIEW   Issues in the Culture Wars of the 1920s

| Issue | Proponent view | Opponent view |
|---|---|---|
| The new morality | Promotes greater personal freedom and opportunities for fulfillment | Promotes moral collapse |
| Evolutionism | A scientific advance linked to notions of progress | A threat to religious belief |
| Jazz | Modern and vital | Unsettling, irregular, vulgar, and primitive |
| Immigration | A source of national strength from ethnic and racial diversity | A threat to the status and authority of old-stock white Protestants |
| Great Migration | A chance for African Americans to find new economic opportunities and gain autonomy and pride | A threat to traditional white privilege, control, and status |
| Prohibition | Promotes social and family stability and reduces crime | Restricts personal liberty and increases crime |
| Fundamentalism | An admirable adherence to traditional religious faith and biblical injunctions | A superstitious creed given to intolerant interference in social and political affairs |
| Ku Klux Klan | An organization promoting community responsibility, patriotism, and traditional social, moral, and religious values | A group of religious and racial bigots given to violent vigilantism and fostering moral and public corruption |
| Mass culture | Increases popular participation in national culture; provides entertainment | Promotes conformity, materialism, mediocrity, spectacle, and relaxation |
| Consumerism | Promotes material progress and higher living standards | Promotes waste, sterility, and self-indulgence |

ing immigrants as radicals, racial inferiors, religious subversives, or criminals, nativists clamored for congressional action. The Emergency Quota Act of 1921 reduced immigration by about two-thirds and established quotas for nationalities on the basis of their numbers in the United States in 1910. Restrictionists, however, demanded more stringent action, especially against the largely Catholic and Jewish immigrants from southern and eastern Europe. Coolidge himself urged that America "be kept American," by which he meant white, Anglo-Saxon, and Protestant.

Congress adopted this racist rationale in the **National Origins Act of 1924,** which proclaimed its objective to be the maintenance of the "racial preponderance" of "the basic strain of our population." This law restricted immigration quotas to 2 percent of the foreign-born population of each nationality as recorded in the 1890 census, which was taken before the mass immigration from southern and eastern Europe. Another provision, effective in 1929, restricted total annual immigration to 150,000, with quotas that nearly eliminated southern and eastern Europeans. The law also completely excluded Japanese immigrants.

Other actions targeted Japanese residents in America. California, Oregon, Washington, Arizona, and other western states prohibited them from owning or leasing land, and in 1922, the Supreme Court ruled that, as nonwhites, they could never become

**National Origins Act of 1924** Law sharply restricting immigration on the basis of immigrants' national origins and discriminating against southern and eastern Europeans and Asians.

**Nisei** U.S. citizens born of immigrant Japanese parents.

*National Origins Quota Act* (1924)

**QUICK REVIEW**

**The New Klan**

◆ National movement claiming millions of members.

◆ Functioned as a fraternal organization providing community activities.

◆ Focused particularly on hatred of Catholics and Jews.

◆ Popular backlash contributed to Klan's collapse by 1930.

Hiram Evans, *The Klan's Fight for Americanism* (1926)

naturalized citizens. Dispirited by the prejudice of the decade, Japanese residents hoped for fulfillment through their children, the **Nisei,** who were American citizens by birth.

Ironically, the Philippines, as a U.S. territory, was not subject to the National Origins Act, and Filipino immigration increased ninefold during the 1920s. Most Filipino newcomers became farm laborers, especially in California, or worked in Alaskan fisheries. Similarly, because the law did not apply to immigrants from the Western Hemisphere, Mexican immigration also grew. Nativists lobbied to exclude Mexicans, but agribusiness interests in the Southwest blocked any restrictions on low-cost migrant labor.

## THE KU KLUX KLAN

Nativism was also reflected in the popularity of the revived Ku Klux Klan, the goal of which, according to its leader, was to protect "the interest of those whose forefathers established the nation." Founded in Georgia in 1915 and modeled on its Reconstruction predecessor, the new Klan was a national, not only a southern, movement and claimed several million members by the mid-1920s. Admitting only native-born white Protestants, the Klan embodied the fears of a traditional culture threatened by social change. Ironically, its rapid spread owed much to modern business and promotional techniques as hundreds of professional recruiters raked in hefty commissions selling Klan memberships to those hoping to defend their way of life.

In part, the Klan was a fraternal order, providing entertainment, assistance, and community for its members. Its picnics, parades, charity drives, and other social and family-oriented activities—perhaps a half-million women joined the Women of the Ku Klux Klan—sharply distinguished the organization from both the small, secretive Klan of the nineteenth century and the still smaller, extremist Klan of the later twentieth century. Regarding themselves as reformers, Klan members supported immigration restriction and Prohibition.

But the Klan also exploited racial, ethnic, and religious prejudices and campaigned against many social groups and what it called "alien creeds." It attacked African Americans in the South, Mexicans in Texas, Japanese in California, and Catholics and Jews everywhere. A twisted religious impulse ran through much of the Klan's organization and activities. It hired itinerant Protestant ministers to spread its message, erected altars and flaming crosses at its meetings, and sang Klan lyrics to the tunes of well-known hymns. The Klan also resorted to violence. In 1921, for example, a Methodist minister who belonged to the Klan murdered a Catholic priest on his own doorstep, and other Klansmen burned down Catholic churches. The leader of the Oregon Klan insisted that "the only way to cure a Catholic is to kill him."

To the Klan, Catholics and Jews symbolized not merely subversive religions but also the ethnic diversity and swelling urban population that challenged traditional Protestant culture. To protect that culture, the Klan attempted to censor or disrupt "indecent" entertainment, assaulted those it accused of adultery, and terrorized doctors who performed abortions.

While the Klan's appeal seemed rooted in the declining countryside, it also attracted urban residents. Chicago had the largest Klan organization in the nation, with 50,000 members, and Houston, Dallas, Portland, Indianapolis, Denver, and the satellite communities ringing Los Angeles were also Klan strongholds. Urban Klansmen were largely lower or lower middle class, many recently arrived from the country and retaining its attitudes; others were long-term urban residents who feared being marginalized by social changes, especially by competition from immigrants and new ideas.

Klan Day at the races

The Klan also ventured into politics, with some success. But eventually it encountered resistance. In the North, Catholic workers disrupted Klan parades. In the South, too, Klan excesses provoked a backlash. After the Klan in Dallas flogged 68 people in a "whipping meadow" along the Trinity River in 1922, respect turned to outrage. Newspapers demanded that the Klan disband, district attorneys began to prosecute Klan thugs, and in 1924 Klan candidates were defeated by a ticket headed by Miriam "Ma" Ferguson, whose gubernatorial campaign called for anti-Klan laws and for the loss of tax exemptions for churches used for Klan meetings. Elsewhere the Klan was stung by revelations of criminal behavior and corruption by Klan leaders, who had been making fortunes pocketing membership fees and selling regalia to followers. The Klan crusade to purify society had bred corruption and conflict everywhere. By 1930, the Klan had nearly collapsed.

## PROHIBITION AND CRIME

Like the Klan, Prohibition both reflected and provoked social tensions in the 1920s. Reformers had long believed that prohibiting the sale of alcohol would improve social conditions, reduce crime and family instability, increase economic efficiency, and purify politics. They rejoiced in 1920 when the Eighteenth Amendment, prohibiting the manufacture, sale, or transportation of alcoholic beverages, took effect. Congress then passed the **Volstead Act,** which defined the forbidden liquors and established the Prohibition Bureau to enforce the law. But many social groups, especially in urban ethnic communities, opposed Prohibition, and the government could not enforce the law where public opinion did not endorse it.

Evasion was easy. By permitting alcohol for medicinal, sacramental, and industrial purposes, the Volstead Act gave doctors, priests, and druggists a huge loophole through which to satisfy their friends' needs. City-dwellers made "bathtub gin," and

**Volstead Act** The 1920 law defining the liquor forbidden under the Eighteenth Amendment and giving enforcement responsibilities to the Prohibition Bureau of the Department of the Treasury.

## AMERICAN VIEWS

### Evangelism and the Search for Salvation

Aimee Semple McPherson defied traditional roles for women in becoming one of the most famous evangelical leaders in the United States. Traveling in her "Gospel Car," she crisscrossed the nation reminding her followers that "Jesus Is Coming Soon" and advising them to "Get Ready." In 1923, she opened the Angelus Temple in Los Angeles—a white-domed building large enough for 5,000 followers of what McPherson called the "Foursquare Gospel." A lighted rotating cross on top of the dome could be seen from fifty miles away—a beacon for those who journeyed to her center of "spiritual energy." A charismatic orator, McPherson embraced the theatrics of Hollywood to stir her crowds and raised vast sums of money, or "love gifts," to finance the Temple and its activities. Playing upon the phrase shareholder, McPherson sold doll-house chairs for $25 each, enabling purchasers to be "chair-holders" in the Temple. Though tainted by a mysterious disappearance in 1926, she remained extraordinarily popular, attracting crowds of thousands who sought salvation during times of change and uncertainty. McPherson died in 1944 from an accidental overdose of sleeping pills.

In this excerpt from one of her autobiographies, McPherson describes the growth of the Angelus Temple and her pioneering use of radio to advance her "success in soul winning."

- **Why** was Aimee Semple McPherson so popular in the 1920s?
- **What** does her success suggest about the role of religion in American life?
- **How** do you think evangelicals like McPherson might have viewed the cult of business that also characterized the decade?

From the days the doors opened on January 1, 1923, a mighty spiritual revival surged into Angelus Temple with ever-increasing power and fervor. Eight thousand converts knelt at the altars in the first six months and fifteen hundred believers were immersed in the baptistry. Hundreds were healed and baptized with the Holy Spirit. One thousand young people convenanted together to serve as the Angelus Temple Foursquare Crusaders. And as the weeks and months passed, new outreaches commenced.

In February, the Prayer Tower opened, where prayer has not ceased as men gather in two-hour shifts during the night and women pray during the day, bringing God thousands of requests which come by mail, telephone, and telegraph from all over the world.

Then came the challenge of the radio! . . . My soul was thrilled with the possibilities this media offered for the spread of gospel. We secured time on a radio station and began broadcasting a few services. But the thought persisted that if Angelus Temple had her own radio station we could broadcast almost all of the meetings!

And God provided through the love gifts of his people for the radio station. In February 1924, KFSG—Kall Four Square Gospel—went on the air, broadcasting the glorious song, "Give the winds a mighty voice, Jesus saves!" . . . Time and time again converted gamblers, dope addicts, bootleggers, and white-slavery victims rose from knees to send thrilling testimonies out over radio station KFSG as well as to the Temple audience. . . . For three years I stayed close by Angelus Temple, preaching and teaching many times a week, conducting a daily "Sunshine Hour" broadcast, writing, editing, publishing, and praying for the sick. . . . The revival swept on and out. Branch churches sprang up in cities and towns. [And the Foursquare gospel] message has become well known around the world.

Source: *Aimee Semple McPherson: The Story of My Life* (Waco, TX: Word Books, 1973).

rural people distilled "moonshine." Scofflaws frequented the speakeasies that replaced saloons or bought liquor from bootleggers and rumrunners, who imported it from Canada, Cuba, or Mexico. The limited resources of the Prohibition Bureau often allowed bootleggers to operate openly.

The ethics and business methods of bootleggers soon shocked Americans, however. The huge profits encouraged organized crime, which had previously concentrated on gambling and prostitution, to develop elaborate liquor-distribution networks. Operating outside the law, crime "families" used violence to enforce contracts, suppress competition, and attack rivals. In Chicago, Al Capone's army of nearly a thousand gangsters killed hundreds. Using the profits from bootlegging and new tools like the automobile and the submachine gun, organized crime corrupted city governments and police forces.

Gradually, even many "drys"—people who had initially favored Prohibition—dropped their support, horrified by the boost the amendment gave organized crime and worried about the general disrespect for law that it promoted. A 1926 poll found that four-fifths of Americans wanted to repeal or modify Prohibition. Yet it remained in force because it was entangled in party politics and social conflict. Democrats called for repeal in their 1928 and 1932 platforms, and in 1933, 36 states ratified an amendment repealing what Herbert Hoover had called a "noble experiment."

## OLD-TIME RELIGION AND THE SCOPES TRIAL

Religion provided another fulcrum for traditionalists attempting to stem cultural change. Protestant fundamentalism, which emphasized the infallibility of the Bible, including the creation story, emerged at the turn of the century as a conservative reaction to religious modernism and the social changes brought by the mass immigration of Catholics and Jews, the growing influence of science and technology, and the secularization of public education. But the fundamentalist crusade to reshape America became formidable only in the 1920s. Evangelists like Billy Sunday and Aimee Semple McPherson attracted thousands to their revivals across America. (See American Views, Evangelism and the Search for Salvation.)

**Interpreting the Past**
*The Scopes Trial as a Harbinger of Change* (pp. 738–739)

Fundamentalist groups, colleges, and publications sprang up throughout the nation, especially in the South. The anti-Catholic sentiment exploited by the Klan was but one consequence of fundamentalism's insistence on strict biblical Christianity. A second was the assault on Darwin's theory of evolution, which contradicted literal interpretations of biblical Creation. Fundamentalist legislators tried to prevent the teaching of evolution in public schools in at least 20 states. In 1923, Oklahoma banned textbooks based on Darwinian theory, and Florida's legislature denounced teaching evolution as "subversive." In 1925, Tennessee forbade teaching any idea contrary to the biblical account of human origins.

Social or political conservatism, however, was not an inherent part of old-time religion. The most prominent antievolution politician, William Jennings Bryan, continued to campaign for political, social, and economic reforms. Never endorsing the Klan, he served on the American Committee on the Rights of Religious Minorities and condemned anti-Semitism and anti-Catholicism. Bryan feared that Darwinism promoted political and economic conservatism.

The controversy over evolution came to a head when the American Civil Liberties Union (ACLU) responded to Tennessee's violation of the constitutional separation of church and state by offering to defend any teacher who tested the antievolution law. John Scopes, a high school biology teacher in Dayton, Tennessee, did so and was arrested. The Scopes trial attracted national attention after Bryan agreed to assist the prosecution and Clarence Darrow, a famous Chicago lawyer and prominent atheist, volunteered to defend Scopes.

Millions of Americans tuned their radios to hear the first trial ever broadcast. The judge, a fundamentalist, sat under a sign urging people to "Read Your Bible Daily." He ruled that scientists could not testify in support of evolution: Because they were not present at the Creation, their testimony would be "hearsay." But he did allow Darrow to put Bryan on the stand as an expert on the Bible. Bryan insisted on the literal truth of every story in the Bible, allowing Darrow to ridicule his ideas and force him to concede that some biblical passages had to be construed symbolically. Though the local jury took only eight minutes to convict Scopes, fundamentalists suffered public ridicule from reporters.

But fundamentalism was hardly destroyed, and antievolutionists continued their campaign. New organizations, such as the Bryan Bible League, lobbied for state laws and an antievolution amendment to the Constitution. Three more states forbade teaching evolution, but by 1929 the movement had faltered. Even so, fundamentalism retained religious influence and would again challenge science and modernism in American life.

**myhistorylab**
**From Then to Now Online**
*Culture Wars*

**WHAT ROLE** did the United States play in international diplomacy in the decade after World War I?

# A NEW ERA IN THE WORLD?

Abroad and at home, Americans in the 1920s sought peace and economic order. Rejection of the Treaty of Versailles and the League of Nations did not foreshadow isolationism. Indeed, in the 1920s, the United States became more deeply involved in international matters than ever before in peacetime. This involvement both produced important successes and sowed the seeds for serious future problems.

## WAR DEBTS AND ECONOMIC EXPANSION

The United States was the world's dominant economic power in the 1920s, changed by the Great War from a debtor to a creditor nation. The loans the United States had made to its allies during the war troubled the nation's relations with Europe throughout the decade. American insistence on repayment angered Europeans, who saw the money as a U.S. contribution to the joint war effort against Germany. Moreover, high American tariffs blocked Europeans from exporting goods to the United States and earning dollars to repay their debts. Eventually, the United States readjusted the terms for repayment, and American bankers extended large loans to Germany, which used the money to pay reparations to Britain and France, whose governments then used the same money to repay the United States. This unstable system depended on a continuous flow of money from the United States.

America's global economic role expanded in other ways as well. Exports, especially of manufactured goods, soared. To expand their markets and avoid foreign tariffs, many U.S. companies became **multinational corporations,** establishing branches or subsidiaries abroad. Ford built assembly plants in England, Japan, Turkey, and Canada. International Telephone and Telegraph owned two dozen factories in Europe and employed more overseas workers than any other U.S. corporation.

Other companies gained control of foreign supply sources. American oil companies invested in foreign oil fields, especially in Latin America, where they controlled more than half of Venezuelan production. The United Fruit Company developed such huge operations in Central America that it often dominated national economies. In Costa Rica, the company had a larger budget than the national government.

Europeans and Latin Americans alike worried about this economic invasion; even Secretary of Commerce Herbert Hoover expressed concerns. Multinationals, he warned, might eventually take markets from American manufacturers and jobs from American workers. Business leaders, however, dismissed such reservations.

**Multinational Corporations** Firms with direct investments, branches, factories, and offices in a number of countries.

Hoover's concerns, moreover, did not prevent him from promoting economic expansion abroad. The government worked to open doors for American businesses in foreign countries, helping them to secure access to trade, investment opportunities, and raw materials. Hoover's Bureau of Foreign Commerce opened 50 offices around the world to boost American business. Hoover also pressed the British to give U.S. corporations access to rubber production in the British colony of Malaya. Secretary of State Charles Evans Hughes negotiated access to Iraqi oil fields for U.S. oil companies. The government also authorized bankers and manufacturers to form combinations, exempt from antitrust laws, to exploit foreign markets.

## REJECTING WAR

Although government officials cooperated with business leaders to promote American strategic and economic interests, they had little desire to use force abroad. Popular reaction against the Great War, strengthened by a strong peace movement, constrained policymakers. Having repudiated collective security as embodied in the League of Nations, the United States nonetheless sought to minimize international conflict and promote its national security. In particular, the State Department sought to restrict the buildup of armaments among nations.

At the invitation of President Harding, delegations from nine nations met in Washington at the Washington Naval Conference in 1921 to discuss disarmament. The conference drafted a treaty to reduce battleship tonnage and suspend the building of new ships for a decade. Japan and the United States also agreed not to fortify their possessions in the Pacific any further and to respect the Open Door in East Asia. Public opinion welcomed the treaty; the U.S. Senate ratified it with only one dissenting vote, and the 1924 Republican platform hailed it as "the greatest peace document ever drawn."

The United States made a more dramatic gesture in 1928, when it helped draft the **Kellogg-Briand Pact.** Signed by 64 nations, the treaty renounced aggression and outlawed war. Without provisions for enforcement, however, it was little more than symbolic. The Senate reserved the right of self-defense, repudiated any responsibility for enforcing the treaty, and maintained U.S. claims under the Monroe Doctrine.

## MANAGING THE HEMISPHERE

Senate insistence on the authority of the Monroe Doctrine reflected the U.S. claim to a predominant role in Latin America. The United States continued to dominate the hemisphere to promote its own interests. It exerted its influence through investments, control of the Panama Canal, invocation of the Monroe Doctrine, and, when necessary, military intervention.

In response to American public opinion, the peace movement, and Latin American nationalism, the United States retreated from the extreme gunboat diplomacy of the Progressive Era, withdrawing troops from the Dominican Republic and Nicaragua. But Haiti remained under U.S. occupation throughout the decade, American troops stayed in Cuba and Panama, and the United States directed the financial policies of other Latin American countries. Moreover, it sent the marines into Honduras in 1924 and back to Nicaragua in 1926. Such interventions could establish only temporary stability while provoking further Latin American hostility.

Latin American resentment led to a resolution at the 1928 Inter-America Conference denying the right of any nation "to intervene in the internal affairs of another." The U.S. delegation rejected the measure, but the anger of Latin Americans prompted the Hoover administration to rescind support for the Roosevelt Corollary (see

**Kellogg-Briand Pact**  A 1928 international treaty that denounced aggression and war but lacked provisions for enforcement.

Chapter 22), and J. Reuben Clark, chief legal officer of the State Department, drafted the Clark Memorandum. Not published until 1930, this document stated that the Roosevelt Corollary was not a legitimate extension of the Monroe Doctrine and thereby helped prepare the way for the so-called Good Neighbor Policy toward Latin America. Still, the United States did not pledge nonintervention and retained the means, both military and economic, to dominate the hemisphere.

# HERBERT HOOVER AND THE FINAL TRIUMPH OF THE NEW ERA

**WHAT FACTORS** contributed to Herbert Hoover's victory in 1928 over his Democratic opponent, Alfred E. Smith? In what ways did Hoover epitomize the policies of the New Era?

As the national economy steamed ahead in 1928, the Republicans chose as their presidential candidate Herbert Hoover, a man who symbolized the policies of prosperity and the New Era. Hoover was not a politician—he had never been elected to office—but a successful administrator who championed rational and efficient economic development.

The Democrats, by contrast, chose a candidate who evoked the cultural conflicts of the 1920s. Alfred E. Smith, a four-term governor of New York, was a Catholic, an opponent of Prohibition, and a Tammany politician tied to the immigrant constituency of New York City. His nomination plunged the nation into the cultural strife that had divided the Democrats in 1924. Rural fundamentalism, anti-Catholicism, Prohibition, and nativism were crucial factors in the campaign.

But Hoover was, in certain ways, the more progressive candidate. Sympathetic to labor, sensitive to women's issues, hostile to racial segregation, and favorable to the League of Nations, Hoover had always distanced himself from what he called "the reactionary group in the Republican party." By contrast, despite supporting factory reform and state welfare legislation to benefit his urban working-class constituents, Smith was essentially conservative and as parochial as his most rural adversaries.

Although many Americans voted against Smith because of his social background, the same characteristics attracted others. Millions of urban and ethnic voters, previously Republican or politically uninvolved, voted for Smith and laid the basis for the new Democratic coalition that would emerge in the 1930s. In 1928, however, with the nation still enjoying the economic prosperity so closely associated with Hoover and the Republicans, the Democrats were routed.

# CONCLUSION

The New Era of the 1920s changed America. Technological and managerial innovations produced giant leaps in productivity, new patterns of labor, a growing concentration of corporate power, and high corporate profits. Government policies, from protective tariffs and regressive taxation to the relaxation of regulatory laws, reflected and reinforced the triumphs of the business elite over traditional cautions and concerns.

The decade's economic developments, in turn, stimulated social change, drawing millions of Americans from the countryside to the cities, creating an urban nation, and fostering a new ethic of materialism, consumerism, and leisure and a new mass culture based on the automobile, radio, the movies, and advertising. This social transformation swept up many Americans but left others unsettled by the erosion of traditional practices and values. The concerns of traditionalists found expression in campaigns for prohibition and against immigration, the revival of the Ku Klux Klan, and the rise of religious fundamentalism. Intellectuals denounced the materialism and conformity they saw in the new social order and fashioned new artistic and literary trends.

But the impact of the decade's trends was uneven. Mechanization increased the productivity of some workers but cost others their jobs; people poured into the cities while others left for the suburbs; Prohibition, intended to stabilize society, instead produced conflict, crime, and corruption; government policies advanced some economic interests but injured others. Even the notion of a "mass" culture obscured the degree to which millions of Americans were left out of the New Era. With no disposable income and little access to electricity, rural Americans scarcely participated in the joys of consumerism; racial and ethnic minorities were often isolated in ghettos and barrios; and many workers faced declining opportunities. Most ominous was the uneven prosperity undergirding the New Era. Although living standards rose for many Americans and the rich expanded their share of the national wealth, more than 40 percent of the population earned less than $1,500 a year and fell below the established poverty level. The unequal distribution of wealth and income made the economy unstable and vulnerable to a disastrous collapse.

# SUMMARY

## WHAT CONTRIBUTED to the economic boom of the 1920s?

**The Economy that Roared**  Following a postwar depression in 1920 and 1921, the American economy boomed through the rest of the decade. Mechanization of production, investment, new industries such as broadcasting and motion pictures and the automobile industry drove the economy. Oligopoly eliminated competition; Americans accepted the idea that size brought efficiency and productivity. While many businesses boomed, "sick" industries such as textiles, coal mining, agriculture and railroads dragged the economy down. Not all Americans shared in the economic boom; the gap between rich and poor widened.

## WHAT WAS the relationship between big business and government in the 1920s?

**The Business of Government**  The Republican surge in national politics also shaped the economy; a business government went hand in hand with a business country. Government regulation was curtailed, business supporters were installed in regulatory agencies, and the Supreme Court became a champion of business. While the Progressive party had little impact on politics, progressivism was not dead but had lost much of its energy and focus.

## WHAT LED to the Great Migration?

**Cities and Suburbs**  By 1920 more Americans lived in urban than rural areas; the massive population movement interacted with technological innovations to reshape cities, build automobile-accessible suburbs, and transform urban life. The South was the most rapidly urbanizing region; however, African Americans left the South for job opportunities in Midwestern and Northern cities; increased racial pride found expression in the Harlem Renaissance. Puerto Ricans and Mexicans moved into U.S. cities creating their own communities. Suburbs grew more rapidly than cities as middle-class enclaves created by automobiles.

## HOW DID new systems of distribution, marketing, and mass communication shape American culture?

**Mass Culture in the Jazz Age**  Fast food chains symbolized a new society and culture; advertising and its focus on increasing consumption shaped the new society. Brand-name goods, mass consumption, and buying on credit became hallmarks of the new American economy. People also spent more on recreation and leisure; radio, the phonograph, and the movies competed with college football, professional baseball, and boxing during the Jazz Age. The social dislocations and America's growing disenchantment with traditional values fueled the new morality among the young; writers of the Lost Generation criticized the new era.

## WHAT EXPLAINS the resurgence of the Ku Klux Klan in the 1920s?

**Culture Wars**  Despite the new mass culture of the 1920's, conflicts divided social groups. Some of these struggles involved reactions against the new currents in American life, including technical and scientific innovation, urban growth, and materialism. Nativism, racism, religion, dislike of modernism and the expanding role of science, and the desire to return to and strengthen traditional rural values were all underlying issues in the culture wars.

## WHAT ROLE did the United States play in international diplomacy in the decade after World War I?

**A New Era in the World?**  The United States was changed by the Great War into a creditor nation. The loans made to the Allies troubled America's relations with Europe as America insisted on repayment; however, high tariffs blocked Europe exporting goods and earning money to repay those debts. America's global economic role expanded and companies became multinational corporations; Europe and Latin America resented this economic invasion. Reaction to the Great War resulted in America, along, with sixty-four other nations, outlawing war in 1928.

## WHAT FACTORS contributed to Herbert Hoover's victory in 1928 over his Democratic opponent, Alfred E. Smith? In what ways did Hoover epitomize the policies of the New Era?

**Herbert Hoover and the Triumph of the New Era**  Herbert Hoover's election as president in 1928 seemed the "final triumph over poverty"; in 1929, the Great Depression would begin.

# WHERE TO LEARN MORE

**F. Scott and Zelda Fitzgerald Museum, Montgomery, Alabama.** The novelist and his wife lived a short while in this house in her hometown. **www.alabamatravel.org/central/szfm.html**

**Herbert Hoover National Historic Site, West Branch, Iowa.** Visitors may tour Hoover's birthplace cottage, presidential library, and museum. **www.hoover.archives.gov**

**Henry Ford Museum and Greenfield Village, Dearborn, Michigan.** Among many fascinating exhibits, "The Automobile in American Life" superbly demonstrates the importance of the automobile in American social history. **www.hfmgv.org**

**Warren G. Harding House, Marion, Ohio.** Harding's home from 1891 to 1921 is now a museum with period furnishings. **www.ohiohistory.org/places/harding**

**Calvin Coolidge Homestead, Plymouth, Vermont.** Operated by the Vermont Division of Historic Sites, the homestead preserves the exact interiors and furnishings from when Coolidge took the presidential oath of office there in 1923. **www.calvin-coolidge.org/pages/homestead** and **www.dhca.state.vt.us/HistoricSites/sites.htm**

# STUDY RESOURCES

## PEARSON myhistorylab

For study resources for this chapter, go to www.myhistorylab.com and choose *The American Journey*. You will find a wealth of study and review material for this chapter, including pre- and post-tests, customized study plan, key term review flash cards, interactive map and document activities, and documents for analysis.

# REVIEW QUESTIONS

1. How did the automobile industry affect the nation's economy and society in the 1920s? In the excerpt from *The Flivver King*, how does Upton Sinclair illustrate the tension between workers and technology even as they both served Henry Ford's vision of mass production and mass consumerism?

2. What factors characterized the boom industries of the 1920s? The sick industries? How accurate is it to label the 1920s the decade of prosperity?

3. What were the underlying issues in the election of 1924? Of 1928? What role did politics play in the public life of the 1920s?

4. What were the chief points of conflict in the culture wars of the 1920s? What were the underlying issues in these clashes? Why were they so hard to compromise?

5. In what ways did the World War experience shape developments in the 1920s?

6. What were the chief features of American involvement in world affairs in the 1920s? To what extent did that involvement constitute a new role for the United States?

## KEY TERMS

**Great Migration** (p. 720)
**Harlem Renaissance** (p. 720)
**Jazz Age** (p. 723)
**Kellogg-Briand Pact** (p. 733)
**League of Women Voters** (p. 718)
**Multinational corporations** (p. 732)
**National Origins Act of 1924** (p. 727)

*Nisei* (p. 728)
**Oligopoly** (p. 713)
**Open-shop** (p. 713)
**Sheppard-Towner Maternity and Infancy Act** (p. 718)
**Volstead Act** (p. 729)
**Welfare capitalism** (p. 713)
**Yellow-dog contracts** (p. 713)

## The Scopes Monkey Trial as a Harbinger of Change

**EXAMINE** the history and impact of Tennessee's Butler Act (1925) and the trial of John T. Scopes that followed. Would contemporary observers consider the jury decision in the Scopes Trial to be the final decision on the issue of teaching evolution in the public schools of America, or did they have an inkling of the future of this issue?

The Roaring '20's was a decade of turmoil and change in the United States on many levels. All this insecurity unsettled American traditionalists, especially religious fundamentalists. In rural states fundamentalists possessed a majority and control of the state legislature. John Washington Butler, a part time preacher and full time farmer served in the Tennessee legislature, had never read anything about evolution, but heard it denied the teachings of the Bible. He formulated a bill to forbid the teaching of evolution in the schools of Tennessee titled "AN ACT prohibiting the teaching of the Evolution Theory in all the Universities, Normals and all other public schools of Tennessee . . ."

The Butler Act provoked an immediate reaction from the American Civil Liberties Union. To challenge the law, John T. Scopes agreed to be arrested and placed on trial. William Jennings Bryan, a prominent fundamentalist Christian, was seeking the Democratic presidential nomination again in the 1928 election and saw this trial as a vehicle to promote his candidacy. Clarence Darrow, nationally famous criminal lawyer, liberal, and agnostic, took the role of the defense as a matter of conviction. A circus of a trial followed.

John T. Scopes was found guilty and fined. The sentence was appealed to the Tennessee Supreme Court, which upheld the Dayton sentence, but set the sentence aside on a legal technicality that the jury had not set the fine levied against Scopes. The Butler Act would not be repealed by the Tennessee state legislature until 1967. The U.S. Supreme Court would declare similar laws to be unconstitutional in an Arkansas case in 1968.

*Through the historical figures of William Jennings Bryan and Clarence Darrow, the Scopes Trial symbolized the cultural battles of the twenties. And when Darrow (leaning against the table) interrogated Bryan on the accuracy of the Bible, the New York Times called the exchange the "most amazing courtroom scene in Anglo-American history."*

### Butler Act, 1925

That it shall be unlawful for any teacher in any of the Universities, Normals and all other public schools of the State which are supported in whole or in part by the public school funds of the State, to teach any theory that denies the story of the Divine Creation of man as taught in the Bible, and to teach instead that man has descended from a lower order of animals.

### H. L. Mencken, Aftermath (of the Scopes Trial), *Baltimore Evening Sun*, September 14, 1925

True enough, even a superstitious man has certain inalienable rights. He has a right to harbor and indulge his imbecilities as long as he pleases, provided only he does not try to inflict them upon other men by force. He has a right to argue for them as eloquently as he can, in season and out of season. He has a right to teach them to his children. But certainly he has no right to be protected against the free criticism of those who do not hold them. He has no right to demand that they be treated as sacred. He has no right to preach them without challenge. . . .

The meaning of religious freedom, I fear, is sometimes greatly misapprehended. It is taken to be a sort of immunity, not merely from governmental control but also from public opinion. A dunderhead gets himself a long-tailed coat, rises behind the sacred desk, and emits such bilge as would gag a Hottentot. Is it to pass unchallenged? If so, then what we have is not religious freedom at all, but the most intolerable and outrageous variety of religious despotism. Any fool, once he is admitted to holy orders, becomes infallible. Any half-wit, by the simple device of ascribing his delusions to revelation, takes on an authority that is denied to all the rest of us.

## Epperson V. Arkansas, 393 U.S. 97 (1968)

In the present case, there can be no doubt that Arkansas has sought to prevent its teachers from discussing the theory of evolution because it is contrary to the belief of some that the Book of Genesis must be the exclusive source of doctrine as to the origin of man. No suggestion has been made that Arkansas' law may be justified by considerations of state policy other than the religious views of some of its citizens. It is clear that fundamentalist sectarian conviction was and is the law's reason for existence. Its antecedent, Tennessee's "monkey law," candidly stated its purpose: to make it unlawful "to teach any theory that denies the story of the Divine Creation of man as taught in the Bible, and to teach instead that man has descended from a lower order of animals." Perhaps the sensational publicity attendant upon the Scopes trial induced Arkansas to adopt less explicit language. It eliminated Tennessee's reference to "the story of the Divine Creation of man" as taught in the Bible, but there is no doubt that the motivation for the law was the same: to suppress the teaching of a theory which, it was thought, "denied" the divine creation of man.

Arkansas' law cannot be defended as an act of religious neutrality. Arkansas did not seek to excise from the curricula of its schools and universities all discussion of the origin of man. The law's effort was confined to an attempt to blot out a particular theory because of its supposed conflict with the Biblical account, literally read. Plainly, the law is contrary to the mandate of the First, and in violation of the Fourteenth, Amendment to the Constitution.

The judgment of the Supreme Court of Arkansas is Reversed.

*John T. Scopes was a part time biology teacher and full time football coach from Dayton, Tennessee.*

"WHAT WOULD THEIR VERDICT BE?"
—*The Daily Star* (Montreal).

*What Would Their Verdict Be?* The Daily Star *(Montreal),* reprinted in the Literary Digest, *July 25, 1925*

# 25

# The Great Depression and the New Deal

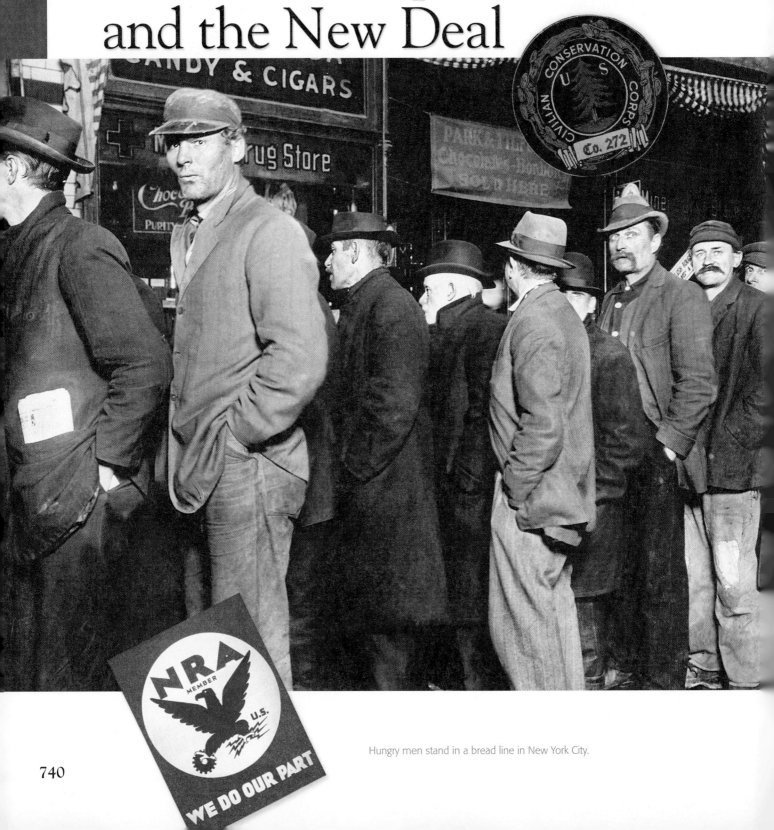

CANDY & CIGARS

Drug Store

PARK & TILF
Chocolate Bonbons
SOLD HERE

Choco
PURITY

CONSERVATION
CIVILIAN CORPS
U S
Co. 272

NRA
MEMBER
U.S.
WE DO OUR PART

Hungry men stand in a bread line in New York City.

**WHAT TRIGGERED** the Great Depression?

**HOW DID** Herbert Hoover respond to the Depression? Why did his policies fail?

**WHAT WERE** the goals of the early New Deal?

**WHAT WERE** the major accomplishments of the Second New Deal?

**WHAT EXPLAINS** labor's resurgence in the 1930s?

**WHY DID** the New Deal lose momentum after 1936?

**HOW DID** Roosevelt respond to the rise of fascism in Europe?

My mother had two small babies on her hands. When I became sickly, Grandmother Josefa took me home with her, and I never returned to my parents. . . . My grandmother's house was located on the "American" side of town, but there was nothing they could do about it because she was there before anybody else. My grandmother worked very hard; I grew up in the Depression.

When it was time for me to go to school I was assigned to [the] Mexican side of town. We were segregated; [the] Anglo children were sent to Roosevelt and the Mexican children who lived closer to Roosevelt [still] had to go down to Harding. I'll admit, there was a lot of discrimination in those years.

During the Depression my grandmother sewed piecework for the WPA. My dad helped out when he could [and] Uncle Ernesto also worked. He used to dig graves.

The Depression years were very, very hard. I remember seeing the people passing on their way to California. . . . It hurt me to see the people in their rickety old cars, their clothes in tatters, escaping from the drought and the dust bowls.

*Oral Testimony,*
*Carlotta Silvas Martin*

On April 27 [1933], according to the New York Times, Paul Schneider, aged forty-four, a sick and crippled Chicago school teacher, shot himself to death. His widow, left with three children, stated that he had not been paid for eight months. . . . Less than a month after Paul Schneider's discouragement drove him to suicide, the militant action of Chicago teachers—patient no more . . . resulted in the payment of $12,000,000 due them for the last months of 1932. Their pay for the five months of 1933 is still owed them. Five hundred of them are reported to be in asylums and sanitariums as a result of the strain. . . .

These are the conditions facing teachers fortunate enough to be employed. What of the unemployed? . . . "We are always hungry," wrote [one unemployed teacher]. "We owe six months' rent. . . . We live every hour in fear of eviction. . . . My sister, a typist, and I . . . have been out of work for two years. . . . We feel discouraged . . . and embittered. We are drifting, with no help from anyone."

*Eunice Langdon,*
*The Nation, August 16, 1933*

I am sitting in the city free employment bureau. It's the women's section. We have been sitting here now for hours. We sit here every day, waiting for a job. There are no jobs. . . .

. . . [W]e don't talk much. . . . There is a kind of humiliation. . . . We look away from each other. We look at the floor.

*Meridel LeSueur, "Women*
*on the Breadlines," 1932*

Dear Mrs. Roosevelt,

I am now 15 years old and in the 10th grade. I have always been smart but I never had a chance as all of us is so poor. I hope to complete my education, but I will have to quit school I guess if there is no clothes can be bought. (Don't think that we are on the relief.) Mother has been a faithful servant for us to keep us together. I don't see how she has made it.

*Mrs. Roosevelt, don't think I am just begging, but that is all you can call it I guess. . . . Do you have any old clothes you have throwed back. You don't realize how honored I would feel to be wearing your clothes.*

Your friend,

M.I.

Star Route One

Albertville, Ala.

January 1, 1936

"Carlotta Silvas Martin: A Mexican American Childhood during the Depression" and "Meridel LeSueur: The Despair of Unemployed Women," both from Susan Ware, *Modern American Women: A Documentary History* (New York: McGraw-Hill Higher Education, 2002), pp. 162–165, 145–146; Eunice Langdon, "The Teacher Faces the Depression," *Nation* 137 (August 16, 1933): 182–187; Letter to Eleanor Roosevelt, January 1, 1936, www.newdeal.feri.org/eleanor/mi0136.htm

PEARSON
myhistorylab

Personal Journeys Online

- **Letter from Eleanor Roosevelt to Walter White, 1936.** Roosevelt writes against lynching.

- Paul Taylor, **"Again the Covered Wagon,"** *Survey Graphic,* July 1935. Article on the migration of "Okies" to California during the Dust Bowl

**CARLOTTA SILVAS MARTIN,** Eunice Langdon, and Meridel LeSueur convey some of the trauma of the Great Depression, but no one voice can capture its devastating effect on Americans. The U.S. economy utterly collapsed, leaving millions of people jobless, homeless, or in continual fear of foreclosure, eviction, even starvation. The decade of hard times constituted a journey into desperation and despair.

The election of Franklin D. Roosevelt, however, lifted spirits and hopes of jobless Americans throughout the nation. They enthusiastically responded to his **New Deal,** taking jobs, as did Carlotta's grandmother, with such programs as the Works Progress Administration (WPA). In unprecedented numbers, they also wrote to both FDR and Eleanor Roosevelt, asking for advice and for assistance for everything from a month's rent money to tide them over to old clothes to wear

to school, as did the 15-year-old girl from Alabama. And they also wrote to thank the president and first lady for their compassionate support and leadership. Throughout all such letters ran a common theme: the belief among poor and unemployed Americans that for the first time there were people in the White House who were interested in their welfare, who wanted to eliminate their hardships, and who would listen to their ideas.

Franklin and Eleanor Roosevelt and the programs of the New Deal brought fresh hope and connected Americans to the White House as never before. And although the federal activism of the 1930s achieved neither full recovery nor systematic reform, it restored confidence to many Americans and permanently transformed the nation's responsibility for the welfare of its citizens. ✦

**New Deal**   The economic and political policies of the Roosevelt administration in the 1930s.

# CHRONOLOGY

**1929** Stock market crashes.

**1932** Farmers' Holiday Association organizes rural protests in the Midwest.

Reconstruction Finance Corporation is created to assist financial institutions.

Bonus Army is routed in Washington, DC.

Franklin D. Roosevelt is elected president.

**1931** Japan invades Manchuria.

**1933** Adolf Hitler comes to power in Germany.

Emergency Banking Act is passed.

The United States recognizes the Soviet Union.

Agricultural Adjustment Administration (AAA) is created to regulate farm production.

National Recovery Administration (NRA) is created to promote industrial cooperation and recovery.

Federal Emergency Relief Act provides federal assistance to the unemployed.

Civilian Conservation Corps (CCC) is established to provide work relief in conservation projects.

Public Works Administration (PWA) is created to provide work relief on large public construction projects.

Civil Works Administration (CWA) provides emergency winter relief jobs.

Tennessee Valley Authority (TVA) is created to coordinate regional development.

**1934** Securities and Exchange Commission (SEC) is established.

Indian Reorganization Act reforms Indian policy.

Huey Long organizes the Share-Our-Wealth Society.

Democrats win midterm elections.

**1935** Supreme Court declares NRA unconstitutional.

Italy attacks Ethiopia.

National Labor Relations Act (Wagner Act) guarantees workers' rights to organize and bargain collectively.

Social Security Act establishes a federal social insurance system.

Banking Act strengthens the Federal Reserve.

Revenue Act establishes a more progressive tax system.

Resettlement Administration is created to aid dispossessed farmers.

Rural Electrification Administration (REA) is created to help provide electric power to rural areas.

Soil Conservation Service is established.

Emergency Relief Appropriation Act authorizes public relief projects for the unemployed.

Works Progress Administration (WPA) is created.

Huey Long is assassinated.

**1936** Supreme Court declares AAA unconstitutional.

Roosevelt is reelected president.

Hitler remilitarizes the Rhineland.

Roosevelt sails to South America as part of Good Neighbor Policy.

Sit-down strikes begin.

**1937** Chicago police kill workers in Memorial Day Massacre.

FDR tries but fails to expand the Supreme Court.

Farm Security Administration (FSA) is created to lend money to small farmers to buy and rehabilitate farms.

National Housing Act is passed to promote public housing projects.

"Roosevelt Recession" begins.

**1938** Congress of Industrial Organizations (CIO) is founded.

Germany annexes Austria.

Fair Labor Standards Act establishes minimum wage and maximum hours rules for labor.

Roosevelt fails to "purge" the Democratic Party.

Republicans make gains in midterm elections.

Munich agreement reached, appeasing Hitler's demand for Sudetenland.

Kristallnacht, violent pogrom against Jews, occurs in Germany.

# HARD TIMES IN HOOVERVILLE

**WHAT TRIGGERED** the Great Depression? The prosperity of the 1920s ended in a stock-market crash that revealed the flaws honeycombing the economy. As the nation slid into a catastrophic depression, factories closed, employment and incomes tumbled, and millions lost their homes, hopes, and dignity. Some protested and took direct action; others looked to the government for relief.

## CRASH!

The buoyant prosperity of the New Era, more apparent than real by the summer of 1929, collapsed in October, when the stock market crashed. During the preceding two years, the market had hit record highs, stimulated by optimism, easy credit, and speculators' manipulations. But after peaking in September, it suffered several sharp checks, and on October 29, "Black Tuesday," panicked investors dumped their stocks, wiping out the previous year's gains in one day. Confidence in the economy disappeared, and the slide continued for months, and then years. The market hit bottom in July 1932. Much of the paper wealth of America had evaporated, and the nation sank into the **Great Depression.**

The Wall Street crash marked the beginning of the depression, but it did not cause it. The depression stemmed from weaknesses in the New Era economy. Most damaging was the unequal distribution of wealth and income. Workers' wages and farmers' incomes had fallen far behind industrial productivity and corporate profits; by 1929, the richest 0.1 percent of American families had as much total income as the bottom 42 percent (see Figure 25–1). With more than half the nation's people living at or below the subsistence level, there was not enough purchasing power to maintain the economy.

A second factor was that oligopolies dominated American industries. By 1929, the 200 largest corporations (out of 400,000) controlled half the corporate wealth. Their power led to "administered prices," prices kept artificially high and rigid rather than determined by supply and demand. Because it did not respond to purchasing power, this system not only helped bring on economic collapse but also dimmed prospects for recovery.

Weaknesses in specific industries had further unbalanced the economy. Agriculture suffered from overproduction, declining prices, and heavy debt; so did the coal and textile industries. These difficulties left the economy dependent on a few industries for expansion and employment, and these industries could not carry the burden. Banking presented other problems. Poorly managed and regulated, banks had contributed to the instability of prosperity; they now threatened to spread the panic and depression.

International economic difficulties spurred the depression as well. Shut out from U.S. markets by high tariffs, Europeans had depended on American investments to manage their debts and reparation payments from the Great War. The stock market crash dried up the flow of American dollars to Europe, causing financial panics and industrial collapse and making the Great Depression global. In turn, European nations curtailed their imports of American goods and defaulted on their debts, further debilitating the U.S. economy. (See Global Perspectives, The Worldwide Collapse.)

Government policies also bore some responsibility for the crash and depression. Failure to enforce antitrust laws had encouraged oligopolies and high prices; failure to regulate banking and the stock market had permitted financial recklessness and irresponsible speculation. Reducing tax rates on the wealthy had also encouraged speculation and contributed to the maldistribution of income. Opposition to labor unions and collective bargaining helped keep workers' wages and purchasing power low. The absence of an effective agricultural policy and the high tariffs that inhibited foreign trade and reduced markets for

**Great Depression**   The nation's worst economic crisis, extending through the 1930s, producing unprecedented bank failures, unemployment, and industrial and agricultural collapse.

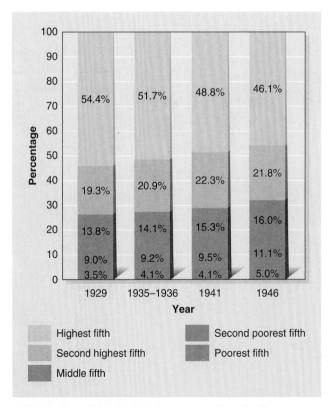

**FIGURE 25–1   Distribution of Income in the United States, 1929–1946**   An unequal distribution of income contributed to the Great Depression by limiting purchasing power. Only slight changes occurred until after World War II, but other factors gradually stabilized the national economy.

Data Source: U.S. Bureau of the Census.

**QUICK REVIEW**

**Causes of the Great Depression**

- Unequal distribution of wealth and income.
- Domination of American economy by oligopolies.
- Weakness in important industries.
- International economic problems.
- Government policies.

agricultural products hurt farmers. In short, the same governmental policies that shaped the booming 1920s economy also led to economic disaster.

State and local fiscal policies also pointed to economic problems for the 1930s. The expansion of public education and road construction led to higher property taxes in communities throughout the nation, and although per capita tax collection at the federal level actually declined between 1920 and 1929, the tax burden in states and cities increased dramatically. Indeed, state and local taxes rose faster than personal incomes in the 1920s. The real estate industry reported a decline as early as 1926, and homeowners steadily protested their higher property taxes.

But the crash did more than expose the weaknesses of the economy. Business lost confidence and refused to make investments that might have brought recovery. Instead, banks called in loans and restricted credit, and depositors tried to withdraw their savings, which were uninsured. The demand for cash caused banks to fail, dragging the economy down further. And the Federal Reserve Board prolonged the depression by restricting the money supply.

## THE DEPRESSION SPREADS

By early 1930, the effects of financial contraction were painfully evident. Factories shut down or cut back, and industrial production plummeted. By 1932, one-fourth of the labor force was out of work (see Figure 25–2). Personal income dropped by more than half between 1929 and 1932. Moreover, the depression began to feed on itself in a vicious circle: Shrinking wages and employment cut into purchasing power, causing business to slash production again and lay off workers, thereby further reducing purchasing power.

The depression particularly battered farmers. Commodity prices fell by 55 percent between 1929 and 1932, stifling farm income. Unable to pay their mortgages, many farm families lost their homes and fields. The dispossessed roamed the byways, highways, and railways of a troubled country.

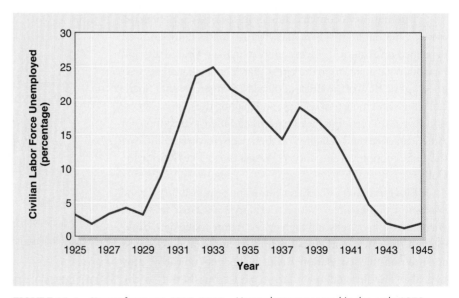

**FIGURE 25–2 Unemployment, 1925–1945** Unemployment soared in the early 1930s, spreading distress and overwhelming charities and local relief agencies. Federal programs improved conditions, but only America's entry into World War II really ended the problem.
Data Source: U.S. Bureau of the Census

Homeless Americans gathered in squalid Hoovervilles like this one in Seattle and struggled to survive.

Urban families were also evicted when they could not pay their rent. Some moved in with relatives; others lived in **Hoovervilles**—the name reflects the bitterness directed at the President—shacks where people shivered, suffered, and starved. Oklahoma City's vast Hooverville covered 100 square miles.

Soup kitchens became standard features of the urban landscape, with lines of the hungry stretching for blocks. But charities and local communities could not meet the massive needs, and neither the states nor the federal government had welfare or unemployment compensation programs.

**Hoovervilles** Shantytowns, sarcastically named after President Hoover, in which unemployed and homeless people lived in makeshift shacks, tents, and boxes.

## "WOMEN'S JOBS" AND "MEN'S JOBS"

The depression affected wage-earning women in complex ways. Although they suffered 20 percent unemployment by 1932, women were less likely than men to be fired. Gender segregation had concentrated women in low-paid service, sales, and clerical jobs that were less vulnerable than the heavy industries where men predominated. But while traditional attitudes somewhat insulated working women, they also reinforced opposition to female employment, especially that of married women. Three-fourths of the nation's school systems refused to hire married women as teachers, and two-thirds dismissed female teachers who married. Many private employers, especially banks and insurance companies, also fired married women. Despite such hostility, the proportion of married women in the workforce increased in the 1930s as women took jobs to help their families survive, and about one-third of working married women provided the sole support for their families.

## FAMILIES IN THE DEPRESSION

"I have watched fear grip the people in our neighborhood around Hull House," wrote Jane Addams as the depression deepened in 1931 and family survival itself seemed threatened.

## GLOBAL PERSPECTIVES

### THE WORLDWIDE COLLAPSE

The Wall Street crash did not immediately provoke widespread alarm at home or abroad. One French observer commented that an "abscess" had been "lanced." British commentators dismissed it as an isolated event and predicted continuing prosperity. President Hoover remained confident well into 1930, even telling a group of religious leaders requesting relief for the unemployed, "You have come sixty days too late. The depression is over."

Still, the stock market collapse did have consequences: It made European borrowing more difficult, especially hurting Germany's failing economy. Without loans from the United States, Germany defaulted on its war debts and faced near bankruptcy. Moreover, the United States accounted for 40 percent of the world's manufactured goods—twice the figure for Germany and England combined in 1929. When the United States slid into depression, the global repercussions were staggering.

The international crisis required global cooperation, but the world's nations responded with various forms of economic nationalism. The United States rejected its role as the lender of the last resort for destitute countries and constructed trade barriers by passing the Smoot-Hawley tariff in 1930. Within months Canada, Mexico, France, Spain, and New Zealand raised their tariffs against American goods. World trade came to a standstill; its volume plummeted by two-thirds between 1929 and 1933.

As the depression deepened, world leaders pointed to external causes and turned to conventional solutions. In the United States, Herbert Hoover claimed that "the hurricane that swept our shores was of European origin" and affirmed the need to balance the budget in hard times. French leaders blamed British monetary policies and blasted the United States for "exporting unemployment" through "mechanization" that replaced workers with machines. The French also regarded a balanced budget as inviolable. In Britain, however, the socialist prime minister, Ramsay MacDonald, faulted capitalism for the collapse, adding "we are not on trial, it is the system under which we live." Britain provided unemployment insurance and public relief. But even MacDonald refused to unbalance the budget to meet the needs of all the jobless. The Japanese finance minister also objected to increased spending for the unemployed.

By 1932, the international crisis had worsened, and the United States and Germany had unemployment rates of 25 and 40 percent, respectively. The German banking system had collapsed in 1931, and the depression helped facilitate the political success of the Nazi Party in 1932. Jobless Germans looted stores and coal yards for food and fuel. As in the United States, working women were targeted as a cause of the depression. One German newspaper declared that "Germany will perish if the women are working and the men are unemployed."

The shockingly high rates of unemployment throughout the world created unprecedented conditions of poverty and despair. And although Americans did not leap from windows during the collapse of the stock market, suicide rates went up in both Germany and the United States during the 1930s. Cases of malnutrition were found in New York, Budapest, and Vienna, among other cities, and relief agencies everywhere were overwhelmed by the needs of the jobless. People lost jobs and homes, creating Hoovervilles in the United States, *bidonvilles* ("tin cities") in France, and the Hungry Mile in Australia. The Great Depression had indeed become global, and, without international cooperation, the unemployed looked to their governments for solutions and support.

- Why did the U.S. depression become a global crisis and how did world leaders respond?

**QUICK REVIEW**

**Gendered Attitudes about Work**

- Women were concentrated in low-paid service, sales, and clerical jobs.
- Traditional attitudes reinforced opposition to female employment.
- Women's responsibilities grew in the face of hard times.

Divorce declined because it was expensive, but desertion increased, and people postponed marriage. Birthrates fell. Husbands and fathers, the traditional breadwinners, were often humiliated and despondent when laid off from work. Unemployed men, sociologists reported, "lost much of their sense of time and dawdled helplessly and dully about the streets," dreading to return home.

Women's responsibilities, by contrast, often grew. The number of female-headed households increased sharply. Not only did some women become wage earners, but their traditional role as homemakers also gained new significance. To make ends meet, many women sewed their own clothing and raised and canned vegetables, reversing the trend toward consumerism. Some also took on extra work at home.

The depression also affected children. Some parents sacrificed their own well-being to protect their children. But children felt the tension and fear, and many went without food. In New York City, 139 people, most of them children, died of starvation and malnutrition in 1933. Boys and girls stayed home from school and church because they lacked shoes or clothing; others gave up their plans for college. As hope faded, family conflicts increased. The California Unemployment Commission concluded that the depression had left the American family "morally shattered. There is no security, no foothold, no future."

## "LAST HIRED, FIRST FIRED"

The depression particularly harmed racial minorities. With fewer resources and opportunities, they were less able than other groups to absorb the economic pain. African Americans were caught in a double bind, reported a sociologist at Howard University in 1932: They were "the last to be hired and the first to be fired." Black unemployment rates were more than twice the white rate, reflecting increased job competition and persistent racism.

Racism also limited the assistance African Americans received. Religious and charitable organizations often refused to care for black people. Local and state governments set higher relief eligibility requirements for blacks than for whites and provided them with less aid. Out of work for longer periods of time and without even modest relief assistance, African Americans were forced to crowd together in already cramped apartments, while still paying exorbitant rents to white landlords. By 1932, most African Americans were suffering acute privation. "At no time in the history of the Negro since slavery," reported the Urban League, "has his economic and social outlook seemed so discouraging."

Hispanic Americans also suffered. As mostly unskilled workers, they faced increasing competition for decreasing jobs paying declining wages. They were displaced even in the California agricultural labor force, which they had dominated. By the mid-1930s, they made up only a tenth of the state's migratory labor force, which increasingly consisted of white people who had fled the South and the Great Plains. Other jobs were lost when Arizona, California, and Texas barred Mexicans from public works and highway construction jobs. Vigilantes threatened employers who hired Mexicans rather than white Americans.

Economic woes and racism drove nearly half a million Mexican immigrants and their American-born children from the United States. Local authorities in the Southwest, with the blessing of the Department of Labor, urged all Mexicans, regardless of their citizenship status, to return to Mexico and free up jobs and relief assistance for white Americans. To intimidate Mexican residents, the U.S. Immigration Service conducted several raids, rounding up people and demanding immediate proof of citizenship.

## PROTEST

Bewildered and discouraged, most Americans reacted to the crisis without protest. Influenced by traditional individualism, many blamed themselves for their plight. But

The Great Depression made more desperate the plight of Mexican Americans; they faced discrimination and feared deportation. As migrant laborers, they also struggled with the forces of nature as they traveled from field to field in search of work. This Mexican migrant worker holds his new baby with his wife standing at the door's edge. They live in this shack on the edge of a frozen pea field in California.

**QUICK REVIEW**

**African Americans and the Depression**

- Black unemployment rates were twice the rate for white people.
- Blacks had less access to state and private aid and relief.
- Blacks faced a bleak economic outlook.

others did act, especially to protect their families. Protests ranged from small desperate gestures like stealing food and coal to more dramatic deeds. In Louisiana, women seized a train to call attention to the needs of their families; in New Jersey, in the "bloodless battle of Pleasantville," 100 women held the city council hostage to demand assistance.

Communists, socialists, and other radicals organized more formal protests. Communists led the jobless into "unemployment councils" that staged hunger marches, demonstrated for relief, and blocked evictions. Socialists built similar organizations, including the People's Unemployment League in Baltimore, which had 12,000 members. Groups of this kind provided protection and assistance. However, local officials often suppressed their protests. In 1932, police fired on the Detroit Unemployment Council as it marched to demand food and jobs, killing four marchers and wounding many more.

Rural protests also broke out. Again, communists organized some of them, as in Alabama, where the Croppers' and Farm Workers' Union mobilized black agricultural laborers in 1931 to demand better treatment. In the Midwest, the Farmers' Holiday Association, organized among family farmers in 1932, stopped the shipment of produce to urban markets, hoping to drive up prices. A guerrilla war broke out as farmers blocked roads and halted freight trains, dumped milk in ditches, and fought bloody battles with deputy sheriffs. Midwestern farmers also tried to prevent foreclosure of their farms. In Iowa, farmers beat sheriffs and mortgage agents and nearly lynched a judge conducting foreclosure proceedings; in Nebraska, a Farmers' Holiday leader warned that if the state did not halt foreclosures, "200,000 of us are coming to Lincoln and we'll tear that new State Capitol Building to pieces."

**HOW DID** Herbert Hoover respond to the Depression? Why did his policies fail?

# HERBERT HOOVER AND THE DEPRESSION

The Great Depression challenged the optimism, policies, and philosophy that Herbert Hoover had carried into the White House in 1929. The president took unprecedented steps to resolve the crisis but shrank back from the interventionist policies activists urged. His failures, personal as well as political and economic, led to his repudiation and to a major shift in government policies.

## THE FAILURE OF VOLUNTARISM

Hoover fought economic depression more vigorously than any previous president, but he believed that voluntary private relief was preferable to federal intervention. The role of the national government, he thought, was to advise and encourage the voluntary efforts of private organizations, individual industries, or local communities.

Hoover obtained pledges from business leaders to maintain employment and wage levels. But most corporations soon repudiated these pledges, slashed wages, and laid off workers. Hoover himself said, "You know, the only trouble with capitalism is capitalists; they're too damn greedy." Still, he rejected government action.

Hoover also depended on voluntary efforts to relieve the misery caused by massive unemployment. He created the President's Organization for Unemployment Relief to help raise private funds for voluntary relief agencies. Charities and local authorities, he believed, should help the unemployed; direct federal relief would expand government power and undermine the recipients' character. He vetoed congressional attempts to aid the unemployed.

The depression rendered Hoover's beliefs meaningless. Private programs to aid the unemployed scarcely existed. Only a few unions, such as the Amalgamated Clothing Workers, had unemployment funds, and these were soon spent. Company plans for unemployment compensation covered less than 1 percent of workers, revealing the charade of

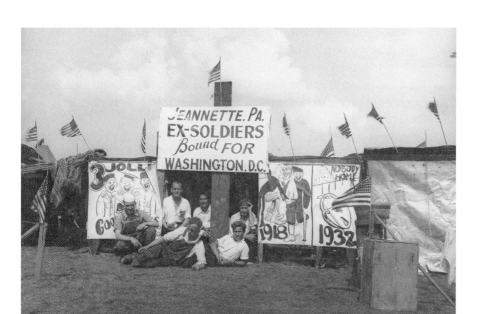

Bonus Army Camp

the welfare capitalism of the 1920s. Private charitable groups like the Salvation Army, church associations, and ethnic societies quickly exhausted their resources.

Nor could local governments cope, and their efforts declined as the depression deepened. By 1932, more than 100 cities made no relief appropriations at all, and the commissioner of charity in Salt Lake City reported that people were sliding toward starvation. Only eight state governments provided even token assistance.

As the depression worsened, Hoover adopted more activist policies. He persuaded Congress to cut taxes to boost consumers' buying power, and he increased the public works budget. The Federal Farm Board lent money to cooperatives and spent millions trying to stabilize crop prices. Unable to control production, however, the board conceded failure by late 1931. More successful was the Reconstruction Finance Corporation (RFC). Established in January 1932, the RFC lent federal funds to banks, insurance companies, and railroads so that their recovery could "trickle down" to ordinary Americans. Hoover still opposed direct aid to the general public, although he finally allowed the RFC to lend small amounts to state and local governments for unemployment relief.

Far more action was necessary, but Hoover remained committed to voluntarism and a balanced budget. Hoover's ideological limitations infuriated Americans who saw him as indifferent to their suffering and a reactionary protector of privileged business interests—an image his political opponents encouraged.

## REPUDIATING HOOVER: THE 1932 ELECTION

Hoover's treatment of the **Bonus Army** symbolized his unpopularity and set the stage for the 1932 election. In 1932, unemployed veterans of World War I gathered in Washington, demanding payment of service bonuses not due until 1945. Hoover refused to meet with them, and Congress rejected their plan. But 10,000 veterans erected a shantytown at the edge of Washington and camped in vacant public buildings. Hoover decided to evict the veterans, but General Douglas MacArthur exceeded his cautious orders and on July 28 led cavalry, infantry, and tanks against the ragged Bonus Marchers. The troops cleared the buildings and assaulted the shantytown, dispersing the veterans and their families and setting their camp on fire.

**QUICK REVIEW**

**The Limits of Voluntarism**

- Business leaders failed to live up to pledges to maintain employment and wage levels.
- Private programs to aid the unemployed scarcely existed.
- Local governments were not equipped to deal with the magnitude of the crisis.

**Bonus Army** Unemployed veterans of World War I gathering in Washington in 1932 demanding payment of service bonuses not due until 1945.

Herbert Hoover, *Speech at New York City* (1932)

Franklin Delano Roosevelt, *Speech at San Francisco* (1932)

**QUICK REVIEW**

**The 1932 Election**

- Republicans renominated Hoover.
- The Democratic platform differed little from the Republican platform.
- Franklin D. Roosevelt's victory was a repudiation of Hoover.

**WHAT WERE** the goals of the early New Deal?

Franklin Delano Roosevelt, *First Inauguration Speech* (1932)

**WHERE TO LEARN MORE**

★ Center for New Deal Studies, Roosevelt University, Chicago, Illinois. www.roosevelt.edu/newdeal/

This assault provoked widespread outrage. The administration tried to brand the Bonus Marchers as communists and criminals, but subsequent investigations refuted such claims. The incident confirmed Hoover's public image as harsh and insensitive.

In the summer of 1932, with no prospects for victory, Republicans renominated Hoover. Confident Democrats selected Governor Franklin D. Roosevelt of New York, who promised "a new deal for the American people."

The 1932 campaign gave scant indication of what Roosevelt's New Deal might involve. The Democratic platform differed little from that of the Republicans, and Roosevelt spoke in vague or general terms. He knew that the election would be a repudiation of Hoover more than an endorsement of himself. Still, observers found clues in Roosevelt's record as governor of New York, where he had created the first state system of unemployment relief and supported social welfare and conservation. More important was his outgoing personality, which radiated warmth and hope in contrast to Hoover's gloom.

FDR carried every state south and west of Pennsylvania. Yet Hoover would remain president for four more months, as the Constitution then required. And in those four months, the depression worsened, spreading misery throughout America. The final blow came in February 1933, when panic struck the banking system. Nearly 6,000 banks had already failed, robbing 9 million depositors of their savings. Desperate Americans rushed to withdraw their funds from the remaining banks, pushing them to the brink. With the federal government under Hoover immobilized, state governments shut the banks to prevent their failure. By March, an eerie silence had descended on the nation. Hoover concluded, "We are at the end of our string."

# LAUNCHING THE NEW DEAL

In the midst of this national anxiety, Franklin D. Roosevelt pushed forward an unprecedented program to resolve the crises of a collapsing financial system, crippling unemployment, and agricultural and industrial breakdown and to promote reform. The early New Deal achieved successes and attracted support, but it also had limitations and generated criticism that suggested the need for still greater innovations.

### ACTION NOW!

On March 4, 1933, Franklin Delano Roosevelt became president and immediately reassured the American people. He insisted that "the only thing we have to fear is fear itself" and he promised "action, and action now!" Summoning Congress, Roosevelt pressed forward on a broad front. In the first three months of his administration, the famous Hundred Days of the New Deal, the Democratic Congress passed many important laws (see Overview, Major Laws of the Hundred Days).

Roosevelt's program reflected a mix of ideas, some from FDR himself, some from a diverse group of advisers, including academic experts dubbed the "brain trust," politicians, and social workers. It also incorporated principles from the progressive movement, precedents from the Great War mobilization, and even plans from the Hoover administration. Above all, the New Deal was a practical response to the depression. FDR had set its tone in his campaign when he declared, "The country needs, and, unless I mistake its temper, the country demands bold, persistent experimentation. . . . Above all, try something."

FDR first addressed the banking crisis. On March 5, he proclaimed a national bank holiday, closing all remaining banks. Congress then passed his Emergency Banking Act,

## OVERVIEW  Major Laws of the Hundred Days

| Law | Objective |
| --- | --- |
| Emergency Banking Act | Stabilized the private banking system |
| Agricultural Adjustment Act | Established a farm recovery program based on production controls and price supports |
| Emergency Farm Mortgage Act | Provided for the refinancing of farm mortgages |
| National Industrial Recovery Act | Established a national recovery program and authorized a public works program |
| Federal Emergency Relief Act | Established a national system of relief |
| Home Owners Loan Act | Protected homeowners from mortgage foreclosure by refinancing home loans |
| Glass-Steagall Act | Separated commercial and investment banking and guaranteed bank deposits |
| Tennessee Valley Authority Act | Established the TVA and provided for the planned development of the Tennessee River Valley |
| Civilian Conservation Corps Act | Established the CCC to provide work relief on reforestation and conservation projects |
| Farm Credit Act | Expanded agricultural credits and established the Farm Credit Administration |
| Securities Act | Required full disclosure from stock exchanges |
| Wagner-Peyser Act | Created a U.S. Employment Service and encouraged states to create local public employment offices |

a conservative measure that extended government assistance to sound banks and reorganized weak ones. Prompt government action, coupled with a reassuring **fireside chat** over the radio by the president, restored popular confidence in the banks. When they reopened on March 13, deposits exceeded withdrawals. In June, Congress created the **Federal Deposit Insurance Corporation (FDIC)** to guarantee bank deposits up to $2,500.

The financial industry was also reformed. The Glass-Steagall Act separated investment and commercial banking to curtail risky speculation. The Securities Act reformed the sale of stocks to prevent the insider abuses that had characterized Wall Street, and in 1934 the **Securities and Exchange Commission (SEC)** was created to regulate the stock market. Two other financial measures in 1933 created the Home Owners Loan Corporation and the Farm Credit Administration, which enabled millions to refinance their mortgages.

### CREATING JOBS

Roosevelt also provided relief for the unemployed. The Federal Emergency Relief Administration (FERA) furnished funds to state and local agencies. Harry Hopkins, who had headed Roosevelt's relief program in New York, became its director and one of the New Deal's most important members. FERA spent over $3 billion before it ended in 1935, and by then Hopkins and FDR had developed new programs that provided work rather than just cash. Work relief, they believed, preserved both the skills and the morale of recipients. In the winter of 1933–1934, Hopkins spent nearly $1 billion to create jobs for 4 million men and women through the Civil Works Administration (CWA). The CWA hired laborers to build roads and airports, teachers to staff rural schools, and singers and artists to give public performances. The Public Works Administration (PWA) provided work relief on useful projects to stimulate the economy

**fireside chats**   Speeches broadcast nationally over the radio in which President Franklin D. Roosevelt explained complex issues and programs in plain language, as though his listeners were gathered around the fireside with him.

**Federal Deposit Insurance Corporation (FDIC)**   Government agency that guarantees bank deposits, thereby protecting both depositors and banks.

**Securities and Exchange Commission (SEC)**   Federal agency with authority to regulate trading practices in stocks and bonds.

through public expenditures. Directed by Harold Ickes, the PWA spent billions from 1933 to 1939 to build schools, hospitals, courthouses, dams, and bridges.

One of FDR's personal ideas, the Civilian Conservation Corps (CCC), combined work relief with conservation. Launched in 1933, the CCC employed 2.5 million young men to work on reforestation and flood-control projects, build roads and bridges in national forests and parks, restore Civil War battlefields, and fight forest fires.

## HELPING SOME FARMERS

Besides providing relief, the New Deal promoted economic recovery. In May 1933, Congress established the Agricultural Adjustment Administration (AAA) to combat the depression in agriculture caused by crop surpluses and low prices. The AAA subsidized farmers who agreed to restrict production. The objective was to boost farm prices to parity, a level that would restore farmers' purchasing power to what it had been in 1914.

Agricultural conditions improved. Farm prices rose from 52 percent of parity in 1932 to 88 percent in 1935, and gross farm income rose by 50 percent. Not until 1941, however, would income exceed the level of 1929, a poor year for farmers. Moreover, some of the decreased production and increased prices stemmed from devastating droughts and dust storms on the Great Plains. The AAA itself harmed poor farmers while aiding larger commercial growers. As southern planters restricted their acreage, they dismissed tenants and sharecroppers, and with AAA payments, they bought new farm machinery, reducing their need for farm labor.

## THE FLIGHT OF THE BLUE EAGLE

The New Deal attempted to revive U.S. industry with the National Industrial Recovery Act (NIRA), which created the National Recovery Administration (NRA). The NRA

A coal miner greeting Franklin D. Roosevelt in West Virginia in 1932. Roosevelt's promise of a New Deal revived hope among millions of Americans trapped in hard times.

## AMERICAN VIEWS

### The Commissioner of the Bureau of Indian Affairs on the New Deal for Native Americans

John Collier, refomer and social worker, served as commissioner of the Bureau of Indian Affairs (BIA) from 1933 until 1945. During his tenure, he radically transformed the agency—long known to be corrupt and hostile to Native Americans—into an organization committed to the preservation of tribal cultures and the restoration of Indian lands. Like other New Dealers, Collier attempted to use the power of the federal government to protect those with limited political power and economic influence—in this case Native Americans.

Collier was extraordinarily successful in promoting the restoration of tribal rights and autonomy and helped ensure that future generations of Indians could reclaim their lands. Yet he was frustrated by Congress's unwillingness to fund the programs he believed necessary for a genuine New Deal for Native Americans. In his 1938 annual report, he calls for greater economic support, arguing that it would be a good investment for the nation. Most important, even as he acknowledges that real changes have occurred since 1933, he points out that there is still much to be done to achieve political autonomy and economic self-sufficiency for American Indians.

- **How** did Collier describe the treatment of Native Americans, and why did white Americans regard Indians as a "problem" to be eliminated?
- **What** were the new goals of the Bureau of Indian Affairs?
- **How** did Collier regard the role of land in Native American society? Why?
- **What** was the greatest challenge Collier saw for Native Americans in 1938?

For nearly 300 years white Americans, in our zeal to carve out a nation made to order, have dealt with the Indians on the erroneous, yet tragic, assumption that the Indians were a dying race—to be liquidated. We took away their best lands; broke treaties, promises; tossed them the most nearly worthless scraps of a continent that had once been wholly theirs. But we did not liquidate their spirit. The vital spark which

kept them alive was hardy. So hardy, indeed, that we now face an astounding and heartening fact.

Actually, the Indians, on the evidence of federal census rolls of the past eight years, are increasing almost twice the rate of the population as a whole.

With this fact before us, our whole attitude toward the Indians has necessarily undergone a profound change. Dead is the centuries-old notion that the sooner we eliminate this doomed race, preferably humanely, the better. . . . No longer can we naively talk of or think of the "Indian problem."

We, therefore, define our Indian policy somewhat as follows: So productively to use the moneys appropriated by the Congress for Indians as to enable them, on good, adequate land of their own, to earn decent livelihoods and lead self-respecting, organized lives in harmony with their own aims and ideals, as an integral part of American life. This will not happen tomorrow; perhaps not in our lifetime; but with the revitalization of Indian hope due to the actions and attitudes of this government during the last few years, that aim is a probability, and a real one. . . . So intimately is all of Indian life tied up with the land and its utilization that to think of Indians is to think of land. The two are inseparable. Upon the land and its intelligent use depends the main future of the American Indian.

The Indian feels toward his land, not a mere ownership but a devotion and veneration befitting that what is not only a home but a refuge. . . . Not only does the Indian's major source of livelihood derive from the land but his social and political organizations are rooted in soil.

Since 1933, the Indian Service has made a concerted effort—an effort which is as yet but a mere beginning—to help the Indian to build back his landholdings to a point where they will provide an adequate basis for a self-sustaining economy, a self-satisfying social organization.

Source: John Collier. Annual Report of the Secretary of the Interior for the Fiscal Year Ended June 30, 1938. From www.historymatters.gmu.edu

sought to halt the slide in prices, wages, and employment by suspending antitrust laws and authorizing industrial and trade associations to draft codes setting production quotas, price policies, wages and working conditions, and other business practices. The codes promoted the interests of business generally and big business in particular, but Section 7a of the NIRA guaranteed workers the rights to organize unions and bargain collectively—a provision that John L. Lewis of the United Mine Workers called an Emancipation Proclamation for labor.

Hugh Johnson became director of the NRA. He persuaded business leaders to cooperate in drafting codes and the public to patronize participating companies. The NRA Blue Eagle insignia and its slogan "We Do Our Part" covered workplaces, storefronts, and billboards. Blue Eagle parades marched down the nation's main streets and climaxed in a massive demonstration in New York City.

Support for the NRA waned, however. Corporate leaders used it to advance their own goals and to discriminate against small producers, consumers, and labor. Businesses also violated the labor rights specified in Section 7a. Defiant employers viewed collective bargaining as infringing their authority. Employers even used violence to smother unions. The NRA did little to enforce Section 7a, and Johnson, strongly probusiness, denounced all strikes. Workers felt betrayed. Roosevelt tried to reorganize the NRA, but the act remained controversial until the Supreme Court declared it unconstitutional in 1935.

## CRITICS RIGHT AND LEFT

The early New Deal did not end the depression. Recovery was fitful and uneven; millions of Americans remained unemployed. Nevertheless, the New Deal's efforts to grapple with problems, its successes in reducing suffering and fear, and Roosevelt's own skills carried the Democratic Party to victory in the 1934 elections. But New Deal policies also provoked criticism, from both those convinced that too little had been achieved and those alarmed that too much had been attempted.

### QUICK REVIEW

**The National Recovery Administration (NRA)**

◆ Sought to halt the slide in prices, wages, and employment.

◆ Tended to help business, often at the expense of labor.

◆ Declared unconstitutional in 1935.

New Deal agricultural programs stabilized the farm economy, but not all farmers benefited. Landowners who received AAA payments evicted these black sharecroppers huddled in a makeshift roadside camp in Missouri in 1935.

Despite the early New Deal's probusiness character, conservatives complained that the expansion of government activity and its regulatory role weakened the autonomy of American business. They also condemned the efforts to aid nonbusiness groups as socialistic, particularly the "excessive" spending on unemployment relief and the "instigation" of labor organizing. These critics attracted little popular support, however, and their selfishness antagonized Roosevelt.

More realistic criticism came from the left. In 1932, FDR had campaigned for "the forgotten man at the bottom of the economic pyramid," and some radicals argued that the early New Deal had forgotten the forgotten man. Communists and socialists focused public attention on the poor, especially in the countryside. In California, communists organized Mexican, Filipino, and Japanese farm workers into the Cannery and Agricultural Workers Union; in Arkansas and Tennessee, socialists in 1934 helped organize sharecroppers into the Southern Tenant Farmers Union, protesting the "Raw Deal" they had received from the AAA. Even without the involvement of socialists or communists, labor militancy in 1934 pressed Roosevelt. The number of workers participating in strikes leaped from 325,000 in 1932 (about the annual average since 1925) to 1.5 million in 1934.

Rebuffing FDR's pleas for fair treatment, employers moved to crush the strikes, often using complaisant police and private strikebreakers. In Minneapolis, police shot 67 teamsters, almost all in the back, as they fled an ambush arranged by employers; in Toledo, company police and National Guardsmen attacked autoworkers with tear gas, bayonets, and rifle fire; in the textile strike, police killed six picketers in South Carolina, and soldiers wounded another 50 in Rhode Island. Against such powerful opponents, workers needed help to achieve their rights. Harry Hopkins and other New Dealers realized that labor's demands could not be ignored.

Four prominent individuals mobilized popular discontent to demand government action to assist groups neglected by the New Deal. Representative William Lemke of North Dakota, an agrarian radical leader of the Nonpartisan League, called attention to rural distress. Lemke objected to the New Deal's limited response to farmers crushed by the depression. In his own state, nearly two-thirds of the farmers had lost their land through foreclosures.

Francis Townsend, a California physician, proposed to aid the nation's elderly, many of whom were destitute. The Townsend Plan called for a government pension to every American over the age of 60, provided that the recipient retired from work and spent the entire pension. This scheme promised to extend relief to the elderly, open jobs for the unemployed, and stimulate economic recovery. Over 5,000 Townsend Clubs lobbied for government action to help the elderly poor.

Father Charles Coughlin, a Catholic priest in the Detroit suburb of Royal Oak, threatened to mobilize another large constituency against the limitations of the early New Deal. Thirty million Americans listened eagerly to his weekly radio broadcasts, which mixed religion with anti-Semitism and demands for social justice and financial reform. Coughlin had condemned Hoover for assisting banks but ignoring the unemployed, and initially he welcomed the New Deal as "Christ's Deal." But after concluding that FDR's policies favored "the virile viciousness of business and finance," Coughlin organized the National Union for Social Justice to lobby for his goals. With support among lower-middle-class, heavily Catholic, urban ethnic groups, Coughlin posed a real challenge to Roosevelt's Democratic Party.

Roosevelt found Senator Huey P. Long of Louisiana still more worrisome. Alternately charming and autocratic, Long had modernized his state with taxation and educational reforms and an extensive public-works program after his election as governor in 1928. Moving to the Senate and eyeing the White House, Long proposed more comprehensive social-welfare policies than the New Deal had envisaged. In 1934, he organized the Share-Our-Wealth Society. His plan to end poverty and unemployment called for

*Documents*

Huey Long, *Share Our Wealth* (1935)

*Documents*

Father Charles E. Coughlin, *A Third Party* (1936)

## QUICK REVIEW

### Critique of the New Deal

- Conservative critics of the expansion of government gained little support.

- Many on the left saw the early New Deal as a "Raw Deal."

- Popular pressure mounted for more aggressive policies.

confiscatory taxes on the rich to provide every family with a decent income, health coverage, education, and old-age pensions. Long's appeal was enormous. Within months, his organization claimed more than 27,000 clubs and 7 million members.

WHAT WERE the major accomplishments of the Second New Deal?

**myhistorylab**

**From Then to Now Online**
*Social Security*

**QUICK REVIEW**

**The Social Security Act**

◆ Provided unemployment compensation, old-age pensions, and aid for dependent mothers and children and the blind.

◆ The law excluded more than a fourth of all workers and did not include health insurance.

◆ Funded by a regressive payroll tax.

# CONSOLIDATING THE NEW DEAL

Responding to the persistence of the depression and political pressures, Roosevelt in 1935 undertook economic and social reforms that some observers have called the Second New Deal. The new measures shifted government action more toward reform even as they still addressed relief and recovery.

## WEEDING OUT AND LIFTING UP

"In spite of our efforts and in spite of our talk," Roosevelt told the new Congress in 1935, "we have not weeded out the overprivileged and we have not effectively lifted up the underprivileged." To do so, he developed "must" legislation. One of the new laws protected labor's rights to organize and bargain collectively. The Wagner National Labor Relations Act, dubbed "Labor's Magna Carta," guaranteed workers the right to organize unions and prohibited employers from adopting unfair labor practices, such as firing union activists and forming company unions. The law also set up the National Labor Relations Board (NLRB) to enforce these provisions, protect workers from coercion, and supervise union elections.

The New Deal enabled photographers and artists to take to the road to capture images of the nation's dispossessed. This photograph by Dorothea Lange of an 18-year old mother and her child in a migrant labor camp in 1937 illustrates both despair and detachment and conveys the hardship of homelessness and deprivation in the Great Depression.

**Social security.**  Of greater long-range importance was the Social Security Act. Other industrial nations had established national social-insurance systems much earlier, but only the Great Depression moved the United States to accept the idea that the federal government should protect the poor and unemployed. Even so, the law was a compromise, framed by a nonpartisan committee of business, labor, and public representatives and then weakened by congressional conservatives. It provided unemployment compensation, old-age pensions, and aid for dependent mothers and children and the blind.

The conservative nature of the law appeared in its stingy benefit payments, its lack of health insurance, and its exclusion of more than one-fourth of all workers, including many in desperate need of protection, such as farm laborers and domestic servants. Moreover, unlike in other nations, the old-age pensions were financed through a regressive payroll tax on both employees and employers rather than through general tax revenues. Thus the new system was more like a compulsory insurance program.

Despite its weaknesses, the Social Security Act was one of the most important laws in American history and Roosevelt was justifiably proud. It provided, he pointed out, "at least some measure of protection to the average citizen and to his family against the loss of a job and against poverty-ridden old age." Moreover, by establishing federal responsibility for social welfare, it inaugurated a welfare system that subsequent generations would expand.

**Money, tax, and land reform.** Another reform measure, the Banking Act of 1935, increased the authority of the Federal Reserve Board over the nation's currency and credit system and decreased the power of the private bankers whose irresponsible behavior had contributed to the depression and the appeal of Father Coughlin. The Revenue Act of 1935 provided for graduated income taxes and increased estate and corporate taxes. Opponents called it the Soak the Rich Tax, but with its many loopholes, it was scarcely that and was certainly not a redistributive measure such as Huey Long had proposed. Nevertheless, it set a precedent for progressive taxation and attracted popular support.

The Second New Deal also responded belatedly to the environmental catastrophe that had turned much of the Great Plains from Texas to the Dakotas into a Dust Bowl (see Map 25–1). Since World War I, farmers had stripped marginal land of its native grasses to plant wheat. When drought and high winds hit the plains in 1932, crops failed, and nothing was left to hold the soil. Dust storms blew away millions of tons of topsoil, despoiling the land and darkening the sky a thousand miles away. Families abandoned their farms in droves. Many of these poor "Okies" headed for California, their plight captured in John Steinbeck's novel, *The Grapes of Wrath* (1939).

In 1935, Roosevelt established the Resettlement Administration to focus on land reform and help poor farmers. Under Rexford Tugwell, this agency initiated soil erosion projects and attempted to resettle impoverished farmers on better land, but the problem exceeded its resources. Congress moved to save the land, if not its people, by creating the Soil Conservation Service in 1935.

## EXPANDING RELIEF

If reform gained priority in the Second New Deal, relief remained critical. With millions still unemployed, Roosevelt pushed through Congress in 1935 the Emergency Relief Appropriation Act, authorizing $5 billion—at the time the largest single appropriation in American history—for emergency public employment. Roosevelt created the Works Progress Administration (WPA) under Hopkins, who set up work relief programs to assist the unemployed and boost the economy. Before its end in 1943, the WPA gave jobs to 9 million people (more than a fifth of the labor force) and spent nearly $12 billion. Three-fourths of its expenditures went on construction projects that could employ manual labor: The WPA built 125,000 schools, post offices, and hospitals; 8,000 parks; nearly 100,000 bridges; and enough roads and sewer systems to circle the earth 30 times. The WPA laid much of the basic infrastructure on which the nation still relies.

The WPA also developed work projects for unemployed writers, artists, musicians, and actors. "Why not?" said FDR. "They are human beings. They have to live." WPA programs allowed people to use their talents while surviving the depression, increased popular access to cultural performances, and established a precedent for federal support of the arts.

The National Youth Administration (NYA), another WPA agency, gave part-time jobs to students, enabling 2 million high school and college students to stay in school, learn skills, and do productive work. At the University of Nebraska, NYA students built

**Exploring America**
*The Dust Bowl*

*Documents*

Carey Mc Williams, *Okies in California* (1939)

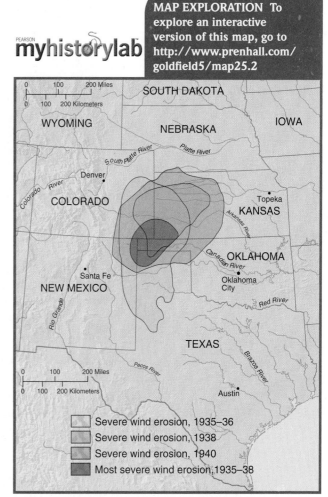

MAP EXPLORATION To explore an interactive version of this map, go to http://www.prenhall.com/goldfield5/map25.2

Severe wind erosion, 1935–36
Severe wind erosion, 1938
Severe wind erosion, 1940
Most severe wind erosion, 1935–38

MAP 25–1 **The Dust Bowl** Years of overcultivation, drought, and high winds created the Dust Bowl, which most severely affected the southern Great Plains. Federal relief and conservation programs provided assistance, but many residents fled the area, often migrating to California.

**Why was** this drought particularly damaging to people in the region?

Eleanor Roosevelt campaigns with FDR in Fremont, Nebraska, in 1935. A visible activist for social and economic reform, she was also politically important in building the powerful Roosevelt coalition. "Previously," said the journalist Ruby Black, "a President's wife acted as if she didn't know that a political party existed."

an observatory; at Duke University, law student Richard M. Nixon earned 35 cents an hour doing research in the library. Lyndon Johnson, a Texas NYA official, believed that "if the Roosevelt administration had never done another thing, it would have been justified by the work of this great institution for salvaging youth."

*Documents*

*Republican Party Platform* (1936)

## THE ROOSEVELT COALITION AND THE ELECTION OF 1936

The 1936 election gave Americans an opportunity to judge FDR and the New Deal. Conservatives alarmed at the expansion of government, business people angered by regulation and labor legislation, and wealthy Americans furious with tax reform decried the New Deal. But they were a minority. Even the presidential candidate they supported, Republican Governor Alf Landon of Kansas, endorsed much of the New Deal, criticizing merely the inefficiency and cost of some of its programs.

The programs and politicians of the New Deal had created an invincible coalition behind Roosevelt. Despite ambivalence about large-scale government intervention, the New Deal's agricultural programs reinforced the traditional Democratic allegiance of white southerners while attracting many western farmers. Labor legislation clinched the active support of the nation's workers. Middle-class voters, whose homes had been saved and whose hopes had been raised, also joined the Roosevelt coalition.

So did urban ethnic groups, who had benefited from welfare programs and appreciated the unprecedented recognition Roosevelt's administration gave them. African Americans voted overwhelmingly Democratic for the first time. Women, too, were an important part of the Roosevelt coalition, and Eleanor often attracted their support as much as Franklin did.

This political realignment produced a landslide. Roosevelt polled 61 percent of the popular vote and the largest electoral vote margin ever recorded, 523 to 8. Democrats also won huge majorities in Congress. Roosevelt's political coalition reflected a mandate for himself and the New Deal; it would enable the Democrats to dominate national elections for three decades.

# THE NEW DEAL AND AMERICAN LIFE

The landslide of 1936 revealed the impact of the New Deal on Americans. Industrial workers mobilized to secure their rights, women and minorities gained increased, if still limited, opportunities to participate in American society, and southerners and westerners benefited from government programs they turned to their own advantage. Government programs changed daily life, and ordinary people often helped shape the new policies.

**WHAT EXPLAINS** labor's resurgence in the 1930s?

## LABOR ON THE MARCH

The labor revival in the 1930s reflected both workers' determination and government support. Workers wanted to improve their wages and benefits as well as to gain union recognition and union contracts that would allow them to limit arbitrary managerial authority and achieve some control over the workplace. This larger goal provoked opposition from employers and their allies and required workers to organize, strike, and become politically active. Their achievement was remarkable.

The Second New Deal helped. By guaranteeing labor's rights to organize and bargain collectively, the Wagner Act sparked a wave of labor activism. But if the government ultimately protected union rights, the unions themselves had to form locals, recruit members, and demonstrate influence in the workplace.

At first, those tasks overwhelmed the American Federation of Labor (AFL). Its reliance on craft-based unions and reluctance to organize immigrant, black, and women workers left it unprepared for the rush of industrial workers seeking unionization. More progressive labor leaders saw that industry-wide unions were more appropriate for unskilled workers in mass-production industries. Forming the Committee for Industrial Organization (CIO) within the AFL, they campaigned to unionize workers in the steel, auto, and rubber industries, all notoriously hostile to unions. AFL leaders insisted that the CIO disband and then in 1937 expelled its unions. The militants reorganized as the separate **Congress of Industrial Organizations.** (In 1955, the two groups merged as the AFL-CIO.)

**Congress of Industrial Organizations (CIO)** An alliance of industrial unions that spurred the 1930s organizational drive among the mass-production industries.

The split roused the AFL to increase its own organizing activities, but it was primarily the new CIO that put labor on the march. It inspired workers previously neglected by organized labor. The CIO's interracial union campaign in the Birmingham steel mills, said one organizer, was "like a second coming of Christ" for black workers, who welcomed the union as a chance for social recognition as well as economic opportunity. The CIO also employed new and aggressive tactics, particularly the sit-down strike, in which workers, rather than picketing outside the factory, simply sat inside the plant, thereby blocking both production and the use of strikebreakers.

U.S. Senate, *Investigation of Strikebreaking* (1939)

The CIO won major victories despite bitter opposition from industry and its allies. The issue was not wages but labor's right to organize and bargain with management. Sit-down strikes paralyzed General Motors in 1937 after it refused to recognize the United Auto Workers. GM tried to force the strikers out of its Flint, Michigan, plants by turning off the heat, using police and tear gas, threatening strikers' families,

Bob Stinson, *Flint-Sit-Down Strike* (1936)

and obtaining court orders to clear the plant by military force. But the governor refused to order National Guardsmen to attack, and the strikers held out, aided by the Women's Emergency Brigade, working-class women who picketed the building, heckled the police, and smuggled food to the strikers. After six weeks, GM signed a contract with the UAW. Chrysler soon followed suit. Ford refused to recognize the union until 1941, often violently disrupting organizing efforts.

Steel companies also used violence against unionization. In the Memorial Day Massacre in Chicago in 1937, police guarding a plant of the Republic Steel Company fired on strikers and their families, killing ten people as they tried to flee. A Senate investigation found that Republic and other companies had hired private police to attack workers seeking to unionize, stockpiled weapons and tear gas, and corrupted officials. Federal court orders finally forced the companies to bargain collectively.

New Deal labor legislation, government investigations and court orders, and the federal refusal to use force against strikes helped the labor movement secure basic rights for American workers. Union membership leaped from under 3 million in 1932 to 9 million by 1939, and workers won higher wages, better working conditions, and more economic democracy.

## WOMEN AND THE NEW DEAL

New Deal relief programs had a mixed impact on working women. Formal government policy required equal consideration for women and men, but local officials so flouted this requirement. Women on relief were restricted to women's work—more than half worked on sewing projects, regardless of their skills—and were paid scarcely half what men received. WPA training programs also reinforced traditional ideas about women's work; black women, for example, were trained to be maids, dishwashers, and cooks. Although women constituted nearly one-fourth of the labor force, they obtained only 19 percent of the jobs created by the WPA, 12 percent of those created by the FERA, and 7 percent of those created by the CWA. The CCC excluded women altogether. Still, relief agencies provided crucial assistance to women during the depression.

Other New Deal programs also had mixed benefits for women. Many NRA codes mandated lower wage scales for women than for men, which officials justified as reflecting long-established customs. But by raising minimum wages, the NRA brought relatively greater improvement to women, who were concentrated in the lowest paid occupations, than to male workers. The Social Security Act did not cover domestic servants, waitresses, or women who worked in the home, but it did help mothers with dependent children.

Still more significant, the Social Security Act reflected and reinforced prevailing notions about proper roles for men and women. The system was based on the idea that men should be wage earners and women should stay at home as wives and mothers. Accordingly, if a woman worked outside the home and her husband was eligible for benefits, she would not receive her own retirement pension. And if a woman had no husband but had children, welfare authorities would remove her from work-relief jobs regardless of whether she wanted to continue to work, and would give her assistance from the Aid to Dependent Children (ADC) program, which was also created under the Social Security Act. These new programs, then, while providing much-needed assistance, also institutionalized a modern welfare system that segregated men and women in separate spheres and reaffirmed the then popular belief that the success of the family depended on that separation.

Women also gained political influence under the New Deal. Appointed to many positions in the Roosevelt administration, progressive women helped develop and implement New Deal social legislation. Secretary of Labor Frances Perkins was the first woman cabinet member and a key member of the network; other women were in the Treasury Department, the Children's Bureau, and relief and cultural programs.

---

**QUICK REVIEW**

**A New Deal for Labor**

- The Wagner Act stimulated labor activism
- The CIO organized workers in the steel, auto, and rubber industries
- Union membership rose from 3 million in 1932 to 9 million in 1939

*Documents*

**Mrs. Henry Weddington,** *Letter to President Roosevelt* (1938)

*Documents*

**Meridel Le Sueur,** *Women on the Breadlines* (1932)

Eleanor Roosevelt was their leader. Described by a Washington reporter as "a cabinet member without portfolio," she roared across the social and political landscape of the 1930s, pushing for women's rights, demanding reforms, traveling across the country, writing newspaper columns and speaking on the radio, developing plans to help unemployed miners in West Virginia and abolish slums in Washington, and lobbying both Congress and her husband. FDR used her as his eyes and ears and sometimes his conscience. Indeed, Eleanor Roosevelt had become not merely the most prominent first lady in history but a force in her own right and a symbol of the growing importance of women in public life.

## MINORITIES AND THE NEW DEAL

Despite the move of African Americans into the Democratic Party, the New Deal's record on racial issues was limited. Although Roosevelt deplored racial abuses, he never pushed for civil rights legislation, fearing to antagonize southern congressional Democrats whose support he needed. For similar reasons, many New Deal programs discriminated against African Americans. And racist officials discriminated in allocating federal relief. Atlanta, for instance, provided average monthly relief checks of $32.66 to white people but only $19.29 to black people.

Nonetheless, disproportionately poor and unemployed African Americans did benefit from the New Deal's welfare and economic programs. W. E. B. DuBois asserted that "large numbers of colored people in the United States would have starved to death if it had not been for the Roosevelt policies," adding that the New Deal served to sharpen their sense of the value of citizenship by making clear the "direct connection between politics and industry, between government and work, [and] between voting and wages." And key New Dealers campaigned against racial discrimination. Eleanor Roosevelt prodded FDR to appoint black officials, wrote articles supporting racial equality, and flouted segregationist laws. Attacked by white racists, she was popular in the black community. Harry Hopkins and Harold Ickes also promoted equal rights. As black votes in northern cities became important, pragmatic New Dealers also began to pay attention to black needs.

African Americans themselves pressed for reforms. Civil rights groups protested discriminatory policies, including the unequal wage scales in the NRA codes and the CCC's limited enrollment of black youth. African Americans demonstrated against racial discrimination in hiring and their exclusion from federally financed construction projects.

In response, FDR took more interest in black economic and social problems. He prohibited discrimination in the WPA in 1935, and the NYA adopted enlightened racial policies. Roosevelt also appointed black people to important positions, including the first black federal judge. Many of these officials began meeting regularly at the home of Mary McLeod Bethune of the National Council of Negro Women. Dubbed the Black Cabinet, they worked with civil rights organizations, fought discrimination in government, influenced patronage, and stimulated black interest in politics.

The New Deal improved economic and social conditions for many African Americans. Black illiteracy dropped because of federal education projects, and the number of black college students and graduates more than doubled, in part because the NYA provided

With an appointment in the National Youth Administration, the educator Mary McLeod Bethune was the highest-ranking African-American woman in the Roosevelt administration. She advised FDR on all racial matters and envisioned "dozens of Negro women coming after me, filling positions of trust and strategic importance."

### QUICK REVIEW

**Impact of the New Deal on Women**

- Despite their numbers in the workforce, women received proportionately fewer New Deal jobs than men.
- The increase in the minimum wage brought relatively greater improvements to workers in the lowest-paying jobs, most of whom were women.
- Women gained political influence under the New Deal.

### QUICK REVIEW

**African Americans and the New Deal**

- Many New Deal programs discriminated against African Americans.
- Key New Dealers campaigned against discrimination.
- African Americans pressed for reforms.
- New Deal improved economic and social conditions for many African Americans.

student aid to black colleges. New Deal relief and public health programs reduced black infant mortality rates and raised life expectancy rates. Conditions for black people continued to lag behind those for white people, and discrimination persisted, but the black switch to the Roosevelt coalition reflected the New Deal's benefits.

Native Americans also benefited from the New Deal. The depression had imposed further misery on a group already suffering from poverty, wretched health conditions, and the nation's lowest educational level. Many New Deal programs had limited applicability to Indians, but the CCC appealed to their interests and skills. More than 80,000 Native Americans received training in agriculture, forestry, and animal husbandry, along with basic academic subjects. CCC projects, together with those undertaken by the PWA and the WPA, built schools, hospitals, roads, and irrigation systems on reservations.

New Deal officials also refocused government Indian policy, which had undermined tribal authority and promoted assimilation by reducing Indian landholding and attacking Indian culture. Appointed commissioner of Indian affairs in 1933, John Collier prohibited interference with Native American religious or cultural life, directed the Bureau of Indian Affairs to employ more Native Americans, and prevented Indian schools from suppressing native languages and traditions.

Collier also persuaded Congress to pass the Indian Reorganization Act of 1934, often called the Indians' New Deal. The act guaranteed religious freedom, reestablished tribal self-government, and halted the sale of tribal lands. It also provided funds to expand Indian landholdings, support Indian students, and establish tribal businesses. But social and economic problems persisted on the isolated reservations, and white missionaries and business interests attacked Collier's reforms as atheistic and communistic. And not all Native Americans supported Collier's reforms, asserting that he, too, stereotyped Indians and their culture, and labeling his efforts as "back-to-the-blanket" policies designed to make Native American cultures historical commodities. (See American Views, The Commissioner of the Bureau of Indian Affairs on the New Deal for Native Americans.)

Hispanic Americans received less assistance from the New Deal. Relief programs aided many Hispanics in California and the Southwest but ignored those who were not citizens. Moreover, local administrators often discriminated against Hispanics, especially by providing higher relief payments to Anglos. Finally, by excluding agricultural workers, neither the Social Security Act nor the Wagner Act gave Mexican Americans much protection or hope. Farm workers remained largely unorganized, exploited, and at the mercy of agribusinesses.

## THE NEW DEAL: NORTH, SOUTH, EAST, AND WEST

"We are going to make a country," President Roosevelt declared, "in which no one is left out." And with that statement, along with his belief that the federal government must take the lead in building a new "economic constitutional order," FDR ensured that his New Deal programs and policies fanned out throughout the nation.

**The New Deal in the South.**    The New Deal's agricultural program boosted farm prices and income more in the South than any other region. By controlling cotton production, it also promoted diversification; its subsidies financed mechanization. The resulting modernization helped replace an archaic sharecropping system with an emergent agribusiness. The rural poor were displaced, but the South's agricultural economy advanced.

The New Deal also improved southern cities. FERA and WPA built urban sewer systems, airports, bridges, roads, and harbor facilities. Whereas northern cities had already constructed such facilities themselves—and were still paying off the debts these had incurred—the federal government largely paid for such modernization in the South, giving its cities an economic advantage.

Federal grants were supposed to be awarded to states in proportion to their own expenditures, but while southern politicians welcomed New Deal funds, they refused to contribute their share of the costs. Nationally, the federal proportion of FERA expenditures was 62 percent; in the South, it was usually 90 percent and never lower than 73 percent.

The federal government had a particularly powerful impact on the South with the **Tennessee Valley Authority (TVA),** launched in 1933 (see Map 25–2). Coordinating activities across seven states, the TVA built dams to control floods and generate hydroelectric power, produced fertilizer, fostered agricultural and forestry development, encouraged conservation, improved navigation, and modernized school and health systems. Private utility companies denounced the TVA as socialistic, but most southerners supported it. Its major drawback was environmental damage that only became apparent later. Over a vast area of the South, it provided electricity for the first time.

The New Deal further expanded access to electricity by establishing the Rural Electrification Administration (REA) in 1935. Private companies had refused to extend power lines into the countryside because it was not profitable, consigning 90 percent of the nation's farms to drudgery and darkness. The REA revolutionized farm life by sponsoring rural nonprofit electric cooperatives. By 1941, 35 percent of American farms had electricity; by 1950, 78 percent.

**Tennessee Valley Authority**   Federal regional planning agency established to promote conservation, produce electric power, and encourage economic development in seven southern states.

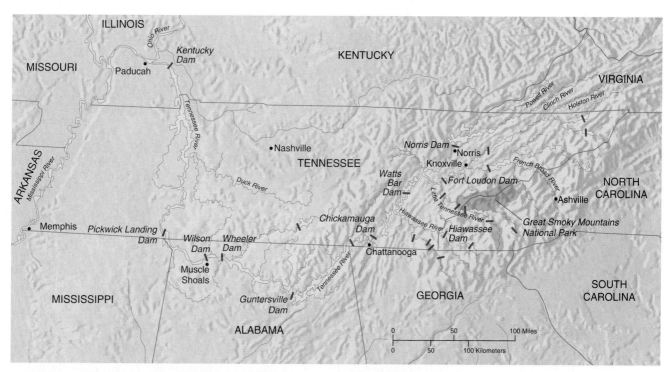

MAP 25–2   **The Tennessee Valley Authority**   By building dams and hydroelectric power plants, the TVA controlled flooding and soil erosion and generated electricity that did much to modernize a large region of the Upper South.

**What economic** and social impact did the Tennessee Valley Authority have on the Upper South?

**The New Deal in the West.**    The New Deal also changed the West. Westerners received the most federal money per capita in welfare, relief projects, and loans. Like southerners, they accepted federal aid and clamored for more.

The Bureau of Reclamation, established in 1902, emerged as one of the most important government agencies in the West. It built huge dams to control the western river systems and promote large-scale development. By furnishing capital and expertise, the government subsidized and stimulated western economic development, particularly the growth of agribusiness.

Westerners welcomed such assistance but rarely shared the federal goals of rational resource management. Instead, they often wanted to continue to exploit the land and resented federal supervision as colonial control. In practice, however, the government worked in partnership with the West's agribusinesses and timber and petroleum industries.

## THE NEW DEAL AND PUBLIC ACTIVISM

Despite Hoover's fear that government responsibility would discourage local initiative, the 1930s witnessed an upsurge in activism. New Deal programs, in fact, often encouraged or empowered groups to shape public policy. Moreover, because the administration worried about centralization, some federal agencies fostered what New Dealers called "grassroots democracy." The AAA set up committees that ultimately included more than 100,000 people to implement agricultural policy and held referendums on crop controls; local advisory committees guided the various federal arts projects; federal management of the West's public grasslands mandated cooperation with associations of livestock raisers.

At times, local administration of national programs enabled groups to exploit federal policy for their own advantage. Wealthy planters shaped AAA practices at the expense of poor tenant farmers; local control of TVA projects excluded black people. But federal programs often allowed previously unrepresented groups to contest traditionally dominant interests. Often seeing greater opportunities for participation and influence in federal programs than in city and state governments, community groups campaigned to expand federal authority. In short, depression conditions and New Deal programs actually increased citizen involvement in public affairs.

# EBBING OF THE NEW DEAL

**WHY DID** the New Deal lose momentum after 1936?

After his victory in 1936, Roosevelt committed himself to further reforms. But determined opponents, continuing economic problems, and the president's own misjudgments blocked his reforms and deadlocked the New Deal.

## CHALLENGING THE COURT

Roosevelt regarded the Supreme Court as his most dangerous opponent. During his first term, the Court had declared several important measures unconstitutional. Indeed, most of the justices were elderly conservatives, appointed by Republicans and unsympathetic to an activist federal government. It seemed that the Court would also strike down the Second New Deal.

Emboldened by the 1936 landslide, Roosevelt decided to restructure the federal judiciary. In early 1937, he proposed legislation authorizing the president to name a new justice for each one serving past the age of 70. Additional justices, he said, would increase judicial efficiency. But his real goal was to appoint new justices more sympathetic to the New Deal.

His Court plan led to a divisive struggle. The proposal was perfectly legal: Congress had the authority, which it had used repeatedly, to change the number of justices on the Court. But Republicans and conservative Democrats attacked the plan as a scheme to "pack" the Court and subvert the separation of powers among the three branches of government. Some conservatives called the president a dictator, but even many liberals expressed reservations about the plan or FDR's lack of candor in proposing it.

The Court itself undercut support for FDR's proposal by upholding the Social Security and Wagner acts and minimum-wage legislation. Moreover, the retirement of a conservative justice allowed Roosevelt to name a sympathetic successor. Congress rejected Roosevelt's plan.

Roosevelt's challenge to the Court hurt the New Deal. It worried the public, split the Democratic Party, and revived conservatives. Opponents promptly attacked other New Deal policies, from support for unions to progressive taxation. Henceforth, a conservative coalition of Republicans and southern Democrats in Congress blocked FDR's reforms.

## MORE HARD TIMES

A sharp recession, beginning in August 1937, added to Roosevelt's problems. The New Deal's deficit spending had reflected his desire to alleviate suffering, not a conviction that it would stimulate economic recovery. As the economy improved in 1936, Roosevelt decided to cut federal expenditures and balance the budget. But private investment and employment remained stagnant, and the economy plunged.

In 1938, Roosevelt reluctantly increased spending. New appropriations for the PWA and other government programs revived the faltering economy, but neither FDR nor Congress would spend what was necessary to end the depression. Only the vast expenditures for World War II would bring full recovery.

## POLITICAL STALEMATE

The recession interrupted the momentum of the New Deal and strengthened its opponents. In late 1937, their leaders in Congress issued a "conservative manifesto" decrying New Deal fiscal, labor, and regulatory policies. Holding seniority in a Congress malapportioned in their favor, they blocked most of Roosevelt's reforms. None of his must legislation passed a special session of Congress in December. In 1938, Congress rejected tax reforms and reduced corporate taxes. The few measures that passed were heavily amended.

To protect the New Deal, Roosevelt turned again to the public, with whom he remained immensely popular. In the 1938 Democratic primaries, he campaigned against the New Deal's conservative opponents. But FDR could not transfer his personal popularity to the political newcomers he supported. What his foes attacked as a purge failed. Roosevelt lost further political leverage when the Republicans gained 75 seats in the House and seven in the Senate and 13 governorships.

The 1938 elections did not repudiate the New Deal, for the Democrats retained majorities in both houses of Congress. But the Republican revival and the survival of the conservative southern Democrats guaranteed that the New Deal had gone as far as it ever would. With Roosevelt in the White House and his opponents controlling Congress, the New Deal ended in political stalemate.

# GOOD NEIGHBORS AND HOSTILE FORCES

Even before FDR's conservative opponents derailed the New Deal, the president felt their impact in the area of foreign policy. Isolationists in Congress counseled against any U.S. involvement in world affairs and appealed to the growing national disillu-

**HOW DID** Roosevelt respond to the rise of fascism in Europe?

sionment with America's participation in the Great War to support their position. Moreover, Roosevelt himself, although not an isolationist, believed that the gravity of the nation's economic depression warranted a primary focus on domestic recovery, and in the early years of his presidency, took few international initiatives.

The actions he did take related directly to salvaging America's desperate economy. As the depression worsened in 1933, American businesses searched for new markets throughout the world, and key business leaders informed FDR that they would welcome the opportunity to expand trade to the Soviet Union. Moscow was also eager to renew ties to the United States, and President Roosevelt extended formal recognition of the Soviet Union in November 1933.

Enhancing trade opportunities and rescuing the economy from the damage wrought by high tariffs figured prominently in Roosevelt's policies in the Western Hemisphere. In large measure, Roosevelt merely extended the Good Neighbor policy begun by his predecessor. Hoover had abandoned the U.S. policy of interventionism, and by the time he left office in March 1933, all U.S. troops had been removed from Latin America. Still, the Great Depression strained U.S.-Latin American relations, sending economic shock waves throughout Central and South America and, in several instances, helping propel to power ruthless dictators who ruled with iron fists and U.S. support.

To symbolize that the United States was a "good neighbor," FDR visited the Caribbean in 1934, receiving an enthusiastic reception, and in 1936, he broke new ground by becoming the first U.S. president to sail to South America. He also worked to encourage trade by reducing tariffs.

## NEUTRALITY AND FASCISM

Outside the hemisphere, during his first term as president, Roosevelt generally followed the policy of avoiding involvement in Europe's political, economic, and social problems. But the aggressive actions of Adolf Hitler in Germany ultimately led Roosevelt to a different position, and in the latter part of the decade, he faced the task of educating the American public, still resentful of U.S. participation in World War I, about the fascist danger that was spreading in Europe.

**fascist government** A government subscribing to a philosophy of dictatorship that merges the interests of the state, armed forces, and big business.

Hitler came to power in 1933, shortly before FDR entered the White House, and he pledged to restore German pride and nationalism in the aftermath of the Versailles Treaty. As the leader of the National Socialist Workers Party, or Nazis, Hitler established a **fascist government**—a one-party dictatorship closely aligned with corporate interests, committed to a "biological world evolution," and determined to establish a new empire, the Third Reich. He vowed to eliminate Bolshevik radicalism and purify the German "race" through the elimination of those he deemed undesirable, especially targeting Jews, the group Hitler blamed for most, if not all, Germany's ills.

Others aided the spread of fascism. Italian leader Benito Mussolini, who had assumed power in 1922 and envisaged emulating the power and prestige of the Roman Empire, brutally attacked Ethiopia in 1935. The following year, a young fascist military officer, Francisco Franco, led an uprising in Spain, and with the assistance of Italy and Germany, successfully ousted the Spanish Republic and its loyalist supporters by 1939 to create an authoritarian government. Meanwhile, Hitler implemented his plan of conquest: He remilitarized the Rhineland in 1936, and in 1938 he annexed Austria.

The aggressive actions of Germany and Italy failed to eclipse U.S. fears of becoming involved in another European war. Congress passed Neutrality Acts designed to continue

On November 9, 1938, Nazi Germany launched an attack on Jews, destroying their businesses and burning their synagogues. This street scene in Berlin shows the shattered windows of Jewish businesses. Nazi leader Joseph Goebbels recorded the event, known as Kristallnacht, in his diary: "Yesterday: Berlin. There, all proceeded fantastically. One fire after another. It is good that way. . . . 100 dead. But no German property damaged."

America's trade with its world partners but prohibit the president from taking sides in the mounting European crisis.

**Appeasement and more neutrality.**   After annexing Austria, Hitler pushed again in 1938 when he demanded the Sudetenland from Czechoslovakia. The French and the British refused to stand up to Hitler, following instead a policy of appeasement. Meeting in Munich in September 1938, the leaders of England and France abandoned their security obligations to the Czechs, yielding the Sudetenland to Hitler in exchange for a weak promise of no more annexations. In America, too, the sentiment was for peace at all costs.

Isolationism compounded by anti-Semitism and by the divisions between the leaders of the American Jewish community combined to ensure that the United States would not become a haven for Jews suffering under Nazi brutality. News of Nazi atrocities against Austrian Jews in 1938 shocked the American press, and Hitler's violent pogrom, known as *Kristallnacht* ("Night of the Broken Glass"), conducted against Jews throughout Germany in November 1938, added fresh proof of Nazi cruelty. Although the United States recalled its ambassador from Berlin to protest the pogrom (in response, Germany recalled its ambassador from Washington), it did not alter its restrictive immigration-quota system, the 1924 National Origins Act, to provide refuge for German Jews.

As Europe edged closer to war, the relationship between the United States and Japan, periodically tense in the twentieth century, became more strained. Japan resented U.S. economic interests in East Asia and was offended by the policy of excluding Japanese immigrants. The United States regarded Japan's desires for empire as threatening but also needed Japan as a trading partner, especially in the economically depressed 1930s. Consequently, in September 1931, when Japan seized Manchuria, the United States did little more than denounce the action. Again in 1937, after Japanese troops attacked Chinese forces north of Beijing and outright war began between Japan and China, the United States merely condemned the action.

## EDGING TOWARD INVOLVEMENT

After the Munich agreement, President Roosevelt moved away from domestic reform toward preparedness for war, fearful that conflict in Europe was unavoidable and determined to revise the neutrality laws. In his State of the Union address in January 1939, FDR explained that America's neutrality laws might "actually give aid to an aggressor and deny it to the victim." By the fall of that year, he had won support for changes in the laws that would enable the United States to provide important assistance to Britain and France in the winter of 1939–1940. Hitler's defiance of the Munich agreement in Czechoslovakia, overrunning Prague by March 1939, merely anticipated his next move toward Poland and also convinced the British and the French that war was imminent.

These Spring Days It's Hard to Keep Your Mind on Your Work!

In this political cartoon about Franklin D. Roosevelt's promise of neutrality, Roosevelt and a congressman watch Hitler and Mussolini light a powder keg.

# CONCLUSION

The Great Depression and the New Deal mark a major divide in American history. The depression cast doubt on the traditional practices, policies, and attitudes that underlay not only the nation's economy but also its social and political institutions and relationships. The New Deal brought only partial economic recovery. However, its economic policies, from banking and securities regulation to unemployment compensation, farm price supports, and minimum wages, created barriers against another depression. The gradual adoption of compensatory spending policies expanded the government's role in the economy. Responding to the failures of private organizations and state and local governments, the federal government assumed the obligation to provide social welfare.

Roosevelt also expanded the role of the presidency. As his White House took the initiative for defining public policy, drafting legislation, lobbying Congress, and communicating with the nation, it became the model for all subsequent presidents. Not only was the president's power increased, but Roosevelt made the federal government, rather than state or local governments, the focus of public interest and expectations.

By the end of the 1930s, as international relations deteriorated, FDR was already considering a shift, as he later said, from Dr. New Deal to Dr. Win-the-War. Reluctant to move beyond public opinion that did not want war and limited by neutrality legislation, FDR cautiously led the nation toward war—this time against an enemy far more threatening than the Great Depression. Ironically, only then would President Roosevelt end the depression that had ravaged the nation for nearly a decade.

# SUMMARY

**WHAT TRIGGERED** the Great Depression?

**Hard Times in Hooverville**   The prosperity of the 1920s ended in a stock market crash that revealed the flaws in the economy. As the nation slid into a catastrophic depression, factories closed, employment and incomes tumbled, and millions lost their homes, hopes, and dignity. Some protested and took direct action; others looked to the government for relief. The stock market crash of 1929 marked the beginning of the Great Depression but did not cause it. Contributing factors were the uneven distribution of wealth and income; industries dominated by oligarchies; overproduction in agriculture and other industries; declining prices; government policies; and European debts.

**HOW DID** Herbert Hoover respond to the Depression? Why did his policies fail?

**Herbert Hoover and the Depression**   President Hoover took unprecedented steps to resolve the growing economic crises, but he believed that voluntary private relief was preferable to federal intervention. The scope of the depression over-whelmed anything that private individuals and agencies could manage; Hoover blundered by refusing to admit a more activist approach was needed. The Reconstruction Finance Corporation lent funds that could "trickle down" to the public. The treatment of the Bonus Army symbolized Hoover's unpopularity and set the stage for the election of Franklin D. Roosevelt.

**WHAT WERE** the goals of the early New Deal?

**Launching the New Deal**   In the midst of national anxiety, Franklin D. Roosevelt pushed forward an un-precedented program to resolve the crisis of a collapsing financial system, crippling unemployment, and agricultural and industrial breakdown and to promote reform. After initially addressing the banking crisis, the New Deal went on to establish relief agencies and promote economic recovery. The New Deal achieved successes and attracted support but it also had limitations and generated criticism that suggested the need for still greater innovations.

**WHAT WERE** the major accomplishments of the Second New Deal?

**Consolidating the New Deal**   In 1935 Roosevelt undertook additional economic and social reforms. Labor's right to organize and bargain collectively was addressed, the path-breaking Social Security Act was passed, and the Works Progress Administration was created. The administration also responded to the environmental crises that had turned the Great Plains into a dustbowl and driven the "Okies" to California. The 1936 election gave Americans an opportunity to judge the New Deal and Roosevelt. Political realignment resulted: Former Republican constituents voted Democratic and produced a landslide victory for the president.

**WHAT EXPLAINS** labor's resurgence in the 1930s?

**The New Deal and American Life**   The election of 1936 revealed the impact the New Deal had on Americans. Industrial workers mobilized to secure their rights; women and minorities gained increased, if still limited, opportunities to participate in American society; and Southerners and Westerners benefited from government programs like the TVA that they turned to their own advantage. Government programs changed daily life, and ordinary people often helped shape the new policies.

**WHY DID** the New Deal lose momentum after 1936?

**Ebbing of the New Deal**   After his 1936 election, Roosevelt committed himself to further reforms, but his misjudgment blocked some efforts and deadlocked others. Regarding the Supreme Court as an adversary, Roosevelt attempted to restructure the federal judiciary; his attempt to "pack" the court hurt the New Deal. A 1937 recession caused by the New Deal's lack of aggressiveness caused the administration to adopt Keynesian economic theories and have the government use deficient spending to increase demand and production.

**HOW DID** Roosevelt respond to the rise of fascism in Europe?

**Good Neighbors and Hostile Forces**   While isolationists in Congress counseled against involvement in foreign affairs, fascism was spreading in Europe and Asia. In his first term Roosevelt followed a policy of neutrality; after the Munich crisis, Hitler's intentions toward the world and Germany's Jewish citizens had become more defined and threatening. America's relationship with Japan continued to deteriorate; by 1939, the "epidemic of world lawlessness" was edging the United States toward involvement.

# WHERE TO LEARN MORE

**Center for New Deal Studies, Roosevelt University, Chicago, Illinois.** The center contains political memorabilia, photographs, papers, and taped interviews dealing with Franklin D. Roosevelt and the New Deal; it also sponsors an annual lecture series about the Roosevelt legacy. **www.roosevelt .edu/newdeal/**

**Franklin D. Roosevelt Home and Presidential Library, Hyde Park, New York.** The Roosevelt home, furnished with family heirlooms, and the spacious grounds, where FDR is buried, personalize the president and provide insights into his career. The nearby library has displays and exhibitions about Roosevelt's presidency, and the Eleanor Roosevelt Wing is dedicated to her career. **www.fdrlibrary.marist.edu**

**Eleanor Roosevelt National Historic Site, Hyde Park, New York.** These two cottages, where Eleanor Roosevelt worked and, after 1945, lived, contain her furniture and memorabilia. Visitors can also watch a film biography of ER and tour the grounds of this retreat where she entertained personal friends and world leaders. **www.nps.gov/elro.**

**New Deal Network.** A valuable guide to the study of the Great Depression and the New Deal with a rich collection of photographs and documents. **www.newdeal.feri.org**

# STUDY RESOURCES

## myhistorylab

For study resources for this chapter, go to www .myhistorylab.com and choose *The American Journey*. You will find a wealth of study and review material for this chapter, including pre- and post-tests, customized study plan, key term review flash cards, interactive map and document activities, and documents for analysis.

# REVIEW QUESTIONS

1. Why did President Hoover's emphasis on voluntarism fail to resolve the problems of the Great Depression in the United States?

2. Describe the relief programs of the New Deal. What were they designed to accomplish? What were their achievements and their limitations?

3. What were the major criticisms of the early New Deal? How accurate were those charges?

4. How did the policies of the New Deal shape the constituency and the prospects of the Democratic Party in the 1930s?

5. Describe the conflict between management and labor in the 1930s. What were the major issues and motivations? How did the two sides differ in resources and tactics, and how and why did these factors change over time?

6. How did the role of the federal government change in the 1930s? What factors were responsible for the changes?

## KEY TERMS

**Bonus Army** (p. 751)
**Congress of Industrial Organizations (CIO)** (p. 761)
**Fascist government** (p. 768)
**Federal Deposit Insurance Corporation (FDIC)** (p. 753)
**Fireside chat** (p. 753)

**Great Depression** (p. 745)
**Hoovervilles** (p. 747)
**New Deal** (p. 743)
**Securities and Exchange Commission (SEC)** (p. 753)
**Tennessee Valley Authority (TVA)** (p. 765)

# 26
# World War II

"above and beyond the call of duty"

DORIE MILLER
Received the Navy Cross
at Pearl Harbor, May 27, 1942

American soldiers landing on the coast of France at Normandy on June 6, 1944 (D-Day).

THE DILEMMAS OF NEUTRALITY  (*page 777*)

**WHY WERE** most Americans reluctant to get involved in World War II?

HOLDING THE LINE  (*page 784*)

WHY DID the Allies choose to focus on defeating Germany before Japan?

MOBILIZING FOR VICTORY  (*page 788*)

**WHAT STEPS** did the U.S. government take to organize the economy for war?

THE HOME FRONT  (*page 791*)

HOW DID the war affect the place of women in American society?

WAR AND PEACE  (*page 796*)

**WHY DID** the Allies win the war?

*December, 1942*

*The scene [under the stadium] at The University of Chicago would have been confusing to an outsider, if he could have eluded the security guards and gained admittance. He would have seen only what appeared to be a crude pile of black bricks and wooden timbers. . . .*

*Finally, the day came when we were ready to run the experiment. We gathered on a balcony about 10 feet above the floor of the large room in which the structure had been erected. Beneath us was a young scientist, George Weil, whose duty it was to handle the last control rod that was holding the reaction in check. . . .*

*Finally, it was time to remove the control rods. Slowly, Weil started to withdraw the main control rod. On the balcony, we watched the indicators which measured the neutron count and told us how rapidly the disintegration of the uranium atoms under their neutron bombardment was proceeding.*

*At 11:35 A.M., the counters were clicking rapidly. Then, with a loud clap, the automatic control rods slammed home. The safety point had been set too low.*

*It seemed a good time to eat lunch. During lunch everyone was thinking about the experiment but nobody talked much about it.*

*At 2:30, Weil pulled out the control rod in a series of measured adjustments. Shortly after, the intensity shown by the indicators began to rise at a slow but ever-increasing rate. At this moment we knew that the self-sustaining [nuclear] reaction was under way.*

*The event was not spectacular, no fuses burned, no lights flashed. But to us it meant that release of atomic energy on a large scale would be only a matter of time.*

Enrico Fermi, in *The First Reactor* (Washington, DC: U.S. Department of Energy, 1982).

## myhistorylab
PEARSON

**Personal Journeys Online**

- Patricia Cain Koehler, A Woman Shipyard Worker Recalls Her Experience, 1943.

- Leon Overstreet, A Construction Worker on the Manhattan Project, 1943.

- Bill Mauldin, A cartoonist creates "Willie" and "Joe" as typical American G.I.s, 1943-45.

- Patricia Cain Koehler, writing in the *Oregon Historical Quarterly* (Fall 1990), recounted her experiences as a young woman helping to build aircraft carriers during World War II.

- Leon Overstreet was a construction worker who helped to build Manhattan Project facilities. He was interviewed for S. L. Sanger, *Working on the Bomb: An Oral History of World War II Hanford* (1995)

- Bill Mauldin explains the origins of his cartoon G.I.s Willie and Joe. From Studs Terkel, *The Good War* (1985)

ENRICO FERMI was describing the first controlled nuclear chain reaction—the critical experiment from which atomic weapons and atomic power would soon develop. Fermi had emigrated to escape the growing political repression of Fascist Italy. In 1942, after the United States joined the ongoing global conflict of World War II, Fermi was put in charge of nuclear fission research at the University of Chicago and played a leading role in efforts to develop an atomic bomb. The following year found Fermi, other atomic scientists, and their families at Los Alamos, a science city that the government built hurriedly on a high plateau in northern New Mexico, where isolation was supposed to ensure secrecy and help the United States win the race with Nazi Germany to develop atomic weapons.

The Fermis were not the only family to give Los Alamos a multinational flavor. Laura remembered that it was "all one big family and all one big accent. . . . Everybody in science was there, both from the United States and from almost all European countries." The internationalism of Los Alamos mirrored the larger war effort. Japan's attack on Pearl Harbor in December 1941 thrust the United States into a war that spanned the globe. America's allies against Japan in the Pacific and East Asia included Great Britain, Australia, and China. In Europe, its allies against Nazi Germany and Fascist Italy included Great Britain, the Soviet Union, and more than 20 other nations. The scientists racing to perfect the atomic bomb knew that victory was far from certain. Germany and

Japan had piled one conquest on another since the late 1930s, and they continued to seize new territories in 1942. Allied defeat in a few key battles could have resulted in a standoff or an Axis victory. A new weapon might end the war more quickly or make the difference between victory and defeat.

The war's domestic impacts were as profound as its international consequences. The race to build an atomic bomb was only one part of a vast effort to harness the resources of the United States to the war effort. The war highlighted racial inequalities, gave women new opportunities, and fostered growth in the South and West. By devastating the nation's commercial rivals, compelling workers to retrain and factories to modernize, World War II left the United States dominant in the world economy. It also increased the size and scope of the federal government and built an alliance among the armed forces, big business, and science that helped shape postwar America.

# THE DILEMMAS OF NEUTRALITY

Americans in the 1930s wanted no part of another overseas war. Despite two years of German victories and a decade of Japanese aggression against China, opinion polls in the fall of 1941 showed that a majority of voters still hoped to avoid war. President Roosevelt's challenge was to lead the United States toward rearmament and support for Great Britain and China without alarming a reluctant public.

**WHY WERE** most Americans reluctant to get involved in World War II?

## THE ROOTS OF WAR

The roots of World War II can be found in the aftereffects of World War I. The peace settlement created a set of small new nations in eastern Europe that were vulnerable to aggression by their much larger neighbors, Germany and the Soviet Union (more formally, the Union of Soviet Socialist Republics, or USSR). Italy and Japan thought that the Treaty of Versailles had not recognized their stature as world powers. Many Germans were convinced that Germany had been betrayed rather than defeated in 1918. In the 1930s, economic crisis undermined an already shaky political order. Economic hardship and political instability fueled the rise of right-wing dictatorships that offered territorial expansion by military conquest as the way to redress old rivalries, dominate trade, and gain access to raw materials.

Japanese nationalists believed that the United States, Britain, and France had treated Japan unfairly after World War I, despite its participation against Germany. They believed that Japan should expel the French, British, Dutch, and Americans from Asia and create a **Greater East Asia Co-Prosperity Sphere,** in which Japan gave the orders and other Asian peoples complied. Seizing the Chinese province of Manchuria to expand an East Asian empire that already included Korea and Taiwan emboldened Japan's military in 1931. A full-scale invasion of China followed in 1937.

Italian aggression embroiled Africa and the Mediterranean. The Fascist dictator Benito Mussolini had sent arms and troops to aid General Francisco Franco's right-wing rebels in Spain. The three-year civil war, which ended with Franco's victory in 1939, became a bloody testing ground for new German military tactics and German and Italian ambitions against democratic Europe.

**Greater East Asia Co-Prosperity Sphere**  Japanese nationalists believed that Japan should expel the French, British, Dutch, and Americans from Asia and create this sphere in which Japan would give the orders and other Asian peoples would comply.

# CHRONOLOGY

**1931** Japan invades Manchuria.

**1933** Hitler takes power in Germany.

**1935** Congress passes first of three neutrality acts.

Italy invades Ethiopia.

**1936** Germany and Italy form the Rome-Berlin Axis.

Civil war erupts in Spain.

**1937** Japan invades China.

**1938** Germany absorbs Austria.

Munich agreement between Germany, Britain, and France.

**1939** Germany and the Soviet Union sign a nonagression pact.

Germany absorbs Czechoslovakia.

Germany invades Poland; Great Britain and France declare war on Germany.

**1940** Germany conquers Denmark, Norway, Belgium, the Netherlands, and France.

Japan, Germany, and Italy sign the Tripartite Pact.

Germany bombs England in the Battle of Britain.

The United States begins to draft men into the armed forces.

Franklin Roosevelt wins an unprecedented third term.

**1941** The United States begins a lend-lease program to make military equipment available to Great Britain and later the Soviet Union.

The Fair Employment Practices Committee is established.

Germany invades the Soviet Union.

Roosevelt and Churchill issue the Atlantic Charter.

Japan attacks U.S. military bases in Hawaii.

**1942** American forces in the Philippines surrender to Japan.

President Roosevelt authorizes the removal and internment of Japanese Americans living in four western states.

Naval battles in the Coral Sea and off the island of Midway blunt Japanese expansion. U.S. forces land in North Africa.

Soviet forces encircle a German army at Stalingrad.

The first sustained and controlled nuclear chain reaction takes place at the University of Chicago.

**1943** U.S. and British forces invade Italy, which makes terms with the Allies.

Race conflict erupts in riots in Detroit, New York, and Los Angeles.

The landing of Marines on Tarawa initiates the island-hopping strategy.

U.S. war production peaks.

Roosevelt, Churchill, and Stalin confer at Tehran.

**1944** Allied forces land in Normandy.

The U.S. Navy destroys Japanese sea power in the battles of the Philippine Sea and Leyte Gulf.

The Battle of the Bulge is the last tactical setback for the Allies.

**1945** Roosevelt, Stalin, and Churchill meet at Yalta to plan the postwar world.

The United States takes the Pacific islands of Iwo Jima and Okinawa.

Franklin Roosevelt dies; Harry S Truman becomes president.

Germany surrenders to the United States, Great Britain, and the Soviet Union.

The United Nations is organized at an international meeting in San Francisco.

Potsdam Conference

Japan surrenders after the detonation of atomic bombs over Hiroshima and Nagasaki.

## QUICK REVIEW

### The Roots of War

- Roots of war found in aftermath of World War I.
- Peace settlement created small new nations vulnerable to aggression.
- Germany, Japan, and Italy were angry and unsatisfied with Treaty of Versailles.
- Economic hardship and political instability gave rise to right-wing dictatorships.

In Germany, Adolf Hitler mixed the desire to reassert national pride and power after the defeat of World War I with an ideology of racial hatred. Coming to power by constitutional means in 1933, Hitler quickly consolidated his grip by destroying opposition parties and made himself the German Führer, or absolute leader. Proclaiming the start of a thousand-year Reich ("empire"), he combined the historic German interest in eastward expansion with a long tradition of racialist thought about German superiority.

Special targets of Nazi hatred were the Jews, who were prominent in German business and professional life but soon faced persecution aimed at driving them from the country. In 1935, the Nuremberg Laws denied civil rights to Jews and the campaign against them intensified. On November 9, 1938, in vicious attacks across Germany that became known as *Kristallnacht* ("Night of the Broken Glass"), Nazi thugs rounded up, beat, and murdered Jews, smashed property, and burned synagogues. The Nazi government began expropriating Jewish property and excluded Jews from most employment.

Germany and Italy formed the Rome-Berlin Axis in October 1936 and the Tripartite Pact with Japan in 1940, leading to the term **Axis Powers** to describe the aggressor nations. Hitler's Germany was the most repressive. The Nazi concentration camp began as a device for political terrorism, where socialists and other dissidents and "antisocials"— homosexuals and beggars—could be separated from "pure" Germans. Soon the systematic discrimination and concentration camps would evolve into massive forced-labor camps and then into hellish extermination camps.

**Axis Powers**  The opponents of the United States and its allies in World War II.

## HITLER'S WAR IN EUROPE

After annexing Austria through a coup and seizing and slicing up Czechoslovakia, Germany demonstrated the worthlessness of the Munich agreement by invading Poland on September 1, 1939. Britain and France, Poland's allies, declared war on Germany but could not stop the German war machine. Western journalists covering the three-week conquest of Poland coined the term ***Blitzkrieg,*** or "lightning war," to describe the German tactics. Armored divisions with tanks and motorized infantry punched holes in defensive positions and raced forward 30 or 40 miles per day. Dive bombers blasted defenses. Portable radios coordinated the tanks, trucks, and motorcycles. Ground forces with horse-drawn artillery and supply wagons encircled the stunned defenders.

***Blitzkrieg***  German war tactic in World War II ("lightning war") involving the concentration of air and armored firepower to punch and exploit holes in opposing defensive lines.

Hitler's greatest advantage was the ability to attack when and where he chose. From September 1939 to October 1941, Germany marched from victory to victory (see Map 26–1). Striking from a central position against scattered enemies, Hitler chose the targets and timing of each new front: eastward to smash Poland in September 1939; northward to conquer Denmark and Norway in April and May 1940; westward to defeat the Netherlands, Belgium, and France in May and June 1940, an attack that Italy also joined; southward into the Balkans, enlisting Hungary, Romania, and Bulgaria as allies and conquering Yugoslavia and Greece in April and May 1941. Hitler also launched the Battle of Britain in the second half of 1940. German planes bombarded Britain mercilessly, in an unsuccessful effort to pound the British into submission.

The raspy-voiced Adolf Hitler had a remarkable ability to stir the German people. He and his inner circle made skillful use of propaganda, exploiting German resentment over the country's defeat in World War I and, with carefully staged mass rallies, such as this event in 1938, inspiring an emotional conviction of national greatness.

PEARSON
**myhistorylab**    MAP EXPLORATION  To explore an interactive version of this map, go to
http://www.prenhall.com/goldfield5/map26.1

Axis states and annexed areas
Axis allies
Axis occupied
Sudetenland

**MAP 26–1    Axis Europe, 1941, on the Eve of Hitler's Invasion of the Soviet Union**    After almost two years of war, the Axis powers controlled most of Europe, from the Atlantic Ocean to the Soviet border through annexation, military conquest, and alliances. Failure to force Britain to make peace caused Hitler to look eastward in 1941 to attempt the conquest of the Soviet Union.

**How was** Germany's central location in Europe both a strength and a weakness?

Hitler gambled once too often in June 1941. Having failed to knock Britain out of the war, he invaded the Soviet Union. The attack caught the Red Army off guard. Germany and the USSR had signed a nonaggression pact in 1939, and the Soviets had helped to dismember Poland. Hitler hoped that smashing the USSR and seizing its vast resources would make Germany invincible. Before desperate Soviet counterattacks and a bitter winter stopped the German columns, they had reached the outskirts of Moscow and expected to finish the job in the spring.

## TRYING TO KEEP OUT

For more than two years after the invasion of Poland, strong sentiment against intervention shaped public debate and limited President Roosevelt's ability to help Britain and its allies. Much of the emotional appeal of neutrality came from disillusionment with the American crusade in World War I, which had failed to make the world safe for democracy. Many opponents of intervention wanted the United States to protect its traditional spheres of interest in Latin America and the Pacific. The aviator Charles A. Lindbergh spoke for many when he argued that the best way to ensure the safety of the United States was to conserve resources to defend the Western Hemisphere. Non-interventionists spanned the political spectrum from left-leaning labor unions to conservative business tycoons like Henry Ford. The country's ethnic variety also complicated U.S. responses. Nazi aggression ravaged the homelands of Americans of Polish, Czech, Greek, and Norwegian ancestry. More than 5 million German Americans remembered the anti-German sentiment of World War I, while many of the 4.6 million Italian Americans admired Mussolini. Any move to intervene in Europe had to take these different views into account, meaning that Roosevelt had to move slowly and carefully in his effort to align the United States on the side of Britain.

## EDGING TOWARD INTERVENTION

Still, Roosevelt's appeals to democratic values gained support in 1939 and 1940. Radio broadcasts from England describing London under German bombing heightened the sense of imperiled freedom. The importance of open markets also bolstered interventionism. U.S. business leaders had little doubt that Axis victories would bring economic instability and require crushing defense budgets to protect Fortress America.

Because 85 percent of the American people agreed that the nation should fight only if it was directly attacked, Roosevelt had to chip away at neutrality, educating, arguing, and taking one step at a time. The first step came in October 1939. A month-long congressional debate inspired millions of letters and telegrams in favor of keeping an arms embargo in place against warring nations. Nevertheless, the lawmakers reluctantly allowed arms sales to belligerent nations on a "cash-and-carry" basis, to avoid expanding European debts. In control of the Atlantic, France and Britain were the only expected customers.

Isolationism and anti-Semitism help to explain why the United States accepted only a few thousand Jewish refugees. American law strictly limited the numbers of Europeans who could enter the United States, and Congress in 1939 declined to authorize the entry outside the quotas of 20,000 Jewish children. Bureaucrats at the State Department blocked entry to "undesirables," such as left-wing opponents of Hitler, and were unsympathetic to Jewish refugees. In 1939, officials turned the passenger ship *St. Louis* away from Miami and forced its 950 German Jewish refugees back to Europe. The consequences of these restrictions would prove tragic later in the war, as the Nazis began systematic genocide of European Jews.

**The collapse of France and U.S. rearmament.** Despite the efforts of non-interventionists, in 1940 the United States edged closed to involvement in the war. In May, the Roosevelt administration established the National Defense Advisory Commission and the Council of National Defense to deal with strategic planning for war. The sudden defeat of France, which had survived four years of German attacks in World

**QUICK REVIEW**

**Germany Conquers Europe**

- September 1939: Poland.
- April and May 1940: Denmark and Norway.
- May and June 1940: Netherlands, Belgium, and France.
- April and May 1941: Yugoslavia and Greece.

Charles Lindbergh, *Radio Address* (1941)

War I, made the new war seem far more serious. In the summer of 1940, Congress voted to expand the army to 2 million men, build 19,000 new warplanes, and add 150 ships to the navy. Lawmakers approved the nation's first peacetime draft in September, requiring 16.5 million men between the ages of 21 and 35 to register for military service on October 16.

In the same month, the United States concluded a destroyer deal with Britain. The British were desperate for small, maneuverable warships to guard imports of food and war materials against German submarines. The Americans had long wanted additional air and naval bases to guard the approaches to North America. Roosevelt met both needs by trading 50 old destroyers for the use of bases on British territories in the Caribbean, Bermuda, and Newfoundland.

**The Election of 1940.**  In the presidential election of 1940, the big campaign issue was therefore whether FDR's unprecedented try for a third term represented arrogance or a legitimate concern for continuity in a time of peril. The election was tighter than in 1932 or 1936, but Roosevelt received 55 percent of the vote. The president pledged that no Americans would fight in a foreign war. But if the United States were attacked, he said privately, the war would no longer be "foreign."

## THE BRINK OF WAR

After the election, FDR and his advisers edged the United States toward stronger support of Britain and put pressure on Japan. In January 1941, Roosevelt proposed the lend-lease program, which allowed Britain to "borrow" military equipment for the duration of the war.

The **Lend-Lease Act** triggered intense political debate. Congress finally passed the measure in March 1941, authorizing the president to lease, lend, or otherwise dispose of arms and other equipment to any country whose defense was considered vital to the security of the United States. The program proved invaluable in aiding Great Britain, to which the United States extended unlimited credit, and later in assisting the Soviet Union.

FDR soon began an undeclared war in the North Atlantic, instructing the navy to report sightings of German submarines to the British. In September, the U.S. destroyer *Greer* clashed with a German submarine. Portraying the incident as German aggression, Roosevelt proclaimed a "shoot on sight" policy for German subs and ordered American ships to escort British convoys to within 400 miles of Britain. In reply, German submarines torpedoed the destroyer *Kearny* on October 17 and sank the destroyer *Reuben James*, with the loss of more than 100 lives, on October 30. The United States was now approaching outright naval war with Germany.

**The Atlantic Charter.**  With U.S. ships on a war footing in the North Atlantic, Roosevelt and the British prime minister, Winston Churchill, met secretly off Newfoundland in August 1941 to map out military strategy and postwar goals. They agreed that the defeat of Germany was their first priority, and Japan was secondary. Their joint proclamation, known as the **Atlantic Charter,** provided a political umbrella for American involvement in the war. Echoing Woodrow Wilson, Roosevelt insisted on a commitment to oppose territorial conquest, support self-government, promote freedom of the seas, and create a system of economic collaboration. Churchill signed to keep Roosevelt happy, but the document papered over sharp differences between

**Documents**

Franklin Delano Roosevelt, *Annual Message to Congress* (1941)

**Lend-Lease Act**  Program begun in 1941 through which the U.S. transferred military equipment to Britain and other World War II allies.

**QUICK REVIEW**

**Undeclared War**

♦ March 1941: Lend-lease program approved by Congress.

♦ FDR ordered Navy to offer support to Britain.

♦ August 1941: Atlantic Charter lays out British and American war aims.

**Atlantic Charter**  Statement of common principles and war aims developed by President Franklin Roosevelt and British Prime Minister Winston Churchill at a meeting in August 1941.

## GLOBAL PERSPECTIVES

### RATIONING IN BRITAIN

When World War II broke out, Britain depended on imports for the basic necessities of life— two-thirds of its food, all of its petroleum, all of its rubber, all of its tea.

The British government began to ration gasoline in September 1939 and added butter, sugar, meat, and paper to the list of rationed products early in 1940. By the end of the war, half of all foodstuffs were on strict rationing. The Ministry of Food encouraged Britons to make do with foods that could be grown at home, such as potatoes and carrots, "bright treasure dug from the good British earth." One Ministry of Food advertisement tried to put a good light on shortages:

> The fishermen are saving lives
> By sweeping seas for mines,
> So you'll not grumble, 'What no fish?'
> When you have read these lines.

Clothing was also controlled because cotton was an import and wool was needed for military uniforms. Styles became simpler by government decree. To save cloth, there would be no wide lapels or turned-up cuffs. Skirts became narrower and shorter.

Shortages continued even after the Allies won the Battle of the Atlantic in 1943 and pushed German submarines away from the vital convoy routes. Until the last year of the war, the average German had a better standard of living than the average Briton. At the same time, many members of the British working class welcomed rationing because it equalized consumption among rich and poor and ensured that the wealthy would not monopolize resources.

Because World War II exhausted the British economy, rationing remained in force long after victory. Clothing came off the list in 1949, but meat only in 1954—a year after the coronation of Queen Elizabeth II ushered in a new era in British history and long after the American economy was launched into a postwar boom.

- Rationing in the United States was a way to fine-tune the war economy and engage everyday Americans in the war effort, but in Britain it was a necessity for survival. How might this difference have affected the ways in which the two nations approached the postwar world?

U.S. and British expectations about the future of world trade and European colonial possessions.

**Events in the Pacific.**   The final shove came in the Pacific rather than the Atlantic. In 1940, as part of its rearmament program, the United States decided to build a "two-ocean navy." This decision antagonized Japan, prodding it toward a war that most U.S. leaders hoped to postpone or avoid. Through massive investment and national sacrifice, Japan had achieved roughly 70 percent of U.S. naval strength by late 1941. However, America's buildup promised to reduce the ratio to only 30 percent by 1944. Furthermore, the United States was restricting Japan's vital imports of steel, iron ore, and aluminum in an effort to curb its military aggression. In July 1941, after Japan occupied French Indochina, Roosevelt froze Japanese assets in the United States, blocked shipments of petroleum products, and began to build up U.S. forces in the Philippines. These actions caused Japan's rulers to consider war against the United States while Japan still had a petroleum reserve. Both militarily and economically, it looked in Tokyo as if 1942 was Japan's last chance for victory.

Japanese war planners never seriously considered an invasion of the United States or expected a decisive victory. They hoped that attacks on American Pacific bases would shock the United States into letting Japan have its way in Asia or at least win time to create impenetrable defenses in the central Pacific.

## DECEMBER 7, 1941

On December 7, 1941, the Japanese navy launched a surprise attack on American bases in Hawaii. The Japanese fleet sailed a 4,000-mile loop through the empty North Pacific, avoiding merchant shipping and American patrols. Before dawn on December 7, six Japanese aircraft carriers launched 351 planes in two bombing strikes against Pearl Harbor. When the smoke cleared, Americans counted their losses: eight battleships, eleven other warships, and nearly all military aircraft damaged or destroyed, and 2,403 people killed. They could also count their good fortune. Dockyards, drydocks, and oil storage tanks remained intact because the Japanese admiral had refused to order a third attack. And the American aircraft carriers, at sea on patrol, were unharmed. They proved far more important than battleships as the war developed. Within hours, the Japanese attacked U.S. bases at Guam, Wake Island, and in the Philippines.

Speaking to Congress the following day, Roosevelt proclaimed December 7, 1941, "a date which will live in infamy." He asked for and got a declaration of war against Japan. Hitler and Mussolini declared war on the United States on December 11, following their obligation under the Tripartite Pact. On January 1, 1942, the United States, Britain, the Soviet Union, and 23 other nations subscribed to the principles of the Atlantic Charter and pledged not to negotiate a separate peace.

**WHERE TO LEARN MORE**

★ National Museum of the Pacific War, Fredericksburg, Texas.
www.nimitz-museum.org

**WHY DID** the Allies choose to focus on defeating Germany before Japan?

**Allies** In World War I, these were Britain, France, Russia, and other belligerent nations (but not the United States, which insisted upon being merely an associated nation) fighting against the Central Powers. In World War II, the Allies fighting the Axis Powers included the United States as well as the Soviet Union, Great Britain, France, China, and other nations.

**Eastern Front** The area of military operations in World War II located east of Germany in eastern Europe and the Soviet Union.

# HOLDING THE LINE

Japan's armies quickly conquered most of Southeast Asia; its navy forced the United States onto the defensive in the central Pacific. As it turned out, Japan's conquests reached their limit after six months, but in early 1942, this was far from clear. At the same time, in Europe, Allied fortunes went from bad to worse. Again, no one knew that German and Italian gains would peak at midyear. Decisive turning points did not come until November 1942, a year after the United States entered the war, and not until the middle of 1943 could the **Allies**—the United States, Britain, the Soviet Union, China, and other nations at war with Germany, Japan, and Italy—begin with confidence to plan for victory.

## STOPPING GERMANY

In December 1941, the United States plunged into a truly global war that was being fought on six distinct fronts. In North Africa, the British were battling Italian and German armies that were trying to seize the Suez Canal, a critical transportation link to Asia. Along the 1,000-mile **Eastern Front,** Soviet armies held defensive positions as German forces, pushing deeply into Soviet territory, reached the outskirts of Moscow and Leningrad (now St. Petersburg). In the North Atlantic, German submarines stalked merchant ships carrying supplies to Britain. In China, Japan controlled the most productive provinces but could not crush Chinese resistance. In Southeast Asia, Japanese troops attacked the Philippines, the Dutch East Indies (now Indonesia), New Guinea, Malaya, and Burma. In the central Pacific, the Japanese fleet confronted the U.S. Navy. With the nation facing danger across both the Atlantic and Pacific oceans, Roosevelt helped Americans understand the global nature of the conflict by calling it the "second world war."

The Japanese attack on Pearl Harbor shocked the American people. Images of burning battleships confirmed the popular image of Japan as sneaky and treacherous and stirred a desire for revenge. The attack rendered the United States incapable of resisting Japanese aggression in Southeast Asia in early 1942, but it failed to achieve its goal of destroying U.S. naval power in the Pacific.

**The Eastern Front and the Battle of Stalingrad.**   The Eastern Front held the key to Allied hopes in Europe. In 1941, Germany had seized control of 45 percent of the Soviet population, 47 percent of its grain production, and more than 60 percent of its coal, steel, and aluminum industries. Hitler next sought to destroy the Soviet capacity to wage war, targeting southern Russia, an area rich in grain and oil. The German thrust in 1942 was also designed to eliminate the British from the Middle East.

The turning point of the war in Europe came at Stalingrad (present-day Volgograd), an industrial center on the western bank of the Volga River. After initially aiming at the city, German armies turned south toward the Russian oil fields, leaving a dangerous strong-point on their flank that the German command decided to capture. In September and October 1942, German, Italian, and Romanian soldiers fought their way house by house into the city. For both Hitler and Stalin, the city became a test of will that outweighed even its substantial military importance.

The Red Army delivered a counterstroke on November 18 that cut off 290,000 Axis soldiers. Airlifts kept the Germans fighting for more than two additional months, but they surrendered in February 1943. This was the first German mass capitulation, and it came at immense human cost to both sides. The Soviet army suffered more deaths in this battle than the United States did in the entire war.

Behind the victory was an extraordinary revival of the Soviet capacity to make war. In the desperate months of 1941, the Soviets dismantled nearly 3,000 factories and rebuilt them far to the east of the German advance in the midst of Siberian winter. By the time the two armies clashed at Stalingrad, the Soviets were producing four times as many tanks and warplanes as the Germans, portending the outcome of the battles to come.

## THE SURVIVAL OF BRITAIN

After the failure of German air attacks in 1940, the British struggled to save their empire and supply themselves with food and raw materials. In World War I, German submarines (known as U-boats, from *Unterseeboot*) had nearly isolated Great Britain. In 1940 and 1941, they tried again. Through the end of 1941, German "tonnage warfare" sank British, Allied, and neutral merchant vessels faster than they could be replaced.

**The Battle of the Atlantic.**   The British fought back in what came to be known as the **Battle of the Atlantic.** Between 1939 and 1944, planning and rationing cut Britain's need for imports in half. At sea, the British organized protected convoys. Merchant ships sailing alone were defenseless against submarines. Grouping the merchant ships with armed escorts "hardened" the targets and made them more difficult to find in the wide ocean. Roosevelt's destroyer deal of 1940 and U.S. naval escorts in the western Atlantic in 1941 contributed directly to Britain's survival.

Nevertheless, German submarines dominated the Atlantic in 1942. The balance shifted only when Allied aircraft began to track submarines with radar, spot them with searchlights as they maneuvered to the surface, and attack them with depth charges. New sonar systems allowed escort ships to measure submarines' direction, speed, and depth. By the spring of 1943, American shipyards were launching ships faster than the Germans could sink them.

**North Africa.**   British ground fighting in 1942 centered in North Africa, where the British operated out of Egypt and the Italians and Germans from the Italian colony of Libya. By October 1942, Field Marshal Erwin Rommel's German and Italian forces were within striking distance of the Suez Canal. At El Alamein, however, General Bernard Montgomery forced the enemy to retreat in early November and lifted the danger to the Middle East.

## RETREAT AND STABILIZATION IN THE PACIFIC

Reports from eastern Asia after Pearl Harbor were appalling. The Japanese attack on the Philippines (see Map 26–2) had been another tactical surprise that destroyed most American air power on the ground and isolated U.S. forces. In February, a numerically inferior Japanese force seized British Singapore, until then considered an anchor of Allied strength, and then pushed the British out of Burma. In a three-month siege, they overwhelmed Filipino and U.S. defensive positions on the Bataan peninsula outside Manila; thousands of their captives died of maltreatment on their way to prisoner-of-war camps in what is remembered as the Bataan Death March. On May 6, the last American bastion, the island fortress of Corregidor in Manila Bay, surrendered. The Japanese fleet

**MAP EXPLORATION**  To explore an interactive version of this map, go to
http://www.prenhall.com/goldfield5/map26.2

MAP 26–2  **World War II in the Pacific, from Pearl Harbor to Midway**  The first six months after the Japanese attack on Pearl Harbor brought a string of Japanese victories and conquests in the Pacific, the islands southeast of Asia, and the British colonies of Malaya and Burma. Japan's advance was halted by a standoff battle in the Coral Sea, a decisive U.S. naval victory at Midway, and the length and vulnerability of Japanese supply lines to the most distant conquests.

**How was** Japan able to mount a series of victories in the Pacific after their attack?

was virtually undamaged at the end of April, and the Japanese army was triumphant in conquest of European and American territories in Southeast Asia.

**The Battles of the Coral Sea and Midway.**  The first check to Japanese expansion came on May 7–8, 1942, in the Battle of the Coral Sea, where U.S. aircraft carriers halted a Japanese thrust toward Australia and confirmed that the U.S. Navy could fight effectively. In June, the Japanese struck at the island of Midway, 1,500 miles northwest of Honolulu. Their goal was to destroy American carrier forces. Having cracked Japanese radio codes, U.S. forces were aware of the plan. On the morning of June 4, the Japanese and American carrier fleets faced off across 175 miles of ocean, each sending planes to search out the other. U.S. Navy dive bombers found the Japanese fleet and sank or crippled three aircraft carriers in five minutes; another damaged Japanese carrier sank later in the day. The Battle of Midway ended Japanese efforts to expand in the Pacific.

# MOBILIZING FOR VICTORY

**WHAT STEPS** did the U.S. government take to organize the economy for war?

Barbara Wooddall and Charles Taylor, *Letters to and from the Front* (1941–1944)

War changed the lives of most Americans. Millions of men and women served in the armed forces, and millions more worked in defense factories. In order to keep track of this staggering level of activity, the number of civilian employees of the federal government quadrupled to 3.8 million, a much greater increase than during the New Deal. The breadth of involvement in the war effort gave Americans a common purpose that softened the divisions of region, class, and national origin while calling attention to continuing inequalities of race.

## ORGANIZING THE ECONOMY

The need to fight a global war brought a huge expansion of the federal government. Congress authorized the president to reorganize existing government departments and create new agencies. The War Manpower Commission allocated workers among vital industries and the military. The War Production Board invested $17 billion for new factories and managed $181 billion in war-supply contracts, favoring existing corporations because they had experience in large-scale production.

    The Office of Price Administration (OPA) fought inflation with price controls and rationing. By slowing price increases, the OPA helped convince Americans to buy the war bonds that financed half the war spending. Americans also felt the bite of the first payroll deductions for income taxes as the government secured a steady flow of revenues and soaked up some of the high wages that would have pushed inflation. In total, the federal budget in 1945 was $98 billion, eleven times as large as in 1939, and the national debt had increased more than sixfold.

    Industry had reluctantly begun to convert from consumer goods to defense production in 1940 and 1941. Existing factories retooled to make war equipment, and huge new facilities turned out thousands of planes and ships.

    Most defense contracts went to such established industrial states as Michigan, New York, and Ohio, but the relative impact was greatest in the South and West, where the war marked the takeoff of what Americans would later call the Sunbelt.

    The output of America's war industries was staggering (see Figure 26–1). One historian estimates that 40 percent of the world's military production was coming from the United States by 1944. Equally impressive is the 30 percent increase in the productivity of U.S. workers between 1939 and 1945. Surging farm income pulled agriculture out of its long slump. Organized labor offered a no-strike pledge for the duration, assuring that no one could accuse unions of undermining the war effort but limiting the economic gains of some workers

**QUICK REVIEW**

**Government and the Economy**

◆ War brought a huge expansion of the federal government.

◆ Office of Price Administration (OPA) oversaw price controls and rationing.

◆ Under government pressure, industry shifted to defense production.

During the course of World War II, the government limited the consumption of a number of products to reserve supplies of products for the war effort and to prevent demand from pushing up the prices of scarce consumer goods. Shoppers like this woman at a grocery store counter used ration stamps to obtain their share of controlled products.

and damping the militancy of the CIO. Nevertheless, over-all per capita income doubled, and the poorest quarter of Americans made up some of the ground lost during the Great Depression.

## THE ENLISTMENT OF SCIENCE

The war reached into scientific laboratories as well as shops and factories. At the center of the scientific enterprise was Vannevar Bush, former dean at the Massachusetts Institute of Technology. As head of the newly established Office of Scientific Research and Development, Bush guided spending to develop new drugs such as antibiotics, blood-transfusion procedures, weapons systems, radar, sonar, and dozens of other military technologies. The scale of research and development dwarfed previous scientific work and set the pattern of massive postwar federal support for science.

The most costly scientific effort was the development of radar, or radio detection and ranging devices. Building on British research on microwaves, the United States put $3 billion into the Radiation Laboratory at MIT. Increasingly compact and sophisticated radar systems helped to defeat the German and Japanese navies and to give the Allies control of the air over Europe. Radar research and engineering laid the basis for microwave technology, transistors, and integrated circuits after the war.

As early as 1939, Albert Einstein had written to FDR about the possibility of such a weapon and the danger of falling behind the Germans. In late 1941, Roosevelt established the **Manhattan Project.** By December 2, 1942, scientists proved that it was possible to create and control a sustained nuclear reaction.

The Manhattan Project moved from theory to practice in 1943. The physicist J. Robert Oppenheimer directed the young scientists at Los Alamos in designing a nuclear-fission bomb. The Manhattan Project ushered in the age of atomic energy. The first bomb was tested on July 16, 1945. The explosion astonished even the physicists; Oppenheimer quoted from Hindu scriptures in trying to comprehend the results: "Now I am become Death, destroyer of worlds."

## MEN AND WOMEN IN THE MILITARY

World War II required a more than thirtyfold expansion of the U.S. armed forces from their 1939 level of 334,000 soldiers, sailors, and Marines. By 1945, 8.3 million men and women were on active duty in the army and army air forces and 3.4 million in the navy and Marine Corps, totals exceeded only by the Soviet Union. In total, some 350,000 women and more than 16 million men served in the armed forces; 292,000 died in battle, 100,000 survived prisoner-of-war camps, and 671,000 returned wounded.

**FIGURE 26–1  Making War: The United States Mobilizes, 1939–1945**  The U.S. economic mobilization for World War II reached its peak in 1943, the year in which the Allies prepared for the offensives against Germany and Japan that they hoped would end the war. The number of men and women in uniform continued to grow until 1945.

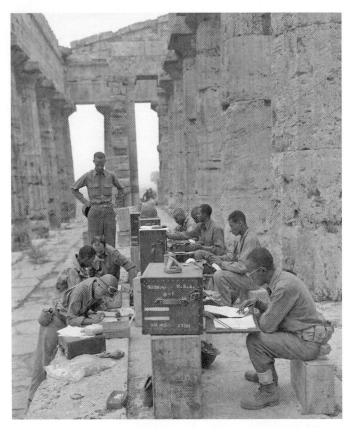

African Americans served in the military large numbers during World War II. Here a signals company has set up operations in the ruins of an ancient temple in southern Italy.

**WHERE TO LEARN MORE**

★ Los Alamos County Historical
   Museum and Bradbury Science
   Museum, Los Alamos, New Mexico.
   www.lanl.gov/museum

*Documents*

Albert Einstein, *Letter to President
Roosevelt* (1939)

**Manhattan Project**   The effort, using
the code name Manhattan Engineer District, to develop an atomic bomb under
the management of the U.S. Army
Corps of Engineers during World War II.

*Documents*

Bernice Brode, *Tales of Los Alamos* (1943)

Sterling A. Brown, *Out of Their Mouths*
(1942)

**Native Americans in the military.**   Twenty-five thousand American Indians served in the armed forces. Most were in racially integrated units, and Harvey Natcheez, of the Ute tribe, was the first American to reach the center of conquered Berlin. Because the Navajo were one of the few tribes that had not been studied by German anthropologists, the Army Signal Corps decided that their language would be unknown to the Axis armies. Roughly 400 members of the tribe were "code-talkers" who served in Marine radio combat-communication teams in the Pacific theater, transmitting vital information in Navajo.

**African Americans in the military.**   Approximately 1 million African Americans served in the armed forces during World War II. African American leaders had pressed for a provision in the Selective Service Act to bar discrimination "against any person on account of race or color." But as it had since the Civil War, the army organized black soldiers in segregated units and often assigned them to the menial jobs, such as construction work, and excluded them from combat until manpower shortages forced changes in policy.

The average black soldier encountered discrimination on and off the base. Towns adjacent to army posts were some-times open to white soldiers but off-limits to blacks. At some southern bases, German prisoners of war watched movies from the first rows along with white GIs while African American soldiers watched from the back. Military courts were quick to judge and harshly punish black GIs. It took racially based riots at army bases in North Carolina and Georgia to open up equal (although segregated) access to base recreation facilities.

Despite the obstacles, all-black units, such as the 761st Tank Battalion and the 99th Pursuit Squadron, earned distinguished records. More broadly, the war experience helped to invigorate postwar efforts to achieve equal rights, as had also been true after World War I.

**Women in the military.**   The nation had a different—but also mixed—reaction to the women who joined the armed forces as army and navy nurses and as members of the WACS (Women's Army Corps), WAVES (Navy), SPARS (Coast Guard), and Marine Corps Women's Reserve. The armed services tried not to change established gender roles. Military officials told Congress that women in uniform could free men for combat. Many of the women hammered at typewriters, worked switchboards, inventoried supplies. Others, however, worked close to combat zones as photographers, code analysts, weather forecasters, radio operators, and nurses. WAC officers battled the tendency of the popular press to call females in the service "girls" rather than "women" or "soldiers" yet emphasized that military service promoted "poise and charm."

The greatest departure from expected roles was the work of the 1,074 members of the Women's Airforce Service Pilots (WASPS), a civilian auxiliary of the Army Air Forces. Many of the WASPS had learned to fly as civilians. From 1942 to 1944, they fer-ried military aircraft across the country, towed targets for antiaircraft practice, and tested new planes. Nevertheless, WASPS were not allowed to carry male passengers, and the group was dissolved when the supply of male pilots caught up with demand.

# THE HOME FRONT

The war inexorably penetrated everyday life. Residents in war-production cities had to cope with throngs of new workers. Especially in 1941 and 1942, many were unattached males—young men waiting for their draft call and older men without their families. Military and defense officials worried about sexually transmitted diseases and pressured cities to shut down their vice districts. At the same time, college officials scrambled to fill their classrooms, especially after the draft age dropped to 18 in 1942. Many colleges and universities responded to federal requests with special training programs for future officers and engineering and technical training for military personnel.

HOW DID the war affect the place of women in American society?

## FAMILIES IN WARTIME

Many Americans put their lives on fast forward. Men and women often decided to beat the clock with instant matrimony. Couples who had postponed marriage because of the depression could afford to marry as the economy picked up. War intensified casual romances and heightened the appeal of marriage as an anchor in troubled times. Altogether, the war years brought 1.2 million "extra" marriages, compared to the rate for the period 1920–1939.

The war's impact on families was gradual. The draft started with single men, then called up married men without children, and finally tapped fathers in 1943. Left at home were millions of "service wives," whose compensation from the government was $50 per month.

The war had mixed effects on children. "Latchkey children" of working mothers often had to fend for themselves, but middle-class kids whose mothers stayed home could treat the war as an interminable scout project, with salvage drives and campaigns to sell war bonds. In the rural Midwest children picked milkweed pods to stuff life jackets; in coastal communities, they participated in blackout drills. Seattle high schools set aside one class period a day for the High School Victory Corps, training boys as messengers for air-raid wardens, while girls knitted sweaters and learned first aid.

## LEARNING ABOUT THE WAR

The federal government tried to keep civilians of all ages committed to the war. It encouraged scrap drives and backyard victory gardens and created colorful posters to warn against espionage, inspire women to join the effort, and promote rationing and car-pooling. The government also managed news about the fighting. Censors screened soldiers' letters. Early in the war, they blocked publication of most photographs of war casualties, although magazines such as *Life* were full of strong and haunting images. Worried about flagging commitment, censors later authorized photographs of enemy atrocities to motivate the public.

War films revealed the nation's racial attitudes, often drawing distinctions between "good" and "bad" Germans but uniformly portraying Japanese as subhuman and repulsive. The most successful films dramatized the courage of the Allies.

**Exploring America**
*Propaganda*

## WOMEN IN THE WORKFORCE

As draft calls took men off the assembly line, women changed the composition of the industrial workforce. The war gave them new job opportunities that were embodied in the image of Rosie the Riveter. Women made up one-quarter of West Coast shipyard workers and nearly half of Dallas and Seattle aircraft workers. Most women in the shipyards were clerks and general helpers. The acute shortage of welders and other skilled workers, however, opened thousands of lucrative journeyman positions to them. Aircraft companies, which compounded the labor shortage by stubborn "whites only"

Virginia Snow Wilkinson, *From House-wife to Shipfitter* (1943)

As millions of men entered the armed forces, millions of women went to work. By 1943, federal agencies were actively recruiting women workers. Those who took production-line jobs in shipyards and aircraft factories, such as the woman shown here, received the greatest attention.

hiring, developed new power tools and production techniques to accommodate the smaller average size of women workers, increasing efficiency for everyone on the production line.

By July 1944, 19 million women held paid jobs, up 6 million in four years. Women's share of government jobs increased from 19 to 38 percent; they typed and filed in offices, but they also wrote propaganda for the Office of War Information and analyzed intelligence data for the office of Strategic Service. Women's share of manufacturing jobs went from 22 to 33 percent, many of them as W.O.W.s or Woman Ordnance Workers. Mirroring the sequence in which the military draft took men, employers recruited single women before turning to married women in 1943 and 1944. The federal government assisted female entry into the labor force by funding daycare programs that served 600,000 children. Some women worked out of patriotism. Many others, however, needed to support their families and already had years of experience in the workforce. As one of the workers recalled of herself and a friend, "We both had to work, we both had children, so we became welders, and if I might say so, damn good ones."

Americans did not know how to respond to the growing numbers of working women. The country needed their labor, but many worried that their employment would undermine families. Employment recruitment posters showed strong, handsome women with rolled-up sleeves and wrenches in hand, but *Life* magazine reassured readers that women in factories could retain their sex appeal. Men and women commonly assumed that women would want to return to the home after victory.

## ETHNIC MINORITIES IN THE WAR EFFORT

Mexican American workers made special contributions to the war effort. As defense factories and the military absorbed workers, western farms and railroads faced an acute shortage of workers. In the 1930s, western states had tried to deport Mexican nationals who were competing for scarce jobs. In 1942, however, the United States and Mexico negotiated the *bracero* program, under which the Mexican government recruited workers to come to the United States on six-to-twelve month contracts. More than 200,000 Mexicans worked on U.S. farms under the program, and more than 100,000 worked for western railroads. Although *bracero* workers still faced discrimination, the U.S. government tried to improve working conditions because it wanted to keep public opinion in Latin America favorable to the Allied cause.

The war was a powerful force for the assimilation of Native Americans. Forty thousand moved to off-reservation jobs; they were a key labor force for military supply depots throughout the West. The average cash income of Indian households tripled during the war. Many stayed in cities at its end. The experience of the war accelerated the fight for full civil rights. Congress had made Indians citizens in 1924, in part to recognize their contributions in World War I, but several states continued to deny them the vote. Activists organized the National Congress of American Indians in 1944 and began the efforts that led the U.S. Supreme Court in 1948 to require states to grant voting rights.

African Americans, too, found economic advancement through war jobs. Early in the mobilization, labor leader A. Philip Randolph of the Brotherhood of Sleeping Car Porters worked with Walter White of the NAACP to plan a "Negro March on Washington" to protest racial discrimination by the federal government. To head off a major embarrassment, Roosevelt issued Executive Order 8802 in June 1941, barring racial discrimination in defense contracts and creating the **Fair Employment Practices Committee** (FEPC); the order coined a phrase that reverberated powerfully through the coming decades: "No discrimination on grounds of race, color, creed, or national origin."

The FEPC's small staff resolved fewer than half of the employment-discrimination complaints, and white resistance to black coworkers remained strong. In Mobile, New Orleans, and Jacksonville, agreements between shipyards and segregated unions blocked skilled black workers from high-wage jobs. Nevertheless, African American membership in labor unions doubled, and wartime prosperity raised the average black income from 41 percent of the white average in 1939 to 61 percent by 1950, particularly because labor shortages raised farm wages.

Outside the workplace, African American women found that many voluntary service groups were racially segregated. In response, they formed the Women's Army for National Defense. They did their part by selling war bonds, helping with civil defense, and organizing USO clubs for black soldiers.

Many African Americans saw themselves as engaged in a "Double V" effort for victory against tyranny abroad and victory over racism at home. Economic gains helped. So did the fact that many were able to vote for the first time, either because they had moved to northern states where voting was not racially limited or because they were servicemen serving overseas. The economic and political changes helped to build a base for the civil rights movement that gained momentum in the postwar decades.

## Clashing Cultures

As men and women migrated in search of work, they also crossed or collided with traditional boundaries of religion, region, and race. Some of the most troublesome conflicts arose from African

A. Philip Randolph, *Why Should We March?* (1942)

Earl B. Dickerson, *The Fair Employment Practices Committee* (1941–1943)

**Fair Employment Practices Committee (FEPC)** Federal agency established in 1941 to curb racial discrimination in war production jobs and government employment.

The Government worked hard to encourage hispanics to support the war effort, both for their contributions and to maintain good relations with Mexico and other Latin American nations.

American migration out of the South accelerated in the early 1940s. Many of the migrants headed for well-established black neighborhoods in northern cities. Others created new African American neighborhoods in western cities. White southerners and black northerners with different ideas of racial etiquette found themselves side by side in West Coast shipyards. In the Midwest, black migrants from the South and white migrants from Appalachia crowded into cities such as Cincinnati and Chicago, competing for the same high-wage jobs and scarce apartments.

Tensions between black and white residents exploded in at least 50 cities in 1943 alone. New York's Harlem neighborhood erupted in a riot after rumors of attacks on black servicemen. In Detroit, the issue was the boundary between white and black territory. In June 1943, an argument over the use of Detroit's Belle Isle Park set off three days of violence: Twenty-five black people and nine white people died in the most serious racial riot of the war.

Tensions were simultaneously rising between Mexican Americans and Anglos. As the Mexican community in Los Angeles swelled to an estimated 400,000, newspapers published anti-Mexican articles. On June 6, 1943, off-duty sailors and soldiers attacked Latinos on downtown streets and invaded Mexican American neighborhoods. The main targets were so-called *pachucos*—young Chicanos who wore flamboyant "zoot suits" with long, wide-shouldered jackets and pleated, narrow-cuffed trousers, whom the rioters considered delinquents or draft dodgers. The attacks dragged on for a week of sporadic violence against black people and Filipinos as well as Latinos. The assaults were poignantly ironic because 750,000 Mexican Americans served in the armed forces and were the most decorated group relative to their numbers.

## INTERNMENT OF JAPANESE AMERICANS

On February 19, 1942, President Roosevelt authorized the secretary of war to define restricted areas and remove civilian residents who were threats to national security. The primary targets were 112,000 Japanese Americans in California and parts of Washington, Oregon, and Arizona. Japanese immigrants and their children in the western states had experienced 40 years of hostility because of racial prejudice, fear of the growing power of Japan, and jealousy of their business success. The outbreak of war triggered anti-Japanese hysteria and gave officials an excuse to take action against enemy aliens (immigrants who retained Japanese citizenship) and their American-born children.

Most West Coast Japanese were unable to leave because of ties to families and businesses. At the end of April 1942, Japanese in the coastal states were given a week to organize their affairs and report to assembly centers at fairgrounds and armories, where they were housed for several weeks before being moved again to ten internment camps in isolated locations in the western interior (see American Views, Internment of Japanese Americans: Life in Camp Harmony). Here, they were housed in tarpaper barracks, hemmed in by barbed-wire fences, and guarded by military police. The victims reacted to the hardship and stress in different ways. Several thousand second-generation Japanese Americans renounced their citizenship in disgust. But many others demonstrated their loyalty by cooperating with the authorities, finding sponsors who would help them move to other parts of the country, or joining the 442nd Regimental Combat Team, the most decorated American unit in the European war.

Although the U.S. Supreme Court sanctioned the removals in *Korematsu v. United States* (1944), the nation officially recognized its liability for lost property with the Japanese Claims Act of 1948. The nation acknowledged its broader moral responsibility in 1988, when Congress approved redress payments to each of the 60,000 surviving evacuees.

The internment of West Coast Japanese contrasted with the situation of German Americans and Italian Americans. The government interned approximately 11,000

**QUICK REVIEW**

**Race Riots**

♦ 1943: Violent confrontations between blacks and whites in at least fifty cities.

♦ Detroit, June 1943: Most serious riot of the war results in thirty-four deaths.

♦ Los Angeles, June 6, 1943: Sailors and soldiers attack young Chicanos.

*Documents*

*Japanese Relocation Order* (1942)

*Documents*

*Korematsu v. United States* (1944)

In 1942, the federal government removed Japanese Americans from parts of four western states and interned them in isolated camps scattered through the West.

German nationals and German Americans who were explicitly seen as individual threats. Until November 1942, it imposed curfews and travel restrictions on Italians and Italian Americans on the West Coast, but it interned fewer than 2,000. Both numbers were tiny fractions of the total populations.

## THE END OF THE NEW DEAL

Roosevelt's New Deal ran out of steam in 1938. The war had reinvigorated his political fortunes by focusing national energies on foreign policy, over which presidents have the greatest power. After the 1942 election left Congress in the hands of Republicans and conservative southern Democrats, lawmakers ignored proposals that war emergency housing be used to improve the nation's permanent housing stock, abolished the National Resources Planning Board, curtailed rural electrification, and crippled the Farm Security Administration. Roosevelt himself declared, at a 1943 press conference, that "Dr. Win-the-War" had replaced "Dr. New Deal."

The presidential election of 1944 raised few new issues of substance. The Republicans nominated Governor Thomas Dewey of New York, who had made his reputation as a crime-fighting district attorney. The Democrats renominated Roosevelt for a fourth term. Missouri Senator Harry S Truman, a tough investigator of American military preparedness, replaced liberal New Dealer Henry Wallace as Roosevelt's running mate. The move appeased southern Democrats and moved the ticket toward the political center.

The most important issue was a fourth term for Roosevelt. Supporters argued that the nation could not afford to change leaders in the middle of a war, but Dewey's vigor and relative youth (he was 20 years younger than FDR) pointed up the president's failing health and energy. Voters gave Roosevelt 432 electoral votes to 99, but the narrowing gap in the popular vote—54 percent for Roosevelt and 46 percent for Dewey—made the Republicans eager for 1948.

# WAR AND PEACE

In January 1943, the U.S. War Department completed the world's largest office building, the Pentagon. The building housed 23,000 workers along 17.5 miles of corridors. The building provided the space in which military planners could coordinate the tasks of raising and equipping the armed forces that would strike directly at Germany and Japan. Indeed, while Congress was chipping away at federal programs, the war effort was massively expanding the government presence in American life. The gray walls of the Pentagon symbolized a U.S. government that was outgrowing its prewar roots.

## TURNING THE TIDE IN EUROPE

The unanswered military question of 1942 and 1943 was when the United States and Britain would open a second front against Germany by attacking across the English Channel. U.S. leaders wanted to justify massive mobilization with a war-winning campaign and to strike across Europe to occupy the heart of Germany. Stalin needed a full-scale invasion of western Europe to divert German forces from the Eastern Front, where Soviet troops were inflicting 90 percent of German battle casualties.

The Allies spent 1943 hammering out war aims and strategies. Meeting in Casablanca in January 1943, Roosevelt and Churchill demanded the unconditional surrender of Italy, Germany, and Japan. The phrase meant that there would be no deals that kept the enemy governments or leaders in power and was an effort to avoid the mistake of ending World War I with Germany intact. Ten months later, the Allied leaders huddled again. At Tehran, the United States and Britain promised to invade France within six months. "We leave here," said the three leaders, "friends in fact, in spirit, in purpose."

The superficial harmony barely survived the end of the war. Roosevelt's ideal of self-determination for all peoples, embodied in the Atlantic Charter, seemed naive to Churchill, who wanted the major powers to carve out realistic spheres of influence in Europe. Stalin wanted control of eastern Europe to protect the Soviet Union against future invasions and assumed that realistic statesmen would understand.

**The Campaign in North Africa.** The United States entered the ground war in Europe with Operation TORCH. Soon after the British victory at El Alamein, British and American troops under General Dwight Eisenhower landed in French Morocco and Algeria on November 8, 1942, against little opposition. (see Map 26–3). These were territories that the Germans had left under a puppet French government after the French military collapse in 1940. German troops that remained in North Africa taught U.S. forces hard lessons in tactics and leadership, but their stubborn resistance ended in May 1943, leaving all of Africa in Allied hands.

**The Invasion of Italy.** The central Mediterranean remained the focus of U.S. and British action for the next year, despite the fact that the hard-pressed Soviets were desperate for their allies to attack the heart of German power in northern Europe. However, the British feared military disaster from a premature landing in across the English Channel and proposed strikes in southern Europe, which Churchill inaccurately called the "soft underbelly" of Hitler's empire. U.S. Army Chief of Staff George Marshall and President Roosevelt agreed to invade Italy in 1943, in part so that U.S. troops could participate in the ground fighting in Europe. Allied forces overran Sicily in July and August, but the Italian mainland proved more difficult. When Sicily fell, the Italian king and army forced Mussolini from power and began to negotiate peace with Britain and America (but not the Soviet Union). In September, the Allies announced an armistice with Italy, and Eisenhower's troops landed south of Naples on September 9. Germany responded by occupying the rest of Italy.

**MAP EXPLORATION** To explore an interactive version of this map, go to
http://www.prenhall.com/goldfield5/map26.3

mistorylab

**MAP 26–3   World War II in Europe, 1942–1945**   Nazi Germany had to defend its conquests on three fronts. Around the Mediterranean, American and British forces pushed the Germans out of Africa and southern Italy, while guerrillas in Yugoslavia pinned down many German troops. On the Eastern Front, Soviet armies advanced hundreds of miles to drive the German Army out of the Soviet Union and eastern Europe. In June 1944, U.S. and British landings opened the Western Front in northern France for a decisive strike at the heart of Germany.

**What were** the turning points in the war in Europe?

## AMERICAN VIEWS

### The Internment of Japanese Americans in 1942

*I*n the spring of 1942, the U.S. army ordered Japanese Americans in four western states relocated to internment camps distant from the Pacific Coast. Monica Itoe Stone describes the experience of her Seattle family as they were transferred to temporary quarters—at the state fairgrounds, renamed "Camp Harmony" by the military—before they were moved again to Idaho.

- **How** do the expectations of *issei* (immigrants who had been born in Japan) differ from those of *nisei* (their American-born children, including the author of this memoir)?
- **Why** did the U.S. army wait five months after Pearl Harbor before beginning the internment?
- **Does** the management of the assembly and internment suggest anything about stereotypes of Japanese Americans?

General DeWitt kept reminding us that E day, evacuation day, was drawing near. "E day will be announced in the very near future. If you have not wound up your affairs by now, it will soon be too late."

. . . On the twenty-first of April, a Tuesday, the general gave us the shattering news. "All the Seattle Japanese will be moved to Puyallup by May 1. Everyone must be registered Saturday and Sunday between 8 A.M. and 5 P.M."

Up to that moment, we had hoped against hope that something or someone would intervene for us. Now there was no time for moaning. A thousand and one details must be attended to in this one week of grace. Those seven days sputtered out like matches struck in the wind, as we rushed wildly about. Mother distributed sheets, pillowcases and blankets, which we stuffed into seabags. Into the two suitcases, we packed heavy winter overcoats, plenty of sweaters, woolen slacks and skirts, flannel pajamas and scarves. Personal toilet articles, one tin plate, tin cup and silverware completed our luggage. The one seabag and two suitcases apiece were going to be the backbone of our future home, and we planned it carefully.

Henry went to the Control Station to register the family. He came home with twenty tags, all numbered "10710," tags to be attached to each piece of baggage, and one to hang from our coat lapels. From then on, we were known as Family \#10710. [On the day set for relocation] we climbed into the truck. . . . As we coasted down Beacon Hill bridge for the last time, we fell silent, and stared out at the delicately flushed, morning sky of Puget Sound. We drove through bustling Chinatown, and in a few minutes arrived on the corner of Eighth and Lane. This area was ordinarily lonely and deserted but now it was gradually filling up with silent, labeled Japanese. . . .

Just as American military planners had feared, the Italian campaign soaked up Allied resources. The mountainous Italian peninsula was one long series of defensive positions, and the Allies repeatedly bogged down. The Allies only managed to gain control of two-thirds of Italy before German resistance crumbled in the final weeks of the war.

**Soviet Advances and the Battle of Kursk.**   Meanwhile, the Soviets recruited, rearmed, and upgraded new armies, despite enormous losses. They learned to outfight the Germans in tank warfare and rebuilt munitions factories beyond German reach. They also made good use of 17.5 million tons of U.S. lend-lease assistance. As Soviet soldiers recaptured western Russia and Ukraine, they marched in 13 million pairs of American-made boots and ate U.S. rations. They traveled in 78,000 jeeps and 350,000 Studebaker, Ford, and Dodge trucks.

The climactic battle of the German-Soviet war erupted on July 5, 1943. The Germans sent 3,000 tanks against the Kursk salient, a huge wedge that the Red Army had pushed into their lines. In 1941 and 1942, such a massive attack would have forced the Soviets to retreat, but now Soviet generals had prepared a defense with 3,000 tanks of their

**QUICK REVIEW**

**The Beginning of the End**
- Allies gained footholds in North Africa.
- Allies took control of much of Italy.
- German's last offensive in Russia turned back.

Finally at ten o'clock, a vanguard of Greyhound busses purred in and parked themselves neatly along the curb. The crowd stirred and murmured. The bus doors opened and from each, a soldier with rifle in hand stepped out and stood stiffly at attention by the door. . . .

Newspaper photographers with flash-bulb cameras pushed busily through the crowd. One of them rushed up to our bus, and asked a young couple and their little boy to step out and stand by the door for a shot. They were reluctant, but the photographers were persistent and at length they got out of the bus and posed, grinning widely to cover their embarrassment. We saw the picture in the newspaper shortly after and the caption underneath it read, "japs good-natured about evacuation." Our bus quickly filled to capacity. . . . The door closed with a low hiss. We were now the Wartime Civil Control Administration's babies.

About noon we crept into a small town . . . and we noticed at the left of us an entire block filled with neat rows of low shacks, resembling chicken houses. Someone commented on it with awe, "Just look at those chicken houses. They sure go in for poultry in a big way here." Slowly the bus made a left turn, drove through a wire-fenced gate, and to our dismay, we were inside the oversized chicken farm. . . .

The apartments resembled elongated, low stables about two blocks long. Our home was one room, about 18 by 20 feet, the size of a living room. There was one small window in the wall opposite the one door. It was bare except for a small, tinny wood-burning stove crouching in the center. . . .

I stared at our little window, unable to sleep. I was glad Mother had put up a makeshift curtain on the window for I noticed a powerful beam of light sweeping across it every few seconds. The lights came from high towers placed around the camp where guards with Tommy guns kept a twenty-four hour vigil. I remembered the wire fence encircling us, and a knot of anger tightened in my breast. What was I doing behind a fence like a criminal? If there were accusations to be made, why hadn't I been given a fair trial? Maybe I wasn't considered an American anymore. My citizenship wasn't real, after all. Then what was I? I was certainly not a citizen of Japan as my parents were. On second thought, even Father and Mother . . . had little tie with their mother country. In their twenty-five years in America, they had worked and paid their taxes to their adopted government as any other citizen.

Of one thing I was sure. The wire fence was real. I no longer had the right to walk out of it. It was because I had Japanese ancestors. It was also because some people had little faith in the ideas and ideals of democracy.

Source: Monica Itoi Sone, *Nisei Daughter* (Seattle: University of Washington Press, 1979).

---

own. With 1 million men actively engaged on each side for more than two weeks, Kursk was the largest pitched battle of the war. It marked the end of the last great German offensive, leaving Germany capable of a fighting retreat but too weak to have any hope of winning the war and expecting an American and British attack across the English Channel.

## OPERATION OVERLORD

On **D-Day**—June 6, 1944—the western Allies landed on the coast of Normandy in northwestern France. Six divisions went ashore from hundreds of attack transports carrying 4,000 landing craft. Dozens of warships and 12,000 aircraft provided support. One British and two American airborne divisions dropped behind German positions. When the sun set on the "longest day," the Allies had a tenuous toehold in France. Americans had been waiting for the news. In Montgomery, Alabama, flags appeared along the streets and traffic halted at 5:00 P.M. for buglers from nearby bases and the high school to sound the "call to the colors." At 6:00 P.M. all movie projectors were stopped to allow time for prayer.

**D-Day** June 6, 1944, the day of the first paratroop drops and amphibious landings on the coast of Normandy, France, in the first stage of Operation OVERLORD during World War II.

*Documents*

Ernie Pyle, *The Toughest Beachhead in the World* (1944)

**Operation OVERLORD**   U.S. and British invasion of France in June 1944 during World War II.

The next few weeks brought limited success. The Allies secured their beachheads and poured more than a million men and hundreds of thousands of vehicles ashore in the first six weeks. However, the German defenders kept them pinned along a narrow coastal strip. **Operation OVERLORD,** the code name for the entire campaign across northern France, met renewed success in late July and August. U.S. troops improved their fighting skills through "experience, sheer bloody experience." They finally broke through the German lines around the town of St.-Lô and then drew a ring around the Germans that slowly closed on the town of Falaise. The Germans lost a quarter of a million troops.

The German command chose to regroup closer to Germany rather than fight in France. The Allies liberated Paris on August 25; Free French forces (units that had never surrendered to the Nazis) led the entry. The drive toward Germany was the largest U.S. operation of the war. The only impediments appeared to be winter weather and pushing forward enough supplies for the rapidly advancing armies.

The story was similar on the Eastern Front, where the Soviets relentlessly battered one section of the German lines after another. By the end of 1944, the Red Army had entered the Balkans and reached central Poland. The Soviets had suffered as many as 27 million military and civilian deaths and sustained by far the heaviest burden in turning back Nazi tyranny (see Table 26–1).

## VICTORY AND TRAGEDY IN EUROPE

In the last months of 1944, massive air strikes finally began to reduce German war production, which had actually increased during 1943 and much of 1944. The Americans flew daylight raids from air bases in Britain with heavily armed B-17s ("Flying Fortresses") and B-24s, ("Liberators") to destroy factories with precision bombing. On August 17, 1943, however, Germans shot down or damaged 19 percent of the bombers that attacked the aircraft factories of Regensburg and the ball-bearing factories of Schweinfurt. The Americans had to seek easier targets.

American, British, and Canadian forces opened the long-awaited second front against Germany on June 6, 1944—D-Day–when tens of thousands of troops landed on the coast of Normandy in France. The landings were the largest amphibious operation ever staged. Although the Germans had expected the landings farther north, their defenses pinned the Allies to a narrow beachhead for several weeks.

## Table 26–1
### Military and Civilian Deaths in World War II

| Nation | Victims (millions) |
| --- | --- |
| USSR | 27 |
| China | 10–20 |
| Germany and Austria | 6 |
| Poland | 6 |
| Japan | 2.7 |
| Yugoslavia | 1.7 |
| Romania | 0.7 |
| France | 0.6 |
| Great Britain | 0.5 |
| Hungary | 0.5 |
| Italy | 0.4 |
| Czechoslovakia | 0.4 |
| United States | 0.3 |

Gradually, however, the balance shifted. P-51 escort fighter helped B-17s over-fly Germany in relative safety after mid-1944. Thousand-bomber raids on railroads and oil facilities began to cripple the German economy. The raids forced Germany to devote 2.5 million workers to air defense and damage repair and to divert fighter planes from the front lines. The air raids cut German military production by one-third through 1944 and destroyed the transportation system. Politics, rather than military need, governed the final great action of the European air war. British and U.S. bombers in February 1945 staged a terror raid on the nonindustrial city of Dresden, packed with refugees, filled with great art, and undefended by the Germans; a firestorm fueled by incendiary bombs and rubble from blasted buildings killed tens of thousands of civilians.

**The Battle of the Bulge and the collapse of Germany.**  Even as the air bombardment intensified, Hitler struck a last blow. Stripping the Eastern Front of armored units, he launched 25 divisions against thinly held U.S. positions in the Ardennes Forest of Belgium on December 16, 1944. He hoped to split U.S. and British forces by capturing the Belgian port of Antwerp. The attack surprised the Americans, and taking advantage of snow and fog that grounded Allied aircraft, the Germans drove a 50-mile bulge into U.S. lines. Although the Americans took substantial casualties, the German thrust literally ran out of gas beyond the town of Bastogne. The Battle of the Bulge never seriously threatened the outcome of the war, but pushing the Germans back through the snow-filled forest gave GIs a taste of the conditions that marked the war in the Soviet Union.

The Nazi empire collapsed in the spring of 1945. American and British divisions crossed the Rhine in March and enveloped Germany's industrial core. The Soviets drove through eastern Germany toward Berlin. On April 25, American and Soviet troops met on the Elbe River. Hitler committed suicide on April 30 in his concrete bunker deep under devastated Berlin, which surrendered to the Soviets on May 2. The Nazi state formally capitulated on May 8.

**WHERE TO LEARN MORE**

United States Holocaust Memorial Museum, Washington, D.C.
www.ushmm.org

**Holocaust**   The systematic murder of millions of European Jews and others deemed undesirable by Nazi Germany.

**The Holocaust.**   The defeat of Germany revealed appalling evidence of the evil at the heart of the Nazi ideology of racial superiority. After occupying Poland in 1939, the Nazis had transformed concentration camps into forced-labor camps, where overwork, starvation, and disease killed hundreds of thousands of Jews, Gypsies, Poles, Russians, and others the Nazis classed as subhuman. As many as 7 million labor conscripts from eastern and western Europe provided forced labor in fields, factories, mines, and repair crews, often dying on the job from overwork and starvation.

The "final solution" to what Hitler thought of as the "Jewish problem" went far beyond slave labor. The German army in 1941 had gained practice with death by slaughtering hundreds of thousands of Jews and other civilians as it swept across Russia. In the fall of that year, Hitler decided on the total elimination of Europe's Jews. The elite SS, Hitler's personal army within the Nazi Party, in 1942 set out to do his bidding. At Auschwitz, Treblinka, and several other death camps, the SS organized the efficient extermination of up to 6 million Jews and 1 million Poles, Gypsies, and others who failed to fit the Nazi vision of the German master race. Prisoners arrived by forced marches and cattle trains. Those who were not worked or starved to death were herded into gas chambers and then incinerated in huge crematoriums.

The evidence of genocide—systematic racial murder—is irrefutable. Allied officials had begun to hear reports of mass murder midway through the war, but memories of the inaccurate propaganda about German atrocities in World War I made many skeptical. Moreover, the camps were located in the heart of German-controlled territory, areas that Allied armies did not reach until 1945. At Dachau in southwestern Germany, American forces found 10,000 bodies and 32,000 prisoners near death through starvation. Soviet troops who overran the camps in Poland found even more appalling sights—gas chambers as big as barns, huge ovens, the dead stacked like firewood. For more than half a century, the genocide that we now call the **Holocaust** has given the world its most vivid images of inhumanity.

The Nazi regime sent slave laborers to weak to continue working on its V-2 rocket project to the Nordhausen concentration camp to die of starvation. When U.S. troops liberated the camp in April 1945, they found more than 3,000 corpses.

# THE PACIFIC WAR

In the Pacific, as in Europe, the United States used 1943 to probe enemy conquests and to build better submarines, bigger aircraft carriers, and superior planes. Washington divided responsibilities in the Pacific theater. General Douglas MacArthur operated in the islands that stretched between Australia and the Philippines. Admiral Chester Nimitz commanded in the central Pacific. The Allies planned to isolate Japan from its southern conquests. The British moved from India to retake Burma. The Americans advanced along the islands of the southern Pacific to retake the Philippines. With Japan's army still tied down in China, the Americans then planned to bomb Japan into submission.

Racial hatred animated both sides in the Pacific war and fueled a "war without mercy." Americans often characterized Japanese soldiers as vermin. Political cartoons showed Japanese as monkeys or rats, and some Marines had "Rodent Exterminator" stenciled on their helmets. In turn, the Japanese depicted themselves as the "leading race" with the duty to rule the rest of Asia. Japan treated Chinese, Filipinos, and other conquered peoples with contempt and brutality, and the record of Japanese atrocities is substantial. Japanese viewed Americans as racial mongrels and called them demons. Each side expected the worst of the other and frequently lived up to expectations.

The Pacific campaigns of 1944 are often called **island hopping.** Planes from American carriers controlled the air, allowing the navy and land forces to isolate and capture the most strategically located Japanese-held islands while bypassing the rest.

**Island hopping** The Pacific campaigns of 1944 that were the American naval versions of the *Blitzkrieg.*

MacArthur used a version of the bypass strategy in the Solomon Islands and New Guinea, leapfrogging past Japanese strong points. The invasion of the Philippines repeated the approach by landing on Leyte, in the middle of the island chain. The Philippine campaign also destroyed the last offensive capacity of the Japanese fleet. The Japanese home islands were left with no defensive screen against an expected invasion.

During 1943 and 1944, the United States also savaged the Japanese economy. Submarines choked off food, oil, and raw materials bound for Japan and island bases. By 1945, imports to Japan were one-eighth of the 1940 level. Heavy bombing of Japan began in early 1944, using the new long-range B-29. Japan's dense wooden cities were more vulnerable than their German counterparts, and Japanese air defenses were much weaker. A fire-bomb raid on Tokyo on the night of March 9, 1945, killed 124,000 people and left 1 million homeless; it was perhaps the single biggest mass killing of all time. Overall, conventional bombing destroyed 42 percent of Japan's industrial capacity. By the time the United States captured the islands of Iwo Jima and Okinawa in fierce fighting (April–June 1945) and neared the Japanese home islands, Japan's position was hopeless.

# SEARCHING FOR PEACE

At the beginning of 1945, the Allies sensed victory. Conferring from February 4 to 11 in the Ukrainian town of Yalta, Roosevelt, Stalin, and Churchill planned for the postwar world. The most important American goal was to enlist the Soviet Union in finishing off the Pacific war. Americans hoped that a Soviet attack on Manchuria would tie down enough Japanese troops to reduce U.S. casualties in invading Japan. Stalin repeated his intent to declare war on Japan within three months of victory in Europe, in return for a free hand in Manchuria.

In Europe, the Allies had decided in 1944 to divide Germany and Austria into French, British, American, and Soviet occupation zones and to share control of Berlin. The Red Army already controlled Bulgaria, Romania, and Hungary, countries that had helped the Germans; Soviet officials were installing sympathetic regimes there. Soviet armies also controlled Poland. The most that Roosevelt could coax from Stalin was a

**Yalta Conference**    Meeting of U.S. President Franklin Roosevelt, British Prime Minister Winston Churchill, and Soviet Premier Joseph Stalin held in February 1945 to plan the final stages of World War II and postwar arrangements.

## QUICK REVIEW

### Preparations for Victory

- February 1945: Allies debate plans for postwar world at Yalta.
- Soviets solidified their hold on Eastern Europe.
- July 26, 1945: Potsdam Declaration fails to produce a definitive response from Japan.

**Potsdam Declaration**    Statement issued by the United States during a meeting of U.S. President Harry Truman, British Prime Minister Winston Churchill, and Soviet Premier Joseph Stalin in which the United States declared its intention to democratize the Japanese political system and reintroduce Japan into the international community.

vague pledge to allow participation of non-communists in coalition governments in eastern Europe. Stalin also agreed to join a new international organization, the United Nations (UN), whose foundations were laid at a conference in San Francisco in the spring of 1945. The new organization was intended to correct the mistakes of World War I, when the United States had stayed aloof from the League of Nations and had relied on international treaties without mechanisms of enforcement. American leaders wanted the UN to provide a framework through which the United States could coordinate collective security against potential aggressors while retaining its own military strength as the primary means to preserve the peace.

Conservative critics later charged that the western powers "gave away" eastern Europe at the **Yalta Conference.** In fact, the Soviet Union gained little that it did not already control.

**Truman and Potsdam.**    On April 12, two months after Yalta, Roosevelt died of a cerebral hemorrhage. Harry Truman, the new president, was a shrewd politician, but his experience was limited; Roosevelt had not even told him about the Manhattan Project. Deeply distrustful of the Soviets, Truman first ventured into personal international diplomacy in July 1945 at a British-Soviet-American conference at Potsdam, near Berlin. Most of the sessions debated the future of Germany. The leaders endorsed the expulsion of ethnic Germans from eastern Europe and moved the borders of Poland 100 miles west into historically German territory. Truman also made it clear that the United States expected to dominate the occupation of Japan. Its goal was to democratize the Japanese political system and reintroduce Japan into the international community, a policy that succeeded. The **Potsdam Declaration** on July 26 summarized U.S. policy and gave Japan an opening for surrender. However, the declaration failed to guarantee that Emperor Hirohito would not be tried as a war criminal. The Japanese response was so cautious that Americans read it as rejection.

The ruins of Hiroshima in the aftermath of the atomic bomb. Atomic bombs, dropped first on Hiroshima and then on Nagasaki in August 1945, instantly destroyed most of each city. Now one airplane could wreak the kind of devastation that massive fire-bombing raids had inflicted on cities such as Hamburg and Tokyo, adding new terror to the idea of total war.

## OVERVIEW     The Decision to Use the Atomic Bomb

Americans have long argued about whether the use of atomic bombs on the Japanese cities of Hiroshima and Nagasaki was necessary to end the war. Several factors probably influenced President Truman's decision to use the new weapon.

| | |
|---|---|
| **Military necessity** | After the war, Truman argued that the use of atomic bombs was necessary to avoid an invasion of Japan that would have cost hundreds of thousand of lives. Military planners expected Japanese soldiers to put up the same kind of suicidal resistance in defense of the home islands as they had to American landings in the Philippines, Iwo Jima, and Okinawa. More recently, historians have argued that the Japanese military was near collapse and an invasion would have met far less resistance than feared. |
| **Atomic diplomacy** | Some historians believe that Truman used atomic weapons to overawe the Soviet Union and induce it to move cautiously in expanding its influence in Europe and East Asia. Truman and his advisers were certainly aware of how the bomb might influence the Soviet leadership. |
| **Domestic politics** | President Roosevelt and his chief military advisers had spent billions on the secret atomic bomb project without the full knowledge of Congress or the American public. The managers of the Manhattan Project may have believed that only proof of its military value would quiet critics and justify the huge cost. |
| **Momentum of war** | The United States and Britain had already adopted wholesale destruction of German and Japanese cities as a military tactic. Use of the atomic bomb looked like a variation on fire bombing, not the start of a new era of potential mass destruction. In this context, some historians argue, President Truman's choice was natural and expected. |

**The atomic bomb.**     Secretary of State James Byrnes now urged Truman to use the new atomic bomb, tested just weeks earlier. Japan's ferocious defense of Okinawa had confirmed American fears that the Japanese would fight to the death. Thousands of suicide missions by kamikaze pilots who tried to crash their planes into U.S. warships seemed additional proof of Japanese fanaticism. Prominent Americans were wondering if unconditional surrender was worth another six or nine months of bitter fighting. In contrast, using the bomb to end the conflict quickly would ensure that the United States could occupy Japan without Soviet participation, and the bomb might intimidate Stalin (see Overview, The Decision to Use the Atomic Bomb). In short, a decision not to use atomic weapons was never a serious alternative in the summer of 1945.

In early August, the United States dropped two of the three available nuclear bombs on Japan. On August 6, at Hiroshima, the first bomb killed at least 80,000 people and poisoned thousands more with radiation. A second bomb, three days later at Nagasaki, took another 40,000 lives. Japan ceased hostilities on August 14 and surrendered formally on September 2. The world has wondered ever since whether the United States might have defeated Japan without resorting to atomic bombs, but recent research shows that the bombs were the shock that allowed the emperor and peace advocates to overcome military leaders who wanted to fight to the death.

## HOW THE ALLIES WON

The Allies won with economic capacity, technology, and military skill. The ability to outproduce the enemy made victory certain in 1944 and 1945, but it was the ability to outthink and outmaneuver the Axis powers that staved off defeat in 1942 and 1943.

*Documents*

Harry S. Truman, *Statement on the Atomic Bomb* (1945)

**WHERE TO LEARN MORE**

★ National Museum of the U.S. Air Force, Dayton, Ohio.
www.wpafb.af.mil/museum

**WHERE TO LEARN MORE**

★ National Museum of the Pacific War, Fredericksburg, Texas.
www.nimitz-museum.org

**From Then to Now Online**

*Nuclear Weapons*

In the spring of 1942, an unbroken series of conquests had given the Axis powers control of roughly one-third of the world's production of industrial raw materials, up from only 5 percent in 1939. But while Germany and Japan struggled to turn these resources into military strength, the Soviet Union accomplished wonders in relocating and rebuilding its manufacturing capacity after the disasters of 1941. The United States, meanwhile, rearmed with astonishing swiftness, accomplishing in one year what Germany had thought would take three. By 1944, the United States was outproducing all of its enemies combined; over the course of the war, it manufactured two-thirds of all the war materials used by the Allies.

The United States and the Soviet Union not only built more planes and tanks than the Axis nations, but they also built better ones. The Soviets developed and mass-produced the T-34, the world's most effective tank. American aircraft designers soon jumped ahead of the Germans. The United States and Britain gained the lead in communication systems, radar, code-breaking capability, and, of course, atomic weapons. Even behind the lines the Allies had the technical advantage. The U.S. and British forces that invaded France were fully motorized, and Soviet forces increasingly so, while the German army still depended on horses to draw supply wagons and artillery.

The Allies learned hard lessons from defeat and figured out how to outfight the Axis. Hitler's generals outsmarted the Soviet military in 1941, Japan outmaneuvered the British and Americans in the first months of the Pacific war, and the German navy came close to squeezing the life from Great Britain in 1942. In 1943 and 1944, the tables were turned. The Russians reexamined every detail of their military procedures and devised new tactics that kept the vast German armies off guard and on the defensive. New ways to fight U-boats in the Atlantic devastated the German submarine service and staved off defeat. Americans in the Pacific utilized the full capacity of aircraft carriers, while Japanese admirals still dreamed of confrontations between lines of battleships.

Finally, the Allies had the appeal of democracy and freedom. The Axis nations were clearly the aggressors. Germany and Japan made bitter enemies by exploiting and abusing the people of the countries they conquered, from Yugoslavia and France to Malaya and the Philippines, and incited local resistance movements. The Allies were certainly not perfect, but they fought for the ideals of political independence and were welcomed as liberators as they pushed back the Axis armies.

## CONCLUSION

The United States ended the war as the world's overwhelming economic power. It had put only 12 percent of its population in uniform, less than any other major combatant. For every American who died, 20 Germans and dozens of Soviets perished. Having suffered almost no direct destruction, the United States was able to dictate a postwar economic trading system that favored its interests.

Nevertheless, the insecurities of the war years influenced the United States for decades. A nation's current leaders are often shaped by its last war. Churchill had directed strategy, and Hitler, Mussolini, and Truman had all fought in World War I and carried its memories into World War II. The lessons of World War II would similarly influence the thinking of presidents from Dwight Eisenhower in the 1950s to George H. W. Bush in the 1990s. Even though the United States ended 1945 with the world's mightiest navy, biggest air force, and only atomic bomb, memories of the instability that had followed World War I made its leaders nervous about the shape of world politics.

One result in the postwar era was conflict between the United States and the Soviet Union, whose only common ground had been a shared enemy. After Germany's defeat, their wartime alliance gave way to hostility and confrontation in the Cold War. At home, international tensions fed the pressure for social and political conformity. The desire to enjoy the fruits of victory after 15 years of economic depression and sacrifice made the postwar generation sensitive to perceived threats to steady jobs and stable families. For the next generation, the unresolved business of World War II would haunt American life.

# SUMMARY

**WHY WERE** most Americans reluctant to get involved in World War II?

**The Dilemmas of Neutrality** In the late 1930s President Roosevelt's challenge was to lead the United States toward rearmament and support nations at war with fascism without alarming the public. The roots of World War II were to be found in the after-effects of the first World War; as Germany marched from victory to victory from 1939 to 1941, strong isolationist sentiment in America shaped public debate and limited attempts to help Britain and the Soviet Union. The swift collapse of France and radio broadcasts describing the bombing of London frightened Americans; the Lend Lease Act, an undeclared naval war, and the Atlantic Charter drew America closer to war. The final shove came in the Pacific with the attack on Pearl Harbor; in December 1941 America entered World War II.

**WHY DID** the Allies choose to focus on defeating Germany before Japan?

**Holding the Line** Despite the popular desire to defeat Japan, the Allies planned to defeat Germany first. The Soviet Union held the Eastern front in the Battle of Stalingrad; the British fought back in the Battle of the Atlantic; German troops in North Africa were forced to retreat; Japanese expansion came to a halt at the Battle of the Coral Sea and Battle of Midway. By the end of 1942 the tide was turning; in mid-1943 the Allies could begin to plan for victory with confidence.

**WHAT STEPS** did the U.S. government take to organize the economy for war?

**Mobilizing for Victory** The need to fight a global war brought a huge expansion of the federal government; price controls and rationing fought inflation, industry mobilized for defense production, and the Manhattan Project ushered in the age of atomic energy. The war penetrated every facet of everyday life; women and minorities changed the composition of the industrial work force. The government saw Japanese Americans as threats and interned them in camps throughout the West. The war required more than a thirtyfold expansion of the U.S. military; soldiers came from across the American spectrum. While women in the military received unequal treatment, African Americans fared worse.

**HOW DID** the war affect the place of women in American society?

**The Home Front** The war penetrated almost all aspects of everyday life, from family life, to education, to work. The federal government tried to keep civilians of all ages committed and involved in the war effort. As the draft called men to war, women changed the composition of the industrial workforce. Ethnic minorities were drawn into the national effort. The migration of men and women searching for work produced increased opportunities for cultural clashes. The one group excluded from the national war effort were Japanese Americans living on the west coast who were forced to endure internment. Finally, the war brought an end to the New Deal.

**WHY DID** the Allies win the war?

**War and Peace** Plans for ending the war were drawn up at Casablanca and Tehran; Italy was invaded in 1943; Operation Overlord opened the second front in Europe; in 1944 Germany was being battered from the east and west. As Allied troops entered Germany and discovered the death camps, the extent of what is now called the Holocaust became clear. Through the island hopping campaign in the Pacific, American forces neared the Japanese home islands; in 1945 President Truman chose to use the atomic bomb to end the war with Japan. The postwar world would prove to be a challenge; the Yalta and Potsdam conferences divided Europe into spheres that would last for almost fifty years.

# WHERE TO LEARN MORE

**National Museum of the U.S. Air Force, Dayton, Ohio.** Visitors can walk among World War II fighter planes and bombers, including the B-29 that dropped the atomic bomb on Nagasaki, and learn about the role of aviation in the war. **www.wpafb.af.mil/museum**

**National Museum of the Pacific War, Fredericksburg, Texas.** In the birthplace of Admiral Chester Nimitz, this new museum is an excellent introduction to the war with Japan. **www.nimitz-museum.org**

**Los Alamos County Historical Museum and Bradbury Science Museum, Los Alamos, New Mexico.** The museum traces the origins of atomic energy for military and civilian uses. Nearby is the Los Alamos County Historical Museum, which gives the feel of everyday life in the atomic town. **www.lanl.gov/museum**

**United States Holocaust Memorial Museum, Washington, DC.** The Holocaust Museum gives visitors a deeply moving depiction of the deadly impact of Nazi ideas in the 1930s and 1940s. The museum's website at **www.ushmm.org** also explores virtually every facet of the Holocaust experience for Jews during World War II.

# STUDY RESOURCES

## PEARSON myhistorylab

For study resources for this chapter, go to www.myhistorylab .com and choose *The American Journey.* You will find a wealth of study and review material for this chapter, including pre- and posttests, customized study plan, key term review flash cards, interactive map and document activities, and documents for analysis.

# REVIEW QUESTIONS

1. What motivated German, Italian, and Japanese aggression in the 1930s? How did Great Britain, the USSR, and other nations respond to the growing conflict?

2. What arguments did Americans make against involvement in the war in Europe, and how deep was anti-intervention sentiment? Why did President Roosevelt and many others believe it necessary to block German and Japanese expansion? What steps did Roosevelt take to increase U.S. involvement short of war?

3. What was the military balance in early 1942? What were the chief threats to the United States and its allies? Why did the fortunes of war turn in late 1942?

4. Assess how mobilization for World War II altered life in the United States. How did the war affect families? How did it shift the regional balance of the economy? What opportunities did it open for women?

5. Did World War II help or hinder progress toward racial equality in the United States? How did the experiences of Japanese Americans, African Americans, and Mexican Americans challenge American ideals?

6. What factors were decisive in the defeat of Germany? How important were Soviet efforts on the Eastern Front, the bomber war, and the British-American landings in France?

7. What was the U.S. strategy against Japan, and how well did it work? What lay behind President Truman's decision to use atomic bombs against Japanese cities?

8. What role did advanced science and technology play in World War II? How did the scientific lead of the United States affect the war's outcome?

## KEY TERMS

**Allies** (p. 784)
**Atlantic Charter** (p. 782)
**Axis Powers** (p. 779)
**Battle of the Atlantic** (p. 786)
**Blitzkrieg** (p. 779)
**D-Day** (p. 799)
**Eastern Front** (p. 784)
**Fair Employment Practices Committee** (p. 793)

**Greater East Asia Co-Prosperity Sphere** (p. 777)
**Holocaust** (p. 802)
**Island hopping** (p. 803)
**Lend-Lease Act** (p. 782)
**Manhattan Project** (p. 789)
**Operation OVERLORD** (p. 800)
**Potsdam Declaration** (p. 804)
**Yalta Conference** (p. 804)

# 27

# The Cold War at Home and Abroad

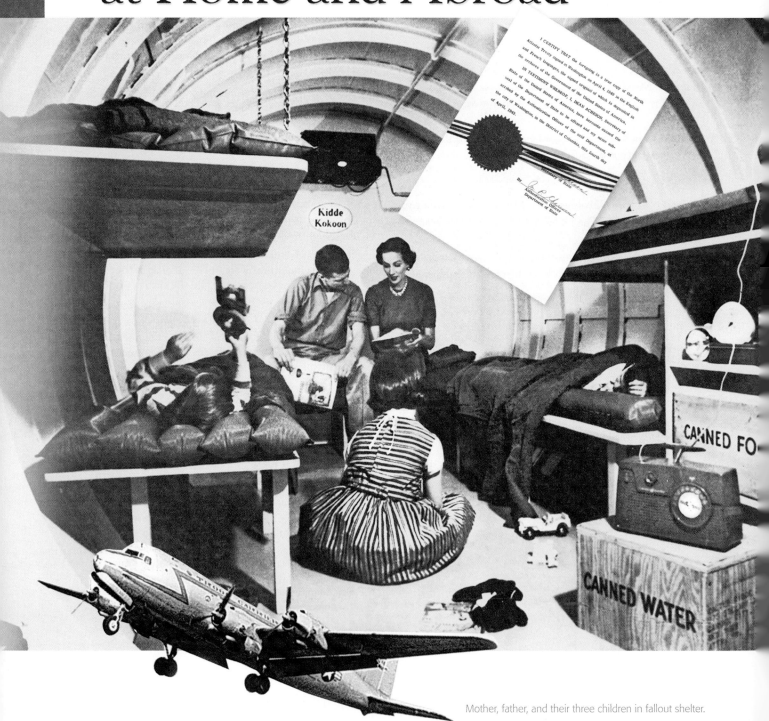

Mother, father, and their three children in fallout shelter.

## LAUNCHING THE GREAT BOOM *(page 813)*

**WHAT WAS** the catalyst for the economic boom that began in 1947?

## TRUMAN, REPUBLICANS, AND THE FAIR DEAL *(page 818)*

**HOW WAS** Harry Truman able to win the 1948 presidential election?

## CONFRONTING THE SOVIET UNION *(page 821)*

**WHAT WERE** the origins of the Cold War?

## COLD WAR AND HOT WAR *(page 825)*

**HOW DID** the Korean War shape American domestic politics?

## THE SECOND RED SCARE *(page 831)*

**WHY DID** fear of communism escalate in the years following World War II?

*My eyes popped when I got to town hall because the lobby and the stairs leading up to the hearing room were loaded with people. The upstairs hallway was jammed and the room was packed. People were standing along the walls. I remember there were a lot of children, toddlers— some in strollers—and many babies held by men and women. We expected there would be quite a turnout. But the extent of the crowd was a big surprise to me. . . . The meeting itself was rather brief. There were some speeches. No screaming and yelling the way people do at town meetings today. Everyone was quiet, anxious. I remember one guy in uniform, holding a baby, made a strong statement. These people were desperate. It was very moving. When the decision was announced, the crowd broke into applause.*

*Levittown was the last place on the planet I thought I would be living. But, as it turned out, we moved there because the house was such a good buy. . . . We loved living there. I came into work and told [Newsday managing editor Alan] Hathway that I would be eating crow for the rest of my days.*

Bernadette Rischer Wheeler, in "Levittown at Fifty: Long Island Voices," at www.lihistory.com/specsec/hsvoices.htm; originally published in *Newsday*.

## PEARSON
## myhistorylab

### Personal Journeys Online

- "This Is How I Keep House," McCalls, April 1949. The routine of a typical Levittown housewife.

- Eric Hodgins, *Mr. Blandings Builds His Dream House* (1946). A fictional New York advertising agent buys a house in the far edge of suburbia.

- Atlanta Housing Council, "Proposed Areas for Expansions of Negro Housing in Atlanta, Georgia," Papers of the Atlanta Urban League, Atlanta University Center, Atlanta, Georgia. Reprinted in Andrew Wiese and Becky Nicolaides, *The Suburb Reader* (2006). Atlanta Housing Council, suggests ways to continue residential segregation in a growing city.

**BERNADETTE WHEELER** was a reporter for *Newsday*, the daily newspaper for the Long Island suburbs of New York, who covered the birth of the new community of Levittown. She remembers the meeting on May 21, 1947, when the local governing board approved construction of the new subdivision. The size of the crowd indicated the severity of the housing shortage after World War II and the intense desire of Americans to return to normal life. After years of hardship, they defined American ideals in terms of economic opportunity and the chance to enjoy national prosperity.

This compelling desire to enjoy the promise of American life after years of sacrifice helps explain why Americans reacted so fiercely to new challenges and threats. They watched as congressional conservatives and President Truman fought over the fate of New Deal programs. More worrisome was the confrontation with the Soviet Union that was soon being called the **Cold War.** Triggered by the Soviet Union's imposition of communist regimes throughout eastern Europe, the Cold War grew into a global contest in which the United States tried to counter Soviet influence around the world. The Cold War would shape the United States and the world for a generation. ✦

## CHRONOLOGY

| | |
|---|---|
| **1944** Servicemen's Readjustment Act (GI Bill) is passed. | **1949** North Atlantic Treaty Organization is formed. |
| **1945** United Nations is established. | Communist Chinese defeat Nationalists. |
| **1946** Employment Act creates Council of Economic Advisers. | Soviet Union tests an atomic bomb. |
| George Kennan sends his "long telegram." | Department of Defense is established. |
| Winston Churchill delivers his "iron curtain" speech. | **1950** Senator McCarthy begins his Red hunt. |
| **1947** Truman Doctrine is announced. | Alger Hiss is convicted of perjury. |
| Truman establishes a federal employee loyalty program. | Internal Security Act (McCarran Act). |
| Kennan explains containment policy in an anonymous article in *Foreign Affairs*. | NSC-68 is drafted and accepted as U.S. policy. |
| Marshall Plan begins providing economic aid to Europe. | Korean War begins. |
| HUAC holds hearings on Hollywood. | **1951** Senate Internal Security Subcommittee begins hearings. |
| Taft-Hartley Act rolls back gains of organized labor. | Truman relieves MacArthur of his command. |
| National Security Act creates National Security Council and Central Intelligence Agency. | Julius and Ethel Rosenberg are convicted of conspiring to commit espionage. |
| **1948** Communists stage coup in Czechoslovakia. | Truce talks begin in Korea. |
| Berlin airlift overcomes Soviet blockade. | **1952** United States tests the hydrogen bomb. |
| Truman orders desegregation of the armed forces. | Eisenhower is elected president. |
| Selective Service is reestablished. | |
| Truman wins reelection. | |

# LAUNCHING THE GREAT BOOM

When World War II ended, Americans feared that demobilization would bring a rerun of the inflation and unemployment that had followed World War I. Indeed, in the first 18 months of peace, rising prices, strife between labor and management, and shortages of everything from meat to automobiles confirmed their anxiety. But in fact, 1947 and 1948 ushered in an economic expansion that lasted for a quarter-century. The resulting prosperity would finance a military buildup and an activist foreign policy. It also supported continuity in domestic politics from the late 1940s to the mid-1960s.

**WHAT WAS** the catalyst for the economic boom that began in 1947?

**Cold War** The political and economic confrontation between the Soviet Union and the United States that dominated world affairs from 1946 to 1989.

## RECONVERSION CHAOS

Japan's sudden surrender took the United States by surprise. The Pentagon, already scaling back defense spending, canceled $15 billion in war contracts in the first two days after the Japanese surrender. Public pressure demanded that the military release the nation's 12 million service personnel as rapidly as possible. GIs in Europe and the South Pacific waited impatiently for their turn on slow, crowded troop ships. Even at the rate of 25,000 discharges a day, it took a year to get all of them back to civilian life.

Veterans came home to shortages of food and consumer goods. High demand and short supply meant inflationary pressure, checked temporarily by continuing the Office of Price Administration until October 1946. Meanwhile, producers, consumers, and retailers scrambled to evade price restrictions and scarcities.

A wave of strikes made it hard to retool factories for civilian products. Inflation squeezed factory workers, who had accepted wage controls during the war effort. Since 1941, prices had risen twice as fast as base wages. In the fall of 1945, more and more workers went on strike to redress the balance; the strikes interrupted the output of products from canned soup to copper wire. By January 1946, some 1.3 million auto, steel, electrical, and packinghouse workers were off the job. Strikes in these basic industries shut other factories down for lack of supplies. Presidential committees crafted settlements that allowed steel and auto workers to make up ground lost during the war, but they also allowed corporations to pass on higher costs to consumers.

## ECONOMIC POLICY

The economic turmoil of 1946 set the stage for two major and contradictory efforts to deal more systematically with peacetime economic readjustment. The Employment Act of 1946 and the Taft-Hartley Act of 1947 represented liberal and conservative approaches to the peacetime economy.

The Employment Act was an effort by congressional liberals to ward off economic crisis by fine-tuning government taxation and spending. It started as a proposal for a full-employment bill that would ensure everyone's "right to a useful and remunerative job." Watered down in the face of business opposition, it still defined economic growth and high employment as national goals. It also established the **Council of Economic Advisers** to assist the president.

In the short term, the Employment Act aimed at a problem that did not materialize. Economists had predicted that the combination of returning veterans and workers idled by canceled defense work would bring depression-level unemployment of 8 to 10 million. In fact, more than 2 million women provided some slack by leaving the labor force outright. Federal agencies hastened their departure by publishing pamphlets asking men the pointed question, "Do you want your wife to work after the war?" In addition, a savings pool of $140 billion in bank accounts and war bonds created a huge demand for consumer goods and workers to produce them. Total employment rose rather than fell with the end of the war, and unemployment in 1946–1948 stayed below 4 percent.

From the other end of the political spectrum, the **Taft-Hartley Act** climaxed a ten-year effort by conservatives to reverse the gains made by organized labor in the 1930s. The act passed in 1947 because of anger about continuing strikes. Many middle-class Americans were convinced that organized labor needed to be curbed.

In November 1946, Republicans capitalized on the problems of reconversion chaos, labor unrest, and dissatisfaction with Truman. Their election slogan was simple: "Had enough?" The GOP won control of Congress for the first time since the election of 1928, continuing the political trend toward the right that had been apparent since 1938.

Adopted by the now firmly conservative Congress, the Taft-Hartley Act was a serious counterattack by big business against large unions. It outlawed several union tools as "unfair labor practices." It barred the closed shop (the requirement that all workers hired in a given company or plant be union members) and blocked secondary boycotts (strikes against suppliers or customers of a targeted business). The federal government could postpone a strike by imposing a cooling-off period, which gave companies time to stockpile their products. Officers of national unions had to swear that they were not Communists or Communist sympathizers, even though corporate executives had no similar obligation. The bill passed over Truman's veto.

**QUICK REVIEW**

**Post-war Economic Problems**
- Military spending and military service came to an abrupt halt.
- Veterans came home to shortages in food and consumer goods.
- Inflation contributed to labor unrest.

**Council of Economic Advisers** Board of three professional economists established in 1946 to advise the president on economic policy.

**Taft-Hartley Act** Federal legislation of 1947 that substantially limited the tools available to labor unions in labor-management disputes.

**QUICK REVIEW**

**The Taft-Hartly Act (1947)**
- Effort to reverse gains made by labor in the 1930s.
- Public anger over strikes made passage of the act possible.
- Many middle-class Americans believed labor had gone too far.

## THE GI BILL

Another landmark law for the postwar era passed Congress without controversy. The Servicemen's Readjustment Act of 1944 was designed to ease veterans back into the civilian mainstream. Popularly known as the **GI Bill of Rights,** it was one of the federal government's most successful public assistance programs. Rather than pay cash bonuses to veterans, as after previous wars, Congress tied benefits to specific public goals. The GI Bill guaranteed loans of up to $2,000 for buying a house or farm or starting a business, a substantial sum at a time when a new house cost $6,000. The program encouraged veterans to attend college with money for tuition and books plus monthly stipends.

The GI Bill democratized American higher education by making college degrees accessible to men with working-class backgrounds. It brought far more students into higher education than could otherwise have enrolled. In the peak year of 1947, veterans made up half of all college students. Veterans helped convert the college degree, once available primarily to the socially privileged, into a basic business and professional credential. However, the GI tide unfortunately crowded women out of classrooms. Women's share of bachelor's degrees dropped from 40 percent in 1940 to 25 percent in 1950.

**GI Bill of Rights** Legislation in June 1944 that eased the return of veterans into American society by providing educational and employment benefits.

## ASSEMBLY-LINE NEIGHBORHOODS

Americans faced a housing shortage after the war. In 1947, fully 3 million married couples were unable to set up their own households. Most doubled up with relatives while they waited for the construction industry to respond. Hunger for housing was fierce. Eager buyers lined up for hours and paid admission fees to tour model homes or to put their names in drawings for the opportunity to buy.

The solution started with the federal government and its Veterans Administration (VA) mortgage program. By guaranteeing repayment, the VA allowed veterans to get home-purchase loans from private lenders without a downpayment. Neither the VA program nor the New Deal–era Federal Housing Administration (FHA) mortgage insurance program, however, could do any good unless there were houses to buy. Eyeing the mass market created by the federal programs, innovative private builders devised their own solution. In 1947, William Levitt, a New York builder who had developed defense housing projects, built 2,000 houses for veterans on suburban Long Island. His basic house had 800 square feet of living space in two bedrooms, living room, kitchen, and bath, a 60-by-100-foot lot, and an unfinished attic waiting for the weekend handyman. There were 6,000 **Levittown** houses by the end of 1948 and more than 17,000 by 1951.

**Levittown** Suburban Long Island community of postwar rental houses built by William Levitt for veterans of World War II.

Other successful builders worked on the same scale. They bought hundreds of acres of land, put in utilities for the entire tract, purchased materials by the carload, and kept specialized workers busy on scores of identical houses. Work crews in the Los Angeles suburb of Lakewood started a hundred houses a day as they moved down one side of the street and back up the other, digging foundation trenches, pouring concrete, and working through the dozens of other stages of home building.

From 1946 through 1950, the federal government backed $20 billion in VA and FHA loans, approximately 40 percent of all home-mortgage debt. Housing starts neared 2 million in the peak year of 1950. By the end of the 1940s, 55 percent of American households owned their homes. The figure continued to climb until the 1980s, broadening access to the dream of financial security for many families. All during this time, the suburban population grew much faster than the population of central cities, and the population outside of metropolitan areas actually declined. (see Figure 27–1).

**QUICK REVIEW**

**Housing Shortages**
- Americans faced housing shortages after the war.
- The VA mortgage program allowed veterans to purchase homes without a down payment.
- Builders responded with mass-produced housing.

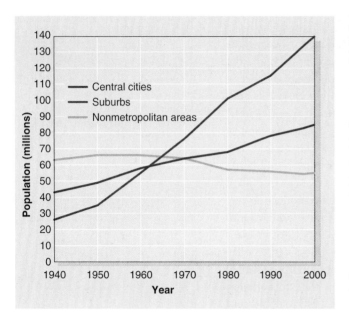

**FIGURE 27–1    The Suburbanizing Nation**    In the decades after World War II, Americans moved in unprecedented numbers to new communities surrounding established cities in the early 1960s, the combined population of suburban areas passed the populations of large central cities and of smaller towns and rural areas.

**Redlining**   The withholding of home purchase loans and insurance coverage from innercity older neighborhoods by federal housing agencies and private industry.

**Isolation and discrimination.**    Unfortunately, the suburban solution to the housing shortage came with costs. The vast new housing tracts tended to isolate women and children from traditional community life. Moreover, they were of little benefit to African Americans. As the migration of black workers and their families to northern and western cities continued after the war, discrimination excluded them from new housing. Federal housing agencies and private industry worsened the problem by **redlining** older neighborhoods, which involved withholding home-purchase loans and insurance coverage from inner-city areas that were deemed too risky as investments.

Thus public and private actions kept African Americans in deteriorating inner-city ghettos.

## STEPS TOWARD CIVIL RIGHTS

The urgent need for decent housing helped to motivate African Americans to demand full rights as citizens. The wartime experience of fighting for freedom abroad while suffering discrimination at home steeled a new generation of black leaders to close the gap between America's ideal of equality and its performance. As had also been true after World War I, some white Americans held the opposite view, hoping to reaffirm racial segregation. A wave of racist violence surged across the South after the war; special targets were black veterans who tried to register to vote. However, many white Americans felt uneasy about the contradiction between a crusade for freedom abroad and racial discrimination at home.

In this era of rapid change and racial tension, the Truman administration recognized the importance of upholding civil rights for all Americans. Caught between

Jackie Robinson, the first black player in modern major league baseball, joined the Brooklyn Dodgers in 1947. He was both personally courageous and an outstanding player. Here he steals home against the Chicago Cubs in 1952.

pressure from black leaders and the fear of alienating southern Democrats, the president in 1946 appointed the Committee on Civil Rights, whose report developed an agenda for racial justice that would take two decades to put into effect. The NAACP had already begun a campaign of antisegregation lawsuits, which the Justice Department now began to support. The administration ordered federal housing agencies to modify their racially restrictive policies and prohibited racial discrimination in federal employment. Federal committees began to push for desegregation of private facilities in the symbolically important city of Washington, DC. In an important decision in the case of *Shelley v. Kraemer* (1948), the Supreme Court held that clauses in real estate deeds that forbid selling or renting to minorities could not be enforced in the courts.

The president also ordered "equality of treatment and opportunity" in the armed services in July 1948. The army in particular dragged its feet, hoping to limit black enlistees to 10 percent of the total. Manpower needs and the record of integrated units in the war in Korea from 1950 to 1953 persuaded the reluctant generals. Over the next generation, African Americans would find the military an important avenue for career opportunities.

Changes in national policy were important for ending racial discrimination, but far more Americans were interested in lowering racial barriers in professional team sports. Americans had applauded individual black champions, such as boxer Joe Louis and sprinter Jesse Owens, but team sports required their members to travel, practice, and play together. The center of attention was Jack Roosevelt ("Jackie") Robinson, a gifted African American athlete, who opened the 1947 baseball season as a member of the Brooklyn Dodgers. Robinson broke the color line that had reserved the modern major leagues for white players. His ability to endure taunting and hostility and still excel on the ballfield opened the door for other African Americans and Latinos. In the segregated society of the 1940s, Robinson found himself a powerful symbol of racial change.

## CONSUMER BOOM AND BABY BOOM

The housing boom was a product of both pent-up demand and a postwar "family boom." Americans celebrated the end of the war with weddings; the marriage rate in 1946 surpassed even its wartime high. Many women who left the labor force opted for marriage, and at increasingly younger ages. By 1950, the median age at which women married would be just over 20 years—lower than at any previous time in the twentieth century. The United States ended the 1940s with 7 million more married couples than at the decade's start.

New marriages jumpstarted the "baby boom," as did already married couples who decided to catch up after postponing childbearing during the war. In the early 1940s, an average of 2.9 million children per year were born in the United States; in 1946–1950, the average was 3.6 million. Those 3.5 million "extra" babies needed diapers, swing sets, lunch boxes, bicycles, and schoolrooms (see Figure 27–2).

Fast-growing families also needed to stock up on household goods. Out of an average household income of roughly $4,000 in 1946 and 1947, a family of four had $300 to $400 a year for furnishings and appliances.

Americans were eager to enjoy the most modern appliances and houses. Manufacturers promoted streamlined kitchens to make life easier for housewives and their families.

FIGURE 27–2   **The Postwar Baby Boom: The U.S. Birthrate 1930–2000**   The baby boom after World War II was the product of high marriage rates and closely spaced children. The generation of Americans born between 1945 and 1960 has strongly affected American society and politics as its members went to school and college, entered the workforce, started their own families, and now have begun to plan for retirement in the twenty-first century.

# TRUMAN, REPUBLICANS, AND THE FAIR DEAL

**HOW WAS** Harry Truman able to win the 1948 presidential election?

WHERE TO LEARN MORE

Harry S Truman National Historical Site, Library, and Museum, Independence, Missouri. www.nps.gov/hstr

**Dixiecrats**   States' Rights Democrats.

From new products to new homes to new jobs, the economic gains of the postwar years propelled Americans toward the political center. After 15 years of economic crisis and world war, they wanted to enjoy prosperity.

Recognizing this attitude, Harry Truman and his political advisers tried to define policies acceptable to moderate Republicans as well as to Democrats. This meant creating a bipartisan coalition to block Soviet influence in western Europe and defending the core of the New Deal's social and economic agenda at home.

This political package is known as the strategy of the "vital center," after the title of a 1949 book by Arthur Schlesinger, Jr. The book linked anti-communism in foreign policy with efforts to enact inclusive social and economic policies to extend freedom abroad and at home. The vital center reflected the political reality of the Cold War years, when Democrats had to prove that they were tough on communism before they could enact domestic reforms. The approach defined the heart of the Democratic Party for 20 years and found full expression in the administrations of John Kennedy (1961–1963) and Lyndon Johnson (1963–1969).

## TRUMAN'S OPPOSITION

Truman had unexpected luck in his campaign for a full term as president in 1948. Besides the Republicans, he faced new fringe parties on the far right and far left that allowed him to position himself in the moderate center.

Truman's opponents represented the left-leaning American Progressive Party, the **Dixiecrats** (officially the States' Rights Democrats), and the Republicans. The Progressive candidate was Henry Wallace, who had been FDR's vice president from 1941 to 1945, before being dumped in favor of Truman; more recently, he had been Truman's secretary of commerce. The Dixiecrat, Governor Strom Thurmond of South Carolina, had bolted the Democratic Party over civil rights. The most serious challenger was the Republican, Thomas Dewey, who had run against Roosevelt in 1944.

Harry Truman greets supporters and railroad workers in Pittsburgh at the start of an 18-state campaign tour in June 1948. Truman's grassroots campaign and down-home style helped him pull out an unexpected victory in November 1948.

Tom Dewey had a high opinion of himself. He had been an effective governor of New York and represented the moderate eastern establishment within the Republican Party. Fortunately for Truman, Dewey lacked the common touch. Smooth on the outside, he alienated people who should have been his closest supporters. He was a bit of a snob and was an arrogant campaigner, refusing to interrupt his morning schedule to talk to voters.

Dewey was also saddled with the results of the Republican-controlled "do-nothing" 80th Congress (1947–1948). Truman used confrontation with Congress to rally voters who had supported the New Deal. He introduced legislation that he knew would be ignored, and he used his veto even when he knew Congress would override it. All the while he was building a list of campaign issues by demonstrating that the Republicans were obstructionists. Vote for me, Truman argued, to protect the New Deal, or vote Republican to bring back the days of Herbert Hoover.

**QUICK REVIEW**

**1948: Candidates for President**

- Harry Truman (Democrat).
- Thomas Dewey (Republican).
- Henry Wallace (Progressive).
- Strom Thurmond (States' Rights Democrat, or Dixiecrat).

## GLOBAL PERSPECTIVES

### GUNNAR MYRDAL, RACE RELATIONS, AND COLD WAR LEADERSHIP

*In 1938, the Swedish social scientist Gunnar Myrdal came to the United States at the invitation of the Carnegie Foundation to study relations between white and black Americans—what people at the time called the "Negro problem." Six years later, he published* An American Dilemma, *a 1,000-page volume with hundreds of additional pages of supporting data. Studying the problems of race relations as a stranger, Myrdal was struck by the basic national values derived from English law and Christian belief, values and opportunities that he termed the "American Creed."*

Not since Reconstruction has there been more reason to anticipate fundamental changes in American race relations, changes which will involve a development toward the American ideals. . . . America, relative to all the other branches of Western civilization, is moralistic and "moral-conscious." . . .

America feels itself to be humanity in miniature. When in this crucial time the international leadership passes to America, the great reason for hope is that this country has a national experience of united racial and cultural diversity and a national theory, if not a consistent practice, of freedom and equality for all. What America is constantly reaching for is democracy at home and abroad. The main trend in its history is the gradual realization of the American Creed.

In this sense the Negro problem is not only America's greatest failure but also America's incomparably great opportunity for the future. If America should follow its own deepest convictions, its well-being at home would be increased directly. At the same time, America's prestige and power would be increased directly. . . . America can demonstrate that justice, equality and cooperation are possible between white and colored people.

Myrdal's challenge became an important consideration during the Cold War. Washington policymakers realized that the peoples of Africa, Asia, and Latin America were paying close attention to how the nation's white majority treated its black and Hispanic citizens. This concern for America's global reputation helped make otherwise reluctant leaders into supporters of the black civil rights movement and fair treatment of Mexican migrant workers. The admission of multiracial Hawaii as the fiftieth state in 1959 was a challenge to segregationists and was seen as a "bridge to Asia" that carried the message that the United States was welcoming to all peoples.

Gunnar Myrdal, *An American Dilemma* (New York: McGraw-Hill, 1964), pp. lxi, lxx, 1021. (Originally published in 1944)

- Does the idea of an American Creed help us to understand the international roles of the United States in the twenty-first century?

### WHISTLE-STOPPING ACROSS AMERICA

The 1948 presidential campaign mixed old and new. For the last time, a major candidate crisscrossed the nation by rail and made hundreds of speeches from the rear platforms of trains. For the first time, national television broadcast the two party conventions, although the primitive cameras showed the handful of viewers little more than talking heads.

Truman ran on both character and issues. He was a widely read and intelligent man who cultivated the image of a backslapper. He covered 31,700 miles in his campaign train and gave ten speeches a day. Republicans belittled the small towns and cities he visited, calling them "whistle stops." Democrats made the term a badge of pride for places like Laramie, Wyoming, and Pocatello, Idaho.

Truman brought the campaign home to average Americans. He tied Dewey to inflation, housing shortages, and fears about the future of Social Security (an issue that Democrats would continue to use into the next century). In industrial cities, he hammered at the Taft-Hartley Act. In the West, he pointed out that Democratic administrations had built dams and helped to turn natural resources into jobs. He called the Republicans the party of privilege and arrogance. The Democrats, he said, offered opportunity for farmers, factory workers, and small business owners.

Truman got a huge boost from Dewey's unwillingness to fight. Going into the fall with a huge lead in the public opinion polls, Dewey sought to avoid mistakes. Wallace and Thurmond each took just under 1.2 million votes. Dewey received nearly 22 million popular votes and 189 electoral votes, but Truman won more than 24 million popular votes and 303 electoral votes (see Map 27–1).

## TRUMAN'S FAIR DEAL

Truman hoped to build on the gains of the New Deal. In his State of the Union address in January 1949, he called for a Fair Deal for all Americans. He promised to extend the New Deal and ensure "greater economic opportunity for the mass of the people." Over the next four years, however, conservative Republicans and southern Democrats forced Congress to choose carefully among Truman's proposals, accepting those that expanded existing programs but rejecting new departures. The result was a set of disconnected measures rather than the consistent program that Truman had advocated.

With the Housing Act of 1949, the federal government reaffirmed its concern about families who had been priced out of the private market. The act provided money for local housing agencies to buy, clear, and resell land for housing. The intent was to clear "substandard and blighted areas" and replace them with affordable modern apartments. The program never worked as intended because of scanty appropriations, poor design of the replacement housing, and local decisions that concentrated public housing in segregated minority neighborhoods, but it established the goal of decent housing for all Americans.

In 1950, Congress revitalized the weak Social Security program. Benefits went up by an average of 80 percent, and 10.5 million additional people received old-age and survivors' insurance. Most of the new coverage went to rural and small-town people, thus consolidating the broad support that has made it politically difficult to change Social Security ever since, even in the face of projected shortages in the twenty-first century.

Congress rejected other Fair Deal proposals that would remain on the national agenda for decades. A Senate filibuster killed a permanent Fair Employment Practices Commission to fight racial discrimination in hiring, halting progress toward civil rights. The medical establishment blocked a proposal for national health insurance as "socialistic." The overall message from Truman's second term was clear: Americans liked what the New Deal had given them but were hesitant about new initiatives.

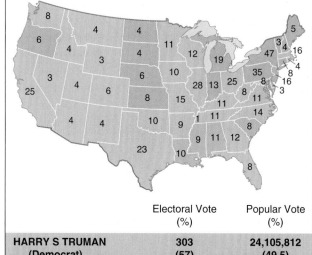

| | Electoral Vote (%) | Popular Vote (%) |
|---|---|---|
| **HARRY S TRUMAN** (Democrat) | **303** **(57)** | **24,105,812** **(49.5)** |
| Thomas E. Dewey (Republican) | 189 (36) | 21,970,065 (45.1) |
| Strom Thurmond (States' Rights) | 39 (7) | 1,169,063 (2.4) |
| Henry A. Wallace (Progressive) | – | 1,157,172 (2.4) |
| Other candidates (Socialist, Prohibition, Socialist Labor, Socialist Workers) | – | 272,713 (.6) |

**MAP 27–1  The Election of 1948**  Harry Truman won a narrow victory in the presidential election of 1948 by holding many of the traditionally Democratic states of the South and West and winning key industrial states in the Middle West. His success depended on the coalition of rural and urban interests that Franklin Roosevelt had pulled together in the 1930s.

**Why do** you think industrial states in the Midwest supported Harry S Truman in the 1948 presidential election?

American Medical Association, *Campaign against Compulsory Health Insurance* (1949)

# CONFRONTING THE SOVIET UNION

In 1945, the United States and the Soviet Union were allies, victorious against Germany and planning the defeat of Japan. By 1947, they were engaged in a diplomatic and economic confrontation and soon came close to war over the city of Berlin. The business tycoon

**WHAT WERE** the origins of the Cold War?

*Documents*

Kenneth MacFarland, *The Unfinished Work* (1946)

**W** WHERE TO LEARN MORE

★ United Nations Headquarters, New York, New York.
www.un.org

**International Monetary Fund (IMF)**
International organization established in 1945 to assist nations in maintaining stable currencies.

**World Bank**   Designed to revive postwar international trade, it drew on the resources of member nations to make economic development loans to governments for such projects as new dams or agricultural modernization.

**QUICK REVIEW**

New International Organizations

- United Nations.
- International Monetary Fund (IMF).
- World Bank.

and presidential adviser Bernard Baruch characterized the conflict in April 1947 as a "cold war," and newspaper columnist Walter Lippmann quickly popularized the term.

Over the next 40 years, the United States and the Soviet Union contested for economic, political, and military influence around the globe. The heart of Soviet policy was to control eastern Europe as a buffer zone against Germany. The centerpiece of American policy was to link the United States, western Europe, and Japan into an alliance of overwhelming economic power. For the United States, the Cold War was simultaneously an effort to promote democracy in Europe, maintain a favorable military position in relation to the Soviet Union, and preserve its leadership of the world economy.

Each side in the Cold War thought the worst of the other. Behind the conflicts were Soviet insecurity about an aggressive West and American fear of Communist expansionism. Americans and Soviets frequently interpreted each other's actions in the most threatening terms, turning miscalculations and misunderstandings into crises. A U.S. public that had suffered through nearly two decades of economic depression and war reacted to international problems with frustration and anger. The emotional burdens of the Cold War warped and narrowed a generation of American political life around the requirements of anticommunism.

## THE END OF THE GRAND ALLIANCE

The Yalta Conference of February 1945 had recognized military realities by marking out rough spheres of influence. The Western allies had the better of the bargain. Defeated Italy and Japan, whose reconstruction was firmly in Western hands, had far greater economic potential than Soviet-controlled Bulgaria, Romania, or Hungary. In addition, the British, French, and American occupation zones in western Germany held more people and industrial potential than the Russian zone in eastern Germany.

As the victorious powers tried to put their broad agreements into operation, they argued bitterly about Germany and eastern Europe. Was the Soviet Union to dominate eastern Europe as its protective buffer, or was the region to be open to Western economic and political influence? For Poland, Truman and his advisers claimed that Yalta had assumed open elections on the American model. The Soviet Union claimed that Yalta had ensured that any Polish government would be friendly to Soviet interests and acted to guarantee that this would be so.

Facing Soviet intransigence over eastern Europe, Truman decided that the United States should "take the lead in running the world in the way the world ought to be run." One technique was economic pressure. The State Department "mislaid" a Soviet request for redevelopment loans. The United States and Britain objected to Soviet plans to take industrial equipment and raw materials from the western occupation zones in Germany, compensation that the Soviets thought they had been promised.

The United States also tried to involve the Soviet Union and eastern Europe in new international organizations. The Senate approved American membership in the newly organized United Nations (UN) with only two opposing votes, a sharp contrast to its rejection of the League of Nations in 1920. The Washington-based **International Monetary Fund (IMF)** and the **World Bank** were designed to revive international trade. The IMF stabilized national currencies against the short-term pressures of international trade. The World Bank drew on the resources of member nations to make economic development loans to governments for such projects as new dams or agricultural modernization. These organizations ensured that the reviving world economy would revolve around the industrial and technological power of the United States, and they continue to dictate the economic policy of many developing nations into the twenty-first century.

In 1946, the United States presented a plan in the United Nations to control atomic energy. Bernard Baruch suggested that an international agency should oversee all uranium production and research on atomic explosives. The Baruch plan emphasized enforcement and inspections that would have opened the Soviet nuclear effort to American interference, an unacceptable prospect for a nation trying to catch up with the United States by building its own atomic bombs.

While UN delegates debated the future of atomic energy, American leaders were becoming convinced of Soviet aggressiveness. In February 1946, George Kennan, a senior American diplomat in Moscow, sent a "long telegram" to the State Department. He depicted a Soviet Union driven by expansionist Communist ideology. The Soviets, he argued, would constantly probe for weaknesses in the capitalist world. The best response was firm resistance to protect the Western heartlands.

Truman's foreign-policy advisers shared the belief in an aggressive Soviet Union, and the president himself saw the world as a series of either-or choices. Added to military apprehension were worries about political and economic competition. Communist parties in war-ravaged Europe and Japan were exploiting discontent. In Asia and Africa, the allegiance of nationalists who were fighting for independence from European powers remained in doubt. America's leaders worried that much of the Eastern Hemisphere might fall under Soviet control.

Were Truman and his advisers right about Soviet intentions? The evidence is mixed. In their determination to avoid another Munich, Truman and his foreign-policy circle ignored examples of Soviet caution and conciliation. The Soviets withdrew troops from Manchuria in northern China and acquiesced in America's control of defeated Japan. They allowed a neutral but democratic government in Finland and technically free elections in Hungary and Czechoslovakia (although it was clear that Communists would do well there). They demobilized much of their huge army and reduced their forces in eastern Europe.

However, the Soviet regime also acted to justify American fears. The Soviet Union could not resist exerting influence in the Middle East. It pressured Turkey to give it partial control of the exit from the Black Sea. It retained troops in northern Iran until warned out by the United States. The Soviets were ruthless in support of Communist control in Eastern Europe in 1946 and 1947; they aided a Communist takeover in Bulgaria, backed a coup in Romania, and undermined the last non-Communist political opposition in Poland. U.S. policymakers read these Soviet actions as a rerun of Nazi aggression and determined not to let a new totalitarian threat undermine Western power.

## THE TRUMAN DOCTRINE AND THE MARSHALL PLAN

Whatever restraint the Soviet Union showed was too late or too little. Early in 1947, Truman and his advisers acted decisively. The British could no longer afford to back the Greek government that was fighting a civil war against Communists, and U.S. officials feared that a Communist takeover in Greece would threaten the stability of Italy, France, and the Middle East. Truman coupled his case for intervention in Greece with an appeal for aid to neighboring Turkey, which lived under the shadow of the Soviet Union. On March 12, he told Congress that the United States faced a "fateful hour" and requested $400 million to fight Communism in Greece and Turkey and secure the free world. Congress agreed, and the United States became the dominant power in the eastern Mediterranean.

Framing the specific request was a sweeping declaration that became known as the **Truman Doctrine.** The president pledged to use U.S. economic power to help free nations everywhere resist internal subversion or aggression. "It must be the policy of the

George F. Kennan, *Long Telegram* (1946)

Clark Clifford, *Memorandum to President Truman* (1946)

Henry Wallace, *Letter to President Truman* (1946)

**Truman Doctrine**   President Harry Truman's statement in 1947 that the United States should assist other nations that were facing external pressure or internal revolution.

Harry S Truman, *The Truman Doctrine* (1947)

George Marshall, *The Marshall Plan* (1947)

**Marshall Plan**  Secretary of State George C. Marshall's European Recovery Plan of June 5, 1947, committing the United States to help in the rebuilding of post-World War II Europe.

**WHERE TO LEARN MORE**

★ General Douglas MacArthur Memorial, Norfolk, Virginia.
www.macarthurmemorial.org

## QUICK REVIEW

### Post-war Foreign Policy

- Truman launched the nation into a global battle against communism.
- The U.S. pledged to help countries that faced external pressure or internal revolution.
- The U.S. played a decisive role in the rebuilding of Europe.

George F. Kennan, *Containment* (1947)

**containment**  The policy of resisting further expansion of the Soviet bloc through diplomacy and, if necessary, military action, developed in 1947–1948.

United States," he said, "to support free peoples who are resisting attempted subjugation by armed minorities or by outside pressures. . . . I believe that our help should be primarily through economic and financial aid, which is essential to economic stability and orderly political processes."

Meanwhile, Europe was sliding toward chaos. Germany was close to famine after the bitter winter of 1946–1947. Western European nations were bankrupt and unable to import raw materials for their factories. Overstressed medical systems could no longer control tuberculosis and other diseases. Communist parties had gained in Italy, France, and Germany.

The U.S. government responded with unprecedented economic aid. Secretary of State George C. Marshall announced the European Recovery Plan on June 5, 1947. What the press quickly dubbed the **Marshall Plan** committed the United States to help rebuild Europe. The United States invited Soviet and eastern European participation, but under terms that would have reduced Moscow's control over its satellite economies. The Soviets refused, fearing that the United States wanted to undermine its influence, and instead organized their eastern European satellites in their own association for Mutual Economic Assistance, or Comecon, in 1949. In western Europe, the Marshall Plan was a success. Aid totaled $13.5 billion over four years. It met many of Europe's economic needs and quieted class conflict. The Marshall Plan expanded American influence through cooperative efforts. Because Europeans spent much of the aid on U.S. goods and machinery, and because economic recovery promised markets for U.S. products, business and labor both supported it. In effect, the Marshall Plan created an "empire by invitation," in which Americans and Europeans jointly planned Europe's recovery.

U.S. policy in Japan followed the pattern set in Europe. As supreme commander of the Allied Powers, General Douglas MacArthur acted as Japan's postwar dictator. He tried to change the values of the old war-prone Japan through social reform, democratization, and demilitarization. At the end of 1947, however, the United States decided that democracy and pacifism could go too far. Policymakers were fearful of economic collapse and political chaos, just as in Europe. The "reverse course" in occupation policy aimed to make Japan an economic magnet for other nations in East Asia, pulling them toward the American orbit and away from the Soviet Union.

George Kennan summed up the new American policies in the magazine *Foreign Affairs* in July 1947. Kennan argued that the Soviet leaders were committed to a long-term strategy of expanding Communism. The proper posture of the United States, he said, should be an equally patient commitment to "firm and vigilant **containment** of Russian expansive tendencies." Kennan warned that the emerging Cold War would be a long conflict, with no quick fixes.

## SOVIET REACTIONS

The bold American moves in the first half of 1947 put the Soviet Union on the defensive. In response, Soviet leaders orchestrated strenuous opposition to the Marshall Plan by French and Italian Communists. East of the Iron Curtain, Hungarian Communists expelled other political parties from a coalition government. Bulgarian Communists shot opposition leaders. Romania, Bulgaria, and Hungary signed defense pacts with the Soviet Union.

In early 1948, the Soviets targeted Czechoslovakia. For three years, a neutral coalition government there on the model of Finland had balanced trade with the West with a foreign policy friendly to the Soviet Union. In February 1948, while Russian forces assembled on the Czech border, local Communists took advantage of political bumbling by other members of the governing coalition. Taking control through a technically legal process, they pushed aside Czechoslovakia's democratic leadership and turned the nation into a dictatorship and Soviet satellite within a week.

The climax of the Soviet reaction came in divided Berlin, located 110 miles inside the Soviet Union's East German occupation zone. The city was divided into four sectors: one controlled by the Soviets and three by the United States, Britain, and France. On June 4, 1948, Soviet troops blockaded surface traffic into Berlin, cutting off the U.S., British, and French sectors. The immediate Soviet aim was to block Western plans to merge their three German occupation zones into an independent federal republic (West Germany). Rather than abandon 2.5 million Berliners or shoot their way through, the Western nations responded to the **Berlin blockade** by airlifting supplies to the city. Stalin decided not to intercept the flights. After 11 months, the Soviets abandoned the blockade, making the Berlin airlift a triumph of American resolve.

## AMERICAN REARMAMENT

The coup in Czechoslovakia and the Berlin blockade shocked American leaders and backfired on the Soviets. The economic assistance strategy of 1947 now looked inadequate. Congress responded in 1948 by reinstating the military draft and increasing defense spending.

The United States had already begun to modernize and centralize its national security apparatus, creating the institutions that would run foreign policy in the second half of the century. The National Security Act of July 1947 created the **Central Intelligence Agency (CIA)** and the **National Security Council (NSC).** The CIA handled intelligence gathering and covert operations. The NSC assembled top diplomatic and military advisers in one committee. In 1949, legislation also created the Department of Defense to oversee the army, navy, and air force (independent from the army since 1947). The civilian secretary of defense soon began to exercise influence on foreign policy equal to that of the secretary of state.

In April 1949, ten European nations, the United States, and Canada signed the North Atlantic Treaty as a mutual defense pact. American commitments to the **North Atlantic Treaty Organization (NATO)** included military aid and the deployment of U.S. troops in western Europe. After 1955, its counterpart would be the Warsaw Pact for mutual defense among the Soviet Union and its European satellites.

Two years later, the United States signed similar but less comprehensive agreements in the western Pacific: the ANZUS Pact with Australia and New Zealand and a new treaty with the Philippines. Taken together, peacetime rearmament and mutual defense pacts amounted to a revolution in American foreign policy.

**Berlin blockade**   Three-hundred-day Soviet blockade of land access to United States, British, and French occupation zones in Berlin, 1948–1949.

**Central Intelligence Agency (CIA)** Agency established in 1947 that coordinates the gathering and evaluation of military and economic information on other nations.

**National Security Council (NSC)** The formal policymaking body for national defense and foreign relations, created in 1947 and consisting of the president, the secretary of defense, the secretary of state, and others appointed by the president.

**North Atlantic Treaty Organization (NATO)**   Organization of ten European countries, Canada, and the United States whom together formed a mutual defense pact in April, 1949.

**From Then to Now Online**
*NATO*

# COLD WAR AND HOT WAR

The first phase of the Cold War reached a crisis in the autumn of 1949. Two key events seemed to tilt the world balance against the United States and its allies. In September, Truman announced that the Soviet Union had tested its own atomic bomb. A month later, the Communists under Mao Zedong (Mao Tse-tung) took power in China. The following summer, civil war in Korea sucked the United States into a fierce war with Communist North Korea and China.

**HOW DID** the Korean War shape American domestic politics?

## THE NUCLEAR SHADOW

Experts in Washington had known that the Soviets were working on an A-bomb, but the news dismayed the average citizen. As newspapers and magazines scared their readers with artists' renditions of the effects of an atomic bomb on New York or Chicago, the shock tilted U.S. nuclear policy toward military uses. In 1946, advocates of civilian control had won a small victory when Congress established the Atomic Energy Commission (AEC). The

Berlin was still a devastated city in 1948. When the Soviet Union closed off ground access to the British, French, and American occupation zones, the city became a symbol of the West's Cold War resolve. Allied aircraft lifted in food, fuel, and other essentials for West Berliners for nearly a year until the Soviets ended the blockade.

AEC tried to balance research on atomic power with continued testing of new weapons. Now Truman told the AEC to double the output of fissionable uranium and plutonium for "conventional" nuclear weapons. A more momentous decision soon followed. Truman decided in January 1950 to authorize work on the "super" bomb—the thermonuclear fusion weapon that would become the hydrogen bomb (H-bomb).

Nuclear weapons proliferated in the early 1950s. The United States repeatedly tested nuclear fission weapons in Nevada and exploded the first hydrogen bomb in the South Pacific in November 1952. Releasing 100 times the energy of the Hiroshima bomb, the detonation tore a mile-long chasm in the ocean floor. Great Britain became the third nuclear power in the same year. The Soviet Union tested its own hydrogen bomb only nine months after the United States.

The nuclear arms race and the gnawing fear of nuclear war multiplied the apprehensions of the Cold War. Under the guidance of the Federal Civil Defense Administration, Americans learned that they should always keep a battery-powered radio and tune to 640 or 1240 on the AM dial for emergency information when they heard air raid sirens. Schoolchildren learned to hide under their desks when they saw the blinding flash of a nuclear detonation.

More insidiously, nuclear weapons development generated new environmental and health problems. Soldiers were exposed to posttest radiation with minimal protection. Nuclear tests in the South Pacific dusted fishing boats with radioactivity and forced

## QUICK REVIEW

### Nuclear Weapons

- Truman ordered in the Atomic Energy Commission to double the production of materials for nuclear weapons.
- The U.S. began work on the hydrogen bomb.
- The U.S. tested the first hydrogen bomb in 1952.

islanders to abandon contaminated homes. Las Vegas promoted tests in southern Nevada as tourist attractions, but radioactive fallout contaminated large sections of the West and increased cancer rates among "downwinders" in Utah. Weapons production and atomic experiments contaminated vast tracts in Nevada, Washington, and Colorado and left huge environmental costs for later generations.

## THE COLD WAR IN ASIA

Communist victory in China's civil war was as predictable as the Soviet nuclear bomb but no less controversial. The collapse of Jiang Jieshi's Nationalist regime was nearly inevitable, given its corruption and narrow support. Nevertheless, Americans looked for a scapegoat when Jiang's anti-Communist government and remnants of the Nationalist army fled to the island of Taiwan off China's southern coast.

Advocates for Jiang, mostly conservative Republicans from the Midwest and West, were certain that Truman's administration had done too little. Critics looked for scapegoats. Foreign Service officers who had honestly analyzed the weakness of the Nationalists were accused of Communist sympathies and hounded from their jobs. The results were tragedy for those unfairly branded as traitors and damage to the State Department, a weakness that would haunt the United States as it became entangled in southeast Asia in the 1950s and 1960s.

## NSC-68 AND AGGRESSIVE CONTAINMENT

The turmoil of 1949 led to a comprehensive statement of American strategic goals. In April 1950, the State Department prepared a sweeping report known as **National Security Council Paper 68 (NSC-68).** The document described a world divided between the forces of "slavery" and "freedom" and assumed that the Soviet Union was actively aggressive, motivated by greed for territory and a "fanatic faith" in Communism. To defend civilization itself, said the experts, the United States should use as much force as needed to resist Communist expansion anywhere and everywhere.

The authors of NSC-68 intended to extend the Truman Doctrine and convince Americans of the threat of the Cold War. They also thought in terms of military solutions. In the original containment policy, Truman and his advisers had hoped to contain the Soviets by diplomacy and by integrating the economies of Europe and Japan with that of the United States. Now that the Soviets had the atomic bomb, however, the American atomic shield might be neutralized. Instead, NSC-68 argued that the United States needed to press friendly nations to rearm and make its former enemies into military allies. It also argued that the nation needed expensive conventional forces to defend Europe on the ground and to react to crises as a "world policeman." NSC-68 thus advocated nearly open-ended increases in the defense budget (which, in fact, tripled between 1950 and 1954).

The thinking behind the report led the United States to approach the Cold War as a military competition and to view political changes in Africa and Asia as parts of a Soviet plan. The need for a flexible military response became the centerpiece of a U.S. policy of active intervention that led eventually to the jungles of Vietnam in the 1960s. And the report's implied strategy of bankrupting the Communists through competitive defense spending helped destroy the Soviet Union at the end of the 1980s.

## WAR IN KOREA, 1950–1953

The success of Mao and the Chinese Communists forced the Truman administration to define national interests in eastern Asia and the western Pacific. Most important was Japan, still an industrial power despite its devastating defeat. The United States had

*National Security Council Memorandum Number 68* (1950)

**National Security Council Paper 68 (NSC-68)**   Policy statement that committed the United States to a military approach to the Cold War.

**QUICK REVIEW**

**American Strategy**

◆ U.S. experts believed that America needed to use force to oppose communism around the world.

◆ They argued that the U.S. should pressure allies to rearm.

◆ They argued for the introduction of conventional forces in Europe.

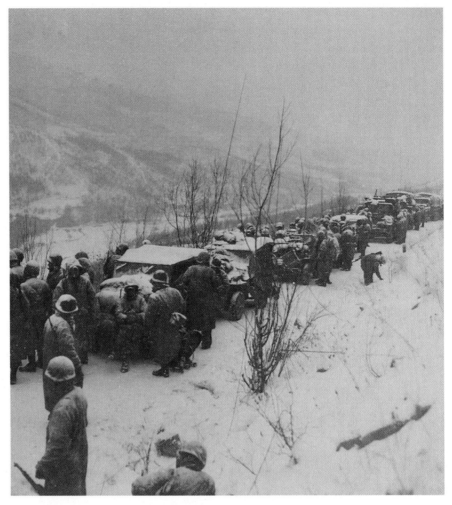

United Nation forces in Korea fought the weather as well as Communist North Koreans and Chinese. Baking summer heat alternated with fierce winters. Snow and cold were a major help to the Chinese when they surprised United States forces in November 1950 and drove American troops such as these southward.

denied the Soviet Union any part in the occupation of Japan in 1945 and had shaped a more democratic nation that would be a strong and friendly trading partner. Protected by American armed forces, Japan would be part of a crescent of offshore strong points that included Alaska, Okinawa, the Philippines, Australia, and New Zealand.

Two questions remained at the start of 1950. One was the future of Taiwan and the remnants of Jiang's regime. Some American policymakers wanted to defend Jiang against the Communists. Others assumed that his tattered forces would collapse and allow Mao to complete the Communist takeover of Chinese territory. The other question was Korea, whose own civil war would soon bring the world to the brink of World War III.

The Korean peninsula is the closest point on the Asian mainland to Japan. With three powerful neighbors—China, Russia, and Japan—Korea had always had to fight for its independence. From 1910 to 1945, it was an oppressed colony of the Japanese Empire. As World War II ended, Soviet troops moved down the peninsula from the north and American forces landed in the south, creating a situation similar to that in Germany. The 38th parallel, which Russians and Americans set as the dividing line between their zones of occupation, became a *de facto* border. The United States in 1948 recognized an independent South Korea, with its capital at Seoul, under a conservative government led by Syngman Rhee. Rhee's support came from large landowners and from a police force trained by the Japanese before 1945. The Soviets recognized a separate North Korea, whose Communist leader, Kim Il Sung, advocated radical social and political change. Both leaders saw the 38th parallel as a temporary barrier and hoped to unify all Koreans under their own rule. Each crushed political dissent and tried to undermine the other with economic pressure and commando raids.

As early as 1947, the United States had decided that Korea was not essential to American military strategy. Planners assumed that U.S. air power in Japan could neutralize unfriendly forces on the Korean peninsula. In January 1950, Secretary of State Dean Acheson carefully excluded Korea from the primary "defensive perimeter" of the United States but kept open the possibility of international guarantees for Korean security.

On June 25, 1950, North Korea, helped by Soviet equipment and Chinese training, attacked South Korea. The invasion began the **Korean War,** which lasted until 1953 (see Map 27–2). Truman and Acheson believed that Moscow lay behind the invasion. In fact, Kim originated the invasion plan because he seemed to be losing the civil war in the south, and he spent a year persuading Stalin to agree to it. Stalin hoped that the conquest of South Korea would force Japan to sign a favorable treaty with the USSR.

American leaders thought that the explosion of a hot war after five years of world tension demanded a military response. As the South Korean army collapsed, Truman committed American ground troops from Japan on June 30. The United States also had the good fortune of securing an endorsement from the United Nations. Because the Soviet Union was boycotting the UN (hoping to force the seating of Mao's People's Republic of China in place of Jiang's government), it could not use its veto when the Security Council asked UN members to help South Korea. The Korean conflict remained officially a United Nations action. Although U.S. Generals Douglas MacArthur, Matthew Ridgway, and Mark Clark ran the show as the successive heads of the UN command, 21 other nations committed military resources in a true multinational coalition.

## THE POLITICS OF WAR

Fortunes in the first year of the Korean conflict seesawed three times. The first U.S. combat troops were outnumbered, outgunned, and poorly trained. They could not stop the North Koreans. By early August, the Americans clung to a narrow toehold around the port of Pusan on the tip of the Korean peninsula. As reinforcements arrived, however, MacArthur transformed the war with a daring amphibious counterattack at Inchon, 150 miles behind North Korean lines. The North Korean army was already overextended and exhausted. It collapsed and fled north.

The temptation to push across the 38th parallel and unify the peninsula under Syngman Rhee was irresistible. MacArthur and Washington officials disregarded warnings by China that it would enter the war if the United States tried to reunite Korea by force. U.S. and South Korean troops rolled north, drawing closer and closer to the boundary between North Korea and China.

MAP EXPLORATION  To explore an interactive version of this map, go to http://www.prenhall.com/goldfield5/map27.2

MAP 27–2   **The Korean War**   After rapid reversals of fortune in 1950 and early 1951, the war in Korea settled into stalemate. Most Americans agreed with the need to contain Communist expansion but found it deeply frustrating to fight for limited objectives rather than total victory.

**Was a** stalemate the inevitable end to the Korean War? Why or why not?

**Korean War**  Pacific war started on June 25, 1950, when North Korea, helped by Soviet equipment and Chinese training, attacked South Korea.

Chinese forces attacked MacArthur's command in late October but then disappeared. MacArthur dismissed the attacks as a token gesture. In fact, they were a final warning. On November 26, the Chinese struck the overextended American columns. They had massed 300,000 troops without detection by American aviation. Their assault drove the UN forces into a two-month retreat that again abandoned Seoul.

Despite his glaring mistake, MacArthur remained in command until he publicly contradicted national policy. In March 1951, with the UN forces again pushing north, Truman prepared to offer a ceasefire that would have preserved the separate nations of South and North Korea. MacArthur tried to preempt the president by demanding that China admit defeat or suffer the consequences. He then published a direct attack on the administration's policy of limiting the Asian war to ensure the security of Europe. President Truman had no choice. To protect civilian control of the armed forces, he relieved MacArthur of his command on April 11, 1951.

In Korea itself, U.S. and South Korean forces stabilized a strong defensive line that cut diagonally across the 38th parallel. Here the conflict settled into trench warfare. What had started as a civil war was now an international conflict between the two sides in the larger Cold War.

Stabilization of the Korean front ushered in two years of truce negotiations beginning in July 1951, for none of the key actors wanted a wider war. Negotiations stalled over thousands of Chinese prisoners of war who might not want to return to China. The political decision to turn free choice for POWs into a symbol of resistance to Communism left Truman's administration bogged down in a grinding war. Nearly half of the 140,000 U.S. casualties came after the truce talks started. The war was a decisive factor behind the Republican victory in the November 1952 elections and dragged on until June 1953, when an armistice returned the peninsula roughly to its prewar political division, a situation that endured into the twenty-first century.

**Consequences of the Korean War.**   The war in Korea was a preview of Vietnam 15 years later. American leaders propped up an undemocratic regime to defend democracy. Both North Koreans and South Koreans engaged in savage political reprisals as the battlefront shifted back and forth. American soldiers found it hard to distinguish between allied and enemy Koreans. American emphasis on massive firepower led U.S. forces to demolish entire villages to kill single snipers. The air force tried to break North Korean resistance by pouring bombs on cities, power stations, factories, and dams; General Curtis LeMay estimated that the bombings killed a million Koreans.

The Korean War had global consequences. It helped to legitimize the United Nations and set a precedent for its peace-keeping role in places like the Middle East. In Washington, it confirmed the ideas underlying NSC-68, with its call for the United States to expand its military and to lead an anti-Communist alliance. Two days after the North Korean invasion, President Truman ordered the Seventh Fleet to interpose between mainland China and the Nationalist Chinese on Taiwan, a decision that guaranteed 20 years of hostility between the United States and China. In the same month, the United States began to aid France's struggle to retain control over its Southeast Asian colony of Indochina, which included Laos, Cambodia, and Vietnam.

In Europe, the United States now pushed to rearm West Germany as part of a militarized NATO and sent troops to Europe as a permanent defense force. It increased military aid to European governments and secured a unified command for the national forces allocated to NATO, a step that made West German rearmament acceptable to other nations of western Europe that remembered 1940. Rearmament also stimulated German economic recovery and bound West Germany to the political and economic institutions of the North Atlantic nations. In 1952, the European Coal and Steel

**QUICK REVIEW**

**Impact of the Korean War**

◆ Preview of American involvement in Vietnam 15 years later.

◆ Helped legitimize the UN.

◆ Confirmed the analysis of NSC-68 in the minds of many American officials.

Community marked an important step toward economic cooperation that would evolve into the European Union by the end of the century. Dwight Eisenhower, who had led the Western allies in the invasion of France and Germany, became the new NATO commander in April 1951; his appointment symbolized the American commitment to western Europe.

# THE SECOND RED SCARE

The Korean War reinforced the second Red Scare, an assault on civil liberties that stretched from the mid-1940s to the mid-1950s and dwarfed the Red Scare of 1919–1920. The Cold War fanned fears of Communist subversion on American soil. Legitimate concerns about espionage mixed with suspicions that Communist sympathizers in high places were helping Stalin and Mao. The scare was also a weapon that the conservative wing of the Republican Party used against the men and women who had built Roosevelt's New Deal (see Overview, The Second Red Scare).

**WHY DID** fear of communism escalate in the years following World War II?

Efforts to root out suspected subversives operated on three tracks. National and state governments established loyalty programs to identify and fire suspect employees. The courts punished members of suspect organizations. Congressional and state legislative investigations followed the whims of committee chairs. Anti-Communist crusaders often relied on dubious evidence and eagerly believed the worst. They also threatened basic civil liberties.

## THE COMMUNIST PARTY AND THE LOYALTY PROGRAM

The Communist Party in the United States was in rapid decline as a political factor after World War II. Nevertheless, Republicans used Red-baiting as a campaign. In 1944 they tried to frighten voters about "commydemocrats" by linking FDR, CIO labor unions, and Communism. Democrats slung their own mud by trying to convince voters that Hitler preferred the Republicans. Two years later, Republican campaigners told the public that the basic choice was "between Communism and Republicanism." Starting a 30-year political career, a young navy veteran named Richard Nixon won a southern California congressional seat by hammering on his opponent's connections to supposedly Communist-dominated organizations.

President Truman responded to the Republican landslide with Executive Order 9835 in March 1947, initiating a loyalty program for federal employees. It authorized the attorney general to prepare a list of "totalitarian, Fascist, Communist, or subversive" organizations and made membership or even "sympathetic association" with such groups grounds for dismissal. The loyalty program applied to approximately 8 million Americans working for the federal government or defense contractors; similar state laws affected another 5 million.

*Documents*

*The Truman Loyalty Order* (1947)

Federal employees worked under a cloud of fear. Would the cooperative store they had once patronized or the protest group they had joined in college suddenly appear on the attorney general's list? Would someone complain that they had disloyal books on their shelves? Loyalty boards asked about religion, racial equality, and a taste for foreign films. They also tried to identify homosexuals, who were thought to be targets for blackmail by foreign agents. The loyalty program resulted in 1,210 firings and 6,000 resignations under Truman and comparable numbers during Dwight Eisenhower's first term from 1953 to 1956.

## NAMING NAMES TO CONGRESS

Congress was even busier than the executive branch. The congressional hunt for subversives had its roots in 1938, when Congressman Martin Dies, a Texas Democrat,

## OVERVIEW  The Second Red Scare

| Type of Anti-Communist Effort | Key Tools | Results |
|---|---|---|
| Employee loyalty programs | U.S. attorney general's list of subversive organizations | Thousands of federal and state workers fired, careers damaged |
| Congressional investigations | HUAC | Employee blacklists, investigation of writers and intellectuals, Hollywood Ten |
| | McCarran Committee Army-McCarthy hearings | |
| Criminal prosecutions | Trials for espionage and conspiracy to advocate violent overthrow of the U.S. government | Convictions of Communist Party leaders (1949), Alger Hiss (1950), and Rosenbergs (1951) |

**House Un-American Activities Committee (HUAC)** Originally intended to ferret out pro-Fascists, it later investigated "un-American propaganda" that attacked constitutional government.

Ronald Reagan, *Testimony Before the House Un-American Activities Committee* (1947)

created the Special Committee on Un-American Activities. Originally intended to ferret out pro-Fascists, the Dies Committee evolved into the permanent **House Committee on Un-American Activities (HUAC)** in 1945. It investigated "un-American propaganda" that attacked constitutional government.

One of HUAC's juiciest targets was Hollywood. Hollywood's reputation for loose morals, foreign-born directors, Jewish producers, and left-leaning writers aroused the suspicions of many congressmen. HUAC sought to make sure that no un-American messages were being peddled through America's most popular entertainment.

When the hearings opened in October 1947, studio executives Jack Warner of Warner Brothers and Louis B. Mayer of MGM assured HUAC of their anti-Communism. So did the popular actors Gary Cooper and Ronald Reagan. By contrast, eight screenwriters and two directors—the so-called Hollywood Ten— refused to discuss their past political associations, citing the free-speech protections of the First Amendment to the Constitution. HUAC countered with citations for contempt of Congress. The First Amendment defense failed when it reached the Supreme Court, and the Ten went to jail in 1950. Other actors, writers, and directors found themselves on the Hollywood blacklist, banned from jobs where they might insert Communist propaganda into American movies.

At the start of 1951, the new Senate Internal Security Subcommittee went into action. The McCarran Committee, named for the Nevada senator who chaired it, targeted diplomats, labor union leaders, professors, and schoolteachers. Both committees turned their investigations into rituals. The real point was not to force personal confessions from witnesses but to badger them into identifying friends and associates who might have been involved in suspect activities.

State legislatures imitated Congress by searching for "Reducators" among college faculty in such states as Oklahoma, Washington, and California. Harvard apparently used its influence to stay out of the newspapers, cutting a deal in which the FBI fed it information about suspect faculty, whom the university quietly fired. More common was the experience of the economics professor fired from the University of Kansas City after testifying before the McCarran Committee. He found it hard to keep any job once his name had been in the papers. A local dairy fired him because it thought its customers might be uneasy having a radical handle their milk bottles.

### SUBVERSION TRIALS

In 1948, the Justice Department indicted the leaders of the American Communist Party under the Alien Registration Act of 1940. Eleven men and women were convicted in

## AMERICAN VIEWS

### Integrating the Army in Korea

Racial integration of the armed forces became official policy in 1948, but President Truman's directive was not fully implemented until after the war in Korea. Two veterans of that war—white G.I. Harry Summers and black officer Beverly Scott—recall some of the steps toward integration.

- **What** do these recollections say about the pervasiveness of racism in mid-century American life?
- **How** has the experience of minority soldiers changed from the 1950s to the 1990s?

**Harry Summers:** When they first started talking about integration, white soldiers were aghast. They would say, How can you integrate the army? How do you know when you go to the mess hall that you won't get a plate or a knife or a spoon that was used by a Negro? Or when you go to the supply room and draw sheets, you might get a sheet that a Negro had slept on? . . .

I remember a night when your rifle company was scheduled to get some replacements. I was in a three-man foxhole with one other guy, and they dropped this new replacement off at our foxhole. The other guy I was in the foxhole with was under a poncho, making coffee. It was bitterly cold. And pitch dark. He got the coffee made, and he gave me a drink, and he took a drink, and then he offered some to this new replacement, who we literally couldn't see, it was that dark.

And the guy said, "No, I don't want any."

"What the hell are you talking about, you don't want any? You got to be freezing to death. Here, take a drink of coffee."

"Well," he said, "you can't tell it now, but I'm black. And tomorrow morning when you find out I was drinking out of the same cup you were using, you ain't gonna be too happy."

Me and this other guy kind of looked at each other. "You silly son of a bitch," we told him, "here, take the goddam coffee."

**Beverly Scott:** The 24th Regiment was the only all-black regiment in the division, and as a black officer in an all-black regiment commanded by whites I was always super sensitive about standing my ground. Being a man. Being honest with my soldiers. . . .

Most of the white officers were good. Taken in the context of the times, they were probably better than the average white guy in civilian life. But there was still that patronizing expectation of failure. White officers came to the 24th Regiment knowing or suspecting or having been told that this was an inferior regiment.

[In September 1951, members of the regiment were integrated into other units.]

I was transferred to the 14th [Regiment] and right away I experienced some problems. People in the 14th didn't want anybody from the 24th. I was a technically qualified communications officer, which the 14th said they needed very badly, but when I got there, suddenly they didn't need any commo officers.

Then their executive officer said, "We got a rifle platoon for you. Think you can handle a rifle platoon?"

What the hell do you mean, can I handle a rifle platoon? I was also trained as an infantry officer. He know that. I was a first lieutenant, been in the army six years. . . . If I had been coming in as a white first lieutenant the question never would have been asked.

Source: Rudy Tomedi, *No Bugles, No Drums: An Oral History of the Korean War* (New York: John Wiley, 1993).

1949 of conspiring to advocate the violent overthrow of the United States government through their speech and publications.

The case of Alger Hiss soon followed. In 1948, a former Communist, Whittaker Chambers, named Hiss as a Communist with whom he had associated in the 1930s. Hiss, who had held important posts in the State Department, first denied knowing Chambers but then admitted to having known him under another name. He continued to deny any involvement with Communists and sued Chambers for slander. As proof, Chambers revealed microfilms that he had hidden inside a pumpkin on his Maryland farm, and Congressman Richard Nixon quickly announced the discovery. Tests seemed

Richard Nixon (right) and the chief investigator for the House Committee on Un-American Activities inspect microfilm of the "pumpkin papers." Hidden inside a pumpkin on the Maryland farm of committee informant Whittaker Chambers, the papers helped convict Alger Hiss of perjury. Nixon's role in pursuing Hiss launched a political career that took him to the White House.

to show that the "pumpkin papers" were State Department documents that had been copied on a typewriter Hiss had once owned. With the new evidence, the Justice Department indicted Hiss for perjury—lying under oath. A first perjury trial ended in deadlock, but a second jury convicted Hiss in January 1950.

Another important case was that of Julius and Ethel Rosenberg. In 1950, the British arrested nuclear physicist Klaus Fuchs, who confessed to passing atomic secrets to the Soviets when he worked at Los Alamos in 1944 and 1945. The "Fuchs spy ring" soon implicated the Rosenbergs, New York radicals of strong beliefs but limited sophistication. Convicted in 1951 on the vague charge of conspiring to commit espionage, they were sent to the electric chair in 1953 after refusing to buy a reprieve by naming other spies.

As with Alger Hiss, the government had a plausible but not airtight case. After their trial, the Rosenbergs became a cause for international protest. Their small children became pawns and trophies in political demonstrations, an experience recaptured in E. L. Doctorow's novel *The Book of Daniel* (1971). There is no doubt that Julius Rosenberg was a convinced Communist. It is likely that he was part of Soviet spy ring, but he probably did not pass atomic secrets. Ethel Rosenberg was charged, in the words of FBI director J. Edgar Hoover, "as a lever" to pressure her husband into naming his confederates.

## SENATOR MCCARTHY ON STAGE

The best-remembered participant in the second Red Scare was Senator Joseph McCarthy of Wisconsin. Crude, sly, and ambitious, McCarthy had ridden to victory in the Republican landslide of 1946. He burst into national prominence on February 9, 1950. In a rambling speech in Wheeling, West Virginia, he latched on to the issue of

Documents

Joseph R. McCarthy, *Speech Delivered to the Women's Club of Wheeling, West Virginia* (1950)

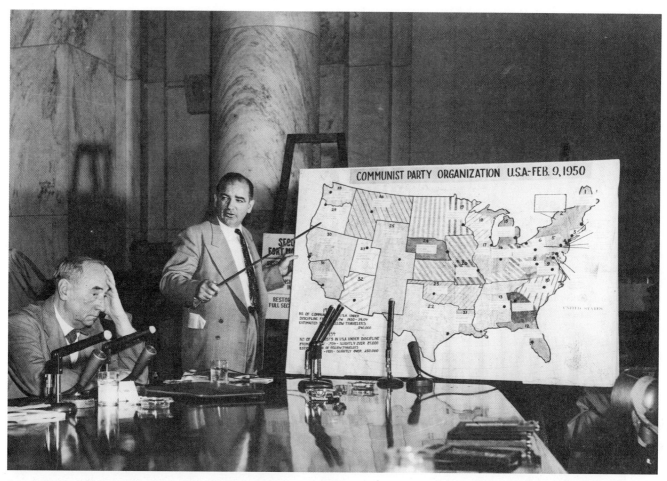

Senator Joe McCarthy used press releases and carefully managed congressional committee hearings to attack suspected Communists, although he had almost no hard information. At the Army-McCarthy hearings in June 1954, he clashed with attorney Joseph Welch. Here Welch listens as McCarthy points to Oregon on a map that supposedly showed Communist Party organization in the United States.

Communist subversion. Although no transcript of the speech survives, he supposedly stated, "I have here in my hand a list of 205 that were known to the Secretary of State as being members of the Communist Party and who, nevertheless, are still working and shaping the policy of the State Department." In the following days, the 205 Communists changed quickly to 57, to 81, to 10, to 116. McCarthy's rise to fame climaxed with an incoherent six-hour speech to the Senate. Over the next several years, his speeches were aimed at moving targets, full of multiple untruths. He threw out so many accusations, true or false, that the facts could never catch up.

The Senate disregarded McCarthy, but the public heard only the accusations, not the lack of evidence. Senators treated McCarthy as a crude outsider in their exclusive club, but voters in 1950 turned against his most prominent opponents. Liberal politicians ran for cover; conservatives were happy for McCarthy to attract media attention away from HUAC and the McCarran Committee. In 1951, McCarthy even called George Marshall, then serving as secretary of defense, an agent of Communism. The idea was ludicrous. Marshall was one of the most upright Americans of his generation, the architect of victory in World War II, and a key contributor to the stabilization of Europe. Nevertheless, McCarthy was so popular that the Republicans featured him at their 1952 convention and their presidential candidate, Dwight Eisenhower, conspicuously failed to defend Marshall, who had been chiefly responsible for Eisenhower's fast-track career.

*Documents*

Joseph McCarthy, *Telegram to President Truman following the Wheeling [W. Va.] Speech* (1950)

McCarthy's personal crudeness made him a media star but eventually undermined him. Given control of the Senate Committee on Government Operations in 1953, he investigated dozens of agencies from the Government Printing Office to the Army Signal Corps. Early in 1954, he investigated an army dentist with a supposedly subversive background. The back-and-forth confrontation led to two months of televised hearings. The cameras brought political debates into living rooms and put McCarthy's bullying style on trial. "Have you no decency?" asked the army's lawyer, Joseph Welch, at one point.

The end came quickly. McCarthy's "favorable" rating in the polls plummeted. The U.S. Senate finally voted 67 to 22 in December 1954 to condemn McCarthy for conduct "unbecoming a Member of the Senate." When he died in 1957, he had been repudiated by the Senate and ignored by the media that had built him up.

## UNDERSTANDING MCCARTHYISM

**McCarthyism** Anti-Communist attitudes and actions associated with Senator Joe McCarthy in the early 1950s, including smear tactics and innuendo.

The antisubversive campaign that everyone now calls **McCarthyism,** however, died a slower death. Legislation, such as the Internal Security Act (1950) and the Immigration and Nationality Act (1952), remained as tools of political repression. HUAC continued to mount investigations as late as the 1960s.

In retrospect, at least four factors made Americans afraid of Communist subversion. One was the legitimate concern about atomic spies. The Soviet Union had developed an extensive espionage network in the early 1940s. More than a few U.S. officials passed on secret information, although there was not the vast interlocking

American State department official Alger Hiss taking an oath before the House Committee on Un-American Activities in Washington in 1948. Hiss denied he was a member of a Communist cell, but was later convicted of perjury in 1950.

conspiracy that some critics feared. A second was an undercurrent of anti-Semitism and nativism, for many labor organizers and Communist Party members (like the Rosenbergs) had Jewish and eastern European backgrounds. Third was southern and western resentment of the nation's Ivy League elite. Most general, finally, was a widespread fear that the world was spinning out of control. Many people sought easy explanations for global tensions. It was basically reassuring if Soviet and Chinese Communist successes were the result of American traitors rather than of Communist strengths.

Partisan politics mobilized the fears and resentments into a political force. From 1946 through 1952, the conservative wing of the Republican Party used the Red Scare to attack New Dealers and liberal Democrats. HUAC, the McCarran Committee, and McCarthy were all tools for bringing down the men and women who had been moving the United States toward a more active government at home and abroad. The Republican elite used McCarthy until they won control of the presidency and Congress in 1952, and then abandoned him.

The broader goal of the second Red Scare was conformity of thought. Many of the professors and bureaucrats targeted for investigation had indeed been Communists or interested in Communism, usually in the 1930s and early 1940s. Most saw it as a way to increase social justice, and they sometimes excused the failures of Communism in the Soviet Union. Unlike the handful of real spies, however, they were targeted not for actions but for ideas. The investigations and loyalty programs were efforts to ensure that Americans kept any left-wing ideas to themselves.

# CONCLUSION

Despite the turmoil and injustice of the second Red Scare and deep worries about nuclear war, the United States emerged from the Truman years remarkably prosperous. It was also more secure from international threats than many nervous Americans appreciated. The years from 1946 to 1952 set the themes for a generation that believed that the United States could do whatever it set its mind to: end poverty, land an astronaut on the moon, thwart Communist revolutions in other countries. There was a direct line from Harry Truman's 1947 declaration that the United States would defend freedom around the world to John Kennedy's 1961 promise that the nation would bear any burden necessary to protect free nations from Communism. As the world moved slowly toward greater stability in the 1950s, Americans were ready for a decade of confidence.

# SUMMARY

**WHAT WAS** the catalyst for the economic boom that began in 1947?

**Launching the Great Boom** Americans feared demobilization would bring inflation and unemployment, but the immediate postwar years ushered in an economic expansion that would last a quarter century; the resulting prosperity would finance a military buildup and activist foreign policy. Veterans benefited from VA mortgages and the GI Bill of Rights; the need for family housing fueled a boom and suburbs expanded; the housing boom was a product of the consumer and baby booms. The first steps toward civil rights for African Americans were taken; the crusade for freedom abroad had contrasted with the racial discrimination faced at home.

**HOW WAS** Harry Truman able to win the 1948 presidential election?

**Truman, Republicans, and the Fair Deal** The economic gains of the postwar years propelled Americans toward the political center; after depression and war they wanted prosperity. In his campaign for a full term as president in 1948, Truman faced third-party candidates in addition to Republican Thomas Dewey. Truman appealed to average Americans and his victory astounded the pollsters. The Fair Deal showed that Americans liked what the New Deal had given them but were hesitant about major new initiatives.

**WHAT WERE** the origins of the Cold War?

**Confronting the Soviet Union** By 1947 the former allies were involved in a conflict that came to be known as the Cold War. Both sides assumed the other's ill will, spent vast amounts on military forces and atomic weapons, and competed for political advantage around the globe. As the "iron curtain" divided Europe, the Marshall Plan committed the United States to aid European recovery. The announcement of the Truman Doctrine brought Soviet reactions climaxing in the Berlin blockade; the formation of the CIA, NSC, and signing mutual defense pacts such as NATO amounted to a revolution in American foreign policy.

**HOW DID** the Korean War shape American domestic politics?

**Cold War and Hot War** The news that the Soviet Union and China had developed nuclear bombs helped begin the "arms race" and the fear of nuclear war multiplied the apprehensions of the Cold War. America's strategic goals were outlined in NSC-68: America would use force to counter communist aggression: The first use of this policy was in Korea. North Korea, helped by Soviet equipment and Chinese training, attacked South Korea. The Korean War, which lasted until 1953, had global consequences and was a preview of another war to come.

**WHY DID** fear of communism escalate in the years following World War II?

**The Second Red Scare** The Korean War reinforced the second Red Scare, an assault on civil liberties that dwarfed the Red Scare of 1919–1920. The Cold War fanned fears of Communist subversion on American soil. Legitimate concerns about espionage mixed with suspicions that Communist sympathizers in high places were helping China and the Soviet Union. Loyalty programs and the Congressional hunt for subversives such as that by Senator Joseph McCarthy showed how deep the fear of Communists was in the country.

# WHERE TO LEARN MORE

**Harry S Truman National Historical Site, Library, and Museum, Independence, Missouri.** The museum has exhibits on Truman's political career and U.S. history during his administration. Also in Independence is the Harry S Truman Courtroom and Office, with exhibits on his early career. **www.nps.gov/hstr**

**General Douglas MacArthur Memorial, Norfolk, Virginia.** The MacArthur Memorial in downtown Norfolk commemorates the career of a key figure in shaping the postwar world. **www.macarthurmemorial.org**

**United Nations Headquarters, New York, New York.** A tour of the United Nations complex in New York is a reminder of the new organizations for international cooperation that emerged from World War II. **www.un.org**

# STUDY RESOURCES

## PEARSON myhistorylab

For study resources for this chapter, go to www.myhistorylab .com and choose *The American Journey*. You will find a wealth of study and review material for this chapter, including pre- and post-tests, customized study plan, key term review flash cards, interactive map and document activities, and documents for analysis.

# REVIEW QUESTIONS

1. As described in the opening of the chapter, what housing choices were available after World War II? How did these choices reshape American cities? How did the postwar readjustment create a suburban society?

2. What were the key differences between Harry Truman and congressional Republicans about the legacy of the New Deal? Why did regulating labor unions become a central domestic issue in the late 1940s? Why did Truman manage to win the presidential election of 1948 despite starting as an underdog?

3. How did the postwar years expand opportunity for veterans and members of the working class? How did they limit opportunities for women? How did they begin to challenge racial inequities in American society?

4. What foreign policy priorities did United States set after 1945? To what extent did the United States achieve its most basic objectives? How did mutual mistrust fuel and deepen the Cold War?

5. How did the Cold War change character in 1949 and 1950? What were key actions by the Soviet Union and China, and how did the United States respond? What was the effect of the chaotic fighting in Korea on U.S. domestic politics and diplomacy?

6. What factors motivated an increasingly frantic fear of domestic subversion in the late 1940s and early 1950s? Who were the key actors in the second Red Scare? What was its long-term impact on American society?

7. How did the continuation and expansion of the nation's global commitments after 1945 affect life in the United States?

## KEY TERMS

**Berlin blockade** (p. 825)
**Central Intelligence Agency** (p. 825)
**Cold War** (p. 812)
**Containment** (p. 824)
**Council of Economic Advisers** (p. 814)
**Dixiecrats** (p. 818)
**GI Bill of Rights** (p. 815)
**House Committee on Un-American Activities (HUAC)** (p. 832)
**International Monetary Fund (IMF)** (p. 822)
**Korean War** (p. 829)
**Levittown** (p. 815)
**Marshall Plan** (p. 824)
**McCarthyism** (p. 836)
**National Security Council** (p. 825)
**National Security Council Paper 68 (NSC-68)** (p. 827)
**North Atlantic Treaty Organization (NATO)** (p. 825)
**Redlining** (p. 816)
**Taft-Hartley Act** (p. 814)
**Truman Doctrine** (p. 823)
**World Bank** (p. 822)

# 28

# The Confident Years

Singer Elvis Presley sings Hillbilly Heartbreak on stage in Hollywood, California during a performance in 1956.

WE INSIST!
MAX ROACH'S - FREEDOM NOW SUITE

FEATURING ABBEY LINCOLN
COLEMAN HAWKINS, OLATUNJI
CANDID

> *The first day I was able to enter Central High School [in Little Rock, Arkansas, September 23, 1957], what I felt inside was terrible, wrenching, awful fear. On the car radio I could hear that there was a mob. I knew what a mob meant and I knew that the sounds that came from the crowd were very angry. So we entered the side of the building, very, very fast. Even as we entered there were people running after us, people tripping other people. There has never been in my life any stark terror or any fear akin to that. I'd only been in the school a couple of hours and by that time it was apparent that the mob was just overrunning the school. Policemen were throwing down their badges and the mob was getting past the wooden sawhorses because the police would no longer fight their own in order to protect us. So we were all called into the principal's office, and there was great fear that we would not get out of this building. We were trapped. And I thought, Okay, so I'm going to die here, in school. . . . Even the adults, the school officials, were panicked, feeling like there was no protection. . . . [A] gentleman, who I believed to be the police chief, said . . . "I'll get them out." And we were taken to the basement of this place. And we were put into two cars, grayish blue Fords. And the man instructed the drivers, he said, "Once you start driving, do not stop." And he told us to put our heads down. This guy revved up his engine and he came up out of the bowels of this building, and as he came up, I could just see hands reaching across this car, I could hear the yelling, I could see guns, and he was told not to stop. "If you hit somebody, you keep rolling, 'cause the kids are dead." And he did just that, and he didn't hit anybody, but he certainly was forceful and aggressive in the way he exited this driveway, because people tried to stop him and he didn't stop. He dropped me off at home. And I remember saying, "Thank you for the ride," and I should've said, "Thank you for my life."*

Melba Patillo Beals, in Henry Hampton and Steve Frayer, eds., *Voices of Freedom: An Oral History of the Civil Rights Movement from the 1950s through the 1980s* (New York: Bantam, 1990).

### PEARSON myhistorylab

**Personal Journeys Online**

- **Diane Nash, Interview in Mathew Allman, *The New Negro*, 1961. The civil rights sit-in movement in Nashville in 1960.**

- **Suzette Miller, in Staughton Lynd, *Nonviolence in America*, 1966. Grass roots civil rights efforts in Mississippi in 1961.**

**MELBA PATTILLO** was one of the nine African American students who entered previously all-white Central High in the fall of 1957. Her enrollment in the high school, where she managed to last through a year of harassment and hostility, was a symbolic step in the journey toward greater racial equality in U.S. society.

Melba Pattillo's life after Little Rock also reveals something about the increasing economic opportunities available to most Americans. She graduated from San Francisco State University, earned a master's degree from Columbia University, and worked as a television reporter and writer. The prosperous years from 1953 to 1964 spread the economic promise of the 1940s across American society. Young couples could afford large families and new houses. Labor unions grew conservative because cooperation with big business offered immediate gains for their members.

Despite challenges at home and abroad, Americans were fundamentally confident during the decade after the Korean War. They expected corporations to use scientific research to craft new products for eager customers and medical researchers to conquer diseases. When the USSR challenged U.S. preeminence and launched the first artificial space satellite in 1957, Americans responded with shock followed by redoubled efforts to regain what they considered their rightful world leadership in science and technology. ◆

## CHRONOLOGY

| | |
|---|---|
| **1953** | CIA-backed coup returns Shah Reza Pahlevi to power in Iran. |
| | Soviet Union detonates hydrogen bomb. |
| **1954** | Vietnamese defeat the French; Geneva conference divides Vietnam. |
| | United States and allies form SEATO. |
| | Supreme Court decides *Brown v. Board of Education of Topeka*. |
| | CIA overthrows the government of Guatemala. |
| | China provokes a crisis over Quemoy and Matsu. |
| **1955** | Salk polio vaccine is announced. |
| | Black citizens boycott Montgomery, Alabama, bus system. |
| | Soviet Union forms the Warsaw Pact. |
| | AFL and CIO merge. |
| **1956** | Interstate Highway Act is passed. |
| | Soviets repress Hungarian revolt. |
| | Israel, France, and Britain invade Egypt. |
| **1957** | U.S. Army maintains law and order in Little Rock after violent resistence to integration of Central High School. |
| | Soviet Union launches *Sputnik,* world's first artificial satellite. |
| **1958** | United States and Soviet Union voluntarily suspend nuclear tests. |
| **1959** | Fidel Castro takes power in Cuba. |
| | Nikita Khrushchev visits the United States. |
| **1960** | U-2 spy plane shot down over Russia. |
| | Sit-in movement begins in Greensboro, North Carolina. |

| | |
|---|---|
| **1961** | Bay of Pigs invasion fails. |
| | Kennedy establishes the Peace Corps. |
| | Vienna summit fails. |
| | Freedom rides are held in the Deep South. |
| | Berlin crisis leads to construction of the Berlin Wall. |
| **1962** | John Glenn orbits the earth. |
| | Cuban missile crisis brings the world to the brink of nuclear war. |
| | Michael Harrington publishes *The Other America*. |
| **1963** | Civil rights demonstrations rend Birmingham. |
| | Civil rights activists march in Washington. |
| | Betty Friedan publishes *The Feminine Mystique*. |
| | Limited Test Ban Treaty is signed. |
| | Ngo Dinh Diem is assassinated in South Vietnam. |
| | President Kennedy is assassinated. |
| **1964** | Civil Rights Act is passed. |
| | Freedom Summer is organized in Mississippi. |
| | Office of Economic Opportunity is created. |
| | Gulf of Tonkin Resolution is passed. |
| | Wilderness Act marks new direction in environmental policy. |
| **1965** | Medical Care Act establishes Medicare and Medicaid. |
| | Elementary and Secondary Education Act extends direct federal aid to local schools. |
| | Selma-Montgomery march climaxes era of nonviolent civil rights demonstrations. |
| | Voting Rights Act suspends literacy tests for voting. |

# A DECADE OF AFFLUENCE

Americans in the 1950s believed in the basic strength of the United States. Television's *General Electric Theater* was third in the ratings in 1956–1957. Every week, its host, Ronald Reagan, a popular Hollywood lead from the late 1930s, stated, "At General Electric, progress is our most important product." It made sense to his viewers. Large, technologically sophisticated corporations were introducing new marvels: Orlon sweaters and Saran Wrap, long-playing records, and Polaroid cameras. As long as the United States defended free enterprise, Reagan told audiences on national speaking tours, the sky was the limit.

## WHAT'S GOOD FOR GENERAL MOTORS

Dwight Eisenhower presided over the prosperity of the 1950s. Both Democrats and Republicans had courted him as a presidential candidate in 1948. Four years later, he picked the Republicans because he wanted to make sure that the party remained committed to NATO and collective security in Europe rather than retreat into isolationism. He easily defeated the Democratic candidate, Adlai Stevenson, the moderately liberal governor of Illinois.

**Eisenhower and the politics of the middle.**    Over the next eight years, Eisenhower claimed the political middle for Republicans. Satisfied with postwar America, Eisenhower accepted much of the New Deal but saw little need for further reform. In a 1959 poll, liberals considered him a fellow liberal and conservatives thought him a conservative. Eisenhower's first secretary of defense, "Engine Charlie" Wilson, had headed General Motors. At his Senate confirmation hearing, he proclaimed, "For years, I thought what was good for the country was good for General Motors and vice versa." Wilson's statement captured a central theme of the 1950s. Not since the 1920s had Americans been so excited about the benefits of big business.

**The new prosperity.**    The economy in the 1950s gave Americans much to like. Between 1950 and 1964, output grew by a solid 3.2 percent per year.

American workers in the 1950s had more disposable income than ever before. Their productivity, or output per worker, increased steadily. Average compensation per hour of work rose faster than consumer prices in nine of eleven years from 1953 to 1964. Rising productivity made it easy for corporations to share gains with large labor unions. In turn, labor leaders lost interest in making radical changes in American society.

For members of minority groups with regular industrial and government jobs, the 1950s were also economically rewarding. Detroit, Dayton, Oakland, and other industrial cities offered them factory jobs at wages that could support a family. Black people worked through the Urban League, the National Association of Colored Women, and other race-oriented groups to secure fair-employment laws and jobs with large corporations. Many Puerto Rican migrants to New York found steady work in the Brooklyn Navy Yard. Mexican American families in San Antonio benefited from maintenance jobs at the city's military bases. Steady employment allowed black people and Latinos to build strong community institutions and vibrant neighborhood business districts.

However, there were never enough family-wage jobs for all of the African American and Latino workers who continued to move to northern and western cities. Many Mexican Americans were still migrant farm laborers and workers in nonunionized sweatshops. Minority workers were usually the first to suffer from the erosion of some industrial jobs and the shift of other jobs to new suburban factories that were isolated from minority neighborhoods. Black unemployment crept upward to twice the white rate, laying the seeds of frustration that would burst forth in the 1960s.

Native Americans faced equally daunting prospects. To cut costs and accelerate assimilation, Congress pushed the policy of termination between 1954 and 1962. The government sold tribal land and assets, distributed the proceeds among tribal members, and terminated its treaty relationship with the tribe. Applied to such tribes as the Klamaths in Oregon and the Menominees in Wisconsin, termination gave thousands of Indians one-time cash payments but cut them adrift from the security of tribal organizations.

## RESHAPING URBAN AMERICA

If Eisenhower's administration opted for the status quo on many issues, it nevertheless reshaped U.S. cities around an agenda of economic development. In 1954, Congress transformed the public housing program into urban renewal. Cities used federal funds to replace low-rent businesses and run-down housing on the fringes of their downtowns with new hospitals, civic centers, sports arenas, office towers, and luxury apartments.

**PEARSON**
**myhistorylab**
**Exploring America**
*The Consumer Society: 1950–1960*

Urban renewal temporarily revitalized older cities in the Northeast and Midwest that were already feeling the competition of the fast-growing South and West.

Only a decade later, the same cities would top the list of urban crisis spots, in part because of accumulating social costs from urban renewal. The bulldozers often leveled minority neighborhoods in the name of downtown expansion. Urban renewal displaced Puerto Ricans in New York, African Americans in Atlanta and Norfolk, Mexican Americans in Denver.

The Eisenhower administration also revolutionized American transportation. By the early 1950s, Americans were fed up with roads designed for Model A Fords: They wanted to enjoy their new V-8 engines and the 50 million new cars sold between 1946 and 1955. The solution was the **Federal Highway Act of 1956,** creating a national system of interstate and defense highways.

**Federal Highway Act of 1956**
Measure that provided federal funding to build a nationwide system of interstate and defense highways.

Although the first interstate opened in Kansas in 1956, most of the mileage came into use in the 1960s and 1970s. Interstates halved the time of city-to-city travel. They were good for General Motors, the steel industry, and the concrete industry, requiring the construction equivalent of 60 Panama Canals. The highways promoted long-distance trucking at the expense of railroads. They also wiped out hundreds of homes per mile when they plunged through large cities. As with urban renewal, the bulldozers most often plowed through African American or Latino neighborhoods, where land was cheap and white politicians could ignore protests. Some cities, such as Miami, used the highways as barriers between white and black neighborhoods.

Interstates accelerated suburbanization. The beltways or perimeter highways that began to ring most large cities made it easier and more profitable to develop new subdivisions and factory sites than to reinvest in city centers. Federal grants for sewers and other basic facilities further cut suburban costs. Continuing the pattern of the late 1940s, suburban growth added a million new single-family houses per year.

## COMFORT ON CREDIT

Prosperity transformed spending habits. The 1930s had taught Americans to avoid debt. The 1950s taught them to buy on credit. The value of consumer debt, excluding home mortgages, tripled from 1952 to 1964.

Daly City, south of San Francisco, typified the mass-produced suburbs that housed the growing postwar middle class. It was the inspiration for the satirical song, "Little Boxes."

## GLOBAL PERSPECTIVES

### CONSUMER SOCIETY IN EUROPE

In 1958, the French comedian Jacques Tati made the film Mon Oncle ("My Uncle"), depicting the plight of a befuddled middle-aged Frenchman trying to cope with the high-tech lifestyle of his sister and her businessman husband. Their house is angular and modern, unlike his rickety walk-up apartment. Their chairs are modern, low-slung, and uncomfortable. Their kitchen is full of sleek and mysterious appliances. Their money comes from a plastics factory whose production line also baffles the hapless hero.

The film was an early reaction to the headlong development of consumer society in western Europe. In the late 1940s, Europe was still a miserable place, with war damage to be repaired and shortages of basic goods. Fifteen years later, it was a showplace of prosperity and modern design. Both Italians and Germans talked about their "economic miracle." German industrial production rose by 250 percent in the 1950s, and the rest of western Europe was not far behind. Just as in the United States, a booming domestic economy raised wages and consumption.

Americans experienced the European boom through a wave of new, stylishly designed products that began to appear in upscale stores—household appliances from Germany, typewriters from Italy and Switzerland, textiles from Finland, elegant furniture from Denmark, sports cars from Germany, England, and Italy. The millionth Volkswagen Beetle rolled off the assembly line in 1955; the total number of Beetles eventually topped that of the Model T Ford. For average Europeans, the boom meant a new apartment or duplex in a suburban "new town," money to buy an automobile, and enough left over for a vacation. Meanwhile, new glass-sheathed office buildings shoved their way into old city centers.

By the early 1960s, European filmmakers could depict a continent that was no longer lagging behind the United States. One of the points of Ian Fleming's James Bond novels and films, such as Goldfinger (1964), was brand-name snobbery. Red Desert (1964) dramatized its story of personal alienation against a backdrop of Italian industry depicted in the stark primary colors of modern design. Blow-Up (1966) gave Americans a window into fashionable swinging England.

According to historian Lizabeth Cohen, the United States after World War II became a "consumer's republic" that defined mass consumption as the solution to social and economic problems. During America's confident years, western Europe was not far behind.

- How did European prosperity fit into the aims of U.S. foreign policy after World War II?

---

New forms of marketing facilitated credit-based consumerism. The first large-scale suburban shopping center was Northgate in Seattle, which assembled all the elements of the full-grown mall—small stores facing an interior corridor between anchor department stores and surrounded by parking. By the end of the decade, developers were building malls with 1 million square feet of shopping floor. At the start of the 1970s, the universal credit card (Visa, MasterCard) made shopping even easier.

Surrounding the new malls were the servants and symbols of America's car culture. Where cities of the early twentieth century had been built around public transportation—streetcars and subways—those of the 1950s depended on private automobiles. Interstate highways sucked retail business from small-town main streets to interchanges on the edge of town. By shopping along highways rather than downtown, suburban whites also opted to minimize contact with people of other races.

The spread of automobiles contributed to increased leisure travel. The tacit pact between large corporations and labor unions meant that more workers had two-week vacations and time to take to their families on the road. Between 1954 and 1963, the number of visits to National Parks doubled to more than 100 million and visits to National Forests nearly tripled. Route 66 from Chicago to Los Angeles was celebrated in song. On television from 1956 to 1963, variety show hostess Dinah Shore tied the nation's best-selling car to the appeal of vacationing as she belted out the jingle "Drive your Chevrolet through the USA, America's the greatest land of all."

## THE NEW FIFTIES FAMILY

Family life in the Eisenhower years departed from historic patterns. Prosperity allowed children to finish school and young adults to marry right after high school. Young women faced strong social pressure to pursue husbands rather than careers. In a decade when the popular press worried about "latent homosexuality," single men were suspect. The proportion of single adults reached its twentieth-century low in 1960. At all social levels, young people married quickly and had an average of three children spaced closely together, adding to the number of baby boomers whose needs would influence American society into the twenty-first century. Strong families, said experts, defended against Communism by teaching American values.

**The impact of television.**   Television was made to order for the family-centered fifties. By 1960, fully 87 percent of households had sets (see Figure 28–1). Popular entertainment earlier had been a communal activity; people saw movies as part of a group, cheered baseball teams as part of a crowd. TV was watched in the privacy of the home.

Situation comedies were the most successful programs. Viewers liked continuing characters who resolved everyday problems in half an hour. Most successful shows depicted the ideal of family togetherness. The families on *The Adventures of Ozzie and Harriet* (1952–1966), *Father Knows Best* (1954–1962), and *Leave It to Beaver* (1957–1962) were white, polite, and happy.

Middle class women in the 1950s faced conflicting pressures and messages. The popular media idealized the woman whose life revolved around her house and family. As this magazine cover suggests, however, that image was as much a myth as a reality. Despite real limitations on available careers, increasing numbers of women entered the labor force and made necessary contributions to their families' incomes—while daydreaming about getting help with never-ending household tasks.

*Day Dreaming* by Constantin Alajalov. © 1959 SEPS; Licensed by Curtis Publishing Co., Indianapolis, Ind. All rights reserved. www.curtispublishing.com

**Stay-at-home moms and working women.**   The 1950s extended the stay-at-home trend of the postwar years. Women gave up some of their earlier educational gains. Their share of new college degrees and professional jobs fell. Despite millions of new electrical appliances, the time spent on housework increased. Magazines proclaimed that proper families maintained distinct roles for dad and mom, and mom was urged to find fulfillment in a well-scrubbed house and children.

In fact, far from allowing women to stay home as housewives, family prosperity in the 1950s often depended on their earnings. The number of employed women reached new highs. By 1960, nearly 35 percent of all women held jobs, including 7.5 million mothers with children under 17 (see Figure 28–2). The pressures of young marriages, large families, and economic needs interacted to erode some of the assumptions behind the idealized family and laid the groundwork for dramatic social changes in the 1960s and 1970s.

**QUICK REVIEW**

**Family Life**

♦ Young women faced pressure to marry early and forego careers.

♦ Young people married young and had an average of three children.

♦ Television took on a central role in family life.

## INVENTING TEENAGERS

Teenagers in the 1950s joined adults as consumers of movies, clothes, and automobiles. Advertisers tapped and expanded the growing youth market by promoting a distinct "youth culture," an idea that became omnipresent in the 1960s and 1970s. Many cities matched their high schools to the social status of their students: college-prep curricula for

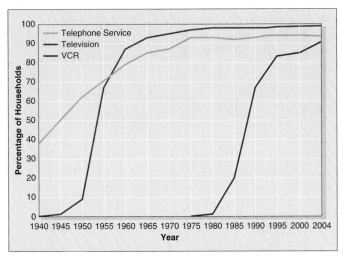

**FIGURE 28–1    Households with Telephones, Televisions, and VCRs**    American life in the twentieth century was transformed by a sequence of electronic consumer goods, from telephones to laptop computers. Entertainment items (televisions and videocassette recorders) spread even more rapidly among consumers than did the home telephone.
Data Source: *Statistical Abstract of the United States.*

**QUICK REVIEW**

**Teenagers**

◆ Teenagers became consumers in the 1950s.

◆ Advertisers directed their message at the youth market.

◆ Teenagers developed a shared culture.

middle-class neighborhoods, vocational and technical schools for future factory workers, and separate schools or tracks for African Americans and Latinos. In effect, the schools trained some children to be doctors and officers and others to be mechanics and enlisted men.

All teenagers shared rock-and-roll, a new music of the mid-1950s that adapted black urban rhythm-and-blues for a white mass market. Rhythm-and-blues was the hard-edged and electrified offspring of traditional blues and gospel music. In turn, rock music augmented its black roots by drawing vitality from poor white southerners familiar with country and western music (Buddy Holly, Elvis Presley), Hispanics (Richie Valens), and, in the 1960s, the British working class (the Beatles). Record producers played up the association between rock music and youthful rebellion.

Technological changes helped rock split off from adult pop music. Portable phonographs and 45-rpm records let kids listen to rock-and-roll in their own rooms. Car radios and transistor radios (first marketed around 1956) let disc jockeys reach teenagers outside the home. The result was separate music for young listeners and separate advertising for teenage consumers, the roots of the teenage mall culture of the next generation.

Outside the realm of mass entertainment, the Beats were coming together in San Francisco, where novelists like Jack Kerouac, poets like Gary Snyder, artists, and musicians drifted in and out of the City Lights bookstore. They attracted national attention in 1955 when Allen Ginsberg first chanted his poem "Howl," with its blistering attack on stifling materialism.

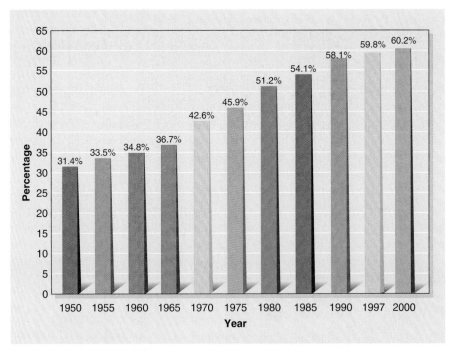

**FIGURE 28–2    Working Women as a Percentage of All Women, 1950–2000**    The proportion of American women who are part of the labor force (working or looking for work) has increased steadily since 1950, with the fastest increase between 1965 and 1985.

## TURNING TO RELIGION

Leaders from Dwight Eisenhower to FBI Director J. Edgar Hoover advocated churchgoing as an antidote for Communism. Regular church attendance grew from 48 percent of the population in 1940 to 63 percent in 1960. *Newsweek* talked about the "vast resurgence of Protestantism," and *Time* claimed that "everybody knows that church life is booming in the U.S."

The situation was more complex. Growing church membership looked impressive at first, but the total barely kept pace with population growth. In some ways, the so-called return to religion was new. Congress created new connections between religion and government when it added "under God" to the Pledge of Allegiance in 1954 and required currency to bear the phrase "In God We Trust" in 1955.

Radio and television preachers added a new dimension to religious life. Another strand in the religious revival was found in the revitalized evangelical and fundamentalist churches. During the 1950s, the theologically and socially conservative Southern Baptists passed the Methodists as the largest Protestant denomination. The evangelist Billy Graham continued the grand American tradition of the mass revival meeting.

African American churches were community institutions as well as religious organizations. With limited options for enjoying their success, the black middle class joined prestigious churches. Black congregations in northern cities swelled in the postwar years. Prestigious black churches thrived and often supported extensive social service programs. In southern cities, churches were centers for community pride and training grounds for the emerging civil rights movement.

Other important changes to come in American religion had their roots in the 1950s and early 1960s. Boundaries between many Protestant denominations blurred as church leaders emphasized national unity, paving the way for the ecumenical movement and denominational mergers. Supreme Court decisions sowed the seeds for later political.

In his first years as a star, Elvis Presley brought new energy to the world of popular music. Frank Driggs/Archive Photos

Movie actor James Dean died in an automobile accident shortly after completing *Rebel Without a Cause.* His tragic death and his depiction of alienated youth made him a symbol of dissatisfaction with the middle-class 1950s.

## THE GOSPEL OF PROSPERITY

Writers and intellectuals often marveled at the prosperity of Eisenhower's America. For scholars and journalists who had grown up during the Great Depression, the lack of economic hardship was the big story.

At times in these years, production and consumption outweighed democracy in the American message to the world. Officially, Americans argued that abundance was a natural by-product of a free society. In fact, it was easy to present prosperity as a goal in itself, as Vice President Richard Nixon did when he represented the United States at a technology exposition in Moscow in 1959. The U.S. exhibit included 21 models of automobiles and a complete six-room ranch house. In its "miracle kitchen," Nixon engaged Soviet Communist Party chairman Nikita Khrushchev in a carefully planned "kitchen debate." The vice president claimed that the "most important thing" for Americans was "the right to choose": "We have so many different manufacturers and many different kinds of washing machines so that the housewives have a choice."

## THE UNDERSIDE OF AFFLUENCE

The most basic criticism of the ideology of prosperity was the simplest—that affluence concealed vast inequalities. Michael Harrington had worked among the poor before writing *The Other America* (1962). He reminded Americans about the "underdeveloped nation" of 40 to 50 million poor people who had missed the last two decades of prosperity.

If Harrington found problems at the bottom of U.S. society, C. Wright Mills found dangers in the way that the Cold War distorted American society at the top. *The Power Elite* (1956) described an interlocking alliance of big government, big business, and the military. The losers in a permanent war economy, said Mills, were economic and political democracy. His ideas would reverberate in the 1960s during the Vietnam War.

Other critics targeted the alienating effects of consumerism and the conformity of homogeneous suburbs. Although much of the antisuburban rhetoric was based on intellectual snobbery rather than research, it represented significant dissent from the praise of affluence.

There was far greater substance to the increasing dissatisfaction among women, who faced conflicting images of the perfect woman in the media. On one side was the comforting icon of Betty Crocker, the fictional spokeswoman for General Mills who made housework and cooking look easy. On the other side were sultry sexpots like Marilyn Monroe and the centerfold women of *Playboy* magazine, which first appeared in 1953. Women wondered how to be both Betty and Marilyn. In 1963, Betty Friedan's book *The Feminine Mystique* recognized that thousands of middle-class housewives were seething behind their picture windows. It followed numerous articles in *McCall's, Redbook,* and the *Ladies' Home Journal* about the unhappiness of college-educated women who were expected to find total satisfaction in kids and cooking. Friedan repackaged the message of the women's magazines along with the results of a survey of her Smith College classmates, who were then entering their forties. What Friedan called "the problem that has no name" was a sense of personal emptiness.

**QUICK REVIEW**

**Critique of the Ideology of Prosperity**

◆ Some critics argued that affluence concealed inequality.

◆ Others were concerned about the alienating effects of consumerism.

◆ Many women became dissatisfied with their assigned role in society.

The United States exhibit at a technology exposition in Moscow in 1959 displayed a wide range of American consumer goods, from soft-drink dispensers to sewing machines. It included a complete six-room ranch house with an up-to-date kitchen where, in a famous encounter dubbed the "kitchen debate," Vice President Richard Nixon and Soviet Communist Party chairman Nikita Khrushchev disputed the merits of capitalism and Communism.

# FACING OFF WITH THE SOVIET UNION

Americans got a reassuring new face in the White House in 1953, but not new policies toward the world. As had been true since 1946, the nation's leaders weighed every foreign policy decision for its effect on the Cold War. The United States pushed ahead in an arms race with the Soviet Union, stood guard on the borders of China and the Soviet empire, and judged political changes in Latin America, Africa, and Asia for their effect on the global balance of power.

**WHAT IMPACT** did Dwight Eisenhower's foreign policy have on U.S. relations with the Soviet Union?

## WHY WE LIKED IKE

In the late twentieth century, few leaders were able to master both domestic policy and foreign affairs. Some presidents, such as Lyndon Johnson, were more adept at social problems than diplomacy. By contrast, Richard Nixon and George H. W. Bush were more interested in the world outside the United States.

Dwight Eisenhower was also a "foreign-policy president." As a general, he had understood that military power should serve political ends. He had helped to hold together the alliance that defeated Nazi Germany and built NATO into an effective force in 1951–1952. He then sought the Republican nomination, he said, to ensure that the United States would keep its international commitments. He sealed his victory in 1952 by emphasizing his foreign-policy expertise, telling a campaign audience that "to bring the Korean war to an early and honorable end . . . requires a personal trip to Korea. I shall make that trip . . . I shall go to Korea."

What makes Eisenhower's administration hard to appreciate is that many of its accomplishments were things that did not happen. Eisenhower refused to dismantle the social programs of the New Deal. He exerted American political and military power around the globe but avoided war. Preferring to work behind the scenes, he knew how to delegate authority and keep disagreements private.

In his "hidden-hand" presidency, Eisenhower sometimes masked his intelligence. It helped his political agenda if Americans thought of him as a smiling grandfather. He was the first president to have televised news conferences and knew how to manipulate them. The "Ike" whose face smiled from "I Like Ike" campaign buttons and who gave rambling, incoherent answers at White House press conferences knew exactly what he was doing—controlling information and keeping the opposition guessing. He was easily reelected in 1956, when Americans saw no reason to abandon competent leadership.

## A BALANCE OF TERROR

The backdrop for U.S. foreign policy was the growing capacity for mutual nuclear annihilation. The rivalry between the United States and the USSR was played out within a framework of deterrence, the knowledge that each side could launch a devastating nuclear attack. The old balance of power had become a balance of terror.

The Eisenhower administration's doctrine of **massive retaliation** took advantage of America's superior technology while economizing on military spending. Eisenhower and his advisers worried that matching the land armies of China and the Soviet Union would inflate the role of the federal government in American society (see Figure 28–3). Eisenhower compared uncontrolled military spending to crucifying humankind on a "cross of iron." "Every gun that is fired," he warned, "every warship launched, every rocket fired signifies . . . a theft from those who hunger and are not fed, those who are cold and not clothed." The administration concentrated military spending where the nation already had the greatest advantage—on atomic weapons. In response to any serious attack, the United States would direct maximum force against the homeland of the aggressor.

The massive-retaliation doctrine treated nuclear weapons as ordinary or even respectable. It put European and American cities on the frontline in the defense of Germany, for it meant that the United States would react to a Soviet conventional attack on NATO by dropping nuclear bombs on the Soviet Union, which would presumably retaliate in kind. The National Security Council in 1953 made reliance on "massive retaliatory damage" by nuclear weapons official policy.

The doctrine grew even more fearful as the Soviet Union developed its own hydrogen bombs. The chairman of the Atomic Energy Commission terrified the American people by mentioning casually that the Soviets could now obliterate New York City. Dozens of nuclear weapons tests in the late 1950s made the atomic threat immediate.

**massive retaliation**   Popular name for the military doctrine adopted in the 1950s, whereby the U.S. promised to respond to any attack on itself or its allies with massive force, including nuclear weapons.

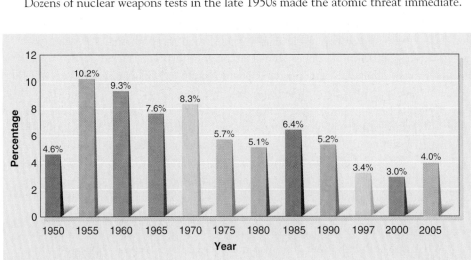

**FIGURE 28–3    Defense Spending as a Percentage of Gross Domestic Product, 1950–2005.**
Defense spending has been an important force for economic development and innovation. The impact of the defense budget on the domestic economy was greatest in the mid-1950s, at the height of the Cold War. Lesser peaks came during the Vietnam War in the late 1960s and the Reagan administration defense buildup in the early 1980s.
Data Source: *Statistical Abstract of the United States.*

The Soviet Union added to the worries about atomic war by launching the world's first artificial satellite. On the first Sunday of October 1957, Americans discovered that *Sputnik*—Russian for "satellite"—was orbiting the earth. Soviet propagandists claimed that their technological "first" showed the superiority of Communism, and Americans wondered if the United States had lost its edge. Schools beefed up science courses and began to introduce the "new math," Congress passed the National Defense Education Act to expand college and postgraduate education, and the new **National Aeronautics and Space Administration (NASA)** took over the satellite program in 1958.

**National Aeronautics and Space Administration (NASA)** Federal agency created in 1958 to manage American space flights and exploration.

## CONTAINMENT IN ACTION

Someone who heard only the campaign speeches in 1952 might have expected sharp foreign-policy changes under Eisenhower, but there was more continuity than change. John Foster Dulles, Eisenhower's secretary of state, had attacked the Democrats as defeatists and appeasers. He demanded that the United States liberate eastern Europe from Soviet control and encourage Jiang Jieshi to attack Communist China. Warlike language continued after the election. In 1956, Dulles proudly claimed that tough-minded diplomacy had repeatedly brought the United States to the verge of war.

In fact, Eisenhower viewed the Cold War in the same terms as Truman. He worried about the "sullen weight of Russia" pushing against smaller nations and saw a world caught between the incompatible values of freedom and communism, but caution replaced campaign rhetoric about "rolling back" Communism. Around the periphery of the Communist nations, from eastern Asia to the Middle East to Europe, the United States accepted the existing sphere of Communist influence but attempted to block its growth, a policy most Americans accepted.

The U.S. worldview assumed both the right and the need to intervene in the affairs of other nations, especially countries in Latin America, Asia, and Africa. Policymakers

Schoolchildren in the 1950s regularly practiced taking cover in case of atomic attack. If there was warning, they were to file into interior hallways, crouch against the walls, and cover their heads with their jackets as protection against flying glass. If they saw the blinding flash of an atomic explosion without warning, they were to "duck and cover" under their school desks.

saw these nations as markets for U.S. products and sources of vital raw materials. When political disturbances arose in these states, the United States blamed Soviet meddling to justify U.S. intervention. If Communism could not be rolled back in eastern Europe, the CIA could still undermine anti-American governments in the third world. The Soviets themselves took advantage of local revolutions even when they did not instigate them; in doing so they confirmed Washington's belief that the developing world was a game board on which the superpowers carried on their rivalry by proxy.

Twice during Eisenhower's first term, the CIA subverted democratically elected governments that seemed to threaten U.S. interests. In Iran, which had nationalized British and U.S. oil companies in an effort to break the hold of Western corporations, the CIA in 1953 backed a coup that toppled the government and helped the young shah, as the reigning monarch was called, to gain control. The shah then cooperated with the United States, but his increasingly repressive regime would lead to his overthrow in 1979 and deep Iranian resentment of the United States. In Guatemala, the leftist government was threatening the United Fruit Company. When the Guatemalans accepted weapons from the Communist bloc in 1954, the CIA imposed a regime friendly to U.S. business (see Map 28–1).

For most Americans in 1953, democracy in Iran was far less important than ending the war in Korea and stabilizing relations with China. Eisenhower declined to escalate the Korean War by blockading China and sending more U.S. ground forces. Instead, he positioned atomic bombs on Okinawa, only 400 miles from China. The nuclear threat, along with the continued cost of the war on both sides, brought the Chinese to a truce that left Korea divided into two nations.

Halfway around the world, there was a new crisis when three U.S. friends—France, Britain, and Israel—ganged up on Egypt. France was angry at Egyptian support for revolutionaries in French Algeria. Britain was even angrier at Egypt's nationalization of the British-dominated Suez Canal. And Israel wanted to weaken its most powerful Arab enemy. On October 29, 1956, Israel attacked Egypt. A week later, British and French forces attempted to seize the canal.

Although the United States had been the first nation to recognize Israel in 1948, the relationship was much less close than it would become. The U.S. forced a quick cease-fire, partly to maintain its standing with oil-producing Arab nations. Because Egypt blocked the canal with sunken ships, the war left Britain and France dependent on American oil that Eisenhower would not provide until they left Egypt. Resolution of the crisis involved one of the first uses of peacekeeping troops under the United Nations flag.

In Europe, Eisenhower accepted the status quo because conflicts there could result in nuclear war. In 1956, challenges to Communist rule arose in East Germany, Poland, and Hungary and threatened to break up the Soviet empire. The Soviets replaced liberal Communists in East Germany while accepting a more liberal leader in Poland. In Hungary, however, reformers took the fatal step of proposing to quit the Warsaw Pact. Open warfare broke out when the Soviet army rolled across the border to preserve the Soviet empire. Hungarian freedom fighters in Budapest used rocks and firebombs against Soviet tanks for several days, while pleading in vain for Western aid. NATO would not risk war with the USSR. Tens of thousands of Hungarians died, and 200,000 fled when the Soviets crushed the resistance.

## GLOBAL STANDOFF

The Soviet Union, China, and the United States and its allies were all groping in the dark as they maneuvered for influence in the 1950s and 1960s. In one international crisis after another, each player misinterpreted the other's motivations and diplomatic signals. Now that documents from both sides of the Cold War are becoming available, historians have realized what dangerously different meanings the two sides gave to their confrontations between 1953 and 1964.

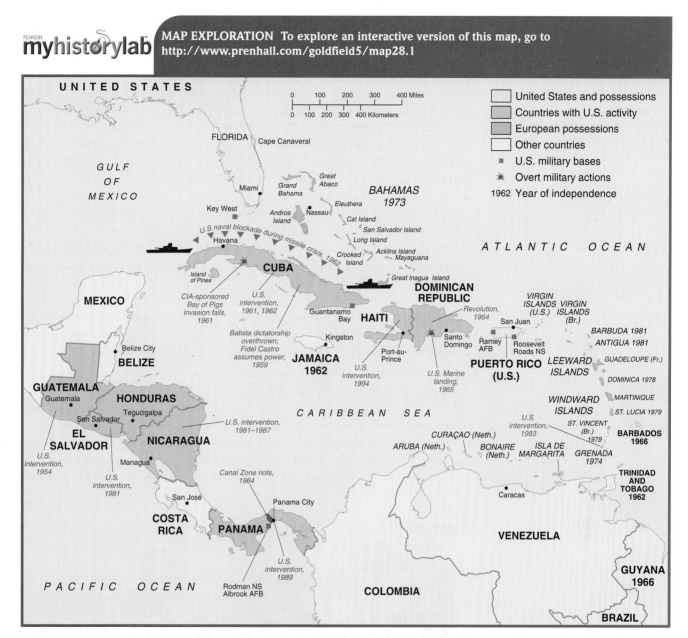

PEARSON
**myhistorylab**    **MAP EXPLORATION**  To explore an interactive version of this map, go to
http://www.prenhall.com/goldfield5/map28.1

MAP 28–1    **U.S. Intervention around the Caribbean since 1954**    The United States has long kept a careful eye on the politics of neighboring nations to the south. In the second half of the twentieth century, the United States frequently used military assistance or force to influence or intervene in Caribbean and Central American nations. The purpose has usually been to counter or undermine left-leaning governments; some interventions, as in Haiti, have been intended to stabilize democratic regimes.

**What was** the effect of U.S. involvement in the Caribbean?

A good example is the U-2 spy plane affair of 1960, which derailed progress toward nuclear disarmament. The Kremlin was deeply worried that West Germany and China might acquire nuclear bombs. Washington wanted to reduce military budgets and nuclear fallout. Both countries voluntarily suspended nuclear tests in 1958 and prepared for a June 1960 summit meeting in Paris, where Eisenhower intended to negotiate a test ban treaty. But on May 1, 1960, Soviet air defenses shot down an American U-2 aircraft over the heart of Russia and captured the pilot, Francis Gary Powers. The cover story for the U-2 was weather research, but the frail-looking black plane was a CIA operation. Designed to soar above the range of Soviet antiaircraft missiles, information obtained by U-2s had assured American officials that there was no missile gap.

When Moscow trumpeted the news of the plane's downing, Eisenhower took personal responsibility in hopes that Khrushchev would accept the U-2 as an unpleasant reality of international espionage. Unfortunately, the planes meant something very different to the Soviets, touching their festering sense of inferiority. They had stopped protesting the flights in 1957, because they saw complaints as demeaning. The Americans thought their silence signaled acceptance. Khrushchev had staked his future on good relations with the United States; when Eisenhower refused to apologize in Paris, Khrushchev stalked out. Disarmament was set back for years because the two sides had such different understandings of the same events.

The most important aspect of Eisenhower's foreign policy was continuity. Despite militant rhetoric, the administration pursued containment as defined under Truman. The Cold War consensus, however, prevented the United States from seeing the nations of the developing world on their own terms. By viewing every independence movement and social revolution as part of the competition with Communism, U.S. leaders created unnecessary problems. In the end, Eisenhower left troublesome and unresolved issues—upheaval in Latin America, civil war in Vietnam, tension in Germany, the nuclear arms race—for his successor, John Kennedy, who wanted to confront international Communism even more vigorously. (see American Views, Two Presidents Assess the Implications of the Cold War).

## QUICK REVIEW

### The U-2 Spy Plane Incident

- May 1, 1960: Soviets shot down American U-2 spy plane.
- Eisenhower took responsibility, hoping to reassure the Soviets.
- The Soviets responded with renewed distrust and hostility.
- The incident set back efforts at disarmament for years.

# JOHN F. KENNEDY AND THE COLD WAR

**WHAT WAS** John F. Kennedy's approach to dealing with the Soviet Union?

John Kennedy was a man of contradictions. Many Americans recall his presidency (1961–1963) as a golden age, but they are more taken by his memory than they were by Kennedy himself. A Democrat who promised to get the country moving again, he presided over policies whose direction was set under Eisenhower. Despite stirring rhetoric

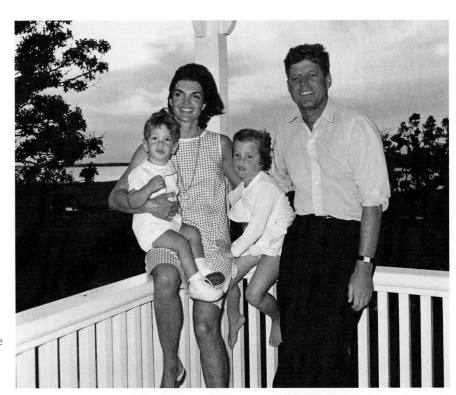

For many Americans in the early 1960s, John and Jacqueline Kennedy and their two children represented the ideal family, although the carefully posed pictures with happy smiles concealed the president's severe health problems and deep rifts in the marriage.

## AMERICAN VIEWS

### Two Presidents Assess the Implications of the Cold War

*I*n speeches two days apart in January 1961, outgoing President Dwight Eisenhower and incoming President John Kennedy offered contrasting interpretations of America's Cold War crusade. Eisenhower spoke with concern about the effects of defense spending on American society. Kennedy promised an unlimited commitment of resources to achieve national goals.

- **Why** did Kennedy define the American mission to the world so broadly?
- **What** changes in the 1950s led Eisenhower to warn about the dangers of pursuing that mission?
- **Do** the selections show basic agreement or disagreement about the goals of national policy?

Dwight D. Eisenhower
Farewell Address, January 18, 1961

Our military organization today bears little relation to that known by any of my predecessors in peace-time. . . . This conjunction of an immense military establishment and a large arms industry is new in the American experience. The total influence—economic, political, even spiritual— is felt in every city, every State house, every office of the federal government. We recognize the imperative need for this development. Yet we must not fail to comprehend its grave implications. . . .

In the councils of government, we must guard against the acquisition of unwarranted influence, whether sought or unsought, by the military-industrial complex. The potential for the disastrous rise of misplaced power exists and will persist. We must never let the weight of this combination endanger our liberties or democratic processes. We should take nothing for granted. Only an alert and knowledgeable citizenry can compel the proper meshing of the huge industrial and military machinery of defense with our peaceful methods and goals.

John F. Kennedy
Inaugural Address, January 20, 1961

Let the word go forth from this time and place, to friend and foe alike, that the torch has been passed to a new generation of Americans—born in this century, tempered by war, disciplined by a hard and bitter peace, proud of our ancient heritage—and unwilling to witness or permit the slow undoing of those human rights to which this nation has always been committed, and to which we are committed today at home and around the world.

Let every nation know, whether it wishes us well or ill, that we shall pay any price, bear any burden, meet any hardship, support any friends, oppose any foe to assure the survival and the success of liberty.

---

about leading the nation toward a **New Frontier** of scientific and social progress, he recorded his greatest failures and successes in the continuing Cold War.

## THE KENNEDY MYSTIQUE

Kennedy won the presidency over Richard Nixon in a cliff-hanging election that was more about personality and style than about substance (see Map 28–2). Both candidates were determined not to yield another inch to Communism. The charming and eloquent Kennedy narrowly skirted scandal for a sexually promiscuous personal life. Well publicized as a hero from World War II, he tempered ruthless ambition with respect for public service. His forthright campaigning allayed voter concern about his Roman Catholicism. Nixon had wider experience and was a shrewd tactician, but he was also self-righteous and awkward.

Television was crucial to the outcome. The campaign featured the first televised presidential debates. In the first session, Nixon actually gave better replies, but his nervousness and a bad makeup job turned off millions of viewers, who admired Kennedy's

**New Frontier**   John F. Kennedy's domestic and foreign policy initiatives, designed to reinvigorate a sense of national purpose and energy.

**WHERE TO LEARN MORE**

John F. Kennedy Library and Museum, Boston, Massachusetts. www.cs.umb.edu/jfklibrary

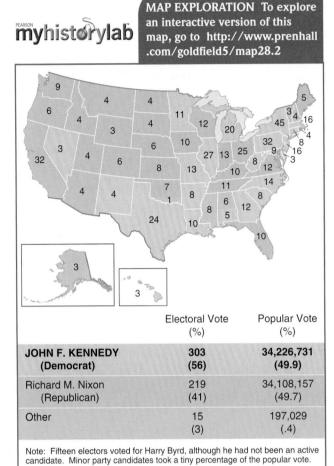

MAP EXPLORATION  To explore an interactive version of this map, go to  http://www.prenhall.com/goldfield5/map28.2

| | Electoral Vote (%) | Popular Vote (%) |
|---|---|---|
| **JOHN F. KENNEDY** (Democrat) | **303** **(56)** | **34,226,731** **(49.9)** |
| Richard M. Nixon (Republican) | 219 (41) | 34,108,157 (49.7) |
| Other | 15 (3) | 197,029 (.4) |

Note: Fifteen electors voted for Harry Byrd, although he had not been an active candidate. Minor party candidates took a tiny percentage of the popular vote.

MAP 28–2  **The Election of 1960**  The presidential election of 1960 was one of the closest in American history. John Kennedy's victory depended on his appeal in northern industrial states with large Roman Catholic populations and his ability to hold much of the traditionally Democratic South. Texas, the home state of his vice-presidential running mate, Lyndon Johnson, was vital to the success of the ticket.

**Why did** most Western states not support Kennedy?

**Bay of Pigs**  Site in Cuba of an unsuccessful landing by fourteen hundred anti-Castro Cuban refugees in April 1961.

energy. Nixon never overcame the setback, but the race was tight, with tiny margins in crucial states giving Kennedy the victory.

Kennedy brought dash to the White House. His beautiful and refined wife, Jackie, made sure to seat artists and writers next to diplomats and businessmen at White House dinners. Kennedy's staff and large family played touch football, not golf. No president had shown such verve since Teddy Roosevelt. People began to talk about Kennedy's "charisma," his ability to lead by sheer force of personality. In fact, the image of a fit, vigorous man concealed the reality that he was battling severe physical ailments that demanded constant medical attention and often left him with debilitating pain.

Behind the glamorous façade, Kennedy remained a puzzle. One day, Kennedy could propose the Peace Corps, which gave thousands of idealistic young Americans a chance to help developing nations; another day, he could approve plots to assassinate Fidel Castro. Visitors who expected a shallow glad-hander were astonished to meet a sharp, hard-working man who was eager to learn about the world.

## KENNEDY'S MISTAKES

Kennedy and Khrushchev perpetuated similar problems. Talking tough to satisfy their more militant countrymen, they repeatedly pushed each other into a corner, continuing the problems of mutual misunderstanding that had marked the 1950s. When Khrushchev promised, in January 1961, to support "wars of national liberation," he was really fending off Chinese criticism. But Kennedy overreacted in his first State of the Union address by asking for more military spending.

Three months later, Kennedy fed Soviet fears of American aggressiveness by sponsoring an invasion of Cuba. At the start of 1959, Fidel Castro had toppled the corrupt dictator Fulgencio Batista, who had made Havana infamous for Mafia-run gambling and prostitution. Castro then nationalized American investments, and thousands of Cubans fled to the United States.

When 1,400 anti-Castro Cubans landed at Cuba's **Bay of Pigs** on April 17, 1961, they were following a plan prepared by the Eisenhower administration. The CIA had trained and armed the invaders and convinced Kennedy that the landing would trigger spontaneous uprisings. But when Kennedy refused to commit U.S. armed forces to support them, Cuban forces captured the attackers.

Kennedy followed the Bay of Pigs debacle with a hasty and ill-thought-out summit meeting with Khrushchev in Vienna in June. Poorly prepared and nearly incapacitated by agonizing back pain, Kennedy made little headway. Coming after Kennedy's refusal to salvage the Bay of Pigs by military intervention, the meeting left the Soviets with the impression that the president was weak and dangerously erratic.

To exploit Kennedy's perceived vulnerability, the Soviet Union renewed tension over Berlin, deep within East Germany. The divided city served as an escape route from Communism for hundreds of thousands of East Germans. Khrushchev now threatened to transfer the Soviet sector in Berlin to East Germany, which had no treaty obligations to France, Britain, or the United States. If the West had to deal directly with East Germany for access to Berlin, it would have to recognize a permanently divided Germany. Kennedy sounded the alarm: He doubled draft calls, called up reservists, and warned families to build fallout shelters.

Rather than confront the United States directly, however, the Soviets and East Germans on August 13, 1961, built a wall around the western sectors of Berlin while leaving the access route to West Germany open. The **Berlin Wall** thus isolated East Germany without challenging the Western allies in West Berlin itself. In private, Kennedy accepted the wall as a clever way to stabilize a dangerous situation.

## GETTING INTO VIETNAM

U.S. involvement in Vietnam, located in Southeast Asia on the southern border of China, dated to 1949–1950. After World War II ended, France had fought to maintain its colonial rule there against rebels who combined Communist ideology with fervor for national independence under the leadership of Ho Chi Minh. Although the United States supported independence of most other European colonies, the triumph of Mao Zedong in China and the Korean War caused policymakers to see Vietnam as another Cold War conflict. The United States picked up three-quarters of the costs. Nevertheless, the French military position collapsed in 1954 after Vietnamese forces overran the French stronghold at Dien Bien Phu. The French had enough, and President Eisenhower was unwilling to join another Asian war. A Geneva peace conference "temporarily" divided Vietnam into a Communist north and a non-Communist south and scheduled elections for a single Vietnamese government.

The United States then replaced France as the supporter of the pro-Western Vietnamese in the south. Washington's client was Ngo Dinh Diem, an anti-Communist from South Vietnam's Roman Catholic elite. U.S. officials encouraged Diem to put off the elections and backed his efforts to construct an independent South Vietnam. Ho meanwhile consolidated the northern half as a communist state that claimed to be the legitimate government for all Vietnam. The United States further reinforced containment in Asia by bringing Thailand, the Philippines, Pakistan, Australia, New Zealand, Britain, and France together in the **Southeast Asia Treaty Organization (SEATO)** in 1954.

Another indirect consequence of the Vienna summit was the growing U.S. entanglement in South Vietnam, where Kennedy saw a chance to take a firm stand and reassert America's commitment to containment. In the countryside, Communist insurgents known as the **Viet Cong** were gaining strength. The anti-Communist leader, Diem, controlled the cities with the help of a large army and a Vietnamese elite that had worked with the French. The United States stepped up its supply of weapons and sent advisers, including members of one of Kennedy's military innovations, the Army Special Forces Group (Green Berets).

U.S. aid did not work. Despite overoptimistic reports and the help of 16,000 U.S. troops, Diem's government by 1963 was losing the loyalty—the "hearts and minds"—of many South Vietnamese. North Vietnamese support for the Viet Cong canceled the effect of U.S. assistance. Diem courted a second civil war by violently crushing opposition from Vietnamese Buddhists. Kennedy's administration tacitly approved a coup on November 1 that killed Diem and his brother and installed an ineffective military junta.

## MISSILE CRISIS: A LINE DRAWN IN THE WAVES

The escalating tensions of 1961 in Southeast Asia, the Caribbean, and Germany were a prelude to the crisis that came closest to triggering a nuclear war. On October 15, 1962, reconnaissance photos revealed Soviets at work on launching sites from which nuclear missiles could hit the United States. Top officials spent five exhausting and increasingly

**Berlin Wall**   Wall erected by East Germany in 1961 that isolated West Berlin from the surrounding areas in Communist-controlled East Berlin and East Germany.

**Southeast Asia Treaty Organization (SEATO)**   Mutual defense alliance signed in 1954 by the United States, Britain, France, Thailand, Pakistan, the Philippines, Australia, and New Zealand.

**Viet Cong**   Communist rebels in South Vietnam who fought the pro-American government established in South Vietnam in 1954.

desperate days sorting through the options. Secretary of Defense Robert McNamara suggested demanding removal of the missiles and declaring a naval "quarantine" against the arrival of further offensive weapons. A blockade would buy time for diplomacy.

Kennedy imposed the blockade on Monday, October 22. While Khrushchev hesitated, Soviet ships circled outside the quarantine line. On Friday, Khrushchev offered to withdraw the missiles in return for a U.S. pledge not to invade Cuba. On Saturday, a second communication nearly dashed this hopeful opening by raising a new complaint about U.S. missiles on the territory of NATO allies. The letter was the result of pressure by Kremlin hard-liners and Khrushchev's own wavering. Kennedy decided to accept the first letter and ignore the second. The United States pledged not to invade Cuba and secretly promised to remove obsolete Jupiter missiles from Turkey. Khrushchev accepted these terms on Sunday, October 28.

Why did Khrushchev risk the Cuban gamble? One reason was to protect Castro as a symbol of Soviet commitment to anti-Western regimes in the developing world. Kennedy had tried to preempt Castroism in 1961 by launching the **Alliance for Progress,** an economic-development program for Latin America that tied aid to social reform. However, the United States had also orchestrated the Bay of Pigs invasion and funded a CIA campaign to sabotage Cuba. High U.S. officials were not contemplating a full-scale invasion, but Castro and Khrushchev had reason to fear the worst.

Khrushchev also hoped to redress the strategic balance. As Kennedy discovered on taking office, the United States actually led the world in the deployment of strategic missiles. The strategic imbalance had sustained NATO during the Berlin confrontation, but 40 launchers in Cuba with two warheads each would have doubled the Soviet capacity to strike at the United States.

Soviet missiles in Cuba thus flouted the Monroe Doctrine and posed a real military threat. Kennedy and Khrushchev had also backed each other into untenable positions. In September, Kennedy had warned that the United States could not tolerate Soviet offensive weapons in Cuba, never dreaming that they were already there. Had Khrushchev acted openly (as the United States had done when it placed missiles in Turkey), the United States would have been hard pressed to object under international law. By acting in secret and breaking previous promises, the Soviets outsmarted themselves. When the missiles were discovered, Kennedy had to act.

In the end, both sides were cautious. Khrushchev backed down rather than fight. Kennedy fended off hawkish advisers who wanted to destroy Castro. The world had trembled, but neither nation wanted war over "the missiles of October."

## SCIENCE AND FOREIGN AFFAIRS

The two superpowers competed through science as well as diplomacy. When Kennedy took office, the United States was still playing catch-up in space technology. Kennedy committed the United States to placing a U.S. astronaut on the moon by 1970. The decision narrowed a multifaceted scientific and military program to a massive engineering project that favored the economic capacity of the United States.

The Soviet Union and the United States were also fencing about nuclear weapons testing. After the three-year moratorium, both resumed tests in 1961–1962. Both nations worked on multiple-targetable warheads, antiballistic missiles, and other innovations that might destabilize the balance of terror.

After the missile crisis showed his toughness, however, Kennedy had enough political maneuvering room to respond to pressure from liberal Democrats and groups like Women Strike for Peace and the Committee for a Sane Nuclear Policy by giving priority to disarmament. In July 1963, the United States, Britain, and the USSR signed the **Limited Test Ban Treaty,** which outlawed nuclear testing in the atmosphere, in outer space,

---

**Alliance for Progress**   Program of economic aid to Latin America during the Kennedy administration.

**QUICK REVIEW**

**U.S. Intervention Abroad**

• Many Americans assumed the U.S. had a right to intervene abroad.

• Eisenhower used the CIA to subvert democratically elected governments in Iran and Guatemala.

• The U.S. replaced France as the supporter of pro-Western Vietnamese in the south.

**WHERE TO LEARN MORE**

★ National Air and Space Museum, Washington, DC.
www.nasm.edu

**Limited Test Ban Treaty**   Treaty, signed by the United States, Britain, and the Soviet Union, outlawing nuclear testing in the atmosphere, in outer space, and under water.

and under water, and invited other nations to join in. France and China, the other nuclear powers, refused to sign, and the treaty did not halt weapons development, but it was the most positive achievement of Kennedy's foreign policy and a step toward later disarmament treaties.

# RIGHTEOUSNESS LIKE A MIGHTY STREAM: THE STRUGGLE FOR CIVIL RIGHTS

Supreme Court decisions are based on abstract principles, but they involve real people. One was Linda Brown of Topeka, Kansas, a third-grader whose parents were fed up with sending her past an all-white public school to attend an all-black school a mile away. The Browns volunteered to help the NAACP challenge Topeka's school segregation by trying to enroll Linda in their neighborhood school, beginning a legal case that reached the Supreme Court. On May 17, 1954, the Court decided **Brown v. Board of Education of Topeka,** opening a new civil rights era. Led by the persuasive power of the new chief justice, Earl Warren, the Court unanimously reversed the 1896 case of *Plessy v. Ferguson* by ruling that sending black children to "separate but equal" schools denied them equal treatment under the Constitution.

WHAT WAS the significance of *Brown v. Board of Education of Topeka?*

**Brown v. Board of Education of Topeka** Supreme Court decision in 1954 that declared that "separate but equal" schools for children of different races violated the Constitution.

## GETTING TO THE SUPREME COURT

The *Brown* decision climaxed a 25-year campaign to reenlist the federal courts on the side of equal rights (see Overview, Civil Rights: The Struggle for Racial Equality). The work began in the 1930s when Charles Hamilton Houston, dean of Howard University's law school, trained a corps of civil rights lawyers. Working on behalf of the NAACP, he hoped to erode *Plessy* by suits focused on interstate travel and professional graduate schools (the least defensible segregated institutions, because states seldom provided alternatives). In 1938, Houston's student Thurgood Marshall, a future Supreme Court justice, took over the NAACP job. He and other NAACP lawyers such as Constance Baker Motley risked personal danger crisscrossing the South to file civil rights lawsuits wherever a local case emerged. In 1949, Motley was the first black lawyer to argue a case in a Mississippi courtroom since Reconstruction.

Efforts in the 1940s and early 1950s, often fueled by the experience of World War II soldiers, had important successes. In *Smith v. Allwright* (1944), the Supreme Court invalidated the all-white primary, a decision that led to increased black voter registration in many southern communities. With new political power, and often with the cooperation of relatively progressive white leaders, blacks fought for specific improvements, such as equal pay for teachers or the hiring of black police officers.

The *Brown* case combined lawsuits from Delaware, Virginia, South Carolina, the District of Columbia, and Kansas. In each instance, students and families braved community pressure to demand equal access to a basic public service. Chief Justice Earl Warren brought a divided Court to unanimous agreement. Viewing public education as central for the equal opportunity that lay at the heart of American values, the Court weighed the consequences of segregated school systems and concluded that separate meant unequal. The reasoning fit the temper of a nation that was proud of making prosperity accessible to all.

*Brown* also built on efforts by Mexican Americans in the Southwest to assert their rights of citizenship. After World War II, Latino organizations such as the League of United Latin American Citizens battled job discrimination and ethnic segregation. In 1946, Mexican American parents sued five Orange County, California school districts that systematically placed their children in separate schools. In the resulting case

## OVERVIEW  Civil Rights: The Struggle for Racial Equality

| Area of Concern | Key Actions | Results |
| --- | --- | --- |
| Public school integration | Federal court cases | *Brown v. Board of Education of Topeka* (1954) Enforcement by presidential action, Little Rock (1957) Follow-up court decisions, including mandatory busing programs |
| Equal access to public facilities | Montgomery bus boycott (1955) Lunch counter sit-ins (1960) Freedom rides (1961) Birmingham demonstrations (1963) March on Washington (1963) | Civil Rights Act of 1964 |
| Equitable voter registration | Voter registration drives, including Mississippi Summer Project (1964) Demonstrations and marches, including Selma to Montgomery march (1965) | Voting Rights Act of 1965 |

of *Mendez v. Westminster*, federal courts prohibited segregation of Mexican-American children in California schools as a violation of the equal protection clause of the Fourteenth Amendment. Eight years later, the Supreme Court forbade Texas from excluding Mexican Americans from juries. These cases provided precedents for the Court's decision in *Brown* and subsequent civil rights cases.

### DELIBERATE SPEED

Racial segregation by law was largely a southern problem, the legacy of Jim Crow laws (see Chapter 17). The civil rights movement therefore focused first on the South, allowing Americans elsewhere to think of racial injustice as a regional issue.

Southern responses to *Brown* revealed regional differences. Few southern communities desegregated schools voluntarily, for to do so undermined the entrenched principle of a dual society. Their reluctance was bolstered in 1955 when the Supreme Court allowed segregated states to carry out the 1954 decision "with all deliberate speed" rather than immediately.

The following year, 101 southern congressmen and senators issued the **Southern Manifesto,** which asserted that the Court decision was unconstitutional. President Eisenhower privately deplored the desegregation decision, which violated his sense of states' rights and upset Republican attempts to gain southern votes. At the same time, many in Washington knew that racial discrimination offered, in the worlds of Dean Acheson, "the most effective kind of ammunition" for Soviet propaganda.

Eisenhower's distaste for racial integration left the Justice Department on the sidelines. Courageous parents and students had to knock on schoolhouse doors, often carrying court orders. Responses varied: school districts in border states, such as Maryland, Kentucky, and Oklahoma, desegregated relatively peacefully; farther south, African American children often met taunts and violence.

The first crisis came in Little Rock, Arkansas, in September 1957. The city school board admitted nine African Americans, including Melba Pattillo, to Central High, while segregationist groups, such as the White Citizens Council, stirred up white fears. Claiming he feared violence, Governor Orval Faubus surrounded Central High with

**Interpreting the Past**
*The Quest for African American Equality: Washington, DuBois, and King*
(pp. 874–875)

**Southern Manifesto**    A document signed by 101 members of Congress from Southern states in 1956 that argued that the Supreme Court's decision in *Brown v. Board of Education of Topeka* itself contradicted the Constitution.

the National Guard and turned the new students away. Under intense national pressure, Faubus withdrew the Guard. The black students entered the school, but a howling mob forced the police to sneak them out after two hours. Fuming at the governor's defiance of federal authority, Eisenhower reluctantly nationalized the National Guard and sent in the 101st Airborne Division to keep order.

Virginians in 1958–1959 tried avoidance rather than confrontation. Massive resistance was a state policy that required local school districts to close rather than accept black students. When court orders to admit 19 black students triggered the shutdown of four high schools and three junior highs in Norfolk, white parents tried to compensate with private academies and tutoring, but it was soon apparent that a modern community could not dismantle public education.

The breakthrough in school integration did not come until the end of the 1960s, when the courts rejected further delays, and federal authorities threatened to cut off education funds. As late as 1968, only 6 percent of African American children in the South attended integrated schools. By 1973, the figure was 90 percent. Attention thereafter shifted to northern communities, whose schools were segregated, not by law, but by the divisions between white and black neighborhoods and between white suburbs and multiracial central cities, a situation known as *de facto* segregation.

## PUBLIC ACCOMMODATIONS

The civil rights movement also sought to integrate public accommodations. Most southern states separated the races in bus terminals and movie theaters. They required

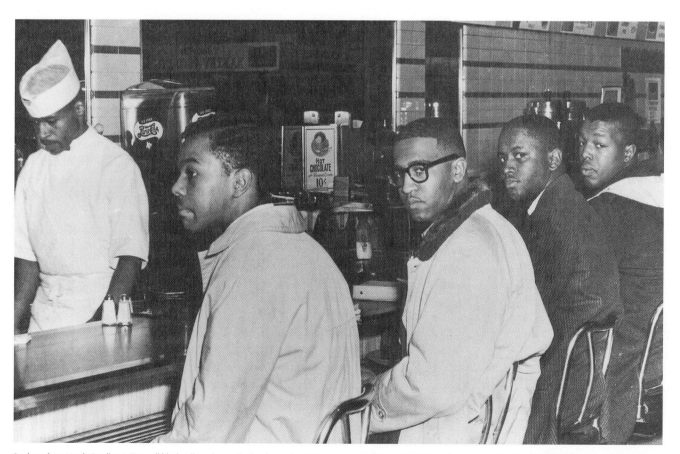

Students from North Carolina A&T, an all-black college, began the lunch-counter sit-in movement in February 1960. Here four students sit patiently in the Greensboro Woolworth's without being served. Participants wore their best clothes and suffered politely through days of verbal and sometimes physical abuse.

**W**  WHERE TO LEARN MORE

★ Martin Luther King, Jr., National Historical Site, Atlanta, Georgia. www.nps.gov/malu

**Southern Christian Leadership Conference (SCLC)** Black civil rights organization founded in 1957 by Martin Luther King, Jr., and other clergy.

## QUICK REVIEW

### The Montgomery Bus Boycott

◆ December 1, 1955: Rosa Parks refused to give up her bus seat to a white passenger and was arrested.

◆ The Women's Political Council organized a boycott of the bus company.

◆ After nearly a year, the Supreme Court ruled the bus segregation law unconstitutional.

**Student Nonviolent Coordinating Committee (SNCC)** Black civil rights organization founded in 1960 and drawing heavily on younger activists and college students.

**Congress of Racial Equality (CORE)** Civil rights group formed in 1942 and committed to nonviolent civil disobedience.

black riders to take rear seats on buses. They labeled separate rest-rooms and drinking fountains for "colored" users. Hotels denied rooms to black people, and restaurants refused them service.

The struggle to end segregated facilities started in Montgomery, Alabama. On December 1, 1955, Rosa Parks, a seamstress who worked at a downtown department store, refused to give up her bus seat to a white passenger and was arrested. Parks acted spontaneously, but she was part of a network of civil rights activists who wanted to challenge segregated buses and was the secretary of the Montgomery NAACP. As news of her action spread, the community institutions that enriched southern black life went into action. The Women's Political Council, a group of college-trained black women, initiated a mass boycott of the privately owned bus company. Martin Luther King, Jr., a 26-year-old pastor, led the boycott. He galvanized a mass meeting with a speech that quoted the biblical prophet Amos: "We are determined here in Montgomery to work and fight until justice runs down like water, and righteousness like a mighty stream."

Montgomery's African Americans organized their boycott in the face of white outrage. A car pool substituted for the buses despite police harassment. As the boycott survived months of pressure, the national media began to pay attention. After nearly a year, the Supreme Court agreed that the bus segregation law was unconstitutional.

Victory in Montgomery depended on steadfast African American involvement. Success also revealed the discrepancy between white attitudes in the Deep South and national opinion. For white southerners, segregation was a local concern best defined as a legal or constitutional matter. For other Americans, it was increasingly an issue of the South's deviation from national moral norms.

The Montgomery boycott won a local victory and made King famous, but it did not propel immediate change. King formed the **Southern Christian Leadership Conference (SCLC)** and sparred with the NAACP about community-based versus court-based civil rights tactics, but four African American college students in Greensboro, North Carolina, started the next phase of the struggle. On February 1, 1960, they put on jackets and ties and sat down at the segregated lunch counter in Woolworth's, waiting through the day without being served. Their patient courage brought more demonstrators; within two days, 85 students packed the store. Nonviolent sit-ins spread throughout the South.

The sit-ins had both immediate and long-range effects. In such comparatively sophisticated border cities as Nashville, Tennessee, sit-ins integrated lunch counters. Elsewhere, they precipitated white violence and mass arrests. King welcomed nonviolent confrontation. SCLC leader Ella Baker, one of the movement's most important figures, helped the students form a new organization, the **Student Nonviolent Coordinating Committee (SNCC).**

The year 1961 brought "freedom rides" to test the segregation of interstate bus terminals. The idea came from James Farmer of the **Congress of Racial Equality (CORE),** who copied a little-remembered 1947 Journey of Reconciliation that had tested the integration of interstate trains. Two buses carrying black and white passengers met only minor problems in Virginia, the Carolinas, and Georgia, but Alabamians burned one of the buses and attacked the riders in Birmingham, where they beat demonstrators senseless and clubbed a Justice Department observer. The governor and police refused to protect the freedom riders. The riders traveled into Mississippi under National Guard protection but were arrested at the Jackson bus terminal. Despite Attorney General Robert Kennedy's call for a cooling-off period, freedom rides continued through the summer. The rides proved that African Americans were in charge of their own civil rights revolution.

# THE MARCH ON WASHINGTON, 1963

John Kennedy was a tepid supporter of the civil rights movement and entered office with no civil rights agenda. He appointed segregationist judges to mollify southern congressmen and would have preferred that African Americans stop disturbing the fragile Democratic Party coalition.

In the face of the slow federal response, the SCLC concentrated for 1963 on rigidly segregated Birmingham. April began with sit-ins and marches that aimed to integrate lunch counters, restrooms, and stores and secure open hiring for some clerical jobs. Birmingham's commissioner of public safety, Bull Connor, used fire hoses to blast demonstrators against buildings and roll children down the streets. When demonstrators fought back, his men chased them with dogs. Continued marches brought the arrest of hundreds of children. King's "Letter from Birmingham City Jail" stated the case for protest: "We have not made a single gain in civil rights without determined legal and nonviolent pressure. . . . Freedom is never voluntarily given by the oppressor; it must be demanded by the oppressed."

The Birmingham demonstrations were inconclusive. White leaders accepted minimal demands on May 10 but delayed enforcing them. Antiblack violence continued, including a bomb that killed four children in a Birmingham church. Meanwhile, the events in Alabama had forced President Kennedy to board the freedom train with an eloquent June 11 speech and to send a civil rights bill to Congress.

On August 28, 1963, a rally in Washington transformed African American civil rights into a national cause. A quarter of a million people, black and white, marched to the Lincoln Memorial. The day gave Martin Luther King, Jr., a national pulpit. His call

**WHERE TO LEARN MORE**

★ Birmingham Civil Rights Institute Museum, Birmingham, Alabama.
www.bcri.bham.al.us

## QUICK REVIEW

**Civil Rights during the Kennedy Administration**

- Kennedy was a tepid supporter of the civil rights movement.
- 1963: activists focused their attention on segregation in Birmingham.
- August 28, 1963: quarter of a million people marched to the Lincoln Memorial in support of civil rights.

On August 28, 1963, Rev. Martin Luther King, Jr., delivered his famous "I Have a Dream" speech to the March on Washington for Jobs and Freedom. The address was a climactic moment in the civil rights movement, encapsulating the optimism of decades of struggle, but the March on Washington also papered over emerging divisions that would become apparent later in the 1960s.

for progress toward Christian and American goals had immense appeal. Television cut away from afternoon programs for his "I Have a Dream" speech.

## RELIGIOUS BELIEF AND CIVIL RIGHTS

Although *Brown* and other civil rights court decisions drew on the secular Constitution, much of the success of the southern civil rights movement came from grassroots Christianity. A century earlier, the abolitionist crusade had drawn much of its power from evangelistic revival movements. Now in the 1950s and 1960s, black southerners drew on prophetic Christianity to forge and act on a vision of a just society. Religious conviction and solidarity provided courage in the face of opposition.

At the same time, most white Christians understood that segregation contradicted the message of the Bible. The two largest religious groups in the South, the Presbyterian Church of the United States and the Southern Baptist Convention, took public stands in favor of desegregation in the mid-1950s. Revival leader Billy Graham shared a pulpit with Martin Luther King, Jr., in 1957 and insisted against local laws that his revival services be integrated. The opponents of civil rights thus lacked the moral support of the South's most fundamental cultural institutions.

In this context, it was no accident that black churches were organizing centers for civil rights work. King named his organization the Southern Christian Leadership Conference with clear intent and purpose. His famous speech in Washington drew on religious imagery and ended: "Free at last! Free at last! Thank God almighty, we are free at last!"

# "LET US CONTINUE"

**HOW DID** Lyndon B. Johnson continue the domestic agenda inherited from the Kennedy administration? In what ways did he depart from it?

**War on Poverty**  Set of programs introduced by Lyndon Johnson between 1963 and 1966 designed to break the cycle of poverty by providing funds for job training, community development, nutrition, and supplementary education.

**WHERE TO LEARN MORE**

Sixth Floor Museum, Dallas, Texas. www.jfk.org

The two years that followed King's speech mingled despair and accomplishment. The optimism of the March on Washington shattered with the assassination of John Kennedy in November 1963. In 1964 and 1965, however, President Lyndon Johnson pushed through Kennedy's legislative agenda and much more in a burst of government activism unmatched since the 1930s. Federal legislation brought victory to the first phase of the civil rights revolution, launched the **War on Poverty,** expanded health insurance and aid to education, and opened an era of environmental protection.

## DALLAS, 1963

In November 1963, President Kennedy visited Texas to raise money and patch up feuds among Texas Democrats. On November 22, the president's motorcade took him near the Texas School Book Depository building in Dallas, where Lee Harvey Oswald had stationed himself at a window on the sixth floor. When Kennedy's open car swung into the sights of his rifle, Oswald fired three shots that wounded Texas Governor John Connally and killed the president. Vice President Lyndon Johnson took the oath of office as president on Air Force One while the blood-spattered Jacqueline Kennedy looked on. Two days later, as Oswald was being led from one jail cell to another, Jack Ruby, a Texas nightclub owner, killed him with a handgun in full view of TV cameras.

Some Americans believe there is more to the story. Why? The sketchy job done by the Warren Commission, appointed to investigate the assassination, also bred doubts. The commission hurried to complete its work before the 1964 election. It sought to assure Americans that Kennedy had not been killed as part of a Communist plot. The Warren Commission calmed fears in the short run but left loose ends that have fueled conspiracy theories.

All of the theories remain unproved. Until they are, logic holds that the simplest explanation is usually the best. Oswald was a social misfit with a grievance against U.S. society. Like Presidents Garfield and McKinley before him, Kennedy died at the hands of one unbalanced man acting alone.

## WAR ON POVERTY

Five days after the assassination, Lyndon Johnson claimed Kennedy's progressive aura for his new administration. "Let us continue," he told the nation, promising to implement Kennedy's policies. In fact, Johnson was vastly different from Kennedy. He was a professional politician who had reached the top through Texas politics and congressional infighting. As Senate majority leader during the 1950s, he had built a web of political obligations and friendships. Johnson's upbringing in rural Texas shaped a man who was endlessly ambitious, ruthless, and often personally crude, but also deeply committed to social equity. He had entered public life with the New Deal in the 1930s and believed in its principles. Johnson, not Kennedy, was the true heir of Franklin Roosevelt.

Johnson inherited a domestic agenda that the Kennedy administration had defined but not enacted. Kennedy's farthest-reaching initiative was rooted in the acknowledgment that poverty was a persistent U.S. problem. Michael Harrington's study *The Other America* became an unexpected bestseller. As poverty captured public attention, Kennedy's economic advisers devised a community action program that emphasized education and job training, a national service corps, and a youth conservation corps. They prepared a package of proposals to submit to Congress in 1964 that focused on social programs intended to alter behaviors that were thought to be passed from generation to generation, thus following the American tendency to attribute poverty to the personal failings of the poor.

Johnson made Kennedy's antipoverty package his own. Adopting Cold War rhetoric, he declared "unconditional war on poverty." The core of Johnson's program was the **Office of Economic Opportunity (OEO).** Established under the direction of Kennedy's brother-in-law R. Sargent Shriver in 1964, the OEO operated the Job Corps for school dropouts, the Neighborhood Youth Corps for unemployed teenagers, the Head Start program to prepare poor children for school, and VISTA (Volunteers in Service to America), a domestic Peace Corps. OEO's biggest effort went to Community Action Agencies. By 1968, more than 500 such agencies provided health and educational services. Despite flaws, the War on Poverty improved life for millions of Americans.

## CIVIL RIGHTS, 1964–1965

Johnson's passionate commitment to economic betterment accompanied a commitment to civil rights. In Johnson's view, segregation not only deprived African Americans of access to opportunity but also distracted white southerners from their own poverty and underdevelopment.

One solution was the **Civil Rights Act of 1964,** which Kennedy had introduced but which Johnson got enacted. The law prohibited segregation in public accommodations, such as hotels, restaurants, gas stations, theaters, and parks, and outlawed employment discrimination on federally assisted projects. It also created the Equal Employment Opportunity Commission (EEOC) and included gender in the list of categories protected against discrimination, a provision whose consequences were scarcely suspected in 1964.

Even as Congress was debating the 1964 law, **Freedom Summer** moved political power to the top of the civil rights agenda. Organized by SNCC, the Mississippi Summer Freedom Project was a voter-registration drive that sent white and black volunteers to the small towns and back roads of Mississippi. The target was a political system that used rigged

**Office of Economic Opportunity (OEO)** Federal agency that coordinated many programs of the War on Poverty between 1964 and 1975.

**WHERE TO LEARN MORE**

★ National Civil Rights Museum, Memphis, Tennessee. www.civilrightsmuseum.org

**Civil Rights Act of 1964** Federal legislation that outlawed discrimination in public accommodations and employment on the basis of race, skin color, sex, religion, or national origin.

**Freedom Summer** Voter registration effort in rural Mississippi organized by black and white civil rights workers in 1964.

"President Lyndon Johnson was a crafty and sometimes ruthless politician, but he also had a deep personal commitment to solving problems of poverty and inequality in American society."

literacy tests and intimidation to keep black southerners from voting. In Mississippi in 1964, only 7 percent of eligible black citizens were registered voters. Local black activists had laid the groundwork for a registration effort with years of courageous effort through the NAACP and voter leagues. Now an increasingly militant SNCC took the lead. The explicit goal was to increase the number of African American voters. The tacit intention was to attract national attention by putting middle-class white college students in the line of fire. Freedom Summer gained 1,600 new voters and taught 2,000 children in SNCC-run Freedom Schools at the cost of beatings, bombings, church arson, and the murder of three project workers.

Another outgrowth of the SNCC effort was the Mississippi Freedom Democratic Party (MFDP), a biracial coalition that bypassed Mississippi's all-white Democratic Party, followed state party rules, and sent its own delegates to the 1964 Democratic convention. To preserve party harmony, President Johnson refused to expel the "regular" Mississippi Democrats and offered instead to seat two MFDP delegates and enforce party rules for 1968. The MFDP walked out, seething with anger.

Freedom Summer and political realities both focused national attention on voter registration. Lyndon Johnson and Martin Luther King, Jr., agreed on the need for federal voting legislation when King visited the president in December 1964 after winning the Nobel Peace Prize. For King, power at the ballot box would help black southerners to take control of their own communities. For Johnson, voting reform would fulfill the promise of American democracy. It would also benefit the Democratic Party by replacing with black voters the white southerners who were drifting toward the anti-integration Republicans.

The target for King and the SCLC was Dallas County, Alabama, where only 2 percent of eligible black residents were registered, compared with 70 percent of white residents. Peaceful demonstrations started in January 1965. By early February, jails in the county seat of Selma held 2,600 black people whose offense was marching to the courthouse to demand the vote. The campaign climaxed with a march from Selma to the state capital of Montgomery.

On Sunday, March 7, 500 marchers crossed the bridge over the Alabama River, to meet a sea of state troopers. The troopers gave them two minutes to disperse and then attacked on foot and horseback "as if they were mowing a big field." The attack drove the demonstrators back in bloody confusion while television cameras rolled.

As violence continued, Johnson addressed a joint session of Congress to demand a voting-rights law. By opening the political process to previously excluded citizens, the Voting Rights Act was as revolutionary and far-reaching as the Nineteenth Amendment, which guaranteed women the right to vote, and the Labor Relations Act of 1935, which recognized labor unions as the equals of corporations.

Johnson signed the **Voting Rights Act** on August 6, 1965. The law outlawed literacy tests and provided for federal voting registrars in states where registration or turnout in 1964 was less than 50 percent of the eligible population. It applied initially in seven southern states. Black registration in these states jumped from 27 percent to 55 percent

**Voting Rights Act** Legislation in 1965 that overturned a variety of practices by which states systematically denied voter registration to minorities.

President Lyndon Johnson signing the Tonkin resolution. This gave him power to escalate the Vietnam War after the Gulf of Tonkin incident in which American vessels had been attacked by the North Vietnamese

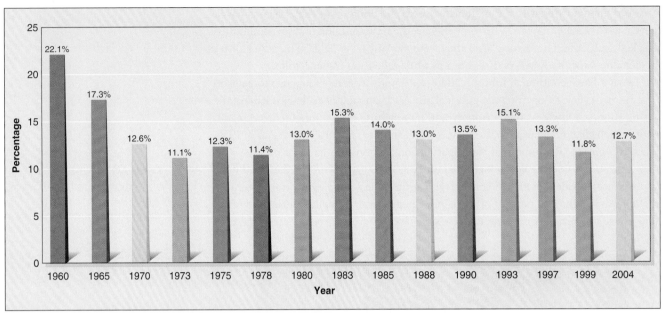

**FIGURE 28–4    Poverty Rate, 1960–2004**    With the improvement of federal health insurance, assistance for the elderly, and antipoverty programs, the proportion of Americans living in poverty dropped dramatically in the later 1960s. It began to inch upward again in the 1980s, when the priorities of the federal government shifted.

Data Source: *Statistical Abstract of the United States.*

within the first year. In 1975, Congress extended coverage to Hispanic voters in the Southwest. The Act required new moderation from white leaders, who had to satisfy black voters, and it opened the way for black and Latino candidates to win positions at every level of state and local government. In the long run, the Voting Rights Act climaxed the battle for civil rights and shifted attention to the continuing problems of economic opportunity and inequality.

## WAR, PEACE, AND THE LANDSLIDE OF 1964

Lyndon Johnson was the peace candidate in 1964. Johnson had maintained Kennedy's commitment to South Vietnam. On the advice of such Kennedy holdovers as Defense Secretary Robert McNamara, he stepped up commando raids and naval shelling of North Vietnam, on the assumption that North Vietnam controlled the Viet Cong. On August 2, North Vietnamese torpedo boats attacked the U.S. destroyer *Maddox* in the Gulf of Tonkin while it was eavesdropping on North Vietnamese military signals. Two days later, the *Maddox* and the *C. Turner Joy* reported another torpedo attack (probably false sonar readings). Johnson ordered a bombing raid in reprisal and asked Congress to authorize "all necessary measures" to protect U.S. forces and stop further aggression. Congress passed the **Gulf of Tonkin Resolution** with only two nay votes, effectively authorizing the president to wage undeclared war.

Johnson's militancy paled beside that of his Republican opponent. Senator Barry Goldwater of Arizona represented the new right wing of the Republican Party, which was drawing strength from the South and West. Goldwater's campaign made Johnson look moderate. Johnson pledged not "to send American boys nine or ten thousand miles from home to do what Asian boys ought to be doing for themselves" while Goldwater proposed an all-out war.

The election was a landslide. Johnson's 61 percent of the popular vote was the greatest margin ever recorded in a presidential election. Democrats racked up two-to-one majorities in Congress. For the first time in decades, liberal Democrats could enact their domestic program without begging votes from conservative southerners or Republicans, and Johnson could achieve his goal of a **Great Society** based on freedom and opportunity for all.

The result was a series of measures that Johnson pushed through Congress before the Vietnam War eroded his political standing and distracted national attention. The National Endowment for the Arts and the National Endowment for the Humanities seemed uncontroversial at the time but would later become the focus of liberal and conservative struggles over the character of American life. The Wilderness Act (1964), which preserved 9.1 million acres from development, would prove another political battlefield in the face of economic pressures in the next century.

The goal of increasing opportunity for all Americans stirred the president most deeply. The Elementary and Secondary Education Act was the first general federal aid program for public schools, allocating $1.3 billion for textbooks and special education. The Higher Education Act funded low-interest student loans and university research facilities. The Medical Care Act created **Medicare,** federally funded health insurance for the elderly, and **Medicaid,** which helped states offer medical care to the poor. The Appalachian Regional Development Act funded economic development in the depressed mountain counties of 12 states from Georgia to New York and proved a long-run success.

It is sometimes said that the United States declared war on poverty and lost. In fact, the nation came closer to winning the war on poverty than it did the war in Vietnam. New or expanded social insurance and income-support programs, such as Medicare, Medicaid, Social Security, and food stamps, cut the proportion of poor people from 22 percent of the American population in 1960 to 13 percent in 1970 (see Figure 28–4). Infant mortality dropped by a third because of improved nutrition and better access to healthcare for mothers and children. Taken together, the political results of the 1964 landslide moved the United States much closer to the vision of an end to poverty and racial injustice.

# CONCLUSION

The era commonly remembered as the 1950s stretched from 1953 to 1964. Consistent goals guided U.S. foreign policy through the entire period, including vigilant anti-Communism and the confidence to intervene in trouble spots around the globe. At home, the Supreme Court's *Brown* decision introduced a decade-long civil rights revolution that reached its emotional peak with the March on Washington and its political climax with the Civil Rights Act (1964) and Voting Rights Act (1965). However, many patterns of personal behavior and social relations remained unchanged. Women faced similar expectations from the early fifties to the early sixties. Churches showed more continuity than change.

But the consistency and stability of the 1950s were fragile. As we shall see the national consensus splintered after 1964. Some members of minority groups turned their backs on integration. Some younger Americans dropped out of mainstream society to join the aptly named counterculture. Others sought the security of religious commitment and community. Perhaps most divisively, "hawks" battled "doves" over Vietnam. If civil rights and Cold War had been the defining issues for the fifties, Vietnam would define the sixties, which stretched from 1965 to 1974.

**Great Society**   Theme of Lyndon Johnson's administration, focusing on poverty, education, and civil rights.

**Medicare**   Basic medical insurance for the elderly, financed through the federal government; program created in 1965.

**Medicaid**   Supplementary medical insurance for the poor, financed through the federal government; program created in 1965.

## QUICK REVIEW

### Achievements of the Great Society

- Reflected Johnson's commitment to reducing poverty.
- Provided federal aid for public schools.
- Established Medicare and Medicaid.
- Reduced percentage of Americans living in poverty.
- Improved health and nutrition of the poor.

**From Then to Now Online**
*Medical Research on Polio and AIDS*

# SUMMARY

**HOW DID** the "Decade of Affluence" alter social and religious life in America?

**A Decade of Affluence** President Eisenhower presided over the prosperity of the 1950s. He claimed the "political middle" and accepted much of the New Deal but saw little need for further reform. During his administration, workers had more disposable income and credit-based consumerism expanded; suburbs and the "car culture" grew. Families were seen as part of the anti-Communist crusade. The "youth culture" emerged, but religious affiliation, the belief in prosperity, and social conformity characterized the era. Vast inequalities were concealed; many had missed out on "affluent America" and many women were unhappy in their "perfect" world.

**WHAT IMPACT** did Dwight Eisenhower's foreign policy have on U.S. relations with the Soviet Union?

**Facing Off with the Soviet Union** The actions of the United States and Soviet Union created a bipolar world: Each was a magnetic pole with countries aligning themselves or attempting to remain neutral. The Soviet launching of the *Sputnik* satellite concerned Americans who thought they were technologically superior. America's worldview of the right and need to intervene in areas that were possible Communist takeover targets resulted in an expansion of containment. "Brinksmanship" characterized this period in the Cold War.

**WHAT WAS** John F. Kennedy's approach to dealing with the Soviet Union?

**John F. Kennedy and the Cold War** John F. Kennedy won over Richard Nixon in a close election in 1960; television was a critical element.

Kennedy's administration dealt with the Bay of Pigs invasion, a new Berlin crisis and the building of the Berlin Wall, growing American involvement in Vietnam, and the Cuban Missile crisis. Kennedy supported science as well as diplomacy; he committed the United States to placing an American astronaut on the moon and signed the Limited Test Ban Treaty which was a step toward later disarmament treaties.

**WHAT WAS** the significance of *Brown v. Board of Education of Topeka*?

**Righteousness Like a Mighty Stream: The Struggle for Civil Rights** The Supreme Court's *Brown* decision made the growing effort to secure equal legal treatment for African Americans a challenge to American society. The first phase of the civil rights struggle built from the Supreme Court's decision in 1954 to a vast gathering at the Lincoln Memorial in 1963. In between African Americans chipped away at racial segregation of schools, universities, and public facilities with boycotts, sit-ins, and lawsuits, forcing segregationists to choose between integration and violent defiance.

**HOW DID** Lyndon B. Johnson continue the domestic agenda inherited from the Kennedy administration? In what ways did he depart from it?

**"Let Us Continue"** After President Kennedy's assassination, Lyndon Johnson inherited a domestic agenda that was based on the knowledge that poverty was a widespread American problem. Johnson's passionate commitment to economic betterment accompanied a commitment to civil rights. War on Poverty and Great Society measures were passed before Johnson's enlargement of the Vietnam War eroded his political standing; the United States moved closer to addressing the effects of poverty and racial injustice than ever before.

# WHERE TO LEARN MORE

**National Air and Space Museum, Washington, DC.** Part of the Smithsonian Institution's complex of museums in Washington, the Air and Space Museum is the richest source for artifacts and discussion of the American space program. **www.nasm.edu.**

**Kansas Cosmosphere, Hutchinson, Kansas.** A rich collection of artifacts and equipment from the U.S. space program. **www.cosmo.org.**

**Sixth Floor Museum, Dallas, Texas.** Occupying the sixth floor of the former Texas School Book Depository building, exhibits examine the life, death, and legacy of John F. Kennedy. **www.jfk.org.**

**Birmingham Civil Rights Institute Museum, Birmingham, Alabama.** This museum and archive deal with the background of southern racial segregation, civil rights activism, and the 1963 demonstrations in Birmingham. **www.bcri.bham.al.us**

**Martin Luther King, Jr., National Historical Site, Atlanta, Georgia.** The birthplace and grave of Reverend King are the nucleus of a park set in the historic black neighborhood of Auburn. **www.nps.gov/malu**

**National Civil Rights Museum, Memphis, Tennessee.** Located in the Lorraine Motel, where Martin Luther King, Jr., was killed, the museum traces the participants, background, and effects of key events in the civil rights movement. **www.civilrightsmuseum.org**

**National Afro-American Museum and Cultural Center, Wilberforce, Ohio.** The exhibit "From Victory to Freedom: Afro-American Life in the Fifties" looks at home, family, music, and religion. **www.ohiohistory.org/places/afroam**

**John F. Kennedy Library and Museum, Boston, Massachusetts.** Exhibits offer a sympathetic view of Kennedy's life and achievements. **www.cs.umb.edu/jfklibrary**

# STUDY RESOURCES

## myhistorylab

For study resources for this chapter, go to www.myhistorylab.com and choose *The American Journey.* You will find a wealth of study and review material for this chapter, including pre- and posttests, customized study plan, key term review flash cards, interactive map and document activities, and documents for analysis.

# REVIEW QUESTIONS

1. What were the sources of prosperity in the 1950s and 1960s? How did prosperity shape cities, family life, and religion? What opportunities did it create for women and for young people? How did it affect the American role in the world? Why did an affluent nation still need a war on poverty in the 1960s?

2. What assumptions about the Soviet Union shaped U.S. foreign policy? What assumptions about the United States shaped Soviet policy? What did American leaders think was at stake in Vietnam, Berlin, and Cuba?

3. Who initiated and led the African American struggle for civil rights? What role did the federal government play? What were the goals of the civil rights movement? Where did it succeed, and in what ways did it fall short?

4. How did the growth of nuclear arsenals affect international relations? How did the nuclear shadow affect U.S. politics and society?

5. In what new directions did Lyndon Johnson take the United States? Were there differences between the goals of the New Frontier and the Great Society?

6. Why was school integration the focus of such strong conflict? How did the work of Mexican Americans and African Americans support the same goal of equal access to education?

7. How did religious belief shape American society in the Eisenhower and Kennedy years?

## KEY TERMS

**Alliance for Progress** (p. 860)
**Bay of Pigs** (p. 858)
**Berlin Wall** (p. 859)
***Brown v. Board of Education of Topeka*** (p. 861)
**Civil Rights Act of 1964** (p. 867)
**Congress of Racial Equality (CORE)** (p. 864)
**Federal Highway Act of 1956** (p. 845)
**Freedom Summer** (p. 867)
**Great Society** (p. 871)
**Gulf of Tonkin Resolution** (p. 870)
**Limited Test Ban Treaty** (p. 860)
**Massive retaliation** (p. 852)
**Medicaid** (p. 871)
**Medicare** (p. 871)
**National Aeronautics and Space Administration (NASA)** (p. 853)
**New Frontier** (p. 857)
**Office of Economic Opportunity (OEO)** (p. 867)
**Southeast Asia Treaty Organization (SEATO)** (p. 859)
**Southern Christian Leadership Conference (SCLC)** (p. 864)
**Southern Manifesto** (p. 862)
**Student Nonviolent Coordinating Committee (SNCC)** (p. 864)
**Viet Cong** (p. 859)
**Voting Rights Act** (p. 869)
**War on Poverty** (p. 866)

## The Quest for African American Equality: Washington, Du Bois, and King

**HOW AND IN** what manner were the goals of Booker T. Washington and W.E.B. DuBois like those of Dr. Martin Luther King, Jr. during the civil rights movement of the 1950s and 1960s? How do the style and techniques of both men compare to those used by Dr. King?

Booker T. Washington was a leading African American educator in the late 19th century. Washington's proposed that African Americans accept the racial separation of Jim Crow laws and the refusal of southern states to grant them voting rights for the time being in exchange for immediate guarantees of economic security and the right to work in industry and agriculture. Against critics angered by his temporary acceptance of Jim Crow, Washington explained that any attempt to challenge segregation would be disastrous for blacks who could later use their enhanced economic status to effect permanent change.

W.E.B. Du Bois was among Washington's strongest critics and a founder of the Niagara Movement. Du Bois was the first black graduate of Harvard University. He was a principal in establishing the National Association for the Advancement of Colored People (NAACP) in 1909 and became its director of publications in 1910. Du Bois argued that segregation should be confronted directly and aggressively and was in complete opposition to a position of accommodation.

The Reverend Dr. Martin Luther King, Jr., was the foremost civil rights leader of the 20th century. King conducted an activist civil rights movement that challenged Jim Crow on both the social and political fronts in the South. King was instrumental in the establishment of a civil rights program that was founded on the philosophy of nonviolent civil disobedience taken from the teachings of both Mahatma Gandhi and Henry David Thoreau.

*A white man directs a black woman away from a waiting room for whites only at a bus station in Dallas, Texas. In the South, the law segregated public transportation facilities by race.*

### Justice John Marshall Harlan, dissenting opinion, Plessy v. Ferguson (1896)

If evils will result from the commingling of the two races upon public highways established for the benefit of all, they will be infinitely less than those that will surely come from state legislation regulating the enjoyment of civil rights upon the basis of race. We boast of the freedom enjoyed by our people above all other peoples. But it is difficult to reconcile that boast with a state of the law which, practically, puts the brand of servitude and degradation upon a large class of our fellow citizens,-our equals before the law. The thin disguise of 'equal' accommodations for passengers in railroad coaches will not mislead any one, nor atone for the wrong this day done . . . .

'People of the United States,' for whom, and by whom through representatives, our government is administered. Such a system is inconsistent with the guaranty given by the constitution to each state of a republican form of government, and may be stricken down by congressional action, or by the courts in the discharge of their solemn duty to maintain the supreme law of the land, anything in the constitution or laws of any state to the contrary notwithstanding.

For the reason stated, I am constrained to withhold my assent from the opinion and judgment of the majority.

## Booker T. Washington, from *Atlanta Compromise Speech,* 1895

The wisest among my race understand that the agitation of questions of social equality is the extremist folly, and that progress in the enjoyment of all the privileges that will come to us must be the result of severe and constant struggle rather than of artificial forcing. No race that has anything to contribute to the markets of the world is long in any degree ostracized. It is important and right that all privileges of the law be ours, but it is vastly more important that we be prepared for the exercise of these privileges. The opportunity to earn a dollar in a factory just now is worth infinitely more than the opportunity to spend a dollar in an opera-house.

## W.E.B. Du Bois, from *Mr. Booker T. Washington and Others* (1903)

The black men of America have a duty to perform, a duty stern and delicate, - a forward movement to oppose a part of the work of their greatest leader. So far as Mr. Washington preaches Thrift, Patience, and Industrial Training for the masses, we must hold up his hands and strive with him, rejoicing in his honors and glorying in the strength of this Joshua called of God and of man to lead the headless host. But so far as Mr. Washington apologizes for injustice, North or South, does not rightly value the privilege and duty of voting, belittles the emasculating effects of caste distinctions, and opposes the higher training and ambition of our brighter minds, — so far as he, the South, or the Nation, does this, - we must unceasingly and firmly oppose them. By every civilized and peaceful method we must strive for the rights which the world accords to men, . . .

## Martin Luther King, Jr., from *I have a Dream Speech,* Washington D.C., August 28, 1963

I have a dream that one day this nation will rise up and live out the true meaning of its creed: "We hold these truths to be self-evident: that all men are created equal."

I have a dream that one day on the red hills of Georgia the sons of former slaves and the sons of former slave owners will be able to sit down together at the table of brotherhood. . . .

I have a dream that one day even the state of Mississippi, a state sweltering with the heat of injustice, sweltering with the heat of oppression, will be transformed into an oasis of freedom and justice. . . .

And when this happens, when we allow freedom to ring, when we let it ring from every village and every hamlet, from every state and every city, we will be able to speed up that day when all of God's children, black men and white men, Jews and Gentiles, Protestants and Catholics, will be able to join hands and sing in the words of the old Negro spiritual, "Free at last! free at last! thank God Almighty, we are free at last!

# 29

# Shaken to the Roots

Peace protesters lean in close to the barrels of guns held by the military police during an anti-Vietnam War protest outside the Pentagon in Washington DC in 1967

*Contact light! O.K., engine stop. . . . Houston, Tranquility Base here. The Eagle has landed! . . . We opened the hatch and Neil, with me as navigator, began backing out of the tiny opening [in the Lunar Module Eagle]. It seemed like a small eternity before I heard Neil say, "That's one small step for man . . . one giant leap for mankind." In less than fifteen minutes I was backing awkwardly out of the hatch onto the surface to join Neil, who, in the tradition of all tourists, had his camera ready to photograph my arrival.*

*I took off jogging to test my maneuverability. The exercise gave me an odd sensation and looked even more odd when I later saw the films of it. With bulky suits on, we seemed to be moving in slow motion. . . . At one point, I remarked that the surface was "Beautiful, beautiful. Magnificent desolation." I was struck by the contrast between the starkness of the shadows and the desert-like barrenness of the rest of the surface. It ranged from dusty gray to light tan and was unchanging except for one startling sight: our LM sitting there with its black, silver and bright yellow-orange thermal coating shining brightly in the otherwise colorless landscape.*

*During a pause in experiments, Neil suggested we proceed with the flag. . . . To our dismay the staff of the pole wouldn't go far enough into the lunar surface. . . . I dreaded the possibility of the American flag collapsing into the lunar dust in front of the television camera.*

Edgar Cortright, ed., *Apollo Expeditions to the Moon* (Washington: NASA SP 350, 1975).

## myhistorylab

### Personal Journeys Online

- *Easy Rider*, 1969. Fantasies of escape from 1960s America in a popular movie.

- Craig McNamara, interview in Joan Morrison and Robert K. Morrison, *From Camelot to Kent State: The Sixties Experience in the Words of Those Who Lived It*, 1987. Antiwar protest and the generation gap in 1968.

- Reies Lopez Tijerina, "Letter from the Santa Fe Jail," reprinted in *A Documentary History of the Mexican Americans*, ed. by Wayne Moquin, 1971. A Hispanic civil rights manifesto from 1969.

- "Bill Gates and Paul Allen Talk," *Fortune*, 132, October 2, 1995, pp. 69–72. Copyright(c) 1995 *Fortune*. Microsoft founders recall the early ways.

BUZZ ALDRIN AND NEIL ARMSTRONG, on July 20, 1969, completed the longest journey that anyone had yet taken. Landing the *Apollo 11* lunar module on the surface of the moon climaxed a five-day trip across the quarter-million miles separating the earth from the moon.

Even with the excitement of *Apollo*'s success, however, the United States was increasingly shaken and divided in the later 1960s and 1970s. Stalemate in Southeast Asia, political changes in third-world countries, and an oil supply crisis in the 1970s challenged U.S. influence in the world. Frustrated by the slow progress toward racial equality, many minority Americans advocated separation rather than integration, helping to plunge the nation's cities into crisis, while other Americans began to draw back from some of the objectives of racial integration.

Political scandals, summarized in three syllables, "Watergate," undercut faith in government. Fifteen years of turmoil forced a grudging recognition of the limits to American military power, economic capacity, governmental prerogatives, and even the ideal of a single American dream. ✦

## CHRONOLOGY

**1962** Rachel Carson publishes *Silent Spring*.

Port Huron Statement launches Students for a Democratic Society.

Supreme Court limits vocal prayer in schools in *Engel v. Vitale*

**1965** Congress approves Wilderness Act.

Malcolm X is assassinated.

Residents of Watts neighborhood in Los Angeles riot.

Immigration Reform Act allows increased immigration from outside Europe

**1967** African Americans riot in Detroit and Newark.

**1968** Viet Cong launches Tet Offensive.

James Earl Ray kills Martin Luther King, Jr.

Lyndon Johnson declines to run for reelection.

SDS disrupts Columbia University.

Sirhan Sirhan kills Robert Kennedy.

Peace talks start between the United States and North Vietnam.

Police riot against antiwar protesters during the Democratic National Convention in Chicago.

Richard Nixon is elected president.

**1969** Neil Armstrong and Buzz Aldrin walk on the moon.

**1970** United States invades Cambodia.

National Guard units kill students at Kent State and Jackson State universities.

Earth Day is celebrated.

Environmental Protection Agency is created.

**1971** *New York Times* publishes the secret Pentagon Papers.

President Nixon freezes wages and prices.

Plumbers unit is established in the White House.

**1972** Nixon visits China.

United States and Soviet Union adopt SALT I.

Operatives for Nixon's reelection campaign break into Democratic headquarters in the Watergate complex in Washington, DC.

**1973** Paris accords end direct U.S. involvement in South Vietnamese war.

United States moves to all-volunteer armed forces.

Watergate burglars are convicted.

Senate Watergate hearings reveal the existence of taped White House conversations.

Spiro Agnew resigns as vice president, is replaced by Gerald Ford.

Arab states impose an oil embargo after the third Arab-Israeli War.

**1974** Nixon resigns as president, is succeeded by Gerald Ford.

**1975** Communists triumph in South Vietnam.

United States, USSR, and European nations sign the Helsinki Accords.

**1976** Jimmy Carter defeats Gerald Ford for the presidency.

**1978** Carter brings the leaders of Egypt and Israel to Camp David for peace talks.

U.S. agrees to transfer control of the Panama Canal to Panama.

**1979** SALT II agreement is signed but not ratified.

OPEC raises oil prices.

Three Mile Island nuclear plant comes close to disaster.

Iranian militants take U.S. embassy hostages.

**1980** Iranian hostage rescue fails.

Soviet troops enter Afghanistan.

Ronald Reagan defeats Jimmy Carter for the presidency.

# THE END OF CONSENSUS

Pleiku is a town in Vietnam 240 miles north of Saigon (now Ho Chi Minh City). In 1965, Pleiku was the site of a South Vietnamese army headquarters and U.S. military base. At 2:00 A.M. on February 7, Viet Cong attacked the U.S. base, killing eight Americans and wounding a hundred. President Johnson ordered retaliatory airstrikes. A month later, Johnson ordered a full-scale air offensive code-named ROLLING THUNDER.

**WHY DID** the national consensus of the 1950s and early 1960s unravel?

The official reason for the bombing was to pressure North Vietnam to negotiate an end to the war. In the back of President Johnson's mind were the need to prove his toughness and the mistaken assumption that China was aggressively backing North Vietnam.

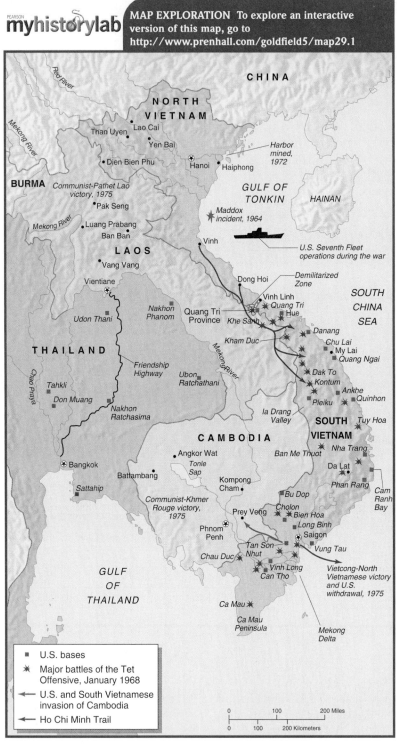

MAP EXPLORATION  To explore an interactive version of this map, go to http://www.prenhall.com/goldfield5/map29.1

**MAP 29–1    The War in Vietnam**   The United States attacked North Vietnam with air strikes but confined large-scale ground operations to South Vietnam and Cambodia. In South Vietnam, U.S. forces faced both North Vietnamese army units and Viet Cong rebels, all of whom received supplies by way of the so-called Ho Chi Minh Trail, named for the leader of North Vietnam. The coordinated attacks on cities and towns throughout South Vietnam during the Tet Offensive in 1968 surprised the United States.

**What were** the shortcomings of American military strategy in Vietnam?

The air strikes pushed the United States over the line from propping up the South Vietnamese government to leading the war effort. A president who desperately wanted a way out of Southeast Asia kept adding U.S. forces. Eventually, the war in Vietnam would distract the United States from the goals of the Great Society and drive Johnson from office. It hovered like a shadow over the next two presidents, set back progress toward global stability, and divided the American people.

## DEEPER INTO VIETNAM

Lyndon Johnson faced limited options in Vietnam (see Map 29–1). The pervasive American determination to contain Communism and Kennedy's previous commitments there hemmed Johnson in. Advisers persuaded him that controlled military escalation—a middle course between withdrawal and all-out war—could secure Vietnam. They failed to understand the extent of popular opposition to the official government in Saigon and the willingness of North Vietnam to sacrifice to achieve national unity.

ROLLING THUNDER put the United States on the up escalator to war. Because an air campaign required ground troops to protect bases in South Vietnam, U.S. Marines landed on March 8. Over the next four months, William Westmoreland, the commander of U.S. forces in South Vietnam, wore away Johnson's desire to contain U.S. involvement. More bombs, a pause, an offer of massive U.S. aid—nothing brought North Vietnam to the negotiating table. On July 28, he finally gave Westmoreland doubled draft calls and an increase in U.S. combat troops from 75,000 to 275,000 by 1966 (see Figure 29–1).

Johnson's decision turned a South Vietnamese war into U.S. war. At the end of 1967, U.S. forces in South Vietnam totaled 485,000; they reached their maximum of 543,000 in August 1969.

The U.S. strategy on the ground was **search and destroy.** As conceived by Westmoreland, sophisticated surveillance and heavily armed patrols were used to locate enemy detachments, which could then be destroyed by air strikes, artillery, and reinforcements carried in by helicopter. The approach made sense when the opposition consisted of North Vietnamese troops and large Viet Cong units.

FIGURE 29–1   **The United States in Vietnam**   American involvement in Vietnam grew slowly during the Kennedy administration from 1961 to 1963, expanded rapidly under Lyndon Johnson from 1964 to 1968, and fell just as rapidly under Richard Nixon from 1969 to 1973. The Nixon Doctrine tried to substitute American weapons and equipment for American military personnel but failed to prevent a North Vietnamese victory in 1975 after United States withdrawal.

Statistical Abstract of the United States.

However, most opponents were not North Vietnamese divisions but South Vietnamese guerrillas. The Viet Cong avoided set-piece battles. Instead, they forced the United States to make repeated sweeps through farms and villages. The enemy was difficult for Americans to recognize among farmers and workers, making South Vietnamese society itself the target. The U.S. penchant for massive firepower killed thousands of Vietnamese and made millions refugees. Because the South Vietnamese government was unable to secure areas after American sweeps, the Viet Cong often reappeared after the Americans had crashed through a district.

The U.S. air war also had limited results. Pilots dropped a vast tonnage of bombs on the Ho Chi Minh Trail, a network of supply routes from North Vietnam to South Vietnam through the mountains of neighboring Laos. Despite the bombing, thousands of

**WHERE TO LEARN MORE**

★ Lyndon B. Johnson National Historical Park, Johnson City, Texas.
www.nps.gov/lypo

**search and destroy**   U.S. military tactic in South Vietnam, using small detachments to locate enemy units and then massive air, artillery, and ground forces to destroy them.

The city of Hue suffered severe damage in the Tet Offensive and its aftermath. Here refugees return to the rubble of bombed-out houses.

Getty Images Inc.—Hulton Archive Photos.

workers converted rough paths into roads that were repaired as soon as they were damaged. The air assault on North Vietnam itself remained "diplomatic," intended to force North Vietnam to stop intervening in the South Vietnamese civil war. Since North Vietnam's leadership considered North and South to be one country, the American goal was unacceptable. Attacking North Vietnam's poorly developed economy, the United States soon ran out of targets.

## VOICES OF DISSENT

At home, protest against the war quickly followed the commitment of U.S. combat forces. The first national antiwar march took place in Washington on April 17, 1965. Twenty-five thousand people picketed the White House, assembled at the Washington Monument for speeches by Senator Ernest Gruening of Alaska (one of the two dissenting votes on the Gulf of Tonkin Resolution) and African American leaders, and walked up the Mall to the Capitol.

One group of opponents consisted of "realists" who argued that the war was a mistake. Foreign policy expert Hans Morgenthau, for example, fully supported anti-Soviet containment in Europe but maintained that the United States had no vital interests in South Vietnam. Policymakers in Washington, he said, were misreading the situation, wasting U.S. lives and resources, and weakening the American presence in regions such as Europe that were truly important to national security.

**From protest to confrontation.**    In 1966 and 1967, antiwar activity changed from respectful protest to direct confrontations with what protesters called the war machine. The tone of the debate became nastier. Johnson and his associates ridiculed the dissenters. Protesters chanted "Hey, hey, LBJ! How many kids did you kill today?" Much of the

In October 1967, 100,000 people marched on the Pentagon to protest the war in Vietnam.

anger was directed at the military draft administered by the **Selective Service System.** In theory, the Selective Service picked the young men who could best serve the nation as soldiers and deferred induction of those with vital skills. As the war expanded, the administration tried to hold the allegiance of the middle class by finding ways to exempt their sons from service in Vietnam. Full-time college enrollment was good for a deferment; so was the right medical diagnosis from the right doctor. As a result, draftees and enlistees tended to be small-town and working-class youth. The resentment created by the draft was an important wedge that began to erode the long-standing alliance between working-class Americans and the Democratic Party.

Military service also deepened the gap between blacks and whites. The black community supplied more than its share of combat soldiers. In 1965, when African Americans made up 11 percent of the nation's population, 24 percent of the soldiers who died in Vietnam were black. This disparity forced the Defense Department to revise its combat assignments so that the racial impact was more equal in later years. Martin Luther King, Jr., joined the protest in 1967. King called the war a moral disaster whose costs weighed most heavily on the poor and a new form of colonialism that was destroying Vietnamese society.

Draft resistance provided a direct avenue for protest against the war. Some young men burned the small paper cards that indicated their selective service classification, causing Congress to enact steep penalties for the act. Several thousand moved to Canada, to spend a decade or more in exile. Thousands of others described their religious and ethical opposition to war in applications for conscientious-objector classification. Much smaller numbers went to jail for refusing to cooperate in any way with the Selective Service System. Resistance mounted throughout the decade. By the end of 1969, over half the men drafted in California were refusing to show up, and prosecutions for draft evasion would peak in 1972 at nearly 5,000.

## NEW LEFT AND COMMUNITY ACTIVISM

The antiwar movement was part of a growing grassroots activism that took much of its tone from the university-based **Students for a Democratic Society (SDS).** Building on the ideas of such 1950s dissenters as C. Wright Mills, SDS tried to harness youthful disillusionment about consumerism, racism, and imperialism. It wanted to counter the trends

**Selective Service System** Federal agency that coordinated military conscription before and during the Vietnam War.

**QUICK REVIEW**

### Opposition to the War

- Antiwar activists and students challenged the "Cold Warriors."
- In 1966 and 1967 antiwar activity intensified.
- Antiwar activists directed their anger against the Selective Service System.

**Students for a Democratic Society (SDS)** The leading student organization of the New Left of the early and mid-1960s.

Writer Ken Kesey and the self-defined Merry Pranksters toured the country in a brightly painted bus, parked here in San Francisco's Golden Gate Park. They sometimes threw open parties where they served punch laced with psychedelic drugs in the hope of inciting radical social change.

**Free Speech Movement (FSM)**
Student movement at the University of California, Berkeley, formed in 1964 to protest limitations on political activities on campus.

**Model Cities Program**   Effort to target federal funds to upgrade public services and economic opportunity in specifically defined urban neighborhoods between 1966 and 1974.

**counterculture**   Various alternatives to mainstream values and behaviors that became popular in the 1960s, including experimentation with psychedelic drugs, communal living, a return to the land, Asian religions, and experimental art.

that seemed to be turning Americans into tiny cogs in the machinery of big government, corporations, and universities. SDS thought of itself as a "New Left" that was free from the doctrinal squabbles that hampered the old left of the 1930s and 1940s.

Many of the original SDS leaders were also participants in the civil rights movement. The same was true of Mario Savio, founder of the **Free Speech Movement (FSM)** at the University of California at Berkeley in 1964. Savio hoped to build a multi-issue "community of protest" around the idea of "a free university in a free society." FSM protests climaxed with a December sit-in that led to 773 arrests and stirred protest on other campuses.

What SDS wanted to do with its grassroots organizing resembled the federal community-action programs associated with the war on poverty. The **Model Cities Program** (1966) invited residents of poor neighborhoods to write their own plans for using federal funds to improve local housing, education, health services, and job opportunities. Model Cities assemblies challenged the racial bias in programs like urban renewal and helped train community leaders.

In the 1970s and 1980s, when SDS was long gone and the Model Cities Program was fading, the lessons of grassroots reform would still be visible in alternative organizations and political movements that strengthened democracy from the bottom up. Activists staffed food cooperatives, free clinics, women's health groups, and drug-counseling centers across the country. Community-based organization was a key element in self-help efforts by African Americans, Asian Americans, and Latinos. Neighborhood associations and community-development corporations that provided affordable housing and jobs extended the "backyard revolution" into the 1980s and beyond. Social conservatives, such as antiabortionists, used the same techniques on behalf of their own agendas.

## YOUTH CULTURE AND COUNTERCULTURE

The popular context for the serious work of the New Left was the growing youth culture and **counterculture.** Millions of young people in the second half of the 1960s expressed their alienation from American society by sampling drugs or chasing the rainbow of a youth culture. The middle-aged and middle-class dubbed the rebellious young "hippies."

The youth culture took advantage of the nation's prosperity. It was consumerism in a tie-dyed T-shirt. A high point was the 1969 Woodstock rock festival in New York State. But Woodstock was an excursion, not a life-altering commitment. Members of the Woodstock Generation were consumers in a distinct market niche, dressing but not living like social reformers or revolutionaries.

Within the youth culture was a smaller and more intense counterculture that added Eastern religion, social radicalism, and evangelistic belief in the drug LSD. San Francisco's Haight-Ashbury district became a national mecca for hippies in 1967's "Summer of Love," and hippie districts sprang up around university campuses across the country.

The cultural rebels of the late 1950s and early 1960s had been trying to combine personal freedom with new social arrangements. Many hippies were more interested in altering their minds with drugs than with politics or poetry. Serious exploration of societal alternatives was left for the minority who devoted themselves to the political work of the New Left, communal living, women's liberation, and other movements.

## SOUNDS OF CHANGE

The youth culture was shaped by films and philosophers, by pot and poets, but above all by music. Many changes in American society are mirrored in the abrupt shift from the increasingly complacent rock-and-roll of the early 1960s to the more provocative albums of mid-decade. The songs were still aimed at popular success, but the musicians were increasingly self-conscious of themselves as artists and social critics.

At the start of the decade, the African American roots of rock-and-roll were unmistakable, but there was no social agenda. Music that criticized American society initially found a much smaller audience through the folk-music revival in a few big cities and university campuses.

Then, in an artistic revolution, the doors opened to a new kind of rock music. The Beatles capitalized on their immense popularity to begin a career of artistic experimentation. They also opened the way for such hard-edged British bands as the Rolling Stones and The Who to introduce social criticism and class consciousness into rock lyrics. San Francisco's new psychedelic-rock scene took its name from drugs, such as LSD, and centered on shows at the Fillmore Auditorium.

Bob Dylan, a folksinger with an acoustic guitar, "went electric" at the Newport, Rhode Island, folk festival in 1965 and further transformed the music scene. Dylan's music was musically exciting and socially critical in a way that expressed much of the discontent of American young people.

## COMMUNES AND CULTS

Out of the half-secular, half-spiritual vision of the counterculture came people who not only dropped out of mainstream institutions but also tried to drop into miniature societies built on new principles. Thousands of Americans in the late 1960s and 1970s formed "intentional communities" or "communes." Their members usually tried to combine individual freedom and spontaneity with cooperative living.

Communes were artificial families, financed by inheritances, food stamps, and handicraft sales. Many suffered from the same inequality between men and women that was fueling the feminist revolt. Like natural families, they were emotional hothouses that often most collapsed because their members had incompatible goals.

However, a number of communes were serious endeavors. Some tried to follow spiritual leadings from Christianity or Buddhism. Thousands of smaller and less conspicuous urban communes whose members occupied large old houses pursued experiments in

## OVERVIEW   Why Were We in South Vietnam?

U.S. leaders offered a number of justifications for U.S. military involvement in Vietnam. Here are some of the key arguments, with points that supported or questioned the explanation.

**To Prop Up a Domino:**   Communist success in South Vietnam would undermine pro-American regimes in adjacent nations, which would topple like a row of dominoes,

| | | |
|---|---|---|
| *Pro* | | The firm U.S. stand contributed to an anti-Communist coup in Indonesia in 1965 and encouraged pro-American interests in Thailand and the Philippines. |
| *Con* | | Detailed knowledge of each nation in Southeast Asia shows that their own histories and internal issues were far more important in determining their futures than was American action in Vietnam. |

**To Contain China:**   China's Communist regime wanted to expand its control throughout Asia.

| | | |
|---|---|---|
| *Pro* | | The People's Republic of China was hostile to the United States, as shown in the Korean War, and had a long history of trying to control Vietnam. |
| *Con* | | North Vietnam had closer ties to the Soviet Union than to China and played the two Communist nations against each other to preserve its independence from China. |

**To Defeat Aggression:**   South Vietnam was an independent nation threatened by invasion.

| | | |
|---|---|---|
| *Pro* | | The major military threat to South Vietnam after 1965 came from the growing presence of the North Vietnamese army, and U.S. military intervention was necessary to counter that invasion. |
| *Con* | | The conflict in South Vietnam originated as a civil war within South Vietnam. Moreover, South and North Vietnam were a single nation, artificially divided in 1954, so that North Vietnam was trying to reunify rather than invade South Vietnam. |

**To Protect Democracy:**   South Vietnam was a democratic nation that deserved U.S. support.

| | | |
|---|---|---|
| *Pro* | | South Vietnam had an emerging middle class and an opportunity to develop democratic institutions. |
| *Con* | | South Vietnam was never a true democracy, ruled first by civilian dictator Ngo Dinh Diem and then a series of military strongmen. |

socialism, environmentalism, or feminism. Such efforts helped to spread the ideas of organic farming, cooperative land ownership, and low-consumption environmentalism that would move into the mainstream.

### THE FEMINIST CRITIQUE

The growing dissatisfaction of many women with their domestic roles helped set the stage for a revived feminism that was another result of the ferment of the 1960s. Important steps in this revival included the Presidential Commission on the Status of Women in 1961; the addition of gender as one of the categories protected by the Civil Rights Act of 1964 (see Chapter 28), and creation of the National Organization for Women (NOW) in 1966.

Mainstream feminism targeted unequal opportunity in the job market. Throughout the mid-1960s and 1970s, activists battled to open job categories to women, who battled for equal pay for everyone with equal qualifications and responsibilities.

*Documents*

National Organization for Women, *Statement of Purpose* (1966)

Changes in sexual behavior paralleled efforts to equalize treatment in the workplace. More reliable methods of contraception, especially birth-control pills introduced in the early 1960s, gave women greater control over childbearing. In some ways a replay of ideas from the 1920s, a new sexual revolution eroded the double standard that expected chastity of women but tolerated promiscuity among men. One consequence was a singles culture that accepted sexual activity between unmarried men and women.

More radical versions of the feminist message came from women who had joined the civil rights and antiwar movements only to find themselves working the copy machine and the coffeemaker while men plotted strategy. Radicals caught the attention of the national media with a demonstration against the 1968 Miss America pageant. Protesters crowned a sheep as Miss America and encouraged women to make a statement by tossing their bras and makeup in the trash.

Women's liberation took off as a social and political movement in 1970 and 1971. Within a few years, millions of women had recognized events and patterns in their lives as discrimination based on gender. The feminist movement, and specific policy measures related to it, put equal rights and the fight against sexism (a word no one knew before 1965) on the national agenda and gradually changed how Americans thought about the relationships between men and women. Feminists focused attention on rape as a crime of violence and called attention to the burdens the legal system placed on rape victims. In the 1980s and 1990s, they also challenged sexual harassment in the workplace, gradually refining the boundaries between acceptable and unacceptable behavior.

## COMING OUT

The new militancy among gay men and lesbians drew on several of the social changes of the late 1960s and 1970s. Willingness to acknowledge and talk about nonstandard sexual behavior was part of a change in public values. Tactics of political pressure came from the antiwar and civil rights movements.

Gay activism spread from big cities to small communities, from the coasts to Middle America. New York police had long harassed gay bars and their customers. When police raided Manhattan's Stonewall Inn in June 1969, however, patrons fought back in a weekend of disorder. The **Stonewall Rebellion** was a catalyst for homosexuals to assert themselves as a political force. San Francisco also became a center of gay life.

With New Yorkers and San Franciscans as examples, more and more gay men and lesbians "came out," or went public about their sexual orientation. They published newspapers, organized churches, and lobbied politicians for protection of basic civil rights such as equal access to employment, housing, and public accommodations. They staged "gay pride" days and marches. In 1974, the American Psychiatric Association eliminated homosexuality from its official list of mental disorders.

# CITIES UNDER STRESS

In the confident years after World War II, big cities had an upbeat image. By the 1970s, however, slums and squalid back streets dominated popular imagery. Movies and television reinforced the message that cities had become places of random and frequent violence.

## DIAGNOSING AN URBAN CRISIS

The nation entered the 1960s with the assumption that urban problems were growing pains. Politicians viewed the difficulties of central cities as by-products of exuberant suburban growth, which left outmoded downtowns in need of physical redevelopment.

*Documents*

The Gay Liberation Front, *Come Out* (1970)

**Stonewall Rebellion**    On June 27, 1969, patrons fought back when police raided the gay Stonewall Inn in New York; the name refers to that event and to the increase in militancy by gay Americans that it symbolizes.

**WHAT CHALLENGES** did cities face in the late 1960s and 1970s?

Ione Malloy, *Southie Won't Go* (1975)

**QUICK REVIEW**

**Urban Problems**

- Minorities and the poor were concentrated in urban centers.
- Postwar black migrants to the north found themselves with limited access to better houses, schools, and jobs.
- Cities faced decaying infrastructure and high taxes.

Central cities had a special burden in caring for the domestic poor. Baltimore, for example, had 27 percent of the Maryland population in 1970 but 66 percent of the state's welfare recipients.

Many urban problems were associated with the "second ghettos" created by the migration of 2.5 million African Americans from southern farms to northern and western cities in the 1950s and 1960s. By 1970, one-third of all African Americans lived in the 12 largest cities, crowding into ghetto neighborhoods dating from World War II.

Postwar black migrants found systems of race relations that limited their access to decent housing, the best schools, and many unionized jobs. Many families arrived just in time to face the consequences of industrial layoffs and plant closures in the 1970s and 1980s.

Central cities faced additional financial problems unrelated to poverty and race. Many of their roads, bridges, fire stations, and water mains were 50 to 100 years old by the 1960s and 1970s, and they were wearing out. Decay of urban utility and transportation systems was a by-product of market forces and public policy. Private developers often borrowed money saved through northeastern bank accounts, insurance policies, and pension funds to finance new construction in sunbelt suburbs. The defense budget pumped tax dollars from the old industrial cities into the South and West.

High local taxes in older cities were one result, for the American system of local government demands that cities and the poor help themselves. By the early 1970s, the average resident of a central city paid roughly twice the state and local taxes per $1,000 of income as the average suburbanite.

## CONFLICT IN THE STREETS

African Americans and Hispanics who rioted in city streets in the mid-1960s were fed up with the lack of job opportunities, with substandard housing, and with crime. The explosion of the Watts neighborhood in Los Angeles fixed the danger of racial unrest in the public mind. Trouble started on August 11, 1965, when a white highway-patrol officer arrested a young African American for drunken driving. Loud complaints drew a crowd, and the arrival of Los Angeles police turned the bystanders into an angry mob that attacked passing cars. Rioting, looting, and arson spread through Watts for two days until the National Guard cordoned off the trouble spots and occupied the neighborhood on August 14 and 15. After Watts, Americans expected "long hot summers" and got them. Scores of cities suffered riots in 1966, including a riot by Puerto Ricans in Chicago that protested the same problems blacks faced. The following year, the worst violence was in Newark, New Jersey, and in Detroit, where 43 deaths and blocks of blazing buildings stunned television viewers.

Few politicians wanted to admit that African Americans and Hispanics had serious grievances. Their impulse was to blame riffraff and outside agitators. This theory was wrong. Almost all participants were neighborhood residents. Except that they were younger, they were representative of the African American population, and their violence came from the frustration of rising expectations. Despite the political gains of the civil rights movement, unemployment remained high, and the police still treated all blacks as potential criminals. The urban riots were political actions to force the problems of African Americans onto the national agenda.

## MINORITY SELF-DETERMINATION

Minority separatism and demands for self-determination tapped the same anger that fueled the urban riots. Drawing on a long heritage of militancy (such as armed resistance during racial riots), activists challenged the central goal of the civil rights movement, which sought full integration and participation in American life. The phrase **Black Power** summed up the new alternative.

The slogans of Black Power, Brown Power, and Red Power spanned goals that ran from civil rights to cultural pride to revolutionary separatism. They were all efforts by minorities to define themselves through their own heritage and backgrounds, not simply by looking in the mirror of white society.

**Expressions of Black Power.**    Black Power translated many ways—control of one's own community through the voting machine, celebration of the African American heritage, creation of a parallel society that shunned white institutions. At the personal level, it was a synonym for black pride.

Black Power also meant increased interest in the **Nation of Islam,** or Black Muslims, who combined a version of Islam with radical separatism. They called for self-discipline, support of black institutions and businesses, and total rejection of whites. The Nation of Islam appealed to blacks who saw no future in integration.

In the early 1960s, Malcolm X emerged as a leading Black Muslim. Growing up as Malcolm Little, he was a street-wise criminal until he converted to the Nation of Islam in prison. After his release, Malcolm preached that blacks should stop letting whites set the terms by which they judged their appearance, communities, and accomplishments. He emphasized the African cultural heritage and economic self-help and proclaimed himself an extremist for black rights. In the last year of his life, however, he returned from a pilgrimage to Mecca willing to consider limited acceptance of whites. Rivals within the movement assassinated him in February 1965, but his ideas lived on in *The Autobiography of Malcolm X*.

The **Black Panthers** pursued similar goals. Bobby Seale and Huey Newton grew up in the Oakland, California, area and met as college students. They saw African American ghettos as internal colonies in need of self-determination. They created the Panthers in 1966, began to carry firearms, and recruited Eldridge Cleaver as the group's chief publicist.

**Black Power** Philosophy emerging after 1965 that real economic and political gains for African Americans could come only through self-help, self-determination, and organizing for direct political influence.

**Nation of Islam** Religious movement among black Americans that emphasizes self-sufficiency, self-help, and separation from white society.

**Black Panthers** Political and social movement among black Americans, founded in Oakland, California, in 1966 and emphasizing black economic and political power.

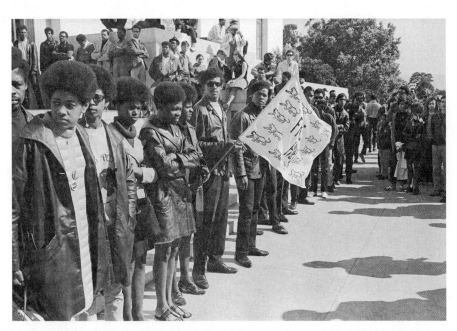

Members of the Black Panthers assemble outside the Alameda County Courthouse in Oakland, California on July, 15, 1968, when Panther leader Huey Newton goes on trial for killing a police officer.

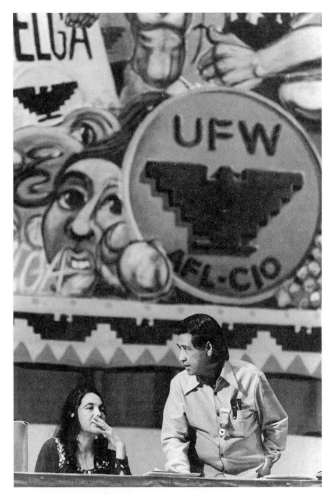

Dolores Huerta and Cesar Chavez confer at the 1973 convention of the United Farm Workers. Chavez and Huerta tried to build a union that welcomed workers of all ethnic backgrounds, but the UFW leaders were largely Hispanic, and the union took much of its symbolism from the Mexican heritage shared by most of its members.

**Exploring America**
*The American Indian Movement*

**American Indian Movement (AIM)**
Group of Native-American political activists who used confrontations with the federal government to publicize their case for Indian rights.

The Panthers asserted their equality. They shadowed police patrols to prevent mistreatment of African Americans and carried weapons into the California State Legislature in May 1967 to protest gun control. The Panthers also promoted community-based self-help efforts, such as a free-breakfast program for school children and medical clinics, and ran political candidates.

In contrast to the rioters in Watts, the Panthers had a political program, if not the ability to carry it through. The movement was shaken when Newton was convicted of manslaughter for killing a police officer and Cleaver fled to Algeria.

**Hispanic activism in the Southwest.** Latinos in the Southwest developed their own Brown Power movement in the late 1960s. Led by Reies López Tijerina, Hispanics in rural New Mexico demanded the return of lands that had been lost to Anglo Americans despite the guarantees of the Treaty of Guadalupe Hidalgo in 1848. Mexican Americans in the 1970s organized for political power in southern Texas communities where they were a majority.

The best-known Hispanic activism combined social protest with the crusading spirit of earlier labor union organizing campaigns. Cesar Chavez organized the multiracial United Farm Workers (UFW) among Mexican American agricultural workers in California in 1965. Chavez was committed both to nonviolent action for social justice and to the labor movement. UFW demands included better wages and safer working conditions, such as less exposure to pesticides.

**Native Americans assert their identity.** Native Americans also fought both for equal access to American society and to preserve cultural traditions through tribal institutions. Congress in 1968 restored the authority of tribal law on reservations. Three years later the Alaska Native Claims Settlement Act granted native Alaskans 44 million acres and $963 million to settle claims for their ancestral lands. Legally sophisticated tribes sued for compensation and enforcement of treaty provisions, such as fishing rights in the Pacific Northwest. Larger tribes established their own colleges, such as Navajo Community College (1969) and Oglala Lakota College (1971).

A second development was media-oriented protests that asserted Red Power. One of the earliest was a series of "fish-ins" in which Indians from Washington state, helped by the multi-tribal National Indian Youth Council, exercised treaty-based fishing rights in defiance of state regulations. Native American students gained national attention by seizing the abandoned Alcatraz Island for a cultural and educational center (1969–1971). Indians in Minneapolis created the **American Indian Movement (AIM)** in 1968 to increase economic opportunity and stop police mistreatment. AIM participated in the cross-country Broken Treaties Caravan, which climaxed by occupying the Bureau of Indian Affairs in Washington in 1972. AIM also allied with Sioux traditionalists on the Pine Ridge Reservation in South Dakota against the tribe's elected government. In 1973, they took over the village of Wounded Knee, where the U.S. Army in 1890 had massacred 300 Indians. They held out for 70 days before leaving peacefully.

## SUBURBAN INDEPENDENCE: THE OUTER CITY

In the mid-1960s, the United States became a suburban nation. The 1970 census found more people living in the suburban counties of metropolitan areas (37 percent) than in

Armed confrontation between militant Indians and state and federal law enforcement at Wounded Knee, S.D. in 1973 recalled the decades of warfare between plains tribes and the U.S. army in the previous century.

central cities (31 percent) or in small towns and rural areas (31 percent). Just after World War II, most new suburbs had been bedroom communities that depended on the jobs, services, and shopping of central cities. By the late 1960s, suburbs were evolving into "outer cities," whose inhabitants had little need for the old central city.

**Suburban economic growth and political influence.**   Suburbs captured most new jobs, leaving the urban poor with few opportunities for employment. In the 15 largest metropolitan areas, the number of central city jobs fell by 800,000 in the 1960s, while the number of suburban jobs rose by 3.2 million. Suburban rings gained a growing share of public facilities intended to serve the entire metropolitan area. As pioneered in California, community colleges served the suburban children of the baby boom.

Suburban political power grew along with economic clout. In 1962, the Supreme Court handed down a landmark decision in the case of *Baker v. Carr.* Overturning laws that treated counties or other political subdivisions as the units to be represented in state legislatures, *Baker* required that legislative seats be apportioned on the basis of population. The principle of "one person, one vote" broke the stranglehold of rural counties on state governments, but the big beneficiaries were not older cities, but fast-growing suburbs. By 1975, suburbanites held the largest block of seats in the House of Representatives. Reapportionment in 1982, based on the 1980 census, produced a House that was even more heavily suburban.

**School busing controversies.**   School integration controversies in the 1970s reinforced a tendency for suburbanites to separate themselves from city problems. In *Swann v. Charlotte-Mecklenburg Board of Education* (1971), the U.S. Supreme Court held that crosstown busing was an acceptable solution to the *de facto* segregation that resulted from residential patterns within a single school district. When school officials around the country failed to achieve racial balance, federal judges ordered their own busing plans. Although integration through busing occurred peacefully in dozens of cities, many white people resented the practice. Working-class students who depended on public schools

*Baker v. Carr*   U.S. Supreme Court decision in 1962 that allowed federal courts to review the appointment of state legislative districts and established the principle that such districts should have roughly equal populations ("one person, one vote").

*Swann v. Charlotte-Mecklenburg Board of Education*   U.S. Supreme Court decision in 1971 that upheld cross-city busing to achieve the racial integration of public schools.

found themselves on the front lines of integration, while many middle-class families switched to private education.

Because the Supreme Court also ruled that busing programs normally stopped at school-district boundaries, suburbs with independent districts escaped school integration. One result was to make busing self-defeating, for it led white families to move out of the integrating school district. Others placed their children in private academies, as happened frequently in the South.

# THE YEAR OF THE GUN, 1968

**HOW DID** the Tet offensive change American public opinion about the war in Vietnam?

In 1968, mainstream Americans increasingly turned against the war in Vietnam, student protest and youth counterculture turned ugly, and political consensus shattered.

## THE TET OFFENSIVE

At the end of 1967, U.S. officials were overconfidently predicting victory. They also fell for a North Vietnamese feint by committing U.S. forces to the defense of Khe Sanh, a strongpoint near the North-South border. The defense was a tactical success for the United States but thinned its forces elsewhere in South Vietnam. Then, at the beginning of Tet, the Vietnamese New Year, the Viet Cong attacked 36 of 44 provincial capitals and the national capital, Saigon. They hit the U.S. embassy and reached the runways of Tan Son Nhut air base. If the United States was winning, the Tet offensive should not have been possible.

As a military effort, the attacks failed. U.S. and South Vietnamese troops repulsed the attacks and cleared the cities. But the offensive was a psychological blow that convinced the American public that the war was quicksand. Television coverage of the Tet battles made the bad publicity worse. At least until Tet, the commentary from network news anchors had supported the U.S. effort, but the pictures undermined civilian morale. Viewers could hear cigarette lighters clicking open to set villages in flames. A handful of images stayed in people's memories—a Buddhist monk burning himself to death in

Gls evacuate a wounded comrade from fighting near the border between Vietnam and Cambodia.

protest; a child with flesh peeled off by napalm; a South Vietnamese official executing a captive on the streets of Saigon.

In the wake of the Tet crisis, General Westmoreland's request for 200,000 more troops forced a political and military reevaluation. Clark Clifford, a dedicated Cold Warrior, was the new secretary of defense. Now he had second thoughts. Twenty "wise men"— the big names of the Cold War—told the president that the war was unwinnable on terms acceptable to America's allies and to many Americans. Most scholars have agreed with this assessment. Tet and its aftermath had shown U.S. military superiority but highlighted the nation's inability to translate tactical advantage into political success in South Vietnam or the United States. The best option, the wise men told LBJ, was disengagement.

## LBJ's Exit

The president was already in political trouble. After other prominent Democrats held back, Minnesota's liberal Senator Eugene McCarthy had decided to challenge Johnson in the presidential primaries. Because he controlled the party organizations in two-thirds of the states, Johnson did not need the primary states for renomination and ignored the first primary in New Hampshire. With enthusiastic college students staffing his campaign, McCarthy won a startling 42 percent of the popular vote and 20 of 24 delegates in the New Hampshire primary. The vote was a protest against Johnson's Vietnam policy rather than a clear mandate for peace. Nevertheless, the vote proved that the political middle would no longer hold. By showing Johnson's vulnerability, New Hampshire also drew Robert Kennedy into the race.

Facing political challenges and an unraveling war, on March 31, 1968, Johnson announced a halt to most bombing of North Vietnam, opening the door for peace negotiations that formally began in May 1969. He then astounded the country by withdrawing from the presidential race. It was a statesmanlike act by a man who had been consumed by a war he did not want, had never understood, and could not end.

## Violence and Politics: King, Kennedy, and Chicago

Johnson's dramatic withdrawal was followed by the violent disruption of U.S. politics through assassination and riot. On April 4, 1968, an ex-convict, James Earl Ray, shot and killed Martin Luther King, Jr., as he stood on the balcony of a Memphis motel. King's death was the product of pure racial hatred, and it triggered a climactic round of violence in black ghettos. Fires devastated the West Side of Chicago and downtown Washington, DC. The army guarded the steps of the Capitol, ready to protect Congress from its fellow citizens.

The shock of King's death was still fresh when another political assassination stunned the nation. On June 5, Robert Kennedy won California's primary election. He was still behind Vice President Hubert Humphrey in the delegate count but coming on strong. As Kennedy walked out of the ballroom at his headquarters in the Ambassador Hotel in Los Angeles, a Jordanian immigrant named Sirhan Sirhan put a bullet in his brain. Sirhan may have wanted revenge for America's tilt toward Israel in that country's victorious Six-Day War with Egypt and Jordan in 1967.

Kennedy's death ensured the Democratic nomination for Humphrey, a liberal who had loyally supported Johnson's war policy. After his nomination, Humphrey faced the Republican Richard Nixon and the Independent George Wallace. Nixon positioned himself as the candidate of the political middle. Wallace appealed to southern whites and working-class northerners who feared black militancy and hated "the ivory-tower folks with pointy heads."

Both got great help from the Democratic Convention, held in Chicago on August 26–29. While Democrats feuded among themselves, Chicago Mayor Richard Daley

## RED SPRING, 1968

Columbia University in New York City was in turmoil in the spring of 1968. Its African American students and its SDS chapter had several grievances. One was the university's cooperation with the Pentagon-funded Institute for Defense Analysis. Another was its plan to build a gymnasium on park land that might better serve the residents of Harlem. Some students wanted changes in university policy, others a confrontation that would recruit new radicals. They occupied five university buildings, including the library and the president's office, for a week in April until police evicted them. A student strike and additional clashes with the authorities lasted until June.

The "battle of Morningside Heights" (the location of Columbia) generated banner headlines in the United States, but it was tame when compared to events in Europe. During the same "red spring," demonstrations and revolts by angry university students and workers created upheaval on both sides of the Iron Curtain.

In the months that followed the Tet crisis, much of the industrial world was in ferment. Students rioted in Italy and Berlin over rigid university systems, the Vietnam War, and the power of multinational corporations. Workers and students

protested against the Franco regime in Spain. In Paris, student demonstrations against the Vietnam War turned into attacks on the university system and the French government. Students fought police in the Paris streets in the first days of May with the approval of a majority of Parisians. Radical industrial workers called a general strike. The government nearly toppled before the disturbance subsided.

Grassroots rebellion also shook the Soviet grip on eastern Europe. University students in Poland protested the stifling of political discussion. Alexander Dubcek, the new leader of the Czech Communist Party, brought together students and the middle class around reforms that caused people to talk about the "Prague Spring"—a blossoming of democracy inside the Soviet bloc. Here the changes went too far. As Czechs pressed for more and more political freedom, the Soviet Union feared losing control of one of its satellites. On August 21, 500,000 troops from the USSR and other Warsaw Pact nations rolled across the border and forced Czechoslovakia back into line.

• What common factors might help explain student unrest on both of the Iron Curtain?

and his police department monitored antiwar protesters. The National Mobilization Committee to End the War in Vietnam drew from the New Left and from older peace activists—sober and committed people who had fought against nuclear weapons in the 1950s and the Vietnam War throughout the 1960s. They wanted to embarrass the Johnson-Humphrey administration by marching to the convention hall on nomination night. Mixed in were the Yippies (the term supposedly stood for Youth International Party, but the idea of hippies making yippie! came first and the word later). The Yippies planned to attract young people to Chicago with the promise of street theater, media events, and confrontation that would puncture the pretensions of the power structure. To the extent they had a program, it was to use the youth culture to attract converts to radical politics.

The volatile mix was ready for a spark. On August 28, the same night that Democratic delegates were nominating Humphrey, tensions exploded in a police riot. Protesters and Yippies had congregated in Grant Park, across Michigan Avenue from downtown hotels. Undisciplined police waded into the crowds with clubs and tear gas. Young people fought back with rocks and bottles. Television caught the hours of violence that ended when the National Guard separated police from demonstrators. For Humphrey, the convention was a catastrophe, alienating liberal Democrats and associating Democrats with disorder in the public mind.

The election was closer than Humphrey had any right to hope (see Map 29–2). Election day gave Wallace 13.5 percent of the popular vote, Humphrey 42.7 percent of

**QUICK REVIEW**

**The 1968 Democratic Convention**

♦ August 26–29: Democrats meet to nominate Hubert Humphrey.

♦ Antiwar protesters march on the convention hall.

♦ Undisciplined police helped precipitate violence between the police and the protesters.

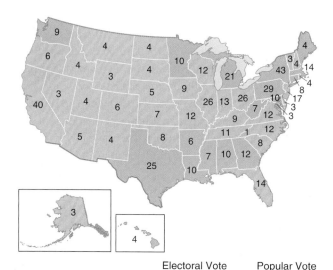

| | Electoral Vote (%) | Popular Vote (%) |
|---|---|---|
| **RICHARD M. NIXON** (Republican) | **301** **(56)** | **31,785,480** **(43.4)** |
| Hubert H. Humphrey (Democrat) | 191 (36) | 31,275,165 (42.7) |
| George C. Wallace (American Independent) | 46 (8) | 9,906,473 (13.5) |
| Other candidates (Dick Gregory, Socialist Labor; Fred Halstead and Paul Boutelle, Socialist Workers; Eugene McCarthy, Peace and Freedom; E. Harold Munn and Rolland E. Fisher, Prohibition) | – | 221,134 (.3) |

MAP 29–2   **The Election of 1968**   Richard Nixon won the presidency with the help of George Wallace, the American Independent Party candidate. Wallace won several southern states, offering an alternative to white southerners unhappy with the Democratic Party but not yet prepared to vote Republican. He also drew northern working-class votes away from Hubert Humphrey and thus helped Nixon to take several midwestern states.

> **What role** did opposition to the war in Vietnam play in determining the outcome of the 1968 election?

the popular vote and 191 electoral votes, and Nixon 43.4 percent of the popular vote and 301 electoral votes.

The Wallace candidacy was a glimpse of the future. The national media saw Wallace in terms of bigotry and a backlash against civil rights, getting only part of the story. Many of Wallace's northern backers were unhappy with both parties. Liberal on economic issues but conservative on family and social issues, many of these working-class voters evolved into "Reagan Democrats" by the 1980s. In the South, Wallace was a transitional choice for conservative voters who would eventually transfer their allegiance from the Democratic to the Republican Party.

# NIXON, WATERGATE, AND THE CRISIS OF THE EARLY 1970s

Nixon's painful public presence and dishonesty have tended to obscure his administration's accomplishments. He reduced tensions in the Cold War. He reluctantly upgraded civil rights enforcement, set goals for minority hiring by federal contractors, and presided over impressive environmental legislation.

WHAT WAS the legacy of Richard Nixon's presidency?

## GETTING OUT OF VIETNAM, 1969–1975

After 1968, things got worse in Southeast Asia before they got better. Nixon had no secret plan to end the war. Opposition intensified with the revelation that U.S. soldiers in March 1968 had slaughtered hundreds of men, women, and children in the South Vietnamese village of My Lai after failing to find any Viet Cong. This crime accentuated the dehumanizing power of war and showed how far the United States was straying from its ideals. Protests at home culminated in 1969 with the Vietnam Moratorium on October 15, when 2 million protesters joined rallies across the country.

Disaffection also mounted in Vietnam. Racial tensions sapped morale on the front lines. Troops lost discipline, took drugs, and hunkered down waiting for their tours of duty to end, and the high command had to adapt its code of justice to keep an army on the job.

Nixon and Vice President Spiro Agnew responded by trying to isolate the antiwar opposition, but Nixon also reduced the role of U.S. ground forces. Nixon claimed that his policies represented "the great silent majority of my fellow Americans." The administration arranged for a "spontaneous" attack by construction workers on antiwar protesters in New York. The hard-hat counterattack was a cynically manipulated symbol, but Nixon and Agnew tapped genuine anger about failure in Asia and rapid change in U.S. society.

The New Left had already split into factions. Many activists continued to focus on peace work, draft resistance, and other efforts to link radical and liberal agendas. About a hundred angry SDS members, however, declared themselves the Weather Underground in 1969. They tried to disrupt Chicago and Washington with window-smashing "days of rage." Three Weatherpeople accidentally blew themselves up with a homemade bomb in New York in 1970. Others robbed a Boston bank to get money for the revolution. Still others bombed a University of Wisconsin building and killed a student.

### "Vietnamization" and the secret war against Cambodia.

Nixon's secretary of defense, Melvin Laird, responded to the antiwar sentiment with "Vietnamization," withdrawing U.S. troops as fast as possible without undermining the South Vietnamese government. In July 1969, the president announced the **Nixon Doctrine.** The United States would help other countries fight their wars with weapons and money but not with soldiers. The policy substituted machines for men. Americans rearmed and enlarged the South Vietnamese army and surreptitiously bombed Communist bases in neutral Cambodia.

The secret war against Cambodia culminated on April 30, 1970, with an invasion. The aim was to smash Viet Cong and North Vietnamese bases to allow time to rebuild the South Vietnamese army. Americans who had hoped that the war was fading away were outraged. At Kent State University in Ohio, the National Guard was called in to maintain order. Taunts, tossed bottles, and the recent record of violence put them on edge. On May 4, one unit fired on a group of young people and killed four of them. At Jackson State University in Mississippi, two students were killed when troops fired on their dormitory.

### Stalemate and cease-fire.

The Cambodian "incursion" extended the military stalemate in Vietnam to U.S. policy. Beginning in December 1969, a new lottery system for determining the order of draft calls by birthdate let two-thirds of young men know they would not be drafted. In December 1970, Congress repealed the Gulf of Tonkin Resolution and prohibited the use of U.S. ground troops outside South Vietnam. Cambodia, however, was already devastated. The U.S. invasion had destabilized its government and opened the way for the bloodthirsty Khmer Rouge, who killed millions of Cambodians in the name of a working-class revolution. Vietnamization continued; only 90,000 U.S. ground troops were still in Vietnam by early 1972. A final air offensive in December smashed Hanoi into rubble and helped to force four and a half years of peace talks to a conclusion.

The cease-fire began on January 27, 1973. It confirmed U.S. withdrawal from Vietnam. North Vietnamese and Viet Cong forces would remain in control of the

**Nixon Doctrine**   President Nixon's new American policy (1969) toward Asia in which the United States would honor treaty commitments but would gradually disengage and expect Asian nations to handle military defense on their own.

### QUICK REVIEW

**The Nixon Doctrine**

- Nixon responded to antiwar protesters by reducing the role of U.S. ground forces in Vietnam.
- "Vietnamization": The withdrawal of U.S. troops as fast as possible without undermining the South Vietnamese government.
- The Nixon Doctrine substituted weapons and money for troops.

territory they occupied in South Vietnam, but they were not to be reinforced or substantially reequipped. The United States promised not to increase its military aid to South Vietnam. There were no solid guarantees for the South Vietnamese government. Immediately after coming to terms with North Vietnam, Nixon suspended the draft in favor of an all-volunteer military.

In 1975, South Vietnam collapsed. Only the U.S. presence had kept its political, ethnic, and religious factions together. For the first two years after the Paris agreement, North Vietnam quietly rebuilt its military capacity. In the spring of 1975, it opened an offensive, and South Vietnamese morale evaporated. Resistance crumbled so rapidly that the United States had to evacuate its embassy in Saigon by helicopter while frantic Vietnamese tried to join the flight.

## NIXON AND THE WIDER WORLD

To his credit, Richard Nixon took U.S. foreign policy in new directions even while he was struggling to escape from Vietnam and Cambodia. Like Dwight Eisenhower before him, Nixon's reputation as an anti-Communist allowed him to improve relations with China and the Soviet Union.

Since 1950, the United States had acted as if China did not exist, refusing economic relations and insisting that the Nationalist regime on Taiwan was the legitimate Chinese government. But the People's Republic of China was increasingly isolated within the Communist world. In 1969, it almost went to war with the Soviet Union. Nixon was eager to take advantage of Chinese-Soviet tension. Secret talks led to an easing of the American trade embargo in April 1971 and a tour of China by a U.S. table-tennis team. Henry Kissinger, Nixon's national security adviser, then arranged for Nixon's startling visit to Mao Zedong in Beijing in February 1972.

Playing the "China card" helped to improve relations with the Soviet Union. The Soviets needed increased trade with the United States and a counterweight to China, the United States was looking for help in getting out of Vietnam, and both countries wanted to limit nuclear armaments. Protracted negotiations led to the **Strategic Arms Limitation Treaty (SALT)** that Nixon signed in Moscow in May 1972. The agreements blocked the creation of extensive antiballistic missiles systems (ABMs) but failed to limit bombers, cruise missiles, or multiple independently targeted warheads on single missiles.

Diplomats used the French word *détente* to describe the new U.S. relations with China and the Soviet Union. *Détente* means an easing of tensions, not friendship or alliance. It facilitated travel between the United States and China. It allowed U.S. farmers to sell wheat to the Soviets. More broadly, *détente* implied that the United States and China recognized mutual interests in Asia and that the United States acknowledged the Soviet Union as an equal in world affairs. *Détente* made the world safer.

**SALT (Strategic Arms Limitation Treaty)**   Treaty signed in 1972 by the United States and the Soviet Union to slow the nuclear arms race.

***détente***   (French for "easing of tension") Used to describe the new U.S. relations with China and the Soviet Union in 1972.

## COURTING MIDDLE AMERICA

Nixon designed domestic policy to help him win reelection. His goal was to solidify his "Middle American" support. The strategy targeted the growing populations of the South and the suburbs, as well as blue-collar voters who were ready to abandon the Democrats for law-and-order Republicans.

The Nixon White House preferred to ignore troubled big cities. Instead, Nixon tilted federal assistance to the suburbs. The centerpiece of his **New Federalism** was General Revenue Sharing (1972), which passed federal funds directly to local governments with no limits on use. By 1980, it had transferred more than $18 billion to the states and more than $36 billion to local governments. Revenue sharing was a suburban-aid program. Its

**New Federalism**   President Richard Nixon's policy to shift responsibilities of government programs from the federal level to the states.

no-strings grants supplemented the general funds of every full-service government, whether a city of 2 million or a suburban town of 500.

Nixon pursued the southern strategy through the symbolism of Supreme Court nominations. His first nominees were Clement Haynsworth of Florida and G. Harrold Carswell of Alabama. Although the Senate rejected both as unqualified, the nominations nonetheless gave Nixon a reputation as a champion of the white South. He hoped to move cautiously in enforcing school desegregation, but a task force led by Secretary of Labor George Shultz crafted an approach that allowed substantial desegregation. In this instance, as elsewhere with his domestic policies, Nixon was inflammatory in speeches but moderate in action, increasing the funding of federal civil rights agencies.

## OIL, OPEC, AND STAGFLATION

**From Then to Now Online**
*Energy Worries*

One of the most troublesome domestic issues was inflation. The cost of living began to outpace wages in the late 1960s. One of the causes was LBJ's decision to fight in Vietnam without tax increases until 1968. An income tax cut in 1969, supported by both parties, made the situation worse. Inflation eroded the value of savings and pensions. It also made U.S. goods too expensive for foreign buyers and generated a trade deficit that placed pressures on the international value of the dollar.

The U.S. economy took another hit from inflation in 1973–1974. The main cause was the sharp increase in the price of energy, an input to every product and service. Angry at U.S. support for Israel in the Arab-Israeli War of October 1973, Arab nations imposed an embargo on oil exports that lasted from October 1973 to March 1974. The shortages eased when the embargo ended, but the **Organization of Petroleum Exporting Countries (OPEC)** had challenged the ability of the industrial nations to dictate world economic policy.

**Organization of Petroleum Exporting Countries (OPEC)**   Cartel of oil-producing nations in Asia, Africa, and Latin America that gained substantial power over the world economy in the mid- to late- 1970s by controlling the production and price of oil.

While Nixon searched for short-term political advantage, underlying problems of the U.S. economy went untreated. After 30 years at the top, the United States could no longer dominate the world economy by itself. The newly found power of OPEC was obvious. Just as important was the surging industrial capacity of Germany and Japan, which now had economies as modern as that of the United States. Declining rates of saving and investment in industrial capacity seemed to put the United States in danger of following the British road to economic obsolescence and second-level status. Indeed, a new term entered the popular vocabulary in 1971: *Stagflation* was the painful combination of stagnant economic growth, high unemployment, and inflation that matched no one's economic theory but everyone's daily experience.

**QUICK REVIEW**

**Causes of Inflation in the Early 1970s**

◆ LBJ's decision to fight in Vietnam without tax increases until 1968.

◆ An income tax cut in 1969.

◆ Increasing oil prices.

## AMERICANS AS ENVIRONMENTALISTS

In the turbulent 1970s, Americans found one issue they could agree on. In the 1970s, resource conservation grew into a multifaceted environmental movement.

**Exploring America**
*Rachel Carson*

After the booming 1950s, Americans had started to pay attention to "pollution," a catchall for the damage that advanced technologies and industrial production did to natural systems. Rachel Carson's *Silent Spring* in 1962 pushed pollution onto the national agenda. Carson, a well-regarded science writer, described the side effects of DDT and other pesticides on animal life. Her book resonated with many suburbanites, who realized that urban sprawl was creating a quiet environmental crisis, providing housing and shopping centers at the cost of bulldozed forests and farms, polluted streams, and smog-choked skies.

Environmentalism gained strength among Americans in 1970. On April 22, 10,000 schools and 20 million other people took part in Earth Day, an occasion first conceived by Wisconsin Senator Gaylord Nelson. Earth Day gained a grassroots following in towns and cities across the country. New York closed Fifth Avenue to automobiles for the day. Companies touted their environmental credentials.

The American establishment had been looking for a safe and respectable crusade to divert the idealism and discontent of the 1960s. Now the mainstream media discovered the ravaged planet. So did a politically savvy president. An expedient proenvironmental stance might attract some of the antiwar constituency. Nixon had already signed the National Environmental Policy Act on January 1, 1970, and later in the year created the **Environmental Protection Agency (EPA)** to enforce environmental laws. The rest of the Nixon administration brought legislation on clean air, clear water, pesticides, hazardous chemicals, and endangered species (see Overview, The Environmental Decades) that made environmental management and protection part of governmental routine.

As Americans became more aware of human-caused environmental hazards, they realized that minority and low-income communities had more than their share of problems. Landfills and waste disposal sites were frequently located near minority neighborhoods. In Buffalo, white working-class residents near the Love Canal industrial site discovered in 1978 that an entire neighborhood was built on land contaminated by decades of chemical dumping. Activists sought to understand the health effects and force compensation, paving the way for Superfund cleanup legislation (see American Views, Grassroots Community Action).

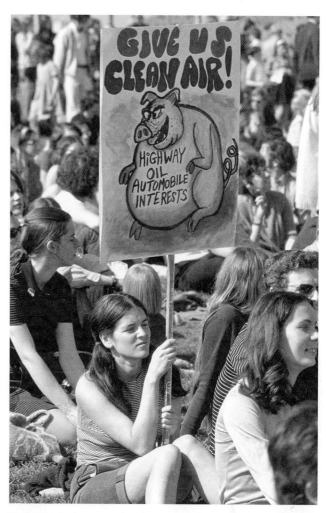

The first Earth Day in 1970 tapped growing concern about the environment. It helped turn the technical field of pollution control into the broad-based environmental movement.

## FROM DIRTY TRICKS TO WATERGATE

The **Watergate** crisis pivoted on Richard Nixon's character. Despite his solid political standing, Nixon saw enemies everywhere and overestimated their strength. Subordinates learned during his first administration that the president would condone dishonest actions—"dirty tricks"—if they stood to improve his political position. In 1972 and 1973, dirty tricks grew from a scandal into a constitutional crisis when Nixon abused the power of his office to cover up wrongdoing and hinder criminal investigations.

The chain of events that undermined Nixon's presidency started with the **Pentagon Papers.** In his last year as secretary of defense, Robert McNamara had commissioned a report on the U.S. road to Vietnam. The documents showed that the country's leaders had planned to expand the war even while they claimed to be looking for a way out. In June 1971, one of the contributors to the report, Daniel Ellsberg, leaked it to the *New York Times.* Its publication infuriated Nixon.

In response, the White House compiled a list of journalists and politicians who opposed Nixon. As one White House staffer, John Dean, put it, the president's men could then "use the available federal machinery [Internal Revenue Service, FBI] to screw our political enemies." Nixon set up a special investigations unit in the White House. Two former CIA employees, E. Howard Hunt and G. Gordon Liddy, became the chief "plumbers," as the group was known because its job was to prevent leaks of information.

Early in 1972, Hunt went to work for CREEP—the Committee to Re-Elect the President—while Liddy took another position on the presidential staff. CREEP had already raised millions and was hatching plans to undermine Democrats with rumors and pranks. Then, on June 17, 1972, five inept burglars hired with CREEP funds were

**Environmental Protection Agency (EPA)**  Federal agency created in 1970 to oversee environmental monitoring and cleanup programs.

### QUICK REVIEW

**Environmentalism**
- In the 1970s resource conversation grew into an environmental movement.
- Nixon created the Environmental Protection Agency (EPA) in 1970.
- Low-income and minority communities had a disproportionate share of environmental problems.

**Watergate**  A complex scandal involving attempts to cover up illegal actions taken by administration officials and leading to the resignation of President Richard Nixon in 1974.

## OVERVIEW    The Environmental Decades

| Administration | Focus of Concern | Legislation |
| --- | --- | --- |
| Johnson | Wilderness and wildlife | Wilderness Act (1964)<br>National Wildlife Refuge System (1966)<br>Wild and Scenic Rivers Act (1968) |
| Nixon | Pollution control and endangered environments | National Environmental Policy Act (1969)<br>Environmental Protection Agency (1970)<br>Clean Air Act (1970)<br>Occupational Safety and Health Act (1970)<br>Water Pollution Control Act (1972)<br>Pesticide Control Act (1972)<br>Coastal Zone Management Act (1972)<br>Endangered Species Act (1973) |
| Ford | Energy and hazardous materials | Toxic Substances Control Act (1976)<br>Resource Conservation and Recovery Act (1976) |
| Carter | Energy and hazardous materials | Energy Policy and Conservation Act (1978)<br>Comprehensive Emergency Response,<br>Compensation, and Liability Act<br>(Superfund) (1980) |
| | Parks and wilderness | Alaska National Interest Lands Conservation<br>Act (1980) |

**Pentagon Papers** Classified Defense Department documents on the history of the United States' involvement in Vietnam, prepared in 1968 and leaked to the press in 1971.

caught breaking into the Democratic National Committee office in Washington's Watergate apartment building. The people involved knew that an investigation would lead back to the White House. Nixon felt too insecure to ride out what would probably have been a small scandal. Instead, he initiated a coverup. On June 23, he ordered his assistant H. R. Haldeman to warn the FBI off the case with the excuse that national security was involved. Nixon compounded this obstruction of justice by arranging a $400,000 bribe to keep the burglars quiet.

The coverup worked in the short run. As mid-level officials from the Justice Department pursued their investigation, the public lost interest in what looked more like slapstick than a serious crime. Nixon's opponent in the 1972 election was South Dakota Senator George McGovern, an impassioned opponent of the Vietnam War. McGovern was honest, intelligent, and well to the left of center on such issues as the defense budget and legalization of marijuana. Nixon wins in a landslide.

The coverup began to come apart with the trial of the Watergate burglars in January 1973. Federal Judge John Sirica used the threat of heavy sentences to pressure one burglar into a statement that implied that higher-ups had been involved. Meanwhile, the *Washington Post* was linking Nixon's people to dirty tricks and illegal campaign contributions. Nixon was aware of many of the actions that his subordinates had undertaken. He now began to coach people on what they should tell investigators, claimed his staff had lied to him, and tried to set up White House Council John Dean to take the fall.

In the late spring and early summer, attention shifted to the televised hearings of the Senate's Select Committee on Presidential Campaign Activities. The real questions, it became obvious, were what the president knew and when he knew it. It seemed to be John Dean's word against Richard Nixon's.

A bombshell turned the scandal into a constitutional crisis. A mid-level staffer told the committee that Nixon had made tape recordings of his White House conversations. Both the Senate and the Watergate special prosecutor, Archibald Cox, subpoenaed the tapes. Nixon refused to give them up, citing executive privilege and the separation of powers. In late October, after he failed to cut a satisfactory deal, he fired his attorney general and the special prosecutor. This "Saturday-night massacre" caused a storm of protest, and many Americans thought that it proved that Nixon had something to hide. In April 1974, he finally released edited transcripts of the tapes, with foul language deleted and key passages missing; he claimed that his secretary had accidentally erased crucial material. Finally, on July 24, 1974, the U.S. Supreme Court ruled unanimously that Nixon had to deliver 64 tapes to the new special prosecutor.

Opposition to the president now spanned the political spectrum from Barry Goldwater to liberal Democrats, and Congress began impeachment proceedings. On July 27, the House Judiciary Committee took up the specific charges. Republicans joined Democrats in voting three articles of impeachment: for hindering the criminal investigation of the Watergate break-in, for abusing the power of the presidency by using federal agencies to deprive citizens of their rights, and for ignoring the committee's subpoena for the tapes. Before the full House could vote on the articles of impeachment and send them to the Senate for trial, Nixon delivered the tapes. One of them contained the "smoking gun," direct evidence that Nixon had participated in the coverup on June 23, 1972, and had been lying ever since. On August 8 he announced his resignation, effective the following day.

## THE FORD FOOTNOTE

Gerald Ford was the first president who had not been elected as either president or vice president. Ford was Nixon's appointee to replace Spiro Agnew, who had resigned and pleaded no contest to charges of bribery and income tax evasion in 1973 as Watergate was gathering steam. Ford was competent but unimaginative. His first major act was his most controversial—the pardon of Nixon for "any and all crimes" committed while president. Since Nixon had not yet been indicted, the pardon saved him from future prosecution. To many Americans, the act looked like a payoff.

Ford's administration presided over the collapse of South Vietnam in 1975, but elsewhere in the world, *détente* continued. U.S. diplomats joined the Soviet Union and 30 other European nations in the capital of Finland to sign the **Helsinki Accords.** The agreements called for increased commerce between the Eastern and Western blocs and for human-rights guarantees. They also legitimized the national boundaries that had been set in eastern Europe in 1945.

At home, the federal government did little new during Ford's two and a half years in office. Ford beat back Ronald Reagan for the Republican presidential nomination, but he was clearly vulnerable.

His Democratic opponent was a political enigma. James Earl Carter, Jr., had been a navy officer, a farmer, and the governor of Georgia. He was one of several new-style politicians who transformed southern politics in the 1970s. Carter and the others left race-baiting behind to talk like modern New Dealers, emphasizing that whites and blacks both needed better schools and economic growth. He appealed to Democrats as someone who could reassemble LBJ's political coalition and return the South to the Democratic Party. In his successful campaign, Carter presented himself as an alternative to party hacks and Washington insiders.

**Helsinki Accords**  Agreement in 1975 among NATO and Warsaw Pact members that recognized European national boundaries as set after World War II and included guarantees of human rights.

## AMERICAN VIEWS

### Grassroots Community Action

In the 1950s, a major chemical company closed a waste dump in Niagara Falls, New York. The site, known as Love Canal, was soon surrounded by a park, school, and hundreds of modest homes. Residents put up with noxious odors and seepage of chemical wastes until 1978, when they learned that the state health department was concerned about the health effects on small children and pregnant women. Over the next two years, residents battled state and federal bureaucracies and reluctant politicians for accurate information about the risks they faced and then for financial assistance to move from the area (often their homes represented their only savings). In October 1980, President Carter signed a bill to move all of the families permanently from the Love Canal area.

One of the leaders of the grassroots movement was housewife Lois Gibbs. The following excerpts from her story show her increasing sophistication as a community activist, starting by ringing doorbells in 1978 and ending with national television exposure in 1980. Although the Love Canal case itself was unusual, community-based organizations in all parts of the country learned the tactics of effective action in the 1960s and 1970s.

- **What** public programs in the 1960s and 1970s gave citizens experience in grassroots action?
- **How** might the Internet change the tactics of community organizing?

**KNOCKING ON DOORS**

I decided to go door-to-door with a petition. It seemed like a good idea to start near the school, to talk to the mothers nearest it. I had already heard that a lot of the residents near the school had been upset about the chemicals for the past couple of years. I thought they might help me. I had never done anything like this. . . . I was afraid a lot of doors would be slammed in my face, that people would think I was some crazy fanatic. But I decided to do it anyway . . . and knocked on my first door. There was no answer. I just stood there, not knowing what to do. It was an usually warm June day and I was perspiring. I thought: What am I doing here? I must be crazy. People are going to think I am. Go home, you fool! And that's just what I did.

It was one of those times when I had to sit down and face myself. I was afraid of making a fool of myself, I had scared myself, and I had gone home. When I got there, I

# JIMMY CARTER: IDEALISM AND FRUSTRATION IN THE WHITE HOUSE

**WHAT FACTORS** limited Jimmy Carter's effectiveness as president?

Jimmy Carter took office with little room to maneuver. Watergate bequeathed him a powerful and self-satisfied Congress and a combative press. OPEC oil producers, Islamic fundamentalists, and Soviet generals followed their own agendas. The American people themselves were fractionalized and quarrelsome, uneasy with the new advocacy of equality for women, uncertain as a nation whether they shared the same values and goals.

## CARTER, ENERGY, AND THE ECONOMY

The biggest domestic problem remained the economy, which slid into another recession in 1978. Another jump in oil prices helped make 1979 and 1980 the worst years for inflation in the postwar era. Interest rates surged past 20 percent as the Federal Reserve tried to reduce inflation by squeezing business and consumer credit. Carter himself was a fiscal conservative whose impulse was to cut federal spending. This course worsened unemployment and alienated liberal Democrats, who wanted to revive the Great Society.

Carter simultaneously proposed a comprehensive energy policy. He asked Americans to make energy conservation the moral equivalent of war—to accept individual sacrifices for the common good. Congress created the Department of Energy but refused to raise taxes

*Documents*

Jimmy Carter, *The "Malaise" Speech* (1979)

sat at the kitchen table with my petition in my hand, thinking. Wait. What if people do slam doors in your face? People may think you're crazy. But what's more important—what people think or your child's health? Either you're going to do something or you're going to have to admit you're a coward and not do it. . . . The next day, I went out on my own street to talk to people I knew. It was a little easier to be brave with them. If I could convince people I knew—friends—maybe it would be less difficult to convince others. . . . I went to the back door, as I always did when I visited a neighbor. Each house took about twenty or twenty-five minutes. . . .

### PHIL DONAHUE AND POLITICAL ACTION

The *Phil Donahue Show* called. They wanted us to appear on their June 18 show. The reaction in the office was different this time, compared to the show in October 1978. In October, everyone was excited. "Phil Donahue—wow!" Now, residents reacted differently. "Donahue. That's great press. Now we'll get the politicians to move!" . . . Now our people looked at the show as a tool to use in pushing the government to relocate us permanently. By this time we

understood how politicians react to public pressure, how to play the political game. We eagerly agreed to go, and found forty other residents to go with us. . . . [After arriving in Chicago] We then planned how we would handle the *Phil Donahue Show*. . . . We had to get the real issues across. Each resident was assigned an issue. One told of the chromosome tests. Another was to concentrate on her multiple miscarriages. Another was to ask for telegrams from across the country to the White House in support of permanent relocation. I coached them to get their point in, no matter the question asked. For example, if Donahue asked what you thought of the mayor, and your assignment was to discuss miscarriages, you should answer: "I don't like the mayor because I have had three miscarriages and other health problems, and he won't help us." Or: "My family is sick, and the mayor won't help us. That's why we need people to send telegrams to the White House for permanent relocation." . . . The residents were great! Each and every one followed through with our plan.

Source: Lois Marie Gibbs, as told to Murray Levine, *Love Canal: My Story* (Albany: State University of New York Press, 1982), pp. 12–13, 161–64.

on oil and natural gas to reduce consumption. However, the Energy Policy and Conservation Act (1978) did encourage alternative energy sources to replace foreign petroleum.

However, antinuclear activism blocked one obvious alternative to fossil fuels. The antinuclear movement had started with concern about the ability of the Atomic Energy Commission to monitor the safety of nuclear-power plants and about the disposal of spent fuel rods. In the late 1970s, activists staged sit-ins at the construction sites of nuclear plants. A near-meltdown at the Three Mile Island nuclear plant in Pennsylvania in March 1979 stalemated efforts to expand nuclear-power capacity.

## CLOSED FACTORIES AND FAILED FARMS

Ford and Carter both faced massive problems of economic transition that undercut their efforts to devise effective government programs. Industrial decay stalked such "gritty cities" as Allentown, Pennsylvania; Trenton, New Jersey; and Gary, Indiana. Communities whose workers had made products in high volume for a mass market found that technological revolutions made them obsolete. Critics renamed the old manufacturing region of the Northeast and Middle West the Rustbelt in honor of its abandoned factories.

Stories of **deindustrialization** were similar in small cities like Springfield, Ohio, and large cities like Cleveland. As high-paying jobs in unionized industries disappeared, sagging income undermined small businesses and neighborhoods. Falling tax revenue

**deindustrialization** The process of economic change involving the disappearance of outmoded industries and the transfer of factories to new low-wage locations, with devastating effects in the Northeast and Middle West, especially in the 1970s and 1980s.

Egyptian President Anwar al-Sadat, U.S. President Jimmy Carter, and Israeli Prime Minister Menachem Begin share a symbolic handshake after the signing of a peace treaty between Egypt and Israel on August 26, 1979. The treaty codified the historic agreement that the leaders had hammered out at Camp David, Maryland, in September 1978.

brought the city to the verge of bankruptcy in 1978; bankers forced public service cuts and tax increases, which meant further job losses.

Plant closures were only one facet of business efforts to increase productivity by substituting machinery for employees. Between 1947 and 1977, American steelmakers doubled output while cutting their workforce from 600,000 to 400,000. High interest rates and a strong dollar made U.S. exports too expensive and foreign imports cheap, forcing American manufacturers to cut costs or perish.

Parallel to the decline of heavy industry was the continuing transformation of American agriculture from small family enterprises to corporate agribusinesses. Agriculture was a national success story in the aggregate, but one accompanied by many human and environmental costs. The early 1970s brought an unexpected boom in farming. Crop failures and food shortages around the world in 1972 and 1973 expanded markets and pushed up prices for U.S. farm products. For a few years, agriculture looked like the best way for the United States to offset the high cost of imported oil. But the boom was over by the 1980s, when global commodity prices slumped. Farmers found themselves with debts they could not cover.

The boom of the 1970s was thus a brief interruption in the long-term transformation of U.S. agriculture. The number of farms slid from 4 million in 1960 to 2.4 million in 1980 and 1.9 million in 2000. Many farmers sold out willingly, glad to escape from drudgery and financial insecurity. Others could not compete in an agricultural system that favored large-scale production by demanding large amounts of capital for equipment and fertilizer. By 2000, fewer than 2 percent of American workers made their living from farming.

## BUILDING A COOPERATIVE WORLD

Despite troubles on the home front, Carter's first two years brought foreign-policy successes that reflected a new vision of a multilateral world. As a relative newcomer to international politics, Carter was willing to work with African, Asian, and Latin American nations on a basis of mutual respect. Carter appointed Andrew Young—an African American from Georgia with long experience in the civil rights movement—as ambassador to the United Nations, where he worked effectively to build bridges to third-world nations. Carter convinced the Senate in 1978 to approve treaties to transfer control of the Panama Canal to Panama by 2000, removing a sore point in relations with Latin America.

Carter's moral convictions were responsible for a new concern with human rights around the globe. He criticized the Soviet Union for prohibiting free speech and denying its citizens the right to emigrate, angering Soviet leaders, who did not expect the human rights clauses of the Helsinki Accords to be taken seriously. Carter was also willing to criticize some (but not all) American allies. He withheld economic aid from South Africa, Guatemala, Chile, and Nicaragua, which had long records of human rights abuses. In Nicaragua, the change in policy helped left-wing Sandinista rebels topple the Somoza dictatorship.

The triumph of the new foreign policy was the **Camp David Agreement** between Egypt and Israel. Carter risked his reputation and credibility in September 1978 to bring Egyptian President Anwar al-Sadat and Israeli Prime Minister Menachem Begin

**Camp David Agreement**  Agreement to reduce points of conflict between Israel and Egypt, hammered out in 1977 with the help of U.S. President Jimmy Carter.

## QUICK REVIEW

### Carter's Foreign Policy Successes

♦ Appointed Andrew Young as ambassador to UN, where he helped build bridges to third-world nations.

♦ Made human rights a key issue in American policy.

♦ Facilitated Camp David Agreement between Egypt and Israel.

The Iran hostage crisis reflected intense anti-American feelings in Iran and provoked an equally bitter anti-Iranian reaction in the United States. Fifty-two of the more than 60 U.S. embassy employees first seized were held for 444 days, giving the United States a painful lesson about the limits on its ability to influence events around the world.

together at Camp David, the presidential retreat. He refused to admit failure and dissuaded the two leaders from walking out. A formal treaty was signed in Washington on March 26, 1979. The pact normalized relations between Israel and its most powerful neighbor and led to Israel's withdrawal from the Sinai Peninsula. It was a vital prelude to further progress toward Arab-Israeli peace in the mid-1990s.

## NEW CRISES ABROAD

In the last two years of Carter's administration, the Cold War sprang back to life around the globe and smothered the promise of a new foreign policy. The Soviets ignored the human-rights provisions of the Helsinki Accords. Soviet advisers or Cuban troops intervened in African civil wars. At home, Cold Warriors who had never accepted détente found it easier to attack Carter than Nixon.

**The failure of SALT II.**    Carter inherited negotiations for SALT II—a strategic arms-limitation treaty that would have reduced both the U.S. and Soviet nuclear arsenals—from the Ford administration. SALT II met stiff resistance in the Senate. Opponents claimed it would create a "window of vulnerability" in the 1980s that would invite the Soviets to launch a nuclear first strike. Carter tried to counter criticism by stepping up defense spending, starting a buildup that would accelerate under Ronald Reagan.

Hopes for SALT II vanished on December 24, 1979, when Soviet troops entered Afghanistan, a technically neutral Muslim nation on the southern border of the Soviet

Union. A pro-Soviet government had fallen into factional strife, while tribespeople, unhappy with modernization, were mounting increasing resistance. One of the factions invited intervention by the Soviets, who quickly installed a client government. The situation resembled the U.S. involvement in South Vietnam. Similar, too, was the inability of Soviet forces to suppress the Afghan guerrillas, who had American weapons and controlled the mountains. In the end, it took the Soviets a decade to find a way out.

**The Iranian Hostage Crisis.**   The final blow to Carter's foreign policy came in Iran. Since 1953, the United States had strongly backed Iran's monarch, Shah Reza Pahlevi. The shah modernized Iran's economy, but his feared secret police jailed and tortured political opponents. U.S. aid and oil revenues helped him build a large army, but the Iranian middle class despised his authoritarianism, and Muslim fundamentalists opposed the Westernizing influence of modernization. A revolution toppled the shah at the start of 1979.

The upheaval installed a nominally democratic government, but the Ayatollah Ruhollah Khomeini, a Muslim cleric who hated the United States, exercised real power. Throughout 1979, Iran grew increasingly anti-American. After the United States allowed the exiled shah to seek medical treatment in New York, a mob stormed the U.S. embassy in Tehran on November 4, 1979, and took more than 60 Americans hostage. They demanded that Carter surrender the shah. The administration tried economic pressure and diplomacy, but Khomeini had no desire for accommodation. When Iran announced in April 1980 that the hostages would remain in the hands of the militants rather than be transferred to the government, Carter ordered an airborne rescue. Even a perfectly managed effort would have been difficult. The hostages were held in the heart of a city

American hostages stand blindfolded among a few of their Iranian captors after the capture of the American embassy in Teheran.

of 4 million hostile Iranians, hundreds of miles from the nearest aircraft carrier and thousands of miles from U.S. bases. Hampered by lack of coordination among the military services, the attempt turned into a fiasco that added to the national embarrassment and a feeling of powerlessness. The United States and Iran finally reached agreement on the eve of the 1980 election. The hostages gained their freedom after 444 days, at the moment Ronald Reagan took office as the new president.

The hostage crisis consumed Jimmy Carter the way that Vietnam had consumed Lyndon Johnson. It gripped the public and stalemated other issues. Carter's tragedy was that "his" Iranian crisis was the fruit of policies hatched by the Eisenhower administration and pursued by every president since then, all of whom had overlooked the shah's despotic government because of his firm anti-Communism.

## CONCLUSION

In the mid-1970s, Americans encountered real limits to national capacity. From 1945 to 1973, they had enjoyed remarkable prosperity. That ended in 1974. Long lines at gas stations showed that prosperity was fragile. Cities and regions felt the costs of obsolete industries. Environmental damage caused many Americans to reconsider the goal of economic expansion.

The nation also had to recognize that it could not run the world. American withdrawal from Vietnam in 1973 and the collapse of the South Vietnamese government in 1975 were defeats; the United States ended up with little to show for a long and painful war. SALT I stabilized the arms race, but it also recognized that the Soviet Union was an equal. The American nuclear arsenal might help deter a third world war, but it could not prevent the seizure of hostages in Iran.

These challenges came amid deep economic and social changes in the United States. The ways Americans made their livings and the range of opportunities they faced were in flux. The nation finished the 1970s more egalitarian than it had been in the early 1960s but also more divided. More citizens had the opportunity to advance economically and to seek political power, but there were deepening fissures between social liberals and cultural conservatives, old and new views about roles for women, rich and poor, whites and blacks. In 1961, John Kennedy had called on his fellow citizens to "bear any burden, pay any price" to defend freedom. By 1980, the nation had neither the economic capacity to pay any price nor the unity to agree on what burdens it should bear.

# SUMMARY

WHY DID the national consensus of the 1950s and early 1960s unravel?

**The End of Consensus** The failure to win an easy victory in Vietnam eroded the nation's confidence and fueled bitter division about the nation's goals. Operation Rolling Thunder in the air and search and destroy missions on the ground were not "winning" the war; protest against the war at home quickly followed America's decision to use combat forces. The tone of the debate over Vietnam turned nastier, much of the anger directed at the draft. The antiwar movement reflected a growing grass-roots activism on college campuses, among women, and the Woodstock generation counterculture.

WHAT CHALLENGES did cities face in the late 1960s and 1970s?

**Cities Under Stress** Exploding metropolitan areas needed money for streets, schools, and sewers. Many urban problems were associated with the creation of "second ghettos" due to immigration in the 1950s and 1960s. A series of riots scarred most big cities during the 1960s; the riots were protests about the problems of ghetto life but were often blamed on "outsiders." Minority separatism tapped into the same anger that caused the riots. The Black Power movement, Hispanic activism in the Southwest, and the American Indian Movement all questioned the American assumption that everyone wanted to be a part of the same homogeneous society, a society increasingly becoming "suburbanized."

HOW DID the Tet offensive change American public opinion about the war in Vietnam?

**The Year of the Gun, 1968** 1968 was a watershed year that forced American society to rethink the role of government. Mainstream Americans began questioning the war in Vietnam after the Tet Offensive; President Johnson was advised that the war was unwinnable on acceptable terms. Facing political challenges, Johnson announced a halt to the bombing of North Vietnam and his withdrawal from the presidential race. The assassinations of Martin Luther King Jr. and Robert Kennedy and the riots at the Democratic National Convention captured America's attention. Richard Nixon gained the presidency in 1968 with a secret plan to end the war and an appeal to middle America.

WHAT WAS the legacy of Richard Nixon's presidency?

**Nixon, Watergate and The Crisis of the Early 1970s** President Nixon had no plan to end the Vietnam War and antiwar sentiment grew; while the Nixon Doctrine and "Vietnamization" made it appear the United States was withdrawing from Southeast Asia, the bombing of Cambodia intensified. The 1973 ceasefire confirmed American withdrawal from Vietnam; in 1975 South Vietnam collapsed. To his credit, Nixon took American foreign policy in new directions, improving relations with the Soviet Union and China, and the president signed numerous laws relating to environmental issues. Nixon abused the power of his office in the Watergate scandal and resigned before he could be impeached; Gerald Ford, who had been appointed vice president, succeeded him.

WHAT FACTORS limited Jimmy Carter's effectiveness as president?

**Jimmy Carter: Idealism and Frustration in the White House** Washington outsider Jimmy Carter's major domestic challenge was the economy. A recession, an energy crisis, the deindustrization of America, and the transformation of the family farm to agribusiness challenged the president upon his election. Carter's moral convictions brought attention to human rights issues abroad. The signing of the Camp David Agreement between Egypt and Israel was a high point; hopes for reducing nuclear arsenals ended when the Soviet Union invaded Afghanistan. The Iranian hostage crisis consumed the Carter administration and helped contribute to Ronald Reagan's 1980 victory.

# WHERE TO LEARN MORE

**Lyndon B. Johnson National Historical Park, Johnson City, Texas.** Johnson's ranch, southwest of Austin, gives visitors a feeling for the open landscape in which Johnson spent his early years. **www.nps.gov/lypo**

**Vietnam Veterans Memorial, Washington, DC.** A simple wall engraved with the names of the nation's Vietnam War dead is testimony to one of the nation's most divisive wars. **www.nps.gov/vive**

**Richard Nixon Library and Birthplace, Yorba Linda, California.** Exhibits trace Nixon's political career and related world events with a sympathetic interpretation. **www.nixonfoundation.org/index.shtml**

**Titan Missile Museum, Green Valley, Arizona.** The Green Valley complex near Tucson held 18 Titan missiles. They were deactivated after SALT I, and the complex is now open to visitors. **www.pimaair.org/titan_01.htm.**

# STUDY RESOURCES

## myhistorylab

# REVIEW QUESTIONS

1. Why did the United States fail to achieve its objectives in Vietnam? What factors limited President Johnson's freedom of action there? How did the Tet Offensive affect U.S. policy? How did antiwar protests in the United States influence national policy?

2. How did racial relations change between 1965 and 1970? What were the relationships between the civil rights movement and minority separatism? What were the similarities and differences between African American, Latino, and Native American activism?

3. In what ways was 1968 a pivotal year for U.S. politics and society? How was it influenced by global events?

4. What were the implications of *détente*? Why did the Cold War reappear in the late 1970s? How and why did U.S. influence over the rest of the world change during the 1970s?

5. How did Richard Nixon's political strategy respond to the growth of the South and West? How did it respond to the shift of population from central cities to suburbs?

6. How did the backgrounds of Presidents Johnson, Nixon, and Carter shape their successes and failures as national leaders?

7. What political and constitutional issues were at stake in the Watergate scandal? How did it change American politics?

8. Why was the space race important for the United States? How did it strengthen the alliance between American science, government, and industry?

## KEY TERMS

American Indian Movement (AIM) (p. 890)
*Baker v. Carr* (p. 891)
Black Panthers (p. 889)
Black Power (p. 889)
Camp David Agreement (p. 904)
Counterculture (p. 884)
Deindustrialization (p. 903)
*Détente* (p. 897)
Environmental Protection Agency (EPA) (p. 899)
Free Speech Movement (FSM) (p. 884)
Helsinki Accords (p. 901)
Model Cities Program (p. 884)
Nation of Islam (p. 889)
New Federalism (p. 897)

Nixon Doctrine (p. 896)
Organization of Petroleum Exporting Countries (Opec) (p. 898)
Pentagon Papers (p. 900)
Strategic Arms Limitation Treaty (SALT) (p. 897)
Search and destroy (p. 881)
Selective Service System (p. 883)
Stonewall Rebellion (p. 887)
Students for a Democratic Society (SDS) (p. 883)
*Swann v. Charlotte-Mecklenburg Board of Education* (p. 891)
Watergate (p. 899)

# The Reagan Revolution and a Changing World

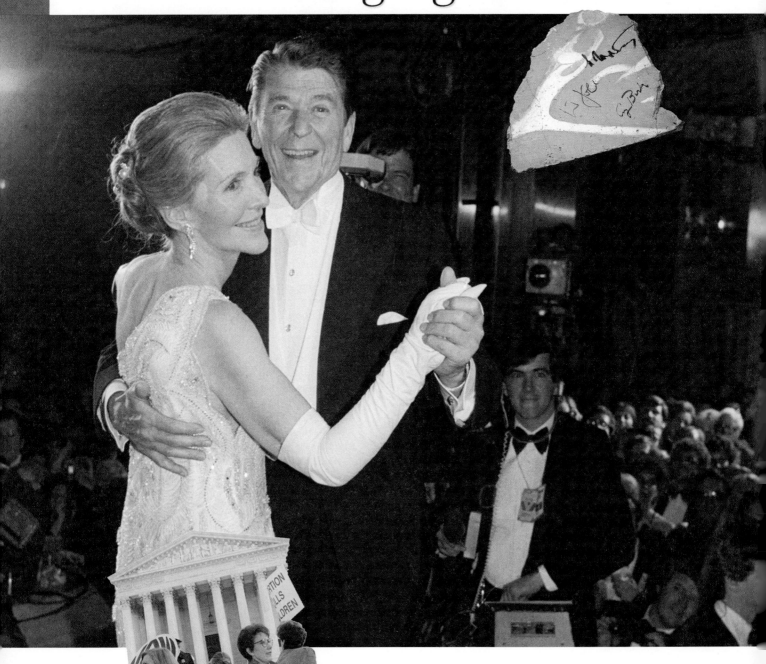

Ronald Reagan and his wife, Nancy, celebrate his inauguration as president.

**REAGAN'S DOMESTIC REVOLUTION** *(page 914)*

**WHAT GROUPS** of traditionally Democratic voters were attracted to Ronald Reagan's message? Why?

**THE SECOND (SHORT) COLD WAR** *(page 924)*

**WHAT WERE** the goals of the Reagan administration's policies in Central America?

**GROWTH IN THE SUNBELT** *(page 931)*

**HOW DID** growth in the Sunbelt shape national politics in the 1980s and 1990s?

**VALUES IN COLLISION** *(page 936)*

**WHAT KEY** social and cultural issues divided Americans in the 1980s and 1990s?

*The Khmer Rouge marched into the city [Phnom Penh, the capital of Cambodia], dressed in black. Young Khmer Rouge [Marxist revolutionary] soldiers, eight or ten years old, were dragging their rifles, which were taller than them. The whole city, more than two million people was forced out of their homes into the streets. My family walked until we reached Mao Tse-Tung Boulevard, the main boulevard in Phnom Penh. All the population of the city was gathered there. The Khmer Rouge were telling everyone to leave the city.*

*Although my two middle children were safe in France, my oldest and youngest daughters were close beside me. Parika was only seven. Mealy, who was nineteen, carried her infant son. I kept my children huddled together. As soon as a parent let go, a child would be lost in the huge crowd. And the Khmer Rouge kept ordering everybody, "You must go forward." They shot their guns in the air. Even during the middle of the night the procession was endless. The Khmer Rouge kept shooting and we kept moving forward.*

*Recently I saw the movie Doctor Zhivago, about the Russian Revolution. If you compare that to what happened in Phnom Penh, the movie is only on a very small scale. Even Killing Fields only gives you part of the idea of what happened in Cambodia. The reality was much more incredible.*

*Each night, when we came back to the village from working in the fields, Mom would say, "Children, let's all go to sleep." She would quietly warn me that the wood had eyes and ears. She'd say, "It's nine o'clock now. Go to sleep. There is nothing else to do but work. All the men are gone in our family." Mom was actually saying for the Khmer Rouge spies to hear, "They are only girls. Don't kill them. We are the only members left of the family." We were lying to them about our identity. It was a horrible game.*

*If you hid your identity, that meant you wanted your past forgotten. We had changed from people who were intellectual, who used to think independently. You became humiliated, allowed to live only as a slave. We were accepted into the United States thanks to my husband's military service. My daughters and I flew to the United States on July 4, 1979. As we landed, I thought, "This is real freedom."*

*I've found that America is a country where people have come from all over the world. You do your job, you get paid like anybody else, and you're accepted. But Cambodians I know in France, like my sister, feel differently. People are not accepted if they are not French. But in America you're part of the melting pot. In 1983, I came to Los Angeles for my daughter Monie's wedding. I decided to stay. Long Beach has the largest concentration of Cambodians in the country. I called the community center in Long Beach. They said they had no job openings. So I decided to get involved in running a store. Donut shops are very American.*

*All that refugees have is our work, our dreams. Do I still hurt from what happened in the past? When I opened my mouth to tell you my story, I don't know where my tears came from. My daughters don't like to talk about the past in Cambodia. They want to forget and think about their future. They ask me why I would talk about the past with anybody. I said, "The past cannot be erased from my memory."*

◆ Celia Noup, in Al Santoli, *New Americans: An Oral History* (New York, 1988).

## myhistorylab
### Personal Journeys Online

- Jubilee Lau, "Chinese and Proud of It," 1996. From Hong Kong to Idaho in the 1980s.

- Richard Rodriguez, Hunger of Memory, 1982. Learning English in an immigrant household.

- Ana Cabellero, 1980s. Mexican American Generations in El Paso. Interview in Al Santoli, *New Americans*, 1988.

◆ **CELIA NOUP** taught school for 20 years in Cambodia, which borders on South Vietnam. In 1975, after a long civil war, the Communist Khmer Rouge insurgents took over Cambodia's capital, Phnom Penh, and forced its inhabitants into the countryside to work in the fields. Four years later, Noup managed to make her way to a refugee camp in neighboring Thailand and then to the United States. Within a decade, she was working from 5:00 A.M. to 7:00 P.M. in her own donut shop near Los Angeles airport and worrying about helping her children buy houses.

Celia Noup's life shows some of the ways that new waves of immigration from Asia, Latin America, and Africa have changed the United States over the last generation. Immigrants fueled economic growth in the 1980s and 1990s with their labor and their drive to succeed in business. They revitalized older neighborhoods in cities from coast to coast and changed the ethnic mix of major cities. And they created new racial tensions that found their way into national political debates about immigration and into open conflict in places such as Miami and Los Angeles.

Noup's story is also a reminder of the drawn-out consequences of the U.S. involvement in Vietnam and the long shadow of the Cold War. The Cambodian civil war was fueled by reactions to the Vietnamese war and the U.S. invasion of Cambodia in 1969. American refugee policy was humanitarian but also political, opening the door to people fleeing Communist regimes but holding it shut against refugees from right-wing dictatorships.

By the end of Ronald Reagan's presidency (1981–1989), new rules governed domestic affairs as well as international relations. In the 1980s Americans decided to reverse the growth of federal government responsibilities that had marked both Republican and Democratic administrations since the 1930s. The backdrop to the political changes were massive readjustments in the American economy that began in the 1970s with the decline of heavy industry and then continued to shift employment from factory jobs to service jobs in the 1980s. The ideology of unregulated markets celebrated economic success, but masked a troubling reality: a widening gap between the rich and poor. The result by 1992 was a nation that was much more secure in the world than it had been in 1980, but also more divided against itself. ◆

## CHRONOLOGY

**1973** *Roe v. Wade*: Supreme Court strikes down state laws banning abortion in the first trimester of pregnancy.

**1980** Ronald Reagan is elected president.

**1981** Economic Recovery and Tax Act, reducing personal income tax rates, is passed.

Reagan breaks strike by air traffic controllers.

AIDS is recognized as a new disease.

**1982** Nuclear freeze movement peaks.

United States begins to finance Contra rebels against the Sandinista government in Nicaragua.

Equal Rights Amendment fails to achieve ratification.

**1983** 241 Marines are killed by a terrorist bomb in Beirut, Lebanon.

Strategic Defense Initiative introduced.

United States invades Grenada.

**1984** Reagan wins reelection.

**1985** Mikhail Gorbachev initiates economic and political reforms in the Soviet Union.

**1986** Tax Reform Act is adopted.

**1987** Congress holds hearings on the Iran-Contra scandal.

Reagan and Gorbachev sign the Intermediate Nuclear Force treaty.

**1988** George H.W. Bush is elected president.

**1989** Communist regimes in eastern Europe collapse; Germans tear down Berlin Wall.

Financial crisis forces federal bailout of many savings and loans.

United States invades Panama to capture General Manuel Noriega.

**1990** Iraq invades Kuwait; and United States sends forces to the Persian Gulf.

West Germany and East Germany reunite.

Americans with Disabilities Act is adopted.

**1991** Persian Gulf War: Operation Desert Storm drives the Iraqis from Kuwait.

Soviet Union dissolves into independent nations.

Strategic Arms Reduction Treaty (START) is signed.

**1992** Acquittal of officers accused of beating Rodney King triggers Los Angeles riots.

# REAGAN'S DOMESTIC REVOLUTION

**WHAT GROUPS** of traditionally Democratic voters were attracted to Ronald Reagan's message? Why?

*Documents*

Ronald Reagan, *First Inaugural Address* (1981)

Political change began in 1980, when Ronald Reagan and running his mate, George H.W. Bush, rode American discontent to a decisive victory in the presidential election (see Map 30–1). Building on a conservative critique of American policies and developing issues that Jimmy Carter had placed on the national agenda, Reagan presided over revolutionary changes in U.S. government and policies. The consequences of his two terms included an altered role for government, powerful but selective economic growth, and a shift of domestic politics away from bread-and-butter issues toward moral or lifestyle concerns.

### REAGAN'S MAJORITY

Ronald Reagan reinvented himself several times on his unusual journey to the White House. A product of small-town Illinois, he succeeded in Hollywood in the late 1930s as a romantic lead actor while adopting the liberal politics common at the time. After World War II, he moved rapidly to the political right as a spokesman for big business. He entered politics with a rousing conservative speech at the 1964 Republican convention and then accepted the invitation of wealthy California Republicans to run for governor in 1966, serving two terms in that office.

With a common touch that made him a favorite for a sizable segment of the public, Reagan tapped into the nostalgia for a simpler America. Although he was 69 when elected, his status as a movie and television personality made him seem up-to-date. His Hollywood background made it easy for him to use popular films to make his points. He once

**WHERE TO LEARN MORE**

Ronald Reagan Boyhood Home, Dixon, Illinois.
www.ronaldreaganhome.com

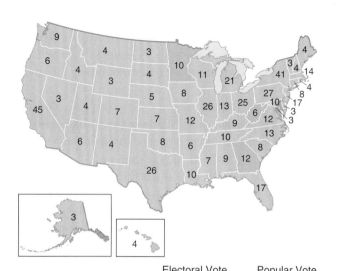

| | Electoral Vote (%) | Popular Vote (%) |
|---|---|---|
| **RONALD REAGAN (Republican)** | **489 (91)** | **43,201,220 (50.9)** |
| Jimmy Carter (Democrat) | 49 (9) | 34,913,332 (41.2) |
| John B. Anderson (Independent) | – | 5,581,379 (6.6) |
| Other candidates (Libertarian) | – | 921,299 (1.1) |

MAP 30–1   **The Election of 1980**   Ronald Reagan won in a landslide in 1980. Independent candidate John Anderson took more votes from Jimmy Carter than from Reagan, but Reagan's personal magnetism was a powerful political force. His victory confirmed the shift of the South to the Republican Party.

**What did** Reagan's victory tell about voters' desire for change in 1980?

threatened to veto legislation by challenging Congress with Clint Eastwood's "Make my day."

Some of Reagan's most articulate support came from anti-Communist stalwarts of both parties, who feared that the United States was losing influence in the world. Despite Jimmy Carter's tough actions in 1979 and 1980 and increased defense spending, such conservatives had not trusted him to do enough. Soviet military buildup, charged the critics, was creating a "window of vulnerability," a dangerous period when the Soviet Union might threaten the United States with a first strike by nuclear weapons.

Other Reagan voters directed their anger at government bureaucracies. Wealthy entrepreneurs from the fast-growing South and West believed that Nixon-era federal offices, such as the Environmental Protection Agency and the Occupational Safety and Health Administration, were choking their businesses in red tape. Many of these critics had amassed new fortunes in oil, real estate, and retailing and hated the taxes that funded social programs.

Christian conservatives worried that social activists were using the federal courts to alter traditional values. Jimmy Carter, a member of the Southern Baptist church, had won a clear majority among white evangelical voters in 1976, but Reagan's contrasting position on school prayer and abortion gave him the edge in 1980 and made him the overwhelming preference of conservative Christian voters in 1984.

Foreign policy activists and opponents of big government would have been unable to elect Reagan without disaffected blue-collar and middle-class voters who deserted the Democrats.

*Documents*

Ronald Reagan, *Speech to the House of Commons* (1982)
Ronald Reagan, *Address to the National Association of Evangelicals* (1983)

Ronald Reagan and his wife, Nancy, celebrate Reagan's inauguration as president.

Reagan's campaign hammered on the question "Are you better off than you were four years ago?" Democrats faced a special dilemma with the deepening tension between working-class white voters and black voters. They needed both groups to win but found white blue-collar voters deeply alienated by affirmative action and busing for school integration.

A further Democratic challenge was Ronald Reagan's personal appeal. The new president won over many Americans by surviving a 1981 assassination attempt in fine spirits. Reagan's popularity compounded the Democrats' inability to excite younger voters. The mid-1980s consistently showed that roughly two-thirds of people in their twenties and early thirties were choosing the Republicans as the party of energy and new ideas, leaving the Democrats to the middle-aged and elderly.

In the election of 1984, Democrats sealed their fate by nominating Walter Mondale, who had been vice president under Carter. Mondale was earnest, honest, and dull. Reagan ran on the theme "It's Morning in America," with the message that a new age of pride and prosperity had begun. Mondale assumed that Americans cared enough about the exploding federal deficit that Reagan's defense spending had produced to accept an across-the-board tax increase. With the economy growing and inflation now in check, most voters did not want Mondale to remind them of long-range financial realities, and Reagan won reelection with 98 percent of the electoral votes. His election confirmed that the American public found conservative ideas increasingly attractive.

## THE NEW CONSERVATISM

Reagan's approach to public policy drew on conservative intellectuals who offered a coherent critique of the New Deal–New Frontier approach to U.S. government. They feared that the antiwar movement had undermined the anti-Communist stance and that social changes were corrupting mainstream values.

**Downsizing the Great Society.**    Worries about big government permeated the critique of domestic policy. Edward Banfield's radical ideas about the failures of the Great Society set the tone of the neoconservative analysis. In *The Unheavenly City* (1968), he questioned the basic idea of public solutions for social problems. He argued that inequality is based on human character and rooted in the basic structure of society; government action can only solve problems that require better engineering, such as pollution control, better highways, or the delivery of explosives to military targets. Government's job, said Banfield, was to preserve public order, not to right wrongs or encourage unrealistic expectations.

**Free market utopians.**    Another strand of conservative argument came from free market utopians. After years of stagflation, Americans were eager to hear that unleashing free markets would trigger renewed prosperity.

The common themes of the conservative critique were simple: Free markets work better than government programs; government intervention does more harm than good; government assistance saps the initiative of the poor. In 1964, three-quarters of Americans had trusted Washington "to do what is right." By 1980, three-quarters were convinced that the federal government wasted tax money. The cumulative effect of the neoconservative arguments was to trash the word "liberal" and convince many Americans that labor unions and minorities were "special interests" but that oil tycoons, defense contractors, and other members of Reagan's coalition were not.

**Conservative political savvy.**    Conservatives promoted their ideology with new political tactics. Targeted mailings raised funds and mobilized voters with emotional

*Documents*

T. Boone Pickens, *My Case for Reagan* (1984)

**QUICK REVIEW**

**The Conservative Critique**

◆ Free markets work better than government programs.

◆ Government intervention does more harm than good.

◆ Government assistance saps the initiative of the poor.

appeals while bypassing the mass media, with their supposed preference for mainstream or liberal policies. Conservative organizers also knew how to use radio call-in shows to spread their message. Such appeals contrasted with the Democrats's reliance on more traditional ways to get out the vote through personal contacts and labor unions. Through the 1980s, Democrats repeatedly found themselves blindsided by creative Republican campaign tactics.

## REAGANOMICS: DEFICITS AND DEREGULATION

The heart of the 1980s revolution was the **Economic Recovery and Tax Act of 1981 (ERTA),** which reduced personal income tax rates by 25 percent over three years. The explicit goal was to stimulate business activity by lowering taxes overall and slashing rates for the rich. Cutting the government's total income by $747 billion over five years, ERTA meant less money for federal programs and more money in the hands of consumers and investors to stimulate economic growth.

Reagan's first budget director, David Stockman, later revealed a second goal. ERTA would lock in deficits by "pulling the revenue plug." Because defense spending and Social Security were untouchable, Congress would find it impossible to create and fund new programs without cutting old ones. If Americans still wanted social programs, they could enact them at the local or state level, but Washington would no longer pay.

The second part of the economic agenda was to free capitalists from government regulations, in the hope of increasing business innovation and efficiency. The **deregulation** revolution built on a head start from the 1970s. A federal antitrust case had split the unified Bell System of AT&T and its subsidiaries into seven regional telephone companies and opened long-distance service to competition. Congress also deregulated air travel in 1978.

**Environmental regulation and federal lands.**   Corporate America used the Reagan administration to attack environmental legislation as "strangulation by regulation." Reagan's new budgets sliced funding for the Environmental Protection Agency. Vice President Bush headed the White House Task Force on Regulatory Relief, which delayed or blocked regulations on hazardous wastes, automobile emissions, and exposure of workers to chemicals on the job.

Most attention, however, went to the controversial appointment of a Colorado lawyer, James Watt, as secretary of the interior. Watt was sympathetic to a western movement known as the **Sagebrush Rebellion,** which wanted the vast federal land holdings in the West transferred to the states for less environmental protection and more rapid economic use. Federal resource agencies sold trees to timber companies at a loss to the Treasury, expanded offshore oil drilling, and expedited exploration for minerals.

**Deregulation of the banking industry.**   The early 1980s also transformed American financial markets. Under new rules, savings and loans began to compete for deposits by offering high interest rates and reinvesting the money in much riskier commercial real estate. By 1990, the result was a financial crisis in which bad loans destroyed hundreds of S&Ls, especially in the Southwest. American taxpayers were left to bail out depositors to the tune of hundreds of billions of dollars to prevent a collapse of the nation's financial and credit system.

With the deregulation of financial markets, corporate consolidations and mergers flourished. Corporate raiders raised money with "junk bonds"—high-interest, high-risk securities—and snapped up profitable and cash-rich companies that could be milked of profits and assets. The merger mania channeled capital into paper transactions rather than investments in new equipment and products. Another effect was to damage the

**Economic Recovery and Tax Act of 1981 (ERTA)**   A major revision of the federal income tax system.

Paul Craig Roberts, *The Supply-Side Revolution* (1984)

**QUICK REVIEW**
***
**Key Components of Reaganomics**
- ◆ Lower personal income tax rates.
- ◆ Increase defense spending.
- ◆ Deregulate industry.

**deregulation**   Reduction or removal of government regulations and encouragement of direct competition in many important industries and economic sectors.

**Sagebrush Rebellion**   Political movement in the Western states in the early 1980s that called for easing of regulations on the economic issue of federal lands and the transfer of some or all of those lands to state ownership.

economies of small and middle-sized communities by transferring control of local companies to outside managers.

In the short term, the national economy boomed in the mid-1980s. Deregulated credit, tax cuts, and massive deficit spending on defense fueled exuberant growth. The stock market mirrored the overall prosperity; the Dow Jones average of blue-chip industrial stock prices more than tripled from August 1982 to August 1987.

## CRISIS FOR ORGANIZED LABOR

The flip side of the economic boom was another round in the Republican offensive against labor unions. Reagan set the tone when he fired more than 11,000 members of the Professional Air Traffic Controllers Organization for violating a no-strike clause in their hiring agreements. He claimed to be enforcing the letter of the law, but the message to organized labor was clear.

**Decline of union membership and blue-collar jobs.**    Organized labor counted a million fewer members at the end of Reagan's administration in 1989 than in 1964, even though the number of employed Americans had nearly doubled. As union membership declined and unions struggled to cope with the changing economy, corporations seized the opportunity to demand wage rollbacks and concessions on working conditions as trade-offs for continued employment, squeezing workers in one plant and then using the settlement to pressure another. Workers in the 1970s and 1980s faced the threat that employers might move a factory to a new site elsewhere in the United States or overseas. Or a company might sell out to a new owner, who could close a plant and reopen without a union contract.

Another cause for shrinking union membership was the overall decline of blue-collar jobs, from 36 percent of the American workforce in 1960 to roughly 25 percent at the end of the 1990s. Unionization of white-collar workers made up only part of the

The working-class family depicted on the television show *Roseanne* offered viewers a glimpse of the problems facing many Americans in an era of economic change marked by deindustrialization and the rise of service jobs.

loss from manufacturing. Unions were most successful in recruiting government workers, such as police officers, teachers, and bus drivers.

**Impact of economic restructuring.**    In the 1950s and 1960s, increasing productivity, expanding markets for U.S. goods, and strong labor unions had made it possible for factory workers to enter the middle class. In an era of deindustrialization, however, companies replaced blue-collar workers with machinery or shifted production to nonunion plants. The corporate merger mania of the 1980s added to instability when takeover specialists loaded old companies with new debt, triggering efforts to cut labor costs, sell off plants, or raid pension funds for cash to pay the interest. Manufacturing employment in the 1980s declined by nearly 2 million jobs, with the expansion of high-tech manufacturing concealing much higher losses in traditional industries.

## AN ACQUISITIVE SOCIETY

The new prosperity fueled lavish living by the wealthy and a fascination with the "lifestyles of the rich and famous." Prime-time soap operas flourished, bringing to the small screen stories of intrigue among the rich folks. With a few exceptions, even the "middle class" in television sitcoms enjoyed lives available only to the top 20 percent of Americans.

The national media in the early 1980s discovered yuppies, or young urban professionals, who were both a marketing category and a symbol of social change. These upwardly mobile professionals supposedly defined themselves by elitist consumerism. Middle-line retailers like Sears had clothed Americans for decades and furnished their homes. With the help of catalog shopping, status-seeking consumers now flocked to such upscale retailers as Neiman-Marcus and Bloomingdale's.

Patricia Morrisroe, *The New Class* (1985)

*"They're museum quality!"*

This 1993 cartoon contrasting a yuppie couple and a family dressed as hippies makes two points. While highlighting the rapid changes in American styles and tastes from the 1970s to the 1990s, it also satirizes the supposed yuppie tendency to value everything as a commodity or "collectible."

Far richer than even such atypical yuppies were wheeler-dealers who made themselves into media stars of finance capitalism. The autobiography of Lee Iacocca, who had helped revive the fortunes of the Chrysler Corporation, was a bestseller in 1984, portraying the corporate executive as hero. *Forbes* magazine began to publish an annual list of the nation's 400 richest people. Long before his television show, real-estate developer Donald Trump made himself a celebrity with a well-publicized personal life and a stream of projects crowned with his name: office tower, hotel, casino. New movements in popular music reacted to the acquisitive 1980s. Punk rock pared rock-and-roll to its basics, lashing out at the emptiness of 1970s disco sound. Hip-hop originated among African Americans and Latinos in New York, soon adding the angry and often violent lyrics of rap. Rap during the 1980s was about personal power and sex, but it also dealt with social inequities and deprivation and tapped some of the same anger and frustration that had motivated black power advocates in the 1960s. When it crossed into mainstream entertainment, it retained a hard-edged "attitude" that undercut any sense of complacency about an inclusive American society.

## MASS MEDIA AND FRAGMENTED CULTURE

On June 1, 1980, CNN Cable News Network gave television viewers their first chance to watch news coverage 24 hours a day. CNN made a global reputation with live reporting on the pro-democracy protests of Chinese students in Beijing in 1989. When American bombs began to fall on Baghdad in January 1991, White House officials watched CNN to find out how their war was going.

Fourteen months after CNN went on the air, another new cable channel, MTV: Music Television, started broadcasting. By the time it reached the key New York and Los Angeles markets in January 1983, MTV's round-the-clock programming of music videos had created a new form of popular art and advertising. With its own programming aimed at viewers aged 18 to 34, MTV inspired Nickelodeon for kids and VH-1 for baby boomers.

CNN, MTV, and the rest of cable television reflected both the fragmentation of American society in the 1980s and 1990s and the increasing dependence on instant communication. As late as 1980, ordinary Americans had few choices for learning about their nation and world: virtually identical newscasts on NBC, CBS, and ABC and similar stories in *Time* and *Newsweek* helped to create a common understanding. Fifteen years later, they had learned to surf through dozens of cable channels in search of specialized programs and were beginning to explore the amazing variety of the World Wide Web (see Chapter 31).

## POVERTY AMID PROSPERITY

Federal tax and budget changes had different effects on the rich and poor (see Figure 30–1). Those in the top fifth increased their share of after-tax income relative to everyone else during the 1980s, and the richest 1 percent saw their share of all privately held wealth grow from 31 percent to 37 percent. The 1981 tax cuts also came with sharp increases in the Social Security tax, which hit lower-income workers the hardest. The tax changes meant that the average annual income of households in the bottom 20 percent *declined* and that many actually paid higher taxes.

Cities and their residents absorbed approximately two-thirds of the cuts in the 1981–1982 federal budget. Provisions for accelerated depreciation (tax write-offs) of factories and equipment in the 1981 tax act encouraged the abandonment of center-city factories in favor of new facilities in the suburbs. One result was a growing jobs-housing mismatch. There were often plenty of jobs in the suburbs, but the poorer people who

## QUICK REVIEW

**Greed is Good?**

◆ Yuppies: young urban professionals.

◆ Corporate dealmakers made themselves into media stars.

◆ New movements in music emerged in response to the acquisitive 1980s.

PEARSON
myhistorylab

**Exploring America**
*Growing Inequality*

most needed the jobs were marooned in city slums and dependent on public transit that seldom served suburban employers.

Federal tax and spending policies in the 1980s decreased the security of middle-class families. As the economy continued to struggle through deindustrialization, average wage rates fell in the 1980s when measured in real purchasing. The squeeze put pressure on traditional family patterns and pushed into the work-force women who might otherwise have stayed home. Many Americans no longer expected to surpass their parents' standard of living.

**Corporate downsizing and white-collar jobs.** Lower-paying office jobs fell under the same sorts of pressure as factory jobs with the increasing reliance of banks, telephone companies, and credit card companies on automation. Increasing numbers of clerical and office workers in organizations of all sorts, from corporations to universities, were "temps" who shifted from job to job. The shift toward temporary and part-time workers not only kept wages low but also allowed less spending on health insurance and other benefits.

The chill of corporate downsizing hit white-collar families most heavily toward the end of the 1980s. Big business consolidations delivered improved profits by squeezing the ranks of middle managers as well as assembly-line workers. With fewer workers to supervise and with new technologies to collect and distribute information, companies could complete their cost cutting by trimming administrators.

**Increase in the poverty rate.** At the lower end of the economic ladder, the proportion of Americans living in poverty increased. After declining steadily from 1960 to a low of 11 percent in 1973, the poverty rate climbed back to the 13 to 15 percent range. Although the economy in the 1980s created lots of new jobs, half of them paid less than poverty-level wages. Most of the nation's millions of poor people lived in households with employed adults. In 1992, fully 18 percent of all full-time jobs did not pay enough to lift a family of four out of poverty, a jump of 50 percent over the proportion of underpaid jobs in 1981.

**The wage gap and the feminization of poverty.** Nor could most women, even those working full-time, expect to earn as much as men. In the 1960s and 1970s, the average working woman earned just 60 percent of the earnings of the average man (see Figure 30–2). Only part of the wage gap could be explained by measurable factors, such as education or experience. The gap narrowed in the 1980s and 1990s, with women's earnings rising to 75 percent of men's by 2003. About half of the change was the result of bad news—the decline of earnings among men as high-wage factory jobs disappeared. The other half was the positive result of better-educated younger women finding better jobs.

Nevertheless, the low earning capacity of women with limited educations meant that women were far more likely than men to be poor. Women constituted nearly two-thirds of poor adults at the end of the 1980s. Only 6 percent of married-couple households were below poverty level, but 32 percent of households headed by a woman without a husband present were poor. The feminization of poverty and American

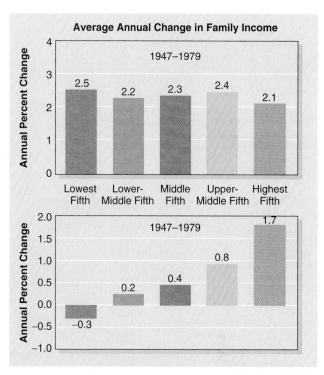

FIGURE 30–1 **Changes in Real Family Income, 1980–1990** In the 1980s, the poor got poorer, the middle class made slight gains, and the most affluent 20 percent of the American people did very well. Tax changes that helped well-off households were one factor. Another factor was the erosion of family-wage jobs in manufacturing.

**From Then to Now Online**
*Women and Office Work*

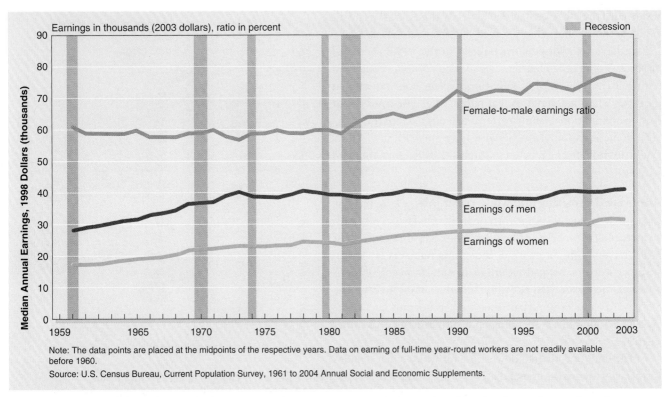

FIGURE 30–2    **Comparison of Men's and Women's Earnings, 1960–2003**    U.S. Census data show that the median earnings of women who worked full time and year round compared to those of men. Since the 1960s, the gap between women and men has narrowed. One reason is better pay for jobs traditionally held by women, but another has been the declining earning power of men without college educations. Nevertheless, the gender gap in earning power remains an important economic issue.

reliance on private support for child rearing also meant that children had a higher chance of living in poverty than adults and that poor American children were worse off than their peers in other advanced nations.

**Homelessness in America.**    Falling below even the working poor were growing numbers of homeless Americans. In the 1980s, several factors made homelessness more visible and pressing. A new approach to the treatment of the mentally ill reduced the population of mental hospitals from 540,000 in 1960 to only 140,000 in 1980. Deinstitutionalized patients were supposed to receive community-based treatment, but many ended up on the streets and in overnight shelters. New forms of self-destructive drug abuse, such as crack addiction, joined alcoholism. A boom in downtown real estate destroyed old skid-row districts with their bars, missions, and dollar-a-night hotels.

These factors tripled the number of permanently homeless people during the early and middle 1980s, from 200,000 to somewhere between 500,000 and 700,000. Twice or three times that many may have been homeless for part of a given year. For every person in a shelter on a given night, two people were sleeping on sidewalks, in parks, in cars, and in abandoned buildings.

## CONSOLIDATING THE REVOLUTION: GEORGE BUSH

In 1988 George H.W. Bush, Reagan's vice president for eight years, won the presidential election with 56 percent of the popular vote and 40 out of 50 states. Bush's view of national and world politics reflected a background in which personal connections

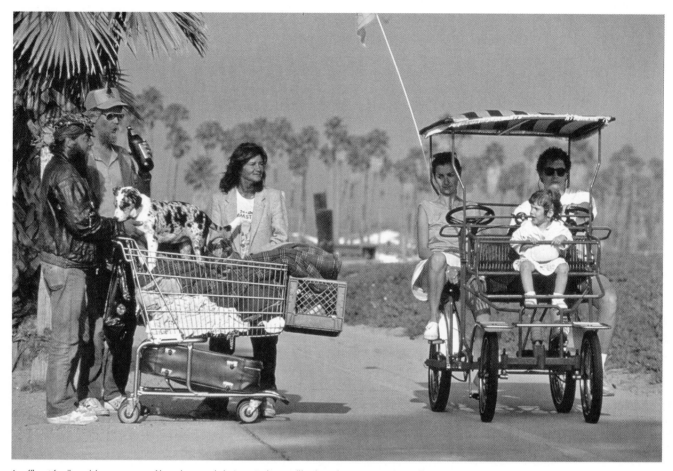

An affluent family pedals past a group of homeless people in Santa Barbara, California. In the 1980s a combination of rising housing prices and the closing of most mental hospitals pushed increasing numbers of Americans onto the streets. Estimates of the number of homeless Americans in the late 1980s ranged from 300,000 to 3 million, depending on the definition of homelessness and the political goals of the estimator.

counted. He was raised as part of the New England elite, built an oil business in Texas, and then held a series of high-level federal appointments.

Michael Dukakis, the Democratic nominee in 1988, was a dry-as-dust, by-the-numbers manager who offered the American people "competence." The Bush campaign director, Lee Atwater, looked for hot-button issues that could fit onto a three-by-five card. Pro-Bush advertisements tapped into real worries among the voters—fear of crime, racial tension, eroding social values. George Bush, despite his background in prep schools and country clubs, came out looking tough as nails, while the Democrats looked inept.

The ads locked Bush into a rhetorical war on crime and drugs that was his major domestic policy. Americans had good cause to be worried about public safety, but most were generally unaware that the likelihood of becoming the target of a violent crime had leveled off and would continue to fall in the 1990s or that crime was far worse in minority communities than elsewhere, in part due to gang- and drug-related activities.

George Bush believed that Americans wanted government to leave them alone. He ignored a flood of new ideas from entrepreneurial conservatives, such as HUD Secretary Jack Kemp. The major legislation from the Bush administration was a transportation bill that shifted federal priorities from highway building toward mass transit and the **Americans with Disabilities Act** (1990) to prevent discrimination against people with physical handicaps. In the areas of crime and healthcare, however, Bush's lack of leadership left continuing problems.

**Americans with Disabilities Act**
Legislation in 1992 that banned discrimination against physically handicapped persons in employment, transportation, and public accommodations.

The same attitude produced weak economic policies. The national debt had amounted to 50 percent of personal savings in 1980 but swelled to 125 percent by 1990. The massive budget deficits of the 1980s combined with growing trade deficits to turn the United States from an international creditor to a debtor nation. After pledging no new taxes in his campaign, Bush backed into a tax increase in 1990. A strong leader might have justified the taxes to the nation, but voters found it hard to forget the president's waffling and attempts to downplay the importance of his decision.

The most conspicuous domestic event of the Bush administration—the "Rodney King riot" of April 1992 in Los Angeles—was a reminder of the nation's inattention to the problems of race and poverty. Rodney King was a black motorist who had been savagely clubbed and kicked by police officers while being arrested after a car chase on March 3, 1991. A nearby resident captured the beating on videotape from his apartment. Early the next year, the four officers stood trial for unjustified use of force before a suburban jury. The televised trial and the unexpected verdict of not guilty on April 29 stirred deep anger that escalated into four days of rioting.

The disorder revealed multiple tensions among ethnic groups and was far more complex than the Watts outbreak of 1965 (see Chapter 29). African Americans from south-central Los Angeles participated, but so did Central American and Mexican immigrants in adjacent districts, who accounted for about one-third of the 12,000 arrests. The disorder spread south to Long Beach and north to the edge of upscale neighborhoods in Westwood and Beverly Hills. Rioters assaulted the downtown police headquarters, city hall, and the *Los Angeles Times* building. As in 1965, some targets were white passers-by and symbols of white authority. But members of competing minority groups were also victims as angry black people targeted hundreds of Korean-owned and Vietnamese-owned shops as symbols of economic discrimination. Four days of disorder left 58 people dead, mostly African Americans and Latinos.

# THE SECOND (SHORT) COLD WAR

**WHAT WERE** the goals of the Reagan administration's policies in Central America?

Ronald Reagan entered office determined to reassert U.S. leadership in world affairs and not to lose the Cold War. After the era of détente, global tensions had started to mount in the late 1970s. They were soon higher than they had been since the 1960s. But by the end of Reagan's two terms, unexpected changes were rapidly bringing the Cold War to an end, and George Bush faced a radically new set of foreign policy issues.

## CONFRONTING THE SOVIET UNION

Who renewed the Cold War after Nixon's diplomacy of *détente* and Carter's early efforts at negotiation? The Soviets had pursued military expansion in the 1970s, triggering the fear that they might stage a nuclear Pearl Harbor. The Soviet Union in 1980 was supporting Marxist regimes in civil wars in Angola, Ethiopia, Nicaragua, and especially Afghanistan, where its 1980 intervention led to a decade of costly and futile military occupation. Given the aging Soviet leadership and the economic weaknesses revealed in the late 1980s, it makes more sense to see the Soviets as muddling along rather than executing a well-planned global strategy.

On the American side, Reagan's readiness to confront "the focus of evil in the modern world" reflected the views of many conservative supporters that the Soviet Union was a monolithic and ideologically motivated foe bent on world conquest. In hindsight, some Reaganites claim that the administration's foreign policy and massive increases in defense spending were part of a deliberate and coordinated scheme to check a Soviet offensive and bankrupt the Soviet Union by pushing it into a new arms race. It is just as likely, however, that the administration's defense and foreign policy initiatives were a set of discrete but effective decisions.

The Reagan administration reemphasized central Europe as the focus of superpower rivalry, just as it had been in the 1950s and early 1960s. To counter improved Soviet armaments, the United States began to place cruise missiles and mid-range Pershing II missiles in Europe in 1983. NATO governments approved the action, but it frightened millions of their citizens.

Escalation of the nuclear arms race reinvigorated the antiwar and antinuclear movement in the United States as well as Europe. Drawing on the experience of the antiwar movement, the nuclear-freeze campaign caught the imagination of many Americans in 1981 and 1982. It sought to halt the manufacture and deployment of new atomic weapons by the great powers. Nearly a million people turned out for a nuclear-freeze rally in New York in 1982. Hundreds of local communities endorsed the freeze or took the symbolic step of declaring themselves nuclear-free zones.

In response, Reagan announced the **Strategic Defense Initiative (SDI),** or Star Wars program, in 1983. SDI was to deploy new defenses that could intercept and destroy ballistic missiles as they rose from the ground and arced through space. Few scientists thought that SDI could work. Many arms control experts thought that defensive systems were dangerous and destabilizing, because strong defenses suggested that a nation might be willing to risk a nuclear exchange.

## RISKY BUSINESS: FOREIGN POLICY ADVENTURES

The same administration that sometimes seemed reckless in its grand strategy also took risks to assert U.S. influence in global trouble spots to block or roll back Soviet influence. Reagan asserted America's right to intervene anywhere in the world to support local groups fighting against Marxist governments. The assumption underlying this assertion, which later became known as the **Reagan Doctrine,** was that Soviet-influenced governments in Asia, Africa, and Latin America needed to be eliminated if the United States was to win the Cold War.

Nevertheless, Reagan kept the United States out of a major war and backed off in the face of serious trouble. Foreign interventions were designed to achieve symbolic victories rather than change the global balance of power. The exception was the Caribbean and Central America, the "backyard" where the United States had always claimed an overriding interest and where left-wing action infuriated Reagan's conservative supporters.

**Intervention and covert activities in Central America.** The Reagan administration attributed political turmoil in Central America to Soviet influence and to arms and agitators from Soviet-backed Cuba. Between 1980 and 1983, the United States sent more military aid to conservative governments and groups in Central America than it had during the previous 30 years. Indeed, Central America became the focus of a secret foreign policy operated by the CIA and then by National Security Council (NSC) staff, since a Democratic Congress was not convinced of the danger. The CIA and the NSC engaged not just in espionage but in direct covert operations. The chief target was Nicaragua, the Central American country where leftist Sandinista rebels had overthrown the Somoza dictatorship in 1979. In the early 1980s, Reagan approved CIA plans to arm and organize approximately 10,500 so-called Contras, from the remnants of Somoza's national guard. From bases in Honduras, the Contras harassed the Sandinistas with sabotage and raids.

The Reagan administration bent the law to support its covert effort to overthrow the Sandinista regime. An unsympathetic Congress blocked U.S. funding for the Contras. In response, CIA director William Casey directed Lieutenant Colonel Oliver North of the National Security Council staff to illegally organize aid from private donors. The arms pipeline operated until a supply plane was shot down in 1986. The Contras failed as a military effort, but the civil war and international pressure persuaded the Sandinistas to allow free elections that led to a democratic, centrist government.

**The war against drugs.**    The American war against drugs was simultaneously shaping U.S. policy in the Caribbean and straining relations with Latin America. As president, George Bush parlayed the war on drugs into war on Panama during his first year in office, extending the American tradition of ousting uncooperative governments around the Caribbean. General Manuel Noriega, the Panamanian strongman, had once been on the CIA payroll. He had since turned to international drug sales in defiance of United States antismuggling efforts. On December 20, 1989, American troops invaded Panama, hunted down Noriega, and brought him back to stand trial in the United States on drug-trafficking charges. A handful of Americans and thousands of Panamanians died, many of them civilians caught in the crossfire.

**Intervention in the Middle East.**    If the results of intervention in Nicaraugua and Panama were mixed, intervention in the Middle East was a failure. In 1982 Israel invaded Lebanon, a small nation to its north, to clear Palestinian guerrillas from its borders and set up a friendly Lebanese government. The Israeli army bogged down in a civil war between Christian Arabs and Muslims. Reagan sent U.S. Marines to preserve the semblance of a Lebanese state and provide a face-saving exit for Israel. In October 1983, a terrorist car bomb killed 241 Marines in their barracks. The remainder were soon gone, confirming the Syrian observation that Americans were "short of breath" when it came to Middle East politics. The debacle in Lebanon undermined U.S.-backed peace initiatives in the Middle East.

**The Iran-Contra Affair.**    Even less effective were the Reagan administration's secret efforts to sell weapons to Iran in return for Iranian help in securing the release of Americans held hostage by pro-Iranian Islamic radicals in Lebanon. The United States in 1985 joined Israel in selling 500 antitank missiles to Iran, then embroiled in a long, bitter war with Iraq. The deal followed stern public pronouncements that the United States would never negotiate with terrorists and considered Iran's religious leaders to be backers of international terrorism. It also violated the official trade embargo against Iran, which had been in place since the U.S. embassy seizure in 1979. In May 1986, National Security adviser Robert McFarlane flew to Iran for more arms-for-hostages talks, carrying a chocolate cake and a Bible autographed by Reagan to present to the Iranian leader Ayatollah Khomeini. When the deals came to light in 1986 and congressional hearings were held in the summer of 1987, Americans were startled to learn that Colonel North had funneled millions of dollars from the arms sales to the Nicaraguan Contras in a double evasion of the law.

As had been true with Watergate, the Iran-Contra affair was a two-sided scandal. First was the blatant misjudgment of operating a secret, bumbling, and unlawful foreign policy that depended on international arms dealers and ousted Nicaraguan military officers. Second was a concerted effort to cover up the illegal and unconstitutional actions. North shredded relevant documents and lied to Congress. In his final report in 1994, Special Prosecutor Lawrence Walsh found that President Reagan and Vice President Bush were aware of much of what had gone on and had participated in efforts to withhold information and mislead Congress.

**U.S. policy in Asia.**   American policy in Asia was a refreshing contrast with practices in Central America and the Middle East. In the Philippines, American diplomats helped push corrupt President Ferdinand Marcos out and opened the way for a popular uprising to put Corazon Aquino in office. In South Korea, the United States similarly helped ease out an unpopular dictator by firmly supporting democratic elections that brought in a more popular but still pro-American government.

## EMBRACING PERESTROIKA

Thaw in the Cold War started in Moscow as Soviet leaders sought to salvage a system under severe economic stress. Mikhail Gorbachev became general secretary of the Communist Party in 1985, when the Soviet Union was trapped in the sixth year of its failed attempt to control Afghanistan. Gorbachev startled Soviet citizens by urging **glasnost**, or political openness, with free discussion of issues and relaxation of controls on the press. He followed by setting the goal of **perestroika**, or restructuring of the painfully bureaucratic Soviet economy that was falling behind capitalist nations. His hope was that market-oriented reforms would help the Soviet Union keep up with the United States.

Gorbachev decided that he needed to reduce the crushing burden of Soviet defense spending if the Soviet Union was to have any chance of modernizing. During Reagan's second term, the Soviets offered one concession after another in a drive for arms control.

Reagan had the vision (or audacity) to embrace the new Soviet position. He cast off decades of belief in the dangers of Soviet Communism and took Gorbachev seriously. He frightened his own staff when he met with Gorbachev in the summer of 1986 and accepted the principle of deep cuts in strategic forces. Reagan explained that when he railed against the evil empire, he had been talking about Brezhnev and the bad old days; Gorbachev and *glasnost* were different.

In the end, Reagan negotiated the **Intermediate Nuclear Force Agreement (INF)** over the strong objections of the CIA and the Defense Department. INF was the first true nuclear-disarmament treaty (see Overview, Controlling Nuclear Weapons: Four Decades of Effort). Previous agreements had only slowed the growth of nuclear weapons; they were "speed limits" for the arms race. The new pact matched Soviet SS-20s with U.S. cruise missiles as an entire class of weapons that would be destroyed, with on-site inspections for verification.

## CRISIS AND DEMOCRACY IN EASTERN EUROPE

As a believer in personal diplomacy, George Bush based much of his foreign policy on his changing attitudes toward Mikhail Gorbachev. He started lukewarm, talking tough to please the Republican right wing. Bush feared that Gorbachev, by instituting reforms that challenged the entrenched Communist Party leaders, was being imprudent: one of the worst things he could say about another leader. Before 1989 was over, however, the president had decided that Gorbachev was OK. For the next two years, the United States pushed the prodemocratic transformation of eastern Europe while being careful not to gloat in public or damage Gorbachev's position at home.

**Glasnost**   Russian for "openness," applied to Mikhail Gorbachev's encouragement of new ideas and easing of political repression in the Soviet Union.

**Perestroika**   Russian for "restructuring," applied to Mikail Gorbachev's efforts to make the Soviet economic and political systems more modern, flexible, and innovative.

**Intermediate Nuclear Force Agreement (INF)**   Disarmament agreement between the U.S. and the Soviet Union under which an entire class of missiles would be removed and destroyed and on-site inspections would be permitted for verification..

Mikhail Gorbachev, holding the child, hosted a summit meeting with President Reagan in Moscow in May 1988. Their smiles ignored the lack of progress toward disarmament beyond the Intermediate Nuclear Force Agreement of the previous year.

## OVERVIEW  Controlling Nuclear Weapons: Four Decades of Effort

| | | |
|---|---|---|
| Limiting the testing of nuclear weapons | Limited Test Ban Treaty (1963) | Banned nuclear testing in the atmosphere, ocean, and outer space. |
| | Comprehensive Test | Banned all nuclear tests, including underground tests. |
| | Ban Treaty (1996) | Rejected by U.S. Senate in 1999. |
| Halting the spread of nuclear weapons | Nuclear Non-Proliferation Treaty (1968) | Pledged five recognized nuclear nations (United States, Soviet Union, Britain, France, China) to pursue disarmament in good faith, and 140 other nations not to acquire nuclear weapons. |
| | Strategic Arms Limitation Treaty (SALT I, 1972) | Limited the number of nuclear-armed missiles and bombers maintained by the United States and Soviet Union. Closely associated with U.S.-Soviet agreement to limit deployment of antiballistic missile systems to one site each. |
| | Strategic Arms Limitation Treaty (SALT II, 1979) | Further limited the number of nuclear-armed missiles and bombers. Not ratified but followed by Carter and Reagan administrations. |
| Reducing the number of nuclear weapons | Intermediate Nuclear Force Agreement (1987) | Required the United States to eliminate 846 nuclear armed cruise missiles, and the Soviet Union to eliminate 1,846 SS-20 missiles. |
| | Strategic Arms Reduction Treaty (START I, 1991) | By July 1999, led to reductions of approximately 2,750 nuclear warheads by the United States and 3,725 warheads by the nations of the former USSR. |
| | Strategic Arms Reduction Treaty (START II, 1993) | Set further cuts in nuclear arsenals. Ratified by Russia in April 2000. Russia withdrew in 2002 after the U.S. abandoned the Anti-Ballistic Missile Treaty. |
| | Strategic Offensive Reductions (2002) | Russia and the United States each agree to deploy no more than 1,700–2,200 strategic nuclear warheads. |

Data Source: Arms Control Association.

**The end of Communist regimes in Eastern Europe.**  The people of eastern Europe overcame both U.S. and Soviet caution. Instead of the careful economic liberalization Gorbachev invisioned, the Warsaw Pact system collapsed. Poland held free elections in June 1989, Hungary adopted a democratic constitution in October, and prodemocracy demonstrations then forced out Communist leaders in other eastern European countries. When East Germans began to flee westward through Hungary, the East German regime bowed to mounting pressure and opened the Berlin Wall on November 9. By the end of 1989, there were new democratic or non-Communist governments in Czechoslovakia, Romania, Bulgaria, and East Germany. These largely peaceful revolutions destroyed the military and economic agreements that had harnessed the satellites to the Soviet economy (the Warsaw Pact and Comecon). The Soviet Union swallowed hard, accepted the loss of its satellites, and slowly withdrew its army from eastern Europe.

**German reunification and the dissolution of the Soviet Union.**  Events in Europe left German reunification as a point of possible conflict. Soviet policy since 1945 had sought to prevent the reemergence of a strong, united Germany that might again threaten its neighbors. West German Chancellor Helmut Kohl removed one obstacle when he reassured Poland and Russia that Germany would seek no changes in the boundaries drawn after World War II. By July 1990, the United States and the Soviet Union had agreed that a reunited Germany would belong to NATO. The decision satisfied France and Britain that a stronger Germany would still be under the influence of the Western allies. In October, the two Germanies completed their political unification, although it would be years before their mismatched economies functioned as one. Reunification was the last step in the diplomatic legacy of World War II.

The final act in the transformation of the Soviet Union began with a failed coup against Mikhail Gorbachev in August 1991. The Soviet Union had held free

The wall that divided East from West Berlin from 1962 to 1989 was a hated symbol of the Cold War. When the Communist government of East Germany collapsed in November 1989, jubilant Berliners celebrated the opening of the wall and the reuniting of the divided city.

WHERE TO LEARN MORE

The Gulf War.
http:archives.cbc.ca/war_conflict/1991_gulf_war/

*Documents*

George Bush, *Address to the Nation Announcing Allied Military Action in the Persian Gulf* (1991)

elections in 1989. Now Gorbachev scheduled a vote on a new constitution that would decrease the power of the central government. Old-line Communist bureaucrats who feared the change arrested Gorbachev in his vacation house and tried to take over the government apparatus in Moscow. Boris Yeltsin, president of the Russian Republic, organized the resistance. Muscovites flocked to support Yeltsin and defied tank crews in front of the Russian parliament building. Within three days, the plotters themselves were under arrest.

The coup hastened the fragmentation of the Soviet Union. Before the month was out, the Soviet parliament banned the Communist Party. Gorbachev soon resigned. Previously suppressed nationalist feelings caused all 15 component republics of the Soviet Union to declare their independence. The superpower Union of Soviet Socialist Republics ceased to exist. Russia remained the largest and strongest of the new states, followed by Ukraine and Kazakhstan. (See Overview, Why Did the Cold War End?)

## THE PERSIAN GULF WAR

On August 2, 1990, President Saddam Hussein of Iraq seized the small neighboring oil-rich country of Kuwait. The quick conquest gave Iraq control of 20 percent of the world's oil production and reserves. President Bush demanded unconditional withdrawal, enlisted European and Arab allies in an anti-Iraq coalition, and persuaded Saudi Arabia to accept substantial U.S. forces to protect it against Iraqi invasion.

The background for Iraq's invasion was a simmering dispute over border oil fields and islands in the Persian Gulf. Iraq was a dictatorship that had just emerged from an immensely costly eight-year war with Iran. Saddam Hussein had depended on help from the United States and Arab nations in this war, but Iraq was now economically exhausted. Kuwait was a small, rich nation whose ruling dynasty enjoyed few friends but plenty of oil royalties. The U.S. State Department had signaled earlier in 1990 that it might support some concessions by Kuwait in its dispute with Iraq. Saddam Hussein read the signal as an open invitation to do what he wanted; having been favored in the past by the United States, he probably expected denunciations but no military response.

The Iraqis gave George Bush a golden opportunity to assert America's world influence. The Bush administration was concerned that Iraq might target oil-rich Saudi Arabia. The importance of Middle Eastern oil helped to enlist France and Britain as military allies and to secure billions of dollars from Germany and Japan. Iraq had antagonized nearly all its neighbors. The collapse of Soviet power and Gorbachev's interest in cooperating with the United States meant that the Soviets would not interfere with U.S. plans.

Bush and his advisers offered a series of justifications for U.S. actions. First, and most basic, were the desire to punish armed aggression and the presumed need to protect Iraq's other neighbors. In fact, there was scant evidence of Iraqi preparations against Saudi Arabia. The buildup of U.S. air power plus effective economic sanctions would have accomplished both protection and punishment. Sanctions and diplomatic pressure might also have brought withdrawal from most or all of Kuwait. However, additional American objectives—to destroy Iraq's capacity to create nuclear weapons and to topple Saddam's regime—would require direct military action.

Bush probably decided on war in October, eventually increasing the number of American troops in Saudi Arabia to 580,000. The United States stepped up diplomatic pressure by securing a series of increasingly tough United Nations resolutions that culminated in November 1990 with Security Council Resolution 678, authorizing "all necessary means" to liberate Kuwait. The president convinced Congress to agree to military action under the umbrella of the UN. The United States ignored compromise plans floated by France and last-minute concessions from Iraq.

**The Persian Gulf War** began one day after the UN's January 15 deadline for Iraqi withdrawal from Kuwait. **Operation Desert Storm** opened with massive air attacks on command centers, transportation facilities, and Iraqi forward positions. The air war destroyed 40 to 50 percent of Iraqi tanks and artillery by late February. The attacks also seriously hurt Iraqi civilians by disrupting utilities and food supplies.

The 40-day rain of bombs was the prelude to a ground attack (see Map 30–2). On February 24, 1991, allied forces swept into Iraq. Americans, Saudis, Syrians, and Egyptians advanced directly to liberate Kuwait. A cease-fire came 100 hours after the start of the ground war. Allied forces suffered only 240 deaths in action, compared to perhaps 100,000 for the Iraqis.

Bush directed Desert Storm with the "Vietnam syndrome" in mind, believing that Americans were willing to accept war only if it involved overwhelming U.S. force and ended quickly. The United States hoped to replace Saddam Hussein without disrupting Iraqi society. Instead, the 100-hour war incited armed rebellions against Saddam in southern Iraq by Shiites, a group within the Muslim religion whose adherents comprise a majority in Iraq, and in the north by the ethnically distinct Kurds. Because Bush and his advisers were unwilling to get embroiled in a civil war or commit the United States to occupy all of Iraq, they stood by while Saddam crushed the uprisings.

**MAP EXPLORATION** To explore an interactive version of this map, go to http://www.prenhall.com/ goldfield5/map30.2

**MAP 30–2   The Persian Gulf War**   Ground operations against Iraq in the Persian Gulf War followed six weeks of aerial bombardment. The ground attack, which met quick success, was a multinational effort by the United States, Britain, France, Saudi Arabia, and other Arab nations threatened by an aggressive Iraq. The war freed Kuwait from Iraqi occupation but stopped before forcing a change in Iraq's government.

**Why did** so many people, including many in the military, believe that the Persian Gulf War would be a protracted conflict with high casualties on the U.S. side?

# GROWTH IN THE SUNBELT

The rise of the **Sunbelt,** which is anchored by Florida, Texas, and California, reflected the leading economic trends of the 1970s and 1980s, including military spending, immigration from Asia and Latin America, and recreation and retirement spending. Corporations liked the business climate of the South, which had weak labor laws, low taxes, and generally low costs of living and doing business.

New factories dotted the southern landscape, often in smaller towns rather than cities. General Motors closed factories in Flint, Michigan, but invested in a new Saturn plant in Spring Hill, Tennessee. In contrast to troubled industrial cities in the Northeast and Midwest, cities like Orlando, Charlotte, Atlanta, Dallas, and Phoenix enjoyed headlong prosperity. Houston, with sprawling growth, business spinoffs from NASA, and purring air-conditioners epitomized the booming metropolitan areas of the South and West.

## THE DEFENSE ECONOMY

The Vietnam buildup and reinvestment in the military during the Carter (1977–1981) and Reagan (1981–1989) administrations fueled the growth of the Sunbelt. Over

**HOW DID** growth in the Sunbelt shape national politics in the 1980s and 1990s?

**Persian Gulf War**   War (1991) between Iraq and a U.S. led coalition that followed Iraq's invasion of Kuwait and resulted in the expulsion of Iraqi forces from that country.

**Operation Desert Storm**   Code name for the successful offensive against Iraq by the United States and its allies in the Persian Gulf War (1991).

**Sunbelt**   The states of the American South and Southwest.

## OVERVIEW  Why Did the Cold War End?

Commentators have offered a number of explanations for the rapid failure of the USSR and the collapse of Soviet power at the end of the 1980s. All of these factors made contributions to the complex unraveling of the Cold War.

| | |
|---|---|
| **Economic exhaustion:** | The United States in the late 1970s embarked on a great modernization and expansion of its military forces. The USSR exhausted its economy and revealed its technical backwardness by trying to keep pace. Gorbachev's policy of *perestroika* was an attempt to reduce the bureaucratic inertia of the economy. |
| **Failure of leadership:** | The Soviet Union in the 1970s and early 1980s was governed by unimaginative bureaucrats. A closed elite that thought only of preserving their privileges and authority could not adapt to a changing world. The policy of *glasnost* was an effort to encourage new ideas. |
| **Intervention in Afghanistan:** | The disastrous intervention in Afghanistan revealed the limits of Soviet military power. It alienated the large Muslim population of the USSR and brought disillusionment with the incompetence of Soviet leaders. |
| **Triumph of democratic ideas:** | As political discussion became more free, the appeal of democratic ideas took on its own momentum, especially in eastern European satellite nations such as East Germany, Czechoslovakia, and Poland. |
| **Power of nationalism:** | The collapse of the Soviet empire was triggered by the resurgence of national sentiments throughout the Soviet empire. National sentiments fueled the breakaway of the eastern European satellite nations such as Hungary, Romania, and Poland. Nationalism also broke up the USSR itself as 14 smaller socialist republics declared independence from the Russian-dominated Union. |

the 40 years from the Korean conflict to the Persian Gulf War, the United States made itself the mightiest military power ever known. Military bases and defense contractors remolded the economic landscape, as mild winters and clear skies for training and operations helped the South and West attract more than 75 percent of military payrolls.

Big cities and small depended on defense spending. Southern California thrived on more than 500,000 jobs in the aircraft industry. A thousand miles away, visitors to Colorado Springs could drive past sprawling Fort Carson and visit the new Air Force Academy, opened in 1958. Sunk deep from view was the North American Air Defense Command headquarters beneath Cheyenne Mountain west of the city.

Defense spending underwrote the expansion of American science and technology. Nearly one-third of all engineers worked on military projects. Large universities, such as MIT, the University of Michigan, the California Institute of Technology, and Stanford, were leading defense contractors. The modern electronics business started in New York, Boston, and the San Francisco Bay area with research and development for military uses, such as guided-missile controls.

### AMERICANS FROM AROUND THE WORLD

Few Americans anticipated the effects of the **Immigration and Nationality Act of 1965,** which transformed the ethnic mix of the United States and helped to stimulate the Sunbelt boom. The new law initiated a change in the composition of the American people by abolishing the national quota system in effect since 1924.

Immigration reform opened the doors to Mediterranean Europe, Latin America, and Asia. Legal migration to the United States surged from 1.1 million in 1960–1964

**QUICK REVIEW**

**The Military and the Economy**

- Reinvestment in the military fueled growth in the Sunbelt.
- Communities of all sizes depended on the military.
- Military spending underwrote the expansion of American science and technology.

**Immigration and Nationality Act of 1965** Federal legislation that replaced the national quota system for immigration with overall limits of 170,000 immigrants per year from the Eastern Hemisphere and 120,000 per year from the Western Hemisphere.

## GLOBAL PERSPECTIVES

### ⌘ DISNEY IN TOKYO AND PARIS ⌘

Tokyo Disneyland opened in 1983 as the first Disney theme park outside the United States. Designed by Walt Disney Imagineering, it copied California's original Disneyland and Florida's Walt Disney World. It includes the classic Disneyland features of Adventureland, Westernland, Tomorrowland, and Fantasyland (complete with a Cinderella Castle that looks just like its Florida counterpart).

Tokyo Disney was been enormously successful from the start. It has consistently attracted huge crowds. For many years was the most popular theme park in the world, and developers have added Tokyo DisneySea to keep visitors coming back.

If Japanese immediately took to Tokyo Disneyland, Europeans were much less excited by the Euro Disney Resort that opened east of Paris in 1992. Critics complained about the strict rules for workers. Intellectuals criticized the invasion of American popular culture into the heart of Europe. It took several years, and new attractions like De la Terre à la Lune (Space Mountain), to bring in enough visitors to put the project in the black.

The contrasting experiences demonstrate the close affinities between American and Japanese pop culture.

Japanese monster movies of the 1950s, including Godzilla, King of Monsters, and his various opponents, earned money in both Japan and the United States. The huge Japanese animation, or anime, industry that developed after World War II drew on Disney cartoon style. It developed into an economic powerhouse of comic books, TV series, video games, and spinoff toys that made fortunes for Sony, Nintendo, and other companies. Pokemon, which began as a children's game for handheld computers, grew into a marketing phenomenon that made the cover of *Time* magazine.

This exchange of entertainment and consumer products has been part of the increasingly close engagement between the economies of the United States and East Asia. Its roots lie in the democratic revival of Japan after World War II and in the opening of political relations between the United States and the People's Republic of China in the 1970s. It has grown into a huge field of investment and exchange of everything from sneakers to steel, comic book artists to centerfielders.

- What are some reasons for the contrasting ways that Japan and France have responded to Disney theme resorts?

---

to nearly 4 million for 1990–1994. Nonlegal immigrants may have doubled the total number of newcomers in the 1970s and early 1980s. Not since World War I had the United States absorbed so many new residents.

Immigration changed the nation's ethnic mix. Members of officially defined ethnic and racial minorities accounted for 25 percent of Americans in 1990 and 30 percent in 2000 (see Table 30–1). Roughly 28 million Americans had been born in other countries according to the 2000 census, or 10.4 percent of the population.

The largest single group of new Americans came from Mexico. The long border has facilitated easy movement from south to north. Especially in the border states of Texas, New Mexico, Arizona, and California, permanent immigrants have mingled with tourists, family members on visits, temporary workers, and other workers without legal permission to enter the United States. Mexican Americans were the largest minority group in many southwestern and western states in the later twentieth century.

The East Coast has especially welcomed migrants from the West Indies and Central America. Many Puerto Ricans, who hold U.S. citizenship, came to Philadelphia and New York in the 1950s and 1960s.

Another great immigration has occurred eastward across the Pacific. Chinese, Filipinos, Koreans, Samoans, and other Asians and Pacific Islanders constituted only 6 percent of newcomers to the United States in 1965 but nearly half of all arrivals in 1990. The number of ethnic Chinese in the United States jumped from a quarter of a million in 1965 to 1,645,000 in 1990.

*Documents*

Cecelia Rosa Avila, *Third Generation Mexican American* (1988)

## Table 30–1

**Major Racial and Ethnic Minorities in the United States**

|  | 1960 Population (in millions) | Percentage of Total | 2000 Population (in millions) | Percentage of Total |
|---|---|---|---|---|
| American Indians | 0.5 | 0.3 | 2.5 | 0.9 |
| Asians and Pacific Islanders | 1.1 | 0.6 | 10.6 | 3.7 |
| African Americans | 18.9 | 10.5 | 34.7 | 12.3 |
| Hispanics | not available |  | 35.3 | 12.5 |

QUICK REVIEW

Immigration

♦ Immigration changed the country's ethnic mix.

♦ The single largest group of new Americans came from Mexico.

♦ In 1990 nearly half of all new arrivals were Asians and Pacific islanders.

The most publicized Asian immigrants were refugees from Indochina after the Communist victory in 1975. The first arrivals tended to be highly educated professionals who had worked with the Americans. Another 750,000 Vietnamese, Laotians, and Cambodians arrived after 1976 by way of refugee camps in Thailand, as did Celia Noup. Most settled on the West Coast.

In addition to southeast Asians, political conflicts and upheavals sent other waves of immigrants to the United States. Many Iranians fled the religious regime that took power in their country in the late 1970s, at the same time that Ethiopians were fleeing a nation shattered by drought, civil war, and doctrinaire Marxism. To escape repression in the Soviet Union, Jews and conservative Christians came to the United States in the 1980s, and the collapse of Communism in the Soviet Union opened the door for more Russians, Ukrainians, Romanians, and other eastern Europeans.

Recent immigrants have found both economic possibilities and problems. On the negative side, legal and illegal immigration has added to the number of nonunion workers. By one estimate, two-thirds of the workers in the Los Angeles garment trade were undocumented immigrants. Most worked for small, nonunion firms in basements and storefronts, without health insurance or pensions. But a positive contrast was the abundance of opportunities for talent and ambition in the expanding economy of the mid-1980s and 1990s. The 130,000 Vietnamese immigrants of 1975 now have an average income above the national figure. Asians and Pacific islanders by 2000 constituted 22 percent of the students in California's public universities. Like earlier European immigrants, many newcomers have opened groceries, restaurants, and other businesses that serve their own group before expanding into larger markets.

## OLD GATEWAYS AND NEW

The new immigration from Asia, Latin America, and the Caribbean had its most striking effects in coastal and border cities. New York again became a great mixing bowl of the U.S. population. By 1990, some 28 percent of the population of New York City was foreign-born, compared to 42 percent at the height of European immigration in 1910.

Just as important was the transformation of southern and western cities into gateways for immigrants from Latin America and Asia. Los Angeles emerged as "the new Ellis Island" that rivaled New York's historic role in receiving immigrants. The sprawling neighborhoods of East Los Angeles make up the second-largest Mexican city in the world. New ethnic communities appeared in Los Angeles suburbs: Iranians in Beverly Hills, Chinese in Monterey Park, Japanese in Gardena, Thais in Hollywood, Samoans in Carson, Cambodians in Lakewood. One hundred languages are spoken among students entering Los Angeles schools.

New York and Los Angeles are world cities as well as immigrant destinations. Like London and Tokyo, they are capitals of world trade and finance, with international banks and headquarters of multinational corporations. They have the country's greatest concentrations of international lawyers, accounting firms, and business consultants. The deregulation of international finance and the explosive spread of instant electronic communication in the 1980s confirmed their importance as global decision centers (see Table 30–2).

Similar factors have turned Miami into an economic capital of the Caribbean. A quarter-million Cuban businessmen, white-collar workers, and their families moved to the United States between 1959 and 1962 to escape Castro's socialist government. By the late 1970s Cubans owned about one-third of the area's retail stores and many of its other businesses. Their success in business made Miami a major Latino market and helped to attract millions of Latin American tourists and shoppers. Access to the Caribbean and South America also made Miami an international banking and commercial center with hundreds of offices for corporations engaged in U.S.–Latin American trade.

Cross-border communities in the Southwest, such as El Paso, Texas, and Juarez, Mexico, or San Diego, California, and Tijuana, Mexico, are "Siamese twins joined at the cash register." Employees with work permits commute from Mexico to the United States. American popular culture flows southward. Bargain hunters and tourists pass in both directions.

Both nations have promoted the cross-border economy. The Mexican government in the mid-1960s began to encourage a "platform economy" by allowing companies on the Mexican side of the border to import components and inputs duty-free as long as 80 percent of the items were re-exported and 90 percent of the workers were Mexicans. The intent was to encourage U.S. corporations to locate assembly plants south of the

## Table 30–2
### Global Cities

| Ranked by Population in 2005 (population in millions) | | Ranked as Economic Decision Centers |
| --- | --- | --- |
| Tokyo, Japan | 35.2 | 1. London |
| Cuidad de Mexico | 19.4 | 2. New York |
| New York | 18.7 | 3. Hong Kong |
| Sao Paulo, Brazil | 18.3 | 4. Paris |
| Mumbai, India | 18.2 | 5. Tokyo |
| Delhi, India | 15.0 | 6. Singapore |
| Shanghai, China | 14.5 | 7. Chicago |
| Kolkata, India | 14.3 | 8. Milan |
| Jakarta, Indonesia | 13.2 | 9. Los Angeles |
| Buenos Aires, Argentina | 12.6 | 10. Toronto |
| Dhaka, Bangladesh | 12.4 | 11. Madrid |
| Los Angeles | 12.3 | 12. Amsterdam |

Sources: UN Department of Economic and Social Affairs/Population Division, *World Urbanization Prospects: The 2005 Revision*; Peter J. Taylor and Robert Lang, "U.S. Cities in the 'World City Network," The Brookings Institution, February 2005.

border. Such *maquila* industries were able to employ lower-wage workers and avoid strict antipollution laws (leading to serious threats to public health on both sides of the border). From the Gulf of Mexico to the Pacific Ocean, 1,800 *maquiladora* plants employed half a million workers. North of the border, U.S. factories supplied components under laws that meshed with the Mexican regulations.

## THE GRAYING OF AMERICA

Retirees were another factor contributing to the growth of the Sunbelt. Between 1965 and 2000, the number of Americans aged 65 and over jumped from 18.2 million to 35 million, or 12.4 percent of the population.

Older Americans have become a powerful voice in public affairs. They tend to vote against local taxes but fight efforts to slow the growth of Social Security, even though growing numbers of the elderly are being supported by a relatively smaller proportion of working men and women. By the 1990s, observers noted increasing resentment among younger Americans, who fear that public policy is biased against the needs of those in their productive years. In turn, the elderly fiercely defend the programs of the 1960s and 1970s that have kept many of them from poverty.

Retired Americans changed the social geography of the United States. Much growth in the South and Southwest has been financed by money earned in the Northeast and Midwest and transferred by retirees.

WHAT KEY social and cultural issues divided Americans in the 1980s and 1990s?

Jesse Jackson, *Common Ground* (1988)

# VALUES IN COLLISION

In 1988, two very different religious leaders sought a presidential nomination. Pat Robertson's campaign for the Republican nomination tapped deep discontent with the changes in American society since the 1960s. A television evangelist, Robertson used the mailing list from his *700 Club* program to mobilize conservative Christians and push the Republican Party further to the right on family and social issues. Jesse Jackson, a civil rights leader and minister from Chicago, mounted a grassroots campaign with the opposite goal of moving the Democratic Party to the left on social and economic policy.

In diagnosing social ills, Robertson pointed to the problems of individual indulgence, while Jackson pointed to racism and economic inequality. Their sharp divergence expressed differences in basic values that divided Americans in the 1980s and beyond. In substantial measure, the conflicts were rooted in the social and cultural changes of the 1960s and 1970s that had altered traditional institutions.

## WOMEN'S RIGHTS AND PUBLIC POLICY

The women's liberation movement of the 1960s achieved important gains when Congress wrote many of its goals into law in the early 1970s. Title IX of the Educational Amendments (1972) to the Civil Rights Act prohibited discrimination by sex in any educational program receiving federal aid. The legislation expanded athletic opportunities for women and slowly equalized the balance of women and men in faculty positions. In the same year, Congress sent the Equal Rights Amendment (ERA) to the states for ratification. The amendment read, "Equal rights under the law shall not be denied or abridged by the United States or by any state on account of sex." More than 20 states ratified in the first few months. As conservatives who wanted to preserve traditional family patterns rallied strong opposition, however, the next dozen states ratified only after increasingly tough battles in state legislatures. The ERA then stalled, three states short, until the time limit for ratification expired in 1982.

**Abortion rights and the conservative backlash.**   In January 1973, the U.S. Supreme Court expanded the debate about women's rights with the case of *Roe v. Wade.* Voting 7 to 2, the Court struck down state laws forbidding abortion in the first three months of pregnancy and set guidelines for abortion during the remaining months. Drawing on the earlier decision of *Griswold v. Connecticut,* which dealt with birth control, the Court held that the Fourteenth Amendment includes a right to privacy that blocks states from interfering with a woman's right to terminate a pregnancy.

These changes came in the context of increasingly sharp conflict over the feminist agenda. Both the ERA and *Roe* stirred impassioned support and equally passionate opposition that pushed the two major political parties in opposite directions. Behind the rhetoric were male fears of increased job competition during a time of economic contraction and concern about changing families. Also fueling the debate was a deep split between the mainstream feminist view of women as fully equal individuals and the contrary conservative belief that women had a special role as anchors of families, an updating of the nineteenth-century idea of separate spheres. The arguments tapped such deep emotion that the two sides could not even agree on a common language, juxtaposing a right to life against rights to privacy and freedom of choice.

**Women in the workforce.**   The most sweeping change in the lives of American women did not come from federal legislation or court cases, but from the growing likelihood that a woman would work outside the home. In 1960, some 32 percent of married women were in the labor force; 40 years later, 61 percent were working or looking for work (along with 69 percent of single women). Federal and state governments slowly responded to the changing demands of work and family with new policies, such as a federal childcare tax credit.

More women entered the workforce as inflation in the 1970s and declining wages in the 1980s eroded the ability of families to live comfortable lives on one income. A second reason for the increase in working women from 29 million in 1970 to 66 million in 2000 was the broad shift from manufacturing to service jobs, reducing demand for factory workers and manual laborers and increasing the need for such "women's jobs" as data-entry clerks, reservation agents, and nurses. Indeed, the U.S. economy still divides job categories by sex. There was some movement toward gender-neutral hiring in the 1970s because of legal changes and the pressures of the women's movement. Women's share of lawyers more than quadrupled, of economists more than tripled, and of police detectives more than doubled. Nevertheless, job types were more segregated by sex than by race in the 1990s.

## AIDS AND GAY ACTIVISM

After the increasing openness about sexual orientation in the 1970s, the character of life in gay communities took an abrupt turn in the 1980s when a new worldwide epidemic emerged. Scientists identified a new disease pattern, **acquired immune deficiency syndrome (AIDS),** in 1981. The name described the symptoms resulting from infection by the human immunodeficiency virus (HIV), which destroys the body's ability to resist disease. HIV is transferred through blood and semen. In the 1980s, the most frequent American victims were gay men and intravenous drug users.

*Roe v. Wade* (1973)

**Roe v. Wade**   U.S. Supreme Court decision in 1973 that disallowed state laws prohibiting abortion during the first three months (trimester) of pregnancy and established guidelines for abortion in the second and third trimesters.

**AIDS (Acquired immune deficiency syndrome)**   A complex of deadly pathologies resulting from infection with the human immunodeficiency virus (HIV).

The AIDS Quilt, displayed in Washington in October 1992, combined individual memorials to AIDS victims into a powerful communal statement. The quilt project reminded Americans that AIDS had penetrated every American community.

A decade later, it was clear that HIV/AIDS was a national and even global problem. By the end of 2005, AIDS had been responsible for 550,000 deaths in the United States, and transmission to heterosexual women was increasing. The U.S. Centers for Disease Control and Prevention estimated roughly 40,000 new cases of HIV infection per year at the beginning of the twenty-first century, bringing the total of infected Americans to around 1,200,000. Once a problem of big cities, HIV infection had spread to every American community and had helped to change American attitudes about the process of dying through the spread of hospices for the care of the terminally ill. Meanwhile, the toll of AIDS deaths in other parts of the world, particularly eastern Africa, dwarfed that in the United States and made it a world health crisis.

By the 1990s, Americans were accustomed to open discussion of gay sexuality, if not always accepting of its reality. Television stars and other entertainers could "come out" and retain their popularity. So could politicians in certain districts. On the issue of gays in the military, however, Congress and the Pentagon were more cautious, accepting a policy that made engaging in homosexual acts, though not sexual orientation itself, grounds for discharge.

## CHURCHES IN CHANGE

Americans take their search for spiritual grounding much more seriously than do citizens of other industrial nations. Roughly half of privately organized social activity (such as charity work) is church related. In the mid-1970s, 56 percent of Americans said that religion was "very important" to them, compared to only 27 percent of Europeans. Moreover, religious belief is an important source of political convictions and basis for political action (see American Views, The Religious Imperative in Politics).

Nonetheless, the mainline Protestant denominations that traditionally defined the center of American belief were struggling after 1970. The United Methodist Church, the Presbyterian Church U.S.A., the United Church of Christ, and the Episcopal Church battled internally over the morality of U.S. foreign policy, the role of women in the ministry, and the reception of gay and lesbian members. They were strengthened by an ecumenical impulse that united denominational branches divided by ethnicity or regionalism. However, they gradually lost their position among American churches, perhaps because ecumenism diluted the certainty of their message. Liberal Protestantism has historically been strongest in the slow-growing Northeast and Midwest.

By contrast, evangelical Protestant churches have benefitted from the direct appeal of their message and from strong roots in the booming Sunbelt. Members of evangelical churches (25 percent of white Americans) now outnumber the members of mainline Protestant churches (20 percent). Major evangelical denominations include Baptists, the Church of the Nazarene, and the Assemblies of God. Fundamentalists, defined by a belief in the literal truth of the Bible, are a subset of evangelicals. So are 8 to 10 million Pentecostals and charismatics, who accept "gifts of the spirit," such as healing by faith and speaking in tongues.

Outsiders knew evangelical Christianity through "televangelists." Spending on religious television programming rsoe from $50 million to $600 million by 1980. The "electronic church" built on the radio preaching and professional revivalism of the 1950s. By the 1970s it reached 20 percent of American households.

Evangelical churches emphasized religion as an individual experience focused on personal salvation. Unlike many of the secular and psychological avenues to fulfillment, however, they also offered communities of faith that might stabilize fragmented lives. The conservative nature of their theology and social teaching in a changing society offered certainty that was especially attractive to many younger families.

Another important change in national religious life has been the continuing Americanization of the Roman Catholic Church following the Second Vatican Council in 1965, in which church leaders sought to respond to postwar industrial society. In the United

*Documents*

*Dissent Within the World Episcopal Church over Gay Rights* (2004)

States, Roman Catholicism moved toward the center, helped by the popularity of John Kennedy and by worldly success that made Catholics the economic peers of Protestants. Even as the tight connection between Catholicism and membership in European immigrant communities gradually faded, Asian and Latino immigrants brought new vigor to many parishes, and many inner-city churches have been centers for social action. Church practice lost some of its distinctiveness; celebrating Mass in English rather than Latin was an important move toward modernization, but it also sparked a conservative counter-effort to preserve the traditional liturgy. Traditional and nontraditional Catholics also disagree about whether priests should be allowed to marry and other adaptations to American culture.

The new globalization of American society simultaneously increased the nation's religious diversity and confirmed the dominant position of Christianity. Many immigrants from Asia and Africa have come with their native religious beliefs. There are now hundreds of Hindu temples and thousands of Buddhist centers. More than a million Muslims now worship in mosques that are found in every major city. In total, the proportion of Americans who identify themselves with non-Christian religions grew from 3 percent in 1990 to 4 percent in 2001. Over the same period, however, the proportion identifying with a Christian group or denomination grew from 86 to 87 percent. Indeed, many recent immigrants are Christians: Roman Catholics from Vietnam and the Philippines, Protestants from Korean, evangelicals from the former Soviet Union, Catholics and evangelicals from Latin America.

## CULTURE WARS

In the 1950s and 1960s, Americans argued most often over foreign policy, racial justice, and the economy. Since the 1980s, they have also quarreled over beliefs and values, especially as the patterns of family life have become more varied. In the course of these quarrels, religious belief has heavily influenced politics as individuals and groups try to shape America around their own, and often mutually conflicting, ideas of the godly society. Americans who are undogmatic in religion are often liberal in politics as well, hoping to lessen economic inequities and strengthen individual social freedom. Religious and political conservatism also tend to go together.

*Documents*

Bill O'Reilly and John Gibson, *The Alleged Attack on Christmas Secular Progressives* (2005)

The division on social issues is related to theological differences within Protestantism. The "conservative" emphasis on personal salvation and the literal truth of the Bible expresses itself in a desire to restore "traditional" social patterns. Conservatives worry that social disorder occurs when people follow personal impulses and pleasures. In contrast, the "liberal" or "modern" emphasis on the universality of the Christian message restates the Social Gospel with its call to build the Kingdom of God through social justice and may recognize divergent pathways toward truth. Liberals worry that greed in the unregulated marketplace creates disorder and injustice.

The cultural conflict also transcends the historic three-way division of Americans among Protestants, Catholics, and Jews. Instead, the conservative-liberal division now cuts through each group.

Conservatives initiated the culture wars, trying to stabilize what they fear is an American society spinning out of control because of lack of self-discipline and sexual indulgence. In fact, the evidence on the sexual revolution is mixed. Growing numbers of teenagers reported being sexually active in the 1970s, but the rate of increase tapered off in the 1980s. The divorce rate began to drop after 1980. Births to teenagers dropped after 1990, and the number of two-parent families increased. There was, however, an astonishing eagerness to talk about sex in the 1990s, a decade when soap-opera story lines and talk shows covered everything from family violence to exotic sexual tastes.

The explosion of explicit attention to sexual behavior set the stage for religiously rooted battles over two sets of issues. One cluster revolved around so-called family values, questioning the morality of access to abortion, the acceptability of

## AMERICAN VIEWS

### The Religious Imperative in Politics

The strong religious faith of many Americans frequently drives them to different stands on political issues. The first of these two documents, a letter by Jerry Falwell to potential supporters of the Moral Majority, reflects the politically conservative outlook of many evangelical Christians. Falwell is pastor of the Thomas Road Baptist Church in Lynchburg, Virginia. He founded the Moral Majority, a conservative religious lobbying and educational organization, in 1979 and served as its president until 1987, the year he wrote the letter reprinted here. The organization was especially important for voter registration efforts among conservative Christians. The second document, from an open letter issued by the Southside United Presbyterian Church in Tucson in 1982, expresses the conviction of other believers that God may sometimes require civil disobedience to oppose oppressive government actions. The letter explains the church's reasons for violating immigration law to offer sanctuary to refugees from repressive Central American regimes supported by the United States.

- **How** do Falwell and the Southside Presbyterian Church define the problems that demand a religious response?
- **Are** there any points of agreement?
- **How** does each statement balance the claims of God and government?

#### FROM THE REVEREND JERRY FALWELL:

I believe that the overwhelming majority of Americans are sick and tired of the way that amoral liberals are trying to corrupt our nation from its commitment to freedom, democracy, traditional morality, and the free enterprise system. And I believe that the majority of Americans agree on the basic moral values which this nation was founded upon over 200 years ago.

Today we face four burning crises as we continue in this Decade of Destiny—the 1980s—loss of our freedom by giving in to the Communists; the destruction of the family unit; the deterioration of the free enterprise system; and the crumbling of basic moral principles which has resulted in the legalizing of abortion, wide-spread pornography, and a drug problem of epidemic proportions.

That is why I went to Washington, D.C., in June of 1979, and started a new organization, The Moral Majority.

Right now you may be wondering: "But I thought Jerry Falwell was the preacher on the Old-Time Gospel Hour television program?"

You are right. For over twenty-four years I have been calling the nation back to God from the pulpit on radio and television. But in recent months I have been led to do more than just preach. I have been compelled to take action.

I have made the commitment to go right into the halls of Congress and fight for laws that will save America.

I will still be preaching every Sunday on the Old-Time Gospel Hour and I still must be a husband and father to my precious family in Lynchburg, Virginia.

But as God gives me the strength, I must do more. I must go into the halls of Congress and fight for laws that will protect the grand old flag for the sake of our children and grandchildren.

#### FROM SOUTHSIDE UNITED PRESBYTERIAN CHURCH:

We are writing to inform you that Southside Presbyterian Church will publicly violate the Immigration and Nationality Act, Section 274 (A).

We take this action because we believe the current policy and practice of the United States Government with regard to Central American refugees is illegal and immoral. We believe our government is in violation of the 1980 Refugee Act and international law by continuing to arrest, detain, and forcibly return refugees to the terror, persecution, and murder in El Salvador and Guatemala.

We believe that justice and mercy require the people of conscience to actively assert our God-given right to aid anyone fleeing from persecution and murder.

We beg of you, in the name of God, to do justice and love mercy in the administration of your office. We ask that "extended voluntary departure" be granted to refugees from Central America and that current deportation proceedings against these victims be stopped.

Until such time, we will not cease to extend the sanctuary of the church. Obedience to God requires this of us all.

Sources: Gary E. McCuen, ed., *The Religious Right* (Hudson, WI, G. E. McCuen, 1989); Ann Crittenden, *Sanctuary* (New York, Weidenfeld & Nicolson, 1988).

homosexuality, and the roles and rights of women. A second set of concerns has focused on the supposed role of public schools in undermining morality through sex education, unrestricted reading matter, nonbiblical science, and the absence of prayer. The Supreme Court decisions in 1962 and 1963 that prohibited vocal prayer and devotional Bible reading in public schools were targets for many.

A culturally conservative issue with great popular appeal in the early 1990s was an effort to prevent states and localities from protecting homosexuals against discrimination. Under the slogan "No special rights," antigay measures passed in Cincinnati, Colorado, and communities in Oregon in 1993 and 1994, only to have the Supreme Court overturn the Colorado law in *Romer v. Evans* (1996). It is important to note that public support for lesbian and gay civil rights varies with different issues (strong support for equal employment opportunity, much less for granting marriage rights to same-sex couples) and whether the issues are framed in terms of specified rights for gays or in terms of the right of everyone to be free from government interference with personal decisions, such as living arrangements and sexual choices.

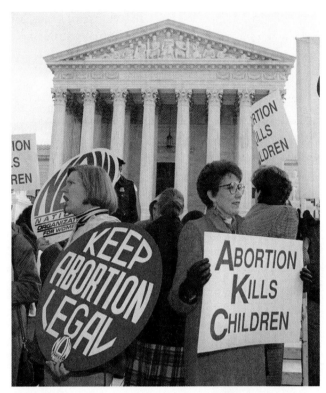

In December 1993, the U.S. Supreme Court heard arguments on whether states could require protesters to remain a certain distance from abortion clinics. These antiabortion and proabortion protesters revealed the deep divisions over this and other issues in the culture wars.

# CONCLUSION

Taken as a whole, the years from 1981 through 1992 brought transformations that redirected the course of American life. Because many changes were associated with national policy choices, it is fair to call this the era of the Reagan revolution. The astonishing collapse of the Soviet Union ended 40 years of Cold War. New political leadership in Washington reversed the 50-year expansion of federal government programs to deal with economic and social inequities. Prosperity alternated with recessions that shifted the balance between regions. Economic inequality increased after narrowing for a generation at the same time that more and more leaders proclaimed that unregulated markets could best meet social needs. Middle-class Latinos and African Americans made substantial gains, while many other minority Americans sank deeper into poverty.

At the same time, it is important to recognize that every revolution has its precursors. Intellectuals have been clarifying the justifications for Reagan administration actions since the 1960s. The Reagan-Bush years extended changes that began in the 1970s, particularly the conservative economic policies and military buildup of the troubled Carter administration. Intervention in the Persian Gulf amplified U.S. policies that had been in place since the CIA intervened in Iran in 1953. The outbreak of violence in Los Angeles after the Rodney King verdict showed that race relations were as tense as they had been in the 1960s.

In 1992, the United States stood as the undisputed world power. Its economy was poised for a surge of growth at the same time that rivals such as Japan were mired in economic crisis. It was the leader in scientific research and the development of new technologies. Its military capacities far surpassed those of any rival and seemed to offer a free hand in shaping the world—capacities that would be tested and utilized in the new century.

# SUMMARY

**WHAT GROUPS** of traditionally Democratic voters were attracted to Ronald Reagan's message? Why?

**Reagan's Domestic Revolution**
Political change began in 1980, when Ronald Reagan and his running mate George H. W. Bush, rode American discontent to a decisive victory in the presidential election. Building on a neoconservative critique of American public policies and issues from the Carter administration, Reagan presided over revolutionary changes in American government and policies. The consequences of his two terms included an altered role for government, powerful but selected economic growth, and a shift of domestic policy toward lifestyle concerns. Reaganomics and a new prosperity contrasted with corporate "downsizing" and an increase in the poverty rate.

**WHAT WERE** the goals of the Reagan administration's policies in Central America?

**The Second (Short) Cold War**
Reagan regarded the Soviet Union as an "evil empire." By the end of 1991 the Soviet Union was gone, Communist regimes had ended in Eastern Europe, and the Berlin Wall had come down. Reagan's foreign policy was marked by the invasion of Granada, assistance to Nicaraguan Contras, and the revelation of the Iran-Contra affair. In 1991, President George H. W. Bush intervened in the Persian Gulf in response to Iraq's invasion of Kuwait; the war fascinated millions who watched it live on television; America won the war but not the peace.

**HOW DID** growth in the Sunbelt shape national politics in the 1980s and 1990s?

**Growth in the Sunbelt** The emergence of the Sunbelt as a center of population and source of conservative voting strength, the immigration "boom," the demographic and ethnic changes in American cities, and the graying of America are all characteristics of America since 1981. Much of the Sunbelt growth has come from retired Americans and new job seekers. Older Americans have now become a powerful voice in public affairs. Immigration has significantly changed the American ethnic mix; while the largest single group of immigrants is Hispanic, immigrants from Asia, Russia, Eastern Europe, and the Middle East are reflected in the 10.4 percent of the population that is foreign-born.

**WHAT KEY** social and cultural issues divided Americans in the 1980s and 1990s?

**Values in Collision** In the 1950s and 1960s Americans argued most often about foreign policy, racial injustice, and the economy. Since that time, they have also quarreled over beliefs and values, especially as patterns in family life have become more varied. In substantial measure these conflicts were rooted in the social and cultural changes of the 1960s and 1970s that had altered traditional institutions. Changes in roles and expectations among women and new openness about gay and lesbian sexuality were particularly powerful in dividing American churches and politics. Abortion rights and the conservative backlash, the increase of women in the work force, and the new "culture wars" were part of modern America.

# WHERE TO LEARN MORE

**Ronald Reagan Boyhood Home, Dixon, Illinois.** The home where Reagan lived from 1920 to 1923 tells relatively little about Reagan himself but a great deal about the small-town context that shaped his ideas. **www.ronaldreaganhome.com**

**The Intermediate Nuclear Force Agreement (INF).** The full-text document of the INF agreement between the United States and the Soviet Union, the first true nuclear-disarmament treaty. **http://www.state.gov/www/global/arms/ treaties/inf1.html**

**The Gulf War.** See video clips from that Canadian Broadcasting Cooperation that provide a running narrative of the military crisis and war. **http:archives.cbc.ca/war_conflict/1991 _gulf_war/.**

# STUDY RESOURCES

## myhistorylab

For study resources for this chapter, go to www.myhistorylab .com and choose *The American Journey.* You will find a wealth of study and review material for this chapter, including pre- and post-tests, customized study plan, key term review flash cards, interactive map and document activities, and documents for analysis.

# REVIEW QUESTIONS

1.  Is it accurate to talk about a Reagan Revolution in U.S. politics? Did Reagan's presidency change the economic environment for workers and business corporations? How did economic changes in the 1980s affect the prospects of the richest and poorest Americans?

2.  How did American ideas about the proper role of government change during the 1980s? What were the basis of these changes?

3.  What caused the breakup of the Soviet Union and the end of the Cold War? Did U.S. foreign policy under Reagan and Bush contribute significantly to the withdrawal of Soviet power from eastern Europe? Did the collapse of the USSR show the strength of the United States and its allies or the weakness of Soviet Communism?

4.  How did the United States use military force during the Reagan and Bush administrations? Did military actions achieve the expected goals?

5.  What were some of the important economic trends that shifted American growth toward the Sunbelt (South and West)? How has immigration from other nations affected the different American regions?

6.  What changes in family roles and sexual behavior became divisive political issues? How have churches responded to cultural changes? What are some of the ways in which churches and religious leaders have tried to influence political decisions?

7.  How did U.S. military involvement in southeast Asia in the 1960s continue to affect American society for decades to come?

## KEY TERMS

Acquired immune deficiency syndrome (AIDS) (p. 937)
Americans with Disabilities Act (p. 923)
Deregulation (p. 917)
Economic Recovery and Tax Act of 1981 (ERTA) (p. 917)
*Glasnost* (p. 927)
Immigration and Nationality Act of 1965 (p. 932)
Intermediate Nuclear Force Agreement (INF) (p. 927)

Operation Desert Storm (p. 931)
Persian Gulf War (p. 931)
*Perestroika* (p. 927)
Reagan Doctrine (p. 925)
*Roe v. Wade* (p. 937)
Sagebrush Rebellion (p. 917)
Strategic Defense Initiative (SDI) (p. 925)
Sunbelt (p. 931)

# 31
# Complacency and Crisis

New York City firefighters walk through the rubble at the World Trade Center, the skeletal remains of the Twin Towers behind them

POLITICS OF THE CENTER  *(page 947)*

**WHAT ISSUES** did Bill Clinton capitalize on in his 1992 presidential campaign?

A NEW ECONOMY?  *(page 953)*

**WHAT ROLE** did new information technology play in the economic boom of the 1990s?

BROADENING DEMOCRACY  *(page 959)*

**WHAT GAINS** did women make in national politics in the 1990s?

EDGING INTO A NEW CENTURY  *(page 967)*

**WHAT WERE** the key elements of George W. Bush's agenda?

PARADOXES OF POWER  *(page 970)*

**HOW DID** the government's response to dissent after 9-11 compare to government policies during World War I?

*I'm a firefighter for the FDNY [Fire Department New York]. I had gotten off the night before. . . . My friend woke me up early that morning to borrow my car to take his sick cat to the vet. . . . I was up so I went to my local bagel store for my coffee and paper . . . when I heard a lady scream a plane had hit the Trade Center. . . . I thought since it was a beautiful day that perhaps a Cessna with the pilot having a heart attack had accidentally done this. . . . I ran home to put the TV on. . . . as soon as I saw what damage was done I knew this wasn't any Cessna. . . . my god people were jumping . . . phone rang it was a fellow from my station and he hadn't turned his TV on yet. . . . I screamed to him to turn his #\*#\* TV on. . . .*

*When the second plane hit . . . I said goodbye and told him I was going in. . . . I jumped in my car and was off to the races. . . . the highway was closed . . . but open for us.*

*. . . I had the gas pedal to the floor as I headed toward the city looking out my window I see both towers burning . . . when I hear a rumble and see the south tower #2 fall. . . . I have to get my gear so I pull off the highway going down the on ramp . . . arriving at the firehouse everyone's in shock and we know we gotta get there now to help. . . . as we're getting ready to leave the 2nd tower fell. . . . we commandeer a bus and we're off. . . .*

*We arrived at a staging area and then finally got the ok to go in. . . . who's in charge? . . . Shoes, papers, and dust are everywhere. . . . we wait til [building] 7 collapses. . . . chief gets us into the site by going thru the financial center and bam there we are. . . . pieces of the outside wall sticking out of the highway. . . . cars on fire . . . buses gutted. . . . I saw numerous acts of courage that day both civilian and uniformed. . . . the looks on the faces of the people coming out of the city that day will haunt me forever . . . everyone was the same color. . . . dust white. . . . women crying. . . . men crying. . . . we . . . must never forget the men and women that died that day. . . . their sacrifice will live on for generations to come. . . .*

John McNamara, Story \#400, The September 11 Digital Archive, 13 April 2002, http://911digitalarchive.org/stories/details/400

**PEARSON**
**myhistorylab**
**Personal Journeys Online**

- **Anthony Fernandez III, "Remembering the Oklahoma City Bombing," 2007.**
  **A search and rescue worker describes the background of the picture on page 899.**

- **Dawn Shurmaitis, 2001. Volunteering in the aftermath of the September 11, 2001 attack.**

◆ **JOHN MCNAMARA** was one of the many off-duty New York City firefighters who rushed to the World Trade Center after the terrorist attack on September 11, 2001. Altogether, 479 police officers, firefighters, and other emergency workers died in the collapse of the towers. Thousands of volunteers rushed to assist rescue efforts or contribute to relief efforts. The total confirmed death toll was 2,752 in New York, 184 at the Pentagon, and 40 in Pennsylvania.

The attacks, masterminded by the Al-Qaeda network of Muslim extremists, ended a decade of prosperity at home and complacency about the place of the United States in the world. In their aftermath, as Americans noticed millions of Muslim neighbors and tried to balance civil liberties against national security, they realized how diverse the nation had become. For most of the 1990s, prosperity had allowed politics to focus on social issues, such as healthcare and education, as well as on bitterly partisan but often superficial battles over personalities and presidential behavior. However, the terrorists attacked buildings that were symbols of the nation's economic and military power. The aftermath deepened a business recession that had followed a decade of growth spurred by new technologies. At the same time, the vulnerability of the targets undermined Americans' sense of security and isolation from world problems, underscored the global reach of terrorism, and made understanding its sources more necessary than ever. ◆

## CHRONOLOGY

| | |
|---|---|
| **1969** | First version of Internet (ARPAnet) launched. |
| **1980** | CNN begins broadcasting. |
| **1991** | World Wide Web launched. |
| **1992** | Bill Clinton elected president. |
| **1993** | Congress approves the North American Free Trade Agreement (NAFTA). |
| | Congress adopts Family Leave Act. |
| **1994** | Independent Counsel Kenneth Starr begins investigation of Bill and Hillary Clinton. Paula Jones files sexual harassment lawsuit against Bill Clinton. |
| | Republicans sweep to control of Congress. |
| | Federal government temporarily shuts down for lack of money. |
| **1995** | United States sends peacekeeping troops to Bosnia. |
| **1996** | Clinton wins a second term as president. |
| **1998** | Paula Jones lawsuit dismissed. |
| | House of Representatives impeaches Clinton. |
| **1999** | Senate acquits Clinton of impeachment charges. |
| | United States leads NATO intervention in Kosovo. |
| **2000** | George W. Bush defeats Al Gore in nation's closest presidential election. |
| **2001** | Congress passes massive ten-year tax reduction. |

| | |
|---|---|
| | United States refuses to agree to Kyoto Treaty to limit global warming. |
| | Terrorists crash airliners into World Trade Center and Pentagon. |
| | U.S. military operations oust Taliban regime in Afghanistan. |
| | Congress passes U.S. PATRIOT Act to combat domestic terror. |
| **2002** | United States and Russia agree to cut number of deployed nuclear warheads. |
| | Congress creates Department of Homeland Security. |
| | United Nations Security Council passes resolution requiring Iraq to allow open inspections of weapons systems. |
| **2003** | U.S. and British troops invade Iraq and topple government of Saddam Hussein. |
| | Supreme Court allows limited forms of affirmative action in university admissions. |
| **2004** | George W. Bush reelected as president. |
| **2005** | Hurricane Katrina devastates New Orleans. |
| | Iraq adopts new constitution. |
| **2006** | Democrats regain narrow edge in Congress. |
| **2008** | John McCain and Barack Obama compete for Presidency. |

# POLITICS OF THE CENTER

In the race for president in 1992, Bill Clinton promised economic leadership and stressed the need for private investment to create jobs. He promised to reduce government bureaucracy and the deficit, touted the value of stable families, and talked about healthcare and welfare reform. His message revealed an insight into the character of the United States in the 1990s. What mattered most were down-to-earth issues, not the distant problems of foreign policy, which seemed to have little urgency after the end of the Cold War.

Bill Clinton's election, first term, and reelection in 1996 showed the attraction of pragmatic policies and the political center in a two-party system. In his first inaugural address in January 1993, Clinton pledged "an end to the era of deadlock and drift and a new season of American renewal."

**WHAT ISSUES** did Bill Clinton capitalize on in his 1992 presidential campaign?

## THE ELECTION OF 1992: A NEW GENERATION

The mid-1990s brought new generation into the political arena. The members of "Generation X" came of voting age with deep worries about the foreclosing of opportunities. They worried that previous administrations had ignored growing economic divisions and let the competitive position of the United States deteriorate. The range of suggested solutions differed widely—individual moral reform, a stronger labor movement, leaner competition in world markets—but the generational concern was clear.

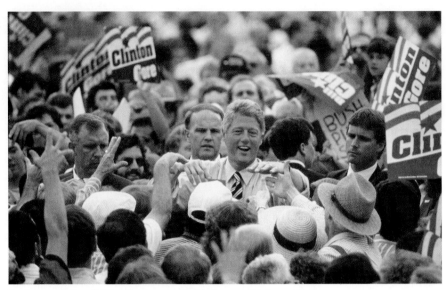

Despite personal flaws, Bill Clinton was enormously effective as a political campaigner.

This generational change made 1992 one of the most volatile national elections in decades. A baby boomer and successful governor of Arkansas who was not widely known nationally, Democrat Bill Clinton decided that George H.W. Bush was vulnerable when more senior Democrats opted to pass on the contest.

Bush, the last politician of the World War II generation to gain the White House, won renomination by beating back the archconservative Patrick Buchanan, who claimed that the last 12 years had been a long betrayal of true conservatism. The Republican National Convention in Houston showed how important cultural issues had become to the Republican Party. The party platform conformed to the beliefs of the Christian right.

The wild card was the Texas billionaire Ross Perot, whose independent campaign started with an appearance on a television talk show. Perot loved flip charts, distanced himself from professional politicians, and claimed to talk sense to the American people. He also tried to occupy the political center. In May, Perot outscored both Bush and Clinton in opinion polls, but his behavior became increasingly erratic. He withdrew from the race and then reentered after floating stories that he was the target of dark conspiracies.

Bush campaigned as a foreign policy expert. He expected voters to reward him for the end of the Cold War, but he ignored anxieties about the nation's direction at home. Clinton hammered away at economic concerns, appealing to swing voters, such as suburban independents and blue-collar Reagan Democrats. He presented himself as the leader of new, pragmatic, and livelier Democrats.

Election day gave the Clinton-Gore ticket 43 percent of the popular vote, Bush 38 percent, and Perot 19 percent. Clinton held the Democratic core of northern and midwestern industrial states and loosened the Republican hold on the South and West (see Map 31–1).

## POLICING THE WORLD

Although Clinton was much more interested in domestic policies, he inherited a confused expectation that the United States could use its military and economic power to keep the world on an even keel and counter ethnic hatred without incurring serious risks to itself. During the administration's first years, U.S. diplomats helped broker an Israel-PLO accord that gave Palestinians self-government in Gaza and the West Bank, only to watch extremists on both sides undermine the accords and plunge Israel into a near–civil war by 2002.

### QUICK REVIEW

**Candidates for President in 1992**

- Republican George H.W. Bush seeking a second term.
- Democrat Bill Clinton: little known governor of Arkansas.
- Independent Ross Perot: Texas billionaire and political maverick.

**Exploring America**
*Globalization*

The United States in 1994 used diplomatic pressure to persuade North Korea to suspend building nuclear weapons, temporarily calming a potentially explosive trouble spot. The world also benefitted from a gradual reduction of nuclear arsenals and from a 1996 treaty to ban the testing of nuclear weapons.

**Bosnia and Kosovo.**   Clinton reluctantly committed the United States to a multinational effort to end the bloody civil war in ethnically and religiously divided Bosnia in 1995. In the early 1990s, the former Communist nation of Yugoslavia, in southeastern Europe, fragmented into five independent nations: Slovenia, Macedonia, Croatia, Bosnia, and Yugoslavia (the name retained by the predominantly Serbian nation with its capital at Belgrade). Bosnia, divided both ethnically and religiously between Christians and Muslims, erupted in bitter civil war. Christian Serbs, supported by Belgrade, engaged in massacres and deportations of Muslim Bosnians with the goal of creating "ethnically clean" Serbian districts. Too late to stop most bloodshed, NATO troops after 1995 enforced a brittle peace accord and a division of territory into Bosnian and Serb sectors under a shaky federated government.

The U.S. military revisited the same part of Europe in 1999, when the United States and Britain led NATO's intervention in Kosovo. The overwhelming majority of people in this Yugoslav province were ethnic Albanians who had chafed under the control of the Serb-controlled Yugoslav government. When a Kosovar independence movement began a rebellion, Yugoslav president Slobodan Milosevic responded with brutal repression that threatened to drive over 1 million ethnic Albanians out of the province. To protect the Kosovars, NATO in March 1999 began a bombing campaign that targeted Yugoslav military bases and forces in Kosovo. In June, Yugoslavia agreed to withdraw its troops and make way for a multinational NATO peacekeeping force with 50,000 troops from Britain, France, Germany, Italy, the Netherlands, and the United States, marking a measured success for U.S. policy.

**The reinvention of NATO.**   To satisfy Russia, the peacekeeping force that entered Kosovo in June was technically a U.S. operation, but it was a reinvented NATO that negotiated with Yugoslavia.

The new NATO is a product of the new Europe of the 1990s. A key step was expansion into the former Soviet sphere in eastern Europe. In 1999, NATO formally admitted Poland, Hungary, and the Czech Republic over the objections of Russia. Three years later, NATO agreed to give Russia a formal role in discussions about a number of its policy decisions, further eroding the barriers of the Cold War, and it added another seven nations of eastern Europe in 2004.

**Clinton's Neoliberalism**   Domestic policy attracted Clinton's greatest interest, and his first term can be divided into two parts. In 1993–1994, he worked with a slim Democratic majority in Congress to modernize the U.S. economy, taking advantage of an economic upturn that lasted for most of the decade. In 1995 and 1996, however, he faced solid Republican majorities, the result of an unanticipated Republican tide in the November 1994 elections.

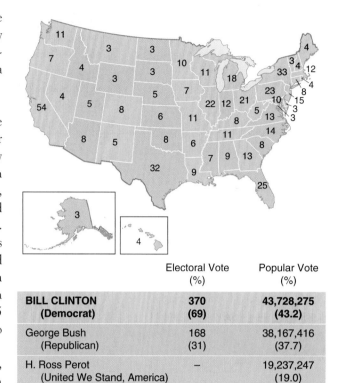

| | Electoral Vote (%) | Popular Vote (%) |
|---|---|---|
| **BILL CLINTON** **(Democrat)** | **370** **(69)** | **43,728,275** **(43.2)** |
| George Bush (Republican) | 168 (31) | 38,167,416 (37.7) |
| H. Ross Perot (United We Stand, America) | – | 19,237,247 (19.0) |

**MAP 31–1   The Election of 1992**   Bill Clinton defeated George H. W. Bush in 1992 by reviving the Democratic Party in the industrial Northeast and enlisting new Democratic voters in the western states, where he appealed both to Hispanic immigrants and to people associated with fast-growing high-tech industries. He won reelection in 1996 with the same pattern of support. However, the coalition was an unstable combination of "Old Democrats," associated with older industries and labor unions, and "New Democrats," favoring economic change, free trade, and globalization.

**What factors** led to George H. W. Bush's downfall in the election of 1992?

**neoliberal** Advocate or participant in the effort to reshape the Democratic party for the 1990s around a policy emphasizing economic growth and competitiveness in the world economy.

## QUICK REVIEW

### Clinton's Agenda

◆ Make the U.S. economy more equitable domestically and competitive internationally.

◆ Reduce the size of government while raising taxes on the wealthy and reducing them on the poor.

◆ Clinton's biggest setback was the failure of comprehensive healthcare legislation.

*Republican Contract with America* (1994)

**Contract with America** Platform proposing a sweeping reduction in the role and activities of the federal government on which many Republican candidates ran for Congress in 1994.

**Temporary Assistance for Needy Families (TANF)** Federal program, utilizing work requirements for and time limits on benefits, created in 1996 to replace earlier welfare programs to aid families and children.

The heart of Clinton's agenda was an effort to make the United States economy more equitable domestically and more competitive internationally. These goals marked Clinton as a **neoliberal** who envisioned a partnership between a leaner government and a dynamic private sector. Steps to "reinvent" government cut federal employment below Reagan administration levels. A new tax bill reversed some of the inequities of the 1980s by increasing taxes on the weathiest 1.2 percent of households. An improved college student-aid program spread benefits to more students by allowing direct federal loans. In early 1993, Clinton pushed through the Family and Medical Leave Act, which provided up to 12 weeks of unpaid leave for workers with newborns or family emergencies and had been vetoed twice by George H.W. Bush.

Clinton's biggest setback was the failure of comprehensive healthcare legislation. The goals seemed simple at first: containment of healthcare costs and extension of basic medical insurance from 83 percent of Americans under age 65 to 100 percent. In the abstract, voters agreed that something needed to be done.

Clinton appointed his wife, Hillary Rodham Clinton, to head the healthcare task force. Many found this an inappropriate role for a first lady. The plan that emerged from the White House ran to 1,342 pages of complex regulations, with something for everyone to dislike. Thus the reform effort went nowhere.

## CONTRACT WITH AMERICA AND THE ELECTION OF 1996

Conservative political ideology and personal animosity against the Clintons were both part of the background for an extraordinary off-year election in 1994, in which voters defeated dozens of incumbents and gave Republicans control of Congress. For most of 1995, the new speaker of the House, Newt Gingrich of Georgia, dominated political headlines as he pushed the **Contract with America,** the official Republican campaign platform for the 1994 elections, which called for a revolutionary reduction in federal responsibilities.

Clinton lay low and let the new Congress attack environmental protections, propose cuts in federal benefits for the elderly, and try to slice the capital-gains tax to help the rich. As Congress and president battled over the budget, congressional Republicans refused to authorize interim spending and forced the federal government to shut down for more than three weeks between November 1995 and January 1996. Gingrich was the clear loser in public opinion, both for the shutdowns and for his ideas. Democrats painted Gingrich and his congressional allies as a radical fringe who wanted to gut Medicare and Medicaid, undermine education, punish legal immigrants, and sell off national parks—core values and programs that most Americans wanted to protect.

After the budget confrontations, 1996 brought a series of measures to reward work—a centrist position acceptable to most Americans. The minimum wage increased. Congress made pension programs easier for employers to create and made health insurance portable when workers changed jobs. After tough negotiations, Clinton signed bipartisan legislation to "end welfare as we know it." **Temporary Assistance to Needy Families (TANF)** replaced Aid to Families with Dependent Children (AFDC). TANF had strict requirements that aid recipients be seeking work or be enrolled in schooling, and it set a time limit on assistance. By 2001, the number of public-assistance recipients had declined 58 percent from its 1994 high, but there are doubts that many of the former recipients have found jobs adequate to support their families.

Clinton's reelection in 1996 was a virtual replay of 1992. His opponent, Robert Dole, represented the World War II generation of politicians. Because the nation was prosperous and at peace, and because Clinton had claimed the political center and sounded like Dwight Eisenhower, the results were never in doubt. Clinton became the first Democratic president to be elected to a second term since Franklin Roosevelt.

The Clinton-Gore ticket took 70 percent of the electoral votes and 49 percent of the popular vote (versus 41 percent for Dole and 9 percent for a recycled Ross Perot). Clinton easily won the Northeast, the industrial Midwest, and the Far West; Hispanic voters alienated by anti-immigrant rhetoric from the Republicans helped Clinton also take the usually Republican states of Florida and Arizona.

The election confirmed that voters liked the pragmatic center. What voters wanted was to continue the reduction of the federal role in domestic affairs that had begun in the 1980s without damaging social insurance programs.

## THE DANGERS OF EVERYDAY LIFE

Part of the background for the sometimes vicious politics of mid-decade was a sense of individual insecurity and fear of violence that coexisted with an economy that was booming in some sectors but still leaving many Americans behind.

**Random violence and domestic terrorism.**  One after another, headlines and news flashes proclaimed terrifying random acts of violence. The greatest losses of life came in Waco, Texas, and in Oklahoma City. On April 19, 1993, federal agents raided the fortified compound of the Branch Davidian cult outside Waco after a 51-day siege. The raid triggered a fire, probably set from inside, that killed more than 80 people. On the second anniversary of the Waco raid, Timothy McVeigh packed a rented truck with explosive materials and detonated it in front of the federal office building in downtown Oklahoma City, presumably as revenge against what he considered an oppressive government. The blast collapsed the entire front of the nine-story building and killed 169 people.

Search and rescue worker Anthony Fernandez and rescue dog Aspen pause during the search through the ruins of the Oklahoma City federal building after its bombing by domestic terrorists in 1995.

In April 1999, two high school students in Littleton, Colorado, took rifles and pipe bombs into Columbine High School to kill 12 classmates, a teacher, and themselves. A national manhunt in 1997 captured Ted Kaczynski, the so-called Unabomber, who since 1978 had mailed more than a dozen bombs to college professors and airlines as protest against an industrialized economy.

**Gun control.**  Workplace assassins, schoolroom murders, and domestic terrorism invigorated efforts to monitor access to firearms. The Brady Handgun Violence Prevention Act, passed in 1994, took its name from James Brady, President Reagan's first press secretary, who was seriously injured in the 1981 attempt to kill the president. The act set up a waiting period and background checks for purchases of firearms from retailers, pawnshops, and licensed firearm dealers.

 **WHERE TO LEARN MORE**

 Oklahoma City National Memorial Center Museum, Oklahoma City, OK.

www.oklahomacitynationalmemorial.org

Gun control was political dynamite, for Americans have drastically differing understandings of the Second Amendment, which states: "A well regulated militia, being necessary to the security of a free State, the right of the people to keep and bear arms, shall not be infringed." The powerful National Rifle Association, the major lobby for gun owners and manufacturers, now argued that the amendment establishes an absolute individual right. Federal courts for many decades interpreted the Second Amendment to apply to the possession of weapons in connection with citizen service in a government-organized militia. In June 2008, however, the Supreme Court in *District of Columbia v. Heller* struck down Washington, D.C.'s absolute ban on the ownership or possession of handguns. The majority in the 5-4 decision argued that the Second Amendment implied an individual right to own firearms. However, it left most state and federal firearms laws intact by allowing restrictions on individual categories of weapons and regulations on acquisition and use that fall short of prohibitions.

**Crime and the war on drugs.**    Conservatives, including many gun-ownership absolutists, put their faith in strict law enforcement as the best route to public security. The 1990s saw numerous states adopt "three-strike" measures that drastically increased penalties for individuals convicted of a third crime. The number of people serving sentences of a year or longer in state and federal prisons grew from 316,000 in 1980 to 740,000 in 1990 and 1,422,000 in 2004, with another 714,000 being held for shorter periods in local jails. By 2007, one in every 99.1 adults was behind bars.

The war on drugs, begun in the 1980s, was the biggest contributor to the prison boom. As the drug war dragged on through the 1990s, the federal government poured billions of dollars into efforts to stop illegal drugs from crossing the Mexican border or from landing by boat or airplane. The United States intervened in South American nations that produced cocaine, particularly Peru and Colombia, aiding local military efforts to uproot crops and battle drug lords. Meanwhile, aggressive enforcement of domestic laws against drug possession or sales filled U.S. prison cells. The antidrug campaign fell most heavily on minorities.

In fact, crime fell steadily for a decade after reaching a peak in 1991. The rate of violent crime (murder, rape, robbery, aggravated assault) fell by 33 percent from 1991 to 2000, including a 36 percent drop in the number of murders. The rate of major property crimes (burglary, larceny-theft, and motor vehicle theft) fell by 30 percent over the same period. Easing fears combined with escalating costs cause some states to rethink the reliance on prison terms.

**Debating the death penalty.**    Governor George Ryan of Illinois was elected in 1998 as a conservative Republican. In January 2003, this small-town businessman emptied death row in the Illinois prison system by commuting the death sentences of 167 convicted murderers to prison terms of life or less. He asserted that his review of individual cases had led him to doubt the justice of the death-penalty system as a whole, which he said is "haunted by the demons of error—error in determining guilt and error in determining who among the guilty deserves to die."

Specific discussion of flaws in the application of the death penalty reveals basic disagreements about the best approach to public order. Thirty-eight of the 50 states impose the death penalty, although sixteen states have not carried out an execution since 1976. The majority of Americans have accepted capital punishment as a flawed but necessary defense for society.

In contrast, a passionate minority thinks that capital punishment is a tool so bent and blunted as to be worse than useless. They point out that the deterrent effect of capital punishment is weak at best; murder rates are often higher in death-penalty states than in similar states without the penalty. They note that African Americans and Latinos receive the death penalty far more often than whites charged with the same crimes. The debate about capital punishment exemplifies the fault lines that divide Americans as they try to balance the demands of justice and public order.

## MORALITY AND PARTISANSHIP

Years of rumors, innuendos, and lawsuits culminated in 1999 in the nation's second presidential impeachment trial. President Clinton's problems began in 1994 with the appointment of a special prosecutor to investigate possible fraud in the **Whitewater**

**QUICK REVIEW**

**Crime and Punishment**

♦ High-profile acts of violence sparked interest in gun control.

♦ Some conservatives argued that the best defense against violence was gun ownership.

♦ The war on drugs led to a prison population boom.

**Whitewater**    Arkansas real estate development in which Bill and Hillary Clinton were investors; several fraud convictions resulted from investigations into Whitewater, but evidence was not found that the Clinton's were involved in wrongdoing.

**QUICK REVIEW**

**From Whitewater to Impeachment**

♦ 1994: Appointment of special prosecutor to investigate possible Whitewater fraud.

♦ Special prosecutor conducts wide-ranging investigation.

♦ January 1998: Accusations of affair between President Clinton and Monica Lewinsky.

♦ Fall 1998: Congressional Republicans pursue impeachment.

development, an Arkansas land promotion in which Bill and Hillary Clinton had invested in the 1980s. The probe by Kenneth Starr, the independent counsel, however, expanded into a wide-ranging investigation that encompassed the firing of the White House travel-office staff early in 1993, the suicide of White House aide Vincent Foster, and the sexual behavior of the president. Meanwhile, Paula Jones had brought a lawsuit claiming sexual harassment by then-governor Clinton while she was a state worker in Arkansas. The investigation of Whitewater brought convictions of several friends and former associates of the Clintons, but no evidence pointing decisively at either Bill or Hillary Clinton.

The legal landscape changed in January 1998, with allegations about an affair between the president and Monica Lewinsky, a former White House intern. Lewinsky admitted to the relationship privately and then to Starr's staff after the president had denied it in a sworn deposition for the Paula Jones case. This opened Clinton to charges of perjury and obstruction of justice.

In the fall of 1998, the Republican leaders who controlled Congress decided that Clinton's statements and misstatements justified initiating the process of impeachment. In December, the majority on the House Judiciary Committee recommended four articles of impeachment, or specific charges against the president, to the House of Representatives. By a partisan vote, the full House approved two of the charges and forwarded them to the Senate. The formal trial of the charges by the Senate began in January 1999 and ended on February 12. Moderate Republicans joined Democrats, thereby ensuring that the Senate would fall far short of the two-thirds majority required for conviction and removal from office (see Overview, Presidential Impeachment).

*Articles of Impeachment against William Jefferson Clinton* (1998)

# A NEW ECONOMY?

Within months of the impeachment trial, Americans had a new worry. In the closing months of 1999, many people stocked up on canned food and kerosene, powdered milk, ammunition, and cash. They were preparing to survive, not foreign invasion or natural disaster, but rather the possible collapse of the global computer network. Europeans called the problem the "millennium bug," Americans the "Y2K" problem (for Year 2000). In fact, almost nothing happened.

**WHAT ROLE** did new information play in the economic boom of the 1990s?

In larger perspective, the Y2K worries illustrate how much the American economy had changed in the preceding decade, and how mysterious the changes seemed. More than ever, it was a global economy. And, unlike any time in the past, it was an economy that depended on electronic computing to manage and transmit vast quantities of data. The impact of the electronic revolution was still being absorbed into the structures and routines of everyday life as Americans put Y2K behind them and looked to a new century.

## THE PROSPEROUS 1990S

From 1992 through 2000, Americans enjoyed nine years of continuous economic expansion. Unemployment dropped from 7.2 percent in 1992 to 4.0 percent at the start of 2000 as American businesses created more than 12 million new jobs. Key states like California rebounded from economic recession with new growth driven by high-tech industries, entertainment, and foreign trade. The stock market soared during the nineties; rising demand for shares in established blue-chip companies and new **Internet** firms swelled the value of individual portfolios, retirement accounts, and pension funds. The rate of home ownership rose after declining for 15 years. Prosperity also trickled down to Americans at the bottom of the economic ladder. The proportion of Americans in poverty dropped to 12 percent in 1999, and the gap between rich and poor began to narrow (slightly) for the first time in two decades.

**Internet**   The system of interconnected computers and servers that allows the exchange of e-mail, posting of Web sites, and other means of instant communication.

## OVERVIEW  Presidential Impeachment

| | | |
|---|---|---|
| Andrew Johnson, 1868 | Charges: | Failure to comply with Tenure of Office Act requiring congressional approval to fire cabinet members. |
| | Political Lineup: | Radical Republicans against Johnson; Democrats and moderate Republicans for him. |
| | Actions: | Tried and acquitted by Senate. |
| | Underlying Issues: | Johnson's opposition to Republican plans for reconstruction of southern states after the Civil War. |
| Richard Nixon, 1974 | Charges: | Obstruction of justice in Watergate investigation, abuse of power of federal agencies for political purposes, refusal to recognize congressional subpoena. |
| | Political Lineup: | Democrats and many Republicans against Nixon. |
| | Actions: | Charges approved by House committee; Nixon resigned before action by the full House of Representatives. |
| | Underlying Issues: | Nixon's construction of a secret government and his efforts to undermine integrity of national elections. |
| Bill Clinton, 1999 | Charges: | Perjury and obstruction of justice in the investigation of sexual-misconduct allegations by Paula Jones. |
| | Political Lineup: | Conservative Republicans against Clinton; Democrats and some moderate Republicans for him. |
| | Actions: | Tried and acquitted by Senate. |
| | Underlying Issues: | Republican frustration with Clinton's ability to block their agenda; deep concern about Clinton's character and moral fitness for presidency. |

The economic boom was great news for the federal budget. Tight spending and rising personal income turned perennial deficits into surpluses for 1998, 1999, and 2000. Reduced borrowing by the U.S. Treasury resulted in low interest rates, which further fueled corporate expansion and consumer spending. In 1997, Clinton signed a deficit-reduction bill that seemed to promise fiscal stability.

Behind the statistics were substantial gains in the efficiency of the U.S. economy. International rivals, especially Japan, experienced severe economic slumps in the mid-1990s. In the United States, in contrast, by the end of the decade the productivity of manufacturing workers was increasing more than 4 percent per year, the highest rate in a generation. Part of the gain was the payoff from the painful business restructuring and downsizing of the 1970s and 1980s. Another cause was improvements in efficiency from the full incorporation of personal computers and electronic communication into everyday life and business practice.

### THE SERVICE ECONOMY

At the beginning of the twenty-first century, the United States was an economy of services. As fewer Americans drove tractors and toiled on assembly lines, more became service workers. The service sector includes everyone not directly involved in producing and processing physical products. Service workers range from lawyers to hair stylists, from police officers who write traffic tickets to theater employees who sell movie tickets. In 1965, services already accounted for more than half of American jobs. By the end of the 1990s, their share rose to more than 75 percent.

Service work varies greatly. At the bottom of the scale are minimum-wage jobs held mostly by women, immigrants, and the young, such as cleaning people, childcare workers, hospital orderlies, and fast-food workers. These positions offer little in terms of advancement, job security, or benefits. In contrast, many of the best new jobs are in information industries. Teaching, research, advertising, mass communications, and professional consulting depend on producing and manipulating information. All of these fields have grown. They add to national wealth by creating and applying new ideas rather than by supplying standardized products and services.

The information economy flourishes in large cities with libraries, universities, research hospitals, advertising agencies, and corporate headquarters. New York's bankers and stockbrokers made Manhattan an island of prosperity in the 1980s. Pittsburgh, with major universities and corporate headquarters, made the transition to the information economy even while its steel industry failed.

The rise of the service economy had political consequences. Rapid expansion of jobs in state and local government triggered popular revolts against state taxes that started in 1978 with passage of California's Proposition 13, which limited property taxes, and continued into the 1990s. Another growth industry was healthcare. Spending on medical and health services amounted to 15 percent of the gross domestic product in 2000, up from 5 percent in 1960. The need to share this huge expense fairly was the motivation for Medicare and Medicaid in the 1960s and the search for a national health insurance program in the 1990s and beyond.

## THE HIGH-TECH SECTOR

The epitome of the "sunrise" economy was electronics, which grew hand-in-glove with the defense budget. The first computers in the 1940s were derived in part from wartime code-breaking efforts. Employment in computer manufacturing rose in the mid-1960s with the expansion of mainframe computing. Large machines from IBM, Honeywell, NCR, and other established corporations required substantial support facilities and staff and were used largely by universities, government agencies, and corporations. In the 1970s, new companies began to build smaller, specialized machines

Seattle in the 1980s and 1990s prospered from the globalizing economy and the rise of the information industries. Only old-timers noticed the disappearance of fish canneries and lumber mills. Taking their place were Boeing, which fueled an international travel revolution; Microsoft, which made Seattle a high-tech capital; and the many foreign companies that used Seattle's port for access to the U.S. market.

**Silicon Valley** The region of California between San Jose and San Francisco that holds the nation's greatest concentration of electronics firms.

for such purposes as word processing. One cluster of firms sprang up outside Boston around Route 128, benefitting from proximity to MIT and other Boston-area universities. California's **Silicon Valley,** north of San Jose, took off with corporate spinoffs and civilian applications of military technologies and benefitted from proximity to Stanford University.

The electronics boom was driven by extraordinary improvements in computing capacity. At the start of the microcomputer era, Intel co-founder Gordon Moore predicted that the number of transistors on a microchip would double every 18 months, with consequent increases in performance and drops in price. "Moore's Law" worked at least through the opening of the new century as producers moved from chips with 5,000 transistors to ones with 50,000,000. The practical result was a vast increase in the capacities and portability of computers, with personal computers and consumer electronics becoming part of everyday life in the 1990s.

## AN INSTANT SOCIETY

**World Wide Web** A part of the Internet designed to allow easier navigation of the network through the use of graphical user interfaces and hypertext links between different addresses.

The spread of consumer electronics helped to create an "instant society." Americans in the 1990s learned to communicate by e-mail and to look up information on the **World Wide Web.** The United States was increasingly a society that depended on instant information and expected instant results.

The Internet grew out of concerns about defense and national security. Its prototype was ARPAnet (for Advanced Research Projects Administration of the Defense Department), intended to be a communication system that could survive nuclear attack. As the Internet evolved into a system that connected universities and national weapons laboratories, the Pentagon gave up control in 1984. Through the 1980s, it was used mainly by scientists and academics to share data and communicate by e-mail. The World Wide Web, created in 1991, expanded the Internet's uses by allowing organizations and companies to create websites that placed political and commercial information only a few clicks away from wired consumers.

Instant satisfaction was one of the principles behind the boom of dotcom businesses in 1998, 1999, and 2000. Many were services that repackaged information for quick access. Others were essentially on-line versions of mail order catalogs, but capable of listing hundreds of thousands of items. Still others were instant-delivery services designed to save consumers a trip to the video store or minimart.

Mobile telephones, or cell phones, were part of the same instant society. They exploited underutilized radio bands and communication satellites to allow wireless conversations among cells—geographic areas linked by special microwave broadcasting towers. Technological changes again drove demand. The chunky car phone built into a vehicle gave way to sleek handheld devices the size of *Star Trek* communicators. Wireless phone companies originally sold their phones as emergency backups and business necessities, just as wired telephones had been sold in the first years of the twentieth century. The 5 million cell phone subscribers of 1990 had exploded to 208 million in 2005.

Meanwhile the twenty-first century Internet had become another inescapable method of communication. Direct travel reservation sites pushed travel agencies out of business. Young people found and kept friends with MySpace and Facebook. Columns of classified ads in newspapers shrank as craigslist expanded. Listings on eBay competed with face-to-face garage sales, and businesses invested in websites rather than Yellow Pages display ads.

## IN THE WORLD MARKET

Instant access to business and financial information accelerated the globalizing of the American economy. With the help of national policy and booming economies overseas, the value of U.S. imports and exports more than doubled, from 7 percent of the gross domestic product in 1965 to 16 percent in 1990—the largest percentage since World War I. Americans in the 1970s began to worry about a "colonial" status, in which the United States exported food, lumber, and minerals and imported automobiles and television sets. By the 1980s, foreign economic competitiveness and trade deficits, especially with Japan, became issues of national concern that continued into the new century, when China and India were emerging as the newest competitors.

The effects of international competition were more complex than "Japan-bashers" acknowledged. Mass-production industries, such as textiles and aluminum, suffered from cheaper and sometimes higher-quality imports, but many specialized industries and services, such as Houston's oil equipment and exploration firms, thrived. Globalization also created new regional winners and losers. In 1982, the United States began to do more business with Pacific nations than with Europe.

**The politics of trade.**    More recent steps to expand the global reach of the U.S. economy were the **North American Free Trade Agreement (NAFTA)** in 1993 and a new worldwide General Agreement on Tariffs and Trade (GATT) approved in 1994. Negotiated by Republican George Bush and pushed through Congress in 1993 by Democratic Bill Clinton, NAFTA combined 25 million Canadians, 90 million Mexicans, and 250 million U.S. consumers in a single "common market" similar to that of western Europe. This enlarged free-trade zone was intended to open new markets and position the United States to compete more effectively against the European Community and Japan. The agreement may have been a holdover from the Bush years, but it matched Clinton's ideas about reforming the American economy.

NAFTA was a hard pill for many Democrats, and it revived the old debate between free traders and protectionists. Support was strongest from businesses and industries that sought foreign customers, including agriculture and electronics. Opponents included organized labor, communities already hit by industrial shutdowns, and environmentalists worried about lax controls on industrial pollution in Mexico. In contrast to the nineteenth-century arguments for protecting infant industries, new industries now looked to foreign markets, whereas uncompetitive, older firms hoped for protected domestic markets. The readjustments from NAFTA have produced obvious pain in the form of closed factories or farms made unprofitable by cheaper imports, while its gains are less visible—a new job here, larger sales there.

The **World Trade Organization (WTO),** which replaced GATT in 1996, became the unexpected target of a global protest movement. Seattle officials, committed to promoting Seattle as a world-class city, lobbied hard to get the 1999 WTO meeting. With finance and foreign affairs ministers and heads of government expected to attend, it would give Seattle world attention. Instead, it gave the city a headache. Fifty thousand protesters converged on the meeting, held from November 30 to December 4, 1999. Most demonstrators were peaceful, but several hundred started a rampage through downtown that triggered a massive overreaction by unprepared police.

The battle of Seattle was part of an international movement. Large demonstrations followed against the International Monetary Fund in Washington in 2000 and against a WTO meeting in Genoa, Italy, in 2001. Protesters were convinced that the WTO is a tool of transnational corporations that flout local labor and environmental protections in the name of "free trade" that benefits only the wealthy nations and their businesses. WTO defenders pointed to the long-term effects of open trade in raising net production in the world economy and thereby making more wealth available for developing nations. Opponents asserted, in turn, that such wealth never reaches the workers and farmers in those nations. American opponents demanded that U.S. firms, such as sportswear companies, that make their products overseas make sure that their overseas workers have decent living conditions and wages.

**North American Free Trade Agreement (NAFTA)**    Agreement reached in 1993 by Canada, Mexico, and the United States to substantially reduce barriers to trade.

**World Trade Organization (WTO)**    International organization that sets standards and practices for global trade, and the focus of international protests over world economic policy in the late 1990s.

## AMERICAN VIEWS

### ⟡ Relief Work in Africa ⟡

In the early twenty-first century, thousands of Americans work in other countries for relief and reconstruction organizations such as the Peace Corps, CARE, and Mercy Corps, and thousands more do similar work under the sponsorship of religious groups. In 2003, Peggy Senger Parsons, an evangelical Quaker minister and trauma counselor from "far off Planet America" spent several months in the small African nation of Burundi, trying to help residents develop strategies for dealing with the impacts of civil war and endemic criminal violence. Here are some excerpts from her blog.

- **What** does Peggy Parsons's experience suggest about the spread of American culture around the world?
- **How** does the level of personal safety in a nation such as Burundi compare to that in the United States?
- **What** questions does Parsons's experience raise about the challenges of building peace and democracy in troubled and divided nations?
- **How** might religiously based work in other countries differ from efforts sponsored by the U.S. government, such as with the Peace Corps? How might it be the same?

We function in Swahili and French, mine bad and hers good. . . . I have been in the company of four children who have been giving me language and cultural tutorials, which I exchanged for introducing them to the Beatles.

Pavement is a subjective concept in Burundi. Traffic is extremely real. We fly in a zig zag pattern through cars, trucks, bicycles, and lots of little children. If you notice a lack of angels in America, it is because they are all in Burundi keeping the babies from being killed on the road. . . . And in four days I am totally immune to the sight of guys with automatic weapons. My host says that he cannot tell a rebel from a Burundi soldier and sometimes neither can they.

We have a night watchman . . . we live in a walled compound and he is there to keep us safe. His only weapon is a whistle. The children tell me that if there is trouble he whistles, and all the nearby watchmen whistle and then come running to help. Then I met Gadi the moneychanger.

He walks around with rolls of money as big as softballs in every pocket and he does not carry a gun. He has a quiet gentle confidence that reminds me of every wiseguy I ever met in Chicago. I do not know what happens if you jump a moneychanger—but it must be bad enough that nobody tries. Some things are very familiar.

My traumatology students are amazing. They have come from great distances and at great sacrifice to study with me. . . . Many of the terms I need to use have no equivalent. I have learned the face that my translator makes when I give her a hard one. She signals for me to stop, and the students confer and when a consensus is reached about a newly coined phrase someone shouts *Voila!* And we have a new psychological term. My students were interviewed on Burundi National Radio. The reporter came on the second day to do a quick filler piece and stayed all afternoon and then asked to join the class. He carries a huge reel-to-reel recorder. The voices of these students went out to 22 million listeners this morning in Burundi, Congo, Rwanda, and Tanzania. They were fabulous explaining the effects of trauma and how they themselves had been helped in the class. On Friday my class thanked me for telling them the truth and for bringing them the best of myself. They compared me to a Jonah "who did not run away but ran towards her call," can't get better pay than that.

I was not prepared for the fact that my trauma class students would be such recent victims [many bearing fresh wounds from beatings or torture]. Thursday there was a bit of shooting outside of the teaching compound. I had to be told what it was—a "thump" and then a "tat, tat, tat." But it was quiet after that and we resume. After a long morning of brain physiology and learning about the left brain functions, my translator said, "Peggy have mercy on them— they say they need to sing." And so they did, all Christian music. I taught them "We Shall Overcome" and told them about Dr. King and we marched around the room singing that "I do believe, deep in my heart, that Burundi will have peace one day."

Protests against the WTO have united environmentalists and labor unions, interests that are often in opposition over domestic issues.

# BROADENING DEMOCRACY

Closely related to the changes in the American economy were the changing composition of the American people and the continued emergence of new participants in U.S. government. Bill Clinton's first cabinet, in which three women and four minority men balanced seven white men, recognized the makeup of the American population and marked the maturing of minorities and women as distinct political constituencies. The first cabinet appointed by George W. Bush in 2001 included four minority men and four women, one of whom was Asian American. In both administrations, the new prominence of women and minorities in the national government followed years of growing success in cities and states.

**WHAT GAINS** did women make in national politics in the 1990s?

### AMERICANS IN 2000

The federal census for the year 2000 found 281,400,000 Americans in the 50 states, District of Columbia, and Puerto Rico (and probably 2–3 million more residents were not counted). The increase from 1990 was 13.2 percent, or 32,700,000. It was the largest ten-year population increase in U.S. history, evidence of the nation's prosperity and its attractiveness for immigrants. More than 12 percent of Americans had been born in other countries, the highest share since 1920 (Table 31–1). One third of all Americans lived in four states: California, Texas, New York, and Florida. These were the key prizes in presidential elections.

The West grew the fastest. Fast growth implies young populations, and the states with the lowest average ages were all western: Utah, Alaska, Idaho, and Texas. The Southwest and South also had the fastest growing metropolitan areas. Among large metro areas with over 500,000 people in 2000, all 20 of the fastest growing of were in the West and Southeast.

In contrast, parts of the American midlands grew slowly. Rural counties continued to empty out in Appalachia and across the Great Plains as fewer and fewer Americans were needed for mining and farming or for the small towns associated with those industries.

## Table 31–1

### Immigrants 1991–2005, by Continent and by Twenty Most Important Countries of Origin

| | |
|---|---|
| Total | 14,083,000 |
| **North America** | 5,657,000 |
| Mexico | 3,127,000 |
| Dominican Republic | 469,000 |
| El Salvador | 359,000 |
| Cuba | 300,000 |
| Haiti | 270,000 |
| Jamaica | 250,000 |
| Canada | 227,000 |
| Guatemala | 183,000 |
| **Asia** | 4,557,000 |
| Philippines | 773,000 |
| India | 729,000 |
| China | 708,000 |
| Vietnam | 576,000 |
| Korea | 267,000 |
| Pakistan | 191,000 |
| Iran | 167,000 |
| **Europe** | 2,067,000 |
| Poland | 234,000 |
| Ukraine | 232,000 |
| Russia | 218,000 |
| United Kingdom | 214,000 |
| **South America** | 912,000 |
| Colombia | 225,000 |
| **Africa** | 697,000 |
| **Oceania** | 76,000 |

Source: *Statistical Abstract of the United States.*

Another important trend was increasing ethnic and racial diversity (Table 31–2). Hispanics were the fastest growing group in the U.S. population. Although immigrants concentrated in the coastal and border states, Hispanics and Asian Americans were also spreading into interior states. Asians and Hispanics who had been in the United States for some time showed substantial economic success. Non-Hispanic whites are now a minority in California at 47 percent, in the District of Columbia, in Hawaii, and in New Mexico.

The changing ethnicity of the American people promises to be increasingly apparent in coming decades. Immigrants tend to be young adults who are likely to form families, and birth rates have been high among Hispanics and Asian Americans. The result is a sort of multiethnic baby boom. Over the coming decades, the effects of ethnic change will be apparent not only in schools but also in the workplace, popular culture, and politics.

## Table 31–2

### States with Highest Proportions of Minority Residents in 2000 (percentage of total population)

| | |
|---|---|
| **Hispanic** | |
| New Mexico | 42% |
| California | 32% |
| Texas | 32% |
| Arizona | 25% |
| Nevada | 20% |
| **Asian and Pacific Islander** | |
| Hawaii | 51% |
| California | 11% |
| Washington | 6% |
| New Jersey | 6% |
| New York | 6% |
| **Black** | |
| Mississippi | 36% |
| Louisiana | 33% |
| South Carolina | 30% |
| Georgia | 29% |
| Maryland | 28% |
| **American Indian** | |
| Alaska | 16% |
| New Mexico | 10% |
| South Dakota | 8% |
| Oklahoma | 8% |
| Montana | 6% |

## WOMEN FROM THE GRASSROOTS TO CONGRESS

The increasing prominence of women and family issues in national politics was a steady, quiet revolution that bore fruit in the 1990s, when the number of women in Congress more than doubled. In 1981, President Reagan appointed Arizona judge Sandra Day O'Connor to be the first woman on the United States Supreme Court. In 1984, Walter Mondale chose New York Congresswoman Geraldine Ferraro as his vice presidential candidate. In 1993 Clinton appointed the second woman to the Supreme Court, U.S. Appeals Court judge Ruth Bader Ginsburg. Clinton appointee Janet Reno was the first woman to serve as attorney general, and Madeleine K. Albright the first to serve as secretary of state. George W. Bush continued to break new ground by naming Condoleezza Rice as his national security advisor in 2001 and as secretary of state in 2005.

Political gains for women at the national level reflected their growing importance in grassroots politics. The spreading suburbs of postwar America were "frontiers" that required concerted action to solve immediate needs like adequate schools and decent

Nancy Pelosi, *Inaugural Address* (2007)

## GLOBAL PERSPECTIVES

### WORKING 24/7 IN BANGALORE

Bangalore is a beautiful city in the highlands of southern India. Its cool climate attracted retired British officials in the days of the British Empire, leaving a legacy of Victorian parks and wide boulevards. After India achieved independence in 1947, the new government made Bangalore a center for scientific research, leaving a legacy of four universities, dozens of technical schools, and a home-grown high-tech industry. In the 1990s, U.S. electronics companies began to establish branches and subsidiaries to take advantage of the concentration of talent, creating a new suburban landscape of technology parks and gated residential neighborhoods with a strong resemblance to Silicon Valley.

The logical extension came in the twenty-first century. Computers and telephone lines have brought Bangalore, Delhi, and other Indian cities into instant contact with American businesses and consumers. Enough U.S. companies have outsourced their customer-service operations to India to become a comic-strip joke.

The development is a logical extension of the global economy. India represents the world's second-largest concentration of English speakers after the United States. Its high-quality educational system produces a million college graduates a year. Many of them are glad to work for U.S. companies at pay that is cheap by U.S. standards but good by comparison with other opportunities in India.

Any kind of routine customer service can be outsourced— telephone catalog sales, billing and debt collection, credit card marketing, help lines for Internet providers, technical support for computer manufacturers. Tens of thousands of simple income tax returns are now processed in India each year. An American accountant scans in a customer's tax information, an Indian accountant logs on and fills out the return, the American accountant prints it out for signature.

The magic of electronics and the 12-hour time differential allow Indians to do specialized work while Americans sleep. Hospitals can transit MRIs to be read in India and get the results the next morning. Publishers can send files to be formatted and proofread while authors and editors sleep. Software companies can transmit code to be debugged overnight.

There is both a light side and a serious side to this 24/7 economy. It is amusing to learn that Indian workers practice American accents and take "phone names" that sound American; CBS reported that one young woman named Sangita becomes "Julia" because Julia Roberts is her favorite actress. But it is also important to understand that distance scarcely matters when an economy's important products take the form of information, and that information flows back and forth across the oceans linking the United States to the world in ways not seen in earlier centuries.

- In twenty-first century, is the English language the most important asset of the American economy?

---

parks. Because pursuit of such community services was often viewed as "woman's work" (in contrast to the "man's work" of economic development), postwar metropolitan areas offered numerous opportunities for women to engage in volunteer civic work, learn political skills, and run for local office. Moreover, new cities and suburbs had fewer established political institutions, such as political machines and strong parties; their politics were open to energetic women. Most women in contemporary politics have been more liberal than men—a difference that political scientists attribute to women's interest in the practical problems of schools, neighborhoods, and two-earner families. But women's grassroots mobilization, especially through evangelical churches, has also strengthened groups committed to conservative social values.

Regional differences have affected women's political gains. The West has long been the part of the country most open to women in state and local government and in business. Westerners have been more willing than voters in the East or South to choose women as mayors of major cities and as members of state legislatures. Many of the skills learned from politics were also useful as women played a growing role in professional and managerial occupations.

In 1991, the nomination of Judge Clarence Thomas, an African American, to the U.S. Supreme Court ensured that everyone knew that the terms of U.S. politics were changing. Because of his conservative positions on social and civil rights issues, Thomas was a controversial nominee. Controversy deepened when law professor Anita Hill accused Thomas of harassing her sexually while she served on his staff at the Equal Employment Opportunity Commission. The accusations led to riveting hearings before a U.S. Senate committee. Critics tried to discredit Hill with vicious attacks on her character, and the committee failed to call witnesses who could have supported her claims. The public was left with Hill's plausible but unproved allegations and Thomas's equally vigorous but unproved denials. The Senate confirmed Thomas to the Supreme Court. Partisans on each side continued to believe the version that best suited their preconceptions and agendas.

Whatever the merits of her charges, Hill's badgering by skeptical senators angered millions of women. In the shadow of the hearings, women made impressive gains in the 1992 election, which pushed women's share of seats in the 50 state legislatures above 20 percent. The number of women in the U.S. Senate jumped from two to seven (and grew further to eleven Democrats and five Republicans in 2007). The number of women serving as federal judges grew from 48 in 1981 to more than 200—roughly a quarter of the total (see Figure 31–1).

Women have influenced national politics as voters as well as candidates and cabinet members. Since the 1980s, voting patterns have shown a gender gap. Women in the 1990s identified with the Democratic Party and voted for its candidates at a higher rate than men. The reasons include concerns about the effect of government spending cuts and interest in measures to support families rather than in conservative rhetoric. This gender gap has helped keep Democrats competitive and dampened the nation's conservative swing on social issues.

## MINORITIES AT THE BALLOT BOX

The changing makeup of the American populace also helped black and Latino candidates for public office to increased success. After the racial violence of the 1960s, many

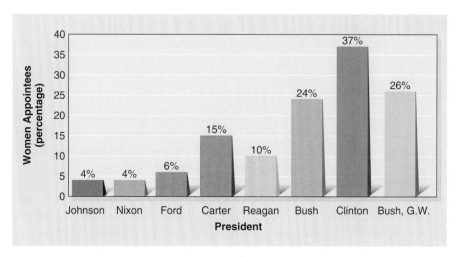

**FIGURE 31–1    Women as a Percentage of Initial High-Level Presidential Appointments: Lyndon Johnson to George W. Bush**    By the 1990s, Americans were willing to accept women in positions that would have been reserved for men only in earlier decades, such as attorney general, secretary of state, and national security advisor.

black people turned to local politics to gain control of their own communities. The first black mayor of a major twentieth-century city was Carl Stokes in Cleveland in 1967. The 1973 election brought victories for Tom Bradley in Los Angeles, Maynard Jackson in Atlanta, and Coleman Young in Detroit. By 1983, three of the nation's four largest cities had black mayors. In 1989, Virginia made Douglas Wilder the first black governor in any state since Reconstruction.

Most mid-sized cities stopped electing city councils by wards or districts during the first half of the twentieth century. Voting at large shifted power away from geographically concentrated ethnic groups. It favored business interests that claimed to speak for the city as a whole but could assign most of the costs of economic growth to older and poorer neighborhoods.

In the 1970s, minority leaders and community activists realized that a return to district voting could convert neighborhood segregation from a liability to a political resource. As amended in 1975, the federal Voting Rights Act allowed minorities to use the federal courts to challenge at-large voting systems that diluted the impact of their votes. Blacks and Mexican Americans used the act to reestablish city council districts in the late 1970s and early 1980s in city after city across the South and Southwest.

The political rebalancing meant that local leaders faced strong pressures to ensure equitable distribution of the benefits and burdens of growth. Newly empowered minorities began to press for a fair share of an expanding economic pie.

At the national level, minorities gradually increased their representation in Congress. Ben Nighthorse Campbell of Colorado, a Cheyenne, brought a Native American voice to the U.S. Senate in 1992. The number of African Americans in the House of Representatives topped 40 after 1992, with the help of districts drawn to concentrate black voters. Even after a series of Supreme Court cases invalidated districts drawn with race as the "predominant factor," however, African Americans held most of their gains, while the number of Latino members of Congress rose to 26 by 2007 (see Figure 31–2).

In struggling for political influence, recent immigrants have added new panethnic identities to their national identities. Hispanic activists revived the term "Chicano" to bridge the gap between recent Mexican immigrants and Latinos whose families had settled in the Southwest before the American conquest in 1848. Great gaps of experience and culture separated Chinese, Koreans, Filipinos, and Vietnamese, but they gained political recognition and influence if they dealt with other Americans as "Asians." Native Americans have similarly downplayed tribal differences in efforts to secure better opportunities for Indians as a group.

## RIGHTS AND OPPORTUNITIES

The increasing presence of Latinos and African Americans in public life highlighted a set of troublesome questions about the proper balance between equal rights and equal opportunities. The debates at the end of the twentieth century replayed many of the questions that European immigration raised at the century's beginning.

**Illegal Immigration and Bilingual Education**    One issue is the economic impact of illegal immigration. Advocates of tight borders assert that illegal immigrants take jobs away from legal residents and eat up public assistance. Many studies, however, find that illegal immigrants fill jobs that nobody else wants. Over the long run, high employment levels among immigrants mean that their tax contributions through sales taxes and Social Security taxes and payroll deductions more than pay for their use of welfare, food stamps, and unemployment benefits, which illegal immigrants are often

*Documents*

*Illegal Immigration* (2007)

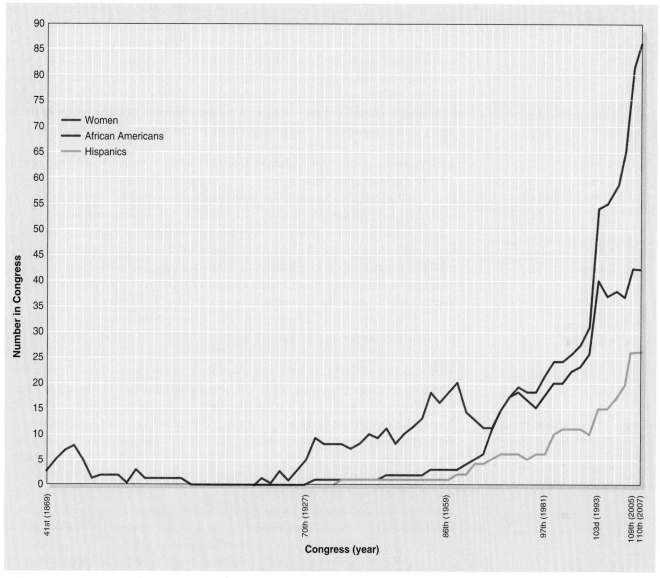

**FIGURE 31–2   Minorities and Women in Congress, 1869–2005**   The number of African Americans, Hispanics, and women serving in the House of Representatives and Senate increased rapidly in the 1980s and early 1990s and more slowly in the middle 1990s. The increases reflected changing attitudes, the impact of the Voting Rights Act, and decades of political activism at the grassroots.

afraid to claim for fear of calling attention to themselves. Nevertheless, high immigration can strain local government budgets even if it benefits the nation as a whole. Partly for this reason, 60 percent of California voters approved **Proposition 187** in 1994, cutting off access to state-funded public education and healthcare for illegal immigrants

A symbolic issue was the degree to which American institutions should accommodate non–English speakers. Referendums in Alaska (1996) and Utah (2000) raised to 26 the number of states that declared English their official language. California voters in 1998 banned bilingual public education, a system under which children whose first language was Spanish or another "immigrant" tongue were taught for several years in that language before shifting to English-language classrooms. Advocates of bilingual education claimed that it eased the transition into American society, but opponents said that it blocked immigrant children from fully assimilating into American life.

**Proposition 187**   California legislation adopted by popular vote in California in 1994, which cuts off state-funded health can education benefits to undocumented or illegal immigration.

**QUICK REVIEW**

**Divisive Issues**

◆ The proper response to illegal immigration.

◆ Degree of accommodation of non-English speakers in U.S. schools.

◆ Affirmative action.

**affirmative action**   A set of policies to open opportunities in business and education for members of minority groups and women by allowing race and sex to be factors included in decisions to hire, award contracts, or admit students to higher education programs.

*University of California v. Bakke*
U.S. Supreme Court case in 1978 that allowed race to be used as one of several factors in college and university admission decisions but made rigid quotas unacceptable.

The issue of illegal immigration simmered in the 1990s, but exploded in the new century. As the total of undocumented immigrants reached 11 to 12 million by best estimates, many Americans became increasingly concerned about a porous southern border. Unlike early eras of concern about immigration that had usually coincided with economic downturns, the new immigration worries came in an era of economic prosperity. In 2007, the president and leaders in both political parties were blindsided when a carefully constructed compromise over immigration policy failed because of public outcry over provisions that many voters interpreted as amnesty for rule-breaking.

**Affirmative Action**   An equally divisive issue was a set of policies that originated in the 1960s as **affirmative action,** a phrase that first appeared in executive orders issued by Presidents Kennedy and Johnson. The initial goal was to require businesses that received federal contracts to "take affirmative action to ensure that applicants are employed, and that employees are treated during employment without regard for their race, creed, color, or national origin." By the 1970s, many states and cities had adopted similar policies for hiring their own employees and choosing contractors and extended affirmative action to women as well as minorities. Colleges and universities used affirmative-action policies in recruiting faculty and admitting students.

As these efforts spread, the initial goal of nondiscrimination evolved into expectations and requirements for active ("affirmative") efforts to achieve greater diversity among employees, students, or contractors. Government agencies began to set aside a small percentage of contracts for woman-owned or minority-owned firms. Cities actively worked to hire more minority police officers and firefighters. Colleges made special efforts to attract minority students. The landmark court case about affirmative action was *University of California v. Bakke* (1978). Alan Bakke was an unsuccessful applicant to the medical school at the University of California at Davis. He argued that the university had improperly set aside 16 of 100 places in its entering class for minority students, thereby engaging in reverse discrimination against white applicants. In a narrow decision, the U.S. Supreme Court ordered Bakke admitted because the only basis for his rejection had been race. At the same time, the Court stated that race or ethnicity could legally be one of several factors considered in college and university admissions as long as a specific number of places were not reserved for minorities.

In 1996, California voters took grassroots action, approving a ballot measure to eliminate state-sponsored affirmative action. One effect was to prohibit state-funded colleges and universities from using race or ethnicity as a factor in deciding which applicants to admit. In the same year, the Supreme Court let stand a lower-court ruling in *Hopwood v. Texas*, which had forbidden the University of Texas to consider race in admission decisions. The number of black freshmen in the University of Texas dropped by half in 1997 and the number of blacks and Hispanics among first-year law students by two-thirds. The results were similar at the University of California at Berkeley, where the number of blacks among entering law students dropped from twenty to one.

In 2003, the Supreme Court affirmed the basic principle of affirmative action in two cases involving admission to the University of Michigan. Aided by supporting statements filed by major corporations and by members of the U.S. military, the Court found that promoting ethnic and racial diversity among students constitutes a compelling state interest, and it approved narrowly tailored affirmative-action programs that weigh race and ethnicity along with other admissions criteria on an individual basis. But four years later, a different majority on the Court rejected public school plans in Seattle and Lexington, Kentucky, that took race into account in deciding how to match students and schools, leaving the larger issue for further court cases.

# EDGING INTO A NEW CENTURY

On the evening of November 7, 2000, CBS-TV made the kind of mistake that journalists dread. Relying on questions put to a sample of voters after they cast their ballots in the presidential contest between Albert Gore, Jr., and George W. Bush, the CBS newsroom first projected that Gore would win Florida and likely the election, then reversed itself and called the election for Bush, only to find that it would be days or even weeks before the votes in several pivotal states, including Florida, could be certified.

**WHAT WERE** the key elements of George W. Bush's domestic agenda?

The inability to predict the outcome in 2000 was an indication of the degree to which Americans were split down the middle in their political preferences and their visions for the future. The United States entered the twenty-first century both divided and balanced, with extremes of opinion revolving around a center of basic goals and values.

## THE 2000 ELECTION

On November 8, 2000, the day after their national election, Americans woke up to the news that neither Republican George W. Bush nor Democrat Albert Gore, Jr., had a majority of votes in the electoral college. For the next five weeks, they woke every day to the same news. Although Gore held a lead in the popular vote (about 340,000 votes out of more than 100 million cast), both candidates needed a majority in Florida to win its electoral votes and the White House. After protracted protests about voting irregularities and malfunctioning voting equipment, politically divided Floridians engaged in an on-again off-again recount in key counties. The U.S. Supreme Court finally preempted the state process and ordered a halt to recounting on December 12 by the politically charged margin of 5 to 4. The result was to make Bush the winner in Florida by a few hundred votes and the winner nationwide by 271 electoral votes to 267 (see Map 31–2).

**QUICK REVIEW**

**Election Controversy**

- Al Gore secured a majority of the popular vote.
- Both sides needed Florida's contested electoral votes to secure election.
- The U.S. Supreme Court voted 5–4 to end the recount in Florida, making George W. Bush the new president.

The outcome of the election showed a nation that was paradoxically divided around a strong center. The votes showed basic differences between the parties. Gore appealed especially to residents of large cities, to women, to African Americans, and to families struggling to make it economically. Bush appealed to people from small towns, to men, and to members of households that had benefitted the most from the prosperity of the Clinton era. These were divisions that had marked the two parties since the 1930s, and their persistence was a reminder of the nation's diversity of opinions and values. The nation also divided regionally, with Gore strong in the Northeast, upper Middle West, and Pacific Coast, Bush in the South, Ohio Valley, Great Plains, and Rocky Mountain states.

At the same time, both Bush, governor of Texas and son of President George H. W. Bush (1989–93), and Gore, vice president for the previous eight years, targeted their campaigns at middle Americans. Each offered to cut taxes, downsize the federal government, and protect Social Security, differing in the details rather than the broad goals. In trying to claim the political middle, they reflected the successful political message of the Clinton administration. Voters also shaved the Republican control of Congress to razor-thin margins, further undermining any chance of radical change in either a conservative or a liberal direction. To those on the political left and right who had hoped for new directions for

In November 2002, Linda Sanchez (left) and Loretta Sanchez celebrate Linda's election to Congress from Los Angeles County. Loretta had won a Congressional seat from Orange County in 1996, and Linda's victory made them the first sisters to serve simultaneously in the House of Representatives.

**MAP EXPLORATION** To explore an interactive version of this map, go to http://www.prenhall.com/goldfield5/map31.2

| | Electoral Vote (%) | Popular Vote (%) |
|---|---|---|
| **GEORGE W. BUSH** (Republican) | **271** **(50.4)** | **50,459,624** **(47.9)** |
| Albert Gore (Democrat) | 266 (49.4) | 51,003,328 (48.4) |
| Ralph Nader (Green) | – | 2,882,985 (2.7) |
| Other candidates | – | 1,066,482 (1.0) |

MAP 31–2    **The Election of 2000**    In the nation's closest presidential election, Democrat Al Gore was most successful in the Northeast and Far West, while George W. Bush swept the South and won most of the Great Plains states. Green Party candidate Ralph Nader took most of his votes from Gore, in an ironic twist, helped to swing the election to Bush.

**What do** the 2000 election results reveal about the divisions that separate Americans today?

the nation, it looked like a formula for paralysis; for the majority of Americans, it looked like stability.

## REAGANOMICS REVISITED

Despite the message of stability, the Bush administration took the Republican return to executive power as an opportunity to tilt domestic policy abruptly to the right. Following the example of Ronald Reagan, Bush made massive tax cuts the centerpiece of his first months in office. By starting with proposals for ten-year cuts so large that two generations of federal programs were threatened, Bush and congressional Republicans forced the Democrats to "compromise" on reductions far higher than the economy could probably support. The resulting cuts to income taxes and estate taxes were projected to total $1,350 billion over the decade, with one-third of the benefits going to families earning more than $200,000. The federal budget quickly plunged into the red, undoing the careful political balancing and fiscal discipline of the Clinton administration. Deficits were $375 billion in 2003, $413 billion in 2004, $319 billion in 2005, and $248 billion in 2006, with more of the same forecast for the rest of the decade.

The Bush team also moved quickly to deregulate the economy. It opened many of the environmental and business regulations of the last two decades to reconsideration—from arsenic standards in drinking water to protection for wetlands to the pollution controls required of electric utilities. In many cases, the administration proposed to rely on the market through voluntary compliance and incentives to replace regulations. Vice President Dick Cheney developed a new production-oriented energy policy in consultation with energy companies but not with environmental or consumer groups. The collapse of the energy-trading company Enron in a hailstorm of criticism over deceptive accounting and shady market manipulations to create an energy crisis in California in early 2000 slowed the push to deregulate. In turn, Enron proved to be the first of many companies that had to restate earnings in 2002, depressing the stock market and raising questions about the ethics of big business and business accounting practices. Stock market declines and the

## Table 31–3

**Economic Inequality: 2003**

| | Percent of Families in Poverty | Median Household Money Income |
|---|---|---|
| White | 10.2 | $45,631 |
| Black | 24.1 | $29,645 |
| Asian | 10.1 | $55,699 |
| Hispanic origin | 21.8 | $32,997 |
| Native born | 11.5 | $44,347 |
| Foreign born | 16.6 | $37,499 |

Source: U.S. Census.

evaporation of retirement savings for many workers raised doubts about the solidity of the 1990s boom and helped to hold down economic growth for a third year.

Education policy, a centerpiece of Bush's image as an innovator from his service as governor of Texas, was another legislative front. Tough battles with Congress resulted in compromise legislation, reminiscent of the 1990s, that included national testing standards, as Bush wanted, balanced by more federal funding. More important for both education and religion was the narrow decision by the Supreme Court in *Zelman v. Simmons-Harris* (2002) to uphold the use of taxpayer-funded assistance, or vouchers, to help students attend religious schools. By declaring that both religious and secular institutions can compete for government money as long as it is channeled through individuals who made "true private choices" about how to spend it, the court continued a two-decade trend to narrow the constitutional prohibition on the "establishment of religion."

## DOWNSIZED DIPLOMACY

Strong conservatives had long criticized subordinating U.S. authority and freedom of action to international agreements. The new Bush administration heeded this criticism and brought a revolutionary approach to foreign affairs. The administration repeatedly adopted unilateral or bilateral policies in preference to the complexities of negotiations with an entire range of nations.

In his first 18 months, Bush opted out of a series of treaties and negotiations on global issues, sometimes despite years of careful bargaining. In each case he pointed to specific flaws or problems, but the goal was to reduce restrictions on U.S. business and its military. The administration undercut efforts to implement the Convention on Biological Warfare because of possible adverse effects on drug companies. It refused to sign on to efforts to reduce the international trade in armaments, declined to acknowledge a new International Criminal Court that is designed to try war criminals, and ignored an international compact on the rights of women in deference to cultural conservatives. Most prominently, it refused to accept the Kyoto Agreement, aimed at combating the threat of massive environmental change through global warming resulting from the carbon dioxide released by fossil fuels, dismissing a growing scientific consensus on the problem.

In the field of arms control, Bush entered office with the intention of ending the 1972 treaty that had limited the deployment of antimissile defenses by the United States and Russia in order to stabilize the arms race. The treaty had been a cornerstone of national security policy. Despite the objection of Russia, however, he formally withdrew from the treaty in December 2001. In its place he revived Ronald Reagan's idea of a Strategic Defense Initiative with proposals for new but unproven technologies to protect the United States against nuclear attacks by "rogue states." This argument was supported in 2002 by North Korea's revelation that it was pursuing a nuclear weapons program, even though it had agreed not to do so in 1994. Bush also decided not to implement the START II treaty, which had been one of the major accomplishments of his father's term as president. In its place, he worked directly to improve relations with Russia and negotiated a bilateral agreement to reduce substantially the number of nuclear warheads that Russia and the United States actively deploy (while pressing for the development of new tactical nuclear weapons). A new U.S. policy that explicitly claimed the right to act militarily to preempt potential threats confirmed the go-it-alone approach.

*Documents*

Al Gore, *Global Warming* (2006)

George W. Bush used his Texas ranch to escape the pressures of Washington and to cultivate his down-to-earth image.

# PARADOXES OF POWER

**HOW DID** the government's response to dissent after 9-11 compare to government policies during World War I?

Condoleezza Rice, *Secretary of State Defines Transformational Diplomacy* (2006)

George Bush, *Address to the Nation* (2001)

The United States in the twenty-first century faced the paradox of power: the enormous economic, military, and technological capacity that allowed it to impose its will on other nations did not extend to an ability to prevent anti-American actions by deeply enraged individuals.

In the 1990s, the U.S. economy had surged while Japan stagnated, Europe marked time, and Russia verged on economic collapse. The U.S. economy in the early twenty-first century was twice the size of Japan's; California alone had economic capacity equal to France or Britain. America's lead was nurtured by research and development spending equal to that of the next six countries combined. The U.S. military budget exceeded the total military spending of the next dozen nations. The United States had the world's only global navy and a huge edge in military technology.

But the United States remained vulnerable. Huge trade deficits, massive oil imports, and a falling dollar in the early years of the new century underlined its economic vulnerability. Overseas, terrorist attacks by Islamic radicals killed 19 American soldiers at military housing in Saudi Arabia in 1996 and 17 sailors on the destroyer *Cole* while in port in the Arab nation of Yemen in 2000. Bombs at the U.S. embassies in Kenya and Tanzania in 1998 killed more than 200 people. These bombings followed the detonation of explosives in the basement garage of the World Trade Center in New York in February 1993, killing six people. New acts of terror remained a constant threat—realized in an appalling manner on September 11, 2001.

## SEPTEMBER 11, 2001

The men who hijacked four commercial jetliners on the morning of September 11 were part of the Al-Qaeda network of terrorists coordinated by Osama Bin-Laden. A Saudi Arabian businessman who had turned against the United States because of its role in the Gulf War and its support for Israel, Bin-Laden was probably the brains behind the attacks on the U.S. military and on diplomats overseas and the earlier blast at the World Trade Center. Operating from exile in Afghanistan, he now masterminded the new and spectacular assault. The first hijacked plane hit the North Tower of the World Trade Center at 8:46 A.M. eastern time, and the second plane hit the South Tower at 9:30. As flames billowed upward, the South Tower disintegrated at 10:05 and the North Tower at 10:28. Each building took only ten seconds to fall in on itself, but television replays burned the image into the national memory.

The events of September 11 were an enormous shock to the American people, but worries about escalating terrorism were not new. Security specialists such as Defense Secretary William Cohen had been sounding the alarm through the 1990s. The U.S. Commission on National Security/21st Century, appointed by President Clinton, had included detailed warnings in its February 2001 report, although the new administration had ignored its recommendations to reorganize federal homeland security. The problem, however, had been to connect broad concerns to specific threats. After September 11, there were reports of information-gathering failures by the FBI and CIA, to be investigated by a commission appointed by President Bush at the end of 2002. However, it is always enormously difficult to separate and correlate key points in the vast flood of information that flows through law-enforcement and intelligence agencies. It is much easier to read the warnings after an event has occurred than to pick out the essential data before the unexpected happens—something as true about the attack on Pearl Harbor, for example, as about the attack of 9–11.

## SECURITY AND CONFLICT

On September 12, President George W. Bush called the Pentagon and World Trade Center attacks "acts of war." Three days later, Congress passed a Joint Resolution that gave the president sweeping powers "to use all necessary and appropriate force against those nations, organizations, or persons he determines planned, authorized, committed, or aided the terrorist attacks that occurred on September 11, 2001." Only one member voted against the resolution—the same level of agreement that the nation showed after December 7, 1941.

The government response in the United States was a hodge-podge of security measures and arrests. Federal agents detained more than 1,000 terrorist suspects, mostly men from the Middle East, releasing some but holding hundreds without charges, evidence, or legal counsel. President Bush also declared that "enemy combatants" could be tried by special military tribunals, although domestic and international protest caused the administration to agree to more legal safeguards than originally planned. Congress passed the **PATRIOT Act** (Providing Appropriate Tools Required to Intercept and Obstruct Terrorists) in late October, which gave federal authorities substantial new capacity to conduct criminal investigations, in most provisions for the next three to five years. These measures raised a number of concerns about the protection of civil liberties, as noted by the several dozen members of Congress who voted against the act. The law would be renewed in 2006 with a few added provisions to protect basic constitutional and political rights.

In November 2002, Congress approved a massive reorganization of the federal government to improve security at home. The new Department of Homeland Security includes the Immigration and Naturalization Service, Customs Service, Coast Guard, Secret Service, federal airport security workers, bioterrorism experts, and many others. With 170,000 employees, it is the second-largest federal agency, after the Defense Department. In 2004 Congress adopted a package of reforms to improve intelligence gathering and analysis, creating the position of director of national intelligence to oversee the CIA and report directly to the president.

In contrast to the suppression of dissent during World War I or the internment of Japanese Americans during World War II, Americans in 2001 and 2002 were careful on the home front. The leaders and supporters of the War on Terror reacted to dissenting voices, particularly those from a pacifist tradition, with caustic remarks rather than repression. Censorship consisted of careful management of the news and stonewalling of requests under the Freedom of Information Act rather than direct censorship of speech and the press. Violations of civil liberties have affected individuals rather than entire groups. President Bush made an important gesture soon after September 11 by appearing at a mosque and arguing against blanket condemnation of Muslims. Ethnic profiling has resulted in heightened suspicion and surveillance of Muslims, selective enforcement of immigration laws on visitors from 20 Muslim nations, and detention of several hundred U.S. residents of Middle Eastern origin, rather than incarceration of entire ethnic groups.

In the months after 9-11, the military response overseas focused on Afghanistan, where the ruling Taliban regime was harboring Bin-Laden. Afghanistan had been wracked by civil war since the invasion by the Soviet Union in 1979. The Taliban, who came to power after the Soviet withdrawal and civil war, were politically and socially repressive rulers with few international friends. U.S. bombing attacks on Taliban forces began in early October 2001, and internal opposition groups in Afghanistan threw the Taliban out of

Firefighters work in the rubble of one of the World Trade Center towers soon after its destruction on September 11, 2001.

**PATRIOT Act** Federal legislation adopted in 2001, in response to the terrorist attacks of September 11, intended to facilitate antiterror actions by federal law enforcement and intelligence agencies.

power by December. Bin-Laden, however, escaped with the aid of mountainous terrain and the confusion of war. The United States and NATO allies were left with an uncertain commitment to rebuild a stable Afghanistan, which remained an active war zone where resurgent Taliban activity in 2007 and 2008 threatened previous gains. The Al-Qaeda network and sympathetic groups remained active around the world with bombings in places as distant as Indonesia and Kenya.

**From Then to Now Online**
*America's Mission to the World*

## IRAQ AND CONFLICTS IN THE MIDDLE EAST

Even while the United States was intervening in Afghanistan, the administration was extending its attention to other nations that supported or condoned anti-American terrorists or had the potential to produce chemical, biological, or nuclear weapons of mass destruction. George Bush named North Korea, Iran, and Iraq as an "axis of evil" for these reasons, and then focused on Iraq. After the Gulf War, Iraq had grudgingly accepted a United Nations requirement that it eliminate such weapons, but gradually made UN inspections impossible. This resistance caused Bush to make the overthrow of Iraq's ruthless dictator, Saddam Hussein, the center of foreign policy. In effect, he declared one small, possibly dangerous nation to be the greatest menace the United States faced. In the meantime, North Korea created a further crisis by actively pursuing its atomic weapons program with the threat of additional war. However, it did enter into talks with China, Japan, Russia, South Korea, and the United States and agreed in 2007 to suspend its nuclear weapons program under international supervision and took initial steps toward compliance in 2008—an example of the potential of persistent and patient diplomacy.

In addition to the direct fallout from the Persian Gulf War, the background to the deep-seated tensions in the Middle East included U.S. support of Israel amidst the deterioration of relations between Israel and the Arab Palestinians in territories occupied by Israel since 1967. The United States has consistently backed Israel since the 1960s. The cornerstones of U.S. policy have been the full endorsement of Israel's right to exist with secure borders and agreement on the right of Palestinians to a national state—in effect, a policy of coexistence. The United States helped to broker an Israel-Egypt peace agreement in 1977 and agreements pointing toward an independent Palestinian state in the 1990s. But hardline Israeli governments have repeatedly taken advantage of U.S. support from the 1980s in Lebanon (see Chapter 30) to the present.

In 2001–2002, the United States watched from the sidelines as the Israeli-Palestinian agreements for transition to a Palestinian state fell apart. Palestinian extremists and suicide bombers and an Israeli government that favored military responses locked each other into a downward spiral that turned into civil war. As a result, many Arabs identify the United States as an enemy of Arab nations and peoples. Israel's decision in 2005 to withdraw from the Gaza Strip and transfer authority there to the Palestinian government was a step toward resolution that unfortunately led to radical takeover there in 2007-08. The deep and long unsolvable Israel-Palestinian conflict helps to explain anti-American terrorism among Arabs, and sometimes other Muslims.

In the spring and summer of 2002, the administration escalated threats of unilateral intervention to change the Iraqi regime and began preparations for a second war in the Persian Gulf region. On October 10, Congress authorized preemptive military action against Iraq. However, international pressure from unenthusiastic allies and from other Arab nations persuaded Bush to put diplomacy ahead of war and devote two months to making his case at the United Nations. On November 8, the UN Security Council unanimously adopted a compromise resolution that gave Iraq three and a half months to allow full and open inspections before military action might be considered. In the following months, UN inspectors searched Iraqi military sites while the United States built up forces in the Middle East in preparation for war. On March 17, 2003, Bush suspended further diplomatic efforts, and on March 19 a full scale U.S.-British invasion of Iraq began.

The war to overthrow Saddam Hussein was a success as a large-scale military operation. On May 1, 2003, President Bush declared "mission accomplished"—that U.S. and British forces now controlled Iraq and major combat operations in Iraq were over.

Peace proved far more difficult than war. Reconstruction of damaged bridges, roads, water systems, and electrical systems took far longer than expected and many basic services were still fragile or nonexistent four years after the U.S. invasion. Meanwhile, American troops and relief workers were the continuing targets of car bombs, booby-trapped highways, mortar attacks, and similar guerrilla resistance. By July 2008, more than 4,100 U.S. soldiers had died in Iraq, over 90 percent of them after the president declared victory.

By 2007, a consensus had emerged among both critics of the war and realistic supporters that the United States had overthrown Saddam without any clear plan for next steps. Because of decisions by Secretary of Defense Donald Rumsfeld, the occupation force was inadequate in size from the start—a deficiency that a "surge" of additional U.S. forces in 2007 could not fully remedy. U.S. officials dismantled the Iraqi army and police, putting 650,000 unemployed but armed men onto the streets. The decision to shut down state industries and purge members of Saddam's political party from low-level government jobs like schoolteachers created massive unemployment. The result was the decimation of Iraq's middle class, a collapse of living standards, and the creation of roughly two million refugees who fled Iraq's new chaos for neighboring nations.

The aftermath of the war also created political problems for George Bush. A systematic search found no active production facilities or stockpiles for chemical, nuclear, or biological weapons of mass destruction. In October 2004, the final report

George W. Bush, *Address to the Nation on the Iraq Invasion* (2003)

*National Failure toward Veterans of the Iraq War* (2007)

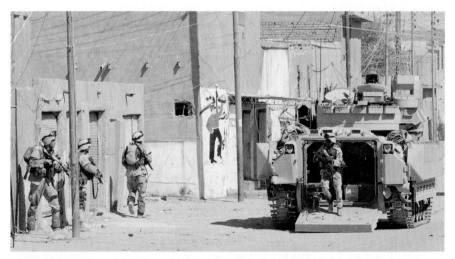

After the defeat of the Iraqi army in 2003, U.S. forces faced continuing challenges and casualties from a stubborn resistance from anti-American insurgents.

of the U.S. bomb hunters concluded that Saddam has disbanded his chemical and nuclear weapons efforts after 1991, refuting one of the basic justifications for the war. The continuing necessity to mobilize National Guard and reserve units met heavy criticism. The need to keep an occupying army in Iraq stretched the military close the breaking point at exactly the same time that the Taliban showed renewed strength in Afghanistan.

## 2004 AND AFTER

Wars past and present were the pivotal issue in the 2004 election. George W. Bush argued for staying the course with the same administration. Democratic candidate John Kerry had a liberal voting record as a Massachusetts senator and decorations for meritorious service in Vietnam, but central to the Republican campaign were attacks on the veracity of his war record. A wild card was the issue of same sex marriage. Courts in Massachusetts and politicians in Oregon and San Francisco decided that legal marriage could not be denied to same sex couples. Their actions mobilized religious and cultural conservatives and led to successful ballot measures banning same sex marriage in 11 states. Bush won a solid although not overwhelming victory that helped Republicans extend their lead in Congress. Commentators liked to talk about a nation divided on issues of morality between Democratic "Blue states" and Republican "red states" (colors drawn from television maps of election results). In fact, many states remained closely divided and only three shifted from one party to the other (New Hampshire to Kerry, and Iowa and New Mexico to Bush). Pundits also claimed that Bush used the issue of "moral values," including opposition to same sex marriage, to mobilize voters, but he did not do any better among regular church-goers in 2004 than in 2000.

After the election, Bush reaffirmed his commitment to U.S. presence in Iraq, where a deeply divided nation held elections for a new government early in 2005. Kurds from northern Iraq and Shiite Muslims from southern Iraq voted in large numbers and formed a coalition government. Participation was much lower among Sunni Muslims in central Iraq, who had benefitted most from Saddam Hussein's regime and who were the heart of continued guerrilla resistance to the United States occupation forces. The

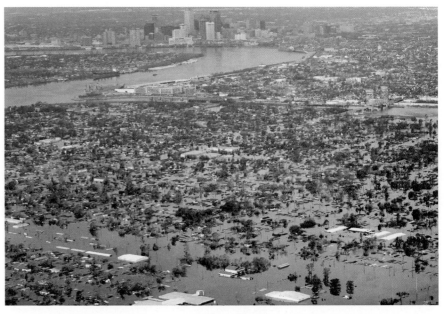

The flooding from Hurricane Katrina devastated huge expanses of low income neighborhoods in New Orleans.

same divisions were evident in October when Iraqis approved a new constitution that met Shiite and Kurdish desires for greater autonomy but left many Sunnis dissatisfied. Those tensions played into the hands of militants who kept the level of violence among Iraqis high. In mid-2007, Congress concluded that the new Iraqi government had failed to meet most of the benchmarks that would have indicated progress toward normalcy in that devastated country, although progress was shown in 2008. Meanwhile, U.S. coalition allies such as Britain were quietly packing and leaving Iraq to its American conquerors.

As the nation worried about the open-ended commitment in Iraq, it received a devastating reminder of vulnerability. At the end of August 2005, hurricane Katrina devastated the Gulf Coast. It first seemed to spare New Orleans, much of which lies below sea level, but its backlash breached levees that protected the city. Much of the city and its surroundings flooded. Tens of thousands of residents who had not evacuated found themselves trapped in homes or huddled in the Superdome. The slowness and inadequacy of the emergency response raised serious doubts about the effectiveness of the Department of Homeland Security and its Federal Emergency Management Agency and revealed the deep fault lines that still separate the poor from the larger society—exacerbated in New Orleans by the fact that most of the poor residents were African American. Two years after the disaster, only 60 percent of the city's pre-Katrina residents had stayed or returned, and large sections of the city had seen only sporadic rebuilding. Behind the growing discussion about whether and how to rebuild New Orleans on its vulnerable site was a larger problem of continuing inequality.

Iraq and Katrina combined to deal Republicans a blow in the 2006 Congressional elections, in which Democrats regained effective control of Congress for the first time in 12 years. The results reflected the reality that the red state/blue state division of 2000 and 2004 had been poised on a knife's edge, ready to tilt toward one party or the other. Through 2007, as candidates of both parties jockeyed for presidential nominations, important domestic issues like immigration policy, health insurance, and the future of social security remained unresolved. Federal courts began to cautiously consider the basic issues of civil liberties raised by the PATRIOT Act and, even more, by

*Documents*

Lou Dobbs, *The Attack on the Middle Class* (2006)

A large FEMA trailer park was erected in August, 2006 in New Orleans, Louisana, almost one year to the day of the first anniversary of Hurricane Katrina (August 29, 2005).

Senator Barack Obama D-Ill. claimed the Democratic presidential nomination in a long-time-coming victory speech in St. Paul, MN on Tuesday, June 3, 2008.

Documents

Barack Obama, *Presidential Campaign Announcement* (2007)
Hillary Clinton, *Speech on Health Care* (2007)
*Dirty Politics in the 2008 Election* (2007)

the unilateral actions of the Bush administration in claiming free rein to deal with persons suspected as terrorists. And there was no clear consensus in Congress or the nation about the best steps in Iraq—whether a quick exit or a long-term U.S. occupation would do more damage to Iraq itself, to the U.S. military, and to U.S. standing in the world.

In September 2008, Americans faced a presidential election campaign with two improbable candidates. The Republicans nominated John McCain, an Arizona senator who had been a prisoner of war during the Vietnam War and who cultivated a reputation as a maverick. Nevertheless, he outlasted more mainstream candidates to win his party's nomination. Democrats had a hard-fought contest between Hillary Rodham Clinton, who hoped to be the first woman nominated for President by a major party, and Barack Obama, an Illinois senator who became the first African American nominee. Whatever the outcome of the election in November, Obama's nomination was a milestone in the long, often painful history of race relations in America.

The outcome of the November, 2008 election was both a sweeping victory for the Democratic party, which expanded its margins in the Senate and House of Representatives, and a milestone in American history. Barack Obama, the first African American candidate nominated by a major political party, won more than two-third of the electoral votes, making gains in previously Republican territory in the South (Virginia, North Carolina, and Florida) and in the West (Nevada, Colorado, New Mexico). He also received strong support from new voters and people under age thirty, promising a solid base for his party in future elections. Meanwhile, Americans waited to see how his thoughtful and disciplined approach to campaigning would translate into the many challenges of governing in the twenty-first century.

# CONCLUSION

If there was a dominant theme that ran through the changes and challenges of the 1990s and early 2000s, it was interconnection. The Internet, e-mail, and cell phones brought instant communication. The national economy was more and more deeply engaged with the rest of the world through trade, investment, travel, and immigration. Corporate mismanagement affected far more people than before because of pensions and savings invested in the stock market.

The nation's growing diversity—closely connected to its internationalized economy—was reflected in the political gains of African Americans and Hispanics, as well as women. The same diversity fueled battles over affirmative action and language politics. It underlay the effort to increase security against terrorism without endangering the civil liberties of Muslim Americans.

Despite what some might have wished, Americans also found that they could not always isolate the nation from the problems and conflicts that wracked much of the rest of the world. The Clinton administration joined international peacekeeping efforts in Bosnia and Kosovo. The Bush administration chose to ignore several international agreements, but still sought the cover of United Nations approval for action against Iraq (although it largely disregarded international opinion in its pursuit of the war).

Beyond its growing military commitments, the United States in the first years of the twenty-first century was deeply connected to the world. Travel, work and study abroad—and foreign tourists, workers, and students in the United States—improved American understanding of other nations. But the ease and volume of travel and trade also brought problems and fears. Many Americans had long worried that the United States was being flooded by illegal immigrants, and the revelation that some of the 9-11 terrorists had learned to fly in U.S. training schools compounded fears of a porous border. A ballooning national debt and fast-growing trade deficits reduced the purchasing power of the dollar and made the economy dependent on investment from abroad. Hovering in the background was the issue of massive climate change—global warming—that was caused or accelerated by the massive use of fossil fuels whose combustion adds carbon dioxide to the atmosphere. As the Nobel Peace Prize committee recognized in 2007, when it honored the work of an international panel of scientists as well as former vice-president Al Gore's efforts to publicize the issue, global warming is a truly international problem that cannot be solved within national boundaries or politics.

The events of September 11 sparked a renewed sense of national unity, at least in the short run. Stories of heroism were inspiring, as was the outpouring of volunteers and contributions for rescue and relief efforts. As the nation slowly settled back into routines, however, the devastation of hurricane Katrina revealed continuing divisions that undercut the full promise of American life. The question that remained was whether Americans could sustain and build an inclusive and unified nation under the pressures of economic uncertainty, threats of terrorism, and war.

# SUMMARY

**WHAT ISSUES** did Bill Clinton capitalize on in his 1992 presidential campaign?

**Politics of the Center** In 1992 voters ranked the economy as their first concern, and Bill Clinton hammered at this in his campaign messages. His elections in 1992 and 1996 showed a move toward the political center; Clinton emerged as a neoliberal. Conservative political ideology and animosity toward the Clintons dominated the headlines; the Contract with America, the budget battle that shut down the federal government, Whitewater, the Clinton scandals, and impeachment filled the political headlines. Domestic terrorism (Waco, Oklahoma City, and Columbine) also grabbed the national spotlight. In foreign affairs, the United States became involved in a multinational effort to restore peace in Bosnia and Kosovo.

**WHAT ROLE** did new information technology play in the economic boom of the 1990s?

**A New Economy?** At the end of the millennium, America had a new worry, the "Y2K" problem, that did not materialize. In the 1990s Americans enjoyed nine years of continuous economic expansion; services became the new underpinning of the economy; and an instant society based on twenty-four hour access gave people immediate satisfaction. The American economy also expanded internationally. The controversial North American Free Trade Agreement went into effect and protestors took on the World Trade Organization in the streets of Seattle which demonstrated as part of a larger worldwide debate over free trade and the role of transnational corporations.

**WHAT GAINS** did women make in national politics in the 1990s?

**Broadening Democracy** The changing composition of the American people is related to the changes in the economy. The growing West, the concentration of one-third of the population in four states, the largest ten-year population increase in history,

and racial and ethnic diversity, are all significance trends. As women have become more influential in national politics, so have minorities; both have contributed to a political rebalancing. Questions about equal rights and equal opportunities (Proposition 187, bilingual education, and affirmative action) have become part of the American dialogue.

**WHAT WERE** the key elements of George W. Bush's domestic agenda?

**Edging into a New Century** The United States began the twenty-first century with a disputed presidential contest between Al Gore, Jr., and George W. Bush. The contest underlined the nation's sharp political divide. The new Bush administration took the Republican return to executive power as an opportunity to tilt domestic policy to the right. The center pieces of the adminstrations domestic agenda were tax cuts, education reform, and deregulation. In foreign policy, the Bush administration favored unilateral or bilateral approaches to international problems, opting out of a number of international agreements.

**HOW DID** the government's response to dissent after 9-11 compare to government policies during World War I?

**Paradoxes of Power** At the beginning of the twenty-first century, the United States was the most powerful nation on earth. Yet, it remained vulnerable. Its economy was threatened by trade deficits, dependence on imported energy, and a falling dollar. Despite the power of its military, terrorist attacks posed a threat to American interests at home and abroad. That threat was realized in the events of September 11, 2001. President Bush responded to the attack by declaring a "war on terrorism." The focus of American efforts soon became the war in Iraq. In the years after Bush's reelection in 2004, the ongoing conflict in Iraq and the inadequate emergency response to hurricane Katrina convinced many Americans that their country was moving in the wrong direction.

# WHERE TO LEARN MORE

**Oklahoma City National Memorial Center Museum, Oklahoma City, OK.** Exhibits about the federal building bombing and its impact on the community. **www.oklahomacitynationalmemorial.org**

# STUDY RESOURCES

## myhistorylab

For study resources for this chapter, go to www.myhistorylab.com and choose *The American Journey*. You will find a wealth of study and review material for this chapter, including pre- and posttests, customized study plan, key term review flash cards, interactive map and document activities, and documents for analysis.

# REVIEW QUESTIONS

1. Was the U.S. political system more polarized and divided in 1992 than in 1980? How did religiously conservative Americans understand issues of foreign relations and economic policy? How did religiously liberal Americans understand the same issues? What was the gender gap in national politics in the 1990s? Why were Republicans unable to appeal to most black and Hispanic voters in 1992?

2. What were Bill Clinton's major policy accomplishments? Do these represent liberal, moderate, or conservative positions?

3. What was the Contract with America? What are other examples of a conservative political trend in the 1990s?

4. What issues were involved in Clinton's impeachment? How does the impeachment compare with the challenges to Presidents Andrew Johnson and Richard Nixon?

5. Did the U.S. economy undergo fundamental changes in the 1990s? What has been the impact of the computer revolution? Of the growing importance of world markets?

6. What new directions did George W. Bush establish for U.S. domestic and foreign policy?

7. How did the terrorist attacks of September 11, 2001, change life in the United States? How did ordinary Americans respond at the time and since the attacks?

8. What or some of the reasons why the experience of the United States in reconstructing Iraq after 2003 has differed from its experience in Japan and Germany after World War II?

## KEY TERMS

**Affirmative action** (p. 966)
**Contract with America** (p. 950)
**Internet** (p. 953)
**Neoliberal** (p. 950)
**North American Free Trade Agreement (NAFTA)** (p. 957)
**PATRIOT Act** (p. 971)
**Proposition 187** (p. 965)

**Silicon Valley** (p. 956)
**Temporary Assistance for Needy Families (TANF)** (p. 950)
*University of California v. Bakke* (p. 966)
**Whitewater** (p. 952)
**World Trade Organization (WTO)** (p. 957)
**World Wide Web** (p. 956)

## The Threat of War to Democratic Institutions

**HOW** has the use of the PATRIOT Act and its later revisions in line with wartime actions of earlier American governments during wartime or times of perceived threat to the United States?

As early as 1798 and the Alien and Sedition Act of the Adams administration, American governments have been willing to suppress civil liberties in the name of national defense. Adams was fearful of French immigrants who added to the voting power of Democratic Republicans and the poisoned pens of Democratic Republicans whose newspaper torn at his public reputation. In the Civil War Lincoln suspended the right of habeas corpus in Maryland and arrested members of Congress who were known secessionists.

In the twentieth century, the events of the 18th and 19th century during war were paralleled during World War One, World War Two, the Cold War, and during the current War on Terror which began on September 11, 2001. In World War II hysteria over the Japanese attack on Pearl Harbor combined with a long standing racism against Asians in West Coast states resulted in the imprisonment of approximately 120,000 Japanese Americans, many native born citizens, under Roosevelt's Executive Order 9066. During the Cold War and the era of Joseph McCarthy Americans lost their jobs, faced government investigation of the most intrusive nature, and public disgrace. Civil libertarians have criticized the PATRIOT Act of 2001 also called *The Uniting and Strengthening America by Providing Appropriate Tools Required to Intercept and Obstruct Terrorism Act of 2001 (Public Law 107-56)*, as an inappropriate curtailment of constitutional rights and a dangerous expansion of executive police powers.

## *. . . to prescribe military areas . . .*

### George W. Bush, President's Statement on H.R. 199, the "USA PATRIOT Improvement and Reauthorization Act of 2005," March 9, 2006

Today, I have signed into law H.R. 3199, the "USA PATRIOT Improvement and Reauthorization Act of 2005," and then S. 2271, the "USA PATRIOT Act Additional Reauthorizing Amendments Act of 2006." The bills will help us continue to fight terrorism effectively and to combat the use of the illegal drug methamphetamine that is ruining too many lives.

The executive branch shall construe the provisions of H.R. 3199 that call for furnishing information to entities outside the executive branch, such as sections 106A and 119, in a manner consistent with the President's constitutional authority to supervise the unitary executive branch and to withhold information the disclosure of which could impair foreign relations, national security, the deliberative processes of the Executive, or the performance of the Executive's constitutional duties.

The executive branch shall construe section 756(e)(2) of H.R. 3199, which calls for an executive branch official to submit to the Congress recommendations for legislative action, in a manner consistent with the President's constitutional authority to supervise the unitary executive branch and to recommend for the consideration of the Congress such measures as he judges necessary and expedient.

## Sedition Act of 1918, May 16, 1918 (repealed 1921)

SECTION 3. Whoever, when the United States is at war, shall willfully make or convey false reports or false statements with intent to interfere with the operation or success of the military or naval forces of the United States, or to promote the success of its enemies, or shall willfully make or convey false reports, or false statements, . . . or incite insubordination, disloyalty, mutiny, or refusal of duty, in the military or naval forces of the United States, or shall willfully obstruct . . . the recruiting or enlistment service of the United States, or . . . shall willfully utter, print, write, or publish any disloyal, profane, scurrilous, or abusive language about the form of government of the United States, or the Constitution of the United States, or the military or naval forces of the United States . . . or shall willfully display the flag of any foreign enemy, or shall willfully . . . urge, incite, or advocate any curtailment of production . . . or advocate, teach, defend, or suggest the doing of any of the acts or things in this section enumerated and whoever shall by word or act support or favor the cause of any country with which the United States is at war or by word or act oppose the cause of the United States therein, shall be punished by a fine of not more than $10,000 or imprisonment for not more than twenty years, or both. . . .

## Franklin D. Roosevelt, Executive Order 9066, February 19, 1942

I hereby authorize and direct the Secretary of War, and the Military Commanders whom he may from time to time designate, whenever he or any designated Commander deems such action necessary or desirable, to prescribe military areas in such places and of such extent as he or the appropriate Military Commander may determine, from which any or all persons may be excluded, and with respect to which, the right of any person to enter, remain in, or leave shall be subject to whatever restrictions the Secretary of War or the appropriate Military Commander may impose in his discretion.

Esther C. Brunauer, an employee of the State Department, testified before the Senate Subcommittee on Foreign Relations to defend herself against allegations made against her by Senator Joseph McCarthy.

The hysteria and fear following the Pearl Harbor attack resulted in the internment of 110,000 Japanese Americans in "War Relocation Centers" located in isolated areas of the West for the duration of the war. In 1944 the U.S. Supreme Court upheld this action by the government with the comment that it was a "pressing public necessity."

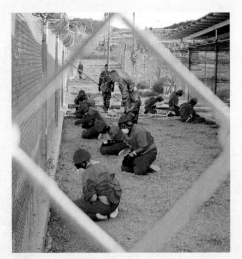

Camp X-ray Detainees – Guantanamo Bay Detention Camp. In his War on Terrorism President Bush deemed it necessary to intern approximately 775 enemy prisoners captured in Afghanistan and elsewhere in a military facility. Bush claimed these prisoners did not possess rights under the terms of the Geneva Conventions. The U.S. Supreme Court ruled against his position in 2006 and ordered the U.S. military to extend international rights granted under the Geneva Conventions to enemy combatants to these individuals.

*. . . help us continue to fight terrorism . . .*

# THE DECLARATION OF INDEPENDENCE

When in the course of human events it becomes necessary for one people to dissolve the political bands which have connected them with another and to assume, among the powers of the earth, the separate and equal station to which the laws of nature and of nature's God entitle them, a decent respect to the opinions of mankind requires that they should declare the causes which impel them to the separation.

We hold these truths to be self-evident, that all men are created equal; that they are endowed by their Creator with certain unalienable rights; that among these are life, liberty, and the pursuit of happiness. That, to secure these rights, governments are instituted among men, deriving their just powers from the consent of the governed; that, whenever any form of government becomes destructive of these ends, it is the right of the people to alter or to abolish it, and to institute a new government, laying its foundation on such principles, and organizing its powers in such form, as to them shall seem most likely to effect their safety and happiness. Prudence, indeed, will dictate that governments long established should not be changed for light and transient causes; and, accordingly, all experience hath shown that mankind are more disposed to suffer, while evils are sufferable, than to right themselves by abolishing the forms to which they are accustomed. But when a long train of abuses and usurpations, pursuing invariably the same object, evinces a design to reduce them under absolute despotism, it is their right, it is their duty, to throw off such government and to provide new guards for their future security. Such has been the patient sufferance of these colonies, and such is now the necessity which constrains them to alter their former systems of government. The history of the present King of Great Britain is a history of repeated injuries and usurpations, all having, in direct object, the establishment of an absolute tyranny over these States. To prove this, let facts be submitted to a candid world:

He has refused his assent to laws the most wholesome and necessary for the public good.

He has forbidden his governors to pass laws of immediate and pressing importance, unless suspended in their operation till his assent should be obtained; and, when so suspended, he has utterly neglected to attend to them.

He has refused to pass other laws for the accommodation of large districts of people, unless those people would relinquish the right of representation in the legislature, a right inestimable to them and formidable to tyrants only.

He has called together legislative bodies at places unusual, uncomfortable, and distant from the depository of their public records, for the sole purpose of fatiguing them into compliance with his measures.

He has dissolved representative houses, repeatedly for opposing, with manly firmness, his invasions on the rights of the people.

He has refused, for a long time after such dissolutions, to cause others to be elected; whereby the legislative powers, incapable of annihilation, have returned to the people at large for their exercise; the state remaining, in the meantime, exposed to all the danger of invasion from without and convulsions within.

He has endeavored to prevent the population of these States; for that purpose, obstructing the laws for naturalization of foreigners, refusing to pass others to encourage their migration hither, and raising the conditions of new appropriations of lands.

He has obstructed the administration of justice by refusing his assent to laws for establishing judiciary powers.

He has made judges dependent on his will alone for the tenure of their offices and the amount and payment of their salaries.

He has erected a multitude of new offices and sent hither swarms of officers to harass our people and eat out their substance.

He has kept among us, in time of peace, standing armies, without the consent of our legislatures.

He has affected to render the military independent of, and superior to, the civil power.

He has combined with others to subject us to a jurisdiction foreign to our Constitution and unacknowledged by our laws, giving his assent to their acts of pretended legislation—

For quartering large bodies of armed troops among us;

For protecting them by mock trial, from punishment for any murders which they should commit on the inhabitants of these States;

For cutting off our trade with all parts of the world;

For imposing taxes on us without our consent;

For depriving us, in many cases, of the benefit of trial by jury;

For transporting us beyond seas to be tried for pretended offences;

For abolishing the free system of English laws in a neighboring province, establishing therein an arbitrary government, and enlarging its boundaries, so as to render it at once an example and fit instrument for introducing the same absolute rule into these colonies;

For taking away our charters, abolishing our most valuable laws, and altering, fundamentally, the powers of our governments.

For suspending our own legislatures and declaring themselves invested with power to legislate for us in all cases whatsoever.

He has abdicated government here by declaring us out of his protection and waging war against us.

He has plundered our seas, ravaged our coasts, burnt our towns, and destroyed the lives of our people.

He is, at this time, transporting large armies of foreign mercenaries to complete the works of death, desolation, and tyranny already begun with circumstances of cruelty and perfidy scarcely paralleled in the most barbarous ages, and totally unworthy the head of a civilized nation.

He has constrained our fellow citizens, taken captive on the high seas, to bear arms against their country, to become the executioners of their friends and brethren, or to fall themselves by their hands.

He has excited domestic insurrections amongst us and has endeavored to bring on the inhabitants of our frontiers, the merciless Indian savages, whose known rule of warfare is an undistinguished destruction of all ages, sexes, and conditions.

In every stage of these oppressions, we have petitioned for redress in the most humble terms; our repeated petitions have been answered only by repeated injury. A prince whose character is thus marked by every act which may define a tyrant is unfit to be the ruler of a free people.

Nor have we been wanting in attention to our British brethren. We have warned them, from time to time, of attempts made by their legislature to extend an unwarrantable jurisdiction over us. We have reminded them of the circumstances of our emigration and settlement here. We have appealed to their native justice and magnanimity, and we have conjured them, by the ties of our common kindred, to disavow these usurpations, which would inevitably interrupt our connections and correspondence. They, too, have been deaf to the voice of justice and consanguinity. We must, therefore, acquiesce in the necessity which denounces our separation, and hold them, as we hold the rest of mankind, enemies in war, in peace, friends.

We, therefore, the representatives of the United States of America, in general Congress assembled, appealing to the Supreme Judge of the world for the rectitude of our intentions, do, in the name and by the authority of the good people of these colonies, solemnly publish and declare, that these united colonies are, and of right ought to be, free and independent states: that they are absolved from all allegiance to the British Crown, and that all political connection between them and the state of Great Britain is, and ought to be, totally dissolved; and that, as free and independent states, they have full power to levy war, conclude peace, contract alliances, establish commerce, and to do all other acts and things which independent states may of right do. And, for the support of this declaration, with a firm reliance on the protection of Divine Providence, we mutually pledge to each other our lives, our fortunes, and our sacred honor.

# The Constitution of the United States of America

We the people of the United States, in order to form a more perfect union, establish justice, insure domestic tranquillity, provide for the common defense, promote the general welfare, and secure the blessings of liberty to ourselves and our posterity, do ordain and establish this Constitution for the United States of America.

### ARTICLE I

SECTION 1. All legislative powers herein granted shall be vested in a Congress of the United States, which shall consist of a Senate and House of Representatives.

SECTION 2. 1. The House of Representatives shall be composed of members chosen every second year by the people of the several States, and the electors in each State shall have the qualifications requisite for electors of the most numerous branch of the State legislature.

2. No person shall be a representative who shall not have attained to the age of twenty-five years, and been seven years a citizen of the United States, and who shall not, when elected, be an inhabitant of that State in which he shall be chosen.

3. Representatives and direct taxes[1] shall be apportioned among the several States which may be included within this Union, according to their respective numbers, which shall be determined by adding to the whole number of free persons, including those bound to service for a term of years, and excluding Indians not taxed, three fifths of all other persons.[2] The actual enumeration shall be made within three years after the first meeting of the Congress of the United States, and within every subsequent term of ten years, in such manner as they shall by law direct. The number of representatives shall not exceed one for every thirty thousand, but each State shall have at least one representative; and until such enumeration shall be made, the State of New Hampshire shall be entitled to choose three, Massachusetts eight, Rhode Island and Providence Plantations one, Connecticut five, New York six, New Jersey four, Pennsylvania eight, Delaware one, Maryland six, Virginia ten, North Carolina five, South Carolina five, and Georgia three.

4. When vacancies happen in the representation from any State, the executive authority thereof shall issue writs of election to fill such vacancies.

5. The House of Representatives shall choose their speaker and other officers; and shall have the sole power of impeachment.

SECTION 3. 1. The Senate of the United States shall be composed of two senators from each State, chosen by the legislature thereof,[3] for six years; and each senator shall have one vote.

---

Note: This version of the Constitution has been edited to conform to present-day punctuation and usage standards. In addition, paragraphs within sections have been numbered for ease of reference.

[1]See the Sixteenth Amendment.

[2]See the Fourteenth Amendment.
[3]See the Seventeenth Amendment.

2. Immediately after they shall be assembled in consequence of the first election, they shall be divided as equally as may be into three classes. The seats of the senators of the first class shall be vacated at the expiration of the second year, of the second class at the expiration of the fourth year, and of the third class at the expiration of the sixth year, so that one third may be chosen every second year; and if vacancies happen by resignation, or otherwise, during the recess of the legislature of any State, the executive thereof may make temporary appointments until the next meeting of the legislature, which shall then fill such vacancies.[4]

3. No person shall be a senator who shall not have attained to the age of thirty years, and been nine years a citizen of the United States, and who shall not, when elected, be an inhabitant of that State for which he shall be chosen.

4. The Vice President of the United States shall be President of the Senate, but shall have no vote, unless they be equally divided.

5. The Senate shall choose their other officers, and also a president pro tempore, in the absence of the Vice President, or when he shall exercise the office of the President of the United States.

6. The Senate shall have the sole power to try all impeachments. When sitting for that purpose, they shall be on oath or affirmation. When the President of the United States is tried, the chief justice shall preside: and no person shall be convicted without the concurrence of two thirds of the members present.

7. Judgment in cases of impeachment shall not extend further than to removal from office, and disqualification to hold and enjoy any office of honor, trust or profit under the United States: but the party convicted shall nevertheless be liable and subject to indictment, trial, judgment and punishment, according to law.

SECTION 4. 1. The times, places, and manner of holding elections for senators and representatives, shall be prescribed in each State by the legislature thereof; but the Congress may at any time by law make or alter such regulations, except as to the places of choosing senators.

2. The Congress shall assemble at least once in every year, and such meeting shall be on the first Monday in December, unless they shall by law appoint a different day.

SECTION 5. 1. Each House shall be the judge of the elections, returns and qualifications of its own members, and a majority of each shall constitute a quorum to do business; but a smaller number may adjourn from day to day, and may be authorized to compel the attendance of absent members, in such manner, and under such penalties as each House may provide.

2. Each House may determine the rules of its proceedings, punish its members for disorderly behavior, and, with the concurrence of two thirds, expel a member.

3. Each House shall keep a journal of its proceedings, and from time to time publish the same, excepting

such parts as may in their judgment require secrecy; and the yeas and nays of the members of either House on any question shall, at the desire of one fifth of those present, be entered on the journal.

4. Neither House, during the session of Congress, shall, without the consent of the other, adjourn for more than three days, nor to any other place than that in which the two Houses shall be sitting.

SECTION 6. 1. The senators and representatives shall receive a compensation for their services, to be ascertained by law, and paid out of the Treasury of the United States. They shall in all cases, except treason, felony, and breach of the peace, be privileged from arrest during their attendance at the session of their respective Houses, and in going to and returning from the same; and for any speech or debate in either House, they shall not be questioned in any other place.

2. No senator or representative shall, during the time for which he was elected, be appointed to any civil office under the authority of the United States, which shall have been created, or the emoluments whereof shall have been increased, during such time; and no person holding any office under the United States shall be a member of either House during his continuance in office.

SECTION 7. 1. All bills for raising revenue shall originate in the House of Representatives; but the Senate may propose or concur with amendments as on other bills.

2. Every bill which shall have passed the House of Representatives and the Senate, shall, before it become a law, be presented to the President of the United States; If he approves he shall sign it, but if not he shall return it, with his objections, to that House in which it shall have originated, who shall enter the objections at large on their journal, and proceed to reconsider it. If after such reconsideration two thirds of that House shall agree to pass the bill, it shall be sent, together with the objections, to the other House, by which it shall likewise be reconsidered, and if approved by two thirds of that House, it shall become a law. But in all such cases the votes of both Houses shall be determined by yeas and nays, and the names of the persons voting for and against the bill shall be entered on the journal of each House respectively. If any bill shall not be returned by the President within ten days (Sundays excepted) after it shall have been presented to him, the same shall be a law, in like manner as if he had signed it, unless the Congress by their adjournment prevent its return, in which case it shall not be a law.

3. Every order, resolution, or vote to which the concurrence of the Senate and the House of Representatives may be necessary (except on a question of adjournment) shall be presented to the President of the United States; and before the same shall take effect, shall be approved by him, or being disapproved by him, shall be repassed by two thirds of the Senate and House of Representatives, according to the rules and limitations prescribed in the case of a bill.

---

[4]See the Seventeenth Amendment.

SECTION 8. 1. The Congress shall have the power

1. To lay and collect taxes, duties, imposts, and excises, to pay the debts and provide for the common defense and general welfare of the United States; but all duties, imposts, and excises shall be uniform throughout the United States.

2. To borrow money on the credit of the United States;

3. To regulate commerce with foreign nations, and among the several States, and with the Indian tribes;

4. To establish a uniform rule of naturalization, and uniform laws on the subject of bankruptcies throughout the United States;

5. To coin money, regulate the value thereof, and of foreign coin, and fix the standard of weights and measures;

6. To provide for the punishment of counterfeiting the securities and current coin of the United States;

7. To establish post offices and post roads;

8. To promote the progress of science and useful arts, by securing for limited times to authors and inventors the exclusive right to their respective writings and discoveries;

9. To constitute tribunals inferior to the Supreme Court;

10. To define and punish piracies and felonies committed on the high seas, and offenses against the law of nations;

11. To declare war, grant letters of marque and reprisal, and make rules concerning captures on land and water;

12. To raise and support armies, but no appropriation of money to that use shall be for a longer term than two years;

13. To provide and maintain a navy;

14. To make rules for the government and regulation of the land and naval forces;

15. To provide for calling forth the militia to execute the laws of the Union, suppress insurrections and repel invasions;

16. To provide for organizing, arming, and disciplining the militia, and for governing such part of them as may be employed in the service of the United States, reserving to the States respectively, the appointment of the officers, and the authority of training the militia according to the discipline prescribed by Congress;

17. To exercise exclusive legislation in all cases whatsoever, over such district (not exceeding ten miles square) as may, by cession of particular States, and the acceptance of Congress, become the seat of the government of the United States, and to exercise like authority over all places purchased by the consent of the legislature of the State in which the same shall be, for the erection of forts, magazines, arsenals, dockyards, and other needful buildings; and

18. To make all laws which shall be necessary and proper for carrying into execution the foregoing powers, and all other powers vested by this Constitution in the government of the United States, or any department or officer thereof.

SECTION 9. 1. The migration or importation of such persons as any of the States now existing shall think proper to admit, shall not be prohibited by the Congress prior to the year one thousand eight hundred and eight, but a tax or duty may be imposed on such importation, not exceeding ten dollars for each person.

2. The privilege of the writ of habeas corpus shall not be suspended, unless when in cases of rebellion or invasion the public safety may require it.

3. No bill of attainder or ex post facto law shall be passed.

4. No capitation, or other direct, tax shall be laid, unless in proportion to the census or enumeration herein-before directed to be taken.[5]

5. No tax or duty shall be laid on articles exported from any State.

6. No preference shall be given by any regulation of commerce or revenue to the ports of one State over those of another: nor shall vessels bound to, or from, one State be obliged to enter, clear, or pay duties in another.

7. No money shall be drawn from the treasury, but in consequence of appropriations made by law; and a regular statement and account of the receipts and expenditures of all public money shall be published from time to time.

8. No title of nobility shall be granted by the United States: and no person holding any office of profit or trust under them, shall, without the consent of the Congress, accept of any present, emolument, office, or title, of any kind whatever, from any king, prince, or foreign State.

SECTION 10. 1. No State shall enter into any treaty, alliance, or confederation; grant letters of marque and reprisal; coin money; emit bills of credit; make any thing but gold and silver coin a tender in payment of debts; pass any bill of attainder, ex post facto law, or law impairing the obligation of contracts, or grant, any title of nobility.

2. No State shall, without the consent of the Congress, lay any imposts or duties on imports or exports, except what may be absolutely necessary for executing its inspection laws: and the net produce of all duties and imposts laid by any State on imports or exports, shall be for the use of the treasury of the United States; and all such laws shall be subject to the revision and control of the Congress.

3. No State shall, without the consent of the Congress, lay any duty of tonnage, keep troops, or ships of war in time of peace, enter into any agreement or compact with another State, or with a foreign power, or engage in war, unless actually invaded, or in such imminent danger as will not admit of delay.

**ARTICLE II**

SECTION 1. 1. The executive power shall be vested in a President of the United States of America. He shall hold his office during the term of four years, and, together with the Vice President, chosen for the same term, be elected, as follows:

2. Each State shall appoint, in such manner as the legislature thereof may direct, a number of electors, equal to the whole number of senators and representatives to which the State may be entitled in the Congress: but no senator or representative, or person holding any office of trust or profit under the United States, shall be appointed an elector.

---

[5]See the Sixteenth Amendment.

The electors shall meet in their respective States, and vote by ballot for two persons, of whom one at least shall not be an inhabitant of the same State with themselves. And they shall make a list of all the persons voted for, and of the number of votes for each; which list they shall sign and certify, and transmit sealed to the seat of the government of the United States, directed to the president of the Senate. The president of the Senate shall, in the presence of the Senate and House of Representatives, open all the certificates, and the votes shall then be counted. The person having the greatest number of votes shall be the President, if such number be a majority of the whole number of electors appointed; and if there be more than one who have such majority, and have an equal number of votes, then the House of Representatives shall immediately choose by ballot one of them for President; and if no person have a majority, then from the five highest on the list the said House shall in like manner choose the President. But in choosing the President, the votes shall be taken by States, the representation from each State having one vote; a quorum for this purpose shall consist of a member or members from two thirds of the States, and a majority of all the States shall be necessary to a choice. In every case after the choice of the President, the person having the greatest number of votes of the electors shall be the Vice President. But if there should remain two or more who have equal votes, the Senate shall choose from them by ballot the Vice President.[6]

3. The Congress may determine the time of choosing the electors, and the day on which they shall give their votes; which day shall be the same throughout the United States.

4. No person except a natural born citizen, or a citizen of the United States, at the time of the adoption of this Constitution, shall be eligible to the office of President; neither shall any person be eligible to the office who shall not have attained to the age of thirty-five years, and been fourteen years a resident within the United States.

5. In case of the removal of the President from office, or of his death, resignation, or inability to discharge the powers and duties of the said office, the same shall devolve on the Vice President, and the congress may by law provide for the case of removal, death, resignation or inability, both of the President and Vice President, declaring what officer shall then act as President, and such officer shall act accordingly until the disability be removed, or a President shall be elected.

6. The President shall, at stated times, receive for his services a compensation which shall neither be increased nor diminished during the period for which he shall have been elected, and he shall not receive within that period any other emolument from the United States, or any of them.

7. Before he enter on the execution of his office, he shall take the following oath or affirmation:—"I do solemnly swear (or affirm) that I will faithfully execute the office of President of the United States, and will to the best of my ability, preserve, protect and defend the Constitution of the United States."

SECTION 2. 1. The President shall be commander in chief of the army and navy of the United States, and of the militia of the several States, when called into the actual service of the United States; he may require the opinion in writing, of the principal officer in each of the executive departments, upon any subject relating to the duties of their respective offices, and he shall have power to grant reprieves and pardons for offenses against the United States, except in cases of impeachment.

2. He shall have power, by and with the advice and consent of the Senate, to make treaties, provided two thirds of the senators present concur; and he shall nominate, and by and with the advice and consent of the Senate, shall appoint ambassadors, other public ministers and consuls, judges of the Supreme Court, and all other officers of the United States, whose appointments are not herein otherwise provided for, and which shall be established by law; but the Congress may by law vest the appointment of such inferior officers, as they think proper, in the President alone, in the courts of laws, or in the heads of departments.

3. The President shall have power to fill up all vacancies that may happen during the recess of the Senate, by granting commissions which shall expire at the end of their next session.

SECTION 3. He shall from time to time give to the Congress information of the state of the Union, and recommend to their consideration such measures as he shall judge necessary and expedient; he may, on extraordinary occasions, convene both Houses, or either of them, and in case of disagreement between them with respect to the time of adjournment, he may adjourn them to such time as he shall think proper; he shall receive ambassadors and other public ministers; he shall take care that the laws be faithfully executed, and shall commission all the officers of the United States.

SECTION 4. The President, Vice President, and all civil officers of the United States, shall be removed from office on impeachment for, and conviction of, treason, bribery, or other high crimes and misdemeanors.

## ARTICLE III

SECTION 1. The judicial power of the United States shall be vested in one Supreme Court, and in such inferior courts as the Congress may from time to time ordain and establish. The judges, both of the Supreme and inferior courts, shall hold their offices during good behavior, and shall, at stated times, receive for their services, a compensation, which shall not be diminished during their continuance in office.

SECTION 2. 1. The judicial power shall extend to all cases, in law and equity, arising under this Constitution, the laws of the United States, and treaties made, or which shall be

---

[6]Superseded by the Twelfth Amendment.

made, under their authority;—to all cases of admiralty and maritime jurisdiction;—to controversies to which the United States shall be a party;[7]—to controversies between two or more States;—between a State and citizens of another State;—between citizens of different States;—between citizens of the same State claiming lands under grants of different States, and between a State, or the citizens thereof, and foreign States, citizens or subjects.

2. In all cases affecting ambassadors, other public ministers and consuls, and those in which a State shall be party, the Supreme Court shall have original jurisdiction. In all the other cases before mentioned, the Supreme Court shall have appellate jurisdiction, both as to law and fact, with such exceptions, and under such regulations as the Congress shall make.

3. The trial of all crimes, except in cases of impeachment, shall be by jury; and such trial shall be held in the State where the said crimes shall have been committed; but when not committed within any State, the trial shall be such place or places as the congress may by law have directed.

SECTION 3. 1. Treason against the United States shall consist only in levying war against them, or in adhering to their enemies, giving them aid and comfort. No person shall be convicted of treason unless on the testimony of two witnesses to the same overt act, or on confession in open court.

2. The Congress shall have power to declare the punishment of treason, but no attainder of treason shall work corruption of blood, or forfeiture except during the life of the person attained.

## ARTICLE IV

SECTION 1. Full faith and credit shall be given in each State to the public acts, records, and judicial proceedings of every other State. And the Congress may by general laws prescribe the manner in which such acts, records and proceedings shall be proved, and the effect thereof.

SECTION 2. 1. The citizens of each State shall be entitled to all privileges and immunities of citizens in the several States.[8]

2. A person charged in any State with treason, felony, or other crime, who shall flee from justice, and be found in another State, shall on demand of the executive authority of the State from which he fled, be delivered up to be removed to the State having jurisdiction of the crime.

3. No person held to service or labor in one State under the laws thereof, escaping into another, shall, in consequence of any law or regulation therein, be discharged from such service or labor, but shall be delivered up on claim of the party to whom such service or labor may be due.[9]

SECTION 3. 1. New States may be admitted by the Congress into this Union; but no new State shall be formed or erected within the jurisdiction of any other State, nor any State be formed by the junction of two or more States, or parts of States, without the consent of the legislatures of the States concerned as well as of the Congress.

2. The Congress shall have power to dispose of and make all needful rules and regulations respecting the territory or other property belonging to the United States; and nothing in this Constitution shall be so construed as to prejudice any claims of the United States, or of any particular State.

SECTION 4. The United States shall guarantee to every State in this Union a republican form of government, and shall protect each of them against invasion; and on application of the legislature, or of the executive (when the legislature cannot be convened) against domestic violence.

## ARTICLE V

The Congress, whenever two thirds of both Houses shall deem it necessary, shall propose amendments to this Constitution, or, on the application of the legislatures of two thirds of the several States, shall call a convention for proposing amendments, which in either case shall be valid to all intents and purposes, as part of this Constitution, when ratified by the legislatures of three fourths of the several States, or by conventions in three fourths thereof, as the one or the other mode of ratification may be proposed by the Congress; Provided that no amendment which may be made prior to the year one thousand eight hundred and eight shall in any manner affect the first and fourth clauses in the ninth section of the first article; and that no State, without its consent, shall be deprived of its equal suffrage in the Senate.

## ARTICLE VI

1. All debts contracted and engagements entered into, before the adoption of this Constitution, shall be as valid against the United States under this Constitution, as under the Confederation.[10]

2. This Constitution, and the laws of the United States which shall be made in pursuance thereof; and all treaties made, or which shall be made, under the authority of the United States, shall be the supreme law of the land; and the judges in every State shall be bound thereby, any thing in the Constitution or laws of any State to the contrary notwithstanding.

3. The senators and representatives before mentioned, and the members of the several State legislatures, and all executive and judicial officers, both of the United States and of the several States, shall be bound by oath or affirmation to support this Constitution; but no religious test shall ever be required as a qualification to any office or public trust under the United States.

---

[7]See the Eleventh Amendment.

[8]See the Fourteenth Amendment, Sec.1.

[9]See the Thirteenth Amendment.

---

[10]See the Fourteenth Amendment, Sec.4.

## Article VII

The ratification of the conventions of nine States shall be sufficient for the establishment of this Constitution between the States so ratifying the same.

Done in Convention by the unanimous consent of the States present the seventeenth day of September in the year of our Lord one thousand seven hundred and eighty-seven, and of the independence of the United States of America the twelfth. In witness whereof we have hereunto subscribed our names.

[Signatories' names omitted]

*Articles in addition to, and amendment of, the Constitution of the United States of America, proposed by Congress, and ratified by the legislatures of the several States, pursuant to the fifth article of the original Constitution.*

### Amendment I

[First ten amendments ratified December 15, 1791] Congress shall make no law respecting an establishment of religion, or prohibiting the free exercise thereof; or abridging the freedom of speech, or of the press; or the right of the people peaceably to assemble, and to petition the government for a redress of grievances.

### Amendment II

A well regulated militia, being necessary to the security of a free State, the right of the people to keep and bear arms, shall not be infringed.

### Amendment III

No soldier shall, in time of peace be quartered in any house, without the consent of the owner, nor in time of war, but in a manner to be prescribed by law.

### Amendment IV

The right of the people to be secure in their persons, houses, papers, and effects, against unreasonable searches and seizures, shall not be violated, and no warrants shall issue, but upon probable cause, supported by oath or affirmation, and particularly describing the place to be searched, and the persons or things to be seized.

### Amendment V

No person shall be held to answer for a capital or otherwise infamous crime, unless on a presentment or indictment of a grand jury, except in cases arising in the land or naval forces, or in the militia, when in actual service in time of war or public danger; nor shall any person be subject for the same offense to be twice put in jeopardy of life or limb; nor shall be compelled in any criminal case to be a witness against himself, nor be deprived of life, liberty, or property, without due process of law; nor shall private property be taken for public use, without just compensation.

### Amendment VI

In all criminal prosecutions, the accused shall enjoy the right to a speedy and public trial, by an impartial jury of the State and district wherein the crime shall have been committed, which district shall have been previously ascertained by law, and to be informed of the nature and cause of the accusation; to be confronted with the witnesses against him; to have compulsory process for obtaining witnesses in his favor, and to have the assistance of counsel for his defense.

### Amendment VII

In suits at common law, where the value in controversy shall exceed twenty dollars, the right of trial by jury shall be preserved, and no fact tried by a jury shall be otherwise reexamined in any court of the United States, than according to the rules of the common law.

### Amendment VIII

Excessive bail shall not be required, nor excessive fines imposed, nor cruel and unusual punishments inflicted.

### Amendment IX

The enumeration in the Constitution of certain rights shall not be construed to deny or disparage others retained by the people.

### Amendment X

The powers not delegated to the United States by the Constitution, nor prohibited by it to the States, are reserved to the States respectively, or to the people.

### Amendment XI [January 8, 1798]

The judicial power of the United States shall not be construed to extend to any suit in law or equity, commended or prosecuted against one of the United States by citizens of another State, or by citizens or subjects of any foreign State.

### Amendment XII [September 25, 1804]

The electors shall meet in their respective States, and vote by ballot for President and Vice President, one of whom, at least, shall not be an inhabitant of the same State with themselves; they shall name in their ballots the person voted for as President, and in distinct ballots the person voted for as Vice President, and they shall make distinct lists of all persons voted for as President and of all persons voted for as Vice President, and of the number of votes for each, which lists they shall sign and certify, and transmit sealed to the seat of the government of the United States, directed to the President of the Senate;—The President of the Senate shall, in the presence of the Senate and House of Representatives, open all the certificates and the votes shall then be counted;—The person having the greatest number of votes for President, shall be the President, if such number be a majority of the whole number of electors appointed; and if no person have such majority, then from the persons having the highest numbers not exceeding three on the list of those voted for as President, the House of Representatives shall choose immediately, by ballot, the President. But in choosing the President, the votes shall be taken by States, the representation from each State having one vote; a quorum for this purpose shall consist of a member or members from two thirds of the States, and a majority of all the States shall be necessary to a choice. And if the House of Representatives shall not choose a President whenever the right of choice shall devolve upon them, before the fourth day of March next following, then the Vice President shall act as President, as in the case of the death or other constitutional disability of the President. The person having the greatest number of votes as Vice President shall be the Vice President, if such number be a majority of the whole number of electors appointed, and if no person have a majority, then from the two highest numbers on the list, the Senate shall choose the Vice President; a quorum for the purpose shall consist of two thirds of the whole number of Senators, and a majority of the whole number shall be necessary to a choice. But no person constitutionally ineligible to the office of President shall be eligible to that of Vice President of the United States.

### Amendment XIII [December 18, 1865]

SECTION 1. Neither slavery nor involuntary servitude, except as a punishment for crime whereof the party shall have been duly convicted, shall exist within the United States, or any place subject to their jurisdiction.

SECTION 2. Congress shall have power to enforce this article by appropriate legislation.

### Amendment XIV [July 28, 1868]

SECTION 1. All persons born or naturalized in the United States, and subject to the jurisdiction thereof, are citizens of the United States and of the State wherein they reside. No State shall make or enforce any law which shall abridge the privileges or immunities of citizens of the United States; nor shall any State deprive any person of life, liberty, or property, without due process of law; nor deny to any person within its jurisdiction the equal protection of the laws.

SECTION 2. Representatives shall be apportioned among the several States according to their respective numbers, counting the whole number of persons in each State, excluding Indians not taxed. But when the right to vote at any election for the choice of electors for President and Vice President of the United States, representatives in Congress, the executive and judicial officers of a State, or the members of the legislature thereof, is denied to any of the male inhabitants of such State, being twenty-one years of age, and citizens of the United States, or in any way abridged, except for participating in rebellion, or other crime, the basis of representation there shall be reduced in the proportion which the number of such male citizens shall bear to the whole number of male citizens twenty-one years of age in such State.

SECTION 3. No person shall be a senator or representative in Congress, or elector of President and Vice President, or hold any office, civil or military, under the United States, or under any State, who having previously taken an oath, as a member of Congress, or as an officer of the United States, or as a member of any State legislature, or as an executive or judicial officer of any State, to support the Constitution of the United States, shall have engaged in insurrection or rebellion against the same, or given aid or comfort to the enemies thereof. But Congress may by a vote of two thirds of each House, remove such disability.

SECTION 4. The validity of the public debt of the United States, authorized by law, including debts incurred for payment of pensions and bounties for services in suppressing insurrection or rebellion; shall not be questioned. But neither the United States nor any State shall assume or pay any debt or obligation incurred in aid of insurrection or rebellion against the United States, or any claim for the loss or emancipation of any slave; but all such debts, obligations, and claims shall be held illegal and void.

SECTION 5. The Congress shall have the power to enforce, by appropriate legislation, the provisions of this article.

### Amendment XV [March 30, 1870]

SECTION 1. The right of citizens of the United States to vote shall not be denied or abridged by the United States or by any State on account of race, color, or previous condition of servitude.

SECTION 2. The Congress shall have power to enforce this article by appropriate legislation.

### Amendment XVI [February 25, 1913]

The Congress shall have power to lay and collect taxes on incomes, from whatever source derived, without apportionment among the several States, and without regard to any census or enumeration.

### Amendment XVII [May 31, 1913]

The Senate of the United States shall be composed of two senators from each State, elected by the people thereof, for six years; and each senator shall have one vote. The electors in each State shall have the qualifications requisite for electors of the most numerous branch of the State legislature.

When vacancies happen in the representation of any State in the Senate, the executive authority of such State shall issue writs of election to fill such vacancies: Provided, That the legislature of any State may empower the executive thereof to make temporary appointments until the people fill the vacancies by election as the legislature may direct.

This amendment shall not be so construed as to affect the election or term of any senator chosen before it becomes valid as part of the Constitution.

### Amendment XVIII[11] [January 29, 1919]

After one year from the ratification of this article, the manufacture, sale, or transportation of intoxicating liquors within, the importation thereof into, or the exportation thereof from the United States and all territory subject to

---

[11]Repealed by the Twenty-first Amendment.

the jurisdiction thereof for beverage purposes is thereby prohibited.

The Congress and the several States shall have concurrent power to enforce this article by appropriate legislation.

This article shall be inoperative unless it shall have been ratified as an amendment to the Constitution by the legislatures of the several States, as provided in the constitution, within seven years from the date of the submission hereof to the States by Congress.

## Amendment XIX [August 26, 1920]

The right of citizens of the United States to vote shall not be denied or abridged by the United States or by any State on account of sex.

Congress shall have the power to enforce this article by appropriate legislation.

## Amendment XX [January 23, 1933]

SECTION 1. The terms of the President and Vice President shall end at noon on the 20th day of January and the terms of Senators and Representatives at noon on the 3d day of January, of the years in which such terms would have ended if this article had not been ratified; and the terms of their successors shall then begin.

SECTION 2. The Congress shall assemble at least once in every year, and such meeting shall begin at noon on the 3d day of January, unless they shall by law appoint a different day.

SECTION 3. If, at the time fixed for the beginning of the term of President, the President-elect shall have died, the Vice President-elect shall become President. If a President shall not have been chosen before the time fixed for the beginning of his term, or if the President-elect shall have failed to qualify, then the Vice President-elect shall act as President until a President shall have qualified; and the Congress may by law provide for the case wherein neither a President-elect nor a Vice President-elect shall have qualified, declaring who shall then act as President, or the manner in which one who is to act shall be selected, and such person shall act accordingly until a President or Vice President shall have qualified.

SECTION 4. The Congress may by law provide for the case of the death of any of the persons from whom, the House of Representatives may choose a President whenever the right of choice shall have devolved upon them, and for the case of the death of any of the persons from whom the Senate may choose a Vice President whenever the right of choice shall have devolved upon them.

SECTION 5. Sections 1 and 2 shall take effect on the 15th day of October following the ratification of this article.

SECTION 6. This article shall be inoperative unless it shall have been ratified as an amendment to the Constitution by the legislatures of three-fourths of the several States within seven years from the date of its submission.

## Amendment XXI [December 5, 1933]

SECTION 1. The Eighteenth Article of amendment to the Constitution of the United States is hereby repealed.

SECTION 2. The transportation or importation into any State, Territory, or possession of the United States for delivery or use therein of intoxicating liquors in violation of the laws thereof, is hereby prohibited.

SECTION 3. This article shall be inoperative unless it shall have been ratified as an amendment to the Constitution by conventions in the several States, as provided in the Constitution, within seven years from the date of the submission thereof to the States by the Congress.

## Amendment XXII [March 1, 1951]

No person shall be elected to the office of the President more than twice, and no person who has held the office of President, or acted as President, for more than two years of a term to which some other person was elected President shall be elected to the office of the President more than once.

But this article shall not apply to any person holding the office of President when this article was proposed by the Congress, and shall not prevent any person who may be holding the office of President, or acting as President, during the term within which this article becomes operative from holding the office of President or acting as President during the remainder of such term.

This article shall be inoperative unless it shall have been ratified as an amendment to the Constitution by the legislatures of three-fourths of the several States within seven years from the date of its submission to the States by the Congress.

## Amendment XXIII [March 29, 1961]

SECTION 1. The District constituting the seat of Government of the United States shall appoint in such manner as the Congress may direct.

A number of electors of President and Vice President equal to the whole number of Senators and Representatives in Congress to which the District would be entitled if it were a State, but in no event more than the least populous State; they shall be in addition to those appointed by the States, but they shall be considered, for the purposes of the election of President and Vice President, to be electors appointed by a State; and they shall meet in the District and perform such duties as provided by the twelfth article of amendment.

SECTION 2. The Congress shall have power to enforce this article by appropriate legislation.

## Amendment XXIV [January 23, 1964]

SECTION 1. The right of citizens of the United States to vote in any primary or other election for President or Vice President, for electors for President or Vice President, or for Senator or Representative in Congress, shall not be denied or abridged by the United States or any State by reason of failure to pay any poll tax or other tax.

SECTION 2. The Congress shall have power to enforce this article by appropriate legislation.

### Amendment XXV [February 10, 1967]

SECTION 1. In case of the removal of the President from office or of his death or resignation, the Vice President shall become President.

SECTION 2. Whenever there is a vacancy in the office of the Vice President, the President shall nominate a Vice President who shall take office upon confirmation by a majority of both Houses of Congress.

SECTION 3. Whenever the President transmits to the President pro tempore of the Senate and the Speaker of the House of Representatives his written declaration that he is unable to discharge the powers and duties of his office, and until he transmits to them a written declaration to the contrary, such powers and duties shall be discharged by the Vice President as Acting President.

SECTION 4. Whenever the Vice President and a majority of either the principal officers of the executive departments or of such other body as Congress may by law provide, transmit to the President pro tempore of the Senate and the Speaker of the House of Representatives their written declaration that the President is unable to discharge the powers and duties of his office, the Vice President shall immediately assume the powers and duties of the office as Acting President.

Thereafter, when the President transmits to the President pro tempore of the Senate and the Speaker of the House of Representatives his written declaration that no inability exists, he shall resume the powers and duties of his office unless the Vice President and a majority of either the principal officers of the executive departments or of such other body as Congress may by law provide, transmit within four days to the President pro tempore of the Senate and the Speaker of the House of Representatives their written declaration that the President is unable to discharge the powers and duties of his office. Thereupon Congress shall decide the issue, assembling within forty-eight hours for that purpose if not in session. If the Congress, within twenty-one days after receipt of the latter written declaration, or, if Congress is not in session, within twenty-one days after Congress is required to assemble, determines by two-thirds vote of both Houses that the President is unable to discharge the powers and duties of his office, the Vice President shall continue to discharge the same as Acting President; otherwise, the President shall resume the powers and duties of his office.

### Amendment XXVI [June 30, 1971]

SECTION 1. The right of citizens of the United States who are eighteen years of age or older to vote shall not be denied or abridged by the United States or by any State on account of age.

SECTION 2. The Congress shall have power to enforce this article by appropriate legislation.

### Amendment XXVII[12] [May 7, 1992]

No law, varying the compensation for services of the Senators and Representatives, shall take effect until an election of Representatives shall have intervened.

---

[12]James Madison proposed this amendment in 1789 together with the ten amendments that were adopted as the Bill of Rights, but it failed to win ratification at the time. Congress, however, had set no deadline for its ratification, and over the years—particularly in the 1980s and 1990s—many states voted to add it to the Constitution. With the ratification of Michigan in 1992 it passed the threshold of 3/4ths of the states required for adoption, but because the process took more than 200 years, its validity remains in doubt.

## Presidential Elections

| Year | Number of States | Candidates | Party | Popular Vote* | Electoral Vote† | Percentage of Popular Vote |
|---|---|---|---|---|---|---|
| 1789 | 11 | GEORGE WASHINGTON | No party designations | | 69 | |
| | | John Adams | | | 34 | |
| | | Other Candidates | | | 35 | |
| 1792 | 15 | GEORGE WASHINGTON | No party designations | | 132 | |
| | | John Adams | | | 77 | |
| | | George Clinton | | | 50 | |
| | | Other Candidates | | | 5 | |
| 1796 | 16 | JOHN ADAMS | Federalist | | 71 | |
| | | Thomas Jefferson | Democratic-Republican | | 68 | |
| | | Thomas Pinckney | Federalist | | 59 | |
| | | Aaron Burr | Democratic-Republican | | 30 | |
| | | Other Candidates | | | 48 | |
| 1800 | 16 | THOMAS JEFFERSON | Democratic-Republican | | 73 | |
| | | Aaron Burr | Democratic-Republican | | 73 | |
| | | John Adams | Federalist | | 65 | |
| | | Charles C. Pinckney | Federalist | | 64 | |
| | | John Jay | Federalist | | 1 | |
| 1804 | 17 | THOMAS JEFFERSON | Democratic-Republican | | 162 | |
| | | Charles C. Pinckney | Federalist | | 14 | |
| 1808 | 17 | JAMES MADISON | Democratic-Republican | | 122 | |
| | | Charles C. Pinckney | Federalist | | 47 | |
| | | George Clinton | Democratic-Republican | | 6 | |
| 1812 | 18 | JAMES MADISON | Democratic-Republican | | 128 | |
| | | DeWitt Clinton | Federalist | | 89 | |
| 1816 | 19 | JAMES MONROE | Democratic-Republican | | 183 | |
| | | Rufus King | Federalist | | 34 | |
| 1820 | 24 | JAMES MONROE | Democratic-Republican | | 231 | |
| | | John Quincy Adams | Independent-Republican | | 1 | |
| 1824 | 24 | JOHN QUINCY ADAMS | Democratic-Republican | 108,740 | 84 | 30.5 |
| | | Andrew Jackson | Democratic-Republican | 153,544 | 99 | 43.1 |
| | | William H. Crawford | Democratic-Republican | 46,618 | 41 | 13.1 |
| | | Henry Clay | Democratic-Republican | 47,136 | 37 | 13.2 |
| 1828 | 24 | ANDREW JACKSON | Democrat | 647,286 | 178 | 56.0 |
| | | John Quincy Adams | National Republican | 508,064 | 83 | 44.0 |
| 1832 | 24 | ANDREW JACKSON | Democrat | 687,502 | 219 | 55.0 |
| | | Henry Clay | National Republican | 530,189 | 49 | 42.4 |
| | | William Wirt | Anti-Masonic | 33,108 | 7 | 2.6 |
| | | John Floyd | | | 11 | |
| 1836 | 26 | MARTIN VAN BUREN | Democrat | 765,483 | 170 | 50.9 |
| | | William H. Harrison | Whig | | 73 | |
| | | Hugh L. White | Whig | | 26 | |
| | | Daniel Webster | Whig | 739,795 | 14 | 49.1 |
| | | W. P. Mangum | Whig | | 11 | |

* Percentage of popular vote given for any election year may not total 100 percent because candidates receiving less than 1 percent of the popular vote have been omitted.
† Prior to the passage of the Twelfth Amendment in 1904, the electoral college voted for two presidential candidates; the runner-up became Vice-President. Data from Historical Statistics of the United States, Colonial Times to 1957 (1961), pp. 682–683, and The World Almanac.

## Presidential Elections (*Continued*)

| Year | Number of States | Candidates | Party | Popular Vote* | Electoral Vote[†] | Percent-age of Popular Vote |
|------|------------------|------------|-------|---------------|---------------|------------------------------|
| 1840 | 26 | WILLIAM H. HARRISON | Whig | 1,274,624 | 234 | 53.1 |
|      |    | Martin Van Buren | Democrat | 1,127,781 | 60 | 46.9 |
| 1844 | 26 | JAMES K. POLK | Democrat | 1,338,464 | 170 | 49.6 |
|      |    | Henry Clay | Whig | 1,300,097 | 105 | 48.1 |
|      |    | James G. Birney | Liberty | 62,300 | | 2.3 |
| 1848 | 30 | ZACHARY TAYLOR | Whig | 1,360,967 | 163 | 47.4 |
|      |    | Lewis Cass | Democrat | 1,222,342 | 127 | 42.5 |
|      |    | Martin Van Buren | Free Soil | 291,263 | | 10.1 |
| 1852 | 31 | FRANKLIN PIERCE | Democrat | 1,601,117 | 254 | 50.9 |
|      |    | Winfield Scott | Whig | 1,385,453 | 42 | 44.1 |
|      |    | John P. Hale | Free Soil | 155,825 | | 5.0 |
| 1856 | 31 | JAMES BUCHANAN | Democrat | 1,832,955 | 174 | 45.3 |
|      |    | John C. Frémont | Republican | 1,339,932 | 114 | 33.1 |
|      |    | Millard Fillmore | American ("Know Nothing") | 871,731 | 8 | 21.6 |
| 1860 | 33 | ABRAHAM LINCOLN | Republican | 1,865,593 | 180 | 39.8 |
|      |    | Stephen A. Douglas | Democrat | 1,382,713 | 12 | 29.5 |
|      |    | John C. Breckinridge | Democrat | 848,356 | 72 | 18.1 |
|      |    | John Bell | Constitutional Union | 592,906 | 39 | 12.6 |
| 1864 | 36 | ABRAHAM LINCOLN | Republican | 2,206,938 | 212 | 55.0 |
|      |    | George B. McClellan | Democrat | 1,803,787 | 21 | 45.0 |
| 1868 | 37 | ULYSSES S. GRANT | Republican | 3,013,421 | 214 | 52.7 |
|      |    | Horatio Seymour | Democrat | 2,706,829 | 80 | 47.3 |
| 1872 | 37 | ULYSSES S. GRANT | Republican | 3,596,745 | 286 | 55.6 |
|      |    | Horace Greeley | Democrat | 2,843,446 | * | 43.9 |
| 1876 | 38 | RUTHERFORD B. HAYES | Republican | 4,036,572 | 185 | 48.0 |
|      |    | Samuel J. Tilden | Democrat | 4,284,020 | 184 | 51.0 |
| 1880 | 38 | JAMES A. GARFIELD | Republican | 4,453,295 | 214 | 48.5 |
|      |    | Winfield S. Hancock | Democrat | 4,414,082 | 155 | 48.1 |
|      |    | James B. Weaver | Greenback-Labor | 308,578 | | 3.4 |
| 1884 | 38 | GROVER CLEVELAND | Democrat | 4,879,507 | 219 | 48.5 |
|      |    | James G. Blaine | Republican | 4,850,293 | 182 | 48.2 |
|      |    | Benjamin F. Butler | Greenback-Labor | 175,370 | | 1.8 |
|      |    | John P. St. John | Prohibition | 150,369 | | 1.5 |
| 1888 | 38 | BENJAMIN HARRISON | Republican | 5,447,129 | 233 | 47.9 |
|      |    | Grover Cleveland | Democrat | 5,537,857 | 168 | 48.6 |
|      |    | Clinton B. Fisk | Prohibition | 249,506 | | 2.2 |
|      |    | Anson J. Streeter | Union Labor | 146,935 | | 1.3 |
| 1892 | 44 | GROVER CLEVELAND | Democrat | 5,555,426 | 277 | 46.1 |
|      |    | Benjamin Harrison | Republican | 5,182,690 | 145 | 43.0 |
|      |    | James B. Weaver | People's | 1,029,846 | 22 | 8.5 |
|      |    | John Bidwell | Prohibition | 264,133 | | 2.2 |
| 1896 | 45 | WILLIAM MCKINLEY | Republican | 7,102,246 | 271 | 51.1 |
|      |    | William J. Bryan | Democrat | 6,492,559 | 176 | 47.7 |

*Because of the death of Greeley, Democratic electors scattered their votes.

# Presidential Elections (*Continued*)

| Year | Number of States | Candidates | Party | Popular Vote* | Electoral Vote[†] | Percentage of Popular Vote |
|---|---|---|---|---|---|---|
| 1900 | 45 | WILLIAM McKINLEY | Republican | 7,218,491 | 292 | 51.7 |
| | | William J. Bryan | Democrat; Populist | 6,356,734 | 155 | 45.5 |
| | | John C. Woolley | Prohibition | 208,914 | | 1.5 |
| 1904 | 45 | THEODORE ROOSEVELT | Republican | 7,628,461 | 336 | 57.4 |
| | | Alton B. Parker | Democrat | 5,084,223 | 140 | 37.6 |
| | | Eugene V. Debs | Socialist | 402,283 | | 3.0 |
| | | Silas C. Swallow | Prohibition | 258,536 | | 1.9 |
| 1908 | 46 | WILLIAM H. TAFT | Republican | 7,675,320 | 321 | 51.6 |
| | | William J. Bryan | Democrat | 6,412,294 | 162 | 43.1 |
| | | Eugene V. Debs | Socialist | 420,793 | | 2.8 |
| | | Eugene W. Chafin | Prohibition | 253,840 | | 1.7 |
| 1912 | 48 | WOODROW WILSON | Democrat | 6,296,547 | 435 | 41.9 |
| | | Theodore Roosevelt | Progressive | 4,118,571 | 88 | 27.4 |
| | | William H. Taft | Republican | 3,486,720 | 8 | 23.2 |
| | | Eugene V. Debs | Socialist | 900,672 | | 6.0 |
| | | Eugene W. Chafin | Prohibition | 206,275 | | 1.4 |
| 1916 | 48 | WOODROW WILSON | Democrat | 9,127,695 | 277 | 49.4 |
| | | Charles E. Hughes | Republican | 8,533,507 | 254 | 46.2 |
| | | A. L. Benson | Socialist | 585,113 | | 3.2 |
| | | J. Frank Hanly | Prohibition | 220,506 | | 1.2 |
| 1920 | 48 | WARREN G. HARDING | Republican | 16,143,407 | 404 | 60.4 |
| | | James M. Cox | Democrat | 9,130,328 | 127 | 34.2 |
| | | Eugene V. Debs | Socialist | 919,799 | | 3.4 |
| | | P. P. Christensen | Farmer-Labor | 265,411 | | 1.0 |
| 1924 | 48 | CALVIN COOLIDGE | Republican | 15,718,211 | 382 | 54.0 |
| | | John W. Davis | Democrat | 8,385,283 | 136 | 28.8 |
| | | Robert M. La Follette | Progressive | 4,831,289 | 13 | 16.6 |
| 1928 | 48 | HERBERT C. HOOVER | Republican | 21,391,993 | 444 | 58.2 |
| | | Alfred E. Smith | Democrat | 15,016,169 | 87 | 40.9 |
| 1932 | 48 | FRANKLIN D. ROOSEVELT | Democrat | 22,809,638 | 472 | 57.4 |
| | | Herbert C. Hoover | Republican | 15,758,901 | 59 | 39.7 |
| | | Norman Thomas | Socialist | 881,951 | | 2.2 |
| 1936 | 48 | FRANKLIN D. ROOSEVELT | Democrat | 27,752,869 | 523 | 60.8 |
| | | Alfred M. Landon | Republican | 16,674,665 | 8 | 36.5 |
| | | William Lemke | Union | 882,479 | | 1.9 |
| 1940 | 48 | FRANKLIN D. ROOSEVELT | Democrat | 27,307,819 | 449 | 54.8 |
| | | Wendell L. Willkie | Republican | 22,321,018 | 82 | 44.8 |
| 1944 | 48 | FRANKLIN D. ROOSEVELT | Democrat | 25,606,585 | 432 | 53.5 |
| | | Thomas E. Dewey | Republican | 22,014,745 | 99 | 46.0 |
| 1948 | 48 | HARRY S. TRUMAN | Democrat | 24,105,812 | 303 | 49.5 |
| | | Thomas E. Dewey | Republican | 21,970,065 | 189 | 45.1 |
| | | J. Strom Thurmond | States' Rights | 1,169,063 | 39 | 2.4 |
| | | Henry A. Wallace | Progressive | 1,157,172 | | 2.4 |

## Presidential Elections (*Continued*)

| Year | Number of States | Candidates | Party | Popular Vote* | Electoral Vote[†] | Percentage of Popular Vote |
|------|------|------------|-------|------------|------------|-----------|
| 1952 | 48 | DWIGHT D. EISENHOWER | Republican | 33,936,234 | 442 | 55.1 |
|      |    | Adlai E. Stevenson | Democrat | 27,314,992 | 89 | 44.4 |
| 1956 | 48 | DWIGHT D. EISENHOWER | Republican | 35,590,472 | 457* | 57.6 |
|      |    | Adlai E. Stevenson | Democrat | 26,022,752 | 73 | 42.1 |
| 1960 | 50 | JOHN F. KENNEDY | Democrat | 34,227,096 | 303[†] | 49.9 |
|      |    | Richard M. Nixon | Republican | 34,108,546 | 219 | 49.6 |
| 1964 | 50 | LYNDON B. JOHNSON | Democrat | 42,676,220 | 486 | 61.3 |
|      |    | Barry M. Goldwater | Republican | 26,860,314 | 52 | 38.5 |
| 1968 | 50 | RICHARD M. NIXON | Republican | 31,785,480 | 301 | 43.4 |
|      |    | Hubert H. Humphrey | Democrat | 31,275,165 | 191 | 42.7 |
|      |    | George C. Wallace | American Independent | 9,906,473 | 46 | 13.5 |
| 1972 | 50 | RICHARD M. NIXON[‡] | Republican | 47,165,234 | 520** | 60.6 |
|      |    | George S. McGovern | Democrat | 29,168,110 | 17 | 37.5 |
| 1976 | 50 | JIMMY CARTER | Democrat | 40,828,929 | 297*** | 50.1 |
|      |    | Gerald R. Ford | Republican | 39,148,940 | 240 | 47.9 |
|      |    | Eugene McCarthy | Independent | 739,256 | | |
| 1980 | 50 | RONALD REAGAN | Republican | 43,201,220 | 489 | 50.9 |
|      |    | Jimmy Carter | Democrat | 34,913,332 | 49 | 41.2 |
|      |    | John B. Anderson | Independent | 5,581,379 | | |
| 1984 | 50 | RONALD REAGAN | Republican | 53,428,357 | 525 | 59.0 |
|      |    | Walter F. Mondale | Democrat | 36,930,923 | 13 | 41.0 |
| 1988 | 50 | GEORGE H. W. BUSH | Republican | 48,901,046 | 426**** | 53.4 |
|      |    | Michael Dukakis | Democrat | 41,809,030 | 111 | 45.6 |
| 1992 | 50 | BILL CLINTON | Democrat | 43,728,275 | 370 | 43.2 |
|      |    | George Bush | Republican | 38,167,416 | 168 | 37.7 |
|      |    | H. Ross Perot | United We Stand, America | 19,237,247 | | 19.0 |
| 1996 | 50 | BILL CLINTON | Democrat | 45,590,703 | 379 | 49.0 |
|      |    | Robert Dole | Republican | 37,816,307 | 159 | 41.0 |
|      |    | H. Ross Perot | Reform | 7,866,284 | | 8.0 |
| 2000 | 50 | GEORGE W. BUSH | Republican | 50,459,624 | 271 | 47.9 |
|      |    | Albert Gore, Jr. | Democrat | 51,003,328 | 266 | 49.4 |
|      |    | Ralph Nader | Green | 2,882,985 | | 2.7 |
| 2008 | 50 | BARACK OBAMA | Democrat | 64,239,421 | 364 | 52.5 |
|      |    | John McCain | Republican | 56,626,340 | 162 | 46.2 |

*Walter B. Jones received 1 electoral vote.
† Harry F. Byrd received 15 electoral votes.
‡ Resigned August 9, 1974: Vice President Gerald R. Ford became President.
** John Hospers received 1 electoral vote.
*** Ronald Reagan received 1 electoral vote.
**** Lloyd Bentsen received 1 electoral vote.

**affirmative action**   A set of policies to open opportunities in business and education for members of minority groups and women by allowing race and sex to be factors included in decisions to hire, award contracts, or admit students to higher education programs.

**Alliance for Progress**   Program of economic aid to Latin America during the Kennedy administration.

**Allies**   In World War I, Britain, France, Russia, and other nations fighting against the Central Powers but not including the United States.

**Allies**   In World War I, these were Britain, France, Russia, and other belligerent nations (but not the United States, which insisted upon being merely an associated nation) fighting against the Central Powers. In World War II, the Allies fighting the Axis Powers included the United States as well as the Soviet Union, Great Britain, France, China, and other nations.

**American Federation of Labor (AFL)**   Union formed in 1886 that organized skilled workers along craft lines and emphasized a few workplace issues rather than a broad social program.

**American Indian Movement (AIM)**   Group of Native-American political activists who used confrontations with the federal government to publicize their case for Indian rights.

**Americans with Disabilities Act**   Legislation in 1992 that banned discrimination against physically handicapped persons in employment, transportation, and public accommodations.

**Atlanta Compromise**   Booker T. Washington's policy accepting segregation and disfranchisement for African Americans in exchange for white assistance in education and job training.

**Atlantic Charter**   Statement of common principles and war aims developed by President Franklin Roosevelt and British Prime Minister Winston Churchill at a meeting in August 1941.

**Australian ballot**   Secret voting and the use of official ballots rather than party tickets.

**Axis Powers**   The opponents of the United States and its allies in World War II.

**Baker v. Carr**   U.S. Supreme Court decision in 1962 that allowed federal courts to review the appointment of state legislative districts and established the principle that such districts should have roughly equal populations ("one person, one vote").

**Battle of the Atlantic**   The long struggle between German submarines and the British and U.S. navies in the North Atlantic from 1940 to 1943.

**Battle of the Little Bighorn**   Battle in which Colonel George A. Custer and the Seventh Cavalry were defeated by the Sioux and Cheyennes under Sitting Bull and Crazy Horse in Montana in 1876.

**Bay of Pigs**   Site in Cuba of an unsuccessful landing by fourteen hundred anti-Castro Cuban refugees in April 1961.

**Berlin blockade**   Three-hundred-day Soviet blockade of land access to United States, British, and French occupation zones in Berlin, 1948–1949.

**Berlin Wall**   Wall erected by East Germany in 1961 that isolated West Berlin from the surrounding areas in Communist-controlled East Berlin and East Germany.

**black codes**   Laws passed by states and municipalities denying many rights of citizenship to free blacks after the Civil war.

**Black Panthers**   Political and social movement among black Americans, founded in Oakland, California, in 1966 and emphasizing black economic and political power.

**Black Power**   Philosophy emerging after 1965 that real economic and political gains for African Americans could come only through self-help, self-determination, and organizing for direct political influence.

**Blitzkrieg**   German war tactic in World War II ("lightning war") involving the concentration of air and armored firepower to punch and exploit holes in opposing defensive lines.

**Bolshevik**   Member of the Communist movement in Russia that established the Soviet government after the 1917 Russian Revolution.

**Bonus Army**   Unemployed veterans of World War I gathering in Washington in 1932 demanding payment of service bonuses not due until 1945.

**Brown v. Board of Education of Topeka**   Supreme Court decision in 1954 that declared that "separate but equal" schools for children of different races violated the Constitution.

**Bureau of Reclamation**   Federal agency established in 1902 providing public funds for irrigation projects   in arid regions.

**Camp David Agreement**   Agreement to reduce points of conflict between Israel and Egypt, hammered out in 1977 with the help of U.S. President Jimmy Carter.

**carpetbaggers**   Northern transplants to the South, many of whom were Union soldiers who stayed in the South after the war.

**Central Intelligence Agency (CIA)**   Agency established in 1947 that coordinates the gathering and evaluation of military and economic information on other nations.

**Central Powers**   Germany and its World War I allies in Austria, Turkey, and Bulgaria.

**chain migration**   Process common to many immigrant groups whereby one family member brings over other family members, who in turn bring other relatives and friends and occasionally entire villages.

**Chisholm Trail**   The route followed by Texas cattle raisers driving their herds north to markets at Kansas railheads.

**Civil Rights Act of 1964**   Federal legislation that outlawed discrimination in public accommodations and employment on the basis of race, skin color, sex, religion, or national origin.

**Cold War** The political and economic confrontation between the Soviet Union and the United States that dominated world affairs from 1946 to 1989.

**collective bargaining** Representatives of a union negotiating with management on behalf of all members.

**Colored Farmer's Alliance** An organization of Southern black farmers formed in Texas in 1886 in response to the Southern Farmer's Alliance, which did not accept black people as members.

**Committee on Public Information (CPI)** Government agency during World War I that sought to shape public opinion in support of the war effort through newspapers, pamphlets, speeches, films, and other media.

**Compromise of 1877** The Congressional settling of the 1876 election which installed Republican Rutherford B. Hayes in the White House and gave Democrats control of all state governments in the South.

**Congress of Industrial Organizations (CIO)** An alliance of industrial unions that spurred the 1930s organizational drive among the mass-production industries.

**Congress of Racial Equality (CORE)** Civil rights group formed in 1942 and committed to nonviolent civil disobedience.

**Congressional Reconstruction** Name given to the period 1867–1870 when the Republican-dominated Congress controlled Reconstruction era policy.

**conservation** The efficient management and use of natural resources, such as forests, grasslands, and rivers, as opposed to preservation or uncontrolled exploitation.

**containment** The policy of resisting further expansion of the Soviet bloc through diplomacy and, if necessary, military action, developed in 1947–1948.

**Contract with America** Platform proposing a sweeping reduction in the role and activities of the federal government on which many Republican candidates ran for Congress in 1994.

**counterculture** Various alternatives to mainstream values and behaviors that became popular in the 1960s, including experimentation with psychedelic drugs, communal living, a return to the land, Asian religions, and experimental art.

**Coxey's Army** A protest march of unemployed workers, led by Populist businessman Jacob Coxey, demanding inflation and a public works program during the depression of the 1890s.

**Dawes Act** An 1887 law terminating tribal ownership of land and allotting some parcels of land to individual Indians with the remainder opened for white settlement.

**D-Day** June 6, 1944, the day of the first paratroop drops and amphibious landings on the coast of Normandy, France, in the first stage of Operation OVERLORD during World War II.

**Declaration of London** Statement drafted by an international conference in 1909 to clarify international law and specify the rights of neutral nations.

**deindustrialization** The process of economic change involving the disappearance of outmoded industries and the transfer of factories to new low-wage locations, with devastating effects in the Northeast and Middle West, especially in the 1970s and 1980s.

**deregulation** Reduction or removal of government regulations and encouragement of direct competition in many important industries and economic sectors.

**détente** (French for "easing of tension") Used to describe the new U.S. relations with China and the Soviet Union in 1972.

**disfranchisement** The use of legal means to bar individuals or groups from voting.

**Dixiecrats** States' Rights Democrats.

**dollar diplomacy** The U.S. policy of using private investment in other nations to promote American diplomatic goals and business interests.

**Eastern Front** The area of military operations in World War II located east of Germany in eastern Europe and the Soviet Union.

**Economic Recovery and Tax Act of 1981 (ERTA)** A major revision of the federal income tax system.

**Eighteenth Amendment** Constitutional revision, adopted in 1919, that prohibited the production and sale of alcohol in the United States.

**Environmental Protection Agency (EPA)** Federal agency created in 1970 to oversee environmental monitoring and cleanup programs.

**Espionage Act** Law whose vague prohibition against obstructing the nation's war effort was used to crush dissent and criticism during World War I.

**Exploring America** ???

**Fair Employment Practices Committee (FEPC)** Federal agency established in 1941 to curb racial discrimination in war production jobs and government employment.

**Farmers' Alliance** A broad mass movement in the rural South and West during the late nineteenth century, encompassing several organizations and demanding economic and political reforms.

**fascist government** A government subscribing to a philosophy of dictatorship that merges the interests of the state, armed forces, and big business.

**Federal Deposit Insurance Corporation (FDIC)** Government agency that guarantees bank deposits, thereby protecting both depositors and banks.

**Federal Highway Act of 1956** Measure that provided federal funding to build a nationwide system of interstate and defense highways.

**Federal Reserve Act** The 1913 law that revised banking and currency by extending limited government regulation through the creation of the Federal Reserve System.

**Federal Trade Commission** Government agency established in 1914 to provide regulatory oversight of business activity.

**Field Order No. 15**  Order by General William T. Sherman in January 1865 to set aside abandoned land along the southern Atlantic coast for forty-acre grants to freedmen, rescinded by President Andrew Johnson later that year.

**Fifteenth Amendment**  Passed by Congress in 1869, guaranteed the right of American men to vote, regardless of race.

**fireside chats**  Speeches broadcast nationally over the radio in which President Franklin D. Roosevelt explained complex issues and programs in plain language, as though his listeners were gathered around the fireside with him.

**Fourteenth Amendment**  Passed by Congress in 1866, guaranteed every citizen equality before the law by prohibiting states from violating the civil rights of their citizens, thus outlawing the black codes.

**free silver**  Philosophy that the government should expand the money supply by purchasing and coining all the silver offered to it.

**Free Speech Movement (FSM)**  Student movement at the University of California, Berkeley, formed in 1964 to protest limitations on political activities on campus.

**Freedmen's Bureau**  Agency established by Congress in March 1865 to provide social, educational, and economic services, advice, and protection to former slaves and destitute whites; lasted seven years.

**Freedom Summer**  Voter registration effort in rural Mississippi organized by black and white civil rights workers in 1964.

**fundamentalists**  Religious conservatives who believe in the literal accuracy and divine inspiration of the Bible.

**Gentlemen's Agreement**  A diplomatic agreement in 1907 between Japan and the United States curtailing but not abolishing Japanese immigration.

**GI Bill of Rights**  Legislation in June 1944 that eased the return of veterans into American society by providing educational and employment benefits.

**Gilded Age**  Term applied to late-nineteenth-century America that refers to the shallow display and worship of wealth characteristic of that period.

**Glasnost**  Russian for "openness," applied to Mikhail Gorbachev's encouragement of new ideas and easing of political repression in the Soviet Union.

**Gospel of Wealth**  Thesis that hard work and perseverance lead to wealth, implying that poverty is a character flaw.

**grandfather clause**  Rule that required potential voters to demonstrate that their grandfathers had been eligible to vote; used in some Southern states after 1890 to limit the black electorate.

**Grange**  The National Grange of the Patrons of Husbandry, a national organization of farm owners formed after the Civil War.

**Granger laws**  State laws enacted in the Midwest in the 1870s that regulated rates charged by railroads, grain elevator operators, and other middlemen.

**Great Depression**  The nation's worst economic crisis, extending through the 1930s, producing unprecedented bank failures, unemployment, and industrial and agricultural collapse.

**Great Migration**  The mass movement of African Americans from the rural South to the urban North, spurred especially by new job opportunities during World War I and the 1920s.

**Great Migration**  The mass movement of African Americans from the rural South to the urban North, spurred especially by new job opportunities during World War I and the 1920s.

**Great Society**  Theme of Lyndon Johnson's administration, focusing on poverty, education, and civil rights.

**Great Uprising**  Unsuccessful railroad strike of 1877 to protest wage cuts and the use of federal troops against strikers; the first nationwide work stoppage in American history.

**Greater East Asia Co-Prosperity Sphere**  Japanese nationalists believed that Japan should expel the French, British, Dutch, and Americans from Asia and create this sphere in which Japan would give the orders and other Asian peoples would comply.

**Greenback Party**  A third party of the 1870s and 1880s that garnered temporary support by advocating currency inflation to expand the economy and assist debtors.

**Gulf of Tonkin Resolution**  Request to Congress from President Lyndon Johnson in response to North Vietnamese torpedo boat attacks in which he sought authorization for "all necessary measures" to protect American forces and stop further aggression.

**Harlem Renaissance**  A new African-American cultural awareness that flourished in literature, art, and music in the 1920s.

**Helsinki Accords**  Agreement in 1975 among NATO and Warsaw Pact members that recognized European national boundaries as set after World War II and included guarantees of human rights.

**Holocaust**  The systematic murder of millions of European Jews and others deemed undesirable by Nazi Germany.

**Homestead Act**  1862 law providing 160 acres of free land to anyone who would live on and farm the land for five years.

**Hoovervilles**  Shantytowns, sarcastically named after President Hoover, in which unemployed and homeless people lived in makeshift shacks, tents, and boxes.

**horizontal integration**  The merger of competitors in the same industry.

**House Un-American Activities Committee (HUAC)**  Originally intended to ferret out pro-Fascists, it later investigated "un-American propaganda" that attacked constitutional government.

**Hull House**  Chicago settlement house that became part of a broader neighborhood revitalization project led by Jane Addams.

**Immigration and Nationality Act of 1965** Federal legislation that replaced the national quota system for immigration with overall limits of 170,000 immigrants per year from the Eastern Hemisphere and 120,000 per year from the Western Hemisphere.

**imperialism** The policy and practice of exploiting nations and peoples for the benefit of an imperial power either directly through military occupation and colonial rule or indirectly through economic domination of resources and markets.

**initiative** Procedure by which citizens can introduce a subject for legislation, usually through a petition signed by a specific number of voters.

**Intermediate Nuclear Force Agreement (INF)** Disarmament agreement between the U.S. and the Soviet Union under which an entire class of missiles would be removed and destroyed and on-site inspections would be permitted for verification..

**International Monetary Fund (IMF)** International organization established in 1945 to assist nations in maintaining stable currencies.

**Internet** The system of interconnected computers and servers that allows the exchange of e-mail, posting of Web sites, and other means of instant communication.

**Interstate Commerce Act** The 1887 law that expanded federal power over business by prohibiting pooling and discriminatory rates by railroads and establishing the first federal regulatory agency, the Interstate Commerce Commission.

**Interstate Commerce Commission (ICC)** The first federal regulation agency, established in 1887 to oversee railroad practices.

**Irreconcilables** Group of U.S. senators adamantly opposed to ratification of the Treaty of Versailles after World War I.

**Island Hopping** The Pacific campaigns of 1944 that were the American naval versions of the *Blitzkrieg*.

**Jazz Age** The 1920s, so called for the popular music of the day as a symbol of the many changes taking place in the mass culture.

**Jim Crow laws** Segregation laws that became widespread in the South during the 1890s.

**Kellogg-Briand Pact** A 1928 international treaty that denounced aggression and war but lacked provisions for enforcement.

**Knights of Labor** Labor union founded in 1869 that included skilled and unskilled workers irrespective of race or gender.

**Korean War** Pacific war started on June 25, 1950, when North Korea, helped by Soviet equipment and Chinese training, attacked South Korea.

**Ku Klux Klan** Perhaps the most prominent of the vigilante groups that terrorized black people in the South during the Reconstruction era, founded by the Confederate veterans in 1866.

**laissez-faire** The doctrine that government should not intervene in the economy, especially through regulation.

**League of Nations** International organization created by the Versailles Treaty after World War I to ensure world stability.

**League of Women Voters** League formed in 1920 advocating for women's rights, among them the right for women to serve on juries and equal pay laws.

**Lend-Lease Act** Program begun in 1941 through which the U.S. transferred military equipment to Britain and other World War II allies.

**Levittown** Suburban Long Island community of postwar rental houses built by William Levitt for veterans of World War II.

**Liberty Bonds** Interest-bearing certificates sold by the U.S. government to finance the American World War I effort.

**Limited Test Ban Treaty** Treaty, signed by the United States, Britain, and the Soviet Union, outlawing nuclear testing in the atmosphere, in outer space, and under water.

**Lost Cause** The phrase many white Southerners applied to their Civil War defeat. They viewed the war as a noble cause but only a temporary setback in the South's ultimate vindication.

**lynching** Execution, usually by a mob, without trial.

**Mahanism** The ideas advanced by Alfred Thayer Mahan, stressing U.S. naval, economic, and territorial expansion.

**Manhattan Project** The effort, using the code name Manhattan Engineer District, to develop an atomic bomb under the management of the U.S. Army Corps of Engineers during World War II.

**Marshall Plan** Secretary of State George C. Marshall's European Recovery Plan of June 5, 1947, committing the United States to help in the rebuilding of post-World War II Europe.

**massive retaliation** Popular name for the military doctrine adopted in the 1950s, whereby the U.S. promised to respond to any attack on itself or its allies with massive force, including nuclear weapons.

**McCarthyism** Anti-Communist attitudes and actions associated with Senator Joe McCarthy in the early 1950s, including smear tactics and innuendo.

**Medicaid** Supplementary medical insurance for the poor, financed through the federal government; program created in 1965.

**Medicare** Basic medical insurance for the elderly, financed through the federal government; program created in 1965.

**Model Cities Program** Effort to target federal funds to upgrade public services and economic opportunity in specifically defined urban neighborhoods between 1966 and 1974.

**muckraking** Journalism exposing economic, social, and political evils, so named by Theodore Roosevelt for its "raking the muck" of American society.

**Mugwumps** Elitist and conservative reformers who favored sound money and limited government and opposed tariffs and the spoils system.

**Multinational Corporations**  Firms with direct investments, branches, factories, and offices in a number of countries.

**Nation of Islam**  Religious movement among black Americans that emphasizes self-sufficiency, self-help, and separation from white society.

**National Aeronautics and Space Administration (NASA)**  Federal agency created in 1958 to manage American space flights and exploration.

**National American Woman Suffrage Movement**  The organization, formed in 1890, that coordinated the ultimately successful campaign to achieve women's right to vote.

**National Association for the Advancement of Colored People (NAACP)**  Interracial organization co-founded by W. E. B. Du Bois in 1910 dedicated to restoring African-American political and social rights.

**National Origins Act of 1924**  Law sharply restricting immigration on the basis of immigrants' national origins and discriminating against southern and eastern Europeans and Asians.

**National Security Council (NSC)**  The formal policymaking body for national defense and foreign relations, created in 1947 and consisting of the president, the secretary of defense, the secretary of state, and others appointed by the president.

**National Security Council Paper 68 (NSC-68)**  Policy statement that committed the United States to a military approach to the Cold War.

**nativism**  Favoring the interests and culture of native-born inhabitants over those of immigrants.

**neoliberal**  Advocate or participant in the effort to reshape the Democratic party for the 1990s around a policy emphasizing economic growth and competitiveness in the world economy.

**New Deal**  The economic and political policies of the Roosevelt administration in the 1930s.

**New Federalism**  President Richard Nixon's policy to shift responsibilities of government programs from the federal level to the states.

**New Freedom**  Woodrow Wilson's 1912 program for limited government intervention in the economy to restore competition by curtailing the restrictive influences of trusts and protective tariffs, thereby providing opportunities for individual achievement.

**New Frontier**  John F. Kennedy's domestic and foreign policy initiatives, designed to reinvigorate a sense of national purpose and energy.

**New Nationalism**  Theodore Roosevelt's 1912 program calling for a strong national government to foster, regulate, and protect business, industry, workers, and consumers.

**Niagara Movement**  African-American group organized in 1905 to promote racial integration, civil and political rights, and equal access to economic opportunity.

**Nineteenth Amendment**  Constitutional revision that in 1920 established women citizens' right to vote.

**Nisei**  U.S. citizens born of immigrant Japanese parents.

**Nixon Doctrine**  President Nixon's new American policy (1969) toward Asia in which the United States would honor treaty commitments but would gradually disengage and expect Asian nations to handle military defense on their own.

**North American Free Trade Agreement (NAFTA)**  Agreement reached in 1993 by Canada, Mexico, and the United States to substantially reduce barriers to trade.

**North Atlantic Treaty Organization (NATO)**  Organization of ten European countries, Canada, and the United States whom together formed a mutual defense pact in April, 1949.

**Office of Economic Opportunity (OEO)**  Federal agency that coordinated many programs of the War on Poverty between 1964 and 1975.

**oligopoly**  An industry, such as steel making or automobile manufacturing, that is controlled by a few large companies.

**Omaha Platform**  The 1892 platform of the Populist party repudiating laissez-faire and demanding economic and political reforms to aid distressed farmers and workers.

**Open Door**  American policy of seeking equal trade and investment opportunities in foreign nations or regions.

**open-shop**  Factory or business employing workers whether or not they are union members; in practice, such a business usually refuses to hire union members and follows antiunion policies.

**Operation OVERLORD**  U.S. and British invasion of France in June 1944 during World War II.

**Pan American Union**  International organization originally established as the Commercial Bureau of American Republics by Secretary of State James Blaine's first Pan-American Conference in 1889 to promote cooperation among nations of the Western Hemisphere through commercial and diplomatic negotiations.

**PATRIOT Act**  Federal legislation adopted in 2001, in response to the terrorist attacks of September 11, intended to facilitate antiterror actions by federal law enforcement and intelligence agencies.

**Pendleton Civil Service Act**  A law of 1883 that reformed the spoils system by prohibiting government workers from making political contributions and creating the Civil Service Commission to oversee their appointment on the basis of merit rather than politics.

**Pentagon Papers**  Classified Defense Department documents on the history of the United States' involvement in Vietnam, prepared in 1968 and leaked to the press in 1971.

**Perestroika**  Russian for "restructuring," applied to Mikail Gorbachev's efforts to make the Soviet economic and political systems more modern, flexible, and innovative.

**Platt Amendment**  A stipulation the United States had inserted into the Cuban constitution in 1901 restricting Cuban autonomy and authorizing U.S. intervention and naval bases.

**Plessy v. Ferguson** Supreme Court decision holding that Louisiana's railroad segregation law did not violate the Constitution as long as the railroads or the state provided equal accommodations.

**pogroms** Government-directed attacks against Jewish citizens, property, and villages in tsarist Russia beginning in the 1880s; a primary reason for Russian Jewish migration to the United States.

**poll taxes** Taxes imposed on voters as a requirement for voting.

**Populist Party** A major third party of the 1890s formed on the basis of the Farmers' Alliance and other reform organizations.

**Populist party** A major third party of the 1890s, formed on the basis of the Southern Farmers' Alliance and other organizations, mounting electoral challenges against Democrats in the South and the Republicans in the West.

**Potsdam Declaration** Statement issued by the United States during a meeting of U.S. President Harry Truman, British Prime Minister Winston Churchill, and Soviet Premier Joseph Stalin in which the United States declared its intention to democratize the Japanese political system and reintroduce Japan into the international community.

**preparedness** Military buildup in preparation for possible U.S. participation in World War I.

**Preservation** Protecting forests, land, and other features of the natural environment from development or destruction, often for aesthetic appreciation.

**Progressive Era** An era in the United States (roughly between 1900 and 1917) in which important movements challenged traditional relationships and attitudes.

**Prohibition Party** A venerable third party still in existence that has persistently campaigned for the abolition of alcohol but has also introduced many important reform ideas into American politics.

**prohibition** A ban on the production, sale, and consumption of liquor, achieved temporarily through state laws and the Eighteenth Amendment.

**Proposition 187** California legislation adopted by popular vote in California in 1994, which cuts off state-funded health can education benefits to undocumented or illegal immigration.

**Reagan Doctrine** The policy assumption that Soviet-influenced governments in Asia, Africa, and Latin America needed to be eliminated if the U.S. was to win the Cold War.

**recall** The process of removing an official from office by popular vote, usually after using petitions to call for such a vote.

**Red Scare** Post-World War I public hysteria over Bolshevik influence in the United States directed against labor activism, radical dissenters, and some ethnic groups.

**Redeemers** Southern Democrats who wrested control of governments in the former Confederacy, often through electoral fraud and violence, from Republican, beginning in 1870.

**Redlining** The withholding of home purchase loans and insurance coverage from innercity older neighborhoods by federal housing agencies and private industry.

**referendum** Submission of a law, proposed or already in effect, to a direct popular vote for approval or rejection.

**Reservationists** Group of U.S. senators opposing approval of the Treaty of Versailles, without significant amendments.

**Roosevelt Corollary** President Theodore Roosevelt's policy asserting U.S. authority to intervene in the affairs of Latin American nations; an expansion of the Monroe Doctrine.

**Sagebrush Rebellion** Political movement in the Western states in the early 1980s that called for easing of regulations on the economic issue of federal lands and the transfer of some or all of those lands to state ownership.

**SALT (Strategic Arms Limitation Treaty)** Treaty signed in 1972 by the United States and the Soviet Union to slow the nuclear arms race.

**Sand Creek Massacre** The near annihilation in 1864 of Black Kettle's Cheyenne band by Colorado troops under Colonel John Chivington's orders to "kill and scalp all, big and little."

**scalawags** Southern whites, mainly small landowning farmers and well-off merchants and planters, who supported the Southern Republican party during Reconstruction.

**search and destroy** U.S. military tactic in South Vietnam, using small detachments to locate enemy units and then massive air, artillery, and ground forces to destroy them.

**Second Treaty of Fort Laramie** The treaty acknowledging U.S. defeat in the Great Sioux War in 1868 and supposedly guaranteeing the Sioux perpetual land and hunting rights in South Dakota, Wyoming, and Montana.

**Securities and Exchange Commission (SEC)** Federal agency with authority to regulate trading practices in stocks and bonds.

**Sedition Act of 1918** Broad law restricting criticism of America's involvement in World War I or its government, flag, military, taxes, or officials.

**segregation** A system of racial control that separated the races, initially by custom but increasingly by law, during and after Reconstruction.

**Selective Service Act of 1917** The law establishing the military draft for World War I.

**Selective Service System** Federal agency that coordinated military conscription before and during the Vietnam War.

**self-determination** The right of a people or a nation to decide its own political allegiance or form of government without external influence.

**Settlement House** A multipurpose structure in a poor neighborhood that offered social welfare, educational, and homemaking services to the poor or immigrants usually under private auspices and directed by middle-class women.

**Seventeenth Amendment** Constitutional change that in 1913 established the direct popular election of U.S. senators.

**sharecropping**  Labor system that evolved during and after Reconstruction whereby landowners furnished laborers with a house, farm animals, and tools and advanced credit in exchange for a share of the laborers' crop.

**Sheppard-Towner Maternity and Infancy Act**  The first federal social welfare law, passed in 1921, providing federal funds for infant and maternity care.

**Sherman Antitrust Act**  The first federal antitrust measure, passed in 1890; sought to promote economic competition by prohibiting business combinations in restraint of trade or commerce.

**Silicon Valley**  The region of California between San Jose and San Francisco that holds the nation's greatest concentration of electronics firms.

**Sixteenth Amendment**  Constitutional revision that in 1913 authorized a federal income tax.

**Slaughterhouse cases**  Group of cases resulting in one sweeping decision by the U.S. Supreme Court in 1873 that contradicted the intent of the **Fourteenth Amendment** by decreein that most citizenship rights remained under state, not federal, control.

**Social Darwinism**  The application of Charles Darwin's theory of biological evolution to society, holding that the fittest and wealthiest survive, the weak and the poor perish, and government action is unable to alter this "natural" process.

**Social Gospel movement**  Movement created by reform-minded Protestant ministers seeking to introduce religious ethics into industrial relations and appealing to churches to meet their social responsibilities.

**Solid South**  The one-party (Demo-cratic) political system that dominated the South from the 1890s to the 1950s.

**sound money**  Misleading slogan that referred to a conservative policy of restricting the money supply and adhering to the gold standard.

**Southeast Asia Treaty Organization (SEATO)**  Mutual defense alliance signed in 1954 by the United States, Britain, France, Thailand, Pakistan, the Philippines, Australia, and New Zealand.

**Southern Christian Leadership Conference (SCLC)**  Black civil rights organization founded in 1957 by Martin Luther King, Jr., and other clergy.

**Southern Farmer's Alliance**  The largest of several organizations that formed in the post-Reconstruction South to advance the interests of beleaguered small farmers.

**Southern Homestead Act**  Largely unsuccessful law passed in 1866 that gave black people preferential access to public lands in five southern states.

**Southern Manifesto**  A document signed by 101 members of Congress from Southern states in 1956 that argued that the Supreme Court's decision in *Brown v. Board of Education of Topeka* itself contradicted the Constitution.

**spheres of influence**  Regions dominated and controlled by an outside power.

**Stonewall Rebellion**  On June 27, 1969, patrons fought back when police raided the gay Stonewall Inn in New York; the name refers to that event and to the increase in militancy by gay Americans that it symbolizes.

**Strategic Defense Initiative (SDI)**  President Reagan's program, announced in 1983, to defend the U.S. against nuclear missile attack with untested weapons systems and sophisticated technologies.

**Student Nonviolent Coordinating Committee (SNCC)**  Black civil rights organization founded in 1960 and drawing heavily on younger activists and college students.

**Students for a Democratic Society (SDS)**  The leading student organization of the New Left of the early and mid-1960s.

**subtreasury plan**  A program promoted by the Southern Farmer's Alliance in response to low cotton prices and tight credit. Farmers would store their crop in a warehouse until prices rose, in the meantime borrowing up to 80 percent of the value of the stored crops from the government at a low interest rate.

**Sunbelt**  The states of the American South and Southwest.

**Sussex Pledge**  Germany's pledge during World War I not to sink merchant ships without warning, on the condition that Britain also observe recognized rules of international laws.

**Swann v. Charlotte-Mecklenburg Board of Education**  U.S. Supreme Court decision in 1971 that upheld cross-city busing to achieve the racial integration of public schools.

**sweatshops**  Small, poorly ventilated shops or apartments crammed with workers, often family members, who pieced together garments.

**Taft-Hartley Act**  Federal legislation of 1947 that substantially limited the tools available to labor unions in labor-management disputes.

**Teller Amendment**  A congressional resolution adopted in 1898 renouncing any American intention to annex Cuba.

**Temporary Assistance for Needy Families (TANF)**  Federal program, utilizing work requirements for and time limits on benefits, created in 1996 to replace earlier welfare programs to aid families and children.

**tenements**  Four- to six-story residential dwellings, once common in New York, built on tiny lots without regard to providing ventilation or light.

**Tennessee Valley Authority**  Federal regional planning agency established to promote conservation, produce electric power, and encourage economic development in seven southern states.

**Treaty of Versailles**  The treaty ending World War I and creating the League of Nations.

**Truman Doctrine**  President Harry Truman's statement in 1947 that the United States should assist other nations that were facing external pressure or internal revolution.

**trusts**  A combination of corporations cooperating in order to reduce competition and control prices.

**Underwood-Simmons Tarriff Act**  The 1913 reform law that lowered tariff rates and levied the first regular federal income tax.

**Union Leagues** Republican party organizations in Northern cities that became an important organizing device among freedmen in Southern cities after 1865.

**United States v. Cruikshank** Supreme Court ruling of 1876 that overturned the convictions of some of those responsible for the Colfax Massacre, ruling that the Enforcement Act applied only to violations of black rights by states, not individuals.

**University of California v. Bakke** U.S. Supreme Court case in 1978 that allowed race to be used as one of several factors in college and university admission decisions but made rigid quotas unacceptable.

**vertical integration** The consolidation of numerous production functions, from the extraction of the raw materials to the distribution and marketing of the finished products, under the direction of one firm.

**Viet Cong** Communist rebels in South Vietnam who fought the pro-American government established in South Vietnam in 1954.

**Volstead Act** The 1920 law defining the liquor forbidden under the Eighteenth Amendment and giving enforcement responsibilities to the Prohibition Bureau of the Department of the Treasury.

**Voting Rights Act** Legislation in 1965 that overturned a variety of practices by which states systematically denied voter registration to minorities.

**War Industries Board (WIB)** The federal agency that reorganized industry for maximum efficiency and productivity during World War I.

**War on Poverty** Set of programs introduced by Lyndon Johnson between 1963 and 1966 designed to break the cycle of poverty by providing funds for job training, community development, nutrition, and supplementary education.

**Watergate** A complex scandal involving attempts to cover up illegal actions taken by administration officials and leading to the resignation of President Richard Nixon in 1974.

**welfare capitalism** A paternalistic system of labor relations emphasizing management responsibility for employee well-being.

**Whitewater** Arkansas real estate development in which Bill and Hillary Clinton were investors; several fraud convictions resulted from investigations into Whitewater, but evidence was not found that the Clinton's were involved in wrongdoing.

**Wobblies** Popular name for the members of the Industrial Workers of the World (IWW).

**Women's Christian Temperance Union (WCTU)** Women's organization whose members visited schools to educate children about the evils of alcohol, addressed prisoners, and blanketed men's meetings with literature.

**World Bank** Designed to revive postwar international trade, it drew on the resources of member nations to make economic development loans to governments for such projects as new dams or agricultural modernization.

**World Trade Organization (WTO)** International organization that sets standards and practices for global trade, and the focus of international protests over world economic policy in the late 1990s.

**World Wide Web** A part of the Internet designed to allow easier navigation of the network through the use of graphical user interfaces and hypertext links between different addresses.

**Wounded Knee Massacre** The U.S. Army's brutal winter massacre in 1890 of at least two hundred Sioux men, women, and children as part of the government's assault on the tribe's Ghost Dance religion.

**Yalta Conference** Meeting of U.S. President Franklin Roosevelt, British Prime Minister Winston Churchill, and Soviet Premier Joseph Stalin held in February 1945 to plan the final stages of World War II and postwar arrangements.

**yellow press** A deliberately sensational journalism of scandal and exposure designed to attract an urban mass audience and increase advertising revenues.

**yellow-dog contracts** Employment agreements binding workers not to join a union.

Inc.–Hulton Archive Photos; Library of Congress. Photos: p. 241: Jane Braddick Petticolas (1791-1852) "View of the West Front of Monticello and Garden" 1825, watercolor on paper, 13 5/8 x 18 1/18 inches. Edward Owen/Monticello/Thomas Jefferson Foundation, Inc.; p. 242: (c) Walters Art Museum, Baltimore/Bridgeman Art Library; p. 247: Courtesy of the Library of Congress; p. 248: Courtesy of the Library of Congress; p. 251: Courtesy of the Library of Congress; p. 253: Corbis/Bettmann; p. 255: Picture Desk, Inc./Kobal Collection.

**Chapter 10** CO photos: (c) Bettmann/CORBIS; Courtesy, American Antiquarian Society; Getty Images, Inc.- Photodisc.; National Museum of American History, Smithsonian Institution; National Numismatic Collection/Smithsonian Institution; Collection of The New-York Historical Society, Negative # 26275; (c) Bettmann/CORBIS; Courtesy of the Library of Congress; The Boston Athenaeum. Photos: p. 270: Collection of The New-York Historical Society, Negative # 26275; p. 271: First State Election in Detroit, Michigan, 1837, c. 1837. Thomas Mickell Burnham. Gift of Mrs. Samuel T. Carson. Photograph (c) 1991 The Detroit Institute of Arts; p. 272: Courtesy of the Library of Congress; p. 273: Corbis/Bettmann; p. 274: The Granger Collection, New York; p. 277: The Granger Collection, New York; p. 281: Courtesy of the Library of Congress; p. 285: The Cincinnati Historical Society; p. 290: Corbis/Bettmann. IP photos: Courtesy of the Library of Congress; The Granger Collection, New York.

**Chapter 11** CO photos: The Granger Collection, New York; Corbis/Bettmann; Wilberforce House (c) Hull Museums; Wilberforce House (c) Hull Museums.; Library of Congress; (c) Dorling Kindersley; The Granger Collection, New York; Carl G. von Iwonski, Block House, New Braunfels. Daughters of the Republic of Texas Library. Yanaguana Society Collection; Boston Anthenaeum; Library of Congress. Photos: p. 302: Library of Congress; p. 304: Collection of The New-York Historical Society; p. 306: Courtesy of the Library of Congress; p. 308: From the Collection of the Louisiana State Museum; p. 311: Library of Congress and Smith College, Sophia Smith Collection, Northampton, Massachusetts; p. 318: The Granger Collection, New York.; p. 319: Courtesy of the Library of Congress.

**Chapter 12** CO photos: The Granger Collection, New York; Map of Proposed route of Erie Canal, 1811 Negative Number 420757, (c) Collection of the New-York Historical Society, New York City.; The Granger Collection; Library of Congress; (c)Bettmann/CORBIS; (c) Stapleton Collection/CORBIS; Getty Images Inc.–Hulton Archive Photos; Courtesy of the Library of Congress; Frederick Douglass (1817?-95). Oil on canvas, c1844, attr. to E. Hammond. The Granger Collection. Photos: p. 330: Collection of The New-York Historical Society, Negative # 34684; p. 331: (c) Bettmann/CORBIS; p. 336: Courtesy of the Library of Congress; p. 339: Family Group, Joesph H. Davis, American, 1811-1865, Graphite pencil and watercolor on paper, Sheet: 24.8 x 41 cm (9 3/4 x 16 1/8 in.), Museum of Fine Arts, Boston, Gift of Maxim Karolik for the proposed M. and M. Karolik Collection of American Watercolors, (c) 2003 Museum of Fine Arts, Boston; p. 342: Corbis/Bettmann; p. 346: Richard Nowitz Photography; p. 347: Library of Congress; p. 355: (c) Bettmann/CORBIS. IP photos: Library of Congress; Getty Images, Inc Bridgeman; Library of Congress.

**Chapter 13** CO photos: Butler Institute of American Art, Youngstown, OH, USA/Gift of Joseph G. Butler III 1946/Bridgeman Art Library.; Courtesy of the Lane County Historical Museum; Getty Images Inc.–Hulton Archive Photos; Peter Anderson (c) Dorling Kindersley; Lynton Gardiner (c) Dorling Kindersley, Courtesy of The American Museum of Natural History; Photo by Lynton Gardiner, Courtesy Dept. of Library Services, American Museum of Natural History.; (c) Christie's Images Inc. 2004; Art Resource, N.Y.; Nathaniel Currier, "General Winfield Scott at the Siege of Vera Cruz, March 1847," 1847. Lithograph. The Granger Collection. Photos: p. 366: The Old Print Shop Inc. Kenneth M. Newman; p. 370: Shirt, about 1860s, unknown Sioux artist Deer skin, hair, quills, feathers, paint Denver Art Museum Collection: Native Arts acquisition funds, 1947.235 (c) Photo by the Denver Art Museum. All Rights Reserved.; p. 371: The Denver Public Library, Western History Department; p. 373: North Wind Picture Archives; p. 374: Alfred Jacob Miller, "The Interior of Fort Laramie," 1858-60. The Walters Art Museum, Baltimore.; p. 375: Courtesy of the Library of Congress; p. 381: Courtesy of the Lane County Historical Museum; p. 385: Smithsonian American Art Museum, Washington, DC/Art Resource, NY.

**Chapter 14** CO photos: Courtesy of the Library of Congress; (c) COR-BIS; Getty Images, Inc.- Photodisc.; Southworth, Albert Sands(1811-1894), and Hawes, Josiah Johnson (1808-1901), Harriet Beecher Stowe. Daguerreotype. 4-1/4in x 3-1/4in. The Metropolitan Museum of Art, Gift of I.N. Phelps Stokes, Edward S. Hawes, Alice Mary Hawes, and Marion Augusta Hawes, 1937.; (c) Bettmann/CORBIS; (c)CORBIS;

Library of Congress. Photos: p. 394: Courtesy of Elliot Koeppel, www.malakoff.com; p. 397: Courtesy of the Library of Congress; p. (c) Bettmann/CORBIS; p. 401: The Newberry Library; p. 402: The Granger Collection, New York; p. 405: Library of Congress; p. 407: Abraham Lincoln Presidental Library & Museum (ALPLM); p. 410: The Granger Collection, New York.

**Chapter 15** CO photos: Theodor Kaufmann (American, b. 1814),"On to Liberty," 1867. Oil on canvas, 36" x 56" (91.4 x 142.2 cm). The Metropolitan Museum of Art, Gift of Erving and Joyce Wolf, 1982. (1982.443.3) Photograph (c) 1982 The Metropolitan Museum of Art; United States Department of the Interior; Dave King/Dorling Kindersley (c) Confederate Memorial Hall, New Orleans; Dave King (c) Confederate Memorial Hall, New Orleans.; National Archives and Records Administration; Dave King/Dorling Kindersley (c) Confederate Memorial Hall, New Orleans; (c) Confederate Memorial Hall, New Orleans.; Library of Congress; (c) CORBIS; Getty Images Inc.–Hulton Archive Photos; Center of Military History, U.S. Army; (c) Bettmann/CORBIS; Courtesy of the Library of Congress. Photos: p. 428: Courtesy of the Library of Congress; p. 433: Center of Military History, U.S. Army; p. 434: Boston Public Library/Rare Books Department–Courtesy of the Trustees.; p. 437: Theodor Kaufmann (American, b. 1814),"On to Liberty," 1867. Oil on canvas, 36" x 56" (91.4 x 142.2 cm). The Metropolitan Museum of Art, Gift of Erving and Joyce Wolf, 1982. (1982.443.3) Photograph (c) 1982 The Metropolitan Museum of Art; p. 439: Manuscripts, Archives and Rare Books Division, Schomberg Center for Research in Black Culture, The New York Public Library. Astor, Lenox and Tilden Foundations; p. 444: Courtesy of the Library of Congress; p. 447: Culver Pictures, Inc.; p. 450: (c) Bettmann/CORBIS; p. 451: National Archives and Records Administration; p. 455: Courtesy of the Library of Congress; p. 457: Courtesy of the Library of Congress; p. 459: Courtesy of the Library of Congress.

**Chapter 16** CO photos: Courtesy of the Library of Congress; Library of Congress; Courtesy of the Library of Congress; Courtesy of Special Collections, Musselman Library, Gettysburg College, Gettysburg, PA.; The Granger Collection, New York.; (c) CORBIS; The Granger Collection, New York. Photos: p. 469: The Granger Collection; p. 472: The Granger Collection; p 476: The Granger Collection, New York.; p. 79: Courtesy of the Library of Congress; p. p. 481: Courtesy of the Library of Congress; p. 483: The Granger Collection, New York; p. 485: Courtesy of the Library of Congress; p. 487: Courtesy of the Library of Congress. IP photos: Library of Congress; Austin History Center, Austin Public Library/PICA 05496.

**Chapter 17** CO photos: Courtesy of the Library of Congress; The Granger Collection, New York.; Collection of The New-York Historical Society. negative number 51391.; Prentice Hall School Division; SHOM-BURG CENTER Center/Art Resource, NY; Courtesy of The North Carolina Division of Archives and History; T. E. Armitstead Collection, University of South Alabama Archives; Collection of The New-York Historical Society. negative number 51391. Photos: p. 505: T. E. Armitstead Collection, University of South Alabama Archives; p. 507: Valentine Museum/Richmond History Center; p. 509: Courtesy of the Library of Congress; p. 512: Courtesy of the Library of Congress; p. p. 514: The Granger Collection, New York.; p. 516: North Carolina Mutual Life Insurance Company.

**Chapter 18** CO photos: George Eastman House; Getty Images Inc.–Hulton Archive Photos; (c) Rykoff Collection/CORBIS; (c) Schenectady Museum; Hall of Electrical/CORBIS; The Granger Collection, New York.; (c) Rykoff Collection/CORBIS; Ford Motor Company. Photos: p. 530: W. Louis Sonntag, Jr., "The Bowery at Night", watercolor, 1895. Copyright Museum of the City of New York. 32.275.2; p. 531: Ford Motor Company; p. 533: Courtesy of the Library of Congress; p. 534: Culver Pictures, Inc.; p. 535: (left) Getty Images Inc.–Hulton Archive Photos, (right) 22 Baxter Street Court. The Jacob A. Riis Collection, Museum of the City of New York.; p. 537: The Granger Collection, New York.; p. 543: Courtesy of the Library of Congress; p. 545: Courtesy of The Bancroft Library. University of California, Berkeley.; p. 548: Brown Brothers.

**Chapter 19** CO photos: The Granger Collection, New York; Dave King/Dorling Kindersley (c) Confederate Memorial Hall, New Orleans; Lynton Gardiner (c) Dorling Kindersley, Courtesy of The American Museum of Natural History; Frederic S. Remington, "The Cheyenne", 1901, cast 1904. Bronze, 20-1/2 x 23-1/4 x 8. Amon Carter Museum, Fort Worth, Texas. (1997.140); (c) Dorling Kindersley; (c) Judith Miller/Dorling Kindersley/Cowan's Historic Americana Auctions; The Granger Collection, New York; Chinese mining laborers, Idaho, 76-119.2/A, Idaho State Historical Society.; Library of Congress. Photos: p. Union Pacific Historical Collection; p. 566: Denver Public Library, Western History

# A

## J

Jackson, Jesse, 936
Jackson, Maynard, 964
Jackson State University, 896
Japan, rivalry with Russia, 668–69
Japanese Americans, internment of, 794–95, 798–99
Japanese Association of America, 542
Japanese immigrants, 540–41
    land ownership and, 727
Jazz, international journey of, 725
Jazz Age, 722
    advertising, 722–23
    leisure and entertainment in, 723–24
    mass culture in, 722–26
    morality in, 724
    writers in, 725–26
Jell-O, 552
Jewish immigrants, 541
Jews
    Holocaust, 802
    *Kristallnacht,* 778
    Nazi anti-Semitism, World War II and, 769–70
Jieshi, Jiang, 853
Jim Crow laws, 514
Job Corps, 867
Jobs, creating, 753–54
Johnson, Andrew
    impeachment of, 595
    Tenure of Office Act and, 479
Johnson, Hiram, 637
Johnson, James Weldon, 721
Johnson, Lyndon B., 760, 867–69
    exit of, 893
    Vietnam War and, 880–82
Johnson C. Smith University, 470
Jones, Paula, 953
Jordan Marsh, 552
Julian, George W., 485
*The Jungle* (Sinclair), 710

## K

Kaczynski, Ted. *See* Unabomber
Kansas
    cow towns in, 573
    settlers in, 577
Kansas Pacific Railroad, 573
Keating-Owen Act, 646
Kellogg-Briand Pact, 733
Kemp, Jack, 923

Kennan, George, 823
Kennedy, Jacqueline, 856, 858
Kennedy, John F., 818, 856–61
    Bay of Pigs, 858
    Berlin Wall, 859
    Cold War, assessment of, 857
    Cold War and, 856–61
    Cuban Missile Crisis and, 859–60
    Dallas, 1963, 866–67
    mistakes by, 858–59
    mystique of, 857–58
    science and foreign affairs, 860–61
    Vietnam and, 859
Kennedy, Robert, 864, 893
    assassination of, 893
Kent State University, 896
Kern-McGillicuddy Act, 646
Kerry, John, 974
Khmer Rouge, 896, 912
Khomeini, Ayatollah Ruhollah, 906
Khrushchev, Nikita, 850, 860
King, Rodney, riot, 924
King Jr., Martin Luther, 864–66, 868, 875
    assassination of, 893
Kissinger, Henry, 897
Knights of Labor, 537
Know-Nothing Party, 545
Kohl, Helmut, 929
Korean War, 827–29
    consequences of, 830
    integrating Army in Korea, 833
    map, 829
    politics of, 829–31
*Korematsu v. United States,* 794
Kosovo, 949
*Kristallnacht,* 769
Ku Klux Klan, 515, 728–29
    women of, 728
Ku Klux Klan Act of 1871, 484
Kyoto Agreement, 969

## L

Labor
    changes in force, 1870-1910, 528
    child, 532
    crisis for organized, 918–19
    Great Depression and, 746–47

    in mining industry, 570–73
    New Deal and, 761–62
    relations, during World War I, 687–88
    Roosevelt, Theodore and, 638
*Ladies' Home Journal,* 850
Ladies' Memorial Associations, 509
La Follette, Robert M., 637, 697, 703, 718
Laissez-faire policies, 594
Lakotas, 562
Landon, Alf, 760
Land ownership
    for African Americans, 470–71
    Japanese immigrants and, 727
*Landsmanshaften,* 541
Langdon, Eunice, 742
Lansing, Robert, 682
La Orden de Hijos de America (The Order of the Sons of America), 721
*Las Gorras Blancas,* 579
Latchkey children, 791
Latin America
    American role in, 733–34
    Cuba, as U.S. protectorate, 669–71
    dollar diplomacy, 672–73
    Panama Canal, 671–72
    Puerto Rico, 669
    Roosevelt Corollary, 672
    U.S. imperialism and, 669–74
    Wilsonian interventions, 673–74
League of Nations, 696
    battle over, 697–99
League of United Latin American Citizens (LULAC), 721
League of Women Voters, 718
Lease, Mary E., 604
*Leave It to Beaver,* 847
Lee, Robert E., 521
Legislation
    protective, for women and children, 627–29
Legislative Reference Bureau, 637
Leisure activities, growth of, 553–54
Leisure and entertainment, in Jazz Age, 723–24
Lemke, William, 757
Lend-Lease Act, 782